SUCCESSFUL MANAGER'S HANDBOOK

www.personneldecisions.com

Also published by Personnel Decisions International

Successful Executive's Handbook:
Development Suggestions for Today's Executives

Successful Manager's Handbook (Japanese language version)

Suggestions de développement et ressources
à l'usage des managers d'aujourd'hui

Entwicklungsvorschläge für erfolgreiches Management

Supplement to the Successful Manager's Handbook:
Readings, Seminars and Training Courses (available in the UK)

Development FIRST: Strategies for Self-Development

Development FIRST Workbook

Leader As Coach: Strategies for Coaching & Developing Others

Leader As Coach Workbook

Presentations: How to Calm Down, Think Clearly,
and Captivate Your Audience

HANDBOOK SERIES

SUCCESSFUL MANAGER'S HANDBOOK

DEVELOPMENT SUGGESTIONS FOR
TODAY'S MANAGERS

SUSAN H. GEBELEIN
LISA A. STEVENS
CAROL J. SKUBE
DAVID G. LEE
BRIAN L. DAVIS
LOWELL W. HELLERVIK

PUBLISHED BY
PERSONNEL DECISIONS INTERNATIONAL CORPORATION
OFFICES THROUGHOUT
NORTH AMERICA, EUROPE,
ASIA, AND AUSTRALIA

PDI PERSONNEL DECISIONS INTERNATIONAL

www.personneldecisions.com

Book Design and Production: Barbara Redmond Design
Editorial Services: Joan E. Kremer, Jane Eastham, Gwen W. Stucker
Illustrations: John Bush

This book is bound by the otabind process so that it will lie flat when opened. The spine gap is a feature of the otabind method.

ISBN: 0-938529-20-X.

CONTENTS

———

CONTENTS

———

ACKNOWLEDGMENTS

We would like to recognize and thank those who helped make this book possible. The *Successful Manager's Handbook* (Sixth Edition) is a result of true partnerships within and outside of PDI.

Thank you for your help.

Kshanika Anthony	Nicolas Mazur
Val Arnold, Ph.D.	Kristie Nelson-Neuhaus
Stanley Birnbaum	Donna Neumann
Lydie Bonnet-Semelin	David B. Peterson, Ph.D.
Adriana Cento	Joanne Provo, Ph.D.
Kathryn Chen	Peter Ramstad
Gordy Curphy, Ph.D.	Diane Rawlings, Ph.D.
Terri Elofson	Ann Ribbens
Tamar Fox	Ursula Schullerus
Dee Gaeddert	Steven Semler
Jocelyne Gessner, Ph.D.	William Shepherd, Ph.D.
Ken Hedberg	Marc Sokol, Ph.D.
Cori Hill	Linda Strmel
Douglas W. Jack	Elyse Sutherland, Ph.D.
Luc Janin, Ph.D.	Paul Van Katwyk, Ph.D.
Michael Jarrett, Ph.D.	Elizabeth Weixel
Teresa Jensen	Deborah Wischow
Bridget Lane	PDI Client Partners
LeRoy Martin	

ABOUT THIS BOOK

Today's organizations are experiencing an ever-accelerating rate of change and information flow amidst fierce competition and a tight labor market. Managers are being called upon to do more with less, keep pace with the current information explosion and technological revolution, and display breadth and depth in more areas than their predecessors ever did. Developing and leveraging human capital has never been more important than it is now.

Sixteen years have passed since Personnel Decisions International (PDI) published its first edition of the *Successful Manager's Handbook*. During this time, skills that once seemed optional—creating strategic advantage, promoting global perspective, leveraging individual and cultural diversity, to name a few—have become as important as the core management skills of, for example, building relationships or establishing plans. Other managerial skills that were basically nonexistent sixteen years ago, such as managing technology, have become requirements for survival in today's business world.

This new edition of the *Successful Manager's Handbook* focuses on what it takes to be a successful and effective manager in the new millennium.

How this handbook can be helpful

Managers are busy. And finding practical, on-the-job activities and advice can be difficult and time-consuming. Ideas may not come easily when you're thinking of your own situation. You may not know how to get started, what is required in a certain area, whom you should ask for advice, or what it takes to reach the next level.

This handbook can help—it's like having a management development consultant at your side to provide advice on development activities and resources specifically suited to you and those you are coaching. Whether you are using one of PDI's processes such as The PROFILOR® or an in-house program, or an offering from another vendor, you can apply the information in the handbook to further your development and that of your employees. The handbook is designed to be a user-friendly tool you can use in a number of ways. For example:

- Look for action steps for your development plan, or for someone you are coaching or mentoring.

- Search for ideas and activities for your long-term career development.

- Refer people to specific sections or chapters as you help them with their development.

- Familiarize yourself with or advise others on the competency and performance expectations for managers.

Don't attempt to read the handbook as you would a novel. Rather, when you use this handbook, it is useful to:

1. Review the Table of Contents on page v to identify the skill areas that interest you.

2. Skim the introductory text of the chapter to pinpoint relevant content areas.

3. Study the suggestions in those content areas.

4. Tailor the ideas and suggestions to fit your situation.

5. Supplement ideas for development by referring to the recommended books and seminars in the Resources by Chapter section at the end of the handbook.

What you will find in this handbook

The content of this handbook is organized around PDI's latest research on four critical leadership performance dimensions: Thought Leadership, Results Leadership, People Leadership, and Self Leadership. Within these broad dimensions, you will find nine core factors—Strategy, Judgment, Business Knowledge, Planning and Execution, Motivation and Courage, Leadership, Interpersonal, Communication, and Self-Management. Within each factor are the specific skills or competencies that comprise that factor. These managerial competencies are derived from a number of PDI's broad service areas, including assessment, development, coaching, and training disciplines. A Wheel of Leadership Success, which represents these broad dimensions, factors, and competencies, is shown below.

One chapter of this handbook is devoted to each competency area. Each chapter contains tips and development suggestions for learning new skills and fine-tuning existing ones. Books and seminars for each competency are listed in the Resources by Chapter section at the end of the handbook.

PDI LEADERSHIP SUCCESS WHEEL

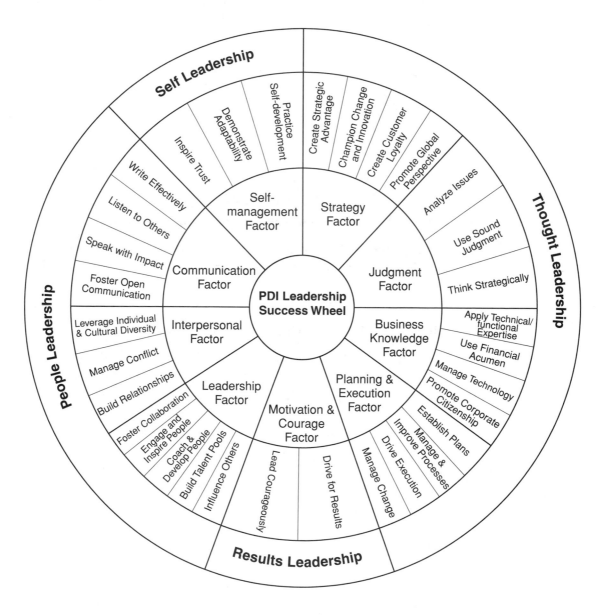

HERE IS A CAPSULE PREVIEW OF THE CONTENTS OF THE HANDBOOK:

STRATEGY FACTOR

Chapter 1: Create Strategic Advantage

Successful managers know that strategy is not stagnant; it is an emergent process that focuses on competitive advantage, competitive differentiation, sustainable advantage, and barriers to entry. We provide suggestions and guidelines for creating strategic advantage, including understanding the critical success factors of your organization and your competitors, identifying current and future customers, and defining strategies to capitalize on strengths and market opportunities.

Chapter 2: Champion Change and Innovation

Today's managers need to do far more than simply manage change; they need to passionately champion both change and innovation to stay ahead of the competition. We discuss how to create original and innovative solutions, be resourceful by taking what is and making it better, and encourage innovation in others.

Chapter 3: Create Customer Loyalty

Managers are responsible for orchestrating customer-focused strategies that build and sustain customer commitment and loyalty—the cornerstone to business success. We outline ways to understand the customer, manage the customer relationship, and build a customer-focused team.

Chapter 4: Promote Global Perspective

The ability to operate within the global economy is no longer optional. Even if your organization is not directly affected by the global economy, your customers or suppliers are more than likely feeling the impact. The global economy influences issues affecting strategy, innovation, intercultural awareness, and technology, to name a few. We provide suggestions for thinking globally in your business and enhancing your international mind-set.

Judgment Factor

Chapter 5: Analyze Issues

In today's fast-paced environment, managers are faced with a myriad of issues each day—some are straightforward and uncomplicated, yet many others are complex and require focused, systematic analysis. We offer common-sense guidelines for improving your analytical skills, including diagnosing the root cause, gathering and integrating critical information for analysis, and detecting flaws in reasoning.

Chapter 6: Use Sound Judgment

Making decisions is a critical part of every manager's job. Decision making involves judging objective as well as subjective data; it relies on a mix of analysis and judgment; it requires comfort with complexity, risk, and ambiguity. We outline suggestions for improving both the process and the outcome of your decisions.

Chapter 7: Think Strategically

The need to think strategically is no longer a requirement for just the executive suite of an organization; managers must also adopt a strategic mind-set to be successful in today's complex business environment. Strategic thinking is characterized by the ability to visualize what might or could be, as well as by a day-to-day strategic approach to issues and challenges. We outline suggestions that will help you to develop a strategic mind-set and apply these skills to more effectively lead your team.

Business Knowledge Factor

Chapter 8: Apply Technical/Functional Expertise

Managers are often first promoted because of their strong technical and functional expertise. While managers do not need the same high level of technical knowledge and skills as that of their staff, they do need to have sufficient knowledge to address strategic issues. We discuss how to stay current and leverage technical innovations, industry trends, and functional knowledge.

Chapter 9: Use Financial Acumen

Managers are responsible for understanding and monitoring the financial performance of their unit. We discuss budgets and forecasts, the key financial indicators necessary to measure business performance, and methods to identify and evaluate alternatives for achieving financial targets.

Chapter 10: Manage Technology

What do managers need to know about technology? Simply stated, leaders needs to be able to use the basic technology necessary to their jobs, discern the proper role for technology to play in their work, and understand how to implement new technology. We provide a process for staying current in this rapidly changing field.

Chapter 11: Promote Corporate Citizenship

Stewardship and corporate citizenship are no longer just "nice to have." We discuss ways to create partnerships between business and the community, understand community issues relevant to the business, and strengthen your commitment to corporate citizenship.

PLANNING AND EXECUTION FACTOR

Chapter 12: Establish Plans

Without an effective plan, a manager's strategic vision is merely a dream. Managers need to be able to translate their broad vision and goals into both long- and short-range plans that are appropriately comprehensive, realistic, and effective at meeting their goals. We outline the components of effective plans and show you how to adapt your plans to respond to changes and unanticipated problems.

Chapter 13: Manage and Improve Processes

Managers need to constantly figure out ways of doing work better, smarter, and faster. Those who don't will find it difficult to stay competitive in the marketplace. We provide suggestions for leading and managing process-improvement efforts and continuous learning.

Chapter 14: Drive Execution

Effectiveness in managing people starts with managing oneself. But it does not end there. This chapter covers both ends of the spectrum. We offer tried-and-true strategies of time management followed by guidelines for effective delegation and meeting management.

Chapter 15: Manage Change

Managers are responsible for the effective implementation of planned organizational change, or change management, as it is commonly labeled. Whether you are managing a change for a single team or across a large multinational corporation, the fundamental requirements are similar. We outline the change-management process, which includes successful communication strategies, involving others in the implementation of the change, and monitoring and reinforcing progress and success.

MOTIVATION AND COURAGE FACTOR

Chapter 16: Drive for Results

Successful managers focus on achieving results through and with others. They set high standards of performance, pursue aggressive goals, and persist in the face of obstacles. They help their team do the same. We share tips to help you and your team maintain a focus on results.

Chapter 17: Lead Courageously

Today's leaders must demonstrate principled leadership, personal courage, and decisiveness. They must be willing to endure difficulty, take risks, and live their values despite discomfort. Principled leaders confront others when necessary, but do so in a respectful way. We show you how to clarify what is important to you, act consistent with your principles, and address tough issues promptly and courageously.

LEADERSHIP FACTOR

Chapter 18: Influence Others

The ability to influence others, with or without authority, has become increasingly important in today's flatter, more matrixed organizations. Managers will continue to encounter situations that demand solid influencing skills. We cover suggestions for presenting a compelling case for your position, garnering support from others, negotiating persuasively, and creating win/win outcomes.

Chapter 19: Build Talent Pools

It's been said that a manager is only as good as his or her people. Your success and the success of your group depend in large part on the talent you are able to attract and retain. We give you some of the latest thinking on attracting and selecting the right people, and provide staffing suggestions to maximize the talent on your team.

Chapter 20: Coach and Develop People

Managers can maximize their human capital investments by placing a high priority on coaching and developing others. Coaching is not a one-way street where managers have all the answers, but rather is a partnership where both people share responsibility. We discuss PDI's five coaching strategies, which are: forge a partnership, inspire commitment, grow skills, promote persistence, and shape the environment.

Chapter 21: Engage and Inspire People

One of the hallmarks of an effective manager is to both get results and generate a high level of morale among employees. Creating and communicating a vision that is aligned with the strategy and direction of the larger organization is the first step in achieving this goal. Clarifying others' involvement in the vision, inspiring a sense of energy and ownership, creating an environment of high performance, and recognizing the efforts of others define the subsequent steps. We give you suggestions for each of these areas.

Chapter 22: Foster Collaboration

Effective leaders work with others to create the conditions for team effectiveness. They know when and how to use teams; they know that sometimes a team approach is not the best choice. They also provide the tools, systems, and resources that create a supportive environment for collaboration. We provide suggestions to help you create this environment.

INTERPERSONAL FACTOR

Chapter 23: Build Relationships

Managers must rely on others in order to achieve their goals. The greater the commitment you have to developing and maintaining respectful, productive relationships with others, the larger the payoff in terms of motivation, commitment, and support. We offer specific suggestions for building relationships with people at all levels of the organization, and discuss ways to develop and leverage your network.

Chapter 24: Manage Conflict

Effective managers realize that conflict is a part of any dynamic business organization. They create stronger working relationships and encourage creative solutions by effectively working through conflicts. We offer ideas for improving your conflict management style, communicating constructively during conflict, and facilitating conflict discussion and resolution.

Chapter 25: Leverage Individual and Cultural Diversity

No doubt, today's workforce has become more diverse. Today's managers are faced with the challenge of balancing the wants and needs of a highly diverse workforce, as it is increasingly common for people of different ages, cultures, first languages, learning styles, and educational backgrounds to be working side by side. We provide suggestions and insights for effectively leveraging individual and cultural diversity.

Communication Factor

Chapter 26: Foster Open Communication

Open communication. Sometimes it seems like the very idea is utopian. Yet trust and solid working relationships are based on a manager's willingness and ability to communicate openly. We show you how to create an environment where communication is open and direct, encouraged, rewarded, and relevant.

Chapter 27: Speak with Impact

Even the most competent leaders fall short of managerial excellence if they are unable to speak with clarity and conviction. Managers need to effectively express themselves in a variety of settings—one-on-one interactions, group meetings, and formal presentations. We give you targeted suggestions to develop and fine-tune your speaking skills in each of these settings.

Chapter 28: Listen to Others

Listening to others—including employees, managers, peers, and customers—is a core, foundational skill for effective managers. The ability to listen is key to developing relationships, making decisions, and solving problems. Like all communication skills, listening improves quickly with practice and technique. We help you to evaluate your current skills, and offer tips for strengthening this core skill.

Chapter 29: Write Effectively

The need for clarity, simplicity, and accuracy in written communication is obvious. With the influx of the Internet and e-mail, writing has become a part of every manager's job. We provide suggestions for avoiding common mistakes, editing your work and the work of others, and choosing a style appropriate to your audience and delivery method.

SELF–MANAGEMENT FACTOR

Chapter 30: Inspire Trust

How does a manager go about building trust? By being consistent, communicating honestly, following through on commitments, to name a few. Trusted leaders create an atmosphere of integrity, marked by fair and respectful behavior. We discuss the key components of creating an environment where uncompromising integrity is the norm.

Chapter 31: Demonstrate Adaptability

In addition to developing comfort with ambiguity and a fast pace, thriving in a managerial position requires juggling the demands of personal and work-related activities as well as finding an appropriate balance between the needs of the organization, others, and self. We cover some of the major aspects of demonstrating adaptability: dealing with stress, ambiguity, change, resiliency, and work/life balance.

Chapter 32: Practice Self-Development

As the pace of change continues to intensify in today's business environment, managerial success now requires a serious commitment to ongoing learning and self-development. We outline PDI's Development FIRST™ process to help you proactively drive your own development and establish a cycle of continuous learning.

Create a Plan for Your Growth and Development

A basic plan or roadmap can help guide you to achieve your personal and career goals. The plan you choose will depend on your desired destination.

A Career Plan, or longer-term roadmap, takes into account your personal mission and overall goals from both a personal and professional standpoint. It charts your desired future roles and responsibilities, and defines how you will get there.

A sample Career Plan is shown on page xix. This very abbreviated Career Plan does not incorporate the necessary "life planning" element that is part of a more comprehensive career plan. For additional career planning and tools, contact PDI Career Management Services.★

A Development Plan is a medium-range plan that outlines the approach you will use to accomplish the shorter-term development goals outlined in your career plan. You will find a sample Development Plan on pages xx.

A Learning Plan is a short-range plan that outlines your learning objectives and specifically defines what you will actually do to change your behavior in the next six months to a year. To maintain focus and increase your likelihood for success, limit yourself to two or three of the objectives listed in your Development Plan. A sample Learning Plan, modeled after PDI's Development FIRST™ process, is shown on pages xxii.

Final Thoughts

We at PDI are interested in your feedback. Please give us your feedback on this edition of the handbook:

- What was helpful?

- What would you like to see more or less of in future editions?

- What one area was the most useful for you?

- How are you using this book? Are you using it for your personal development or for development planning with the people you are coaching?

Send your comments directly to Kristie Nelson-Neuhaus at Kristie.Nelson-Neuhaus@personneldecisions.com. We look forward to hearing from you!

CAREER PLAN

Personal Mission Statement:

Short-term Career Goals (1–2 years)

Long-term Career Goals (3–5 years)

Short-term Development Goals

Strengths to Leverage:	*Development Needs to Address:*
•	•
•	•
•	•

Long-term Development Goals

Strengths to Leverage:	*Development Needs to Address:*
•	•
•	•
•	•

*For more information about Career Management Services, contact Client Relations, Personnel Decisions International, 2000 Plaza VII Tower, 45 South Seventh Street, Minneapolis, Minnesota 55402-1608, 800/332-2336 or 612/915-7600.

SAMPLE DEVELOPMENT PLAN

BUILDING ON STRENGTHS

STEP 1 STRENGTHS TARGETED	STEP 2 ACTION PLANS	STEP 3 INVOLVEMENT OF OTHERS	STEP 4 TARGET DATES
STRENGTH: FOSTER COLLABORATION Objectives: • Involve others more in shaping plans. • Promote teamwork among groups.	1. Conduct a debriefing with customer focus team to find if I've missed anyone necessary to the discussion on new quality standards.	Customer focus team	7/15
	2. Keep a list of interested people to involve in discussions. (If I don't understand why someone should be included, I'll talk with them).	None	7/15
	3. Each time I meet with my staff, ask about problems in coordination with other groups.	Staff	ongoing; evaluate quarterly
	4. Develop and conduct study to determine teamwork issues among groups; feed back information to team.	H.R. person, staff, team leaders	10/15
STRENGTH: COACH AND DEVELOP Objectives: • Increasing my skill in identifying the skills of my direct reports.	1. Volunteer to be trained as an assessor for in-house development centers.	Boss	7/1
	2. Participate in training for assessment.	Assessment staff	8/15
	3. Serve as an assessor in two centers.	Boss	Sept.–Dec.
	4. Use assessment skills with my own staff for career development discussions.	Staff	Nov.–Dec.
STRENGTH: ANALYZE ISSUES Objectives: • Coach others to understand complex concepts and relationships.	1. Give feedback to relevant staff members. Agree to work with them on this.	Sara and James	7/20
	2. Have them present their analysis of issues to me, including factors involved, possible consequences, alternative views, and anticipated side effects.	Sara and James	8/1
	3. Help them identify role models to observe and interview.	Sara and James	ongoing; evaluate quarterly
	4. Give positive reinforcement of improvements.	Sara and James	ongoing; evaluate quarterly

ADDRESSING DEVELOPMENT NEEDS

STEP 1 DEVELOPMENT NEEDS TARGETED	STEP 2 ACTION PLANS	STEP 3 INVOLVEMENT OF OTHERS	STEP 4 TARGET DATES
DEVELOPMENT NEED: MANAGE CONFLICT Objectives: • Know what battles are worth fighting.	1. Ask for feedback about when I have misjudged this. What did I do? What were consequences?	Boss, trusted peer	8/15
	2. Identify when others are telling me (verbally or non-verbally) that I'm pushing too hard. Stop and check if the issue is that important.	None	ongoing
	3. Ask my boss or peer to strategize with me to develop a less alienating way to have my point heard.	Boss, peer	ongoing
	4. Identify issues where I should simply back off.	None	ongoing; evaluate quarterly
DEVELOPMENT NEED: BUILD RELATIONSHIPS Objectives: • Establish networks with people in the industry.	1. Talk with others about best industry organizations.	Boss, peers	7/1
	2. Determine how to get involved in the organization.	Boss, other members	1/30
	3. Identify ways in which that involvement can be useful.	Other members	2/30
	4. Use network to bring in information and points of view from others outside the company.	Industry organizations	ongoing; evaluate quarterly
DEVELOPMENT NEED: DRIVE EXECUTION Objectives: • Empower others with more authority.	1. Shadow managers known for empowering others.	Peers/colleagues	8/15
	2. Based on those observations, ask for additional feedback from direct reports.	Direct reports	9/15
	3. Listen to tape on delegation.	None	10/1
	4. Determine three things I can do differently.	Direct reports	10/1
	5. Ask for feedback after I have begun implementing changes.	Direct reports	10/30

PERSONAL LEARNING PLAN

Name __Waldo Austin_____ Date _____

1. FOCUS ON CRITICAL PRIORITIES.
What do I want to change or develop?
What development priorities give me the greatest leverage?

◇ Be more effective in influencing peers and upper management, especially around department priorities, strategic direction, and major decisions.

2. IMPLEMENT SOMETHING EVERY DAY.

What situations, people, or events signal that right now is the time to put new behaviors into action? *Every time I see the following situation(s)...*	What new behavior will I try? Where will I push my comfort zone? *...I will take the following development action:*
1. Every meeting with peers and upper-level managers where I make a comment or suggestion and then someone else raises a new topic.	1. Speak up and persist with my idea; ask what others think about my suggestions.
2. Every time I feel frustrated or find myself squelching my own opinions in meetings and conversations with peers.	2. State my position at least one more time and ask for a response or for more information from people, rather than staying quiet or backing down.
3. When I find out that an important decision is about to be made.	3. Within 48 hours, find out who the important players are and discuss my views with at least two key decision makers.
4. Before important meetings with my manager or peers.	4. Talk to at least two of the significant players beforehand so that I know their concerns and can lobby for my position.
5. Every meeting with my team.	5. Anticipate emerging problems and issues by asking my team for what they see happening. I'll bring relevant issues to my manager with my recommendations for how to respond.

3. REFLECT ON WHAT YOU HAVE LEARNED.
What will I do each day to consider what worked, what didn't work, and what I want to do next time?

◇ Review my development and business objectives first thing in the morning when I review my calendar for the day.

◇ Record insights and questions in my to-do list as they occur and transfer the most useful ones to my learning log each week following the weekly staff meeting.

4. SEEK FEEDBACK AND SUPPORT.
How will I draw on other people to track my progress, gather advice and feedback, and support my learning?

Seek feedback and information:
◇ Track the number of times my ideas are implemented in peer group.
◇ Ask Cindy and Dale for feedback after each team meeting.
◇ Talk to my manager after critical meetings where I'm trying to be influential.

Seek resources and support:
◇ Training course on influencing skills next quarter, if I'm not making adequate progress.
◇ Monthly lunch with people who are good at influencing and have political savvy.
◇ Ask my manager and my mentor for support in getting invited to key meetings, especially on the Alpha project.
◇ Review the sections I underlined in *Successful Manager's Handbook* every month or so.
◇ In six months, talk to my manager about getting on the strategic task force.

5. TRANSFER LEARNING TO THE NEXT LEVEL.
How will I periodically evaluate my progress?
Considering my goals and organizational priorities, how will I update my development strategy and learning plan?
How will I leverage what I have already learned?

◇ Review my development progress each quarter when I look at quarterly business results.
◇ Discuss my progress and current development priorities with my manager at our quarterly review meeting. Ask for her perceptions and insights.
◇ Redo The PROFILOR® in one year.

STRATEGY
FACTOR

———

Creating strategic and competitive advantage used to be reserved for the executive suite of an organization. The impact of the global marketplace, the influx of e-commerce and other technological applications, and intense competition in the marketplace have changed this practice in dramatic ways.

Operating from a strategic perspective is now a core skill for most managers. Most companies are becoming global enterprises, or at least must learn to "think globally." Additionally, creating customer loyalty by providing superior customer service and developing strong customer relationships is a key element for long-term business success. And the new rules of managerial success now include the ability to champion change and innovation.

The chapters in this section present suggestions for improving your skills in the following four key areas:

Chapter 1 – Create Strategic Advantage: Understands the organization's vision, goals, and strategies; aligns strategic priorities of one's own unit with that of the larger organization; knows the strengths and weaknesses of competitors; determines the team's critical success factors; evaluates and pursues initiatives, investments, and opportunities based on their fit with broader strategies; capitalizes on strengths and counters competitive threats.

Chapter 2 – Champion Change and Innovation: Approaches problems with curiosity and open-mindedness; generates innovative ideas and solutions; stimulates creativity and innovation in others; challenges the way it has always been done; champions new ideas and initiatives; supports those who initiate change and take risks.

Chapter 3 – Create Customer Loyalty: Understands the customer's requirements, expectations, and needs; delivers on commitments to customers; provides value and ensures exceptional customer experiences; seeks feedback from customers; effectively recovers from mistakes; removes barriers to customer service; builds a customer-focused team.

Chapter 4 – Promote Global Perspective: Analyzes the globalization of the business; anticipates the impact of trends and world events on the organization; possesses a global mind-set and encourages others to develop the same; knows how to conduct business, market products and services, and manage employees in other countries.

I
CREATE
STRATEGIC ADVANTAGE

———

- *Understand the organization's vision, goals, and strategies*
- *Analyze impacts on the business*
- *Bring cross-functional and cross-business knowledge to bear on issues*
- *Know the strengths and weaknesses of competitors*
- *Convey a thorough understanding of your area's strengths, weaknesses, opportunities, and threats*
- *Identify your team's critical success factors*
- *Pursue initiatives to capitalize on strengths and market opportunities, and to counter competitive threats*
- *Evaluate and pursue initiatives, investments, and opportunities based on their fit with broader strategies*
- *Align strategic priorities of your group with the direction and strategic priorities of the broader organization*

Introduction

Successful leaders know that strategy is not stagnant. It is an emergent process that focuses on the constant themes of competitive advantage, competitive differentiation, sustainable advantage, and barriers to entry. When a strategic opportunity arises, it's important first to recognize it as such and second to be able to do something about it quickly.

Creating strategic advantage requires a deep understanding of your own organization's strengths and weaknesses, its competitive strategy, and its current and potential customers. In addition, it requires bold and insightful knowledge of current and future competitors.

Effective managers know and capitalize on their organization's strengths. They create strategy that builds on the organization's areas of greatest strength, rather than strategy that relies on the strength of weaker areas. Effective leaders depend on data to support their strategic conclusions. They are not satisfied with today's strengths; they know the bar will be higher next time.

This chapter presents specific steps you and your team can take to position yourselves for the best possible strategic advantage.

VALUABLE TIPS

- Identify the key people or talent groups you need for your strategy to work. Focus on attracting, deploying, developing, and retaining these people.

- Use action-learning teams to identify marketplace opportunities and possible threats.

- Adopt the practice of questioning and challenging the analyses and findings of groups that have worked in an area for a long time.

- Meet with someone who was involved in setting the organization's goals and strategies to learn as much as you can about the rationale for choosing those options.

- Talk with leaders in the organization to understand the organization's approach to strategy and the reasons for the chosen approach.

- Think like your competitors. If you were to compete against you, what would you do? Where are you most vulnerable?

- Determine how the industries of your customers are changing and what impact that has on your strategy.

- Identify the best customers in your industry. Are these your customers? If they are, why? If not, why not?

- Check any tendency you and your colleagues have to talk disparagingly about competitors. Seek instead to identify what makes them good.

- Learn about your competitors as individuals. Get to know their educational background, their track record, where they have worked, their typical mode of operation, and how they achieved competitive advantage in the past.

- Include in your decision-making criteria one that evaluates options in light of the organization's key strategic issues.

- Identify assumptions that underlie the business model of your industry and figure out how the model would change—or is changing—should those assumptions change.

- Read about the organization's vision and strategies as described in industry analysts' research reports on your company.

- Obtain from your corporate communications department newspaper or magazine articles that profile or discuss your company.

- Ask peers what they measure and why so you can learn critical variables that underlie business processes.

- Anticipate how your competitors will respond to your strategic moves before you make any move in the marketplace.

- Identify any technological advances in your industry that you need to implement to ensure strategic advantage.

- Develop a plan to overcome a main weakness of your area that keeps you from adequately addressing a strategic issue.

- Read industry and technical publications looking for changes or trends that indicate new opportunities to meet customer needs.

- Keep a list of business goals, strategies, and action steps where you can see it easily and often.

Understand the organization's vision, goals, and strategies

Without a clear understanding of your organization's vision, goals, and strategies, you will be unable to set a clear direction for your group to support these goals. Too many organizations have business areas and teams pulling in their individual directions, rather than in a unified direction.

To develop a better understanding of your organization's mission and goals, consider these suggestions:

- Learn about your corporate strategy. Recognize that corporate strategy involves three core issues: the customers you serve, the organization's core competencies, and how the organization leverages these competencies to offer value to the customer and sustain strategic advantage.
  - Obtain a copy of your organization's mission, vision, goals, and strategies. Many organizations make this material easily available to their employees. The public version of this information is typically available in the annual report, through the communications department, and from investor relations.
  - Read or listen to presentations the CEO has made to the board, investors, Wall Street, and others. CEO presentations at the beginning and end of years typically communicate direction and progress toward both short-term business goals and longer-term strategic initiatives.
  - Read your organization's annual report, particularly the CEO's message to stockholders. This message typically includes a clear statement of company goals, recent progress toward longer-term objectives, and future challenges.

- Talk with people who were involved in setting the goals and strategies to learn about the options that were discussed and the rationale for the options selected.

- Talk with leaders in the organization to understand the organization's approach to strategy and the reasons for that approach. Approaches may differ in degree of planning and the role of analysis. Knowing about the different approaches can be particularly helpful when the organization's strategy appears difficult to figure out.

- Use strategic theorist Michael Treacy's work to understand the strategy. He describes three types of strategies:
  - *A total-cost strategy* emphasizes operating excellence. Operations are standardized, simplified, tightly controlled, and centrally controlled. Low cost, efficiency, and speed are optimized. Management systems are focused on integrated, reliable, high-speed transactions and compliance to norms.

- *A best-product or technical-excellence strategy* focuses on the core processes of innovation, product development, and market expansion. This strategy emphasizes product excellence rather than cost. Its business structure is flexible, so it can respond to entrepreneurial efforts. Its management systems are results-driven and measure product success, and its culture encourages creativity, innovation, and outside-the-box thinking.
- *A total-solution strategy* concentrates on customer intimacy. It focuses on the core processes of relationship management, solution development, and results management. Its structure moves decision making down in the organization to be close to the customer, and its management systems are geared toward developing specific relationship and customer-service competencies.

- Meet with a seasoned manager to share his or her knowledge of the organization's history, evolution of the company's mission, and the origin of the company's strengths and weaknesses. Discuss key success factors for the business. Ask a lot of questions to help you understand what has happened and why.

- Ask your manager to fill you in on corporate planning sessions that he or she has attended. Get his or her perspective on the company's strategies, goals, strengths, and weaknesses.

- To get an external perspective of the organization's vision and strategies, obtain from your stockbroker research reports on your company prepared by industry analysts. Contact your corporate communications department for copies of recent newspaper or magazine articles that profile or discuss your company.

- Examine the organization's corporate visions, goals, and strategies and identify relevant business-unit and product-line visions, goals, and strategies.

- Make sure that you and your employees attend company meetings in which strategies and results are discussed. Doing so keeps you on top of changes that are likely occurring and gives your employees a clearer idea of how they fit into the big picture.

- Obtain from your corporate communications department a recent copy of your company's executive briefing to security analysts, published in *Wall Street Transcripts*. This document can give you an overview of the organization's future direction and goals.

- Develop contacts with other departments to learn more about their strategic issues and new developments.

Analyze impacts on the business

Organization and business-unit strategy is not static. In fact, in most industries, the lifetime of strategy has been dramatically reduced by upheavals in businesses and industries. Therefore, to remain competitive, it is essential to constantly scan the environment to understand changes that may affect your organization and its strategy.

Forces within and outside the industry impact businesses. By researching the latest developments in your industry and related industries, talking with people, reading industry reports and business publications, utilizing consulting expertise in the areas of interest, and using action-learning teams, you can regularly assess the following common forces of change:

- *Industry changes:*
  - What are the biggest challenges in the industry? Where is your organization in relation to these challenges?
  - What are the largest changes occurring within the industry? How do these changes impact your organization? How ready is your organization?
  - How is the business model of your industry changing? What assumptions underlie the business model? What would happen if these assumptions were no longer true? For example, what if television were available at no cost? What if there were no health insurance organizations?
  - What are the greatest industry constraints to growth? How is your organization addressing these constraints?

- *Globalization:*
  - In what ways has the global economy impacted your organization? What changes do you anticipate?
  - What competitors are in or will enter the global marketplace?
  - What is the impact of global media on your business?

- *Technology change:*
  - What are the latest technological advances? Is your organization current with this technology or, better yet, in the forefront of its development?
  - What impact has technology had on your products and services, work processes, quality, and people?
  - What changes in technology are anticipated? How will they affect your industry?

- *Customers:*
  - How are the expectations of your customers changing?
  - How are the industries of your customers changing? How have those changes affected the requirements from your customers?
  - What are the expectations of the best customers in the industry? Are they your customers? Why or why not?
  - Is the organization expected to target new markets? What impact will that have on meeting customers' needs?

- *Competitive advantage:*
  - What is your current source of competitive advantage? How sustainable is this?
  - What actions are being taken to maintain this advantage or create new advantage?

- *Human capital:*
  - What do you anticipate will be the impact of human capital shortages on the success of your business strategy? Many organizations are limited in what they can accomplish because they are missing key people resources.
  - How will changing demographics affect your workforce, products and services, marketing strategies, etc.?

- *Government regulation:*
  - How do government regulations affect your organization?
  - How will government regulation affect the organization in the new markets you plan to enter?
  - What is the impact of job regulations locally, nationally, and internationally?
  - How do you manage a worldwide organization that must deal with local rules and regulations?

  If your industry is subject to regulation by federal, state, or local agencies, make an effort to stay current with new or pending legislation. Read industry and government reports to learn more about specific regulations governing such areas as safety, quality standards, training, advertising, labeling, and pricing.

Bring cross-functional and cross-business knowledge to bear on issues

Today's business challenges are complex. Effective leaders know what is going on in other parts of the organization and are able to bring cross-functional knowledge to bear on issues and opportunities. Rather than narrowly focusing on their own functional or geographic area, effective managers make it their business to develop a wide-angle perspective of the company as a whole.

Few developments or changes involve just one function or one area of knowledge. For example, the design and implementation of a new computerized inventory system to speed up distribution, and thereby improve customer service, requires the input of people with different types of expertise—systems designers, programmers, inventory managers, distribution personnel, customers, other users, and technical trainers.

This example illustrates the need to develop cross-functional or cross-disciplinary knowledge, as well as the importance of maintaining good working relationships with peers who have expertise in other areas. At the very least, having a basic knowledge of what people in other functions do can help you put together more effective teams and coordinate their efforts to maximum advantage.

To develop your understanding of other disciplines that interact with or affect your group, consider the following suggestions:

- Learn the business from the perspectives of people in other functional areas. Take advantage of the times you work with experts in other fields. Ask people from other functions about:
  - How they see the business. How is their perspective the same as or different from yours?
  - Their customers, their expectations, and their challenges.
  - Their goals and strategies. Learn why they are important.

- Listen to people from other functions talk about problems, issues, and opportunities from their point of view. Pay attention to what they notice and talk about. What knowledge and experience are they using? How is it different from yours?

- Ask peers what they measure and why. Metrics typically point to the critical variables that underlie effective business processes. Spend some time in other areas so you can get a feel for the work, the people, the pace, other resources, etc.

- Become an "armchair traveler" by reading internal and external publications that deal with your organization. Company newsletters are especially useful for providing information about what other divisions or business units are doing, including special accomplishments, products under development, new contracts, project completions, and management promotions.

- Form cross-disciplinary teams to work on complex or recurring problems, and to pursue business opportunities. Provide an open forum to enable experts in other areas to contribute their ideas to the team.

- Conduct learning sessions as part of the work the cross-functional team does together. Regularly ask the team what they are learning. Listen to what the different functional people learn. Is it the same? Different? To solidify the learning and also help you to better understand the function, determine what they will do with the learning.

- Seek out assignments in different functional areas and in both line and staff positions. To prepare for a general manager assignment, it is very helpful to have experience in two or more functional areas to increase your direct understanding of the different functions. It is also typically useful to have both line and staff experience. While line experience provides good solid strategy and execution experience, staff assignments hone individual and organizational skills of influencing without authority, and help develop your organizational savvy, cross-boundary competence, and interpersonal skills.

Know the strengths and weaknesses of competitors

Strong competitors are key to the long-term health and viability of your business. Just as demanding customers challenge you and your organization to continually improve, strong competition requires that you carefully and aggressively craft strategies that will result in sustainable competitive advantage. To do that, you need to understand your competition.

Consider that you have three groups of competitors: current competitors, future competitors in your industry, and potential competitors in different industries. It is important to keep your eye on all three so you do not miss something important.

Typically, the greatest threat is from unexpected competition, and the greatest competition comes from places where you do not expect it. Competition from different industries changes the business model of the industry and, therefore, has a huge impact on the industry.

To identify your company's future and potential competitors, determine:

- Who are your primary competitors in each business and region?

- How have these competitors changed in the last three years?

- Who will be your competitors in the future? As you follow your strategy? As you get larger? As you move geographically?

- Where may new competition come from? What companies? What industries?

The following suggestions can help you learn their strengths and weaknesses:

- Create a detailed profile of your company's top five to ten competitors. This will provide the basis from which to develop strategies for gaining competitive advantage. To create the profile, use corporate reports, industry analyses, and publications like *Standard and Poors*, to answer the following questions about each competitor:

- What are their strengths and weaknesses?
  - How have these changed in the last year or two?
  - What can they do well that you envy? What can you do well that they envy?

- What is their strategy?
  - Are they using customer intimacy, technical excellence, or efficiency?
  - What are the strengths and weaknesses relative to their strategy?

- Are there any indicators of a change in strategy?
  - Where are they investing?
  - Who have they recently hired in key positions?

- How are they differentiated in the marketplace?
  - What is their advantage? Is it sustainable?
  - What can you tell about where they see their future advantage?
  - Who are their customers? Why do they buy from them?
  - Are their customers "better" than yours in some significant way?

- What is the strength of their management team?
  - Who are they? What does that tell you?

- What people strengths and vulnerabilities do they have?

- Use an action-learning team or a cross-business unit team to map the competitive space, figure out what competitors are up to, or anticipate threats from unknown companies or industries. Obtaining new perspectives from this analysis can be quite valuable.

- Identify which competitors you need to watch most closely. Develop strategies to get information about your competitors on an ongoing basis.

- Listen to how you and your colleagues talk. Notice if you and they talk disparagingly about competitors or assume that you are on top of the competition. It is dangerous to underestimate competitors.

- Learn to think like your competitors. If you were to compete against you, what would you do? Where are you most vulnerable?

- Find out specifically whom you are up against. Learn about your competitors as individuals. Get to know their educational background, their track record, where they have worked, their typical mode of operation, and how they achieved competitive advantage in the past.

- Anticipate how your competitors will respond to your strategic moves. Consider this step as a regular part of your planning and analysis process before any move in the marketplace. Remember this lesson from chess: Anticipate many moves ahead to gain advantage.

- Ask your planning group to identify the strategic approach each of your primary competitors uses. With this information, you can anticipate their moves more accurately.

Convey a thorough understanding of your area's strengths, weaknesses, opportunities, and threats

Successful managers are keenly aware of their own area's strengths and weaknesses. To maintain that awareness, they regularly identify and assess the elements of key business processes, their supporting processes and systems, and their people. When considering a change in direction, effective leaders identify the constraints to that strategy's success and ways to address those constraints.

Effective leaders also constantly search for opportunities for sustained competitive advantage and are always on the lookout for competitor moves that threaten that advantage. They know that they must constantly add value for their customers; they assume that customer expectations will continue to increase. Therefore, to stay ahead of the competition, they avidly pursue an understanding of their current and potential customers and their industries.

To convey a thorough understanding of your area's strengths, weaknesses, opportunities, and threats, use the following suggestions:

- Regularly identify the strengths and weaknesses of your strategy, your business processes, and your approach to customers.

- Identify strategic opportunities in the marketplace where customer needs are not being met. Conduct PDI's Customer Review Process with key customers to identify unmet and future needs and to develop stronger customer loyalty.

- Use an action-learning team composed of potential leaders in the organization to conduct an analysis of areas of concern. This will provide a fresh look at the organization.

- Use action-learning teams to also identify opportunities and threats in the marketplace. Adopt the practice of questioning and challenging the analyses and findings of groups that have worked in an area for a long time. People sometimes unintentionally get stale, cut corners, or neglect to question long-held assumptions, resulting in important strategic mistakes.

- Understand people constraints to the success of your strategy. Identify the key staff or talent groups you need for your strategy to work. Focus on attracting, deploying, developing, and retaining these people.

- Review critiques of your organization and its strategy in the media, business publications, and investor community.

- Set the expectation with your management team that they will do regular assessments of their business processes. Ask to see these assessments. Periodically review progress on areas for improvement.

- Use the following process to assess strengths and weaknesses:
  1. Clearly identify the value you provide to your customers. Why should they use you?
  2. Understand your vision, goals, and strategies. What is your plan or vision for the business? What are your strategies to continue to add value for your customers?
  3. Identify the business processes at which the organization needs to excel in order to achieve its goals. What do the organization's strengths need to be to achieve your goals? Typically, you need to look at:

  Human infrastructure:
    - What are the strengths and weaknesses of your management team?
    - What do people need to do to make the value chain work? What roles are needed?
    - What skills, abilities, and attributes are needed for these roles?
    - What are the strengths and weaknesses of people in these roles? Of others available in the organization?
    - What people are available externally, if necessary?

  Technological infrastructure:
    - What technology is needed? What is available now?
    - What are the strengths and weaknesses of current technology in relation to what is needed?

  Customer relationships:
    - What are the strengths and weaknesses of customer relationships?
    - What kinds of customer relationships are needed for your strategy to work?
    - What is the probability that these relationships can be developed or maintained at the level needed?

  Financial infrastructure:
    - What financial support is needed?
    - What are the strengths and weaknesses of the financial support available?

Supplier/vendor relationships:
- What are the relationships needed?
- What are the strengths and weaknesses of the existing relationships?
- How can you develop the relationships you need?

Business processes:
- What are the business processes? How clearly are they documented, understood, and followed? How clear is the ownership of the processes?
- What are the strengths and weaknesses of the business processes?
- How are they measured?
- What can be done to improve them?

Leadership processes:
- What are the strengths and weaknesses of your leadership processes?
- What needs to be done to improve these processes?

Teaming processes:
- What are the strengths and weaknesses of your teams or team processes?
- What is needed from the organization's teams?
- What can be done to ensure these outcomes?

Develop evaluation processes for each element in the business process. Regularly assess the process and the people involved. Use this assessment as a guide for development and performance improvement.

- For the human infrastructure: Use performance management processes, objective assessment processes when the roles and expectations change, and 360-degree assessment when feedback from those in the environment is most helpful and accurate.

- For technology infrastructure: Use internal or external assessment processes that tightly link technology assessment with the strategy needs of the business.

- For customer relationships: Use PDI's Customer Review Process to get information directly from customers about the relationship.

- For leadership, team, development processes, etc.: Use an assessment process that measures your organization against best practices.

Identify your team's critical success factors

Teams are effective when they focus on what is most important—that is, the critical success factors or necessary aligned behaviors. There are activities that need to be done—and done well—to achieve your goals.

To focus on your team's critical success factors, take the following steps:

- Identify your team's critical success factors and clearly understand your customers' requirements by using the following process:

  1. Chart the business processes for which your team is responsible. Identify the pivotal parts of the process. Then ask each team member to identify his or her primary job responsibilities in a way that shows his or her contribution to the goals of the team. For example, "answering customer calls in a way that makes them feel they are taken care of" is a better description of the activity than just "answering phones." And "providing accurate, timely sales forecasts to marketing" is better for this purpose than just "forecasting sales."

  2. Compile your team's lists into one master list. Add appropriate items from your review of past successes and failures. Then ask team members to weigh the importance of each responsibility relative to the strategic goals and the needs of your important stakeholders (especially customers). Use a scale of 1 to 5, as follows:

     5 = absolutely necessary
     4 = critically important
     3 = important
     2 = preferred
     1 = not important

  3. Review the rank-ordered list from others' perspectives. Would your customers agree with this priority? Use actual information from customers, rather than guess what they may think. Would your manager or management team agree? How about your divisional or corporate executives? Does this prioritization support the strategic direction of your larger organization? Make any necessary changes to the list based on this review.

- Keep your list of key success factors on hand at all times. Use it to help you make decisions from a more strategic point of view, and to ensure that your team is always keeping its focus on the "20 percent that makes 80 percent of the difference."

- Whenever you propose something new, identify the key success factors for this new endeavor and determine how they will be achieved. Then you can manage the "right stuff."

Pursue initiatives to capitalize on strengths and market opportunities, and to counter competitive threats

Countless initiatives vie for attention in organizations. Successful leaders focus the energy of their organization on the key initiatives that will have the greatest strategic impact. Whether the initiative focuses on leveraging strengths to gain market share, investing in new technology that will pay off in the future, or countering competitive threats, the key to strategic success is the ability to analyze the current situation, determine how to gain sustainable competitive advantage, and execute the plan.

When a strategic opportunity arises, it's important first to recognize it as such and second to do something about it quickly.

To identify and pursue such opportunities, use the following process:

1. Identify your current key strategic opportunities by answering these questions with your team:
   - What are the key drivers of customers' decisions today?
   - What do we anticipate will be the key drivers in the future?
   - What role will technology play in changing the industry?
   - In what ways are our customers' customers changing? What is happening in their industry and in their customers' industry?
   - Where will our future competition come from?

2. Review your own and your competitors' value chains by answering the following questions:
   - How do our products and services compare with our competitors'? What are our strengths and weaknesses?
   - What activities and processes give us a competitive advantage? What do we have or do that is special and cannot be easily duplicated?
   - What activities and processes give our competitors an advantage?
   - What are the major differences among our competitors?
   - Which barriers to entry will no longer exist in five years?
   - What have the industry's chief limitations been in the past?
   - What influence will legislation and public policy have on our industry?
   - What are our competitors doing differently now or are likely to do in the future to capitalize on these opportunities? (These are the threats.)
   - What competitive threats must we address?
   - How can we leverage our strengths to gain sustainable advantage?

3. Ask your team to evaluate this information and determine where opportunities lie. Identify the information you need to know to determine which opportunities you should pursue.

4. Based on the analysis, decide what strategies and actions will have the greatest impact.

5. Identify areas in which you are vulnerable. For example, if you know that your competitors are investing heavily in technology and you are not, you may soon be in trouble.
   - If you are a knowledge-based business, be aware that your greatest threat is probably not having the people you need with the skills you need when you need them. Therefore, anticipate this problem and develop a human-capital strategy that will address recruitment, selection, deployment, development, and retention issues before they cause you even more problems.

Evaluate and pursue initiatives, investments, and opportunities based on their fit with broader strategies

The purpose of strategy is to help to keep the eye on the ball. Effective leaders use strategy on a regular basis to help them decide where to invest critical time and energy—an organization's most limited resources. To stay focused on what's important, use these suggestions:

- Write down the business goals, strategies, and action steps, and display them in a place easily accessible to you. If they are in a form longer than one page, shorten them.

- Develop a theme or phrase for you and your team that quickly and simply states your focus. Examples include: "Fast, but friendly"; "Keep it simple"; and "Local and global." Use this theme as a short-cut reminder in discussions—e.g., "Does this meet our 'local and global' criteria?"

- Identify the strategic issues. These may be specific goals, constraints to success, or critical business processes. When you are making decisions, check to see if the decision involves any of the strategic issues. For example, if a strategic issue is to develop leadership talent from within the organization, keep that in mind as a criteria for new hires. This means that you would want to hire people who have potential, not those who can just do the current job.

- Ask teams to establish criteria for their decision making that include the important strategic issues. For example, if a strategic issue is that the organization needs to improve its processes, then a criterion for decision making may be, "What does this do to improve processes?"

- Post criteria for evaluation that you want teams to use when they are making decisions.

- When decisions are made, include the rationale for the decision. Basing your rationale on strategic issues will help people to view those issues as important.

Align strategic priorities of your group with the direction and strategic priorities of the broader organization

Unless you are at the top of the organization, others set the vision and direction of the organization. Your responsibility is to bring the corporate vision, goals, and strategies down to the next level. You and your team or business unit can then develop a vision, goals, and strategies consistent with the level above.

If you are part of a business line or functional group, your vision, goals, and strategies will reflect those of the business or function above you.

If you are in the process of creating and confirming the vision, goals, and strategies for your group, consider the following steps:

1. Obtain copies of the corporate and/or business line's vision, goals, and strategies. If you were not involved in their development, talk with people who were involved to better understand the direction.

2. Share your understanding of the vision, goals, and strategies with your team. Provide the background information so the direction makes sense. It is often useful for the team to know the strategic options discussed to help to give a richer understanding of the direction chosen.

3. Discuss your expectations with the group, including the methodology you want to use to arrive at the vision, goals, and strategies for your part of the organization. It helps to provide some reading or model of strategy creation so team members approach the task using a similar methodology. Otherwise, considerable time is spent trying to agree on how you will carry out the process itself.

4. Once you have decided the vision, goals, and strategies for the business unit or team, review them against the criteria your team should be using to ensure accomplishment of the corporate and business unit goals. Look for alignment. Where alignment is missing, determine if there is good reason for the lack. You will want to discuss this with your manager.

If you already have goals and strategies, consider this process:

1. Review the team or business goals and strategies against the corporate or business unit goals and strategies. Where is the alignment? Where are there differences?

2. Determine how to resolve those areas that lack alignment.
   - You may want to discuss the lack of alignment and the reasons for it with your manager. This discussion may result in agreement that there are some goals you need to have that are not in alignment, or it may result in the need to change the goals.
   - You may want to discuss the lack of alignment with peers, explain your rationale, and see if they are willing to support it. Most likely you will need their support in some way, so it's a good idea to get their agreement ahead of time.

3. On an ongoing basis, monitor the team's work for consistency with the plan and the priorities.

4. Ensure that your resources are aligned and adequate to achieve the goals.

Your business strategy needs to be a living and guiding focus for what you and your team do.

RESOURCES

The resources for this chapter begin on page 622.

2
CHAMPION CHANGE AND INNOVATION

PART 1: DEVELOP PERSONAL CREATIVITY
- *Increase your mental flexibility*
- *Determine when to use creative thinking*
- *Approach problems with curiosity and open-mindedness*
- *Make use of existing information*
- *Generate innovative ideas and solutions*
- *Find ways to extend and apply innovative ideas to enhance business results*
- *Think positively when faced with obstacles*

PART 2: ENCOURAGE INNOVATION IN OTHERS
- *Encourage innovation in your department*
- *Use logical and intuitive approaches*
- *Use brainstorming to generate innovative ideas*
- *Stimulate creative ideas and experimentation in others*

PART 3: CHAMPION CHANGE INITIATIVES
- *Challenge the way it has always been done*
- *Champion new ideas and initiatives*
- *Support those who initiate change*
- *Encourage others to take appropriate risks*
- *Motivate others to welcome change*

Introduction

In the 21st century, the demand for change and innovation is challenging and enormous. Fierce competition abounds from both traditional competitors and brand new entries. Shorter time cycles, larger mergers, instant communication, and more rigorous customer requirements are all common. The boundaries of markets and industries are increasingly colliding. Top competitors one month become of little concern the next, when a tiny dot-com business or industry revolutionaries make your business model obsolete.

Shortages of skilled employees have resulted in fundamental changes in the relationships between employees and employers. People work at an organization as long as it benefits them. When it no longer does, they move on. Gone are the days when a traditional autocratic management style is tolerated. Employees are extremely valuable. It is the leader's job to attract and keep good employees.

The result is tremendous pressure on managers to lead their part of the organization through these changes, to challenge their teams to continually improve, and to stay on top of the competitive game. At the same time, the ability to generate and successfully implement creative solutions is essential in business today, when an organization's survival and success depend on how it responds to a changing world with the right value equation recognized by the market. Success involves not only coming up with original and innovative solutions, but also being resourceful by taking what is and making it better.

Effective leaders need to do far more than simply manage change; they need to passionately champion both change and innovation. This chapter presents processes you can use to champion change and innovation in your organization.

VALUABLE TIPS

- Distinguish between and respect the two phases of your creative process: voicing creative ideas, where the quantity of suggestions prevails (diverging process), and sorting out the answers, where the quality of the suggestions prevails (converging process).

- In the creativity phase, suspend your critical judgment—that part of you that says, "It won't work." Instead think in positive terms: "It may work because...."

- Talk about the situation with someone from a different discipline.

- Talk with others in the organization, colleagues outside the organization, and friends to see how they have addressed similar situations or problems.

- Generate as many options as you can during both the problem-identification phase and the alternatives-generation phase of the problem-solving process.

- If you run out of ideas, take a break. Later, redefine the problem and look at it from a different perspective.

- Don't be satisfied with your first idea. Push yourself to generate other ideas before committing to one.

- To get your creative juices flowing and reduce your self-criticism, practice coming up with what may at first seem like "way-out" ideas.

- When considering alternatives, ask yourself and others "why not?" instead of "why?"

- Avoid prematurely censoring ideas, and don't be concerned about whether ideas are flowing in a logical sequence.

- Identify the change champions in your organization and work with them to support and initiate change.

- Use a multifunctional task group to identify opportunities for change.

- Through books or courses, learn about a change model that can help you understand how people change and, therefore, how you can better lead and manage change.

- Communicate your vision of the change to others so they can more easily understand and buy into the change.

- Expect resistance to change; develop strategies to deal with it.

- Educate others about change and how people typically react to it.

- Treat resistance to change as a problem to solve, not as a character flaw.

- Read material different from the kind you typically read. For example, if you usually read journals in your field, read biographies of artists or research from another field.

- To further stimulate your creativity, try drawing problems instead of writing them down.

- To loosen yourself up, try a warm-up activity, such as spending ten minutes enumerating solutions to a question like, "What can you do with a thousand paper clips?"

PART 1:
DEVELOP PERSONAL CREATIVITY

Increase your mental flexibility

Mental flexibility is the ability to adjust to new information and to consider a broad range of alternatives when addressing a challenge. People who think inflexibly generally hold to policy, display rigidity in analyzing issues by discarding alternatives before thinking them through, and believe that each situation has only one right answer. To become more flexible, follow these guidelines:

- Listen to other people's opinions and suggestions. First identify all the positive aspects of their viewpoint before taking a more critical approach.

- Watch for snap reactions. Rather than assuming that the first alternative that enters your mind is the best solution, write it down and then consider other opinions.

- Try to build on other people's opinions by adopting a "yes and..." instead of a "yes, but..." attitude.

- Once you have defined a problem and generated solutions, challenge yourself to think how you would defend the problem from the opposite point of view.

- Practice mental flexibility by doing brainteasers, such as the ones presented later in this chapter, to help get into the habit of challenging your assumptions.

- Ask trusted coworkers to provide feedback on situations in which you tend to be overly opinionated or rigid in your thinking. Most people have specific problem areas. Recognizing the fact that you are becoming inflexible is the first step in initiating change.

Determine when to use creative thinking

Before diving into a creative challenge-solving process, first evaluate whether the situation at hand would be best solved through a creative-thinking process or through more traditional means. Use the following guidelines to determine when you should employ a creative-thinking process:

USE CREATIVE PROBLEM SOLVING WHEN	USE TRADITIONAL PROBLEM SOLVING WHEN
• Problems keep recurring. • You want to do things differently. • Problems are ambiguous. • You are not sure how to evaluate the problem. • Facts are unknown; feelings abound. • Causes are unknown. • Unpredictable and risky solutions are acceptable. • Something that has not been a problem has become one.	• Problems seldom recur. • You want to do things better. • Problems are well defined. • All essential criteria for evaluating the problem are known. • Facts are central to the process. • Causes are definite and defined. • Corrective solutions are acceptable. • The standard "way it has always been done" is no longer working.

Approach problems with curiosity and open-mindedness

Creative people engage in undisciplined, open-minded, and uncritical thinking in the initial stages of the problem-solving process. Remaining open-minded allows you to generate more alternatives.

To increase your use of creative approaches, try the following suggestions:

• Realize that how you view a situation often corresponds to how you approach it. Develop a more positive mind-set; don't think in terms of problems to solve, but challenges to meet and exceed. Examine what you've done in the past few weeks when faced with new situations. Did you look at these as unpleasant or disruptive, or as an adventure or challenge?

• Look at your style to see if there are certain kinds of situations that excite you, that make you curious and enthusiastic, and others that are unappealing. What are the differences? Frame those situations that don't stimulate you such that they resemble those that do.

• When generating ideas, spend more time in the initial stages of challenge-formulation. Broadly scan the alternatives, challenging yourself to view the problem from at least three different perspectives—for example, from the views of your customers, your suppliers, and your competitors. By spending more time defining the problem in a multitude of ways, you will be able to generate a broader range of possible solutions.

- Use the "W" questions (why, where, what, who, when, and how) more in approaching situations. They'll increase your understanding of the challenge and its relation to other issues. These links can lead you to greater enthusiasm and satisfaction.

- Constantly expose yourself to new ideas and trends. Build your intellectual curiosity by developing your knowledge of the world around you. Get into the habit of reading newspapers and periodicals for current events, technical journals for new developments in your field, and books for ideas relating to your work and life.

- Don't miss opportunities to meet and talk with people from backgrounds and cultures different from yours. Because their perspectives are likely to be quite different from yours, they can show you a fresh perspective that will enrich your own.

Make use of existing information

Innovation does not necessarily require doing, making, or thinking something that did not exist before. For example, if your task is to create a training program, don't "reinvent the wheel" or copy those that already exist. This can be a waste of time or unethical. Instead, learn as much as you can about how others have done the task. Then use their ideas, along with your own, to design a unique but solid program that suits your particular needs. To put this concept into practice, follow these guidelines:

1. Choose an area related to your job that you think would benefit from innovation, such as a time-consuming process that may be a bottleneck.

2. Obtain information about the situation from available resources.
   - Attend trade shows or conferences.
   - Talk with people who are knowledgeable in your chosen area and capitalize on their ideas. For instance, call your local university and talk with a subject-matter expert.
   - Talk with people who have dealt with the same issue and learn what they have done. For example, approach people working in a (noncompetitive) business sector different from yours to exchange your respective practices.

3. Analyze what you have learned in order to see what will work in your situation. Look at your resources and develop your implementation strategy. Convince others that your proposal will be an improvement. Then implement it.

Generate innovative ideas and solutions

One of your challenges as a manager is to help your group "think outside the box" about the problems they encounter. Managers often need to take the lead in this activity by demonstrating alternative solutions that are possible and feasible. Consider the following suggestions for coming up with fresh perspectives and innovative approaches.

- Try the following brainteaser activities (answers appear at the end of this chapter):
  1. In the illustration below, connect all of the nine dots using four consecutive straight lines. Follow these two requirements:
     - The end of one line must touch the beginning of the next.
     - When drawing the lines, don't lift your pen or pencil from the paper.

  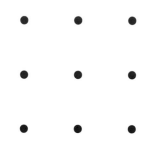

  2. Complete the following series in a creative way.

- Think of yourself as a creative genius. One of the greatest impediments to creativity is believing that you aren't creative. Believing that you are creative will help you be creative.

- Change your scene. A different physical environment may be all it takes to generate innovative ideas.

- Approach the problem differently. For example, instead of putting your problem on paper in written form, draw it out. Drawing can stimulate images, concepts, and intuition, while writing lends itself to facts, numbers, and logic. Chart your problem and illustrate different aspects of it; turn it into a motion picture in your mind.

- Engage in an activity that forces you to operate outside your comfort zone.

- Argue the other side. This may move you to commit to your original idea all the more strongly, or it may cause you to modify your idea or abandon it completely.

- Believe that a solution is possible. When you're faced with a problem, your confidence may wane. Snap out of it! Believe that every step you take will bring you closer to an effective solution.

- Turn your ideas into action. Be relentless about putting your ideas into practice. See what works and what doesn't. You'll not only enjoy what you've conjured up and exert a more positive influence, but you'll be more creative in the future.

- Form cross-functional teams. Make them also cross-cultural whenever you can. Involve people from other functions who have different styles from the rest of your team. Avoid hierarchy in the group.

- View risk taking and failure as an exciting form of learning.

Find ways to extend and apply innovative ideas to enhance business results

Innovative and creative ideas are needed to solve business problems, but they are the critical and necessary ingredient to identifying and creating both enhanced current products and services and creating blockbuster new, innovative ones.

To apply innovative ideas to enhance business results, try the following suggestions:

- Clearly understand the priority of product development and product excellence in your competitive business strategy. If you intend to be successful because you have the best products, and your customers will buy and stay with you because you continue to have the most innovative products, then you need to place the primary priority on stimulating creative ideas that meet or anticipate customer needs, and on bringing these new services and products to market regularly and quickly.

- When product development is a priority, ensure that management systems and processes exist to support it. This includes support for research and development and product marketing; establishing and disbanding high-performance teams to create new services and products and bring them to market; and incentive plans that reward creativity, innovation, product introduction, and new product success. Make sure, also, that developing the scalable infrastructure to support the new products or services is a high priority.

- Establish knowledge-sharing and learning systems so that teams and people can learn from one another rapidly and thus move quickly from idea conception to product creation. Ask your management team to ensure that people are using lessons learned rather than making the same mistakes repeatedly.

- When a new product or service is created, deliberately identify line extensions. While the first product is being introduced, initiate the process for developing and managing the line extensions.

- Decide what percentage of revenue should come from new products. Then manage the business processes to support this direction.

Think positively when faced with obstacles

When you feel that a task is impossible or that an obstacle cannot be overcome, stop yourself from thinking these negative thoughts; they close down your mental processes and prevent you from being resourceful.

You can overcome your feeling of being stuck by using the following techniques:

- Acknowledge that you are stuck; once you realize that your problem-solving processes are blocked, there are a number of techniques you can use to get past the block.

- Think positively. Instead of telling yourself that the task is impossible, tell yourself that you have reached a momentary impasse and that a solution does exist and will eventually come to you. Adopt a "can-do" attitude. Remind yourself that if the task were easy to solve, it wouldn't be a challenge.

- View the obstacle as an opportunity to find a new approach. You'll be in a much better position to create or improve methods when the current ones aren't working.

- Take a break from the problem and return to it later with a fresh perspective.

- Avoid censoring your ideas. Suspend your critical judgments until later.

- Conceptualize the problem, redefine it, and look at it from a different perspective.

- Imagine how the most resourceful person you know would react to the same situation.

- Ask for help. When a new perspective on the problem is required, others may be able to help you develop this perspective. Seek ideas and suggestions from people with perspectives or backgrounds different from your own.

PART 2:
ENCOURAGE INNOVATION IN OTHERS

Encourage innovation in your department

Successful leaders encourage innovation by creating a climate in which individuals feel free to present their ideas without fear of criticism. To foster this type of climate, over the next month, implement two or three techniques for generating new ideas in group discussion.

Following are examples of these techniques:

- Set aside time at your regular staff meeting to discuss new, innovative ideas. Stress the fact that ideas need not be fully thought out.

- Promote a climate in which people initially encourage, rather than criticize, new ideas. Ask people to first discuss what they like, rather than what they dislike, about an idea.

- Initiate two or three sessions dedicated to brainstorming on a particular issue or question. These need not be formal sessions; if a problem arises during a staff meeting, suggest that the group brainstorm to generate as many solutions as possible.

- Reward people for their ideas by thanking them and telling others about their good ideas. Champion their ideas and help to implement them. Success and the belief that one's good ideas will be acted upon go a long way toward encouraging innovation.

- Foster the attitude that innovative thinking is a part of everyone's job, regardless of function and level of responsibility.

As people's fear of criticism diminishes, you will see your department's climate change and hear people voice more new ideas.

Use logical and intuitive approaches

Both logical and intuitive thinking are necessary for creating the optimum climate for innovation. Logical thinking is a sequential process, while intuitive thinking tends to be holistic. Idea-stimulation techniques can also be classified in these ways. To maximize innovative solutions, make sure you and your team members utilize both ways of thinking and generating ideas.

Logical approaches: A logical, or linear, approach provides structure and a logical sequence of steps for generating alternative solutions. Following are some examples of linear approaches:

- *Matrix analysis.* This approach uses a two- or three-dimensional matrix to help identify where to look further for new ideas.

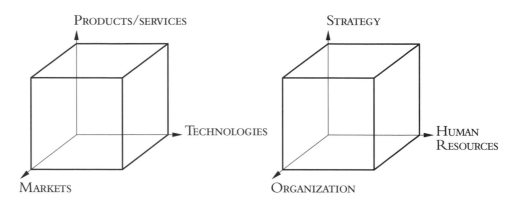

The way to use it is to list on each axis the items pertaining to the category, from core (close to the origin, lower back corner) to peripheral (toward the arrow). After having completed the list for all three axes, it's easy to identify a number of combinations that have not yet been used.

- *Attribute listing.* This is a simple process in which you define all the attributes or components of a procedure or product that you wish to improve. Then, you look at each attribute for possible ways to improve it.

For example, a telephone has the following attributes, in addition to many others:
- Receiver
- Casing or body of the phone
- Mechanism for dialing

Each of these attributes has been improved over the years, including:
- Receivers have been improved with headsets, and even eliminated by speakerphones.
- Heavy metals have been replaced by lightweight plastics that are available in a variety of decorative colors and styles.
- Rotary dials have been replaced by touch pads with quick touch-tone dialing.

- *Force-field analysis.* This is a method for exploring the feasibility of possible solutions by identifying a solution's strong points and potential problem areas. This method can help you clarify your vision, identify strengths that can be used to their fullest potential, and pinpoint weaknesses that can be overcome or minimized.

Using the following format, write an objective statement of the problem you wish to solve, and then describe the factors blocking and the factors supporting a successful outcome.

PROBLEM DEFINITION: _____

BLOCKING FACTORS	SUPPORTING FACTORS
FORCES	
NEGATIVE (-)	POSITIVE (+)
1.	1.
2.	2.
3.	3.

Once you have completed this chart, you can analyze the positive and negative forces to identify ways to strengthen the positive forces, weaken the negative forces, or add new positive forces.

- *Reframing questions.* This is a technique that helps you view your problem from a different perspective. It involves asking questions about your problem in a way that lets you examine it from a broader perspective and identify the less-obvious aspects of the problem.

  An example of a reframing question is, "What are the facts of this problem or situation, and how can each of these facts be challenged?" If you apply this question to a delivery problem, for example, you and your team may determine that one of the facts of the situation is that you must ship product, in full, to your customer on Tuesday mornings. By challenging this assumption, you might find that your customer would be equally, or more, satisfied with shipments on Tuesday evenings or Wednesday mornings, which would ease your delivery person's tight schedule.

- *The design tree.* This is a way to map ideas around a concept or idea that you wish to expand upon, such as a technology or a product.

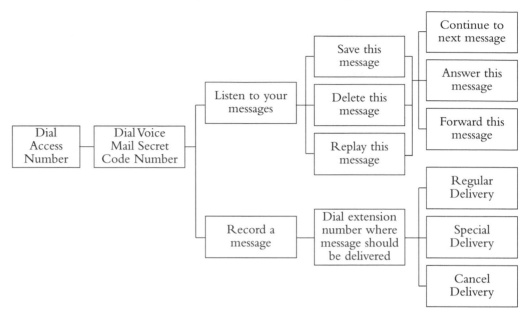

Intuitive approaches: An intuitive approach, on the other hand, looks at the whole instead of the parts. Solutions are often arrived at in one larger step instead of a sequence of steps. Following are some examples of intuitive approaches:

- *Imagery.* This is a method of generating ideas by imagining experiences, scenes, or symbols. After having described and written down in detail their impressions, participants are invited to find links between each of the words on the flip chart (or screen) and the challenge at stake for idea-generating and problem-solving purposes. This method can also be used to clarify or depict aspects of a project or work process.

- *Drawing.* Drawing is an effective way of bringing out intuitive processes through the communication of impressions and symbols, rather than words. Drawing can be used as a technique for putting imagery on paper.

- *Analogies.* Analogies draw similarities or a parallel between two situations or things that would otherwise be dissimilar. This approach serves to make an unfamiliar situation or problem more understandable and can be used to discover new approaches and insights to problems. For example, the invention of Velcro™ was based on the analogy of burdock burrs clinging to clothing.

- *Dreams.* Both daydreams and night dreams may produce images and key words that can be creatively applied to real-world situations.

Use brainstorming to generate innovative ideas

When a number of people gather to solve a problem, their ideas can build on each other. This is especially true in an environment that encourages idea generation. To encourage the sharing of ideas in your organization, conduct brainstorming sessions, using the following guidelines:

1. Organize an informal brainstorming session to discuss new approaches to persistent departmental problems or innovative applications of existing products and/or services. The purpose of the session should be to generate as many novel ideas as possible. Limit the number of participants to seven to ensure the active participation of all members. Find a place to work that will be free of interruptions.

2. Present a clear definition/perimeter of the challenge: what it is about, what it is not about.

3. Set a time limit for the brainstorming to generate a sense of urgency. A group usually runs out of ideas after 30 to 45 minutes of intense brainstorming. Thus, it is preferable to divide the initial challenge into subissues and tackle each of them using a different brainstorming tool.

4. To create the proper environment, announce these ground rules at the beginning of the session:
   - The emphasis is on quantity rather than quality (Phase 1: Creativity). Avoid blocking creative thinking with unnecessary concentration on detail. For the moment, implementation constraints should be ignored. Draw the following picture on a flip chart and make it clear for people where they are:

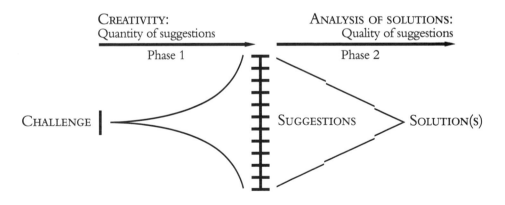

   - No criticism of ideas is allowed. All ideas will be evaluated at a later time in the converging phase (Phase 2: Analysis of solutions).
   - People may add to already-suggested ideas or combine ideas.

5. Appoint a person to record all of the ideas, even ones that have been mentioned before. Use a flip chart so the ideas are in full view of the participants. Record the ideas in a nonsequential fashion to avoid favoring the first or last ideas presented. Whenever a sketch or drawing may clarify a point, invite the individual who produced the idea to make the drawing him- or herself. Use several flip charts at the same time. Hang them on the wall to make the creative production visible to all.

6. Remind participants of the ground rules, and then let loose. Have fun. As a leader, you are responsible for stopping criticism, preventing judgments, and trying to get everyone to participate.

7. At the end of the meeting, or at a later occasion, review the ideas (Phase 2: Analysis of solutions). You can perform this review yourself, get other group members involved, or send the ideas to a preselected committee for evaluation. Your mission at this point is to identify the ideas that could actually be implemented.

When the group is comfortable with this process, you may want to invite individuals from different levels in your department or division to participate. Whenever feasible, invite a client of the challenge to participate as well. A brainstorming session can serve as a communication bridge, helping people to work together as a team.

Stimulate creative ideas and experimentation in others

To switch from a corporate culture that endorses conformity and compliance to one that fosters creativity and initiative, you need to show that you support innovation in others.

Try the following techniques for encouraging creativity in others:

- Allow time for ideas to brew before asking for a solution that can be implemented. Creativity typically is not produced on demand. People need time to think; some daydreaming must be allowed.

- Provide challenges and permit freedom in how tasks are carried out. When employees bring problems to you, ask them to propose the solutions. This will force them to tap into their own creative energy.

- Protect "idea" people. Creative people are often not popular. Others may feel threatened or annoyed by their ideas for change. Their peers may regard them with suspicion, even hostility. Ensure that others understand why idea people are important. Idea generators need a champion and a cheerleader; give them the support they need.

- Tolerate failure. Recognize that creativity and risk taking go hand-in-hand. To maximize creativity, minimize the fear of taking risks.

- Recognize the people who suggest creative solutions by giving them both tangible rewards (adequate workspace, budget, merit salary increases, promotions) and intangible rewards (special attention, public credit for their ideas, challenging tasks).

- Provide innovators with opportunities to network and to learn what others are doing by attending seminars, workshops, and professional meetings. Allow them to have contact with your customers, with others in the organization, and with other economic sectors (via benchmarking, for example).

PART 3:
CHAMPION CHANGE INITIATIVES

Challenge the way it has always been done

Managers can no longer accept "the way it has always been done" as an excuse to avoid making changes. They increasingly need to question status-quo assumptions. To break out of the usual way of doing things, try the following ideas:

- Challenge your employees to find ways of improving business and work processes. Use various forums (staff meetings, private conversations, performance plans) to stimulate and reinforce the need to make continuous improvements.

- Eliminate organizational barriers to innovation. For example:
  - Because specialists may overlook relationships outside their area of expertise, combine people from various areas when you are developing new ideas.
  - Do not overdirect, overobserve, or overreport. These activities will inhibit your employees' ability to be innovative.
  - Reward flexibility. "The way things have always been done" is often a refuge for the inflexible.
  - Remove policy barriers whenever possible. People are often encouraged to analyze their suggestions in terms of existing procedures and policies; thus, they may be discouraged from proposing solutions contrary to current guidelines.
  - Reserve a portion of the budget for implementing innovations. Financial plans frequently do not allow for the cost of promoting an innovation.
  - Identify people who may have hidden agendas or motives for maintaining the status quo. Look for alternative ways to meet their needs.

- Challenge statements that close off alternatives (for example, "It has to be done like this," "They'll never accept…," or "We can't…"). Reward employees who have a "can-do" attitude.

- Support individuals who challenge assumptions and question the way things are done. Unfortunately, organizations typically reward those who avoid rocking the boat. Promote innovation and motivation by actively encouraging questions and positive challenges.

- Be open to the possibility of changing your decisions after you have made them. Listen to new information and gather new data about the solutions you have implemented. Based on this information, decide whether to revisit the decision-making process.

Champion new ideas and initiatives

Successful leaders reach beyond their everyday assignments and responsibilities by identifying and championing new initiatives and improvements within their organization. Successful leaders do not just manage change; they proactively champion it by identifying what needs to be improved and changed.

Some people operate with the belief that "if it's not broken, don't fix it." Change champions operate with the belief that "if it isn't broken, look to see how it can be improved. Things can always be better."

Consider the following suggestions when you need to improve your ability to champion new ideas and change.

- Identify strategic change initiatives:
  - Look at your current and future goals. Then identify the barriers or potential barriers to achieving or exceeding those goals. Identify the one or two changes that would have the greatest impact on these goals.
  - Identify the core assumptions that underlie what and how you and your team work and think. What are the fundamental parts of the business process or business model you use? What would happen if you could change these fundamentals or someone else figured out a way to change them?

  For example, until recently a store was necessary to retail selling. Customers went to a store to buy things. That is no longer true; the Internet has changed retail business. Right now people go to movie theaters to see first-run films. What if you did not need to go to the theater, if you could just order them?

- When doing environmental scans or competitive analyses, or anticipating customer needs, look for directions in the business that will require fundamental changes and/or strategic changes. For example, are your competitors making investments in areas you are not? Are your customers looking to new markets? If so, what are the implications for their requirements? Is new technology being discussed as a remote possibility that will impact your business?

- When you are asked to champion a strategic change identified by others:
  - Find out the reasons for the initiative, the anticipated outcomes, the benefits seen from the point of view of different constituencies, the concerns others have, and the supports and barriers to the change, including people, technology, systems, policies, and readiness.
  - Gain a thorough understanding of what has been done so far and the process used. Often the greatest challenge is not the initiative itself, but how it is being or has been led. If people who thought they should have been involved were not involved early in the process, challenges and resistance will arise.

- Create a clear, compelling vision of the change, the reasons for it, and the benefits to the business and those impacted.

- Identify a team to lead the change with you. Include on the team people who are effective change leaders and supporters and who need to be involved in the change. Ensure that you have a small team for strategizing, planning, and decision making. Involve as many people as you need to implement the change by using task teams and short-term teams for particular parts of the change.

- Identify the people whose support you need to make the change happen or to allow the change to occur. Determine how to get their support and cooperation.

- Take the initiative to share your ideas, conclusions, and reasons for excitement and commitment with other people. Explain what's in it for them.

- Develop the supporting infrastructure and eliminate barriers in the organization that interfere with your initiative. Bring organizational systems into line with your change. For example, make sure the promotion system fits with the performance appraisal system. People should be promoted based on the same criteria by which they are evaluated.

- Develop metrics to measure the success of the initiative. Unless you establish new metrics that include the change, it will not become institutionalized. Carefully analyze the proposed metrics, so you are certain they do not have unintended consequences you don't want.

- If the organization is not ready for your idea, plant seeds. Plan a strategy to get the necessary support over time. Many changes take years to germinate and grow.

Support those who initiate change

Change agents are needed in organizations, yet they also find themselves in difficulty because they challenge the status quo. To develop future leadership talent and to stimulate and support the change and innovation needed in your organization, it's important to encourage and support those who initiate change. This support includes activities such as encouraging people to initiate change, providing knowledge and skills about leading change, helping people to plan and implement change, and being available to coach.

The following suggestions can help you support change-initiators in your organization:

- Provide people with an understanding of why change and improvement is important. Use examples from your own company and the industry of when the organization was successful and unsuccessful in identifying and executing on the needed change.

- Clearly set improvement expectations for your employees. Focus improvements in terms of cost and efficiency, but also innovation. Improvements in cost and efficiency can improve productivity and profitability, but typically do not increase market share or drive product or service development.

- Model strategic change leadership. On each project have at least one employee whose job is to watch you and document the team's process and learning. Watching you will help educate this person about how to lead change; it will also help you learn what you do. The documentation of the team's process will help the team learn, which will result in increased competency among your teams in leading change.

- Depending on how much experience your employee has in leading change, make yourself available to talk over plans and strategies. Help the person think through what he or she wants to do and how to do it. Do not simply give advice; help him or her think through ideas by asking questions, using reflective statements, etc.

- When appropriate, contact people to smooth the way for your employee to talk with them. For example, you might tell a colleague that the employee will be talking with him or her about an idea for an improvement. You might include the fact that the person has a great track record for anticipating client needs.

- Provide introductions and visible support when necessary.

- Practice conversations and presentations with the person, so that they are ready for major presentations or discussions.

- Provide opportunities for them to attend change-management seminars or workshops.

- Give ongoing feedback so that the person knows your perspective of what is going on and his or her skills at leading the change.

- After a meeting and certainly after the project concludes, debrief with the person about what he or she learned.

Encourage others to take appropriate risks

Change does not occur without risk. If you are afraid of taking risks or of rocking the boat, you will have a difficult time leading change yourself and encouraging your employees to champion new ideas and initiatives or to lead change. On the other hand, taking unneeded or large risks is not wise either. Therefore, it is important to strike a balance between wise risk taking and foolhardy behavior.

- When considering a change, think of it as a risk that needs to be assessed and planned for. As with any risk, assess the risk of doing it and not doing it.

    For example, changing the selling model your account managers use may be a risk because they do not know the new model well, it may involve new skills, and it may require a different incentive structure. On the other hand, the current model of selling may have resulted in decreased sales over the last three quarters, loss of key accounts, and loss of key sales managers.

- Identify the possible negative consequences of the change. Whenever possible, determine what you can do so these potential consequences are no longer a risk, or plan for what you will do if the negative consequences occur.

- Tell your staff that you prefer wise risk taking to the status quo. If you are trying to move a conservative group, you may go as far as saying you much prefer action and mistakes to the status quo.

- In assessing risk, look at how skilled the person or team is at recovering from mistakes. Some teams can take greater risks because they are superb at recovery.

- Use force-field analysis or risk-management analysis strategies to assess risk. The risk-management area of your organization can show you the techniques they use to manage risk.

- When mistakes are made, focus on learning from them. Use debriefing sessions. Ask what went well and what people learned.

- Capture learning and use it the next time. For example, when the team begins a new project, ask what they learned about this kind of project the last time. Ask the person who led a "failure or mistake" to consult with the group to help them avoid the same mistakes. This will enable people to save face by becoming experts from their learning experiences.

Motivate others to welcome change

Change is occurring more frequently every day. Organizations often need to move quickly to maximize opportunities. Employees who expect and welcome change will be a step ahead. Use the following suggestions to prepare your staff to expect change and learn to adapt quickly:

- Prepare your organization to expect change as a part of doing business and being successful. To do this:
  - Build in the expectation of continuous improvement. Ask employees about improvements they have identified. Set the clear expectation that spotting opportunities is part of their job.
  - On an annual basis, identify out-dated assumptions, changes in the external environment (for example, with competitors, the market, the economy), and opportunities for change.
  - Frequently reinforce effective performance during the change period.

- In presenting change, take care to emphasize its benefits. When approaching individuals, support the change based on what you know is important to them. Don't be manipulative, but when possible, let people know how the change will help them.

- Demonstrate your own enthusiasm and commitment to the change. When your commitment is obvious to your employees, their motivation and involvement in the success of the change effort are likely to increase.

- Celebrate and communicate successes—even small ones!

- Teach people to remember their successes with change, as a way to build up their resilience.

- Coach your staff on what they need to do to make the change work; knowing these strategies provides employees with their own resource bank for dealing with future changes.

Here are the solutions to the brainteasers:

Brainteaser 1:

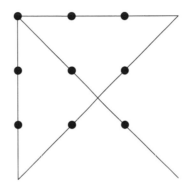

Notice that the problem can't be solved unless you draw outside of the structure. Most people erroneously assume that they are not allowed to draw outside the boundaries of the dots.

Brainteaser 2:

There are no limits to filling out the series, because no rules were established; however, people have a tendency to remain within the framework of what they learned in school (follow the vocabulary progression, think in terms of mathematical series, etc.).

- Cartesian people will offer series like:

$$\frac{\text{A EF KLM STUV etc.}}{\text{BCD GHIJ NOPQR etc.}}$$

Or

$$\frac{\text{A 1 EF 2 KLM 3 etc.}}{\text{BCD 3 GHIJ 4 NOPQR 5 etc.}}$$

- International globetrotters will offer series like:

$$\frac{\text{Americans English French}}{\text{British Canadians Dutch Germans}}$$

- Visual Cartesian people will offer series like:

$$\frac{\text{A EF H I KLMN T V etc. (letters made with lines)}}{\text{BCD G J O PQRS U etc. (letters made with curves)}}$$

- Musicians will recognize the musical scale (ABCDEFG) and could just whistle the ABC song they learned in school, or they may even compose a tune.

- More creative people may draw a picture where the original letters just disappear.

- And so forth.

The same principles apply to problem solving on the job. Many effective solutions are those that require you to think outside the structure, or paradigm, of the situation.

RESOURCES

The resources for this chapter begin on page 624.

3
CREATE CUSTOMER LOYALTY

PART 1: UNDERSTAND THE CUSTOMER
- *Define your customer base*
- *Understand customer requirements, expectations, and needs*
- *Provide value for the customer*
- *Seek feedback from customers*

PART 2: MANAGE THE CUSTOMER RELATIONSHIP
- *Deliver on customer commitments*
- *Ensure exceptional customer experiences*
- *Recover from mistakes*
- *Remove barriers to customer service*
- *Build a network of relationships*
- *Measure performance*

PART 3: BUILD A CUSTOMER–FOCUSED TEAM
- *Hire the right people*
- *Set high standards for customer service*
- *Train for customer focus*
- *Motivate and reward excellence*
- *Work together to serve the customer*
- *Practice what you preach*

INTRODUCTION

Businesses that concentrate on finding and keeping good customers, productive employees, and supportive investors continue to generate superior results. Loyalty is by no means dead. It remains one of the great engines of business success.

— Frederick F. Reichheld

Customer commitment is the cornerstone of business success. Customers are assets and, like other assets, if managed properly, can have a dramatic impact on business performance. Frederick F. Reichheld's work has demonstrated that a mere five percent increase in customer loyalty can produce profit increases of up to 85 percent. Obviously, there are compelling reasons to create customer-focused organizations.

Creating loyal customers results in competitive advantage for your organization. You can gain this advantage by building an organization that engages everyone in continuously improving your customer relationships. If you are actively pursuing a customer-focused mission—asking, "Who is our customer? Are we meeting their requirements and exceeding their expectations?"—the leap to a visionary strategy is shorter than you might imagine. The visionary strategy addresses the questions: "What will be our customers' future needs? How can we meet them? What must we do to gain customer commitment?"

This chapter presents suggestions you can implement to create customer loyalty and build a customer-focused team.

VALUABLE TIPS

- Examine everything you do against these criteria: "Does this contribute to meeting customer needs?" or "What value does this add to the customer?"

- List the requirements you believe your customers have. Then ask your customers what their requirements are. Note the differences.

- Develop standards for products and services that consistently meet customer requirements. Develop standards for customer service that exceed customer expectations.

- Actively review trade and business journals, annual reports, and marketing research on each of your customers to stay abreast of their business.

- Take time every day to ask a customer, "How are we doing?" Actively listen to what they say. Communicate these findings to the appropriate people in your organization.

- Conduct in-depth interviews with key customers to determine how they view your relationship, both its strengths and its weaknesses. What do they think the focus of your relationship should be in the year ahead?

- Interview the customers who have stopped using your products or services. Find out their reasons for leaving. This may help you identify the gaps between their requirements and what you are able to provide.

- Conduct focus groups with potential customers who do not use your products or services. Determine why they don't do business with you and what you can do to win their business.

- Treat your internal customers with care and respect, just as you treat your external customers.

- Use cross-functional teams to improve work processes to more clearly meet customer requirements.

- Meet with your front-line people to solicit their ideas for improving customer service, and discuss how you can support their efforts with customers.

- Conduct a benchmarking visit with organizations that are known for their customer focus.

- Listen to the questions new employees ask about your work processes, service, and so forth. These may be clues to improvement opportunities. Encourage them to challenge the status quo.

- Make it easy for customers to register their complaints with you. After a complaint has been resolved, call the customer to check up on his or her satisfaction level.

- Fully explain and communicate to your employees your commitment to high standards of customer service. Then, be a role model.

- Create a monthly internal newsletter that includes:
  - Tips on dealing with customer requests and complaints
  - Customer-focused policies and procedures
  - Summaries of current customer service readings
  - Recognition of excellent customer service

- In face-to-face interactions, reinforce messages about commitment to customers as often as possible, in addition to including them in the newsletter.

- When hiring, look for good customer-service qualities, such as commitment to excellence, maturity, positive outlook, tolerance, and flexibility.

- Provide special training for all employees on customer service. Include tips on how to handle difficult requests and objections, and how to carry out service-related company policies and work processes.

- Create a "Customer Pleaser of the Month/Week/Day" board to publicly recognize those staff members who provide excellent customer service.

PART I:
UNDERSTAND THE CUSTOMER

Define your customer base

Creating committed customers is the goal of successful organizations. Loyal customers fuel success and growth. They are one of the best measures of corporate performance because loyalty can only be achieved by creating superior value.

In order to create customer value, you must first know who your customers are. The following steps will help you define your customer base:

1. List the individuals or groups that buy or use the products or services you provide. These are your customers.

2. Categorize your customers into groups. For example, are your customers the end users, or do they integrate your products into others before they reach the market? Do you interact directly with the customer, or do you provide your products or services through other channels? (If you work with channel partners, these may be your customers as well.) Do you serve consumers? Do you serve businesses? Your customer segments may be many and varied.

3. Identify your key accounts—those customers who are strategically important to your organization. You may identify an account as strategic because it:
   - Represents a large proportion of your revenue or profit.
   - Has growth potential.
   - Is a key player in the industry.
   - Has the potential to be in an alliance or partnership in the future.

4. Identify the individual contacts you serve in each customer organization. These are the relationships you must manage to create customer loyalty.

5. Determine the specific requirements and expectations these customers have of you. (Don't assume you know; ask.) Be sure to include internal customer expectations as well as external customer expectations.

Understand customer requirements, expectations, and needs

While phrases such as "create value," "meet customer needs," and "deliver on requirements" are heard every day, countless organizations try to meet their own perception of their customer requirements, rather than what the customer's requirements really are. The organization may provide 15 options in a product, while the customer wants one or two. They do not ask the customers directly. They confuse requirements, needs, and value.

The goal should be to consistently meet customers' requirements. (See the model that follows.) Moving up the hierarchy are expectations. Exceeding expectations holds value for the customer because it provides intangibles such as convenience, peace of mind, etc.

Customer needs are those tangibles of product or service that are not currently available, but that, if available, would quickly become requirements. You can anticipate needs by establishing a relationship with a customer that allows you to fully understand who they are and where their business is going. When you understand that, you will begin to see opportunities to work together even before your customer can see them. This is the key to creating loyalty.

THE CUSTOMER RELATIONSHIP HIERARCHY

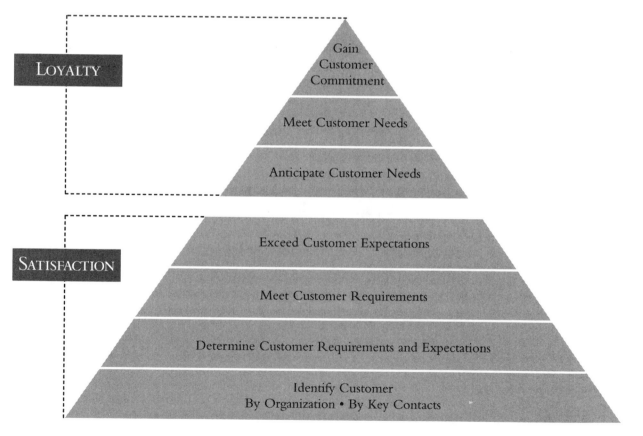

To accurately identify what your customers require and expect of you, follow these suggestions:

- At the outset of a new customer relationship, take time to formally establish the customer's requirements. This becomes the standard that you will consistently meet.

- Talk as well about the customer's expectations. How do they prefer to work with you? What would make their job easier? This becomes the standard you will strive to exceed.

- Be aware that within each customer organization, individuals you deal with may differ in their requirements and expectations of you. It is important to discover these differences as early in the relationship as possible. Therefore, when your customer contacts change, clarify the requirements and expectations of your new contacts to see if anything is different.

- Communicate customer requirements and expectations to everyone in your organization whose work reaches this customer. Tell the team how you won the customer's business, what industry the customer is in, what strategic objectives they are pursuing, and how your services or products help them meet their customer's needs. Then, explain the reasons for their requirements and expectations—and how meeting these standards will help the customer achieve their goals. Even better, invite your customer to join your team meeting to explain the importance of your work to their business.

- Arrange for your team to see the customer's operations—either live or virtually. This experience will clarify how your work plays a role in the customer's success.

- Create several communication channels that will enable you to stay current with your customer's changing requirements and expectations. Seek feedback proactively by frequently asking customer contacts about your performance (via interviews, surveys, focus groups). Also establish channels (hotlines, customer service, help desks) that will allow your customer to call you.

- Be constantly vigilant about your customers' business. This enables you to anticipate their needs and requirements before your competitors do. Research and read about their business/industry and those of their customers to help you identify the trends and forces affecting your customers' businesses. The additional understanding of your customers' customers will help you to add value.

- Keep track of the changes in customer preferences, market demands, and your competitors' offerings or strategies. You need to be able to quickly respond to these changes in order to remain competitive.

- Conduct an environmental scan of customer trends that could affect the products and services you are currently providing. These may also reveal future business opportunities.

Provide value for the customer

One of the most important skills for working directly with customers is the ability to create effective solutions that meet the unique requirements and needs of your customers. When you know who your customers are and what their requirements and expectations are, your organization can respond with products and services that deliver value.

To effectively meet your customers' needs, consider these suggestions:

- Examine everything that is done against the criteria "Does this contribute to meeting our customers' needs?" and "Does it provide added value?"

- Involve customers in designing new products. The majority of new product ideas come from customers, who know how the product can be improved.

- If your customer is proposing a solution rather than describing the problem, probe to understand the problem. This will help you design a solution that meets the customer's underlying need.

- Ask the customer about their long-term goals. Where are they headed in the next year, two years, five years? What do they want to accomplish? How can you help them get there?

- Clarify the customer's definition of "long-term value." Assuming you know what's best or what they consider important could mislead you.

- Make a concerted effort to look at customer problems without preconceived opinions or solutions. Instead, ask questions:
  - What are the customer's goals?
  - Who are their stakeholders?
  - What are the "must haves" in any solution?
  - What long-term considerations must always be addressed when you create a solution?

- Invite customers, suppliers, and distributors to develop effective work processes with you.

- Define and use a structured process to funnel customer feedback into decision making for product enhancements and product development.

- Get more or different people involved with customers. Cross-functional perspective is important to designing creative solutions.

- Design on-line capabilities to provide value-added information and resources. How can the full use of your product or service be enhanced through e-commerce?

- Listen to your customers' feedback and identify additional features that you can easily add to your product or service to increase its value.

- Examine the flexibility and adaptability of your service systems to see if they meet unique or different customer needs. Value-added service offerings can differentiate you from your competitors.

- Stay ahead of the demand for service by enhancing your infrastructure to match your growth curve.

Seek feedback from customers

An executive once said, "Talking to customers tends to counteract the most self-destructive habit of great corporations—that of talking to themselves." Businesses have two choices when it comes to seeking feedback from customers: they can know what's on their minds, or they can choose *not* to know what's on their minds. In only one of these choices do you have a chance to respond. If you choose to know what's on your customers' minds, you create an opportunity to strengthen the relationship. Some customers will tell you before you ask. But in all cases, customers want to be heard.

It's sometimes hard to listen to critical comments. But it's essential to listen, and take the comments seriously. Then ask for more. Probe and clarify to be sure you understand.

To encourage and be more receptive to customers' feedback, consider these suggestions:

- Design feedback systems tailored to each customer segment. For example:
  - For strategic accounts, use a structured, in-depth interviewing process to deepen your understanding of their business needs.
  - For smaller accounts, design a telephone or electronic feedback process that your front-line customer service or inbound sales team can use.
  - For consumers, provide an easily accessible vehicle such as a response section on your Internet site.

- Ask the following key questions when seeking feedback from your customers:
  - How are we serving your needs?
  - How can we improve?
  - What do you like/dislike about our product or service?
  - What qualities are most important to you?
  - How can we serve your needs better?

- Differentiate between feedback tools that enhance the relationship and those that are research tools. If your objective is to enhance the relationship with your customers, provide feedback tools that your own employees can use. If your objective is to gather feedback for research purposes, engage a third party to administer a survey for you.

- Listen beyond specific product needs. This has been shown to be the greatest skill difference between the most successful and least successful salespeople. Listen for:
  - Requirements.
  - Expectations of you and your organization.
  - Frustrations and concerns.
  - What keeps your customer up at night.
  - Hints of dissatisfaction.
  - The underlying need, not just the solution.
  - Their feelings about you and their relationship with you.

- Welcome critical comments. Most customers who leave do so without complaining—and therefore, without ever giving you an opportunity to serve them better. Customers who take time to give you feedback are also saying, "I want this relationship to work, and here is what you can do to keep my business."

- Treat customers' perceptions as reality; they are, in fact, reality for your customer.

- Spend time with customers yourself. There is no substitute for hearing directly from the customer.

- Nurture the relationships with your power users. Listen to their ideas. Research shows that most new product ideas come from this group.

- As you listen to others, ensure that you are listening, not trying to sell or convince them. Refer to Chapter 28: Listen to Others in this handbook for suggestions on improving your listening skills.

- Clarify the indirect messages (the subtext) of any feedback you receive by asking questions.

- Obligate yourself to respond to the concern you hear. Dissatisfied customers tell up to 20 friends that they are unhappy with the way you do business. When problems are resolved, the vast majority will keep doing business with you.

- Check back regularly to see how things are going after you have responded to a customer's comment.

- Conduct post-project debriefings to discuss what went well and what did not. These are great opportunities for gathering customer feedback, as well as evaluating your own performance.

- For long-term customers, consider an annual or quarterly meeting to discuss changing needs, problems, and dissatisfactions, and to generate ideas for improvements. Include all key stakeholders from both your organization and your customer's organization.

For every customer who calls to give you feedback, there are likely to be 20 others who have unresolved problems you don't know about. Therefore, seeking feedback is essential. Initiating a discussion with your customer about how you are doing is far superior to waiting for customers to complain. You still receive the feedback you need to improve your business, but by acting first, you also communicate to your customer how valuable they are to you.

PART 2: MANAGE THE CUSTOMER RELATIONSHIP

Deliver on customer commitments

Customers want, and deserve, quick action. They want to deal with an employee who has all of the information, expertise, and tools necessary to help them—competently and expeditiously. They also expect and deserve efficient follow-through, with no exceptions, on the commitments you have made to them.

Use the following suggestions to increase your and your team's success in delivering on customer commitments:

- Know your customer's requirements. Fully understand the commitments you have made. Be sure you know when, what, how, where, how many, to whom, etc.

- Communicate the commitments to your team. Provide not only the detailed information, but also a context for those who may not deal directly with the customer. Why does the customer need it this way? What are the consequences for them if we fail to meet our commitments?

- If time has passed since the commitments were made and discussed, double-check to be sure nothing has changed.

- Always deliver by the agreed-upon date. Customers expect to receive your product or service as promised.

- Champion the customer's cause inside your organization. Identify other champions with whom you can team up to ensure the organization's response.

- If it appears that you have overcommitted, talk with the customer immediately. Understand their situation fully. Is there any way the customer's need can be met another way?

- Follow up to be sure the commitment was met. Just because it left your organization on time, doesn't necessarily mean the customer received it as expected. Build this follow-up into your process.

- Measure your performance. Establish a tracking system to determine your compliance. In those cases where you have missed the mark, identify where the process gets tied up, and why. If the problem is recurring, find effective ways to remove these roadblocks and inefficiencies.

- Provide the necessary resources for service employees. Give them quick access to the information through software that is designed to provide up-to-date information on all customer transactions.

- Eliminate as many trips as possible to obtain supervisor approval. Provide the parameters within which your employees work, and then give them the latitude to be flexible to meet each customer's needs. When employees give the customer options, they increase the customer's feelings of being accommodated. Ideally, employees should be empowered to do whatever possible to satisfy customers.

- Recognize and reward individuals or teams who consistently meet delivery dates.

Ensure exceptional customer experiences

Every relationship starts with discovery. We learn something about our customer that helps us tailor our actions specifically to meet their needs. They experience us as a responsive, dedicated organization, and when it comes time to evaluate the relationship, they invite us to discover more about them. This is how to manage relationships to achieve customer commitment.

RELATIONSHIP ENGINE

```
          r------------- EVALUATION ------------,
          |                                     |
          v                                     v
DISCOVERY---------> ACTION--------> EXPERIENCE
```

When we seek feedback (discovery) and deliver on our commitments (action), we often assume our job is done. However, orchestrating the experience of the customer is perhaps the most vital step of building relationships. It should not be left to chance.

The following suggestions can help ensure that your customer has an exceptional experience working with your organization:

- Stay attuned to the experiences your customer is having with all parts of your organization. Replace negative or unexpected outcomes with positive ones.

- Before you respond to a customer need, think about the impact the change will have on the customer. Be sure there is a payoff in customer experience for each action you take.

- Implement high-payoff actions first.

- Use as many channels for communicating with customers as possible. This will increase the likelihood that customers will receive your message.

- Understand your customer's "radar screen." Know how they are most likely to pick up information. For example, if you want to use your company newsletter to let customers know how quickly you responded to requests for a new product feature, you will need to know which customers actually read your publication. Any customers who do not read it will not experience the change and will not give you credit for your responsiveness.

- Create customized opportunities for your key accounts to experience your customer focus. With your largest accounts, it is a good investment for you and your team to tailor the interactions to fit those customers' unique needs, based on what you know about their expectations.

- Identify any systemic or organizational barriers that may prevent your employees from creating exceptional experiences for your customers. Brainstorm ways to remove the barriers. Examples of barriers may include:
  - Employees not given enough authority to make quick decisions.
  - Flawed processes that delay production or delivery of product/services.
  - Misaligned reward system that does not reinforce the desired behaviors.

Recover from mistakes

Customers judge the quality of your organization in two ways: how well you deliver on your commitments, and how well you handle exceptions and problems. At some point, every organization is bound to make mistakes in the quality and delivery of its product or service. How you deal with mistakes and complaints, however, can make or break a valued customer relationship.

A good recovery can solidify, rather than weaken, your relationship with the customer. Use the following process to help you rectify mistakes and retain the customer's business:

I JUST WANTED TO RESPOND TO THAT ORDER YOU SENT ME LAST FALL. YOU KNOW, THE ONE LABELED "URGENT."

- Don't wait for the customer to come to you. If you are aware of a problem, be the first to contact your customer.

- Take full responsibility for the mistake. Don't blame another for the problem—another employee, a vendor, an "act of God"—your customer cares little about who is responsible. They care a lot about how the problem will be resolved, so spend your time on that.

- Expedite the recovery process as quickly as possible.

- Empathize with the customer; let the person know you understand that your mistake will cause problems for him or her.

- Atone for the mistake; give the customer a little extra in return for the trouble. Then, follow up with the customer to assure his or her satisfaction.

- Understand the importance of good communication with the customer. Sometimes missing the deadline is not nearly as problematic as not knowing you were going to miss the deadline. Use a "no surprises" motto, so they can plan for the delay.

- Finally, learn from your mistakes. Conduct a postmortem session to investigate the cause of the problem. Then set up process checks to make sure it doesn't happen again.

Remove barriers to customer service

Your employees may be committed to providing exceptional customer service, but may be unable to carry it out because organizational or departmental constraints prohibit them from going the extra mile. Make every attempt to remove the barriers that get in the way of giving your customers top-notch service.

Common barriers and possible solutions include:

BARRIER	POSSIBLE SOLUTIONS
Front-line employees perceive they lack the authority to make decisions to satisfy unhappy customers.	Give front-line employees the proper authority to do what's right for the customer. Change or make exceptions to your current policies, if necessary.
Satisfaction with the status quo.	Raise your standards. Know and communicate what your competitors are doing. Underscore the importance of loyal customers to your success.
Belief that you have a corner on the marketplace.	Recognize that the nature of today's marketplace is dynamic and competitive. Ask what you can do to go beyond what the competition is doing, and then do it.
Concern that the customer will take advantage of lenient customer service policies or pursue legal recourse for poor performance.	Determine the parameters of what constitutes a legitimate customer complaint. Train your staff on ways to identify and handle legally sensitive issues.
Front-line workers overstressed from constantly putting out fires and the heavy workload.	Examine the processes that need improvement. Aggressively work with management to eliminate the source of the problems—the quality issues. Let your front line know that their efforts are valued and respected.
Excess paperwork and red tape for front-line employees and customers.	Streamline your complaint-resolution process. Whenever possible, handle necessary paperwork after the customer leaves or ends the phone call.

Build a network of relationships

We often think of our market in terms of market segments, market share, and market penetration, but the market is actually individual customers—customers with whom we build relationships. It takes time and effort to identify appropriate contacts and develop long-standing relationships. Yet these relationships are true organizational assets. They are a competitive differentiator. While your competition may be able to match or better your products, price, and service, they can never duplicate the history you have with your customers.

To develop professional ties with your customers that go beyond the current transaction, consider these suggestions:

- Review an organizational chart to learn about the business structure of your customer's organization. Identify key individuals at varying levels and functions with whom you would like to build relationships.

- Use your network to gain an introduction to each individual.

- Research your customers and become well versed about their organization and industry. Access their Web site frequently to keep up-to-date. Look specifically for the most recent press releases and earnings reports.

- Make a professional connection by:
  - Listening to customer problems with intensity.
  - Talking to the customer with language that reflects your knowledge of their business.
  - Mentioning articles you have read and sending industry articles they may not have seen.
  - Asking informed questions about their role or their business.
  - Sharing appropriate information about your business or your job.

- Make personal connections in ways appropriate to your and your customer's culture. For example, in the United States:
  - Make direct eye contact.
  - Smile warmly.
  - Make small talk about their weekend, their vacation, etc.
  - Have lunch or dinner, golf, and attend events together.

- Look for positive role models in your organization and your field. Model the behavior of people recognized for their ability to partner with customers. Have a discussion with one or two of these people to find out what they do to build and maintain strong relationships.

- Introduce your colleagues into the customer's organization. Build a web of relationships that is strong enough to withstand transitions of people and roles.

- Create trust and openness with your key customers. Demonstrate a genuine interest in them as people and a firm understanding of the strategic issues they face.

- Talk to your customers about the future direction of your company. It will likely lead to a dialogue about their direction. Look for fit and congruency.

- Build the relationship by conducting in-depth interviews with each contact. This discovery process will uncover opportunities to work with the customer in new ways.

Measure performance

"What gets measured gets managed." This adage certainly applies to creating a customer-focused organization. Organizations that are serious about improving their service to customers measure their performance. In doing so, they also communicate their resolve to all stakeholders: "If customer loyalty is a priority, we will measure it, and we will manage our relationships to achieve it."

You have many choices about putting a measurement plan in place. The following considerations will help you understand the questions you should be asking and make the best use of the process:

- Be clear about your objectives. Is it your intent to:
  - Establish a baseline measure?
  - Provide research tracking and trending?
  - Enhance relationships?
  - Evaluate individual performance?
  - Establish priorities for improvement?
  - Create loyalty?
  - Determine compensation?

- Be clear about what you are measuring:
  - Overall satisfaction?
  - Customer commitment?
  - Transactional excellence?
  - Service quality?
  - Product performance?
  - Competitor analysis?
  - Market penetration?

- Consider all stakeholders when measuring organizational performance:
  - Customers
  - Distributors
  - Employees
  - Internal customers
  - Suppliers
  - Alliance partners
  - Investors
  - Prospects

- Determine the frequency of the process. Will it be an ongoing measurement process, a one-time process, or periodic?

- Choose your method carefully: survey (paper-and-pencil, electronic, telephone), face-to-face interview, or focus group. Success depends on selecting the method that is consistent with the objectives you have established.

- Select measurement tools to fit your objectives: PDI's Customer Review Process, Customer Value Analysis, Balanced Scorecard, Quality Function Deployment (QFD), PDI's TALK2®, and so forth.

- Involve the appropriate internal stakeholders before launching a new measurement process. Many well-intentioned processes have failed because they did not include the right people in the planning phase.

- Shape the message you want to convey through your measurement process. Good measurement tools are designed to communicate a message, as well as gather information. For example, a customer measurement process should convey, "We are committed to enhancing our relationship with you," not, "This is the easiest way for us to get your feedback."

- Make good use of the data you've gathered, and make sure your customers know that. From their perspective, it's better to not ask their opinions at all than to ignore or not use purposefully the valuable feedback they provided in interviews, focus groups, and surveys.

- Analyze the data, identify the necessary actions or improvements to make, and communicate your plan/intention back to the customers.

- Hold periodic debriefing meetings or reviews to assess the systems and processes put in place to meet customer requirements. Discuss what worked well and what needs to be done differently. These periodic reviews are also a good way to catch problems before they become serious.

PART 3:
BUILD A CUSTOMER-FOCUSED TEAM

Hire the right people

Successful managers begin their efforts to enhance customer relationships by hiring the right people. To focus your efforts, determine the specific requirements of the job. Incorporate the requirements and expectations you have solicited from your customers, and then target your interview questions to identify these attributes.

The following suggestions can help you make the right hiring decisions for building a customer-focused team:

- Recognize the characteristics for good customer-relationship management. These include:
  - Good oral communication skills
  - Cooperation and teamwork
  - Even-tempered disposition
  - Sensitivity to and concern for others
  - Problem-solving and decision-making skills
  - Commitment to excellence
  - Enthusiasm and energy
  - Flexibility and adaptability

- Identify the specific skills needed and use these as part of your selection process.

- Use behavioral interviewing techniques to predict how a candidate will behave on the job. During the interviews, ask candidates for specific, real-life examples that demonstrate the specific skills needed for the job.

- Consider involving key customers in the selection of new employees who will serve their account.

- Consider using testing or assessments to identify strong candidates. There are reliable tests for customer service, for example.

Set high standards for customer service

A team that has common standards for providing superior service and that talks about how to continually achieve its goal is more likely to deliver high levels of customer service than teams without these standards and conversations. Communicating the standards to all levels of your organization serves to focus all team efforts on the same expectations for customer service.

To effectively set and communicate your commitment to customer service, try these suggestions:

- Create a statement that encompasses your service commitment. Define it in terms of both employee and customer expectations. Make it a snappy catchphrase that's easy to remember. For example, discount retailer Target Stores' motto is "Fast, Fun, and Friendly."

- Put your service motto on posters and place them strategically throughout halls and open areas frequented by front-line customer-service people.

- Translate the motto into performance standards and behaviors. For each job, identify the specific steps the person in that role must take to achieve the standard.

- Show how each job is an important link in the chain of exceeding customer expectations. Consider using Michael Porter's value-chain assessment to demonstrate this point. Communicate the message that no matter what the job is, it is valued and important.

- Stress the benefits of the team's efforts not only for the entire organization, but also for them as individuals. For example, tie in the fact that better customer service means better business, and thus stronger job security.

- Continually update what you know about customers. Share this information with everyone, especially those who have a lot of customer contact.

- Demonstrate customer focus throughout the organization. Make it a priority for each work group to set customer-focus objectives. Incorporate these objectives into the performance development process for each work group.

- Recognize and reward those who demonstrate high customer-service standards. This will encourage others to change their behaviors accordingly.

Train for customer focus

Once you have hired the best people and you know your standards, get off to the right start with a strong orientation and comprehensive training. The benefits of this approach include higher levels of productivity, enhanced customer relationships and more loyal employees.

The following suggestions will help you provide new employees with effective orientation and training experiences:

- Briefly overview your customer vision and strategies. Outline your standards and expectations for how customer relationships will be managed.

- Design and present a fast-paced, energized program that meets your specific, desired objective.

- During the training, treat employees the way you expect them to treat customers. Role-modeling is a powerful way to influence others.

- Provide an orientation to each part of your business, so employees understand what it takes to meet customer requirements at every step of the process. Create appreciation for how all work groups come together to serve the customer.

- Make the orientation fun. People who enjoy their training will more likely enjoy the job and thus treat customers better.

- Discuss how you build a prospect into a loyal customer. Ask your customer-focus "stars" to describe the role they each play in reaching that goal.

- Demonstrate various ways to handle customers' requests and objections. Model techniques for dealing with tough cases. Get employees involved in their training by role-playing various scenarios, and then having them critique their handling of the "customer."

- Build your new employees' confidence. Show them the effort you made to hire the best. Describe the results that the group can achieve together. Invite a customer to talk about how important your team is to their success.

- Provide on-the-job training. Training does not have to be classroom-based. Look for safe opportunities for people to train and practice on the job.

- Follow up on the training. Create a safe environment for people to apply their learnings. Provide appropriate feedback and coaching as they continue to develop their skills.

Motivate and reward excellence

No matter how competent and self-confident they are, all employees like to know that their efforts are recognized and appreciated. Provide incentives for exceeding customer expectations and rewards for people who demonstrate superior performance. Recognize the small wins and accomplishments the same way you would the major wins. Gather recognition from many sources: customers, senior management, managers, peers, and suppliers. Make the accomplishments widely known.

Consider the following suggestions for motivating and rewarding the excellence of your team members:

- Recognize that the value your employees create for customers is one of the most effective motivators. It taps the strong inner desire of employees to provide excellent service to their customers.

- Realize that positive reinforcement often works best when it is linked to specific rewards. Recognize, however, that not everyone is motivated by the same thing, so tailor your rewards to the individual.

- Create avenues for recognizing excellent performers. Establish continuous programs that are frequently modified.

- Make sure some of your rewards are instant—immediately reinforcing excellent service.

- Obtain feedback from people in the know—your customers. One way to get this valuable information is to provide evaluation cards. For example, in a consumer environment, place these cards near the service desk, or have service employees hand them to your customers. This feedback can be used for giving rewards for good service.

- Ask customers for feedback about what you are doing right. Ask for names of those who are models of excellent customer service. Share this recognition with the organization.

- Encourage employees to recognize each other's excellence. Post a "What Do We Do Well?" chart and a marker in a common area for informal peer recognition.

- Reflect your customers' requirements and expectations in your performance appraisal factors. This will reinforce their importance and allow you to recognize employees for meeting and exceeding the standards.

- Celebrate when goals are achieved. Acknowledge the contributions of less-visible employees, as well as those who have direct customer contact. Behind-the-scenes contributors seldom get the recognition they deserve.

- Recognize attempts to go beyond what the customer expects. Acknowledge these efforts and provide your encouragement.

- Reward people who overcome difficult obstacles to achieve results.

Work together to serve the customer

Everyone in the organization—whether they have front-line customer contact (account managers, customer service representatives, receptionists, salespeople, service technicians, etc.) or whether they rarely see a customer (engineering, operations, finance, etc.)—can provide exceptional feedback on how to improve the organization and thus create more loyal customer relationships. To tap this resource, consider these suggestions:

- Use a process like PDI's TALK2® to conduct in-depth interviews with each of your employees. Discuss opportunities to improve the way customers are being served by your work group. Find out what is working well and how to expand best practices.

- Demonstrate that you take your employees' input seriously by acting on their comments and suggestions.

- Use e-mail or groupware to gather information from employees about what customers are saying or feeling about service.

- Hold regular interdepartmental meetings to get a broader perspective.

- Conduct periodic integration meetings: Gather all the key people who work with a specific customer and have them brainstorm ways to integrate their work/services. This will give your customers the impression that different teams in your organization work together seamlessly. It also prevents your customer from receiving five different calls a day from five different departments within your organization—all asking for the same information.

- Recognize the value of feedback by acknowledging employees' contributions at department meetings or organization-wide meetings.

- Create a "think tank" room where the setting (from music to special furniture to art) encourages people to open up and share their creative energy.

- Use brainstorming sessions with employees to find creative, intuitive solutions to customer problems.

- Recognize the varying priorities of different groups/departments, such as design and manufacturing or sales and operations, and how these priorities may affect the product or service you provide to your customer. Identify ways to gain commitment to total customer focus from all groups. (See Chapter 22: Foster Collaboration in this handbook for additional suggestions.)

Practice what you preach

Great customer-focused organizations practice what they preach. It starts with the behavior of a few and becomes a call to action for all. Showing employees how to focus on customer needs is a good way to teach and motivate them to do it. However, modeling customer-focused behavior is not the only role managers play in creating loyal customers.

The following suggestions will help you lead the way:

- Assume the role of customer-champion. Know what customers require and expect of you. Make sure they receive it.

- Make direct customer contact your priority.

- Think about everything you do from the point of view of the customer. Make this thinking evident to those with whom you work.

- Give others in your organization what they need to meet customer requirements. Make sure their responsibilities to the customer are clear. Ask what they need to carry out these responsibilities. Provide it so they can be accountable.

- Provide cross-training to employees to increase their abilities to solve problems on their own.

- Build an internal network to meet customer requirements. Integrate your efforts with others. Include other departments, levels, and functions.

- Model customer-focused behavior:
  - Be responsive.
  - Return calls or messages from customers and employees within 24 hours.
  - Anticipate and deliver on the needs of your employees.
  - Make decisions with the customer in mind.

- Recognize that your employees' needs for trust, respect, understanding, and appreciation are the same as those of your customers.

- Through your body language, dress, voice, and energy level, send the same positive attitude you want your employees to send to customers.

RESOURCES

The resources for this chapter begin on page 626.

4
PROMOTE GLOBAL PERSPECTIVE

PART 1: THINK GLOBALLY IN YOUR BUSINESS
- *Analyze the globalization of your business*
- *Understand how world events affect your business*
- *Weigh your global competition*
- *Work your globalization strategy*
- *Assess your future global skills*
- *Anticipate trends and impacts on your organization*

PART 2: DEVELOP INTERNATIONAL BUSINESS SAVVY
- *Enhance your international mind-set*
- *Learn the business practices of other cultures*
- *Know how to conduct business in other countries*
- *Market products and services internationally*

PART 3: THINK GLOBALLY ABOUT PEOPLE
- *Help others develop a global mind-set*
- *Know how to manage employees in other countries*
- *Develop cross-cultural knowledge*

Introduction

Today's leaders find themselves in, or working with, organizations that have outgrown their national boundaries. For businesses to be successful, it is critical that managers at all levels think globally. Whether a company is operating as a total global organization—manufacturing in other countries, sourcing materials from other parts of the world, actively marketing its products internationally—or operating locally but facing the need to address competition from abroad, the global economy affects its business.

Global thinking involves thinking on a larger scale and scope about how organizations operate, and considering a growing number of factors when making decisions. Global thinking requires leaders to consider the management of products, people, money, and meaning across boundaries. To do this, leaders must have some experience in understanding other cultures and perspectives. They need access to information and alternate viewpoints. They need a way of understanding what matters to people, whether it's what they want to buy or why they want to work with them.

Managers who think globally consider the present and the future, and look for the balance between processes and outcomes. They listen for the meaning underlying the words, and work at understanding the meaning when it differs from their own. Issues of strategy, innovation, intercultural awareness, and technology all influence global thinking. In the end, however, global thinking is not just thinking "bigger"—it is understanding and managing increasing complexity in your business.

If thinking globally doesn't seem to be imperative in your current position, consider that at the current rate of change, it doubtless will become an issue at some point in your career—and most likely sooner rather than later. Furthermore, even if you are not directly affected by the global economy, you have customers and/or suppliers who are likely feeling the impact. The more you can do now to begin understanding the complex interrelationships of international business, the easier it will be for you to manage in that global economy. The best part is that thinking globally requires you to stretch your understanding of how things fit together, an exercise that makes people better managers no matter how big their universe becomes.

This chapter provides guidelines and suggestions for thinking globally in your business and for developing the skills to manage those implications.

VALUABLE TIPS

- Analyze the degree to which your business is affected by the global economy.

- Question your own assumptions about how business is done and how people should act in other cultures. Expand your sense of what is appropriate to embrace different ways of achieving the same goals.

- Become aware of the natural, common business practices in your own country that are viewed differently in other countries.

- Pay attention when locals object to a product or process. Proceed carefully, balancing their concerns with opportunities for innovation.

- Try to understand other people's ideas from their point of view, rather than making judgments based on your own perspective or culture.

- Ask for coaching from people within your organization who know the culture of the country you'll be working in.

- Read world news in your own periodicals and identify a source to get the news from another nationality's perspective.

- Research the country's laws that affect how you do business in that country.

- Analyze the ways in which your organization is a global organization.

- Recognize that it can take more effort and time to build a trusting relationship with people from another country.

- Plan more face-to-face interactions with global team members early in your relationship.

- Remember that you can respect other points of view without agreeing with them.

- Encourage discussion of international business within your organization, including the difficult issues in dealing with different business practices and cultural norms and values.

- Talk to expatriates about their experiences. Pay careful attention to what surprised them about their opportunity.

- Build bridges together. Talk openly about how each person sees the situation and how you can create the bridge to a new understanding and new ways of working.

- Carefully monitor the way in which you seek understanding of differences. Be open and willing to explain your desire to learn, rather than pushing too quickly for resolution.

- Get in tune with trends in the industry, your organization, and the global landscape. Continually explore how these changes might affect your business. Create and take advantage of developing business opportunities.

- Identify communication technology that will facilitate the global coordination you need to have.

- Identify what aspects of the business need to be global—sourcing, manufacturing, distribution, marketing, sales, etc.

- Determine and communicate a set of core values for your organization that build a common language and a way of doing business throughout the organization.

- Before you work in another country, learn all you can about its language, culture, values, and customs.

- Study how your competition sells its products internationally.

- Develop contacts internationally, and discuss the market, demographics, and cultural norms of their countries.

- When another person is talking, listen carefully to hear his or her values and beliefs. Check out your understanding respectfully and nonconfrontationally, even if the values you hear are very different from your own.

- In international meetings, communicate clearly and completely. Check the accuracy of your assumptions. Slow the speed of your communication to allow others to process differences in accents, terminology, and ideas.

- When dealing with foreign associates, be aware of cultural differences in social and business norms and learn how to modify your behavior when necessary.

- Take a course in cross-cultural studies to understand culture and its impact on people.

- Remember that individuals see themselves as both part of their culture and different from it. Do not assume that all people from a particular culture are exactly alike.

- Study the business practices of successful multinational businesses. Compare these practices with your organization's values and practices. Identify practices that are similar and those that are different, and the reasons why.

- Define your company's global market—the countries where your company does or would like to do business. Determine how your company's products can meet the needs of the people in those countries.

PART 1:
THINK GLOBALLY IN YOUR BUSINESS

Analyze the globalization of your business

Businesses and industries are becoming more global every year. Your customers may be on various continents, your raw materials may come from other parts of the world, new technologies may originate in other countries, or your business may be partially owned by foreign investors.

A useful first step is to understand how your organization is part of the global economy. The following suggestions will help you analyze the globalization of your business:

- Talk with international experts and knowledgeable managers about the international components of your business. Find out:
  - What percentage of revenues and profits comes from foreign markets?
  - In which markets is future growth expected? Are these markets domestic or foreign?
  - Who are your suppliers? From inside or outside your country? Who do you anticipate your suppliers will be in the future? Where will they be located?
  - Where is manufacturing now? In the future? What is the current and future impact on the business of the manufacturing location(s)?
  - Who are your primary domestic and foreign competitors now? In the future? What would be the impact of a change in competitors?
  - Is your company owned or partially owned by foreign investors? What is the impact? What changes do you anticipate?
  - Where is your technology developed and supplied from currently? In the future?
  - What percentage of your organization is located in other countries? Which countries?
  - What percentage of your workforce and managers are foreign nationals?
  - What percentage of managers are managing outside their country of origin?

- Analyze the information you've gathered to spot opportunities and potential problems. You can conduct this analysis in a number of ways:
  - Conduct it yourself with the knowledge you currently have. If you are an experienced manager with some global knowledge, this process may help determine in which areas you need additional help.

- Use your team to gather the information, share it, and draw conclusions together. This approach would capitalize on the expertise of others, plus develop shared knowledge and consensus.
- Ask a team or task force to gather the information, analyze it, and develop recommendations. The task force can present the information to you and/or the other teams in the organization.

Understand how world events affect your business

Whether your business has been involved in the global marketplace for years or has had no contact with other countries, it is affected by world events. The more you understand how world events affect your business, the better prepared you will be to minimize the negative impact and capitalize on the positive.

To further your understanding of the impact that world events can have on your business, consider these suggestions:

- Ask yourself how specific international events, particularly economic developments, will affect your organization or your industry. If you don't know the answers, discuss the events with others in your organization or your network. Ask for the opinions of coworkers from other countries.

- Develop your own perspective of business in the global economy. Watch for patterns and predictors. For example, if a major corporation shifts its national base of production, what kind of fallout can be expected for the industry worldwide and for your organization's place in it?

- Talk with the informal historians in your organization. Ask how major events in the past, such as a fire, major labor strike, war, or natural disaster, affected the organization. This information will help you anticipate some of the effects of major world events on your organization.

- Attend conferences hosted by government agencies that assist organizations interested in international trade. Even if your organization is already trading internationally, these conferences can give you additional insights into how world events are currently affecting the marketplace.

- Allocate a certain amount of time daily or weekly for reading books, periodicals, or other literature that address the global market and evolving world trends.

- Ask experts in international business to help you understand the connections among world events, global business, and your business.

Weigh your global competition

To compete in the global economy, most organizations will find it necessary to increase their global position. The first step in expanding their presence in the global marketplace is to identify and analyze the competitors in that larger market.

To weigh competition your organization faces globally, consider the following process:

1. Determine the information you know and what you will need from business or functional experts. Conduct this analysis with your team or gather a task force to conduct the analysis with you so you do not unintentionally limit your information or analysis. Be sure to look at the following areas in your analysis:
   - Who in the industry has the greatest share of the global market?
   - In which markets is future growth expected?
   - Have foreign competitors targeted your industry as a good one to enter?
   - Have foreign competitors targeted your primary markets?
   - Who are your primary domestic and foreign competitors now? In the future? What will be the impact of a change in competitors?
   - What are the core factors of your success globally?
   - What have been your limitations to success globally?
   - Who in the industry is working with the toughest, most demanding customers?
   - Who in the industry is introducing the most successful new products and line extensions?
   - Who drives the development of technology necessary for your business— you or your competitors? Your supplier of technology?
   - Who is in the position to redefine the industry?
   - Who sets the standard in the industry for quality, customer service, manufacturing excellence, and technological advancement?
   - What trade barriers protect your organization? What is their future?
   - What political trends or events are occurring in the countries in which your business is located that may affect the company?

2. When the analysis is complete, determine which areas you must address now and which must be addressed in the future.

Work your globalization strategy

If your organization is ready for globalization, as one of the opinion- or decision-making leaders, you can help create a vision of what globalization can mean for your business. Be prepared to articulate the strategic imperative to become a global organization.

The following suggestions can help you implement a globalization strategy:

- Identify what needs to be global—sourcing, manufacturing, distribution, marketing, sales, and so forth.
  - Benchmark other organizations to learn effective ways to manage this function, business, or part of the business.
  - Start small, unless you are prepared or need to implement a high-risk strategy because of the competitive threat. Test what works for you before you take the process all over the world.

- Determine the appropriate global-local balance.
  - Benchmark global management in other organizations. Understand their rationale for their particular kind of global management.
  - Present alternative ways to manage globally.
  - Discuss the strengths and weaknesses of each approach.
  - Determine what you want to use for the present.
  - Identify the criteria you will use to determine if the global management approach is working.

- Identify communication technology that will facilitate the global coordination you need to have.
  - Invite the organization's communication technology experts to a staff meeting to present options and possibilities.
  - Discuss your communication needs with potential internal and external providers.

- Determine your entry strategy if you are not already working in particular markets.

- Develop the partnerships (e.g., translation firms, legal assistance, business partners) you need to work globally.

- To determine whether you should enter an alliance, understand your organization's core competencies and processes. Think very seriously before you decide to let another organization be responsible for one of your core competencies; normally, an organization should retain its core competencies and processes and use alliances to support the other processes.

- Regularly review what is working and identify problems. Develop plans to capitalize on what is working and to address the problems.

- Determine a set of organizational core values to communicate throughout the organization that will build a common language and way of doing business with one another.
  - Use a global task force to develop the values.
  - Assure that the values do not reflect only one culture.
  - Ask high-level executives, preferably your CEO, to introduce the values and their rationale to the organization.
  - Obtain a commitment from the executive team to communicate, set expectations, and manage in accordance with the values.
  - Reinforce the values at every opportunity.
  - Use the values to build common direction and processes with your teams.

- Tell stories about successful global projects.

- If you question the importance of becoming more globally oriented, conduct the following analysis:
  - Are your competitors global players?
  - What are your competitors doing globally? Where are they? What markets are they entering? What are they doing that you are not?
  - Where will new competitors come from? How will they compete against you? As a strategic-planning learning experience and to examine these questions:
    1. Divide your staff into teams, with each team taking on the role of a particular competitor. Have the teams come to a meeting prepared to present how they will take 25 to 50 percent of your market share in the next three years.
    2. Ask each team to present its strategy. Have the other teams challenge the presentations and rationale.
    3. Debrief what you learned, and determine what to do as a result.
  - What are your sources of raw materials? What are the chances of these sources staying the same for the next five years? How does the global economy affect your sources of raw materials?
  - Where is manufacturing done? What are the chances that manufacturing locations or sources of labor will stay the same for the next five years?
  - Where and who are your customers? Will they continue to provide large enough growth for the organization? Where may your future customers come from?

Assess your future global skills

As you look to the future, anticipate that competition, complexity, and the pace of business will increase. Competitors will emerge. Old alliances will crumble and new ones will develop. An increase in competition and in collaboration will occur simultaneously, often with the same organizations. Technology will make it possible to accomplish almost everything differently. New organizational structures will arise and will as quickly change. People will need to manage highly complex webs of relationships and develop relationships with different people.

To manage within this competitive environment, you will need to develop a passion for learning, an ability to analyze and synthesize a large amount of disparate information, a willingness and ability to negotiate and work out extraordinarily complex relationships among people and organizations, skills to keep up with and ahead of technology, and the ability to manage complex and changing systems.

To assess your future global skills, consider the degree to which each of the following describes you, using a scale of L=low, M=medium, and H=high.
__ Able to learn information quickly
__ Able to synthesize disparate information
__ Fascinated with learning and understanding
__ Able to master new ways of working quickly
__ Constantly learning
__ Comfortable using communication technology such as voice mail, e-mail, video conferencing, the Internet, and so forth
__ Experiment with new things
__ Follow emerging communication technology
__ Keep up to date with technology
__ Imagine applications of new technology
__ Able to negotiate difficult and complex relationships
__ Speak at least two languages
__ Enjoy learning about different cultures
__ Expert at orchestrating change
__ See challenges as exhilarating and fun
__ Have lots of energy

After you assess yourself, ask those who work with you to provide their points of view on your skills in these areas.

Anticipate trends and impacts on your organization

Continual analysis of your industry, global trends, and technological advances is important to anticipating the future. It is essential that organizations stay ahead of the competition. To anticipate trends and impacts, use the following suggestions:

- Dynamically monitor global business activities, both inside and outside the organization, to avoid being blindsided and to maximize opportunities.

- As you get in tune with trends in the industry, in your organization, and on the global landscape, continually explore how these changes might affect your business. Create and take advantage of developing business opportunities.

- Watch the competition. What moves are they making in response to current trends? Are they somewhere you should be? Are they more experienced than you in particular markets? Learn from their successes and mistakes. How can you keep your organization from making the same mistakes? How can you learn from their successes to leap ahead of them in the future?

- Actively develop your own perspective of business in the global economy. Watch for patterns and predictors. Anticipate and interpret world events.

- Shift your thinking from "where I do business" to "how I do business."

PART 2: DEVELOP INTERNATIONAL BUSINESS SAVVY

Enhance your international mind-set

No matter how involved you are in international business—whether you manage a foreign subsidiary or simply need to be aware of how world events could affect your industry—the first step is to expand your own mind-set about what it means to think globally.

The following suggestions can help you move beyond a domestic business focus and stay abreast of worldwide trends and economic developments:

- Learn how others view your country and its role in the world and in the global economy.

- Keep an open mind in all situations. Step back and observe your feelings, opinions, and assessments about international events or other countries' cultural norms. Before making a judgment, look at other viewpoints and objectively consider the merits of those viewpoints. Not only will this allow you to broaden your mind-set about the complexity of the world, but it will also help you learn specific practices of other cultures.

- Identify people in your organization from other cultures. Discuss both business and social topics with them. Aim to see things from their perspective. Deliberately look for differences in the way they would handle and interpret various situations. Then look for similarities.

- If you work or vacation in another country, record your observations in a journal. What surprises you? What is similar? What is hard to understand?

- Talk and spend time with people from other cultures.

- Rotate staff whenever possible to give people exposure to other cultures. Think creatively to make opportunities available to employees other than managers and executives.

- Stay abreast of world events by reading newspapers and magazines daily. Develop the habit of asking yourself how specific events will or could affect you and your business.

- Join or start a discussion group that analyzes world events and monitors and predicts the impact of those events on people, governments, and business.

- Read newspapers from other countries. Notice the difference in emphasis and interpretation in the different newspapers. Each country's media typically will have an underlying cultural interpretation of events.

- Take a course in world economics that provides an overview of the major world economic systems and how they interact. In particular, watch for examples of how economic events in one system can affect other systems.

- Keep in mind that understanding does not require agreement or approval. Expect to find customs or viewpoints with which you disagree, but still need to understand.

- Examine how other cultures differ from and are similar to your own. Choose one country a month and learn all you can about that country, comparing and contrasting it with your own. Study both its social and cultural norms with objectivity.

- Continue to develop your own perspective of business in the global economy. Watch for patterns and predictors. For instance, if a major corporation shifts its national base of production, what kind of fallout can be expected for the industry worldwide and for your place in it?

Learn the business practices of other cultures

In the United States, business people exchange business cards with hardly a glance at what's on them. In Japan, it's expected that upon receiving someone's business card, you will study it carefully, acknowledge having received it, and perhaps make a comment or ask a polite question about it. During a meeting, you would put the card, along with those of the others at the meeting, in front of you. Such treatment of the business card shows that you respect the individual who gave it to you.

Business practices, as an extension of the culture of a country, vary widely throughout the world. To effectively conduct business with individuals of another country, it's essential to understand the key differences in how business is practiced in the other country versus your own. This knowledge will enable you to better anticipate how other countries will react to your strategies and products.

The following guidelines present ways for you to increase that understanding:

- Observe or study the business practices of successful multinational businesses. Identify similarities and differences among the practices and reasons for them. Compare these practices with your organization's values and practices.

- Talk to expatriates about their experiences. What did they learn about themselves, their culture, the culture of others? What were their frustrations? Their greatest successes? What would they do differently? What should others know?

- Benchmark global businesses.

- Take an expatriate assignment. Whether short- or long-term, an expatriate assignment will allow you to live with cultural differences and observe their effects on business, not just read and theorize about them.

- Join an organizational task force or project team dealing with global issues. Working through a real-life business issue is an action-learning opportunity. Reflect on what you are learning as you work on the assignment.

- Identify people within your organization, industry, or network who are from the country you're researching. Ask them to tell you about business practices of that country. Find out both how to behave and how not to behave.

- Seek advice from a consulting firm that specializes in cross-cultural training for business to teach you the business practices of the countries in which you are or will be doing business. This is particularly useful after you have acquired a more general and conceptual understanding of the culture.

- If your organization has an office in the country you're researching, travel to that office and spend some time with its staff. Observe them as they work with their customers and other business associates. Pay attention to how they behave, what procedures they follow, and what kinds of customs they observe. Note the atmosphere of the meetings, the level of formality and informality, and who leads in any meeting.

- Develop a list of questions to ask and topics to cover about business practices. Role-play several situations with the office staff to make sure you are practicing the customs correctly.

- Attend orientations and briefings held by government agencies about doing business in particular countries.

Know how to conduct business in other countries

How you conduct business in other countries can be very different from how you do business in your own country. From knowing when to give gifts to understanding the protocol of negotiation, different customs can significantly affect your dealings with customers, distributors, suppliers, and colleagues in other countries. Recognizing and handling those differences can be the deciding factor in a successful international business effort.

To help you conduct business internationally, try the following suggestions:

- Before you work in another country (or in your own country with business people from another country), learn all you can about the cultural norms and customs of doing business in that country. For example, what is the cultural norm about coming to appointments on time? Where and when are decisions made—at the meeting at which they are discussed, or at dinner afterward?

- Remember, too, to take into account the regional differences within the country. Just as your own country has regional variations, so do all other countries. These regional differences can become pivotal when they affect business practices.

- Learn enough of the language of the country to be able to use the basic forms of introductions, greetings, and similar exchanges that are used by business people in that country. In addition, learn the 50 or so words that express respect, gratitude, appreciation, and empathy in the language in which you are working.

- Develop international contacts and discuss with them the market, demographics, perceptions, and so on, of the country and the region in which you plan to market your products or services.

- Learn about the national and local laws of the country that relate to your business involvement. For example, if you will be establishing a manufacturing plant in another country:
  - Are there national or local laws related to the use of local suppliers for raw materials to be used?
  - What are the requirements about hiring local citizens?
  - Are there certification or licensing laws that your organization's employees or agents must comply with?
  - What limits, if any, exist on foreign/national composition of management ranks?
  - What are the antipollution laws?
  - What currencies are allowed for transacting business?

- Learn the differences between commissions and salaries in other countries.

- When you are in another country, hire a cultural guide. Check references, and hire a reputable and experienced coach. This should be someone who knows the language and who can coach you on proper conduct. Make it clear up front that you want feedback on your behavior. Your guide will be your teacher.

- Be as flexible as you can; let go of your agenda when necessary. Keep your goals in mind, but remember that the standards and business practices of the country in which you are doing business may require a different route to the achievement of those goals than you had in mind.

- Recognize that it can take a great deal more effort to build a trusting business relationship when you are working with people and businesses from a different culture.

- When checking with others for information about a specific country, don't rely on a single source of information. Use more than one source to avoid biased perceptions.

- When a plan you've developed does not work as expected, analyze the situation. Research what may have gone wrong from a cultural perspective.

- When you select people to work internationally, choose individuals who are curious, flexible, and respectful of other cultures and customs. Provide these people with cultural training and ongoing support.

**Market products
and services
internationally**

One of the biggest problems organizations face in their efforts to market
products and services internationally is learning how to position and
advertise the product so that it fits into the culture of a specific country.
Cultural differences, language differences, and differences in what people
value play a role in marketing products internationally. What plays well in
New York City doesn't necessarily do well in Tokyo. The needs of the people
in Paris differ from those in Lima, Peru.

The following suggestions can help you effectively position your products
or services so they appeal to the cultures involved:

- Identify and define your company's global market—the countries with
  which your company does business or would like to do business.
  Determine how your company's products can meet the needs of the
  people in the countries you identified.

- Assess the countries where you want to do business to determine what
  it takes to market and sell there.
  - Study how the competition sells its products internationally, and evaluate
    how successful their methods have been.
  - Look at publications from those countries to see how nationals advertise
    their products.
  - Know the economy of the country and how people purchase products.
    For example, one organization found that in order to sell cough drops,
    they had to package the drops individually because consumers couldn't
    afford to buy a whole package.
  - Travel to the countries to see for yourself how you might position
    your products and services.

- Look at your competitors.
  - Study your competitors and learn from their successes and mistakes.
  - Go where your competitors are not. Consider this strategy carefully,
    however, especially if you compete with top-notch organizations.
    If you are usually first into a new market, there may be no problem.
    But if your competitor is usually first into a market and is not there,
    make certain you learn the reasons why, and that those reasons have
    been taken into account in your plans for entering the market.
  - Go where your competitors are only when you know you have a
    competitive offering.

- Determine who your future competitors will be. Consider entering markets that you think your future competitors may go into, and gain market share before they actively enter that market.

- Watch carefully to see if your assumptions about future markets are based on your understanding of existing markets. Ask your staff to continuously challenge assumptions.

- Understand your customers. Find out if there is a market for your products. For example, even though it's cheaper, the "huge economy size" will probably be a tough sell in countries where space is at a premium, both in stores and in homes.

- Question the impact of your product on customers. Will it help them? Are there any negative consequences for them?

- Add people to your staff who have personal experience in global markets you plan to enter.

- Assign natives of the country to the team that is responsible for marketing the product in that country, or hire a marketing firm from that country to consult.

- Identify the best way to introduce your product, service, or new marketing campaign to the country involved. For example, one organization sets up symposia to which it invites its key customers in each of the countries in which products are being introduced. An expert from headquarters is brought in to introduce the new product or campaign, which lends credibility and helps to gain the support of those key customers.

- Always remain open to making changes based on your own or other team members' increased understanding of the culture involved. Use internal and external experts as much as possible every step of the way.

PART 3:
THINK GLOBALLY ABOUT PEOPLE

**Help others
develop a
global mind-set**

One of the most important things you can do as a manager is to help others begin to think about the world in a larger context. As you train yourself to think globally, remember to encourage this kind of thinking in your staff and peers. This will be particularly important when you are budgeting, planning, or forecasting for the next year. Introducing the world into your process will help your staff prepare themselves for the global future and make your job easier.

To help others develop a global mind-set, consider the following suggestions:

- Encourage discussion of international business within your organization, including conversations that wrestle with the difficult issues of how to handle differing business practices and cultural norms and values.

- Talk openly about your desire to increase your global knowledge. Find out who else is interested and consistently encourage their efforts.

- Invite speakers to talk with your team about international issues and opportunities. The speakers can be foreign nationals who work at your job site, managers who have recently returned from a global assignment, or people who travel widely.

- Encourage people to share relevant articles, Web sites, or other information in structured ways during team meetings.

- Create a space on a communal bulletin board for relevant international business news.

- Consider a "buddy system" to link members of virtual teams. Have each member pick someone from a different office/country, and encourage them to stay in contact in more informal ways, sharing information about differences in culture and in business practices.

- Include members of your staff in some of the activities you choose to expand your own international business savvy.

- Pay attention to disparaging comments about how people do things differently. It is critical that you act as a role model in valuing working with people in different countries and circumstances. Encourage frank discussions with team members who seem frustrated by working across boundaries.

- Push others to consider whether there is an international or global component to their ideas and suggestions.

- Share books and articles that are helpful. Consider having lunch meetings occasionally to discuss what you've learned.

Know how to manage employees in other countries

With the growth of multinational companies, more people are finding themselves managing staffs of people from other countries—either in that country or remotely, from the organization's headquarters. The following suggestions are helpful in such situations:

- Recognize that the goals and objectives for your staff need to reflect the local business practices and the cultural values and norms. For example, U.S. nationals may be more concerned than others about getting personal credit for success, demonstrating their drive to succeed, or confronting unequal treatment. Some employees from U.S. companies and elsewhere may be willing to work late hours, because they believe it is important, while others believe that spending time with family is more important.

- When writing or interpreting policies, identify the desired outcome and the intention of the policy. Allow the local staff to fine-tune the specific procedures for carrying out the policy. This eliminates situations where the specifics of policies and procedures don't match the local work environment and thus are disregarded. It also encourages the involvement and buy-in of the local staff.

- Learn as much of the local language as you can, especially if you are working in the country involved. Your attempts to learn and use the language of the country will help you build trust and credibility with your staff.

- Learn all that you can about the social and business customs of the country. These customs apply as much to your staff as they do to your customers and business associates.

- Understand the educational system of the country. The U.S. educational system, for example, tends to produce more specialists, while other countries' systems tend to produce more generalists. As a result, the division of tasks may be different—less specialized—in other countries than you might be accustomed to in your own country. For example, one company found that, in its German plant, one position handled the work that was divided among four different specialist positions in its U.S. plants.

- Ask for assistance from your organization's human resources office or your manager about handling international staffs.

- Be clear that you want feedback from the staff regarding your behavior from their cultural viewpoint.

- Find out your organization's reputation for treatment of employees. Is it consistent internationally?

- Recognize the holidays of the countries in which your business is located.

- Build or tap into a network of managers in your organization and industry, as well as in other organizations or industries, who have managed people from other countries. Ask for their advice and support.

- Create different reward systems to accommodate cultural differences.

- Recognize that human-resource practices differ among cultures. Decide how these issues should be handled on a country-by-country basis.

- Pay attention to differences in time zones. Alternate meeting times so that you don't always put the same group at a disadvantage.

- Remember that people in remote locations or "off the beaten path" often feel isolated and left out. Consider the relationship issues that your group takes for granted (e.g., camaraderie, access to resources), and be sensitive and champion ways to provide them more interaction and access.

- Proactively support expatriates and repatriates. Often, they need extra time in moving and getting acclimated, especially when they have families who must adjust as well.

Develop cross-cultural knowledge

Thinking globally means understanding the subtleties of cultural effects. Getting a firm grasp on the variables that affect business in other countries includes knowing how cultures differ from each other. To succeed in a global organization, managers need to know about their own culture and the cultures of people with whom they work or will work. It is essential to learn the key cultural customs and practices that will allow you to work together.

The following suggestions will help you develop that cross-cultural knowledge needed for thinking globally:

- Identify people from other cultures in your organization or network. Ask them for insights about the similarities and differences between your culture and theirs. Identify cultural differences that could be problematic in conducting business. Make sure you also concentrate on the similarities.

- Recognize that business people from other countries may not be the same as other people from those cultures, because business people who work with multinational companies become accustomed to other cultures.

- Avoid generalizing what you learn about one individual to the entire culture from which they come. Think of someone from another culture believing all people from your country behave and think like the one person they met or someone they've seen on television.

- Visit the country or countries on which you are focusing in your work. Talk with people. Learn the proper etiquette in that country. Learn about its social structures and norms. Seek to understand the local and business culture.

- Take a course in cross-cultural studies. Learn not only how specific countries differ from one another, but also how the cultures vary. Learn about similarities as well as differences.

- Do something every day to learn a bit more about the cultures of the countries that interest you. Watch TV programs or videotapes about the country's language and culture. Listen to language/culture tapes while commuting or driving between appointments.

- If you plan to live overseas or work frequently with people from other countries, take foreign language courses designed for business people that include learning about the culture and customs of the country. If you are already living in another country, learn its language.

- Rotate staff whenever possible so that people get exposure to other cultures.

- Participate in cross-cultural communication workshops or training to get a deeper understanding of other cultures.

- Encourage your staff to learn additional languages if they do not already know them. Make language proficiency a requirement for particular positions.

- Write to the embassies of the countries you're interested in and ask for information about the culture of each country, as well as its regional differences.

- Spend time with natives of foreign countries, discussing the differences and similarities of your respective backgrounds.

RESOURCES

The resources for this chapter begin on page 628.

JUDGMENT FACTOR

---

*"Not everything that counts can be measured, and not
everything that can be measured counts."*
— Albert Einstein

Strategic thinking, sound analysis and decision-making skills are a prerequisite for leadership positions. Yet, increasingly, leaders find these skills challenged by the rapid flow of new information, the ongoing stream of thorny business challenges, and the flood of new, complex, and difficult issues. Further complicating these challenges are the double-edged swords of technological advancements, rapid communication, and a global economy.

Consequently, successful leaders need to more effectively identify the issues that matter most to their business area or department, then collect and sift the information, and make sound decisions.

This section presents development activities that address the following three areas of judgment skills:

Chapter 5 - Analyze Issues: Gathers and analyzes the most critical information needed to understand problems; probes and looks past symptoms to determine underlying causes of problems and issues; integrates information from a variety of sources to arrive at optimal solutions; detects inaccuracies or flaws in reasoning; defines reasonable alternatives to resolve problems.

Chapter 6 - Use Sound Judgment: Brings to bear the appropriate knowledge and expertise in making decisions; considers alternative solutions before making decisions; bases decisions on sound logic and rationale; advances problems toward resolution when encountering ambiguity or uncertainty; chooses the best alternative based on consideration of pros, cons, tradeoffs, timing, and available resources; makes timely decisions on problems and issues requiring immediate attention; makes sound decisions on complex functional issues and problems.

Chapter 7 - Think Strategically: Operates from a strategic perspective in own area of business; recognizes the broad implications of issues; shows openness to new ideas and perspectives; shows people, teams, business processes, and outcomes; sees the relationships between people, teams, business processes, and outcomes; considers strategic issues affecting own area when making decisions; creates strategies that balance long- and short-term goals.

5
ANALYZE ISSUES

PART 1: CLARIFY AND DIAGNOSE THE ISSUE
- *Identify issue essentials*
- *Delve under symptoms to find root issues and causes*
- *Analyze issues from multiple perspectives*

PART 2: SOURCE NECESSARY AND CRITICAL INFORMATION FOR ANALYSIS
- *Identify and gather the most relevant information*
- *Obtain relevant information through people and data*
- *Focus on what's critical and important*

PART 3: ANALYZE THE ALTERNATIVES
- *Integrate information and define reasonable alternatives*
- *Recognize broader implications of issues*
- *Fine-tune inductive and deductive thinking skills*
- *Detect inaccuracies or flaws in reasoning*

INTRODUCTION

Strategic issues, competitive challenges, and workplace problems—whether they are interpersonal, interdepartmental, or international in scope—more than ever require a planned, focused analysis to ensure an appropriate conclusion.

Your performance in the workplace depends on how quickly, completely, and accurately you break down and sort through the challenging and complex issues and problems that present themselves.

Thorough, realistic analysis forms the basis for effective decision making, which is now likely to involve more constituencies with shorter timelines than ever before. Such constraints necessitate a mix of systemic and organic analysis to ensure examination of all possible angles of the equation.

This chapter offers common-sense guidelines and ideas for improving analytical skills on the job.

VALUABLE TIPS

- Identify and understand your goal. Then develop a plan for analysis that will achieve the goal.

- Identify what you know. Then identify the information and perspectives you need to gather.

- Identify from whom you need information.

- When you encounter new or recurring issues or opportunities, determine whether you can rely only on the resources and people you are accustomed to using. Identify all possible sources of information and perspective.

- Uncover alternative ways of defining the issue by reformulating or restating it from the different perspectives involved. Consider how the perspective changes the problem.

- When conducting analysis that involves the value chain, include those in the value chain closest to the opportunity or problem.

- Ensure input from those closest to the problem.

- Continue to ask "why" to help discover the root cause of problems.

- Use the most appropriate method of gathering information for the situation. For example, rather than having a meeting, use other methods of gathering information, such as e-mail or voicemail; they take less time and may encourage more objective, complete responses.

- Ask others to list the pros and cons of a given issue in order to identify different perspectives and uncover potential conflicts or ambiguities that need further analysis.

- Double check all data related to important decisions and actions to ensure accuracy and to see if you have neglected salient details.

- Keep a journal of challenges that arise in your area. Review them to identify themes and root causes, and then address those underlying issues.

- Recognize that you will not always have enough information before making some decisions. Plan what to do if the decision does not generate the results you want.

- Conduct post mortems so you can learn from your experience.

PART I:
CLARIFY AND DIAGNOSE THE ISSUE

Identify issue essentials

The first step in analyzing any issue is to identify its scope and parameters. How an issue or opportunity is defined is critical. If you expect to arrive at a successful solution or course of action, you must take time to clearly define the issue.

Clarifying the issue or opportunity also gives you a much better sense of what information needs to be gathered and how it should be evaluated, as well as who should be involved in the process.

When you are confronted with an issue or opportunity, define it by writing down brief responses to the following questions:

- What is the issue or opportunity? Describe it. If it is a problem, when does it occur? Just as important, when does it not occur? Who is involved? What role does each person play? If it is an opportunity, what is the opportunity?

- What is at the core of the issue? If it is a problem, what is its root cause? If it is an opportunity, why is it an opportunity?

- What is the potential impact on me and my role, or my department and its goals? What are the positive elements or consequences of this issue or opportunity? What are the negative elements or consequences?

- What other people and functions are affected or likely to be affected by this issue? Who else may be interested in this opportunity? If an international office or affiliate is involved, how will I address differences in language, in perception of the issue as a problem, and in business culture or expectations?

- What is my goal?

It's wise to be as objective as possible during issue analysis to ensure that all relevant and critical information is carefully considered. If the issue is a problem, define it as a need, not as a solution or next action.

Your first responses to the questions above are likely to be somewhat tentative or general, especially if the issue represents something new, complex, or subtle. As you gather information, review and revise those initial responses to reflect your increased awareness and understanding.

Delve under symptoms to find root issues and causes

If issues and challenges are handled at a surface level, you will find yourself facing them again and again. Identifying the root issues and causes, on the other hand, will let you engage in more effective analysis for lasting change. To bolster your skills in this area, try the following process:

1. Describe the problem. Be careful to describe only the problem—not possible solutions. Describe the problem in terms of needs.

2. Come up with a theory or a guess about why the problem occurs. Include the role that you or your team may play in the problem.

   Here are some ways to find a theory:

   • In a team, have team members tell stories about their experience with the problem. Chart the details. Look for patterns.

   • Draw a picture of the problem. Include the beginning, middle, and consequences.

   • When appropriate, draw a picture of the problem over time. Examine what has happened to it over time.

   • Make a list about the problem that includes when it began, when it occurs, when it does not occur, who is involved, who isn't, when/how it gets better or worse, what impacts the problem, what does not. Look for themes and patterns.

   • Use the Japanese technique of asking the five whys: Identify a problem, including its parts and sequencing. Then, for each statement, ask why. After you answer, ask why to that statement. For example, the problem may be that materials did not arrive on time. Why? The shipper did not know the date. Why? The person thought they had turned it in. Why? They had filled out four forms and thought it was one of them. Why? It is easy to get confused with all the forms and no tracking systems. Why? Funds for the tracking system were not approved. Why? The need seemed less important than other priorities. This example illustrates the power of this process; it surfaced many issues to deal with, rather than one person to blame.

   • Use best-practices lists and models to identify problem causes. Both of these practices help to avoid blind spots and often save time.

Analyze issues from multiple perspectives

A major and recurring obstacle to good analysis is the tendency to look at an issue only in the way it most naturally appears to you, and then to analyze only that view of the issue. But this approach limits your view of the situation, and the ensuing analysis, recommendations, and eventual decision making will contain pronounced biases and preconceived notions of the issue and its parameters.

Instead, analyze issues from multiple perspectives, so that you see it in as many ways as possible. This broader set of perspectives gives you a more accurate understanding of the issue and usually opens up more potential solutions.

To avoid the trap of seeing an issue from only one perspective in the initial stage of analysis, try the following approaches:

- Consider the issue from various stakeholders' perspectives. How would different internal customers view the problem? Your manager? An external customer? The union? A process expert? The CEO?

- Map out the process. It may have a flow, loops, decisions points, etc., rather than simple cause and effect.

- Consider whether the issue represents a change that is actually part of some larger-scale transformation. What could that big picture be, and where could it possibly take the product, department, organization, or industry? To understand the path of change to date, recall how things looked six months ago, a year ago, and three years ago, and then work to extrapolate meaning for the future.

- Find out whether different regions or geographies see the issue differently. A company office in Paris may see a problem in need of fixing, while the Singapore and San Francisco offices are happy with the current state. A problem is defined by and depends on the values, attitudes, and business culture and expectations of the people involved in and affected by it.

- Look at the issue from its political perspective. How might changes affect your customers, vendors, your own people, or senior management? Remember that change represents both power loss and gain, whether it is positional power, referent power, coercive power, or expert power.

- Consider that the issue represents an organism unto itself in some ways. Could it survive without support from other parts of the organization? What is the heart of the issue, and where are the limbs? What climate does it thrive in, and how might it respond to changes in that environment?

PART 2:
SOURCE NECESSARY AND CRITICAL INFORMATION FOR ANALYSIS

Identify and gather the most relevant information

The right information is essential to effective analysis. When you need to analyze an issue or opportunity, your first step is to identify the information you need. Use the following process to help you do this:

1. List what you think you need to know to analyze and resolve the issue. Include information that is important to resolving the issue; avoid listing information that can be easily accessed but is not important. The following suggestions can help you list your information needs:

   - Incorporate other viewpoints. When other people or parts of the organization will be affected, you need to know their perceptions to reach a workable, wise, and accepted result. For example, not everyone in sales will have the same views on the best way to launch a new product or service. In that case, you would ask a few people in various geographic regions and obtain customer and supplier input when appropriate.

   - Build on past experience to avoid reinventing the wheel. Ask:
     - Has the organization faced a similar issue in the past? How can I find out? If it has, who was involved and how was it handled? What were the results? What has changed since then for the organization and in the industry?
     - How have other organizations handled similar issues?
     - Get input from experts inside and outside the organization.

2. Rank the items on your list according to how critical they are to resolving the issue. To avoid wasting time collecting unnecessary or marginally useful information, first pursue information that is likely to yield the most value. Recognize when information is too difficult or time-consuming to access, and gather only the data that is critical to your decision-making process.

3. Determine how, where, and when you will gather the information for your analysis. Your sources might include written materials, live or e-mail-based interviews, group discussions, questionnaires, Internet searches, or direct observation. The sources you use will depend to a large extent on your specific information needs.

   If you are not sure how to obtain the information you need, ask your manager, your peers, or your staff for ideas. They likely use approaches that differ from those you alone would consider.

Obtain relevant information through people and data

When gathering information and perspective from others, ask questions, listen carefully to the information provided, and follow up with summaries and links to ensure that you understand the impact of the information or perspective. Use the following suggestions to help you gather relevant data:

- When interviewing others to gain information, you can increase your efficiency and effectiveness by using these techniques: structuring, open-ended questioning, and active listening.

  - **Structuring** involves establishing an agenda for your interview to ensure that the interview stays on track and you get the information you want. Try these steps:

    1. Before the interview, list the topics to discuss and the information you need.
    2. Write down questions you can ask that will yield the desired information.
    3. At the outset of your meeting, let the person(s) know what you hope to accomplish during your time together.
    4. In many instances, it may help to share your agenda, including the questions you plan to ask. Interviewees who understand your needs are better able to focus their answers to give you the desired information.

  - **Open-ended questioning** involves asking questions that require more than a one- or two-word response. Examples of open-ended questions include those that begin with such phrases as "What do you think…" or "Tell me about…." Avoid closed questions, such as those that begin with "did" or "is" and can be answered with a simple "yes" or "no"; they encourage passive responses.

  - **Active listening** involves paying close attention to what the speaker is saying, rephrasing his or her comments, and then asking whether you have understood them correctly. Take good notes, and summarize the interview by quickly reviewing your notes with the interviewee to ensure that they are correct.

  - **Keep an open mind when you are listening.** Take care not to judge the speaker's suggestions or to convey, either verbally or nonverbally, that you disapprove of the information you are receiving. If you are not open to the information you are soliciting, your speaker will sense that his or her input is not appreciated and will stop trying to communicate with you. A closed interviewer will miss much information and be unable to synthesize it objectively and completely.

FIRST THE THIRTY DAY FORECAST, THEN THE CRACKERS.

BUSH

- Written resources may be relevant to many of the issues you face. These resources might include manuals, books, Web sites, trade journals or other periodicals, and statistical or financial reports.

- Recognize that the amount of research required to solve a problem depends on the complexity and criticality of the problem.

Focus on what's critical and important

Managers can drown in the sea of data available to them. Considering too much detail or information of lesser value can prevent you from making timely decisions. Knowing how to focus on the essential information can greatly increase the efficiency and effectiveness of your analysis.

To determine whether you typically look at an appropriate level of detail in analyzing issues, use the following process:

- Identify the additional information you want by looking at what you know and what you need to know. Separate what you need from what you want by identifying the information that will make a real difference in your analysis.

- Identify the entire business process involved or, when appropriate, the critical path. Understanding the business process will help you see the important components. A critical path accomplishes this goal, and also considers the time sequences.

- Use a team to identify what information is critical.

- Ask a few people for their opinions about what information is most important to gather. The further you are from your area of expertise, the more you will want to rely on others to help you decide the information you need to have.

- If you have received feedback that you do not deal with the most critical issues or spend too much time on less important information, ask people for examples, or verify examples you have identified, so you can better understand the development need.

PART 3:
ANALYZE THE ALTERNATIVES

Integrate information and define reasonable alternatives

Analysis generally involves both quantitative and qualitative operations. The goal is to break down and sort gathered information in a way that will ultimately point you toward reasonable alternatives. The following suggestions can help you develop this skill:

- Integrate information you have into categories or themes. Helpful categories include:
  - "What is" and "what should be" from each perspective.
  - Problem process or phases.
  - People involved.
  - Attempted solutions.
  - Recommended solutions from each perspective.

- Use a model, such as a best-practices model of a business process or a conceptual model, to organize and make sense of the information.

- Find commonalities. With the team or others involved, isolate the issues, perspectives, themes, and patterns that are common to all involved.

- Generate problem definitions that range from narrow viewpoints to all-inclusive ones.

- If you have difficulty analyzing the information, ask others to help. They may be able to see things you cannot. In addition, they can serve as a check of your own perceptions.

- Define the problem in a way that includes all viewpoints.

- Determine criteria for possible solutions. Remember that you are looking for alternatives that will be mutually acceptable.

- Generate alternatives and use your criteria to evaluate them.

Recognize broader implications of issues

Organizations are systems. An issue does not occur in a vacuum. Therefore, to fully grasp the issue, it's essential to understand the systems, processes, and relationships that surround and are part of the issue. Consider these suggestions:

- To understand an issue or opportunity, investigate the following:
  - The business process in which it is nested.
  - The purpose of the business process.
  - The people involved—their roles and responsibilities for parts of the business process and the relationships among them.
  - The goals of the people.

- Recognize that in business, you cannot understand anything in isolation. There is always more than you can see on the surface, so look for it.

- Ask your team, "What might we be missing?" and "What are we assuming?"

- Recognize that any change, favorable or not, will impact the rest of the system. Some of the changes and their consequences you can anticipate, and some you cannot.

- Remember that unintended consequences always arise, no matter how noble and good the idea or change. This is a fact of life, so be sure to look at the downstream impact.

- Consider the people involved, their goals, and their history with one another. It is important to approach this quest for understanding with an open mind. Recognize that two major barriers to understanding are the beliefs that "only the facts count" and "nonsense is anything that doesn't make sense to me." To develop a better understanding of these relationships:
  - Ask the people involved to explain the relationships to you in their own words.
  - Ask others who you believe are insightful about people or organizations to discuss the issue with you.
  - Make a flowchart, map, or network chart to help you visualize the interrelationships and connections.
  - Test your hypotheses with others. You may want to model what will happen if a change is made. In some situations, schematic diagrams outlining the relationship between cause and effect will be effective. Modeling techniques are often facilitated by the use of computer software that can graph interactions and even calculate the quantitative aspects of these relationships. Many resources of this variety are readily available on the Internet.
  - Within the complexity, identify the critical path necessary to achieve your goals.
  - To make the most of complex relationships, find the commonalities and mutual goals that exist among people or groups and leverage these for the benefit of the greater goal.

Fine-tune inductive and deductive thinking skills	When analyzing issues and considering the pros and cons of proposed solutions, you will be better able to make the best decisions if you first check the logic you used to analyze and decide the issue.

People use two types of logic to reach conclusions: inductive and deductive. Inductive thinking moves from the specific to the general; in other words, given that we know specific facts A, B, and C, we can conclude that X happens in general within these sorts of cases. Deductive thinking is the reverse, where logic moves from the general to the specific, i.e., if the concept of X is true, then specific facts A, B, and C will follow as a result. Each of us subconsciously uses both kinds of reasoning every day.

Regardless of whether you use an inductive or a deductive process to reach a conclusion, it's important to check your reasoning to make sure it is logically sound. Try these suggestions:

- When you draw a conclusion from various facts, make sure the facts really support the conclusion. Ask yourself and others if the data could point to any other conclusions as well.

- Conversely, check that your conclusion or generalization is really supported by the facts, not just by your personal beliefs. Also double-check others' conclusions.

- When you arrive at a general conclusion from a situation or series of events, check that the specific changes proposed logically follow or are the only sensible options. For example, if you conclude that quality is important to your customers, you may then assume you have to take particular actions to ensure quality. But before deciding, you need to first evaluate whether these actions are your only options and whether they are the best ones.

Detect inaccuracies or flaws in reasoning	While most business people are sound thinkers, everyone occasionally makes mistakes in logic, assumptions, and conclusions. These flaws occur more frequently when people are operating in uncharted areas, out of their own areas of expertise, or are in a hurry. Consider these suggestions to help yourself and others catch flaws in reasoning and unsupported assumptions and conclusions:

- Use models to help organize your thinking, but at the same time, be aware of how your model will impact your thinking. Identify your mental model as it relates to the issue or problem, or ask another to do so. A mental model is your personal picture or theory about the world, people, teams, and organizations. It is your worldview. For example, you probably have a mental model of how customers should be treated.

This mental model will impact what you see, what you pay attention to, what options you generate, etc. Therefore, to detect flaws in your reasoning, identify your mental model and its possible flaws or impacts. It is easiest to do this by involving other people, because they have different mental models.

- Ask others to challenge your assumptions, the inferences you make from the information gathered, and the options and limitations you see.

- As you listen to people, identify their assumptions that have resulted in their proposed solution or point of view. Ask them for evidence that the assumptions are true.

- Ask people to identify your assumptions. Then identify what information you have that supports the assumptions. If you do not have data to support the conclusion, find it.

- Treat your issue as a legal case. With yourself as the courtroom lawyer, ask a patient, wise, and trusted colleague to play the role of judge, jury, opposing lawyer, and then journalist to track where your reasoning is weak from those angles. What constructive criticism can they offer? Where do they think your analysis or arguments are in need of fine-tuning or renewed focus?

- Check your inferences. In one column, write down the facts you have gathered. In a second column, write down the conclusions you have drawn from the facts, and in a third column, identify alternative conclusions you could draw. If you cannot find alternatives yourself, ask your team or a colleague. How do these additional views impact your view of the issue or problem and the options you see?

RESOURCES

The resources for this chapter begin on page 630.

6
USE SOUND
JUDGMENT

PART 1: MAKE THE DECISION: CONSIDERATIONS AND
HABITS TO KEEP
- *Establish clear goals for decisions*
- *Synthesize analysis with decision objectives*
- *Generate alternatives*
- *Determine criteria for decision making*
- *Consider alternatives and their consequences*
- *Make a decision*
- *Test the practicality of decisions*
- *Collaborate with others in decision making*

PART 2: IMPROVE THE DECISION-MAKING PROCESS
- *Clarify decision-making responsibility and methods*
- *Take responsibility for decisions*
- *Decide in situations of risk, uncertainty, or complexity*
- *Make timely decisions about issues*
- *Curb impulsiveness*

INTRODUCTION

Decision making is a critical part of every manager's job. The consequences of poor decisions are varied, including increased costs, damage to relationships, loss of trust, and inadequate strategy. Effective leaders make sound decisions and guide their teams to use effective decision-making processes.

Decision making involves judging both objective and subjective data; it relies on a mix of analysis and judgment. Sound judgment requires setting clear goals, establishing criteria for decision making, generating alternatives, weighing and analyzing alternatives, balancing task and relationship goals, and making a decision.

This chapter focuses on the process of decision making and provides suggestions for avoiding or overcoming common pitfalls along the way.

VALUABLE TIPS

- Determine whether you have the information necessary to make a sound decision. If not, decide what you need to know and how you can get the information.

- When the decision is important to other people, find out what they think you should know. Listen carefully to their input; it will give you their understanding of the issue, their rationale for their opinion, and often the conclusion or decision they want to reach.

- Deliberately look at the issue from the viewpoint of different constituencies. This will give you a more complete understanding of all aspects of the issue.

- Be concerned if you are reluctant or unable to understand the viewpoint of others. This reaction is an important warning signal, because it will be difficult for you to make a decision that will be received and implemented well if you cannot, at least partially, understand the other points of view.

- Before you make a decision, establish criteria for making the decision. Involve people affected by the decision to help define the criteria.

- Know your goals for the decision. Then determine whether the goals address both the short- and long-term issues and consequences, and both task and relationship elements.

- Ensure that you understand the goals of others by summarizing them and asking for confirmation.

- Consider alternative solutions instead of going with the first option that presents itself. There may be more alternatives than you imagine.

- When you cannot think of alternatives, ask other people. Also use this as a warning sign that you may be restricting your thinking more than is wise.

- Increase your decision options by removing perceived constraints to your options. When you cannot figure out how to remove the constraints yourself, ask others for help.

- List major areas of uncertainty and risk. Strive to resolve, minimize, or eradicate as many as possible.

- Carefully consider possible consequences of each alternative before you make a final decision. Think about the impact on the various stakeholders.

- Before making a hasty decision, ensure that immediate action is required.

- Look at each issue from several angles to get a better perspective and improve your judgment.

PART I:
MAKE THE DECISION:
CONSIDERATIONS AND HABITS TO KEEP

Establish clear goals for decisions

Before making any decision, first determine your goals or objectives for the decision. These serve as the foundation for sound decision making.

Common objectives or goals for decision making include the following:

- To resolve short- and/or long-term issues.

- To resolve issues in a way that the organization can afford.

- To resolve issues so that operations are not disturbed.

- To resolve issues so that those involved find the decision acceptable.

- To resolve issues or make decisions in such a way that relationships among people involved are not harmed.

The goals of most decision-making processes involve both task and relationship aspects of the decision. Sometimes the relationship goal is most important; other times the task objective is. Often, sound decision making must deal with polarities and balance both types of needs.

Synthesize analysis with decision objectives

To make sound decisions, you first need to gather enough information, and to gather it from those involved in the situation and those who will be affected by the decision. Then, you need to analyze that information in light of the goals or objectives you've identified for your decision.

The following guidelines can help ensure that you are appropriately gathering and synthesizing information:

1. Carefully identify, define, and review the issues.

   - What is the problem or issue? Describe the problem or issue in one clear sentence. State it in terms of need rather than a solution.

   - What important, critical facts are known?

   - What is unknown? Who knows that information, or how can it be gathered or determined?

   - When does the problem occur? When is it absent?

   - What is the consequence of the problem or issue?

- What has been tried in the past to deal with the situation? What happened as a result?

- How do people feel about the situation and changes to it?

- What related problems are present? If something changes, what else will likely change with it?

- What assumptions—about people, technology, systems, funding—have been made that might need to be challenged?

2. Organize the information according to its relevance for each of your goals. For example, if one of your goals is to resolve the issue in a way that the organization can afford, then combine all the information you've gathered about the costs of the issue and/or possible solutions so you can clearly see how the information relates to your goal.

3. Consider drafting a mind map that visually shows the relationship of the information you've gathered to each goal. To do so, write the goal in a circle in the center of a blank sheet of paper. Then draw additional circles around the goal circle, and in those circles, write the key points of the information that relate to that particular goal. Some of the information you've gathered may relate to more than one goal. This process will help you see those interrelationships.

4. Analyze the information relevant to each of your goals or objectives. For each goal or objective, ask yourself:

- How does the information affect this goal? Does it support it or present obstacles?

- Do I have all the information I need to ensure that I meet this goal? If not, what do I need and how can I obtain it?

- How does the information give me new perspectives on this goal?

Generate alternatives

Before you actually make a decision, generate as many options as you can for resolving the issue. Involve other people in this process. Doing so will result in more alternatives and more buy-in for the decision.

Use the following suggestions for generating alternatives:

- Brainstorm possible solutions with others. See Chapter 2: Champion Change and Innovation in this handbook for more information on brainstorming techniques.

- Use idea-generating questions, such as, "If we had no resource limitations, what could we do?" or "Technical limitations aside, what would be the best solution?"

- Find out how others have handled similar situations and use those ideas to stimulate alternatives.

- When a team is generating ideas, intervene whenever team members begin to evaluate alternatives. Remind the group that the focus at the moment is to gather as many options as possible, not to critique them. You may have to say this more than once, but it's important because criticism during idea generation can stop the flow of ideas.

- Deliberately try to think of alternatives that different perspectives may see. This approach challenges you to both see the situation and try to solve it from the viewpoints of others.

Determine criteria for decision making

A hallmark of sound decision making is clear criteria for making the decision. Before making a decision, determine the criteria for evaluating the options. The criteria should be drawn from the decision's goals or objectives.

In business situations, the following criteria are common:

- Minimally impacts current operations.

- Is logically sound.

- Helps achieve important business priorities.

- Reflects business priorities.

- Is consistent with values.

- Is acceptable to those involved.

- Can be implemented within the constraints (time, resources, other priorities).

- Incorporates data analysis, intelligent speculation about the future, and related people concerns.

- Considers any and all pros, cons, and risks.

Consider alternatives and their consequences

To make sound decisions, it is important to consider various alternatives and their consequences. Sometimes, an alternative will not work because it affects certain groups so negatively that they set out to modify it or ignore it altogether.

The following process can help you identify the consequences of alternatives:

1. For each alternative, ask how it will be accepted by:

    • Your staff

    • Your manager

    • Other departments

    • Informal leaders in the organization

    • People outside the organization (for example, vendors and customers)

2. Write down the pros and cons for each alternative according to who will support it and who will resist it. A chart like the following can help you structure your analysis:

PERSONS AFFECTED	ALTERNATIVE 1		ALTERNATIVE 2		ALTERNATIVE 3	
	PROS	CONS	PROS	CONS	PROS	CONS
YOUR STAFF						
YOUR MANAGER						
OTHER DEPARTMENTS						
INFORMAL LEADERS						
CUSTOMERS						

3. Analyze this information and use it to make a decision. If there is no clear best option, strike a balance between the options that are most workable and those that are most acceptable. Use this information to construct your implementation plan and to sell the decision and plan to those who need convincing. Naturally, those who disagree the most will require the most attention in the selling and implementation phases.

Make a decision

After you have generated alternative solutions, examined the possible consequences of each option, and determined your criteria for decision making, use the following process to ensure that you evaluate all possible alternatives against the criteria. The chart that follows will help you structure your analysis.

- State the specific problem or issue on the top line of the chart.

- Along the left side, record in order of priority your criteria for evaluating the alternatives.

- Write the alternative solutions across the top of the chart.

- Using a scale from 1 to 5, determine the degree to which each solution meets each criterion you have listed, with 1 being "does not satisfy the criterion" and 5 being "satisfies the criterion very well."

PROBLEM OR ISSUE: _____

CRITERIA	SOLUTION A:	SOLUTION B:	SOLUTION C:
1.			
2.			
3.			
4.			
5.			
6.			
7.			
8.			

Choose the solution that most completely satisfies the important criteria. Then ask yourself the following questions:

- How effectively does this alternative address the core objectives of the decision?

- Can I combine this alternative with another to make it even more effective?

- What will this alternative require in terms of resources (e.g., money, time, technology, people)?

Test the practicality of decisions

Alternatives that look good on paper and initially sound feasible sometimes lack pragmatic sense or do not work when implemented. Here are several ways to test the practicality of your decisions to increase their probability of success:

- Get into the habit of asking yourself at each stage of the decision-making process whether the decision is workable. Consider the specifics of your situation. Think through all possible results of the decision to ensure that you've covered all your bases.

- Before making your final decision, ask those who will be affected to assess the practicality of the decision, the impact of the decision on them, and whether they are likely to accept it. Remember to consider people in other units who may be affected by the changes you initiate. These people can be as instrumental in determining the success of your plan as those within your own group.

- Because many good decisions fail in the execution phase, be sure to develop a sound, specific implementation plan. A good plan needs to detail the correct sequence of steps and assign responsibility for the success of each step. Get input from all groups or departments that will be affected. If you understand how best to implement the change from their points of view, you increase the likelihood that your plan will be accepted and supported.

- Identify potential problems and plan ways to deal with them.

Despite the most careful analysis and planning, there will be times when a seemingly sound solution proves unworkable. In such cases, you need to be flexible, adapting your decision to eliminate efforts that are not working out. Be aware of this, and don't let these situations hinder your future efforts to choose and implement the best solutions.

Collaborate with others in decision making

Because so many perspectives and ideas are considered, the collaborative approach to decision making often produces the best results. In addition, those involved in making the decision are more likely to be committed to carrying out the solution. Thus, the increased time required in the initial decision-making process is often regained during the implementation phase.

Situations will arise, however, when group decision making is not appropriate. When decisions need to be made immediately, when the issue is confidential, or when buy-in is assured, collaborative decision making is not necessary.

The following steps will help you identify appropriate situations for collaborative decision making and how to get others involved in the process:

1. When you first learn that a decision must be made, determine if the decision is solely your own or if it should be made collaboratively. Collaborative decision making is useful when:

   • Other people have information you need.

   • The problem is complex or ambiguous, and you need other people to clarify and define the problem.

   • Other people are needed to implement the decision, and they want to be involved.

   • The situation can be used to train other people in problem analysis or decision making.

2. If you determine that the decision should be made collaboratively, use the group to define the problem, determine criteria for making the decision, look for alternatives, and/or actually make the decision. The group may be the same for each phase of the process, or you may want to use a larger group for getting input and a smaller group for making the decision.

3. When using a collaborative approach to decision making, keep the following in mind:

   • Involve others in the process by talking with them one-on-one, by asking for written input, or by calling a meeting.

   • Collaborative decision making can be effectively accomplished in well-run meetings, especially when participants are informed of the issues in advance.

   • Ask the group to use consensus decision making, rather than taking the majority view. Think of consensus as "Can I live with this?" rather than "Do I like this?"

For more suggestions on involving others in decision making, read Chapter 22: Foster Collaboration in this handbook.

PART 2:
IMPROVE THE DECISION-MAKING PROCESS

Clarify decision-making responsibility and methods

Indecision can often result when it is unclear who is responsible for making a decision. When the decision involves new or uncharted areas, it may be especially uncertain who has the authority to make it.

To help clarify who is responsible for making a decision, use the following process:

1. Talk to your manager to confirm his or her view of who should handle the issue or situation. Discuss his or her views about how the decision should be made, or about the decision-making process itself.

2. If the decision is yours to make, develop a plan for making it.

   • If you have all the necessary information, and those involved will commit to a decision if you make it, then simply make the decision.

   • If you need more information or the involvement of others for commitment, set up a process that involves people appropriately.

   • Remember to involve people whose information or commitment you need, but, whenever possible, also involve those who believe they should be involved.

   • If you involve others, ensure that a decision gets made quickly by using an efficient process. Follow the guidelines in Chapter 14: Drive Execution in this handbook.

If you establish a decision-making team to deal with the issue, use the following method to ensure that the best decision is reached:

1. Enlist the group's help to determine what is known and what needs to be known to make a sound decision. This effort will encourage others to step forward and develop leadership practice and experience. Make sure the group stays on track and distinguishes between information that is really necessary and important and that which is merely nice to know. Create plans and assign responsibilities among group members to gather the information.

2. Once you have obtained the needed information, use it to redefine the problem or opportunity as clearly as possible. At this point, you may decide to have multiple problem definitions.

3. Before making any decisions, generate multiple alternatives. Look for those that satisfy the multiple facets of the problem.

4. Together with the other group members and stakeholders, develop criteria for evaluating alternatives and selecting the best solution.

5. Make the decision, and develop contingency plans in case the solution doesn't work out.

For more suggestions on involving others in decision making, read Chapter 22: Foster Collaboration in this handbook.

Take responsibility for decisions

Sometimes leaders have difficulty accepting responsibility for the decisions they make or need to make. When this happens, the person may become defensive and blame others for decisions that had negative consequences or lacked the approval of others. Or, the person may avoid making decisions or delegate all decisions to others.

If your preferred method is to avoid making decisions or to ask others to do so, the following actions may help:

• List the major areas for which you clearly have decision-making responsibility in your role. Examples of such areas include capital expenditures, staffing, delegating, and policy making. Identify the areas in which you do make decisions and those in which you do not.

For example, you may feel comfortable making decisions on capital expenditures and often make decisions in this area on your own. You may feel less comfortable making policy decisions and may tend to ask for others' opinions immediately.

• For those areas in which you are uncomfortable making a decision, identify the core issue. Fear usually underlies the core issue, such as fear of:
  - Being wrong
  - Displeasing others
  - Executing the decision

Many times simply knowing your underlying concern can enable you to make the decisions you want.

- Once you know what the concern is, you can solve it as a problem. For example, if you are concerned about displeasing others, you can involve them in the decision-making process. If you are concerned about being wrong, you can ask others for their opinions. Keep track of how often your opinion matches those of others you trust.

- Keep a record of decisions you have made and their positive and negative consequences. Include what you did to fix or improve the situation when the consequence was initially negative. Use this record to identify how concerned you need to be about your decision making. This process also helps you see that decisions have both positive and negative consequences. What is most important in making decisions is to work through the issues to reach a realistic and satisfactory solution.

- If you have a tendency to divert your decision-making responsibilities to people higher in the organization, get into the habit of presenting recommended solutions, not problems, to your manager.

- If you make decisions but blame others when the decision is challenged, learn to catch yourself doing this and stop. Instead, when you are criticized, listen carefully and summarize the person's concerns. Do not defend or explain yourself. Then figure out what you want to do about the concerns.

Decide in situations of risk, uncertainty, or complexity

Because uncertainty is always present, every decision involves an element of risk. Sometimes, however, sound alternatives are discarded because they appear too risky or because the decision maker feels uncomfortable with unproven alternatives. Complex or ambiguous issues can multiply the difficulties involved.

Calculated risk taking implies that a decision is made with a thorough understanding of the potential risks and benefits involved. The ability to recognize and take calculated risks is a skill required of all managers.

Some obstacles to deciding on issues involving risk, uncertainty, or complexity are listed below, along with suggestions for overcoming each one.

- *Lack of knowledge about the true risk level of the alternative.* You may feel uneasy about the level of risk because you haven't clearly identified the pros and cons of each alternative. In such cases, write down each alternative and its associated risks and benefits. Then choose the one that provides the greatest benefit, even if it involves some risk. Manage the risk by anticipating as much as possible, planning your actions if problems occur, and dealing with problems as they arise.

- *Discomfort with the consequences of risk taking.* It is not unusual for people to become so uncomfortable about the possible consequences of a risky decision that they avoid taking risks altogether. If you tend to overemphasize the potential negative results of a decision, try the following suggestions:
  - Ask yourself, "What is the worst thing that could happen as a result of this decision? How much impact could this 'worst thing' have on me personally, on the organization, or on the work?" Determine what you could do if the worst-case scenario occurs.
  - Develop a strategy for reducing risks. Some risks can be reduced by good planning or by involving others and gaining their support.
  - If you find yourself concentrating on negative aspects of an alternative and deemphasizing its benefits, substitute positive statements or thoughts for negative ones. This process will help you determine whether the negatives are really as strong as you thought or whether you have been placing too much emphasis on the drawbacks.

- *Discomfort due to unknown risk factors.* In some cases, you may have a vague feeling that a solution carries some unknown risks. Rather than allowing these feelings to keep you from trying the solution, seek to understand what bothers you. Discuss your feelings with someone who may have greater insight or experience. Analyze your implementation process and determine the points at which the process could be halted—the "go/no go" decision points. Inform others of these points so they will not be surprised if you decide to discontinue the process at some point. Then, if the risk becomes too great, stop the process at one of these points.

- *Discomfort in selected areas.* If you analyze the various areas in which you must make decisions—hiring, capital expenditures, work flow, organizational structure, and advertising expenditures, to name a few—you will probably find that you are very comfortable with certain kinds of risks and less comfortable with others. Work at being more courageous and less cautious in your risk-averse areas.

When dealing with areas of discomfort, turn to people in your organization who seem particularly skilled at making decisions that involve these kinds of risks. Talk with these individuals about how they account for risk factors in their decisions, and study the way they make decisions. Then apply what you have learned to your own decision-making process.

Make timely decisions about issues

When managers do not make timely decisions, they may miss deadlines, hold up projects, waste resources, and frustrate people who are counting on them. Some managers want to be certain they have collected enough information; others, concerned about being right, spend a lot of time analyzing that information. Although the intent is positive, the results of stalling can lead to some real negatives, including missed market opportunities and lower morale and motivation.

To tighten up your decision-making timelines, use these guidelines:

- Ask yourself:
  - What information is absolutely necessary?
  - What additional information could be collected? How long would it take?
  - What information would make me feel better, but probably would not cause me to change my decision?

- Avoid "analysis paralysis." Set a deadline to complete your information analysis. Prioritize your greatest concerns, and spend your analysis time on them.

- Rather than insisting on certainty in the decision—which is likely to be impossible in any case—anticipate what you will do if problems arise. Look at whether you might be trying to gather too much data. Although fact finding is necessary, it can become a time drain if taken too far.

- Once you've made a decision, stand by it. Avoid reopening the decision-making process unless new information strongly indicates the need for reconsideration.

Most people do not procrastinate every time they make a decision; rather, they tend to delay decisions under certain circumstances. It's useful to identify those circumstances and determine how you can handle them in the future. The following suggestions can help:

1. Each time you find yourself delaying a decision, ask yourself the reason for the delay. Some of the more common reasons include:

   - Lack of information.

   - Unclear course of action.

   - Lack of time for thought.

   - Fear of negative consequences.

2. Once you've determined why you procrastinate, look for a solution. Plan ways to substitute decisive behaviors for the delaying tactics you wish to eliminate. Following are some possible approaches:

   • For situations in which you lack information, use the information-gathering suggestions in Chapter 5: Analyze Issues of this handbook. Plan for how you will gather the information, and implement your plan immediately.

   • When a course of action is unclear, choose what appears to be the best plan and implement it on a temporary basis. A trial run of the plan may turn up unanticipated benefits. Even if the plan doesn't work, the trial run may produce alternatives that have more credibility than any that could have been generated without the benefit of this experimentation.

   • If you lack sufficient time for focused, concentrated thought, block out time on your schedule for decision making when you are confronted with a major issue. Quiet time is necessary to think effectively about issues and possible solutions. Many people find early morning or late in the day to be the most conducive time for thinking through issues and making important decisions.

   • If you fear negative consequences in making a decision, face your fears. Seek the involvement of those you believe would resist your decision. A participative process is usually better in this kind of situation. If you fear that your plan may fail and that your career may suffer as a result, tell your manager about the risks involved and ask for approval to proceed.

In almost all situations, it helps to designate a time frame for decision making. You may want to create a flowchart of the decision-making process, with deadlines for each part of it. You also might want to request the assistance of someone who can help ensure that you meet your deadlines.

Curb impulsiveness

If you often make decisions and later have to backtrack, or if you realize you should have waited until you had more information, you're probably making decisions impulsively. Impulsiveness can lead to wasted time and effort, resulting in diminished effectiveness or reduced productivity. Knowing the reasons for your tendency to rush can help you avoid it. Consider whether one or more of the following apply to your situation:

- Do you feel pressured into making decisions that you are not ready to make? If so, learn to "buy time" in decision-making situations. When possible, tell the person applying the pressure that you need more time and why; then name a date by which you will announce your decision.

- Are you considering the consequences of not making a decision? Sometimes it is not feasible to get enough data within a specified time frame. Yet, the consequences of making imperfect decisions may be worse for the organization and the people involved than waiting until more information is available.

- Although feelings are an important consideration, might your decision-making process be too emotional? For instance, do you make choices when upset or angry? In those cases, try waiting until you calm down. You can then judge better whether the decision is really the best one or simply one that felt right at the time.

- Do you value quick action at the expense of working more methodically through the issue? If so, try a combination by creating a decision-making plan that will clearly result in action. Write down who will be involved in the decision-making process, the types of information you will need, the criteria you will use to judge solutions, and a time frame for action.

RESOURCES

The resources for this chapter begin on page 632.

7
THINK STRATEGICALLY

- *Evaluate your strategic-thinking skills*
- *Become more open to ideas and perspectives*
- *Enhance your strategic thinking*
- *Recognize the broad implications of issues*
- *See the relationships*
- *Consider strategic issues when making decisions*
- *Balance long-term strategic issues and goals with short-term priorities*

INTRODUCTION

The real voyage of discovery consists not in seeking new lands
but in seeing with new eyes.

— Marcel Proust

Effective leaders are strategic thinkers. They recognize relationships and complexities; they understand the broad implications of issues. Strategic thinkers analyze opportunities and problems from a larger perspective. They anticipate and plan for responses from others.

Strategic thinking is required for, but not limited to, long-term strategic planning. Strategic planning is an event, while strategic thinking is a process and an approach. In some organizations, crafting strategy is the responsibility of executives or higher-level managers. Today most organizations expect that managers will approach their work strategically, whether or not they are directly involved in planning strategy itself.

Strategic thinking is characterized by the ability to visualize what might or could be, as well as by a day-to-day strategic approach to issues and challenges.

This chapter provides suggestions that will help you improve your strategic-thinking skills and use them to more effectively lead your team.

VALUABLE TIPS

- Avoid the temptation to find a quick fix when problems arise.

- Strategize ways in which you can achieve your goals with the support of others, rather than creating dissension.

- Cultivate in yourself these characteristics of strategic thinkers: curiosity, flexibility, future focus, positive outlook, openness to new ideas, and broad knowledge and interests.

- Get into the habit of identifying and challenging the assumptions and beliefs that underlie your thinking, conclusions, and decisions.

- Ask your team members to identify the assumptions behind their recommendations, determine their likelihood of accuracy, and investigate the consequences if their assumptions are wrong.

- Keep strategic issues in mind when approaching day-to-day activities.

- Get a fresh perspective on your company's (or your group's) strategies by looking at them from the viewpoint of a customer or a competitor.

- Read the *Wall Street Journal* and business magazines to learn about the strategies other organizations have implemented to enhance their competitive position.

- Take a course in creative thinking.

- Practice "what-if" thinking. This thinking process can spur more new ideas.

- Listen carefully to new employees. Their fresh viewpoint can serve to challenge your assumptions and work processes.

- Identify and challenge critical factors that hinder even greater performance, quality, or customer service.

- As a team, diagram the workflow or business process to spot interrelationships and dependencies.

- Listen carefully to others who tell you about interrelationships and dependencies.

- Identify employees who are skilled at thinking strategically. Consult with them regularly.

- Think through future implications of plans, and weigh the benefits and risks associated with your actions.

- Volunteer to serve on the strategic planning committee of a community organization to which you belong.

Evaluate your strategic-thinking skills

To evaluate your current strengths as a strategic thinker, answer "yes" or "no" to the following questions:

Evaluation Checklist (Circle the appropriate response.)

- Do you look for multiple ways to define problems?   Yes   No
- Do you look for more than one option or solution?   Yes   No
- Do you look for implications and impacts of behaviors/solutions/actions?   Yes   No
- Do you anticipate other people's concerns?   Yes   No
- Do you usually see connections and interrelationships between things?   Yes   No
- Do you approach work from a systems- and process-oriented point of view?   Yes   No
- Do you figure out ways to get your ideas accepted?   Yes   No
- Do you plan for reactions and responses from others?   Yes   No
- Do you ask for the assumptions that underlie strategies and plans?   Yes   No
- Are you curious about why others see things differently?   Yes   No
- Do others see you as open to the ideas and perspectives of others?   Yes   No
- Do others give you feedback that you are flexible and adaptable?   Yes   No
- Do you regularly change your mind when you are given new information?   Yes   No
- Are you up-to-date on new developments, process improvements, or new technology (for example, new products, new markets, cost-saving measures, etc.) in other parts of your organization, as well as in your own?   Yes   No
- Are you aware of the latest directions and developments in your industry?   Yes   No
- Can you identify your current and future major competitors, including their strengths and weaknesses?   Yes   No
- Do you know what your customers (both internal and external) need and want in terms of products or services?   Yes   No

**Become more
open to ideas
and perspectives**

If you answered "yes" to most of these questions, you possess some of the skills or behaviors required of a strategic thinker. The suggestions presented in this chapter may help you improve those skills. If you answered "no" to most of the questions, this chapter can help you develop a strategic mind-set.

Strategic thinking results from a combination of thinking skills, personality elements, and behaviors. Although people are born with different kinds of intelligence and develop different personalities, they can all adopt some of the behavioral characteristics of strategic thinkers and can practice their thinking skills to develop a more strategic focus. Successful leaders consciously develop and fine-tune their strategic-thinking skills, no matter what their personality or cognitive ability.

To develop a more strategic focus in your daily work, consider the following suggestions:

- Adopt the approach toward life and work that effective strategic thinkers use. This approach involves such characteristics as curiosity, flexibility, future focus, positive outlook, openness to new ideas, and broad knowledge and interests. To adopt this approach:
  - Ask other people for feedback on how well you demonstrate these characteristics. If and when they see you not demonstrating these traits, determine why you are being less open, less flexible, less positively focused than you want to be. Take the necessary action to behave more consistently with your intention to be more strategic in your approach.
  - Learn to catch yourself when you react to new ideas and perspectives in a negative way. Deliberately find something positive or useful about the idea or perspective.
  - Approach other people's ideas with curiosity and an openness to understand them.
  - Constantly ask yourself, "How else can this situation be viewed?"
  - Constantly ask yourself, "How do or will others view this?"

- Recognize that strategic thinking involves the following kinds of thinking:
  - *Critical thinking*—the ability to objectively analyze a situation and evaluate the pros, cons, and implications of any course of action.
  - *Conceptual thinking*—the ability to grasp abstract ideas and put the pieces together to form a coherent picture.
  - *Creative thinking*—the ability to generate options, visualize possibilities, and formulate new approaches.
  - *Intuitive thinking*—the ability to factor hunches into the decision-making equation without allowing them to dominate the final outcome.

Practice these different kinds of thinking by reading books about creativity, intuition, and thinking, and by playing thinking games in newspapers, creativity books, etc. Practicing each type of thinking will increase your ability to use it.

Enhance your strategic thinking

To increase your strategic thinking, you need to challenge your thoughts and assumptions. This may mean simply being more open to feedback and ideas from others, or it may involve more sophisticated skills in challenging your underlying beliefs. Consider the following suggestions:

- Identify and challenge the assumptions and beliefs that underlie your thinking, conclusions, and decisions. For example, your competitive strategy may depend on the assumption that people will continue to need eyeglasses or that it will snow a certain amount in certain parts of the world. What is the evidence those assumptions are correct? What if they are not correct?

- Get into the habit of identifying and challenging underlying assumptions so you can spot possible errors and misjudgments.

- Engage in "what-if" thinking. Consider: "If we do this, how will our competitors respond, what will our customers think, what impact will this have on our suppliers and distributors, or what will our next move be?"

- Listen to new employees. They often challenge the assumptions and work processes. Use these challenges to revitalize and improve business processes.

- Ask your team to identify the critical factors that block or hinder even greater performance, quality, or customer service. What prevents the team from achieving its potential? Which of these factors are considered to be "givens" (things the team believes will always exist)? Realize that these givens are what your competitors will figure out how to change, so begin working on them now. Come up with solutions or alternatives.

- Use pictures and diagrams of workflow or business processes to spot interrelationships and dependencies.

- Think through how your plans will affect your colleagues, customers, employees, and so forth. Decide whether the impact on others matches your intent.

- Consider future implications of plans and weigh the benefits and risks associated with your actions.

- Continually look for alternative ways to work with people that will create better results and better working relationships.

- In a particular situation, challenge yourself to identify three or four options and think about how the people involved will receive them.

- Constantly look for new ideas and new approaches.

- Include expectations for continuous improvement in performance agreements or objectives.

- Learn to play chess, and apply the anticipatory thinking required in chess to your work.

- After you have practiced using strategic thinking, ask for feedback on your skills from your manager or other people who are known to be strong strategic thinkers.

Recognize the broad implications of issues

Leaders who think strategically are able to see the big picture. When dealing with issues, they operate from a systems perspective and see a broad, long-term perspective, rather than taking a narrow view or focusing only on short-term implications. To gain a systems view or broad perspective when issues or opportunities arise, try the following suggestions:

- Identify all the stakeholders potentially involved in the issue. Ask your team to identify the stakeholders.

- In discussing the issue, probe beneath the surface; gather information from the different stakeholders. Ask many open-ended questions. Write down what you are told, so you can grasp the information. Draw a picture of what you hear to help you understand the information in a different way.

- Define problems from the perspective of each stakeholder. If, for some reason, you are not able to talk to the stakeholders directly, ask team members to put themselves in the role of those perspectives and explain the issues from their points of view, straightforwardly and without sarcasm. This is also an excellent exercise to gain better understanding of others.

- Listen carefully to understand the underlying issues. Link the information you receive so you can more fully grasp the issue and understand the connections or interrelationships.

- Identify work processes involved when looking at a problem or opportunity. Use pictures when they help illustrate the process.

- When spotting an opportunity, look at it from a systems perspective. What is the opportunity? Who needs to be involved? Who is affected? What business processes are needed for the opportunity to achieve its potential? What are the constraints to success?

- Identify potential solutions or actions. When considering alternative actions, evaluate how they will affect each stakeholder. How does the action affect other parts of the process?

- Think about whether the action being considered will help achieve your goals or those of the organization. Is it consistent with strategy? How will stakeholders react?

- Use your team and the stakeholders to determine what will be needed for the solution to work. What are the pitfalls? How can potential problems be anticipated?

- Communicate the decision, rationale, and plan to all who were involved in the process of identifying the issues.

See the relationships

Relationships occur between people, but they also occur between business processes. Strategic thinkers see relationships among individuals, among teams, between the organizational teams and the other parts of the value chain (suppliers, distributors, and customers), and between and among work processes. Increase your strategic thinking skills by learning to identify relationships and leverage them for change, improvement, and support. To see these relationships more clearly, consider the following suggestions:

- Chart the business process(es) in your area. The process will identify the teams and people related to you. These are the people with whom you want to develop good working relationships and with whom you will work on improving processes. These also are the people who will be most concerned and usually most helpful to you in accomplishing your goals.

- Identify the people responsible for each part of the business process, both within your team and on other teams. Understand both their work goals and them as people. These are the people you are dependent on; therefore, it is critical that you know what is important to them and that you forge good, solid working relationships.

- Map the business process across all departments and functional areas that influence it. For example, map a core product or service from "order to invoice." Understand how each function adds value to the customer.

- Get to know people in other functional groups. Find out the strategies and goals of these groups. Compare your group's strategies and goals with those of other groups. Identify where the groups are in alignment and where they may be working at cross-purposes.

- Obtain a copy of your company's organization chart. Ask your manager or an experienced peer to explain the major functions of the other groups in the organization. Also ask how these groups affect what your group is doing, and vice versa.

- Identify other groups or functions that might be helped or harmed if you exceed or fall short of your goals.

Consider strategic issues when making decisions

Effective leaders have a vision, goals, and strategies for their part of the business. But if they stopped there, the result would be insignificant, despite their good intentions. For strategic thinking to have impact, it needs to be a way of doing work. Leaders need to take this direction and make it come alive in the everyday world.

The following process can help you incorporate strategic issues into your work decisions:

1. Determine the important strategic issues for your area and for the organization.

2. Use these issues to develop your priorities. For example, if broadening distribution channels is the strategic goal, then your priority is to do all those things necessary to develop, deploy, and retain those alliances.

3. When making a decision, examine whether the situation affects or is affected by a strategic issue. This will help you set your priorities and reinforce them.

Balance long-term strategic issues and goals with short-term priorities

Success depends on successfully executing both the immediate short-term objectives and plans and the long-term strategic plans. One without the other is too dangerous, resulting in too much risk. For example, investors and employee bonus plans for meeting annual goals tend to work against a future orientation of more than one year. But if long-term issues are not addressed, the organization obviously is at risk of not remaining competitive.

To balance both the long- and short-term goals, use the following suggestions:

• Review the work that you and your team have done in the last quarter. Determine whether enough has been accomplished on both short- and long-term issues. If the balance is not right for the priorities of the business, reprioritize how you and your team are spending time.

• If you have attempted reprioritization and it has not worked, consider having some team members assigned to the short-term objectives and others responsible for executing on the long-term issues.

• Ask your teams to look at how they can make progress on long-term issues while addressing the short term. For example, a goal may be to understand more about the industry of the customer. Ask the team to figure out how to make progress on that goal while serving the customer.

- Some managers allow day-to-day activities to capture their attention, while planning and strategy fall by the wayside. If feedback you receive indicates that others have this perception of you, try the following suggestions:
  - Establish goals for yourself about what big-picture work you want to do (e.g., strategic thinking, developing a new approach, or developing bench strength). On a monthly basis, evaluate the progress you have made against your objectives.
  - Keep a log to determine how you spend your time. Evaluate your time allocations to ensure that you are giving proper time and attention to the big picture.
  - When you are faced with many demanding and competing priorities, ask yourself which are the most important ones and make those your first priority. When an urgent matter arises, determine how it fits into your daily plan (is it urgent and important, or simply urgent?) and act accordingly.

RESOURCES

The resources for this chapter begin on page 634.

BUSINESS KNOWLEDGE FACTOR

The information age has exploded. Managers are deluged with an overwhelming amount of new and updated information relating to their profession, their industry, and their competition, to name a few. New technology has created and will continue to create massive changes in the workplace. In short, methods and strategies for conducting business in organizations and the marketplace have become increasingly more complex.

This section explains how increasing your technical, industry, and financial knowledge can help you build your professional competence and increase your contributions to your organization. It outlines additional managerial knowledge and skills requirements demanded by the ever-changing capabilities in technology. Finally, it addresses the increasingly important area of corporate citizenship.

Included in the chapters in this section are development suggestions for the following four business knowledge topics:

Chapter 8 - Apply Technical/Functional Expertise: Keeps up-to-date on technical knowledge and developments; increases knowledge of different functional areas; stays informed about industry practices; provides technical expertise and guidance to others; presents technical information clearly.

Chapter 9 - Use Financial Acumen: Understands how the financial performance of one's own unit contributes to that of the organization; uses budgets and forecasts to manage financial performance; uses financial and investment analyses to make decisions and increase revenue; identifies and uses key financial indicators to measure business performance.

Chapter 10 - Manage Technology: Knows how the IT function is organized; uses IT as a strategic resource; keeps up with new technology and makes decisions about its use; understands how to implement technology; possesses familiarity with basic computer functions, software applications, and Internet-based tools such as e-mail and the Web; recognizes the implications of technology on communication.

Chapter 11 - Promote Corporate Citizenship: Develops collaboration between business and community; understands community issues relevant to the business; encourages the responsible use of resources; supports efforts to improve stewardship; addresses current and future workforce issues.

8
APPLY TECHNICAL/ FUNCTIONAL EXPERTISE

PART 1: MAINTAIN THE TECHNICAL AND INDUSTRY KNOWLEDGE YOU NEED
- *Keep up-to-date on technical knowledge and expertise you need*
- *Keep up-to-date on technical developments*
- *Increase your knowledge of specific processes*
- *Increase your knowledge of functional areas*
- *Stay informed about industry practices*

PART 2: LEVERAGE YOUR EXPERTISE
- *Provide guidance as a technical resource or expert*
- *Present technical information clearly*

INTRODUCTION

Strong technical and functional knowledge and expertise is often a reason many managers were first promoted to their jobs. It is not a prerequisite that managers have strong technical knowledge, yet it can be useful, and it helps build credibility with their staff if they possess some knowledge or skills valued by their direct reports.

Leaders do not need to continually strive for the same high level of technical knowledge and skill as that of their staff. However, at a minimum, leaders do need to have sufficient knowledge to identify and address strategic issues, make sound hiring and capital resource decisions, and address training and development needs.

It is important to distinguish between technical and technological expertise. Technical expertise refers to many kinds of professional expertise, including, but not limited to, knowledge of and experience with technology—technological expertise. Chemists and interior designers, as examples, can both be highly technically skilled in their respective professions, and yet their kind of technical expertise may have little or nothing to do with computers, advanced communications systems, and so forth. A chemist may have a great deal of technical expertise in hands-on experimental laboratory procedures, and an interior designer may possess exceptional technical expertise in fabric types and usages. In this chapter, the term "technical expertise" is used in this broader sense.

This chapter provides suggestions for how to keep up-to-date on technical innovations, increase your knowledge of industry practices and trends, and leverage your technical knowledge and expertise.

VALUABLE TIPS

- Build an informal network of peers in similar organizations through which you can exchange ideas and discuss issues relevant to technical advances in your field.

- Ask for detailed updates from your employees when they are working on highly technical tasks so you can gain better understanding of the subject matter.

- Hire people whose superior technical knowledge will challenge you.

- Understand all the reasons why you need the technical information and expertise. Use this understanding to select the best resources to gain the information.

- Identify the resources for technical expertise available to you, which may include your staff members, cross-functional team members, other managers and peers, trusted external consultants, and so forth.

- When working with people who pride themselves on their professional expertise, show interest in learning and respect for their knowledge. Let them know your areas of expertise and how that might help the business goals.

- Work on cross-functional teams to become more knowledgeable about the functional business processes, issues, and new developments.

- List the three emerging technical advances most likely to have an impact on your field, and develop a plan to learn what you need to know about them and their potential impact.

- Ask your management staff and their teams to present information to you about trends and developments in their areas of expertise. Discuss the implications of these new developments.

- Support funding opportunities for staff to develop their skills and be exposed to new developments.

PART 1:
MAINTAIN THE TECHNICAL
AND INDUSTRY KNOWLEDGE YOU NEED

Keep up-to-date on technical knowledge and expertise you need

Although successful managers do not need the same amount of technical expertise and knowledge as their staff, they do need some. The amount of expertise and knowledge you need depends on your role in the organization, the level of your position, and the expertise available from others.

To keep up-to-date on the knowledge you need, use the following suggestions:

- Assess the level of technical knowledge and expertise you need in your position. In general, the more expertise available from others, the less you need yourself. Therefore, leaders at high levels in an organization often need less technical expertise, because they have many others on whom they can rely.

- Understand the reasons you need the technical information. These may include identifying and addressing strategic issues, making sound decisions and investment choices, hiring the right people, or developing others. This will help to guide the selection of resources you use to gain the information.

- Identify the resources for technical expertise available to you. These may include your staff members, cross-functional team members, other managers and peers, or trusted external consultants.

- Look for areas where you have neither the technical resources you need nor the knowledge yourself. Gain the expertise you need by finding other resources or getting the knowledge yourself.

- Look to company and industry best practices to quickly provide basic standard information, knowledge, and practices.

- Network with others to learn needed information.

- Use resources available through professional associations, Web sites, marketing information, and so forth.

Keep up-to-date on technical developments

Keeping up-to-date with the technical advances in your field is important for your own and your organization's continued growth and development. Following are some suggestions of resources to consult and activities to pursue to help you stay up-to-date:

- Ask your management staff and their teams to present information to you about the trends and developments in their areas of expertise. Join discussions about the implications of these new developments.

- Build an informal network of peers in your own and similar organizations through which you exchange ideas and discuss issues relevant to technical advances and changes in your field.

- Ensure that you or your employees are attending conferences and educational opportunities in which they are exposed to new technology and technical developments.

- Once your strategy team has identified potential competitors from other industries, make a point of learning about the technical foundation of those industries and potential new developments in them.

- Ask customers to educate you and your staff about technical development they see in their industry(ies).

- Support funding opportunities for staff members to develop their skills and be exposed to new developments.

- Aim to take on at least one new project each year that will challenge you to search out new ideas and information.

- Hire people from outside the organization to quickly build capabilities in a particular expertise.

Increase your knowledge of specific processes

Because of specific strategic issues, limited resources, or staff shortages, you may find yourself needing to gain knowledge and expertise outside your own area. Sometimes the need includes learning about other functions, while at other times it may require you to become more expert about particular processes.

For example, due to shortages in technology workers, some managers have had to develop expertise in recruiting and staffing. They found that recruitment could not be left to human resource professionals, because some workers would join the organization due to the attraction of the technology or because of who they would work for. These managers had to become quickly knowledgeable about a more traditional HR area.

When you are faced with learning about other functions or processes, use the following suggestions:

- Arrange for a coach in the content or process area who can help you on an as-needed basis.

- Ask to see any previous process flow maps or documentation.

- Ask the leader of an area of expertise you need what he or she would recommend that you read, observe, or do to learn what you need to know.

- Find out whether a colleague can lend you a resource for a short period of time to cover the need. Express your willingness to reciprocate in the future.

- Read about best practices to understand the best of what is done.

- Seek opportunities to observe, work with, and get feedback from individuals (your supervisor, a colleague, or someone from another part of the company) who are highly skilled in the process.

Increase your knowledge of functional areas

Many positions are part of a broad functional area. Operations may include engineering, design, assembly, material distribution, production planning, and plant management. Employees advance in their careers as they move from specialized positions to jobs in broader functional areas.

Today's business environment has demanded that organizations work and think more and more across functional areas. Increasingly, managers need to know how their function fits with the others and how each adds value to their organization's core business processes.

The following guidelines for professional development within and across functional areas are similar to those for increasing one's technical knowledge; they simply take a broader view. Instead of focusing on your specific position, concentrate on the functional area.

- Observe the actions and practices of those in positions similar or related to yours within your functional area or within other functions in your company. You may want to ask them if you can work with them on tasks, interview them formally or informally to learn their secrets for success, or check in with them on a more regular basis.

- Talk with individuals, both inside and outside your organization, who have expertise in particular areas. View committees, task forces, and department meetings as chances to increase your understanding of functional areas.

- Read reports and documents that describe procedures, practices, and other information related to your and other functional areas.

- Attend courses and seminars that can give you a broader perspective of how your position fits into the functional area, and how your functional area fits into the process.

- Join professional organizations. For example, a materials manager might want to get involved in a professional organization that encompasses additional areas of manufacturing.

Stay informed about industry practices

Beyond the specific technical aspects of your work, which could apply to several industries, you need to keep up-to-date on developments in the industry in which you are doing that work. Industry practices or standards can change. What was considered the norm as you started your career may no longer hold true.

To stay informed about the practices and standards in your industry:

- Read professional newsletters and trade journals. These publications can keep you up-to-date on new developments in the industry in which you work.

- Join one or more industry or professional associations. Attend meetings, conferences, and seminars. Work on program committees. Actively involve yourself in the group.

- Join (or form) a group of professionals from other organizations that get together informally to exchange information on technical advances and discuss issues of common interest. Such affiliations can be based on any number of common bonds—type of business, organization size, manufacturing processes, market, and so on.

- Attend university and industry association educational events to keep abreast of developments.

- Visit other companies and talk with people in similar functions and with their customers. After each visit, detail what you have learned for yourself.

PART 2:
LEVERAGE YOUR EXPERTISE

Provide guidance as a technical resource or expert

One indication of your reputation for technical expertise, and the perception of your approachability, is the extent to which others come to you with questions or ask for your help in resolving technical problems.

The following techniques can help you increase your expertise, and ensure that coworkers benefit from your knowledge:

If you are a manager with some technical expertise or knowledge:

- Offer some portion of your time, be it daily or weekly, to your staff for help with technical issues. Ask others about their work and offer guidance where you can.

- Let yourself be known as an expert in certain areas and continually communicate your availability as a resource.

- Keep in mind that, rather than merely providing a quick solution, you should guide others through technical questions or issues in a way that enables them to solve such problems on their own in the future.

- Examine how you give advice when others come to you for help. Take care not to act "superior" because you know the answer. Also avoid using jargon; or, if you use it, explain the terms.

- Offer to serve as a sounding board for others if they run into technical difficulties, and ask them to do the same for you.

If you do not have technical expertise or the time to help others:

- Make sure you have identified someone in your office as a technical resource. It is essential that you have someone on hand who can help with technical problems or questions. For example, merely relying on a help desk as the technological resource is not sufficient IT support for an entire office.

- Keep in mind that if you are a nontechnical manager, you will usually not be the most qualified person to make a technical decision in your office or workgroup. Your role as a nontechnical manager handling a technical issue, then, would be to:
  - Take a step back and rely upon the expertise of others more skilled in technical matters.
  - Present a set of requirements and constraints to the technical staff, and allow them to make a decision on the technical means to achieve the business ends.

Present technical information clearly

Every function has its own jargon and complex terms. Confusion, frustration, and misunderstandings occur when technical terminology is not explained. Many people hesitate to ask for clarification, so it's important to adopt the habit of speaking in clear, simple language and explaining any technical terms you use.

The following suggestions will help you communicate technical information clearly:

- Identify your audience. If it consists primarily of people with relevant technical expertise, using technical terms and concepts is appropriate, even desirable. The more diverse the group, however, the fewer technical terms you should use.

- Consider how much detail you need to communicate. Is the entire piece likely to be read? If not, open with an executive summary that is a page or less in length. This frees the reader from wading through inessential details to get to the crux of the document. If you can't avoid using technical terms in a document intended for wide distribution, you may want to:
  - Define the terms.
  - Provide a context that makes their meanings apparent.
  - Have your manager or a trusted colleague review your document for the clarity of the message.

- When talking with people about technical information, give illustrations and examples to which your audience can relate.

- Ask others to tell you when you have lapsed into using technical terminology without clarifying the terms.

RESOURCES

The resources for this chapter begin on page 636.

9
USE FINANCIAL ACUMEN

PART 1: USE KEY FINANCIAL INDICATORS TO MEASURE BUSINESS PERFORMANCE
- *Identify the financial indicators top management is emphasizing*
- *Use industry-standard indicators for your function*

PART 2: UNDERSTAND YOUR BUSINESS UNIT'S FINANCIAL CONTRIBUTION
- *Work with a knowledgeable financial advisor as your mentor*
- *Learn to read and interpret annual reports*
- *Determine how major transactions of your business unit are reflected in financial statements*

PART 3: USE FINANCIAL INFORMATION TO COMMUNICATE PERFORMANCE
- *Conduct regular reviews of financial performance*
- *Strive to "make the numbers talk" in oral and written communications*

PART 4: IDENTIFY AND EVALUATE ALTERNATIVES FOR ACHIEVING FINANCIAL TARGETS
- *Identify and analyze assumptions*
- *Generate alternatives*
- *Develop a consistent, logical approach for evaluation*
- *Develop contingency plans*
- *Set and achieve effective financial goals*

PART 5: USE BUDGETS AND FORECASTS TO MANAGE AND IMPROVE FINANCIAL PERFORMANCE

- *Create a budget*
- *Get your budget approved*
- *Create a forecast*
- *Develop an early warning system to spot unusual trends*

PART 6: USE FINANCIAL ANALYSIS TO IDENTIFY OPPORTUNITIES TO INCREASE REVENUE

- *Analyze historical results*
- *Review recent pricing decisions and evaluate their differences*
- *Review sales and profitability at the customer level*
- *Assess the relative profitability of products and product lines*

PART 7: EMPLOY APPROPRIATE INVESTMENT ANALYSIS PROCESSES AND TOOLS

- *Understand your company's investment analysis policies and practices*
- *Identify and document decision-making criteria up front*
- *Review underlying assumptions*
- *Employ appropriate analytical techniques*
- *Perform a sensitivity or "what-if" analysis*
- *Conduct post-audits of previous decisions*

INTRODUCTION

"Money speaks sense in a language all nations understand."
— Aphra Behn (1640-1689) English playwright, poet

In his book *Every Manager's Guide to Business Finance* (AMACOM, 1994), Robert G. Finney recommends that managers who are not financial experts develop the knowledge and skills that will enable them to:

- Understand the financial decisions their company makes.

- Maximize the financial contribution of their unit or team.

- Interface effectively with the financial professional so the needs of their organizations are met.

The primary financial objective of most companies is to maximize shareholder value. Unfortunately, the relationship between what your unit does and how that benefits shareholders is often less than crystal clear. By developing your financial acumen, you will gain a line of sight between the activities and decisions within your unit and shareholder value. To gain that line of sight, you must become conversant in:

- How money flows in and out of the organization.

- How the organization is performing.

- Where and how the company can get more money.

- What controls are needed to safeguard the money.

- How to decide where to invest the money.

Financial experts have many tools to aid in these activities. In your role as a leader, you will be expected to master some of these tools, such as budgets and forecasts. For most tools, such as financial reports and sophisticated investment analysis models, you will be expected to be an educated user, usually not a creator of the tool. That means knowing what a particular tool is capable of doing, when it should be used, what inputs are required, and how to interpret and use the outputs. It also means having the confidence to question the outputs if the results run counter to what your knowledge and experience tell you to expect.

This chapter presents suggestions for developing the financial acumen that successful managers need to make effective business decisions.

VALUABLE TIPS

- Review your company's Web site, speeches, annual report, and press releases to find out which financial indicators the company is emphasizing in communications to investors.

- Make the measures you use for your team consistent with those of the organization.

- Learn to read, interpret, and use data from annual reports.

- Ask a colleague you respect as an expert in financial measures to be your mentor.

- Determine how the major transactions of your unit are reflected in the company's financial statements.

- Conduct regular reviews of financial performance. Investigate significant variances to determine the underlying causes, and then take corrective action.

- Build positive working relationships with your accounting and finance contacts.

- When you present financial data, illustrate the meaning and relationships in the numbers with charts, graphs, and descriptive language.

- Set up early warning systems that alert you to signs of trouble before it is too late to take corrective action.

- Always document your assumptions when preparing any financial information. These assumptions are critical to your plan and analysis.

- Test your assumptions for their accuracy or likelihood as part of your "due diligence" process.

- Develop contingency plans that can be quickly enacted if circumstances change or significant assumptions prove wrong.

- Integrate financial and nonfinancial indicators of performance.

- Become familiar with your company's policies and practices for analyzing new investments.

- When you analyze an investment, start with the most likely scenario. Then, do a "what-if" analysis to gauge the impact of changing the assumptions.

- Continually improve your decision-making process by conducting post-audits of previous decisions.

PART 1:
USE KEY FINANCIAL INDICATORS TO MEASURE BUSINESS PERFORMANCE

Identify the financial indicators top management is emphasizing

Most organizations have several key indicators they use to define and communicate success to the financial markets. Sales growth, net income, cash flow, and earnings per share are among the most frequently emphasized indicators. These indicators usually appear, year after year, in external communications to investors. Because management expects to be held accountable for achieving the stated financial targets, these indicators have a strong and far-reaching influence on management policies and practices, ranging from resource allocation decisions to incentive compensation plans.

By understanding what top management has publicly committed to, you can align your actions and measures with their priorities. Identify the indicators that will allow you to create that alignment by taking the following steps:

- Research the company's Web site, speeches, annual report, and press releases to find out which indicators management has been emphasizing in communications to investors. Key financial indicators can vary substantially by industry and company, but most fall into one of these categories: growth, profitability, liquidity, or productivity.

- Look for disconnects between the organization's indicators and what your unit measures. If your unit is measuring performance on indicators that run counter to the company's stated priorities, reconcile the differences.

- Identify the additional indicators your company uses to help everyone in the organization understand how the goals will be achieved (e.g., sales per square foot, inventory turns, etc.). Review internal financial reports, the corporate balanced scorecard, strategic planning documents, and employee communications to learn about these indicators.

- Learn the meaning of each indicator, how it is calculated, and why it is important.

- Identify the ways in which your unit contributes to these indicators. In light of this data, determine whether your unit is measuring the activities that contribute most to the organization's success in terms of these indicators.

Use industry-standard indicators for your function

Many functions have specific indicators that are widely used and essential to managing performance. For example, most staffing departments measure average time to fill positions, average number of candidates per opening, cost per hire, etc. Manufacturing organizations pay close attention to inventory turns. Other metrics include time to market (manufacturers), growth in same-store sales (retail), order backlogs (aerospace and other heavy industries), and administrative expenses as a percentage of assets (money managers).

To use the right indicators for your area, consider the following suggestions:

- Determine whether your company uses industry-wide metrics, which many companies also report on. These indicators often are thought to foreshadow future performance, and they also enable investors to quickly compare your organization's performance with its competitors. Become conversant in these industry-wide measures: what they are, how they are calculated, what meaning is ascribed to them, and where your organization stands in relation to its competitors.

- Find out which indicators leading companies are tracking. Books, trade organizations and their publications, conferences, and Web sites can all be sources of this information.

- If you are not tracking these indicators now, select the few you think are most important and implement them in your unit.

PART 2: UNDERSTAND YOUR BUSINESS UNIT'S FINANCIAL CONTRIBUTION

Work with a knowledgeable financial advisor as your mentor

If you are like most managers, you want to maximize your unit's contribution to the organization's performance overall. To accomplish that objective, you must first understand exactly *how* your unit contributes.

Specifically, you need to discover:

- What resources your unit uses (and in what quantities).

- What value your unit creates from those resources, and how that value is created.

Once you know the answer to these questions, you can determine the return on investment the organization gets from your unit. This will help you improve your understanding of how your unit fits into the big picture.

One of the best ways to learn more about your unit's role in the organization's performance and how you can improve it is to work with a financial advisor. To do so, consider the following suggestions:

- Seek out an advisor who is familiar with the reports you receive and the typical financial decisions you make in your job. An advisor may be a member of your internal finance team or a respected peer. When you select an advisor, consider whether he or she can tailor explanations to your level of financial acumen and the types of decisions you make.

- Involve your advisor in the assessment of your strengths and development needs, and the creation of your development plan as it relates to financial acumen.

- Ask your advisor to help you review the financial reports you regularly receive. Check your understanding of each report's purpose and contents. Ask your advisor to explain unfamiliar terminology and to point out the more subtle interrelationships between items.

- After you have mastered reading the reports, take time to interpret the statements on your own. Check your interpretations with your financial advisor.

Learn to read and interpret annual reports

Financial statements and other data in annual reports represent the face the company is showing to the public and, in turn, they have significant implications for how the company is managed. To develop your proficiency at reading and interpreting annual reports, use the following suggestions:

- If you are truly a novice at reading financial statements, look into one of the many excellent, easy-to-read tutorials on the subject. John A. Tracy's *How to Read a Financial Report* (John Wiley & Sons, 1999), or Lyn M. Fraser and Aileen Ormiston's *Understanding Financial Statements* (Prentice Hall, 1997) are two good choices. A good source on the Internet is Merrill Lynch at www.research.ml.com/marketing/.

- Obtain the most recent annual report for your company. Review the financial statements, accompanying notes, and management's discussion and analysis section. Answer the following questions:
  - What is your company's current financial health? Is it improving, deteriorating, or relatively stable?
  - How are the results of your unit or organization reflected in the financial statements?
  - What is the company's capital structure? How much and what types of debt is it carrying? What is the ratio of debt to equity? What are the implications of this capital structure for your organization?

- From what perspective does management present operating results and significant events?
- How are investors and other stakeholders (customers, suppliers, creditors, etc.) likely to view the company?

• Obtain annual reports for key competitors. Review the reports with the following questions in mind:
- How is their financial position similar to or different from yours?
- Are there significant differences in cost structure?
- Where are they investing?
- Considering their financial condition, are they likely to take competitive actions such as price cutting, easing or tightening credit terms, or entering new geographic markets?

• Analyze annual reports for major customers, asking:
- What are the most pressing financial needs of our customers and suppliers?
- What implications do these needs have for our organization?
- What does the investment strategy say about future directions and plans?

Determine how major transactions of your business unit are reflected in financial statements

To further understand the financial statements, it is helpful to take major transactions or financial events that you know about and see how they appear in the financial statements. For example, how was the acquisition of a company reflected in the statement, or how was the loss from a weather disaster handled?

Use the following ideas to gain a better understanding of these relationships:

• List the most common transactions conducted in your unit and think through how each would be represented in the financial statements. Check your understanding with your financial advisor or other specialists.

• Review the historical performance of your unit:
- How has your unit's contribution to the organization's results changed over time?
- What have been the major implications of these changes? For example, declining performance may mean fewer resources have been allocated to your unit or financial controls have been stiffened. If performance has been improving, your unit may have gained more freedom to make decisions.

PART 3: USE FINANCIAL INFORMATION TO COMUNICATE PERFORMANCE

Conduct regular reviews of financial performance

Financial reporting systems are fundamentally a measurement and feedback tool. Managers who excel at using financial information to create vivid images of expectations and outcomes know that it can be a powerful force in motivating and improving performance.

To develop or fine-tune your and other people's skills in this area, try these suggestions:

- Develop a standard format for financial performance reviews, focusing on what people need to know to make better decisions.

- Assign various staff members to talk about different aspects of the financial reports. You may want to rotate these assignments or pair knowledgeable staff members with those who are less confident of their financial acumen, so that everyone gains an understanding of each area.

- After each review, conduct a debriefing session to identify opportunities for improving the quality of the presentations.

- If some staff members lag behind others in their financial knowledge, hold a separate session conducted at a slower pace where individuals are encouraged to ask even the most basic questions.

- Review the periodic reports you produce. Consider whether any of these reports could be strengthened by the addition of financial information.

Strive to "make the numbers talk" in oral and written communications

If used correctly, numerical data can serve as an influential support for your recommendations or reports. If used poorly, however, this kind of data will confuse, bore, or even generate suspicion among your audience. Use the following suggestions to make your numbers talk:

- List the key messages found in the data.

- Highlight interrelationships between items. Describe not just what happened, but show why it happened.

- Within reason, make liberal use of charts and graphs. (Slide after slide of anything gets boring.) Refer to your key messages, and then determine the visual format that best supports your assertions. For example, pie charts are effective for illustrating relative proportions of things (such as sales by product line). Line graphs can show changes over time, and bar charts are good for illustrating comparisons with targets or historical data.

- Consider what you want others to know about or do with the data, and provide them with just the essentials. Avoid giving too much detail or nonessential information, which can cause readers or listeners to become confused or lose interest. Reserve the details for backup as needed.

- If you use the same words repeatedly to describe results, use a thesaurus to find alternatives. For example, lower-than-anticipated sales could also be termed "slow," "sluggish," "falling short of expectations," "disappointing," etc. This will help your audience sustain their interest and focus.

To increase your effectiveness when making a presentation containing financial information, use the following tips:

- List the outcomes you desire from the presentation. For example, be clear about what actions you want people to take.

- Consider the audience. What is their level of understanding of the reports and terminology?

- Limit yourself to delivering a few key messages per presentation.

- Develop a clear, compelling logic for your conclusions. Show how the data supports that logic.

- Consider what information and level of detail is appropriate for the situation. Summarize and condense reports so people can focus on what is important for the current purpose (e.g., for planning, decision-making, or taking action).

- At meetings where financial information is discussed, study how others present, assess, challenge, and gain an understanding of the financial information presented. Incorporate their most effective strategies into your own presentations.

- Before giving a presentation containing financial data, practice in front of a respected colleague and ask for feedback.

- Ask a peer or member of your staff who will be attending the presentation to take notes on what was most effective and what could have been stronger, and discuss his or her observations nondefensively.

- If you have a tendency to overdo something, such as giving too much numeric detail when answering questions, think of ways to avoid doing that in your next presentation. For example, ask someone you trust to give you a signal whenever your answer is too long. Eventually, you will find yourself providing the appropriate level of detail.

PART 4:
IDENTIFY AND EVALUATE ALTERNATIVES FOR ACHIEVING FINANCIAL TARGETS

The absence of alternatives clears the mind marvelously.

— Henry Kissinger

Identify and analyze assumptions

All plans are based on fundamental assumptions. To identify and manage potential risks that may prevent you from achieving your targets, identify the assumptions that underlie the plan. For example, common assumptions include, "Our large customers will continue to buy from us," "We'll have adequate materials for manufacturing," or "The new product will be rapidly adopted."

To identify and analyze underlying assumptions, use the following process:

1. Challenge the team to identify the assumptions they are making.

2. Estimate the likelihood that the assumptions may be wrong.

3. Determine the impact on the plan if the assumptions are wrong.

Generate alternatives

In any business, there are multiple ways to achieve a given set of goals, and the most obvious path is not necessarily the best. Before setting on a course of action, make sure you have considered multiple alternatives. By identifying and evaluating alternatives during the planning process, you will be better prepared to cope with changing circumstances or unfulfilled expectations. Use the following process to generate alternatives:

- Take stock of your resources. Conduct a brainstorming session with your staff to identify alternative ways of deploying your resources to achieve financial targets. Ask questions such as:
  - What are our resources (assets, people, etc.)?
  - What resources are currently underutilized?
  - What resources do we have in excess? Can we reduce the excess or find ways to make money from it (e.g., rent out unused space or equipment time)?
  - Thinking outside the box, could any of our resources be used in a totally different way?

- Select the best ideas and put them into action.

- Ask your staff to consider the revenues, expenses, and assets under their control.
  - If they had to increase revenues by 50 percent, how would they do it?
  - If they were forced to reduce expenses or make do with fewer assets, what would they cut first?

Develop a consistent, logical approach for evaluation

To ensure that your evaluation of alternatives results in the best solutions, use a consistent, logical approach when conducting your analysis. The following suggestions can help you develop such an approach:

- Involve your staff and financial support people in developing a set of evaluation criteria. The list should include strategic criteria, financial considerations, and the impact on other initiatives. Disseminate these criteria to all managers in your organization.

- Evaluate significant alternatives against these criteria.

- Beware of a tendency to scour the data you know best (e.g., market share data or expenses) while neglecting areas that are less familiar (e.g., impact on cash flow). Also, be aware of your biases and blind spots, and consider their impact on your judgment.

- Focus on large items and those you can control. Identify the items that truly drive your financial results. Avoid the temptation to review every revenue and expense item in detail. Discuss these key items with your staff and consider how you can leverage them to deliver business results.

Develop contingency plans

Contingency planning is an effective way to manage risk while setting a financial course for your unit. As the pace of change has accelerated, the ability to quickly recognize and respond to changes has become a hallmark of successful organizations.

Use the following suggestions to do your own contingency planning:

- With your staff, review the list of assumptions your plan is based on.

- Scan the external environment for signals of change. List those changes that have a significant probability of occurring and could have a significant impact on your business.

- List the most likely implications of the changes you have identified.

- Brainstorm possible responses to each change, and come to consensus on the best responses.

- Develop a high-level plan for responding to change, and explicitly identify which events will trigger these responses.

Set and achieve effective financial goals

One widely accepted standard for goals is that they should be aggressive, yet achievable. Goals need to be aggressive to ensure maximum possible performance, but they need to be achievable or they will lack credibility for many people in the organization. If people believe goals are unattainable, their motivation, and in turn results, will suffer.

To help you set and achieve effective financial goals, consider the following suggestions:

- Define your standards and communicate them to everyone who is involved in the preparation of budgets and plans.

- Consider historical trends and future projections when setting profitability targets. Set appropriate growth and profitability targets accordingly.

- Take a critical look at your targets. Are any elements at odds with your company's stated mission, vision, or values?

- Link targets to company strategy. Clearly articulating the linkages between your targets and strategic goals will help your staff and organization to achieve the goals.

- Communicate the goals to your unit and translate them into individual action plans. Every manager and staff member should know how to answer the question, "What do I need to do to ensure that we reach our goals?"

- Involve managers and staff in developing contingency plans so they understand the consequences of missing the targets.

PART 5:
USE BUDGETS AND FORECASTS TO MANAGE AND IMPROVE FINANCIAL PERFORMANCE

Create a budget

Planning and monitoring financial performance is an essential component of running a successful business. Many otherwise-successful organizations have failed and many careers have been set back as a result of inadequate attention to these important tasks.

A poorly executed budgeting process can have long-lasting consequences, making it difficult to attract and retain talent, maintain a high level of customer satisfaction, and achieve your business goals. To help prevent your budgeting efforts from becoming overly time consuming, chaotic, or failing to get you the resources you needed, follow this process:

1. Before beginning the budgeting process, review your strategic plan, identify goals and objectives, and determine the resources needed to achieve those objectives.

2. Carefully assess what resources you have and what additional resources you will need during the period to be covered.

3. Review budgets and actual results for the year-to-date and the prior year. Determine what significant variations exist and whether they should be taken into account in the preparation of the new budget.

4. Meet with the controller or finance contact to gain a better understanding of how your unit's budget fits into the organization's budgeting process as a whole. Discuss the timeline and make note of deadlines. Ask about any general guidelines or assumptions you should use (e.g., average salary increases, expected changes in raw material prices, etc.). Also ask if there is any historical financial information or special reports that could aid in the budgeting process.

5. Develop contingency plans for possible conditions of slower growth or business contraction. Ask yourself and your employees the question, "If business conditions become unfavorable, what can we give up, stop doing, or defer?"

6. Assign responsibility for the preparation of team or area budgets to the people responsible for particular projects or budget areas. Provide adequate instructions to people preparing their portion of the budget.

7. Compile all team or group budgets and reconcile differences. At the same time, watch for errors of omission, especially for behind-the-scenes items such as office equipment and supplies.

8. Establish a schedule for periodic budget reviews. Compare your budget to actual numbers and, if necessary, make midcourse corrections in order to meet the budget.

A budget represents both the organization's commitment of resources to your unit and a set of boundaries on your actions. Be sure everyone in your unit knows what the budget is, and what it means to them.

Get your budget approved

A well-thought-out budget is of little value if management fails to approve it. While it is rare for a budget to be approved without adjustments, you can use the following suggestions to increase the odds that your budget will survive the intense scrutiny of higher-level management, controllers, and those who are in direct competition for scarce resources:

• Find out the written and unwritten rules and norms of budgeting in your organization. These vary from company to company and from unit to unit.

• Benefit from the experience of others. Ask colleagues about previous budgeting cycles. Emulate what worked for them, and try to avoid the pitfalls.

• Communicate frequently with your manager and financial support person to avoid unpleasant surprises at approval time.

• As you prepare your budget, consider what you will need to defend it.

• Be aware of your assumptions, and be prepared to back them up with sound logic supported by facts and data.

• Be sure you have used the best available data sources.

• Before submitting your budget, consider how others will perceive it. While some managers believe they should pad their initial budget submission so the essentials will survive the red pen, unrealistic requests can permanently damage your credibility.

• Pay appropriate attention to factors outside your department. For example, initiatives requiring a large cash investment are less likely to be approved if the company's financial position is poor or if another initiative is consuming large amounts of resources.

- Coordinate your budgeting efforts with those who might otherwise compete with your unit for resources. Discuss possible resources that could be shared, consolidated, or more efficiently coordinated. These kinds of efforts benefit each unit participating, as well as the organization as a whole, and demonstrate your abilities to work as a team.

Create a forecast
A forecast is a prediction of future results, based on the best available information and logic. Sales revenues are the most common subjects of forecasts, but you may also be asked to forecast cash flow, operating income, or your balance sheet.

To create accurate forecasts, use these suggestions:

- Begin by asking the following questions:
  - What will this forecast be used for?
  - What downstream activities depend on this forecast (e.g., contracting for the necessary raw materials, developing hiring plans, negotiating lines of credit, etc.)?
  - What is the acceptable margin of error?

- Select a forecasting method that takes into account the nature of your business and the item being forecast.
  - Items that have significant downstream impact, such as sales volumes and product mix, will probably require more sophisticated forecasting models.
  - Work with your manager, staff, and financial support person to determine the variables that should be included in the model.
  - Develop the model and thoroughly test it before relying on it.

- Determine for which items—such as those that are not significant or have a steady growth pattern—you can just take the historical results and add an estimated growth percentage to.

- Review and learn from previous forecasts. Consider the following questions:
  - How were they prepared?
  - What models were used and what were the sources of input data?
  - How accurate was the resulting forecast?

- If previous forecasts were poorly constructed or inaccurate, look for opportunities to improve.
  - Identify the factors that have the greatest impact on results, and make sure your model includes them.
  - Be sure the forecasting model accurately captures the relationships between items. For example, product returns may be a consistent percentage of sales.

- Use the best available data to avoid "garbage in, garbage out." In other words, using poor initial data will inevitably produce an unreliable forecast.

Develop an early warning system to spot unusual trends

Forecasts predict into the unknown. Unexpected events can stall or even derail a forecast, no matter how thoroughly it was researched. Effective managers know this and manage for it by establishing warning systems that notify them when such events appear on the horizon. To develop a warning system for your forecasts, consider the following suggestions:

- Develop a comprehensive list of danger signs that will alert you to unusual or unfavorable trends and immediately trigger further investigation. Show the list to your staff and financial specialists, and ask for their input.

- Ask your staff and financial specialists to flag the danger signs to guarantee that they will not be overlooked. Set clear expectations for how and when these items should be communicated to you. Use the added lead time to take corrective action before problems reach crisis proportions.

- Periodically review and update the list to reflect changing circumstances.

- Integrate financial and nonfinancial indicators of business performance. Nonfinancial indicators can often foreshadow problems before they are reflected in the financial statements. Some examples are customer satisfaction data, market share data, progress on key initiatives, customer traffic, merchandise return rates, capacity utilization statistics, employee turnover, and quality data.

PART 6:
USE FINANCIAL ANALYSIS TO IDENTIFY OPPORTUNITIES TO INCREASE REVENUE

Analyze historical results

For profit-making enterprises, the overarching financial goal is to increase shareholder value. This in turn means the organization has to continually increase revenues and profits. Analyzing historical results can give you a solid base for identifying opportunities and increasing revenue. Consider the following suggestions for analyzing your past data:

- Graph revenues by period for the past two or three years. Look for trends, patterns (e.g., seasonal variations), and unusual variations. Consider the implications for future revenue growth.

- Do the same for each significant expense item, graphing them by period (e.g., monthly) for the past two or three years.

- Analyze each expense as a percentage of sales. Note which expenses have changed significantly as a cost of sales. Investigate the underlying causes.

Review recent pricing decisions and evaluate their differences

Analyzing pricing decisions can help you spot opportunities. Use the following suggestions for doing so:

- Determine the data that went into recent pricing decisions. You may find that the pricing decisions were based on guesses and little data. If so, there may be opportunities for price increases or price consistency.

- If you changed pricing, determine whether the change had the intended effect.

- Determine whether evidence indicates the market may accept higher prices. If you have not lost or had trouble getting some sales because of cost, it's possible that your prices could be higher.

Review sales and profitability at the customer level

Your biggest customers may not necessarily be your most profitable. Ask your financial support person to assist you in gathering the data necessary to analyze the profitability of your customers, starting with your largest accounts. To review this data for opportunities, consider the following:

- Compare sales volumes, pricing, product mix, and margins for top customers. How do they differ? Which customers are most profitable? Least?

- Look for opportunities to shift sales toward higher-margin products.

- Consider whether opportunities exist to sell accessories, add-ons, or other value-added products and services.

- Consider "cost to serve" for customers. Ask your staff to help you identify customers that use more resources (e.g., salespersons' time, after-sale support, additional paperwork, etc.). Look for subtle items in addition to the obvious (e.g., small order size or high return rate). Engage your financial support to estimate the cost of each item. Seek out ways to either reduce these costs or start charging for them.

Assess the relative profitability of products and product lines

Some organizations routinely report profitability at the product level, while others do not. If you are in the latter group, ask your finance department to help you gather the information you need to assess product-line profitability.

To assess the relative profitability of your products and take appropriate action, use the following suggestions:

- Prepare a comparison of all products and services in terms of sales volumes, revenues, and margins.

- If any items are below an acceptable level of profit, take corrective action. Possible actions could include price changes, finding cheaper ways to produce the product, instituting minimum order quantities, or deleting the item.

- Before cutting any products, carefully consider any nonmonetary value provided by the product line. In some cases, it may make sense to retain offerings that appear unprofitable. For example, if you reduce a product offering from five items to the two items that represent 95 percent of sales, customers may become dissatisfied by the perceived lack of choice. In other cases, discontinuing one item may result in a decline in sales of a highly profitable complementary item.

- Periodically repeat this review to judge the success of corrective actions and identify additional opportunities for improvement.

PART 7: EMPLOY APPROPRIATE INVESTMENT ANALYSIS PROCESSES AND TOOLS

Understand your company's investment analysis policies and practices

One of the main functions of a manager is to allocate resources to achieve the unit's goals. Most larger companies have well-defined processes and tools for capital budgeting and investment analysis, to increase the odds that the organization is allocating its resources to the projects and initiatives that will create the greatest value.

By learning how to use these processes and tools, you will enhance your ability to build a compelling business case for investing in your proposed initiatives, giving you an edge in the competition for scarce resources.

The following suggestions can help you understand your company's policies and practices:

- Meet with a controller or financial analyst to review the company's policies and practices for analyzing both capital and noncapital investments.

- Learn what methods your company uses to analyze projects and allocate resources. If you are unfamiliar with these methods, ask your colleague to walk you through an example.

- Review recent capital appropriation requests submitted by your department. Which were not approved, and why? Ask your controller what might have increased the chances of the project being approved.

- Find out the company's "hurdle rate" (the minimum required rate of return) for various types of investments so you can demonstrate that your proposals will generate an acceptable return. For example, one company imposes a 15 percent hurdle rate for laborsaving devices and other investments to increase efficiency, 50 percent for new products, and 20 percent for everything else (e.g., packaging changes). Another company has no minimum return for investments that replace existing assets or are otherwise considered to be an operating necessity, but 15 percent for most other investments.

Identify and document decision-making criteria up front

Identifying decision-making criteria, a step that is often overlooked, will save time and frustration on your part and on the part of financial specialists. Staff members and specialists will be able to avoid spending precious time analyzing proposals that, on their face, do not meet your parameters. Include the following factors when deciding on your criteria:

- *Return:* Most publicly traded companies have established a minimum required rate of return on investment that all capital projects must meet. This hurdle rate expedites the process of allocating scarce capital resources to the most worthy projects. Work with your financial specialists to determine the appropriate hurdle rates for the types of investments your unit makes.

- *Risk:* Determine an acceptable level of variability in the expected returns for proposed projects. In addition, consider what alternatives may be forfeited and what options will remain open if you invest in the proposed project.

- *Strategic fit:* Identify the essential elements of your organization's strategy. How closely must proposed projects fit within those strategies?

Review underlying assumptions

Carefully consider the assumptions on which you base your analyses. If the assumptions are flawed, the analysis is worthless. To review the underlying assumptions, take the following steps:

- Explicitly identify the key assumptions of each analysis.

- Ask which assumptions are standard within your organization (e.g., cost of capital, tax rate, etc.) and which are specific to this particular analysis (e.g., sales volumes, development costs, etc.).

- Consider which assumptions should be included in the sensitivity or "what if" analysis (discussed below).

- Evaluate the plausibility of each assumption. Is it logically sound? Are any of the assumptions inconsistent with one another?

- Look for errors of omission in the assumptions and calculations. Ask your financial specialist if steps have been taken to ensure the analysis is accurate.

- Perform a post-audit on previous projects to uncover factors that may have been overlooked.

Employ appropriate analytical techniques

When analyzing proposals for projects and investments, use the appropriate technique to yield the type of results you need. Choose from the following techniques:

Cost-volume-profit analysis:

Also referred to as break-even analysis, this may be the best analytical tool to use when all of the following conditions are met:

- Costs can be reasonably separated into fixed and variable components.

- All cost-volume-profit relationships are linear.

- Selling price will not vary with changes in volume.

Use this break-even analysis for:

- New product decisions—to determine the sales volume needed to break even, given expected selling price and expected costs.

- Pricing decisions—to determine the increase in volume needed to justify a specific price decrease.

- Modernization or automation decisions—to analyze whether to substitute fixed costs (such as equipment) for variable costs (usually direct labor).

Payback-period analysis:

Payback period is the expected length of time it will take for the cash inflow of the investment to equal the initial cash outflow. It is best used for short-term projects of less than a year, since it does not take into account the "time value of money" (i.e., a dollar available today is more valuable than a dollar available at some future date).

Although discussions about payback periods are common in many organizations, avoid using the payback-period method to the exclusion of other analytical methods. Doing so can give others the impression that you are overly simplistic in money matters.

Net Present Value (NPV):

NPV should be used for projects that will last longer than one year, because it takes the "time value of money" into account. In general, NPV is the preferred method for making capital investment decisions.

To use the NPV:

1. "Discount" future cash flows by an appropriate interest rate to calculate their present value.

2. Subtract the initial cash outlay to arrive at the net present value. If the NPV is a positive number, the project should be accepted according to this criterion.

Internal Rate of Return (IRR):

IRR is another technique that considers the time value of money. The IRR is the interest rate that will yield a net present value of zero, given the expected initial investment and the expected future cash flows.

For more information, check +Value on the Web at www.morevalue.com and www.investorguide.com. These sites provide small business tools (e.g., capital budgeting tools and processes) illustrated by case studies, and financial news stories with interpretations.

Perform a sensitivity or "what-if" analysis

All investment analyses require you to make assumptions. In some cases, the assumptions involve little guesswork or estimation (e.g., investing in a proven labor-saving device). In other cases, the assumptions are softer—best guesses that are highly subjective or based on limited data (e.g., new products or new technologies).

The base-case scenario should involve the set of assumptions that you consider most likely. The base case should be supplemented with several "what-if" analyses to help you see how the outcomes may vary if one or more of the assumptions is significantly off.

To conduct a "what-if" analysis for an investment, take the following steps:

• Explicitly identify the assumptions that underlie the analysis. Ask which assumptions and estimates are "solid" and which are "soft." For each of the soft items, consider how much the actual results could differ from your estimates.

- Perform a sensitivity analysis by altering the assumptions you consider uncertain, one assumption at a time. Determine the impact that changing those factors would have. For example, what if sales volumes are 10 percent lower than your best estimate? What if they are 30 percent higher? Work through some best- and worst-case scenarios.

- Determine the factors that most influence the analysis. A thoughtfully designed spreadsheet will help you promptly identify the most critical variables.

- Identify items that are most prone to estimating errors. If necessary, determine ways to reduce the risk of estimation error. You may want to use alternative estimation methods, such as consensus estimates from experts or trend analysis.

Conduct post-audits of previous decisions

Continuously improve your decision-making process by conducting post-audits of previous decisions. Post-audits are particularly valuable for projects of a recurring nature. They should be conducted according to a predetermined schedule. The process should include the individuals involved in the original decision and answer the following questions:

- How much did actual results differ from expected results?

- Which factors most influenced the outcome?

- Were the most important factors considered in the financial analysis?

- Which factors, initially thought to be significant, had little impact on the outcome?

Document key findings to facilitate continuous improvement. Share best practices with other divisions or functions.

RESOURCES

The resources for this chapter begin on page 638.

10
MANAGE TECHNOLOGY

PART 1: MAKE IT A STRATEGIC PARTNER
- *Know how your IT organization operates*
- *Use IT as a strategic resource*
- *Keep up with technology*
- *Make decisions about new technology*
- *Understand the pros and cons of standardizing technology*
- *Understand the fundamentals of technology implementation*
- *Involve employees when implementing new technology*

PART 2: DEVELOP FAMILIARITY WITH BASIC COMPUTER FUNCTIONS
- *Recognize your own need for computer skills*
- *Perform essential functions*
- *Develop familiarity with software applications*
- *Develop familiarity with the Internet*
- *Use the organization's intranet*
- *Use the language of technology*
- *Provide employees with necessary resources and training*

PART 3: UNDERSTAND THE IMPLICATIONS OF TECHNOLOGY ON COMMUNICATION
- *Understand the advantages of various communication technologies*
- *Enhance the effectiveness of communication technology*
- *Use e-mail effectively*
- *Use electronic calendars effectively*

Introduction

The successful companies of the next decade will be the ones that use digital tools to reinvent the way they work. These companies will make decisions quickly, act efficiently, and directly touch their customers in positive ways....
A digital nervous system will let you do business at the speed of thought—
the key to success in the twenty-first century.

— Bill Gates

The current information technology (IT) revolution is being compared to the great industrial revolution—producing both rapid change and global impact. New technology has created and will continue to create massive changes in the workplace. New technology will continuously enhance our capacity to perform by making tasks more efficient and flexible, allowing us to handle a higher level of complexity, and enabling us to work at any time and any place around the globe.

Many employees, however, have experienced technology falling far short of its promises, becoming as much a barrier as a facilitator of work. All too often, plans focus solely on implementing technology—disregarding the business case supporting the technology, overlooking the process expertise required to implement the technology, and underestimating the training and ongoing support needed to make the technology work. Technology without these other elements can swiftly damage performance and add up to huge costs including unexpected cost overruns.

What do managers need to know about technology? Simply stated, leaders need to be able to use the basic technology necessary for their jobs, and they need to know how to implement technology changes. While a manager may not need to implement technology him- or herself, leaders do need to know the steps and processes necessary to do so. Leaders must appreciate the time-consuming nature and the human aspect of implementing and using new technology. They play a crucial role in changing mind-sets about processes and procedures that may need to change when a technology is implemented. Finally, managers also need to partner with IT professionals to determine whether new technology will actually result in business improvement.

This chapter presents guidelines, techniques, and suggestions to help you master the information and skills you need to have to deal with the technological revolution of this era.

VALUABLE TIPS

- Learn the basic operations of the technologies—especially software programs—most commonly used in your organization, profession, and industry.

- If you do not have an IT liaison for your group, ask for one. Work with this person to better understand the role that technology can play in your area.

- Include an IT liaison in your management meetings and other aspects of the strategic planning and execution of your business.

- When planning and implementing technology, make sure that solid project plans are in place and clear accountabilities have been established.

- In a technology project, make clear the roles and responsibilities of your employees and those of the IT people you are partnering with in the implementation.

- Use industry standards for technology planning and implementation to ensure that estimates are based on known realities, rather than wishful thinking.

- Find a technology coach for yourself.

- Ensure that you and your team use lessons learned from previous technology implementations.

- Make sure that files are backed up on a regular basis. Know your IT group's file backup and restore policies. The IT group may back up network files, but you may need to take personal responsibility for backing up other files.

- Pay attention to virus alerts. Know what to look for in a virus hoax.

- Ensure that antivirus software used in your workplace is assessed regularly and continually updated. An IT group typically does this, but if you work alone or are part of a small organization, you may need to assign someone to this role.

- Conduct an expertise audit to determine the level and variability of technological expertise in your current workforce.

- Use the Internet to gather information on clients, competitors, and your industry. Visit business information sites such as www.hoovers.com, www.fortune.com, or www.fastcompany.com.

- Ask that someone on your staff maintain an inventory of your office's technical resources.

- Use auto-reply and out-of-the-office voice-mail and e-mail assistants to ease communication when you are out of the office.

- Hold frequent meetings with other managers to discuss new developments in technology and how they could affect your workplace.

- Identify one or two people you can turn to in your office with immediate IT needs or questions.

- Regularly communicate with your IT group about the business and its customers. Include IT in any planning that impacts their function or the technology they provide.

- Post a list of important IT contacts, such as a help desk phone number and an emergency after-hours support number.

- Be alert to the fact that your e-mails can be considered legal documents.

- If your office uses electronic calendars, consider PDAs for your employees who need to have their calendar information when they are away from their desk.

PART 1:
MAKE IT A STRATEGIC PARTNER

Know how your IT organization operates

Before you can work effectively with your IT group, you need to know how it is structured. IT departments perform numerous functions and are often organized into several different groups. The IT group can be expected to provide information and support in areas such as IT maintenance policies, security, technical training, software and hardware upgrades, and solving technology-related problems. Consider the following suggestions for learning about your organization's IT function:

- Consult knowledgeable IT professionals, colleagues, and your organization's intranet to learn how your IT group is organized. If available, review the strategic plan to gain a deeper understanding of the overall mission, goals, and issues of the IT group.

- Learn enough of the IT group's processes to know what they will need from your business group to support your efforts.

- Ask your peers within and outside of your organization about how they manage their relationships with their IT group. Find out about successful strategies and tactics and "lessons of experience."

- Make sure someone in your group is responsible for communicating to IT about new employees, successes, problems, and potential problems.

- If IT vendors support systems used in your group, ensure that you know who is responsible for the vendor relationship. Consult this person with issues about the system or for vendor support.

Use IT as a strategic resource

In the last decade, IT has moved from an infrastructure issue to a major strategic function. Today, effective leaders see technology as an integral part of their business success. They use IT professionals as strategic partners and realize that technology can either contribute to the bottom line or can destroy it.

To use IT as a strategic resource, consider the following suggestions:

- Look to partner with IT rather than only use them for help when a problem occurs.

- Regularly communicate with IT about your business and its customers. Include IT in any planning that impacts their function or the technology they provide. Include an IT professional as a part of your management team.

- Educate one another. Ensure that the IT group understands your business and its needs—educate them on how the business really operates. Correspondingly, encourage the IT group to educate you and your staff about the IT function, technology, and related processes. Find out what they need from you and what you can expect of them.

- Spend time with IT people, but realize that there are never enough IT people to go around. Find ways to be efficient with IT staff time, including providing them with the business resources they need to do their work for you correctly.

- Realize that trust and frankness are important characteristics of successful IT partnerships. Develop two-way trust with IT. You need to accurately understand what technology will and will not do. The IT person needs to understand how your business really operates. That way, both of you will have a clearer understanding of what problems the technology is intended to solve and what cannot be solved through the identified technology.

- When partnering with IT, invest capable business resources for planning and implementing projects. Determine when to send your computer expert and when to send your business process expert to a meeting.

Keep up with technology

Staying abreast of technological developments is critical. New products are created daily that were impossible five years ago because the technology did not exist. In the future, whoever drives an industry's technology will likely emerge as the industry leader, as long as the organization does not fail on its other core competencies.

Effective managers, whether or not they are in technical positions, need to keep up with current and future technological advances. To accomplish this, consider the following suggestions:

- Determine when to do your own research and when to rely on your IT group. The size of your company and the IT department will determine the level of IT knowledge you need to have yourself.

- Periodically talk with your organization's technology experts to learn more about their current successes and challenges and the advances they expect in the future.

- If your organization's IT department hosts regular IT conference calls or discussions, inquire about joining or listening in. This will help you keep up-to-date on what is going on in IT.

- Attend technology symposiums. Listen for ideas that could change the way you do business.

- Join informal conversations about technology.

- Read magazines that describe new findings in areas of your business. Also read about new developments currently unrelated to your business— in the future, these developments could easily migrate to your industry.

- Ask your telecommunications, computer, and key software vendors to present to you and your staff their ideas about what will be possible in the next three to five years.

- When appropriate, take part in beta testing of technology. This will expose you to new products and give you a chance to talk informally with some of the developers.

Make decisions about new technology

Many organizations report that they are experiencing a gap between what they are spending versus what they are getting from their technology investments. With technology as important as it is today, leaders need to carefully consider new technology, whether it is purchased from external vendors or internally developed.

Consider the following suggestions for making decisions about technology:

- Involve your IT group, if you have one, in the planning and decision-making process.

- Avoid technology for the sake of technology. Realize that technology is a means to an end, not an end in itself.

- Isolate the real business reason or need for new technology. For example, speed is often the default reason for implementing new technology. In reality, speed is often a secondary reason. The need for a new service capability or a deficiency within present systems might be more typical demands driving technology solutions.

- View design, development, and implementation of new systems as critical business strategies and manage them as such. Ask yourself, "What are the current and future reasons for investing in this technology?" Make a specific determination of the intended outcome, such as competitive distinction, etc.

- Gather business requirements from users before considering solutions. Make sure you thoroughly understand short- and long-term needs of the system, such as compatibility, scalability, integratability with other systems, support, and maintenance. Partner with your IT group in this process; they typically have experience in collecting user requirements.

- Once you have a list of your requirements and needs, prioritize and rank them to establish a set of criteria for the selection process.

- Consult experts within your organization for guidance regarding the types of technology that best meet your business needs. Respect the limits of your own knowledge.

- If you do not have internal resources that can help you with gathering requirements, evaluating technology, or developing implementation plans, contact outside consulting firms that specialize in the technology.

- When considering new technology, identify the risks of both implementing new technology and not implementing it. Consider the risks of different options available. Assess your organization's track record in managing each of the risks involved.

- Ensure that someone on your staff or in the organization is doing good, solid competitive analysis on the technology of your competitors. This information will be critical to understanding your competitive position.

- Always consider the implications of implementing new technology, including employees' reactions and comfort with the change. If you are considering a particular vendor, find out how they will help you transition through change associated with the implementation.

- Remember that if it sounds too easy and too inexpensive, it probably is. Include people who understand technology in any presentations, discussions, and decisions about acquiring or licensing technology.

- Recognize that the development of a system or product is only one aspect of the costs and resources needed. All technology systems and products have ongoing maintenance and support or "life-cycle" costs. Other costs include conversion of data from the old system, managing the change, and training for new processes and procedures. You will also need to plan for upgrades; don't be surprised by the need for them.

Understand the pros and cons of standardizing technology

Information technology capabilities and options are endless. In some organizations, standardization of hardware and software across the company is the norm. In other organizations, each area makes its own decision about what e-mail system or spreadsheet or even operating system to use.

It's important for managers to understand that their decisions about standardization affect not just cross-functional communication, but costs, as well. If you need to make decisions about whether to standardize your hardware and software, consider the following guidelines:

- Work with your IT group to make the decision. IT professionals have a lot of experience seeing the advantages and disadvantages of standardizing technology.

- Learn what the hidden costs are for hardware and software, and how those costs are affected by standardization. Hidden costs can include:
  - Training (employee time and materials). Will training costs be higher if you use a nonstandard technology?
  - Support. Will your support costs be higher if you use a nonstandard product that has no internal support?
  - Trouble-shooting problems. The greater the variety of hardware and software, the more possibilities there are for problems that require time and resources to fix.
  - Testing resources for new implementations. The more combinations of software and hardware there are to test on, the higher the costs will be.

- Recognize the potential disadvantages of using standardized technology solutions.
  - Employees won't be able to use new and better products that are not part of the organization's standards.
  - You will need to wait to use new product features if the company wants to pace version upgrades.
  - People may feel that they are missing out by not having more powerful software to do their work.
  - The initial price tag for standardized solutions may seem higher than necessary, often because the hidden costs are not identified.
  - If departments are charged for standard software and hardware, there may be some resentment over not having control of that expenditure decision.

- Assess the pros and cons of standardization for your situation, and use common sense. Even if your organization requires the use of standard technology, determine when and why you may need to deviate from that for business reasons. Then, assess the risks and needs before making a final decision.

Understand the fundamentals of technology implementation

Choosing the right technology is an important step to achieving business success. The implementation process for introducing new technology is at least equally important. Implementing technology is really organizational change. To make it work, you need to treat it as such. The larger the implementation, the larger the change effort. Consider the following suggestions:

- Realize that, as with other changes, people hold on to what they know—often because it is how they have historically experienced success. Change means risk.

- Learn the fundamentals of change management and apply them to implementing new systems. Often new technology fails to produce the anticipated results because the change-management process was overlooked.

- Apply the discipline of traditional project management, including key aspects such as:
  - Creating a steering committee with representatives from different functions and job positions.
  - Involving stakeholders throughout the process.
  - Communicating often because it is difficult to overcommunicate during a time of transition.
  - Identifying how you will coordinate getting the right people, at the right time, on the right assignment.
  - Paying attention to political or public relations issues.
  - Effectively managing the details.

- In partnership with IT, manage the risks associated with implementing new technology. But realize that the risks are often not fully known when implementation begins. Attempt to identify and manage the risks, but be aware that the risks will change during the entire process.

- Make sure you take the human aspects into account when planning and introducing new technology. Probably the biggest mistake managers make when implementing new technology is to severely underestimate the time and resources needed to effectively manage the human side of such change.

- Include training and support as part of the change-management plan for the new technology. Use industry standards and benchmarking to gain an accurate idea of how much time it will take for the staff to develop the necessary skills to use the new technology and to become competent with it.

- Discuss ways to manage work during the transition period of implementing new technology. Remember to take into account the time for learning new technology when your workgroup acquires it. Expect a learning curve for every employee; learning curves will also vary greatly depending on each individual's comfort level with technology.

- Recognize that there is a big difference between automating an existing, well-running business process and automating a business process that is being created or fixed. The latter takes much more time, is much more unpredictable, and needs to have business as well as IT resources dedicated to its success.

- Understand that the following elements of implementing technology almost always increase the cost of the project:
  - Decreasing the amount of time to finish the design or implementation of technology.
  - Increasing the quality and/or decreasing associated risks.
  - Increasing the scope of the project.

Involve employees when implementing new technology

As with any organization change, you need to involve and inform your employees in the implementation of new technology. To reduce both resistance to change and fears of inadequacy with new technology, consider the following:

- Include your staff in decisions by keeping them informed of which technology options are available. Then ask for and consider all their ideas, feedback, and concerns.

- Be excited and positive about the change, and check that all managers are presenting a positive attitude to their staff. Deal first with managers' doubts and fears.

- Go over all the benefits the new technology will bring to the employees. How will it make their jobs easier, more fun, more exciting, and/or more critical to the business? How might the new skills they acquire now benefit them in the future?

- Review the benefits the new technology will provide to the organization in terms of supporting overall business strategy. State the specific business reason for implementing the technology.

- Provide the time and resources each individual will need to learn the new system, no matter their current level of expertise or comfort with technology, and reassure them of this often. This may require providing overtime pay, formal training classes, a trainer to come on-site, individual development planning, and so forth.

PART 2:
DEVELOP FAMILIARITY WITH BASIC COMPUTER FUNCTIONS

Recognize your own need for computer skills

Gone are the days when leaders did not use computers. In the past, leaders relied on their administrative assistants to access needed computer information and let technology-minded peers run their data analyses and reports. Today, those managers who lack computer skills are finding themselves at a major disadvantage. Computers have moved from an optional tool to a core tool.

Computers offer access to limitless types of information, provide numerous methods for analyzing data, and allow easy distribution of information and data.

To understand how you can use computers to better manage, try the following suggestions:

- Identify information that would help you improve your skills in managing your business. Chances are that much of this information is at your fingertips. Examples of such information include:
    - Company information: sales figures, profit margins, inventory data, performance against goals, cost data, and operational data from various functions and sites.
    - Market information: economic trends, demographic data, and competitor information.
    - Customer information: customer satisfaction surveys, customer profiles, contacts, addresses, and information on past business.
    - Employee information: resumes, performance plans, performance appraisals, and succession planning.
    - Development tools: development recommendations, performance-management processes, or information on how to coach others.

- In addition, learn how various computer programs and applications let you access and work with this information in a number of different ways. Examples include:
    - Text programs: word processing and desktop publishing.
    - Numbers programs: statistics packages, spreadsheet programs, inventory-control systems, and decision-support programs.
    - Image tools: graphics packages, presentation generators, design programs, and drawing programs.
    - Time organizers: calendars, schedulers, project-management programs, and account-management programs.

- Communication tools: electronic mail, on-line conferencing, and networked file-sharing applications.
- Information programs: internal database management programs and external databases accessed through bulletin boards, the company's intranet, the Internet, or commercial on-line services.

Perform essential functions

Computers are now a fact of life for people in organizations. More and more organizational work is done through and with computers. Regardless of the amount of technical expertise your position requires, you undoubtedly will need to have a basic understanding of how to use a personal computer. It is generally essential to master functions such as:

- Saving and retrieving files to a disk or to a network.

- Printing to both a network or local printer.

- Copying and pasting text.

- Accessing programs.

- Retrieving and sending electronic mail (e-mail).

- Using the intranet or Internet to look up business information.

In addition, you may need to perform or find out how your IT handles the following basic maintenance functions. Many of these functions need to be done in a certain way.

- Backing up your hard drive.

- Saving key files to a shared network or removable drive.

- Deleting temporary files and unnecessary e-mail messages.

- Following IT procedures for updating antivirus software and responding to potential computer viruses.

Nearly every job function requires or will soon require these skills to comfortably navigate the organization's information systems. If you are not comfortable performing such tasks, consider the following suggestions:

- Find out your organization's standards. Use company-provided training and documentation to learn these skills.

- Find an internal resource to help you learn the basics and develop greater comfort with your computer. For example, many managers ask their administrative assistants to help them learn basic computer skills. Others rely on peers or direct reports who are particularly interested in technology.

- Use the on-screen help functions to guide you through unfamiliar tasks.

- Consult books or written materials, such as product manuals or easy-to-read reference manuals.

- Enroll in a training class offered by your organization or a computer training company.

- Use an on-line tutorial. Many of these resources include videos and interactive ways to learn.

Develop familiarity with software applications

Chances are your job requires a working knowledge of software for word processing, creating spreadsheets, or generating presentations. Most jobs require familiarity with the following types of software applications and tasks:

- Logging on to a local area network and accessing shared files for use with a word processing program such as Microsoft Word®. Required tasks may include the ability to open, save, write, and edit information in such programs.

- Developing presentations on presentation software such as Microsoft PowerPoint®.

- Using spreadsheets such as Microsoft Excel®, including the use of formulas to calculate data totals.

While these types of programs tend to be universal, other necessary software applications can vary greatly depending on your business. An architectural firm, for example, may require software that can produce three-dimensional images for client presentations, whereas a bank may focus on financial and security software.

Develop familiarity with the Internet

The Internet, and particularly that part of it known as the World Wide Web, is fast becoming one of the business tools of choice. For many organizations, e-commerce has become a core business strategy; most others use the Web as an important source of obtaining and sharing information. Organizations often have an internal intranet and access to the Internet.

However your organization uses the Internet, it is important for you to gain experience with its use, because its use will only increase over time. To increase your familiarity with the Internet:

- Ask your IT help desk who has access to the Web. This will help you know what job functions you can expect to use the Web as a resource. For example, staying up-to-date with what is going on with competitors and customers is one of the huge advantages of the Web.

- Learn how to search for information about an industry, organization, or resource by using a search engine. As a starting point, try searching for your own organization or that of a competitor.

- Ask for a copy of your company guidelines about use of the Internet. Most organizations have them. If they do not exist, ask that the IT group develop them. Many guidelines are available from industry standards groups within IT.

- Find an Internet expert within your group to gain further knowledge on methods for locating key information and tools through the Web. Many people enjoy sharing their latest favorite site or search engine.

Use the organization's intranet

Many organizations use a company intranet to post company information, share information, and facilitate communication. The IT function is typically responsible for establishing and maintaining the intranet. However, usually a cross-functional team is responsible for content and intended use. Consider the following tips for using your intranet:

- If you do not already know, find out the uses of the intranet in your organization. Go into the intranet to learn more about the information that would be useful in your job.

  Most organizations have HR information such as benefits, job postings, and HR policies on their intranet. They also frequently post company information such as stock price, management changes, business successes (new contracts), or competitive information. Some organizations are using their intranet to build organizational capabilities by posting such information as best practices and standard business processes.

- Determine the intended use of your company's intranet. For example, should it be used on a daily basis or on an as-needed basis?

- Assign a team to identify how your group is using the intranet. You might also ask them to identify additional uses of the intranet that would benefit your group or the organization as a whole.

Use the language of technology

The language of technology is entering common conversation. Everyday terms include hardware, software, the Internet and intranet, client-server, mainframe, local area network (LAN), wide area network (WAN), and computer virus. The list continues. To better use the language of technology, try these suggestions:

- If you are unfamiliar with such terminology, or would like to improve your technology vocabulary, read one of the many introductory computer books, access a list of terms through the Internet, or talk with an IT professional in your organization.

- On the other hand, if you are well versed in technological jargon, remember that many others may not be. Fearing that they will be viewed as incompetent, it is unlikely they will reveal their lack of knowledge. If you are unsure of someone's technical knowledge, check for understanding and avoid unnecessary technical jargon.

Provide employees with necessary resources and training

As a manager, you are responsible for ensuring that others have the training and resources they need to use technology tools effectively. Consider the following suggestions:

- Conduct an audit of your current workforce's capabilities and comfort with technology in general, as well as the specific skills necessary for your department. This could be accomplished by conducting interviews, creating and administering a survey, or conducting focus groups. You may want to enlist the help of your IT or human resources functions.

- Provide resources for necessary technical training, either internal or external to your organization.

- Communicate information about computer training classes, both internal and external. Ask your staff what kinds of computer training they would like to see offered, and help them find the training they need.

- Post the numbers of your organization's IT help desk—including the after-hours emergency support.

- Set the model by attending required training and using technology tools yourself.

PART 3:
UNDERSTAND THE IMPLICATIONS OF TECHNOLOGY ON COMUNICATION

Understand the advantages of various communication technologies

New technologies have increased the number of ways we are able to communicate with one another. Before you can choose the appropriate communication vehicle, you need to understand their basic advantages and disadvantages. Use the list below to increase your knowledge of the pros and cons of different communication media.

Face-to-face

Advantages:
- Richest medium—incorporates verbal and nonverbal messages.
- Permits dialogue and spontaneity.
- Supports the integration of both task and relationship aspects of communication.
- Best method for initially building relationships and resolving conflict.

Disadvantages:
- May take more time.
- Success of communication depends on an individual's verbal communication skills.
- Supports a limited number of people.

Recommended Use:

Especially helpful in initially building relationships, forming teams, and discussing conflict or other emotionally laden issues.

E-mail

Advantages:
- Permits lengthy written messages with attachments and graphics.
- Allows a single message to be sent to an unlimited number of people at one time.
- Enables rapid communication across local, national, and global boundaries, both within and outside of the network.
- Allows "asynchronous" communication—parties do not have to communicate with one another at the same time.
- Provides a vehicle for documenting communication with others.

Disadvantages:
- Few people read long e-mails in their entirety.
- Highly dependent on the user's ability to communicate through writing.
- Does not communicate nonverbal messages, thus making it difficult to deal with emotional situations.
- Communication is piecemeal and back-and-forth; real-time question-and-answer sessions are not available.
- Dependent on the functioning of the user's PC, network, and/or Internet access.

Recommended Use:

Helpful when communicating to large groups of people, disseminating a large amount of information to others, and documenting of communication is needed.

Voice mail

Advantages:
- Permits messages to be created and sent to one person or multiple people simultaneously (assuming they are in the same voice-mail network).
- Allows "asynchronous" communication.
- Permits quick access and response from a remote site.

Disadvantages:
- Does not allow two-way communication.
- Nonverbal messages are lost.
- Communication is piecemeal and back-and-forth; real-time question-and-answer sessions are not available.
- Can be confusing if the speaker is unorganized or hasn't thought out his or her ideas beforehand.

Recommended Use:

Helpful when communicating a message that is enhanced through one-way verbal dialogue (versus a less personal written approach).

Audio-conferencing

Advantages:
- Allows for ongoing dialogue and spontaneity in conversation.
- Enables people working from outside of the office or another geographical location to connect into a meeting or discussion.

Disadvantages:
- Less cohesive than in-person meetings.
- Nonverbal messages are lost.
- Written information, such as slide presentations or flipcharts, cannot be conveyed unless sent ahead; if so, changes cannot be made during audio-conference to be visible to all.
- Can be difficult to hear clearly if equipment is not up-to-date.

Recommended Use:

Helpful when team discussions are needed across different locations and video-conferencing is not practical.

Video-conferencing

Advantages:	*Disadvantages:*
- Enables participants to convey both verbal and some nonverbal messages, including using visual aids or other documentation.	- Users may have to choose a point of focus between centering on an individual or zooming out to show the group as a whole. - Spontaneity and developing rapport is more difficult than in person.

Recommended Use:

Helpful when team discussions are needed across different locations.

Newer methods

Satellite broadcasting

Many companies use private satellite broadcasting to provide real-time, interactive communication with large groups of employees. Typically, one presenter or a small group presents information that is broadcast to any number of locations. Viewers can interact through keyboard entry for on-the-spot responses or surveys, or they can call in from any site and be heard by all sites. Its benefits include being able to present the same information company-wide at the same time interactively. Its greatest drawback is the expense of building or renting facilities and equipment.

Electronic data repositories

Electronic data repositories allow users to read and, if authorized, edit documents that are posted to this "bulletin board." This technology allows a group of users (e.g., a project team or a work unit) to access documents via their computer and make or recommend changes that all users in the group can see. It conserves computer disk space by maintaining only a single copy of the file that all people can use as the focal point, and allows for keeping track of who made changes and when to each document in the repository.

Electronic meetings

With software such as Microsoft's NetMeeting®, people can combine audio-conferencing with computer networking in a single meeting. In electronic meetings, participants can view what others display on their computer screens and even edit a document at the same time. This technology allows users to communicate from any place in the world that has Internet and phone connections.

Instant messaging

A number of companies, usually Internet providers, offer a new Internet communication tool called instant messaging. Its greatest benefits include the ability to communicate rapidly back-and-forth in a format that most closely resembles a real conversation, rather than the piecemeal one-way communications offered by e-mail and voice mail. Attachments can be transmitted via instant messaging. Recent enhancements to this method allow for transmission of voice and even live video so participants can see and hear each other as they converse over the Internet.

Voice recognition software

Voice recognition software, another very recent development that has not yet been fully refined, enables the user to verbally dictate communications onto the computer system, which converts it to text that could then be communicated rapidly via e-mail.

When deciding which vehicle to use, take into consideration such factors as efficiency versus impact, the speed and availability of technical resources in your workplace, and the advantages of communicating via a one-way information drop versus a dialogue. The best method may depend on how often you need communicate to the party, how wide a geographical group you need to communicate with, and how fast you need to deliver your message.

Enhance the effectiveness of communication technology

Given the advantages and disadvantages of particular kinds of technology, you can maximize the effectiveness of each by considering the following suggestions:

- When it is important that a team forms and works together quickly, arrange for one of the first meetings to be face-to-face. In addition to getting to know one another, identifying the team's charter, and discussing roles and responsibilities, be sure to discuss specific methods and frequency for communicating with one another.

- Use face-to-face meetings to resolve conflict and to discuss emotional issues.

- Watch the tone of your e-mail and voice-mail messages; anger and other emotions may be unintentionally amplified in these communications.

- Use telephones specifically made for conference calls, so that the people attending a meeting via telephone can hear clearly.

- When using audio-conferencing, introduce everyone on the conference call. Then ask that people identify themselves each time they speak.

- If presentations are to be made via a conference call, ensure that those attending remotely have access to the presentation materials.

- When using your wireless phone, pay attention to the connection. Do not try to conduct important business if the connection is unreliable or if there is static or interference.

Use e-mail effectively

Electronic mail has made it faster, easier, and cheaper for businesses to communicate and transfer information across geographic boundaries. Sending information electronically enables the user to quickly transmit messages back and forth, communicate to a wide user group, and include large amounts of text and/or attached software files. The proliferation of e-mail, however, has often resulted in sloppiness and overuse of the system. Consider the following guidelines:

- E-mail is effective when used to:
  - Gather information.
  - Stay in touch with employees at remote sites.
  - Document a conversation that has already occurred.

- In general, e-mail should not be used:
  - As a tool for feedback.
  - As a substitute for a face-to-face conversation.
  - To persuade or influence others.
  - To announce momentous changes.

- To be an effective user of e-mail, you need to know:
  - How to create short, clear written messages whose meaning cannot be misunderstood.
  - The differences between "reply," "reply all," and "forward."
  - How to create a distribution list.
  - How to create a system for organizing your e-mail messages.
  - How to use features of your system, such as those that let others know when you are out of the office for an extended period of time.
  - How to attach and save file attachments.

In addition, it's important to know the document retention policies set up by your legal department. Electronic documents, including e-mail, can be used as evidence in legal proceedings.

Use electronic calendars effectively

Organizations are increasingly moving to centralized electronic calendar systems that allow for easy scheduling of meetings and conference rooms, storage and sharing of contact information, and efficient tracking of task assignments and group projects. To make the most effective use of electronic calendars, consider the following suggestions:

- If your organization does not currently use electronic calendars, initiate a discussion of the pros and cons of implementing the system. Set up a task force to identify the potential time and cost savings of having such a system.

- If your organization is about to implement such a system, use change-management tactics that will ensure maximum buy-in, use, and benefit of the system.

- Develop policies for handling people's calendars, room scheduling, and resource scheduling. To realize the greatest benefit of this technology, everyone needs to use it consistently.

- Learn how the system works, and make sure all of your employees are trained how to use it properly.

- Discuss how personal time is to be handled on work calendars. For example, if the person's calendar shows free time, can it be assumed that a meeting can be scheduled for that time? Identify protocols that everyone agrees to.

- Determine whether there are reasons for anyone to manage another person's calendar. In some large organizations, administrative assistants manage the electronic calendar of their managers either all the time or when the manager is on vacation.

RESOURCES

The resources for this chapter begin on page 640.

II
PROMOTE
CORPORATE CITIZENSHIP

- *Develop collaboration between business and community*
- *Understand community issues relevant to the business*
- *Seek alternatives to business practices harmful to the environment*
- *Encourage responsible use of resources*
- *Support efforts to improve stewardship*
- *Contribute to community organizations*
- *Address questionable business practices*
- *Address issues and concerns of the current and future workforce*

INTRODUCTION

"Business is part of society. Society is part of business."

— Tom Petzinger

"We are not in business to conduct moral activity. We are not in business to conduct socially responsible activity." Such was the sentiment of the chairman of one of the top U.S. companies in the mid-1980s. That was then—but times are changing. A great awakening is under way in business. No author better articulates how today's leaders are approaching the marketplace than Thomas Petzinger in *The New Pioneers: The Men and Women Who Are Transforming the Workplace and Marketplace* (Simon & Schuster, 1999). The leadership emerging in the 1990s and into the new century brings a different mentality and approach.

In earlier times, stewardship and corporate citizenship may have been thought to be a nice sentiment but unnecessary. Corporate philanthropy used to be linked to building a company's image and improving its relationship with the community in which it operates. Today, attracting and retaining qualified employees is one of the most important reasons for community involvement. People want to work for companies that reflect and support their values. It also helps to boost loyalty and morale, and improve motivation and productivity. Corporate citizenship has become a necessity in today's global society, economy, and environment.

Increasingly, effective leaders are good stewards who make wise and careful use of all resources—personal time and energy, material and physical resources, and other people. They take a holistic view of the community and the business enterprise, recognizing that what happens in one arena in some way inevitably affects the other. With a world population exceeding six billion people, the sense of interconnectedness is more obvious in every arena of life. Responsible partnerships between business enterprises and the communities in which they exist are essential. Therefore, leaders in every type of organization need to take the initiative to participate in the public discussions, debates, and decisions affecting the enterprises of which they are a part. Business leaders can positively participate in and influence the decisions made in the communities in which they live. This impact can help sustain and improve the livability of those communities.

Another mark of good managers, particularly at upper levels, is that they champion corporate citizenship within their organizations. This is important for several reasons. Such involvement strengthens the company's relationship with the community and enhances its reputation. The goodwill of the communities in which an organization is located can be very important for a variety of stakeholders, including current and future employees, customers, and shareholders.

Many leaders exhibit an altruism that prompts them to reach beyond their own particular organizational responsibilities. The most admired leaders are those who are committed to causes beyond their personal egos, and who find small and large ways to contribute to the communities to which they belong.

This chapter offers suggestions that can help you strengthen your commitment to stewardship and corporate citizenship.

VALUABLE TIPS

- Pay attention to the organization's business practices and address those that may be questionable.

- With your staff, brainstorm ways to conserve energy and resources in the areas in which you have control or influence.

- Join with other business and community entities to revitalize part of your city.

- Read a local newspaper regularly to learn about important events in the community.

- Develop strategies to eliminate or reduce harmful impact your organization's materials, products, or processes may have on the environment.

- Maintain a big-picture perspective of how your organization and your community can work together. Identify ways in which you can share resources.

- Initiate and support recycling efforts in your organization. Find out what opportunities are available for recycling paper, glass, plastic, and aluminum in your offices.

- Reduce the amount of colored paper you use. The dyes are harmful to the environment, and the large amounts of bleach used to de-ink the paper pollute the water supply.

- Join in business and education institution partnerships to support and encourage education.

- Read *50 Simple Things Your Business Can Do to Save the Earth* by the Earthworks Group (Earthworks Press, 1991), or similar publications.

- Work cooperatively with environmental groups to protect environmental resources.

- Start or participate in a "2%" or "5%" club in your community. These are companies who regularly contribute a certain amount of pretax profits to community improvement.

- Join a service group or club in your community and volunteer some of your time to support their causes. Encourage your employees to do the same.

- Offer to speak to community organizations that deal with issues about which you especially care.

- Learn about and assist with a community leadership program (which are often organized by local business associations).

- Sponsor work projects with your team, such as working with the elderly in your community, mentoring high school students, or building or rehabilitating homes for the ill-housed.

- Run for local office (city council, school board, recreation and parks board, or the like) and contribute your thinking and leadership.

- Read *The New Pioneers: The Men and Women Who Are Transforming the Workplace and Marketplace*, by Thomas Petzinger, Jr. (Simon & Schuster, 1999).

- Meet once a month with employees in the department to keep informed about their progress, feelings about their work, work/life concerns, and future interests.

- Learn about differences in the workforce through reading, attending workshops, and fostering relationships with people who are different.

- Study labor market trends and determine what needs to be done to manage or adapt to any changes. Government agencies and planning departments are good sources of data.

Develop collaboration between business and community

Increasingly, businesses and communities are finding it mutually beneficial to work together to conserve resources and promote educational and community-support programs.

Effective business leaders are forward looking and able to see across organizational boundaries. They seek and create opportunities for learning, cooperation, collaboration, and synergy between and among various business and community entities.

To help you develop collaboration between business and the community, consider the following suggestions:

• Get to know political and community leaders in your area. Learn about and better understand their issues, agendas, and concerns. Use both formal and informal opportunities to share your perspective on issues of mutual interest.

• Establish frequent communication with local community organizations to form a social contract, and identify the ground rules for effective partnerships. Misunderstandings often arise in the absence of clear guidelines and agreed-upon standards.

• Find an area where your organization can use and complement the resources of a community agency. For example, many communities have excellent resources in childcare, family counseling, and drug and alcohol rehabilitation. You can use the community resources available and build your organization's programs around those resources.

• Work with local high schools and colleges. Offer to speak in classrooms. Invite administrators, instructors, and students into your work environment, and share some of the opportunities, common concerns, needs, and constraints your organization faces. Offer internship and scholarship opportunities.

• Create or sponsor a speaker's bureau of people who can talk about issues of concern to the organization, industry, and community. Offer to send speakers to groups with common interests and concerns. Service groups are often interested in this type of opportunity, and they can be an excellent source of referral.

• Show commitment to the community by making efforts to ensure that your employee demographics are sufficiently diverse and representative of the community.

- When you have products, materials, or office supplies that are no longer needed, donate them to a local agency or charitable organization. Your old lobby chair may be someone else's prize office furnishing.

- Support your local educational, cultural, and healthcare institutions. Remember that monetary contribution is not the only way of support. Consider volunteering your time, energy, and expertise.

- Participate in a community outreach program that helps people learn a new marketable skill or otherwise improve the quality of life.

- Develop and distribute written materials to the public and media, acknowledging your company's commitment to supporting and improving your community and/or the environment. You may also want to dedicate a page on your company's Web site to describing your corporate citizenship policies and efforts.

- Sponsor or support charity efforts in the community through funding. The United Way organization in many U.S. communities is one example.

Understand community issues relevant to the business

Every organization operates within a community and is affected by many internal and external factors associated with that community. Successful leaders are frequently active in addressing the community issues that have an impact on their business or profession.

Initiatives and efforts that benefit both your organization and the community can be worth your serious consideration. Following are some actions to consider:

- Locate and read long-range plans made by one or more community or government agencies. Note projections made by demographers and various organizations regarding the future.

- Be aware of future projects planned in the community and their likely impact on your business—on your present or future employees, customers, and so forth.

- In the United States, read publications such as those published by the Citizens League, Chamber of Commerce, and other civic and neighborhood groups. Check out the "State of the City" and "State of the State" reports to identify strengths and weaknesses of the areas in which you do business.

- Identify the community factors that help and hurt your business, and work with community leaders to address the issues. Examples include:
  - Business climate, including taxation policies
  - Status of housing
  - Traffic
  - Transportation
  - Level of violence
  - Quality of schools
  - Overall infrastructure

- Encourage your employees to serve in the community in some capacity through worthwhile public and private initiatives and organizations.

- Dedicate some of your resources to improving community life. The quality of life in your community can directly affect the success of your business.

Seek alternatives to business practices harmful to the environment

Your organization may use or produce materials, products, or processes that may be harmful to the environment. To develop your awareness in this area and commit to doing business in a way that promotes sustainable development and pollution prevention, consider the following suggestions:

- Learn about the materials, products, and processes your organization uses. Follow up on environmental reports that have been done on your products, or see that such reports are produced. Use your own staff as well as independent agencies to look at the environmental impact of your operations. By using a variety of information sources, you will get a more accurate reading on the risks involved.

- If you determine that your materials, products, or processes may be harmful to the environment, set up a task force to learn about and open the way for alternative methods. Countless examples exist of business leaders who have identified safer materials or production methods for their organizations.

- Bring your scientists and engineers together to work on reducing the potential negative impact that your materials, products, or processes may have on human health and the environment.

- Link environmental efforts with your organization's overall objectives. In the short term, the use of materials and processes harmful to the environment may generate a high financial return. Over the long term, however, this is not the case. After-the-fact clean-ups, such as those required by environmental protection regulations, are always more costly than taking appropriate preventive measures.

- Conduct process-improvement efforts to identify and implement new processes that help to reduce or eliminate the amount of waste and harmful byproducts.

- Conduct periodic evaluations to make sure that all your products and/or services are of high quality, safe, and environmentally friendly.

- If your business requires the use of natural resources, identify ways to replenish the resources you deplete, if possible.

Encourage responsible use of resources

The "greening" of businesses has had a significant positive impact on the environment. Resource conservation efforts are good for the physical environment as well as for public relations, employee morale, and the financial bottom line.

To encourage your organization to be more responsive to resource conservation, consider the following suggestions:

I'M TRYING TO MAKE MY OFFICE AS ENVIRONMENTALLY FRIENDLY AS POSSIBLE.

- Bring in someone from outside the organization that specializes in this type of resource-use analysis. Ask them to study the organization and make recommendations.

- Create a recycling task force with staff members. Brainstorm recycling ideas and programs, and put decisions into action.

- Include tips on recycling and waste reduction in departmental and organizational newsletters and other communications.

- Provide containers for recycling in offices, work areas, lounges, and break rooms.

- Reduce the amount of paper you use by copying documents on both sides of the paper, and by using voice mail and e-mail in lieu of internal memos. Use erasable boards rather than paper flip charts for presentations.

- Conserve energy in your office space by turning off lights when you will be gone for more than ten minutes. In addition, use fluorescent lights in your office space; they use less energy and last longer than incandescent lights.

- Work with the facilities department to identify energy conservation methods available, and then implement the relevant, cost-effective measures.

- Invite an energy expert (from inside or outside the company) to talk with your staff about personal conservation measures that can be taken at work and at home.

Support efforts to improve stewardship

Stewardship involves the effective and efficient use of all human, financial, and material resources of businesses and community agencies. Stewardship begins with a mind-set, a perspective that looks for ways of effectively and efficiently using resources.

Good leaders are good stewards of the environment and the community's and organization's resources. While they may not be able to reshape society directly, they know that they are a part of it and certainly have a stake in it. Therefore, they are dedicated to integrating stewardship into their business strategies.

Some steps you can take to promote good stewardship include the following:

- Evaluate your personal stewardship.
  - Identify one or more ways in which you could be more effective or efficient in your work, and make a change that will produce improvement.
  - Assess whether you are giving satisfactory amounts of time, money, and energy to your important personal, relationship, community, and career priorities. Personal stewardship involves maintaining an adequate life balance, in which all areas receive meaningful and appropriate (not equal) attention.

- Review your staff to see if their capabilities are being fully utilized and if there are other contributions they could, and would like to, make. Try to keep enriching people's jobs.

- Encourage others to be good stewards of their own energy, talents, and time. Ask them to evaluate their own productivity. That is, are they:
  - Sufficiently occupied with priority work, or are delays, tardiness of others, and lack of tools and resources getting in the way?
  - Efficient in their work by spending the proper amount of time and energy getting tasks completed for the value those tasks provide to customers (internal or external)?
  - Effective in spending their time and energy on the highest priority tasks for their respective roles in the organization?

- Look for opportunities to improve the stewardship of community organizations with which you work. Are their people well used? Are adequate percentages of funds and other material resources going to the group being served?

- Create a bulletin board to post upcoming drives or community projects, and provide employees with information on volunteer opportunities available.

- Try to think of ways your business could apply the stewardship principle that would be more supportive of the environment and/or people.

The stewardship principle can be applied to business decisions on small or large scales. For example, one well-known commercial developer in the United States applied the stewardship principle to a series of large-scale suburban developments. The decision was made that instead of following a 50/50 guideline—namely 50 percent of the space for buildings, streets, sidewalks, parking ramps, and roads, and 50 percent for grass, trees, and water—the developments would follow an 80/20 pattern. That is, 80 percent of each area was designed for "green and blue," including adding a small lake to the development, and only 20 percent of each area was used for bricks, mortar, and blacktop. The developer creatively retained more of the natural setting and even added to it while providing an aesthetically pleasing and functionally effective office complex.

Contribute to community organizations

Part of effective corporate citizenship is contributing in an altruistic manner to organizations that improve the quality of life in your community, regardless of any specific or definable positive impact on your business.

Contributions can take a variety of forms; at times they may involve financial support, while at other times they may involve donating your time, energy, and skills to an endeavor. Following are some activities you might consider:

- Join and participate in an active service organization. If your schedule prohibits regular attendance, you may wish to work on a special project within a service club.

- Identify organizations that have significant positive impact on your community, and periodically contribute money to them.

- As a way of passing on inspiration and encouragement to future leaders, contribute your time (for example, as a board member or a volunteer) to a youth, athletic, or cultural endeavor.

- Seek an elective or appointive political or community position. Many such positions (such as school board, city council, planning commission) can be coordinated for a period of time even with a demanding career.

- Match employees' financial contributions to civic organizations.

- Encourage and support the involvement of your employees in community service. Consider allowing them to spend a predetermined amount of work time volunteering.

- Offer community groups access to your company resources (people, equipment, or facilities) for civic and other public activities.

- Set up a corporate foundation to oversee your company's philanthropic activities.

- Commit to allocating a minimum percentage of pretax profits for charity organizations.

Address questionable business practices

Leaders have the opportunity to assure their employees, customers, and other stakeholders that the organization's business practices meet high standards by proactively addressing these issues. Consider the following actions:

- Take personal responsibility to find out what the organization and its suppliers are doing in regard to labor practices, environmental concerns, and so forth. See that questionable practices are brought to the attention of people who will address them.

- Make sure the organization has developed a code of conduct for the business, its practices, and its employees.

- Ensure that clear responsibilities for implementing and monitoring the code of conduct are established.

- Challenge the organization and suppliers to improve their business practices when necessary; insist that the improvements are prerequisite to continued business.

- Encourage discussion of ethical issues and work with your team to address these issues and dilemmas.

Address issues and concerns of the current and future workforce

The stewardship of leaders extends to the people who work for them. In the past, corporate philanthropy was linked to building a company's image and improving its relationship with the community in which it operates. Today, attracting and retaining qualified employees has become one of the most important reasons for community involvement. People want to work for companies that reflect and support their values. Community involvement also helps boost loyalty and morale and improve motivation and productivity.

For the same reasons, organizations are also paying more attention to recognizing, respecting, and responding to their employees' interests and concerns. For instance, during the 1990s, on-site or conveniently located childcare and even preschools became more and more common for U.S. companies. Flexible hours, job sharing, work-at-home, part-time professional employment, and so forth, became more common as well.

One aspect of being an effective leader requires making reasonable accommodation for life requirements and responsibilities beyond the specific work assignment. Do you know what is important to your employees to keep them happy, motivated, and productive? What are the work/life issues and concerns that get in the way? What reasonable accommodation can be made when and where necessary?

To address these issues, take the following steps:

- Review your organization's flexibility in responding to workforce interests and concerns such as:
  - Nontraditional workers, people with disabilities, retirees, and immigrants.
  - Reward systems that respond to the values of economically stable older workers, who may prefer sabbaticals, perks, and time off to salary increases or other financial incentives.
  - Part-time roles as people shift their use of time, including more volunteer and community involvement in some cases.
  - Interest in policies related to issues such as dependent care, wellness, family, and so on.
  - Professionals in dual-career families who may be unwilling to relocate and may do so only with significant incentives and support.
  - Flexible leave policies. With both parents working in many families, there is increasing pressure for both of them to be given leave for childbirth, child-related emergencies, school-related activities, and elder care.
  - In general, reward, recognition, and motivational practices that provide for more options.

- Determine how the organization can be a good corporate citizen for an increasingly diverse workforce. Use or initiate ways the organization can:
  - Foster diversity in your workplace. Strive to have minority employees represented at all levels of the organization.
  - Use communication techniques to assist employees unfamiliar with the common language. This can be especially helpful for immigrant employees.
  - Provide remedial education for those groups that were previously disadvantaged.
  - Design jobs and utilize technology in which a command of the national language is not critical.
  - Establish rewards that are valued by different cultural groups and be flexible about holidays, time off, and leaves.

- Create partnerships between managers and employees to discuss appropriate accommodations to their work and resolve workplace issues.
- Create special career-development programs to better match people with jobs that fit their skills, wants, needs, and values.
- Support community education systems and increase training efforts in basic education.

RESOURCES

The resources for this chapter begin on page 642.

PLANNING AND EXECUTION FACTOR

Volumes have been written about the differences between management and leadership. Some have concluded that management has to do with planning and monitoring work and that leadership is about making change happen. In reality, planning and execution are critical success factors in both management and leadership domains.

Planning, which some think of as a management skill, involves making tough choices and influencing others toward those choices (a leadership skill). Implementing a change process, which many believe falls squarely in the realm of leadership, is also about planning and monitoring what's working (management).

Effectiveness in your role requires that your sights be set on what to do and how to do it. As Peter Drucker writes in *Management* (Harper and Row, 1995,) the manager "must, so to speak, keep his nose to the grindstone while lifting his eyes to the hills."

This section describes the connections among planning, delegating, implementing, and creating an environment where change efforts can be successful. It addresses the management of total quality and process-improvement initiatives—the watchwords of customer focus. This section contains development opportunities for these key competency areas:

Chapter 12 - Establish Plans: Proactively develops goals and objectives to support the organization's strategic vision; identifies specific action steps, accountabilities, and timelines for completion; prepares realistic estimates of resource requirements; balances planning with day-to-day demands; coordinates planning across functions and business units; standardizes work processes to facilitate planning efforts.

Chapter 13 - Manage and Improve Processes: Helps others understand their work from a process perspective; defines and communicates expectations for quality outcomes, process standards, and process-management tools; uses statistical information to identify trends and track progress; analyzes process breakdowns and identifies ways to improve the efficiency of future work; investigates and adopts best practices from within and outside the organization.

Chapter 14 – Drive Execution: Effectively manages time and priorities by focusing on highest priority tasks and working efficiently; delegates responsibilities and appropriate authority to others; monitors the progress of others and holds people accountable; prepares for and facilitates productive meetings.

Chapter 15 – Manage Change: Understands own role in the change process; understands and addresses reactions and resistance to change; effectively communicates change; leverages the involvement of key stakeholders; involves others in decision making and implementation of change; establishes structures and roles to support change.

12
ESTABLISH PLANS

PART 1: DEVELOP PLANS AND PROCESSES
- *Understand your organization's strategic vision*
- *Translate strategy into specific goals and objectives to support the organization's vision*
- *Prepare plans*
- *Prepare realistic estimates of resource requirements*
- *Identify and obtain staff capabilities needed to accomplish objectives*
- *Establish clear, realistic timelines for accomplishing goals*

PART 2: IMPROVE YOUR PLANNING SKILLS
- *Identify specific action steps and accountabilities*
- *Balance planning efforts with day-to-day demands*
- *Involve others in planning*
- *Coordinate across work units*
- *Consult with skilled planners*

PART 3: STANDARDIZE WORK PROCESSES TO FACILITATE PLANNING
- *Document current processes*
- *Identify the appropriate work structures to accomplish goals*

PART 4: ENGAGE IN PROACTIVE PLANNING
- *Identify, test, and confirm assumptions in plans*
- *Anticipate problems, identify risks, and plan for contingencies*

INTRODUCTION

*The telephone pole was approaching. I was attempting
to swerve out of the way when it struck my front end.*

— Accident Report Form

Without plans, strategic vision and goals are merely dreams. Work that
lacks adequate planning often falls short of or entirely misses the desired
goals. The rework required at the end of a poorly planned project can
have significant time and cost implications, not only for the project in
question, but also for other projects in your department or division.

Successful managers know how to establish effective plans and develop
effective processes. They also know how to set up processes that carry
out those plans. Effective leaders begin the planning process with the
organization's vision and goals and end up with specific plans to
achieve these goals. Such leaders know, also, that plans must involve
other people, other units, and the management of potential risks. They
make sure their work schedule supports the entire planning process.

This chapter presents procedures and guidelines for establishing plans
and processes for carrying them out most effectively.

VALUABLE TIPS

- Ensure your department or team goals are consistent with the organization's direction and strategic goals.

- Ask your employees how their goals contribute to the organization's success. If they can't tell you, help them translate strategic goals into specific objectives.

- Identify the critical path to achieving your goals.

- If you are unable to reliably predict how much time things will take, use time estimates from others who are more accurate.

- Use plans to guide your work, recognizing that changes and the unexpected will occur.

- Identify assumptions underlying your direction or planning efforts that, if wrong, will cause major problems.

- Set aside quiet time each day for reviewing plans and updating planning activities.

- Ask employees to align their annual goals with the team's or area's strategic plan. Have them include specific objectives, priorities, and timetables.

- Break large projects into several smaller steps, with deadlines for each step. Track completion of each step to assure the success of the plan.

- If deadlines are missed, find out why and incorporate your learning into the next project plan.

- Involve those affected by a plan in the creation of the plan.

- Communicate changes to members of the team and to those affected.

- Review resource allocation to determine whether you are allocating resources according to your priorities.

- Identify the critical constraints to executing the plan. Develop strategies to deal with the constraints.

- Once you develop your plan, ask others to identify potential problems. Then use their feedback to help determine your contingency plans.

- At least once a year, evaluate the consequences of your plans with an eye toward spotting any trends, such as underestimating timelines, not providing adequate project resources, making assumptions that were wrong, etc. Take action to address issues identified.

PART 1:
DEVELOP PLANS AND PROCESSES

Understand your organization's strategic vision

The strategic vision defines what an organization wants to be and where it wants to go. It includes the organization's strategy for gaining and sustaining competitive advantage. Effective planning requires a deep understanding of the strategic intent and the business processes necessary to achieve these goals. This understanding enables leaders and teams to set departmental goals, strategies, and plans that support the vision.

To better understand and link your organization's strategic vision to your team's work, consider the following steps:

1. Be able to articulate your organization's vision and strategic direction.
   - What industry are we in?
   - What is our sustainable competitive advantage? What is our advantage over our competitors?
   - What business processes are critical to our success?
   - What are our strategic goals?
   - What role does my team or part of the organization play in the success of the organization?

2. If you cannot answer the questions above, ask for help from your manager or coach.

3. Communicate this information to those you supervise, so that they understand the organization's direction. They will need this information to set their own goals and/or guide their teams.

Translate strategy into specific goals and objectives to support the organization's vision

Once you understand the organization's vision, strategy, and goals, you can work with your management team and/or direct reports to identify the vision, strategy, and goals for your work group, and then develop specific plans to accomplish these goals.

Detailed action plans that support the organizational strategy can help you translate the vision and strategy into clear goals and action plans for your department or team; focus the department or team output to best serve the organization's needs; and stay in touch with the big picture, even when day-to-day details threaten to cloud the larger goals. Action plans also allow you to better implement and monitor strategy.

The following suggestions can help you develop aligned and effective strategic plans for your work unit:

- Identify the role you and your team(s) play in achieving the organization's goals by identifying the business processes for which you are accountable.

- Determine what your part of the organization must do to achieve the organization's goals. Include objectives for how to improve the business processes necessary for success.

- Identify the primary constraints to achieving the goals.

- Plan what you will do to address the constraints. Most of your planning time should address these issues, because this is where you are most vulnerable.

- Ask individuals and teams to identify their goals and plans. Give them a template to use in planning to ensure that all pertinent components are addressed.

- Review these individual and team goals and plans to ensure that they are compatible with and in support of the organization's strategy.

- Develop objective measures of success that will tell you when you have achieved an objective or goal.

- Put all of this information into a format that is clear, accessible, and easy to update.

- Be flexible, and be prepared to change your action plans if internal or external factors alter the company's strategic direction.

Prepare plans

Planning involves both the long and short term. Because of rapid changes in technology and the fiercely competitive landscape, long term may mean six months for some businesses and five years for others.

As you do your planning, identify areas in which you need a long-term plan and those in which you can plan only a short time out. For the areas needing a long-term plan, also anticipate the significant changes that may occur and plan for those contingencies.

The guide for any long-range plan should be your company's strategic plan and vision. In addition, consider the following suggestions for preparing longer-term plans:

- Consider using scenario planning. Scenario planning builds three or four descriptions of potential future conditions, and uses those possible futures to define a plan that will succeed regardless of which scenario actually comes to pass.

- Review your department's strategies, objectives, and tactics for compatibility with the organization's strategic plans. If revisions are necessary, discuss the reasons with your colleagues.

- Identify colleagues who appear to have well-defined strategic plans. Ask what process they used to develop objectives and tactics.

- Ask your direct reports to submit an annual work plan for your review, and then work with them to incorporate their ideas into an operational plan for the department.

- Communicate your department's business strategies and objectives to peers in other departments. Seek input on objectives and tactics that might affect them.

- Consider using a software planning tool to organize and monitor the work.

The following process will help you construct plans:

1. Identify the goals that need a plan. Assign responsibility for the plan to an appropriate person or team. Agree to a date by which the plan is to be completed. This will help ensure that you complete your project in a timely way.

2. Create your plan. The following sections are included in most plans:
   - Goals, objectives, and deliverables
   - Business process to achieve the goals and objectives
   - Constraints
   - Tasks
   - Dependencies/others involved
   - Budget
   - Resource requirements
   - Staffing
   - Implementation and change-management plan (target dates, assignment of personnel, monitoring techniques, and so forth)

3. Review the completed plan with your manager to assess its completeness and accuracy.

Prepare realistic estimates of resource requirements

When you are planning, make realistic estimates of required resources to achieve the desired goals efficiently. Without timely access to resources of all types, delays will occur. To ensure that you have adequately assessed your resource needs, follow this process:

1. Review plans and projects already implemented, and compare resources required on a like-sized project. If your previous budgets were off target, determine why, and make appropriate adjustments.

2. List all the resources and supplies that will be required to implement the project or strategy. Gain input from others.

   Be sure to include life-cycle costs, not just the original startup costs of a project. For example, CRM (Customer Relationship Management) software requires an initial investment in change-management consulting, requirements gathering, and building and implementing the system. However, these systems also may have significant ongoing costs for software maintenance and upgrades, as well as review and modification of related business processes.

3. For each resource, identify when it will be needed, the different ways it can be obtained, and what acceptable substitutes exist.

4. If you have a history of misjudging resources, ask someone who is more skilled than you to identify and estimate the resources or to review your work.

5. Establish systems to measure and monitor the productivity of various resources. This will enable you to estimate more accurately your resource needs in the future.

Identify and obtain staff capabilities needed to accomplish objectives

A careful assessment of roles and the tasks that need to be done will help you to staff the project adequately. Be sure to identify critical needs that can't be met with current staff and proactively address those needs. In addition, build in an assumption about the loss of some staff, so that you do not have unexpected barriers to success.

To identify the people who will implement your plan, try the following process:

1. Identify the steps and the roles needed to successfully implement your plan.

2. Determine the pivotal role(s) upon which the project's success depends. Identify the knowledge, skills, and competencies needed for each role.

3. Determine which of the roles may be good developmental opportunities.

4. Identify people for each role. Check for their availability and interest.

5. Determine what support potential candidates need for each role, especially if it is to be used as a developmental assignment. Make sure you can arrange for this support before you put the person in the role.

6. When you give someone a developmental assignment, explain thoroughly what you expect him or her to learn. Discuss what the person needs to be successful in the role. Provide the necessary coaching and support to make the assignment an effective learning opportunity.

Establish clear, realistic timelines for accomplishing goals

Unrealistic plans can create more problems than they solve. For example, an impossible schedule set by one department may eventually affect the schedules of many other departments, causing inefficient use of resources, late introduction to the marketplace of an advertised product, and a general sense that things are out of control. It is essential, therefore, that the planning process includes techniques for evaluating project plans. Following are suggestions to help ensure that your project plans are realistic:

- After developing a plan, ask your team or a trusted peer to challenge your assumptions and identify potential flaws or problems with the schedule. Make changes to address any problems you may have overlooked.

- Involve the various people or groups affected by the plan in its construction. When the plan is complete, ask each person to review it one last time to evaluate how realistic it is. Get everyone's commitment to support the plan.

- Consider involving your customers and/or suppliers in the planning process. Their input may be quite helpful in developing appropriate timelines, and you are more likely to gain their commitment to the process.

- In addition to evaluating individual plans, examine how the timing of one plan affects other plans and projects. Get into the habit of keeping a calendar large enough to chart all of your projects simultaneously. Keeping track of the overall picture is the best way to avoid overcommitting yourself. It also provides a quick reference for monitoring the availability of resources and time.

- Compare your timeline with a completed similar project. What were the initial time estimates for that project? What were the actual time spans needed for each piece? Apply knowledge to your current plan.

PART 2:
IMPROVE YOUR PLANNING SKILLS

Identify specific action steps and accountabilities

"Ready, fire, aim" is the operating style of many leaders and organizations. Getting to the outcome is so important that everyone takes off in that general direction, and sometimes—miraculously—everyone does reach the finish line. More often, however, such an approach results in undesirable outcomes and some people getting lost along the way.

A well-defined plan is an effective management tool. When all the required tasks are specified and assigned, and due dates are clearly communicated, it's easy to check periodically the status of a project to determine whether it's on track. Your staff knows what is expected of them and when, and you know whom to follow up with when you need an update.

To develop specific action plans and accountabilities, try the following guidelines:

- Clarify expectations by discussing them openly. Determine if there are any nonnegotiable items and make sure they are communicated clearly.

- Ask people to summarize expectations for you or write down their specific action steps.

- Evaluate and update your plan on a regular basis, checking off tasks or phases as they're completed. This lets others know what progress is being made and allows them to see how their efforts are contributing to the final goal.

- Set dates for completion of various phases of the project. Be sure that everyone agrees to these dates, including expectations for how to reach them.

- Request status reports from your employees or teams on progress toward goals. Use your experience to determine the reporting frequency.

- Monitor and follow up on progress. By documenting performance against plans (for example, actual versus budgeted labor), you will be better able to evaluate results and develop realistic plans for future projects.

- Intervene and adjust plans when necessary.

Balance planning efforts with day-to-day demands

Managers often become caught up in urgent day-to-day activities and crises, losing sight of the importance of developing strategy and planning. Use the following suggestions to ensure that you spend the time you need for planning:

- Evaluate your priorities by identifying the important, the urgent, and the less important or less urgent. First do those items that are both important and urgent, then handle the important ones. Find someone else to address the urgent but less important tasks.

- When an urgent matter arises, determine how it fits into your daily plan (is it urgent and important, or simply urgent?) and act accordingly.

- Use project-planning software or a Gantt chart to plan complex and multiple projects. These systems typically have a process for identifying the most important priorities.

- Use the 80/20 rule, which states that 80 percent of the value of a group of items is generally concentrated in only 20 percent of the items. Simply put, the 80/20 rule means that you can be 80 percent effective by achieving 20 percent of your goals. Thus, if your daily to-do list contains ten items, under the 80/20 rule, you can expect to be generally 80 percent effective by successfully completing only the two most important items.

- Keep a log to determine how you are spending your time. Evaluate your time allocations to ensure that you are giving proper time and attention to the more strategic issues and important priorities.

Involve others in planning

When making plans, involve the people, teams, and constituencies that care about the outcome, the plan, or the process. Deciding when and how to involve people is an important leadership skill that should always be part of the planning process.

Use the following suggestions to involve others in the planning process:

- Identify the business processes involved in accomplishing the goal. Then identify the process owners for each part of the process. Typically, these people or their representatives should be included in the planning.

- Recognize that most planning processes need to include the people and teams affected by the plan or situation.

- Use a team approach to planning in very complex situations where results are critical, many people are involved, and the plan is not obvious.

- Balance the need for involvement with the need for action and speed.

- Train people in team processes, so that team planning will go more quickly and smoothly.

- Include vendors and suppliers when their commitments are necessary and cannot be assumed—for example, when the project requires that new technology from a sole supplier be ready on time.

- Review the plan with others, gathering information on how the plan might affect them. Ask each person for ideas on how to improve the plan, and incorporate the ideas whenever possible.

Coordinate across work units

To ensure integrated and cooperative implementation, effective leaders coordinate planning efforts within and across work units. This can be easier said than done. It takes a concerted effort to get people together, to create a plan that will work for those involved, and to help people balance competing priorities.

Consider the following suggestions for improving your ability to coordinate across units:

- Make it a habit to involve others when they are needed to coordinate on projects. Bring them into the planning process early.

- Set the expectation with your employees that they will include in the planning process people affected by their plans.

- Even when you do not see a direct connection between your proposed plan and other work units, review your plan from their perspective to determine if they might see a relationship.

- Send a copy of the plan to those involved so they have the option of commenting.

- Coordinate planning efforts with your peers by reviewing major priorities with them. It is better to err on the side of overcommunicating.

- Schedule regular reviews of the plan so that necessary people continue to have the involvement they want and you need.

- Ask your employees to submit work plans for your review. Evaluate their plans for duplication of effort and resource availability, and then put these plans together to build a larger operational plan for your department. Bring employees with overlapping plans together, and ask them to coordinate their efforts to accomplish both sets of goals more efficiently.

- Use project-planning software to coordinate plans.

Consult with skilled planners

Individuals in your organization who are known for their planning skills may be able to help you improve your skills. Consider these suggestions for consulting with skilled planners:

- Observe a skilled planner implement the planning process with a person or group of people. Ask yourself:
  - How does he or she approach the task?
  - What does she or he do?
  - What process does he or she use?
  - What techniques does he or she use?
  - What did I learn from observing the process?
  - What can I incorporate into my own work?

- Review the written plans of skilled planners. Notice what they include in their plans and how they organize them. Learn how the plans were developed and who was involved. Finally, find out how the plans were used in the management process and whether they have proven to be effective.

- Ask for advice on your plans. Review your plans with someone who can offer constructive suggestions for improvement. Ask the person to comment on both the content and format of your plans.

PART 3:
STANDARDIZE WORK PROCESSES TO FACILITATE PLANNING

Document current processes

Documenting processes allows you to develop better plans. If you do not know what the process is, you cannot use it to create action plans. Documented processes also reduce variation, improve quality, save time, and provide more rapid transfer of knowledge to new people on the project.

Consider the following suggestions for documenting processes:

- Ensure that you or one of your staff is knowledgeable about process charting.

- Use standard symbols for more rapid understanding and easier transfer of information.

- Identify the most critical business processes for documentation. Once the most critical are done, move on to others.

- Recognize that business processes change and need to change. Do not expect that once you have documented a process, you are done. Challenge the person or team to make process improvements on a regular basis.

Identify the appropriate work structures to accomplish goals

An organization's structure, which includes the roles and relationships among people in the organization, must be dynamic. What once worked well may no longer serve the current vision and goals. Effective managers regularly review and adjust the structure of their part of the organization to meet changing work processes, changing internal and external needs, and the skills of employees.

The following suggestions can help you review and improve the structure of your own part of the organization:

- First identify the business processes, then work on structure. Without a clear understanding of the value chain and business processes, you will not get the structure right.

- Identify the critical roles needed in the team to perform the business processes of the team. Then look at which roles are linked to one another. This will help you understand which structure makes sense.

- Design your structure with empowerment in mind. Whenever possible, create a structure where people do the whole job.

- Ensure that your organization's structure is current, especially if you have just experienced a reorganization, a downsizing effort, or heavy growth. Reevaluate job descriptions, reporting relationships, and lateral structure to match the new organization and goals. Make necessary changes in a timely and responsive fashion.

- Anticipate that you will increasingly need to determine how to include remote workers and contract workers in the work structure. These alternative staffing methods can work effectively as long as the reporting relationships are clear, the people know to whom they connect and how they connect to the organization, the technological resources are available, and the expectation is clear that these individuals are part of the team.

- Set up a team to evaluate the structure of the organization and make recommendations for changes.

- When developing a new product or initiating an interdepartmental project, create a cross-functional task force. Look for participants at varying levels of the organization.

- When working on recurring problems, staff the team with representatives from groups not previously involved. Use customer input or representation; involve administrative support people; get new perspectives.

PART 4:
ENGAGE IN PROACTIVE PLANNING

Identify, test, and confirm assumptions in plans

All business plans are based on both facts and assumptions. The vulnerability of a strategic direction or of any plan lies in the assumptions upon which it depends. To reduce error and to anticipate problems, identify the underlying assumptions and test their accuracy.

To confirm your assumptions, take the following steps as an individual or with the team:

- Identify the assumptions you have made and ensure that they are accurate. For example, a plan may depend on the assumption that it is possible to hire the needed employees. If that assumption is wrong, the plan will encounter serious problems when the employees needed cannot be hired.

- Determine which assumptions are most critical. If they are wrong, it will have a serious, negative impact on accomplishing your goals.

- Ask others to identify the assumptions, because you may be too close to the situation yourself.

Anticipate problems, identify risks, and plan for contingencies

Anticipating potential problems is an important part of the planning process. If you identify risk areas in the initial stages of planning, you can prepare for problems and mitigate them early. In addition, no matter how well you plan, unanticipated events and consequences will arise. If you are prepared for as many eventualities as possible, the problems you can't anticipate will not interfere as much with the project work.

To develop your ability to anticipate and plan for problems, consider the following suggestions:

- Review the discrepancies between plans and actual performance from the previous three to six months. Which of these problems could and should have been anticipated? What patterns exist in regard to risks that you did not plan for? What can you do differently to anticipate problems?

- As part of your regular planning process, identify the risk areas and develop risk-management plans for them. Do not assume that risks will not occur.

- Use data to anticipate and plan for risks. For example, if the plan relies on a stable team, anticipate what you will do if the team loses a member.

- Use scenario planning to identify three or four different ways a situation may evolve. Determine how you will handle each of these scenarios.

- After a plan is drafted, ask the team what might go wrong. Brainstorming works well to accomplish this. Identify the most likely problems. Then generate ideas for handling them if they do occur.

- Each time you begin work on a project over the next three months, use the following process:
  1. Prepare a breakdown of all tasks and critical decisions points, and then determine the critical path of the project.
  2. Analyze each component to detect areas of risk. Be a negative thinker for the moment; try to think of everything that could go wrong. For example:
     - Information required for effective planning might be unavailable.
     - A technical procedure new to employees might be required.
     - A service group that you use might experience staffing problems.
     - You might lose a key resource at a critical time.
  3. Categorize potential problems into high- and low-risk areas. When doing this, consider both how likely it is that the problem will occur and how damaging it would be.
  4. Prepare several possible approaches for dealing with such problems should they occur.
  5. Introduce safety factors into your planning for high-risk areas:
     - Consider allocating more time and/or funds to these phases.
     - Introduce tough control methods in the high-risk areas.
     - Ensure that you are kept fully informed of all developments, either through actual observation or written reports.

RESOURCES

The resources for this chapter begin on page 644.

13
MANAGE AND
IMPROVE PROCESSES

PART 1: MANAGE QUALITY PROCESSES
- *Help others understand their work from a process perspective*
- *Help others understand the impact of variation and how to manage it*
- *Define and communicate process-management tools and methods*
- *Designate process owners accountable for successful execution*
- *Define and communicate expectations for quality outcomes*
- *Manage quality using statistical information to identify trends and track progress*
- *Ensure currency of process standards and process documentation*

PART 2: IMPROVE PROCESSES
- *Analyze process breakdowns to ensure that lessons are learned*
- *Identify ways to streamline and/or improve efficiency of future work*
- *Integrate input from stakeholders to prioritize process-improvement efforts*
- *Adopt best practices and lessons learned from within and outside the organization*

INTRODUCTION

Competitive pressures continually require organizations to change faster and faster. Whether they are reengineering, or implementing a CRM (Client Relationship Management) program, or figuring out how to get resources from new suppliers to manufacturing sites, leaders need to be highly skilled in understanding business processes and how to change them. Effective leaders manage processes as well as lead people. They are the champions of process improvement and continuous learning.

Leaders constantly need to identify ways to do the work better, smarter, and faster. Those who don't will find it difficult to stay competitive in the marketplace. This chapter focuses on ways that managers can keep up with the pace of change and proactively manage process improvement.

VALUABLE TIPS

- Use cross-functional teams composed of people closest to the work when you are trying to improve processes.

- Assign a process owner to lead a change effort.

- Constantly ask why things are done the way they are currently being done.

- When analyzing process flow, recognize which steps add value and which do not. Get rid of those that do not.

- Ask the various stakeholders of a process how and why things are done. Make no assumptions about anything. Ask the same questions of each stakeholder to see if answers differ.

- When you first assume responsibility for an area, learn how the basic business/work processes operate. Ask to see process charts to get a clear understanding of the work processes in the group.

- Include a mini module on process flow and continuous improvement with initial employee training. This sets the expectation that continuous improvement is an important responsibility, and it also provides some basic skills in process improvement.

- When you are thinking about an improvement or a problem, find out what changes have already been tried. If the changes have failed in the past, consider whether anything is different in the workplace today to make another attempt worthwhile.

- Ask new employees for their initial perceptions of the work flow to get some fresh perspectives.

- Listen and listen well. You never know from where ideas or seeds of change can come.

- Ask your business and work teams to review processes on a regular basis.

- Ensure that either you or your staff stays up-to-date on how technology can be used to improve work processes in your area.

- Remember that, when implementing improvements, things sometimes get worse before they get better.

- Ask the process-improvement team what they need from you to be successful. Your role is to provide resources and support to the team and remove blocks to success.

- Communicate to others in the organization about work being done to improve processes. Keeping information about process changes a secret fuels the rumor mill and leads to skepticism and lack of trust.

- Get feedback from internal and external customers on where a process functions well and where it might be improved.

- Look at the physical layout of your department to see how it might be changed to improve communication or enhance efficiency.

- Look for duplication of effort in your department or across department or functions, and review what can be eliminated.

- Focus on the processes, not the people, when analyzing inefficiencies.

- Celebrate successful process changes.

- Make sure necessary training or retraining is provided when implementing new processes or improving old ones.

PART 1:
MANAGE QUALITY PROCESSES

Help others understand their work from a process perspective

To maintain effective and productive processes, people need to develop an understanding of what processes are and how they work. The following steps can help you develop a process focus with your team:

1. Use your team to analyze the operations performed in your department. Draw a flowchart of the processes and tasks that must be accomplished, along with the information the unit needs to meet its goals. Identify both the formal processes and the way things really are done. Note where hand-offs occur. Include people both inside and outside your work unit who are involved in the process.

2. Review various aspects of the work flows in a systematic way.
   - What initiates work to be done?
   - What is the outcome of the process? Where does the outcome go next?
   - What is the cycle time?
   - What occurs when someone is absent? Does the work halt? Your answer will help highlight where the work is employee-dependent rather than process-based.
   - Do people perceive the process as functioning well or poorly? What might make it better?
   - Is everyone adequately trained to execute the tasks?
   - What effects do internal and external forces have on processes? Consider constraints on time and money, group dynamics, and fluctuations in customer demand.
   - How does work move through the department? Review the physical layout of the area. Notice noise levels, placement of supplies, traffic levels, and other distractions.

3. Demonstrate how metrics are an indicator of process health. Talk about internal and external factors that cause the numerical data to fluctuate positively and negatively.

4. Study your work unit's current structure, such as who reports to whom and what their responsibilities are.
   - How did it come to be structured the way it is today?
   - Do all elements of this design still serve a purpose?
   - Is the structure built around capabilities of managers or employees who are no longer with the organization?

5. Compare and contrast the structure and work flows with other work groups in your organization, such as related divisions or departments. Find out how their work processes are set up, what works well and what doesn't, and why.

Help others understand the impact of variation and how to manage it

Work processes exist to get work done. The clearer and more standardized the process is, the more likely that quality will be consistently high. Therefore, it is important to establish and support standard work processes.

You can use the following suggestions to help your group and organization understand how not sticking to processes can have negative impacts:

- After creating a flowchart with the group, explore what happens when variations are introduced into the process. These variations can include not following established communication steps, accommodating last-minute requests, adjusting for employee absences, and so forth.

- Find specific examples of client impact when people did not follow established processes. Sharing feedback from internal and external customers can be a powerful learning tool. Have the team keep track of these situations, if they are not obvious, so the group can discuss better management of such circumstances.

- Explore the value of saying "no" to requests for variations. Sometimes employees don't feel empowered to refuse extreme requests. You may need to coach them on how to address the customer while still focusing on win/win solutions.

- Log customer requests for variation so you can identify when a customer need requires a new process. It is far better to create new processes to respond to new customer needs than to have each request be a variation itself.

- Show that variations are not cost effective in terms of both quantifiable and nonquantifiable costs. Quantifiable costs relate to rework time, employee overtime, extra equipment maintenance, increased overhead costs, product profit margins, etc. Nonquantifiable costs include longer work hours and cycle times, increased employee frustration, lower productivity, etc.

- Show that many process variations do not allow for easy training or cross-training. In fact, training in areas with high variation can be quite time consuming and reduce productivity of both the trainer and the trainee.

- Explore trends in variations that surface because other work groups may need to improve a process. Are your employees consistently having to change the way things are done to make up for another department's poor planning skills, unrealistic turnaround times, lack of proper training, lack of understanding, or miscommunication? Use this information to help other teams improve their efficiency and effectiveness.

Define and communicate process-management tools and methods

When you standardize your work processes, you will not have to "reinvent the wheel" for each new project or for different kinds of situations. Instead, you can modify the process to fit each new initiative. Training also becomes easier to manage and replicate in a consistent manner.

Problem-solving models, quality-improvement models, models for troubleshooting complaints, and tracking and training tools are useful elements of each employee's toolkit. They provide common languages, tools, and processes to use for work and for process improvement.

Some effective tools for standardizing your work processes include the following:

- *Flowcharts* convey the relationships of one process or person to another via visual descriptions of work cycles. Flowcharts are treelike diagrams that represent the work flow among process components. Standard symbols (such as circles and squares) are used to identify tasks, and lines are used to represent relationships.

  Flowcharts are especially effective when the process relationships are complex and when several tasks occur simultaneously. Using flowcharts, you can identify critical paths that will allow you to track progress.

- *Project planning worksheets* provide overall snapshots of projects. A project planning worksheet breaks a project into specific tasks and steps, estimates the time required and the cost involved for each task or step, and identifies the person or group responsible for carrying the task through to completion.

- *Gantt charts* are graphic representations of the time relationships in a project. A Gantt chart works particularly well for projects that involve simple, repetitive tasks, projects that will not go through many process changes, and projects for which the plan needs to be communicated simply and directly to others. Gantt charts do not work well if the various steps are highly interdependent.

- *Control sheets* can be simple spreadsheets that track issues being addressed. They can list due dates, designate responsibilities, and serve as a useful communication tool to both the manager and the employees.

- *Logs of errors* (or process breakdowns) can keep information about specific incidences. Over time, these occurrences can be reviewed for trends indicating process weaknesses.

- *Work plans* can be used to assign and prioritize work and to communicate estimated time standards for individuals or work groups on a daily, weekly, or monthly basis. They can also be used to track estimated versus actual time to complete jobs. Actual times that differ significantly from estimated times may indicate the need for further analysis of the process for completing that job.

- *Standard operating procedures (SOPs)* spell out, step-by-step, how to complete a task. SOPs are very useful as a training/cross-training tool if staff turnover is high. They also help with activities that are long, complex, or infrequently done.

- *Checklists* can be used when documentation is important or when it is crucial that no step is overlooked.

Standard versions of these tools are available in process-improvement literature and in electronic form. Many organizations have created their own versions of these for internal use. If you do not know where to locate such resources, check with your improvement teams or quality process people, or with a manufacturing or customer service group. They typically use these tools on a regular basis.

In addition to standard tools, standard methods are also useful. A standard method is a specific way in which something is done. The following are common, useful standard methods:

- *Cross-functional teams* consist of people who work in different departments. These teams can come together on a temporary or permanent basis. A temporary team might be formed to develop and implement a whole new process. Permanent teams may arise for processes that are highly dependent on many different groups working cohesively together.

- *Meeting management guidelines* provide a standard way to conduct meetings. These guidelines usually cover creating and distributing an agenda prior to the meeting, brainstorming rules, starting and ending on time, agreements for handling conflict, etc.

- *Brainstorming protocol* provides guidelines for effective brainstorming in groups.

- *Project initiation meetings* trigger the start of a project. Attendees include project owners from various functions, the customer, etc., and are used to clarify requirements, work processes, and ways in which the teams will work together.

- *Vendor meetings* allow you to review vendors' abilities and determine what they need from you. Discuss ways of serving each other better. Vendors can often offer solutions on how to serve certain customer needs better.

- *Customer reviews* provide a standardized process for gathering information from customers to improve customer relationships and satisfaction.

Designate process owners accountable for successful execution

Since the business process is so critical to successful execution and the success of your business, assign the responsibility of process owner to someone. This person may be the manager of the area or someone he or she designates. Process owners are responsible for the health and continuous improvement of the processes they own. Make sure you place ownership in the hands of a major stakeholder.

In organizations where no one owns the business processes, process improvement is reactionary rather than proactive; processes are improved when there are problems, not as a way of working. Today, many people in manufacturing areas are well aware of the importance of process owners and continuous improvement, but leaders of other areas can learn much from the dramatic improvements and increased productivity that have come from the manufacturing areas. The same process principles apply also to marketing, customer service, and financial groups.

Responsibilities of process owners may include the following:

- Create and maintain necessary documentation about the process, including flowcharts, SOPs, and checklists.

- Collect feedback from internal and external customers to monitor potential areas for improvement.

- Communicate to stakeholders to make them aware of process changes.

- Be in charge of following up on any process improvements after they are implemented.

- Suggest where gaps in training may exist around performing the process as effectively as possible.

- Maintain and report on the metrics relating to the process.

- Regularly review and update all documentation and metrics that relate to the process.

- Keep abreast of any trends or technology that could improve the work flow.

Define and communicate expectations for quality outcomes

Quality standards are driven by customer requirements and are influenced by the competition you face. Where there is little competition, simply meeting the requirements of the customer may be good enough, as long as you closely monitor those needs and the competition. In highly competitive environments, however, you must go beyond the requirements and surpass your competitors in ways that your customers value. If you are not proactive in going beyond expectations, you can be sure that your competitors will be.

An important rule of thumb to remember is "Quality In, Quality Out." Begin by defining the quality needed in the end product. Then make sure you get quality goods from your vendors. Lastly, build quality into each step of your processes.

Quality *for* your customers:

- To determine the quality your customers require, ask them questions that elicit the following kinds of information:
  - The purpose and use of the product or service
  - Specifications of the product or service itself
  - Service requirements
  - Quantity needs
  - Time considerations
  - Cost considerations
  - Delivery issues
  - Previous problems or concerns
  - Anticipated future needs

- With the customer, identify both the key requirements and the features that are nice to have, but not essential. This will help to prioritize what is really needed. Then manage with the intention of meeting both sets of requirements.

- It is imperative that you consistently seek feedback from your customers. It's better to find out sooner rather than later that the quality you are providing does not meet the customer's needs.

Quality *from* your vendors:

Vendors and suppliers are the first links in the quality process. As their customer, you can require quality and service from them. To help you develop quality partnerships with your suppliers, use the following guidelines:

- Determine your criteria for quality and service from your vendors, and communicate those expectations. Share the quality standards for your products and services with the vendors and suppliers who will be contributing goods or services to the creation of those products.

- Accept only excellence from your vendors and suppliers.

- Select vendors on the basis of quality, not just price. This becomes increasingly important as more competitors enter the marketplace.

- Develop partnerships with your vendors and suppliers so you can count on each other. Let them know that if they deliver quality products and good service, you will give them your business.

- If you do not have a choice of vendors, determine how to expand your options. Many managers feel stuck because they are getting poor quality products or service from suppliers or vendors, and they think they have nowhere else to go. Work with your team, the organization, and the industry to develop your options.

Quality along the way:

Because the quality of the end product or service depends on the quality of all steps along the way, quality standards should be developed for each step in the process. Use the following suggestions for developing and periodically updating quality standards for your organization's work processes:

- Pursue the possibilities of a Total Quality Management model in your organization, adopting the model (or combination of models) that best fits your organization's products, services, and work processes.

- Get customer input.

- Compare the initial standards with the customer's requirements for quality to ensure that these standards are customer-driven.

- Use teams involved in the work processes to define the quality they need in each step.

- Make your definitions of quality as comprehensive and precise as possible; use statistical data whenever it is useful.

- Set standards that include what is acceptable and what is outstanding.

- Provide feedback to teams and people about how they are doing in meeting or exceeding the standards.

Manage quality using statistical information to identify trends and track progress

Measuring your work against defined standards is essential to a quality process. *What* you measure is determined by your quality criteria or standards. *How* you measure it is determined by the technique that will give you practical, useful information.

To help your measurement practices and techniques truly support your quality processes, you and your team can use the following suggestions:

- Get exposure to a variety of measurement techniques. Train people on these techniques.

- Learn about the acceptable levels of statistical fluctuations in metrics and at what point there should be cause for alarm.

- Read a book on statistical process control.

- Select measurement strategies that are user-friendly and appropriate for the process.

- Be sure to measure the *right* criteria in the *right* way—make sure that the criteria and measures are customer-focused.

- Measure frequently.

- Use both quantitative and qualitative data. Qualitative information may include employee morale, attitude, motivation, level of frustration, etc.

- Make the results visible. Put up weekly or monthly "scorecards" to communicate trends.

- Present the results in an easy-to-read manner so that they can be quickly and easily understood.

- Focus on the key criteria for effectiveness; don't overwhelm people with too much data.

- Use the results to reward people or to stimulate further improvement.

- Ask employees to analyze the information or data and present their own results and next steps for improvement.

- When tracking the effects of process improvements, remember to develop a measurement baseline before you implement your changes.

Ensure currency of process standards and process documentation

Standards and processes exist so that customer needs are met. Process documentation exists so that you can learn from it. If the documentation of these standards and processes is never reviewed, it becomes an administrative burden, rather than a management tool. Reviewing and learning from documentation is a key step toward improvement.

Effective leaders manage processes as well as lead people. The following guidelines will help you to ensure that standards and processes are accomplishing what they are supposed to:

- Establish regular times to review and update standards. Get input from customers, suppliers, distributors, and other internal functions to determine revisions.

- Ensure that process standards stay current by reviewing how well customers' needs are being met. You can do this by getting feedback from internal and external customers using surveys, meetings, etc.

- Review requests for variation and look for trends. This will be one of the indicators that requirements are changing.

- Listen carefully to the marketing group about how they see the market changing and the competitive pressures. Make sure you understand how the marketing group intends to compete in the marketplace. Pay attention to implications for your group.

- Meet with your technology group to understand plans for technology.

- Talk with one of the technology salespeople calling on you to keep you up-to-date on advances in applications relevant to your area.

- Work with process owners to review and update all documents that reflect the steps of the process.

- Put process owners in charge of researching industry benchmarks and ask for regular updates. Networking with others or searching the Internet may be good ways of doing this research.

- Update documentation as often as necessary, including whenever:
  - New technology is employed.
  - Organizational, departmental, or process changes occur.
  - Roles or assignments shift within the team.
  - The need arises to cover illnesses, sabbaticals, unforeseen departures, etc., of staff members.
  - Customers' needs change.
  - Certain functions become obsolete.

- Review whether standards for productivity need to be adjusted due to changes in the work or technology. If standards are tracked manually, see whether they can be automated and if it will save time to do so.

- Standardize the place where documentation is kept, whether on paper or electronically. Make sure these areas are easily accessible. If not, the process of updating becomes tedious, and the timeliness and, therefore, usefulness, of the material may diminish.

PART 2: IMPROVE PROCESSES

"Those who cannot remember the past are condemned to repeat it."
— George Santayana

Analyze process breakdowns to ensure that lessons are learned

Quality and service are moving targets. What is considered exceptional quality today will be routine expectation tomorrow. Because expectations constantly change, continuous improvement is a must. It is important to use process breakdowns and quality problems as an opportunity for learning. The following is an example of a standard process-improvement process:

1. When a problem occurs, determine whether it has happened before and if it will happen again. If the answer is "yes" or "maybe," form a team to examine why it may happen again. The team should focus on three to five levels of "why" to identify clearly the steps in the evolution of the problem.

   Example: A customer does not get a requested nonsmoking hotel room.

   Ask: Has this happened before?
   (Answer: Yes, about two times per day.)
   Will it happen again? (Answer: Most likely.)

   Examine why: Level 1: The hotel did not know the customer wanted a nonsmoking room.
   Level 2: There was no record of the request in the computer.
   Level 3: There was nothing in the special comments section.

   Often, simply asking "why" will identify causes and suggest options.

2. Ask the team to look at the cause of the problem and ask how it could have happened or, if it is a recurring problem, how it can happen.

   Example: Continuing with the example from step 1, asking how the problem happened might generate the following responses:
   - Reservations clerk did not know of the request.
   - Customer only thinks he or she made the request.
   - No nonsmoking rooms were available.
   - Travel agency did not tell the hotel.
   - Customer did not tell the travel agency.
   - Hotel did not put the request into the computer.

3. Next, the team should determine an improvement plan that addresses each possible cause.

> **Example:** Some possible improvement plans for the problem with reserving nonsmoking rooms might be:
> - Survey customers or use available data to determine an adequate percentage of nonsmoking rooms.
> - Standardize the procedure for requesting nonsmoking or smoking rooms when reservations are made.
> - Develop frequent-customer profiles that include room preferences.
> - Put a section on the reservation card that specifically asks for smoking preference, rather than just including it in the special comments section.
> - Educate travel agents through industry meetings about the importance of asking for smoking preference.

4. Take the learning from the analysis and ensure that the team implements the changes.

Communication plays a key role in learning from process breakdowns and process improvements. To ensure that your team, as well as others within the organization, benefit from process-improvement initiatives, consider the following suggestions:
- Ask process-improvement teams to share their insights and changes in process with other teams.
- Post notes from process improvement teams in a common place on the company's intranet so others can learn.
- Keep track of problems and their frequency as they occur. Use a frequency log to track the date/time, problem, root cause, what was done, and what follow-up might be needed. Periodically review this information for trends or common themes. Do these problems occur on the same shift, with the same personnel, days of the week, as a result of lack of training, etc.?
- After large projects, hold a debriefing session with the main stakeholders to identify what went well. Talk about weaknesses and where improvements could be made on future projects.
- Develop a method to share the information throughout the organization— for example, through a newsletter, company-wide e-mail, or the company's intranet. Sharing success stories is a powerful way to build confidence and momentum.
- Offer to speak with other work groups to share lessons in process improvements.
- Develop a set process for recording what is learned and a place for archiving the information.

Identify ways to streamline and/or improve efficiency of future work

Inefficient work processes often result in duplication of effort and frustration among employees. Analyze the work flow within your department and across departments, and identify where your current work process is ineffective or can be done in a smarter way. Look for where you can eliminate or modify inefficient procedures and systems by creating new approaches.

Use the following process to generate and analyze new alternatives. While it is productive to do this on an individual level, it is also critical that you work with your team and create new approaches as a group.

1. Identify procedures that you and your team find outdated, overly time-consuming, or difficult to complete.

2. Find out the purpose of the procedure.

3. Evaluate the procedure in detail, critiquing each step. Identify what is working and what is not.
   - Identify bottlenecks and recurring problems.
   - Identify duplication of effort.
   - Note places where the formal process is often circumvented.
   - Highlight internal and external customer-service problems.
   - Examine the level at which decisions are made.
   - Include what is working well. Examine why.
   - Determine if any steps can be eliminated or combined to save time.

4. Generate as many alternate procedures as possible that would meet the same objective.

5. Review your potential alternatives. It may be possible to combine the best elements of several alternatives to obtain one superior solution.

6. Define and document process and role changes.

7. Plan for change. Include internal and external communication, equipment needs, and training.

8. Set up a system to evaluate how well your solution really works. Continue to evaluate it for improvement.

Set aside time during regular staff meetings to discuss changes and improvements to your unit's work processes and procedures. During these sessions, ask employees to be forward-thinking in their approach to the work. Encourage them to challenge decisions on procedures they feel have become outdated. For example, explore what new technologies may exist to increase efficiency. Stress the need to make continuous improvements in the work process, and solicit ideas for change.

Integrate input from stakeholders to prioritize process-improvement efforts

When you have decided which parts of a process to change, make sure you and your team understand how others outside the team will be affected. To help integrate input from stakeholders, consider the following guidelines:

- You will need to understand the process from beginning to end as it is now and how you want it to look in the future. Using "As Is" (current) and "To Be" (desired) process flowcharts may help explain the change to others.

- When a process is long or complex, it may be wise to meet with people from different functional areas to help organize some of the issues surrounding the change and keep people in the communication loop. How and when you work with these people can affect your ability to make changes. Involve the stakeholders who have a vested interest in what is happening. These may include external customers, internal customers, vendors, etc. Use stakeholder meetings to:
  - Understand the broader, interteam issues.
  - Discuss how the changes will affect various stakeholders.
  - Determine priorities to work on, resources needed, appropriate people, and so on.
  - Identify ways to manage the change to minimize any negative effects.
  - Agree on how to communicate what is happening during the change.
  - Talk about individual or group habits that may need to be addressed.

- When it is necessary to involve a large group, you may first want to do some initial fact-finding in smaller groups or one-on-one meetings. This will help ensure effective use of everyone's time.

- To gain the most value from group meetings convened to discuss process improvements, consider these suggestions:
  - Set an agenda for the meeting ahead of time.
  - At the beginning of the meeting, discuss expectations, parameters for the discussion, and norms for the group.
  - Select a strong facilitator who is respected by the group. Provide facilitator training for those people you want to become facilitators.

Adopt best practices and lessons learned from within and outside the organization

Your own organization is a wealth of information about process improvement and learning. In addition, you can learn a lot from other organizations. An effective leader of system and process improvement makes a point to learn from others, gather best practices, and share learning with others.

To assist you in learning from your own organization and others, try these steps:

- Attend leadership and management development programs that include people from other organizations so that you can learn from their experiences.

- Ensure that teams use best-practices models as a starting place for their work. Then, to gain competitive advantage, improve upon those practices.

- Use your company's intranet to post and exchange information about process improvements. Set up a section or page on which to do this.

- Read articles to keep up with current trends in quality management, particularly those that address issues your company is facing. Such articles are also good sources of stories about good and bad implementations.

- Invite guest speakers from the local community to talk with your team about lessons learned regarding process changes.

- Read up on TQM theory, Deming, and/or Juran. Apply the principles that make good business sense to your company.

RESOURCES

The resources for this chapter begin on page 646.

14
DRIVE
EXECUTION

PART 1: MANAGE YOUR TIME AND PRIORITIES
- *Determine priorities*
- *Deal with higher-priority tasks first*
- *Reduce excessive interruptions*
- *Respond to phone calls and written requests*
- *Process paperwork and electronic documents efficiently*
- *Eliminate unnecessary memos and e-mail*
- *Improve documentation*
- *Organize an effective filing system*
- *Create more efficient workspace*

PART 2: DELEGATE EFFECTIVELY
- *Define delegation*
- *Evaluate your delegation skills*
- *Increase your willingness to delegate*
- *Use the SOS model of delegation*
- *Identify tasks for others to do*
- *Delegate responsibility to appropriate staff*
- *Convey clear expectations for assignments*
- *Give people the latitude to manage their responsibilities*
- *Monitor the progress of others*
- *Hold people accountable*
- *Be accessible to provide assistance and support*

PART 3: MANAGE MEETINGS
- *Establish clear agendas and desired outcomes*
- *Prepare for successful meetings*
- *Conduct effective meetings*
- *Facilitate group discussions*
- *Address disruption and unproductive debate*
- *Follow up after meetings*

PART 4: DEVELOP AN EFFECTIVE STRUCTURE
- *Analyze your current organization structure*
- *Diagnose structural problems by surveying employees*
- *Improve the structure of your organization*
- *Use project teams and task forces effectively*

INTRODUCTION

"Our chief want in life is somebody who will make us do what we can."
— Ralph Waldo Emerson

To be most effective, managers must juggle many priorities, get the job done efficiently, keep costs low, and maintain the highest standards of quality. At the same time, managers are expected to assist their employees in setting priorities, managing their time, and expanding their capabilities.

Successful managers learn to focus on the important issues in their own work and become effective delegators by using a developmental approach to assigning and sharing work. They also know how to manage the details of their work time and space, as well as the details of the time and space for group work and team meetings.

This chapter presents processes and approaches you can use to increase your own time-management and prioritization skills, as well as effectively delegate to your employees work that will increase their skills and productivity. It also presents guidelines for managing successful, productive team meetings.

VALUABLE TIPS

- Track your time for one week to see how you spend it. Check that the way you spend your time is compatible with your goals and values.

- Use techniques to minimize interruptions, such as batching your return phone calls and e-mail replies.

- Post a note on your door to let people know whether you can be interrupted.

- Keep your time-management systems (e.g., electronic calendar, voice-mail greetings, etc.) up-to-date so others will know how and where to reach you.

- When using voice-mail, save time and eliminate errors by leaving clear and concise messages.

- Before leaving work each day, identify the things you need to do the next day.

- Delegate work to the most appropriate person by analyzing the requirements of the task and relating those to the capabilities of your employees.

- Evaluate the workload of your area and how it is currently distributed among staff members. Consider redesigning the work flow and job tasks where appropriate.

- Use delegation as a way to help all employees acquire new skills and knowledge necessary for their development.

- When an employee comes to you with a work problem, ask first how he or she plans to approach it.

- Delegate in ways that meet the needs, learning styles, and abilities of each person (for example, a newly hired employee will probably need more detailed instructions and background information).

- Spend informal time, such as hallway chats, with employees to find out how things are going with work you have delegated to them.

- Ask your staff to set their own milestone dates and then hold to them, except on rare occasions when slippage is clearly justified.

- Set aside time on a regular basis (weekly, biweekly, or monthly) to meet with employees and review progress on work.

- Set up an accountability measure, such as a project chart or an electronic follow-up system, that will allow you to track the progress and accomplishments of your employees.

- If due dates are missed, discuss the consequences and options with the person to whom you assigned the task or project.

- If a delegated assignment does not meet your expectations, don't redo it yourself. Explain why it is not up to standard and what needs to be changed. Then have your employee rework it.

- When presenting an issue that affects work you have delegated (perhaps a change in the scope of a project), ask the employee how he or she plans to handle it. Then let the person own the solution.

- Coordinate the work of other areas of the organization that are affected by decisions and outputs of your group. If coordination is a consistent problem, consider process-mapping the workflow to determine weak areas in the way work is done.

- Consider using project management software to track progress on shared responsibilities or team efforts.

- When the outcomes of a meeting are particularly important, consider using an outside facilitator. This will allow you to focus on the content of the meeting, while the facilitator handles the processes for communication, problem solving, and decision making.

- Publish the agenda for meetings in advance, and advise people of any required preparation.

- Make sure your meetings start and end on time. Don't wait for latecomers.

- Draw your organization chart using several different possible structures, and decide which one would work best.

- Analyze how your organization structure will need to be different one, two, and five years from now.

- Keep abreast of changes in other parts of the organization that may affect the way your department needs to be structured.

- Ask people in other departments for input about how your department could be better structured to improve cooperation.

- Talk to people in similar departments to see how they are organized.

- Establish task forces for specific projects, and then disband them upon completion of the project.

PART I:
MANAGE YOUR TIME AND PRIORITIES

Determine priorities

To manage your time effectively, you must have a clear understanding of your short- and long-term priorities. It is easy to fall into the trap of reacting to the crisis of the day rather than focusing on what is most critical to you and your organization. To get a better sense of your priorities, complete the following exercise:

1. List your primary accountabilities.

2. Rank each responsibility according to importance (A = Most Critical, B = Important; C = Least Critical). To help you decide the rank, ask the following questions:
    - Which of these tasks will be of most benefit to my organization?
    - Which tasks do organizational or departmental priorities suggest are most important?
    - Which of these tasks does my manager consider most important?

3. Adjust your schedule and priorities as necessary to ensure that your daily work aligns with your most critical job responsibilities.

4. Periodically repeat this exercise so that the allocation of your time and energy remains in line with your strategy and objectives.

Deal with higher-priority tasks first

Do you often reach the end of the day feeling as if you've worked hard, but accomplished very little? People frequently spend time on things that reduce the tensions of the moment (the urgent) instead of things that relate directly to achieving goals (the important). To determine whether you are using your time wisely, consider the following:

- Identify your A, B, and C priorities. Do the A priorities first.

- For the next week, keep a detailed record of how you spend your time. Each day, write down what you do and for how long. Analyze your results to determine whether you are devoting the bulk of your time to your high-priority work.

- Concentrate on your most important objectives. Ask yourself, "If I have time to complete only three or four tasks today, which should I plan to do?"

- Look ahead and divide your workload into phases to make it more manageable. Determine what should be done tomorrow, next week, and next month, then plan accordingly.

- Schedule time for essential work. If appointments tend to fill your calendar, leaving no time for other important work, block out time on your calendar.

- Do undesirable but important work early in the day.

- Delegate less important tasks to others or let them go undone.

- Ask yourself, "If I ran this organization, would I pay someone my salary/hourly rate to work on what I am working on right now?"

Reduce excessive interruptions

The nature of managerial work results in frequent interruptions. Too many interruptions, though, can leave you wondering, "Where has the day gone?" To help minimize unnecessary interruptions, try these suggestions:

- Establish the norm that when your door is closed, you are not to be interrupted.

- Set a time during the day or week that is unscheduled or open-door time.

- When someone comes to your door, meet them at the door and deal with the issue while standing at the door, rather than waiting for the person to enter your space. This can save time while ensuring that the issue is addressed.

- If you cannot be disturbed, say so and make an appointment to talk later.

- Keep track of who is interrupting you and how often. If someone is responsible for many of your interruptions, consider talking with the individual about ways to reduce them.

- Using a log or record of how your time is spent, analyze the interruptions. Use a chart to establish a plan for handling each type of interruption. (Refer to the sample on the next page.)
  1. In the first column, list the reasons for your interruptions.
  2. In the second column, list possible solutions.
  3. Implement the most workable solutions.
  4. After you have implemented your plan, keep another log of your interruptions for a week to see if they have decreased.

REASONS FOR INTERRUPTIONS	POSSIBLE SOLUTIONS
People stop by to socialize; they interrupt me because of my accessibility.	Decrease my accessibility. Close my office door when I don't want to be interrupted. Establish set times of day when I am available for informal chats.
Individuals are insecure about making decisions on their own because of lack of experience or confidence, so they come to me more often than necessary.	Establish plans to help these individuals develop their skills and increase their confidence.
People who could make decisions on their own are coming to me for approval.	Delegate more authority. Analyze the topics discussed during the interruptions to determine which areas could be delegated.
People stop me in the hallway to carry on impromptu meetings.	Ask the person to continue the conversation, if necessary, by calling me or setting up a brief meeting.
People lack information.	Establish better means of disseminating information, e.g., project plans, more informational memos/e-mails, and more discussion at staff meetings. Set up group distribution lists on e-mail or voice mail for just-in-time updates.

Respond to phone calls and written requests

Returning phone calls and responding to correspondence are important, yet often cumbersome, responsibilities for most managers. To become more efficient in this area, follow these guidelines:

- Schedule and plan your phone calls in advance. Have an agenda and a mission to stay focused on the purpose of your call. Early morning and late afternoon are often good times to catch people in their offices.

- If you return a phone call and the person is out or unavailable, state some times when you would be available for a return call.

- Use voice mail effectively:
  - Schedule time on your calendar each day to return phone calls instead of responding to each message as it comes in.
  - If possible, change your outgoing message to let callers know if you are in or when you will be returning calls.
  - Check your voice mail several times a day instead of several times an hour. Checking too frequently can distract you from your priorities.
  - When you reach someone's voice mail, speak clearly.
  - Leave a message that explains fully why you are calling. Often, return messages can be left on your voice mail, eliminating the need for telephone tag.

- If an administrative assistant answers your phone, work with that person to ensure that he or she takes clear, complete, and accurate phone messages. In many cases, the question can be answered at this point, or referred to a more appropriate person.

- Respond to notes and memos by writing your response directly on the correspondence. Make a copy for your files only if necessary. Or, if it will save you time and you don't need documentation, respond with a telephone call.

- Use electronic mail when you have to respond quickly to people, especially those in other time zones.

Process paperwork and electronic documents efficiently

To be efficient, you need to recognize and attend to important details while ignoring unimportant ones. The following techniques will help you develop a workable system for dealing with documents:

- Adopt this basic rule from time-management expert Alan Lakein: Handle each piece of paper only once. If you pick up a piece of paper, don't put it down without doing something that will help move it on its way. Use this same guideline for e-mail and other electronic data.

- Each time you process paperwork or electronic documents, identify the pieces that contribute to your most important objectives and responsibilities. These are the ones that count. Learn to handle them skillfully. To do so, try these suggestions:
  - Glance through each piece quickly to get an initial understanding of its contents and impact.
  - Place the documents in the order of their importance.
  - Read carefully, highlighting or underlining key points that are important for you to stay aware of or that will influence future actions.
  - Make notes to yourself or others. If appropriate, cross-reference other documents that relate to this piece.
  - Take action or delegate/redirect the material.
  - If follow-up is necessary, use a tickler file with a follow-up date on the document. Also add a follow-up note to your master calendar.
  - File the document where it will be easy to retrieve.

- If you look at the files you currently have in your office (both paper and electronic), you'd most likely conclude that a huge percentage contain documents you haven't looked at in months. As a general rule, you can probably eliminate files older than six months. Here are some other ways to minimize your files:
  - Remove your name from distribution lists that you don't need to be on.
  - Whenever you are tempted to say, "I'm going to keep this just in case," you can probably throw it away.
  - Practice the art of "waste basketry" to avoid filing and retaining unnecessary information.

Eliminate unnecessary memos and e-mail

Although some written communication is necessary, informal surveys reveal that employees in most organizations spend far more time writing and reading memos and e-mail than is advisable—and at great cost to the organizations. To determine whether the communications you and your staff write promote efficiency, periodically ask yourself the following questions:

- Are the messages short and to the point? If not, make your writing more concise.

- Would a phone call or brief personal visit be effective? Memos and e-mails are typically one-way communications unless you have on-line chat capability; phone calls and discussions allow people to get each other's reactions in real-time, ask questions, and clear up misunderstandings immediately.

- Does the memo or e-mail describe a task that could be done in less time than it takes to write the memo?

Time-management specialist R. Alec Mackenzie recommends that you take an occasional inventory to assess the efficiency of your area's memo-writing or e-mail practices. You might look at your deleted e-mail folder and find it to be a good record of messages written and received. In the last month, how many could have been shorter? How many were unnecessary?

Improve documentation

Information and decisions trusted to memory may easily be forgotten or unavailable when they are needed. To ensure that information is documented and accessible, consider the following suggestions:

- Keep a record of decisions made at meetings by asking someone to take notes of the proceedings. File the meeting minutes for future reference so others who need them can readily locate them (for instance, in a public directory on your company's computer network).

- Document decisions reached by phone or in one-to-one meetings in the same way. If appropriate, send a copy of the documentation to others involved with or affected by the decision so that everyone can review it and make corrections if necessary.

Organize an effective filing system

Brian Tracy, an author in time management, estimates that 30 percent of all work time is spent looking for materials that have been mislaid. Poor filing systems, whether electronic or paper, can even stop the flow of work if they prevent people from finding needed information. To improve your filing systems, try these suggestions:

- Often, administrative personnel are the most skilled at setting up effective filing systems. Thus, you may want to team up with an administrative assistant to streamline your paper or electronic files.

- Establish a filing system for organizing your paper and electronic files. Use a categorization system that fits your needs. The following categories comprise one system you can use or modify:
  - A "review" file—for work generated by others that must be reviewed in a timely way so the work can proceed. Consider focusing on this file at the time in your day when interruptions are minimal and interaction with others is not required to keep projects moving.
  - A "reading" file—for information that does not require a response or carry associated deadlines. Attend to this file in your spare time.
  - A "file" folder—for information that has been processed and should be retained.

- An "action item" file—for lists of tasks to be performed and for work in progress.
- A "delegate" file—for papers concerning activities that could be performed by others.

Make sure the system is understandable to those who do not use it on a daily basis so information can be retrieved even when the person in charge of the files is on vacation or leaves the organization.

Create more efficient workspace

The arrangement of your office and items on your desk can either help or hinder your efficiency. To use your workspace more efficiently, try these suggestions:

- Arrange your work area to maximize your working style. If being able to look out of a window enhances your creativity, allowing you to accomplish more, face your desk toward the window. If you are easily distracted by people walking past your office, position your desk so you can avoid seeing them.

- Eliminate time stealers. If a book or file you refer to once a day is across the room, or under something else, make it more accessible. The minutes you save can be spent more productively.

- Organize your desktop based on the frequency with which you use items.
  - Frequently used items, such as your computer or calendar, need to be right at hand.
  - Items that are not constantly used—perhaps your phone—need to be within reach.
  - Items that are used infrequently, such as periodicals, should not be on your desk. These things can be located where you must get up from your desk to get them.
  - Keep in front of you only what you are currently working on, and remove all else.

PART 2: DELEGATE EFFECTIVELY

Define delegation

Delegation is the process of sharing authority and accountability with others in making decisions and meeting objectives. Delegation is critical for two important reasons.

- First, as a manager, you are responsible for all the work output from your area. You cannot accomplish all of this work alone.

- Second, delegating assignments contributes, more than anything else does, to the development of your staff.

Evaluate your delegation skills

The following checklist provides a quick way to evaluate your current delegation skills. Any "no" answer may signal an area for improvement. To gain additional insight into your delegating skills, you might also want to ask your employees to answer these questions about you.

Evaluation checklist

- The amount of work I delegate has been appropriate—neither too much nor too little.   Yes No

- I have a good understanding of my direct reports' capabilities. Yes No

- I delegate assignments that are challenging without being too much of a stretch.   Yes No

- I convey clear goals and expectations of the assignment.   Yes No

- I ensure that people understand the quality standards of their delegated assignments.   Yes No

- I allow people to use their own style of getting their work done.   Yes No

- I give my employees the appropriate amount of authority.   Yes No

- I am available to assist and support when necessary.   Yes No

- I effectively monitor the progress of others.   Yes No

- I coach people rather than take back a delegated task or responsibility.   Yes No

- I hold people accountable for achieving their goals.   Yes No

- I seek feedback from others on how I can improve my delegation skills.   Yes No

Increase your willingness to delegate

It's not uncommon for managers to resist delegating the work they once did themselves. After all, they were promoted to management because they were very effective at, and probably enjoyed, their assignments and projects. However, to be a successful manager, it is essential that you delegate work to others.

To increase your willingness to delegate, first determine the reasons for your resistance, then identify ways to overcome them. Common reasons for reluctance to delegate include:

- *Insufficient time to explain the task or train someone to do it.* While this is sometimes an acceptable reason for short-term projects, more often it is not. The time you spend teaching employees will save you time and effort in the long run, and it will also help your staff develop new skills and capabilities.

- *Desire for perfection.* If you feel you are the only person who can do certain work well enough, be careful; this is a danger sign. It's unlikely that you are the only person who can do the work. Nor is it likely that you will find anyone who works precisely the same way that you do. Begin by delegating parts of these responsibilities and coaching employees to help them perform to required standards.

- *Personal satisfaction and/or reward from accomplishment.* If you enjoy certain work or receive recognition when you perform it, you may tend to reserve this work for yourself. It is difficult to give up work you really like. Learn to achieve satisfaction from other parts of your job—such as coaching others, doing strategic work, and so forth.

- *Fear of overburdening your group.* When people appear overwhelmed, it's tempting to keep more of the overall workload. However, protecting people in this way will limit their chances to develop problem-solving skills. Furthermore, you risk personal burnout. Focus your energies on assessing the demands on your team and then staffing to meet these demands, rather than doing the work yourself.

- *Concerns about an employee's performance.* Sometimes managers do not delegate to individuals whose performance is not up to standard, believing the delegated work would just come back anyway. But this path perpetuates the cycle of nonperformance. Delegate the work the person can do and provide coaching to close the gaps in performance.

- *Fear of failure.* Some managers worry that if mistakes are made, the consequences will be disastrous. If you share this concern, identify the possible risks with the employee and, if the risks are really large, request contingency plans. Ultimately, you need to be willing to take responsibility for your employees' mistakes on delegated tasks so they can grow and develop.

**Use the
SOS model
of delegation**

The fundamental principle of Personnel Decisions International's SOS model of delegation is that delegating is a thoughtful, practical way to increase the work produced in your area while supporting the development of your staff.

The SOS acronym can help you remember the three key elements of delegating:

- Select

- Observe

- Support

The first phase involves selecting an individual to do the work. It is the process of appropriately matching individuals to assignments.

The second phase is observation, which includes giving people latitude, monitoring their progress, and coaching when necessary. Your level of involvement will depend on the employee's experience and motivation and the importance of the delegated assignment.

The third element is support, which involves taking action to ensure that the employee has what he or she needs to complete the assignment. An effective manager finds the appropriate level of support—neither too much nor too little. The skills, interest level, and motivation of the individual and the specifics of the delegated task will determine the support you provide.

**Identify tasks
for others to do**

To determine which of your activities would be best to delegate, consider this process:

1. List all the work for which you are currently responsible. Then classify each in one of the following categories:
   - You must retain and perform it yourself.
   - You can share it with other people.
   - You can delegate it to other people.

The following chart will help you structure your analysis:

TASK	RETAIN	SHARE	DELEGATE
1.			
2.			
3.			
4.			

2. Now, examine those tasks that you retained. Are you holding on to anything unnecessarily? Could you further develop your staff by passing along some of these duties?

3. Realize that the range of tasks you can delegate is limitless. To expand your range, review the list you just made to see if you are retaining any of the following types of tasks:
   - Decisions that you make most frequently.
   - Functions that can cause you to overspecialize.
   - Less complex tasks that may not be the best use of your time as a manager.
   - Tasks that will increase the number of people who know a certain area or have critical skills related to your operation.
   - All the phases that are needed to solve problems: identification, analysis, issues and alternatives, stakeholder opinions and feelings, solution options. These phases could be individually assigned, or the person could be responsible for the entire effort.
   - Elements of a complex, multistage project.

   These types of tasks are often good candidates for delegation.

Delegate responsibility to appropriate staff

When delegating, it's easy to assign too much work to experienced workers and too little to those who require more assistance. Yet every employee needs responsibility sufficient to challenge his or her abilities. Help employees strike a comfortable balance that leaves them neither overworked nor underchallenged.

To choose the appropriate employee for a particular task, use the following guidelines:

1. Begin by considering any employee who:
   - Currently has the requisite knowledge or skills to do the work.
   - Has a high level of interest in the area, or has asked to do similar work.
   - Has a need to further develop in this particular area.
   - Has the time to do it.

2. Narrow your list of candidates by considering the dynamics of the work:
   - Its visibility and importance.
   - Its interaction with other projects, people, and resources.
   - Its complexity.
   - The amount of teaching time you have available.

3. Once you have a sense for what the work will require, select the best person from your list. Assign the work in a way that allows the employee to capitalize on his or her strengths and also address his or her development needs.

When selecting people for assignments, consider not just their experience, but also their motivation level. A less experienced person who is excited about a project may be more successful than an experienced person who disagrees with the project's purpose or desired outcome. Consider the following suggestions:

• What are the person's goals? What does he or she want (in the short or long term)? What is he or she interested in? How are his or her values connected to the project? Discussing these things with the person may uncover any resistance.

• Encourage the employee. Sometimes people appear unmotivated when the real issue is they think they can't do well on a project. Perhaps they see themselves as inexperienced, struggling in an area, or overwhelmed with other work. Discover and understand their reservations. A manager can be a great motivator in these situations and set the stage at the beginning for successful project work.

• Provide options. Determine which elements of the project are negotiable and which are nonnegotiable. Allow the person as much latitude as possible in shaping the work.

Convey clear expectations for assignments

Even experienced employees can waste time if they don't have clear direction for their work. In the worst cases, they may produce results that bear little or no resemblance to the desired outcome. Such experiences are frustrating to both you and the employee.

When delegating, it's important that your direction is clear and that the employee understands the expectations of the assignment. To provide clear objectives, follow these guidelines:

1. Determine how much involvement the employee will have in deciding the specifics of the assignment. The more experienced the employee, the more involved he or she can be in determining timing, methods, amount of help, and so forth.

2. Write a clear statement of the purpose and goal of the work. Include the following information:
   - The success criteria, i.e., "This project will be successful if…".
   - The completion date.
   - Any specific instructions or guidelines the employee needs to execute the work, such as who can provide background information or administrative support.
   - The level of authority the employee has in doing the works. For example:
     ○ Makes decisions and does the work; lets you know the outcome.
     ○ Makes decisions; tells you before he or she actually does it.
     ○ Makes recommendations; the two of you then decide upon the course of action.
     ○ Comes to you with recommendations and you make the final decision.
     ○ Carries out the project after you tell him or her exactly what to do.
   - Areas of high risk or visibility.
   - Any interim progress reports required.
   - What final reports are required.

3. Discuss the assignment with the employee and answer any questions. Don't end the discussion until you're certain that the employee fully understands your expectations.

4. At the end of the discussion, ask the employee to describe the assignment in his or her own words. This will help you determine whether you have mutual agreement about the assignment.

5. During the course of a project, keep track of any instances of unclear or inadequate direction. Note the cause of each misunderstanding so that you can improve your direction on future assignments. You may wish to ask your employees for feedback on your direction and guidance.

Give people the latitude to manage their responsibilities

Giving employees sufficient latitude goes hand-in-hand with delegating. Managers who retain too much responsibility are often seen as overcontrolling and lacking in respect for others. Use the following suggestions to give your employees enough breathing room to manage their own responsibilities:

- When you establish yearly goals with your employees, ask them the level of involvement they want from you. Ask what you can do to be most helpful. Then follow through with their request whenever possible.

- Look for projects where you can assign complete authority to your employees. Not only will this save you the most time in the long run, but also the project is likely to be more fulfilling for the employee.

- When employees update you on projects and there are problems, encourage your employees to present solutions.

- When determining the amount of latitude to give to an employee, consider his or her experience and motivation. For example, give more latitude to a person who is highly skilled and motivated in a particular area. Conversely, individuals learning a new skill will likely benefit from closer guidance.

- Let your staff go forward with their ideas unless you have a major problem with their plans. Keep in mind that learning from mistakes is one of the most effective and common ways for people to develop.

- Resist the temptation to strive for perfection. On most delegated tasks, learning should take precedence over minute, less vital details. Give employees the benefit of the doubt.

- Periodically discuss with individual employees the amount of latitude you give them. Do you tend to give too much direction on some assignments and too little support on others? In which situations do you give the appropriate amount of latitude? Make necessary course corrections based on your employees' input.

Monitor the progress of others

An important part of delegation, especially in the beginning, is checking the progress on assignments. Monitoring does not mean interfering with or micromanaging an assignment. It does mean checking with an employee periodically during the project to ensure that he or she is proceeding without difficulty. Sometimes questions arise during a project and employees are reluctant to ask for assistance because they don't want to appear incompetent. The following guidelines offer efficient ways to check people's progress:

- Ask employees to write action plans and produce progress reports. Have your employees give a copy to you and keep one for themselves; this will ensure that you both know what is expected. Depending on the person's experience level, you may want to be involved in the planning process to ensure that the progress reports are acceptable.

- With your employees, establish due dates for interim reports and keep a copy of these reports in your file.

- Ask your employees to schedule time and prepare for update meetings with you.

- Take advantage of natural opportunities to monitor and observe others, such as casual conversations, meetings, etc.

- Establish the expectation that you want to hear about problems before they mushroom. When employees tell you about problems, concentrate on how they plan to handle them. Do not criticize the employee or try to solve the problem yourself.

- Keep in mind that employees require different levels of your attention and involvement depending on their experience. Set aside time to work with employees who require personal attention.

Hold people accountable

At times, it may seem easier to do a job yourself rather than hold others accountable. If you find that this is the case for you, consider the following suggestions:

- Beware of the boomerang effect in delegation. This occurs when an employee, with the manager's explicit or implicit acceptance, gives back a task delegated to him or her. An example of this is an employee who tells his manager that he doesn't know how to complete the last section of a report. The manager, who is busy at the time, says, "Just leave it here; I'll finish it." Most likely, this employee will require help with his next project report, too.

- Regular progress reports will help both you and your employee ensure that goals are met. If deadlines are being missed, ask the person for his or her assessment of why this is happening and what will be done to correct the situation.

- If your monitoring and follow-up show that performance is not meeting planned goals, try the following:
  - If the discrepancy is minor, alert the person working on that phase of the project and ask him or her to find ways to get back on track.
  - If the discrepancy is major, invite the person working on the project to discuss the situation with you and to work out a plan to get back on track. Rather than taking the entire task back or assigning it to someone else, get the employee's commitment as to what he or she can complete. Realize that you may need to make recommendations for restructuring the work or obtaining additional resources.

- To keep an individual or a team on track, give consistent feedback. Feedback is essential for monitoring progress; it not only helps employees correct mistakes that could become serious problems, but also reinforces positive behaviors and encourages the development of desirable work habits overall. To improve your level of feedback:
  - Communicate the fact that you are willing to provide feedback. This will encourage employees to consult you.
  - Give feedback in a timely manner.
  - Give both positive and negative feedback, when each is appropriate.

Be accessible to provide assistance and support

One of your primary management responsibilities is to make yourself available to employees to answer their questions and address their concerns. When the press of daily activities tends to make you unavailable, try these suggestions:

- Update your calendar regularly. Give your staff access to your calendar so they can arrange a time to meet with you.

- Coordinate your schedule with your administrative assistant and set up times when you will check in at the office, either by phone or in person. Let your staff know that your assistant has this information.

- Set up regular meetings (for example, weekly, monthly, quarterly) to answer employees' project questions and to get the information that will keep you abreast of their assignments.

- Find ways to be available to employees in remote or international locations. For example, be willing to schedule off-hour phone time with employees in different time zones.

- Take time to contact employees periodically, particularly those you do not see daily. Taking time to talk informally with people conveys a message of support. Also, your employees will be less likely to view you as an absentee manager.

PART 3:
MANAGE MEETINGS

Research indicates that managers spend between 25 percent and 75 percent of their working hours in meetings. Efficient, productive meetings are vital communication and decision-making forums. Inefficient, unproductive meetings waste valuable time.

Establish clear agendas and desired outcomes

Agendas are essential for conducting efficient meetings. They allow group members to prepare for meetings and ensure that all necessary items are addressed. When preparing an agenda, check to see that you have taken the following steps:

1. Establish the desired outcome for the meeting. An outcome is something that each participant will take away from the meeting.

2. State the purpose and desired outcome of the meeting at the top of the agenda. This helps participants determine whether they should attend.

3. State a definite start and stop time for the meeting. Try to limit your meetings to 90 minutes. People tend to lose focus if the meeting lasts longer than this. Set up another meeting if more time is required.

4. Structure the content and process of your meeting to support its outcomes. Determine the type of process and action desired on each agenda item. You are likely to have "information only," "discussion only," and "decisions required" items. This, too, helps people prepare for the meeting and determines the goal to be attained in addressing each item.

5. Establish priorities. Set priorities for each agenda item so that group members focus on the most important items.

6. Determine the order of the agenda items. Most experts recommend placing the most important topics toward the beginning of the agenda; that way, if time runs out, the items left unaddressed are lower priority.

7. Establish time limits on items. Decide on an approximate amount of time for each agenda item. Enforce your time limits on "information only" and "discussion only" items. On "decision required" items, acknowledge when the time limit has been reached; then ask the group to decide whether and how to continue with the item.

The following example illustrates one way to structure an agenda:

GOAL-SETTING KICKOFF MEETING
SEPTEMBER 15, 10:00AM – 11:30AM
Desired Outcome: Communicate and establish criteria for next year's goals

ITEM	PROCESS/ACTION	TIME
1. New goal-setting guidelines	Presentation	10:00 – 10:15
2. Next year's corporate goals	Presentation	10:15 – 10:25
3. Next year's division goals	Discussion: assign responsibility to department heads	10:25 – 10:45
4. Next year's individual goals	Discussion: set dates for completion	10:45 – 11:10
5. Process for completion/review	Discussion: consensus	11:10 – 11:30
6. Adjourn		11:30

Prepare for successful meetings

Setting up meeting facilities. When the logistics of setting up meetings are handled in advance, less time is wasted, and meeting initiators and leaders are able to focus on the meeting agenda. Following is a checklist of important elements to consider when setting up meetings:

☐ **Meeting time.** Choose a time when all necessary facts and people are available. Select a time that will help ensure that the meeting ends at a logical time, such as just before lunch or quitting time.

☐ **Location.** Select a location that is accessible to all who will attend.

☐ **Room size.** Select a room that is the appropriate size for your group—neither so large that participants are far away from the action and each other, nor so small that participants have insufficient room to write or sit comfortably.

☐ **Ventilation and temperature.** Ensure that the room is not too stuffy, drafty, hot, or cold.

☐ **Equipment.** Be sure that all necessary equipment is on hand and set up. Meeting time should not be wasted while someone looks for a flip chart or TV monitor. Check teleconference equipment to ensure that those joining via telephone will hear and be heard. Arrange for any projectors that are needed.

☐ **Furniture arrangement.** If possible, set up the room to maximize group attention and participation. If the group is small, use a semicircular seating arrangement that exactly accommodates the number of people involved. If you must use rows, use several short rows rather than a few long rows so people aren't too spread out and the speaker's eye span will not have to be too wide.

☐ **Seating.** Encourage participants to sit close to the speakers and each other rather than spreading out across the room. This promotes equal participation, including those participants who are teleconferencing.

Organizing the meeting. Your attention to organizational details can greatly affect the efficiency of the meeting and the way in which others evaluate your meeting-management skills. Pay attention to the following steps for organizing meetings:

• Limit the number of participants. Invite only those who are needed for decision making or who require the information that will be presented.

• Prepare an agenda.

- Determine the necessary premeeting communication. Distribute the agenda well in advance so participants can gather materials and prepare their assignments.

- Prepare your overheads, slide show, handouts, and/or flip-chart materials.

- If people will be joining the meeting by teleconference, send or fax copies of any overheads or handouts that will be used ahead of time.

Conduct effective meetings

Conducting meetings effectively takes practice. Refer to the following guidelines for the principles of good meeting management. You may wish to take a copy of these guidelines with you to meetings until you feel they have become a natural part of your management style.

- Start the meeting on time. When people expect meetings to start late, they arrive late. If, on the other hand, they must walk in after a meeting has started, they are more likely to arrive at future meetings on time.

- Begin with a reminder of the time allotted for the meeting and with an assurance that the meeting will end on time.

- Review the agenda and amount of time allotted to each item.

- Create or review norms or process guidelines for the meeting, such as how decisions will be made.

- Appoint a recorder for the meeting who will take minutes and monitor the time. Have the recorder inform the group of the time remaining and whether the meeting is running behind schedule. It's always preferable if the recorder can publicly capture notes on flip-chart paper. This technique ensures more accurate notes and enables smoother decision making.

- As the meeting progresses, record assigned actions, responsibilities, and follow-up dates.

Facilitate group discussions

Meetings are most successful when they involve and encourage participation by all those attending. You can guide the meeting toward its desired outcome and foster effective communication among the participants by using the following facilitation techniques:

- **Listen.** Listening will influence the group's ability to achieve understanding and reach the decisions needed to meet its goals.

- **Ask questions.** Questions are an excellent tool for monitoring and facilitating discussions.

- **Encourage participation by silent members.** Seek to find out what they may know, think, or feel about the topic under discussion. People's commitment to the group's decisions and plans is directly proportional to their sense of contribution to the meeting.

- **Integrate contributions.** Link various points of view and keep the group on target by identifying areas of understanding, agreement, and disagreement.

- **Summarize.** A periodic summary of key ideas or major points will help to keep the group focused and on track with the agenda.

- **Express your concern to the group if the meeting is straying from the agenda or if specific items are taking longer to cover than originally planned.** Come to a mutual agreement about whether and how the group should monitor itself to keep the discussion more limited.

- **Intervene when someone takes too much time.** You can gently interrupt and say something like, "John, thanks for that observation. Now, I'd like to find out what Jane's views are."

Address disruption and unproductive debate

Generally, when meeting participants become disruptive and unproductive, and debate gets the group off its purpose, it is due to one or both of these reasons:

- The group is not following its own norms or process guidelines, or has not yet established norms for working together.

- The dialogue has become so intense that everyone gets pulled into emotional camps without realizing it.

Take time at the beginning of meetings to create a list of norms that all participants can agree upon. This step increases in importance when the meeting will be used for decision making (vs. information distribution) and when the participants will be meeting several times on a topic. Norms are behaviors that will guide the group over the course of its work. Some typical norms are:

- Come prepared.

- Don't interrupt other participants.

- Use consensus for decisions unless you decide on another option.

The facilitator can also help by:

- Calling out what is happening in the group at the moment.

- Asking participants what they want to do about the conflict.

- Calling a time-out if people are behaving in a disruptive manner.

- Reminding the group of its norms.

- Asking a member to summarize the issues.

- Protecting the perspectives of less vocal members.

- Dealing with disruption by inquiring about their concerns, asking for their cooperation, or giving them feedback about their impact on the group.

- Encouraging the contrary point of view. Remember that "group think" can greatly diminish a team's functioning and the quality of its decisions.

- Asking for a proposal about how to move the meeting off the impasse.

Follow up after meetings

Summarizing the meeting at its conclusion and after-meeting follow-up are essential to ensuring the full effectiveness of a meeting. Use these suggestions to summarize and follow up:

- At the end of the meeting, take a few moments to process the meeting. Discuss what went well, what problems came up, and what you can do about the ways in which the group works together.

- After the meeting, distribute copies of meeting minutes and reminders about assignments and deadlines to everyone who attended.

PART 4:
DEVELOP AN EFFECTIVE STRUCTURE

Analyze your current organization structure

The way you structure your organization plays a large part in determining your success as a leader. Although no one structure is the correct way for an organization, the structure does affect productivity, quality, customer satisfaction, employee morale, and budget.

Following are some key steps in planning the structure for your organization:

1. Understand your department's business. Ask yourself:
   - What is our vision?
   - What is our mission?
   - What are our long- and short-term goals?

   If your organization does not have a vision and/or mission statement, consider developing one for your unit. Involve your employees in the process.

2. Analyze the operations performed in your department. One way to do this is to draw a flowchart of the tasks that must be accomplished and the flow of information necessary to meet your goals.

3. Study your work unit's organization—who reports to whom and their responsibilities. Compare the current structure to your analysis of the workflow by asking yourself the following questions:
   - Does the chart reveal duplication of effort in any of the operational steps?
   - Are any employees performing functions not directly related to the accomplishment of departmental goals?
   - Does the work unit lack technical expertise that would help it attain its goals?
   - Does the department possess technical expertise it no longer needs?
   - Do individuals in the work unit have ready access to the information, expertise, or other resources needed to perform their functions?
   - Are too many or too few individuals available to carry the workload for any step of the process?

4. Research the structure of other work units in your organization, or other organizations within your company, such as similar divisions or departments in other plants. Find out how they are set up, and examine the ways in which they are satisfied or dissatisfied with their structure.

5. Review and revise your structure to ensure that it supports your mission and vision.

Diagnose structural problems by surveying employees

If your organization is experiencing serious problems and you are unsure of the causes of these problems, consider conducting a survey or interviewing the key members of your staff to determine if structural problems exist.

Following are important questions to include:

Clarity of responsibilities

- What is the main purpose of your job?

- Who might be unclear about your function and why do you think the confusion exists?

- What overlapping responsibilities exist between any part of your operation and any other part(s) of the division/department? If there is overlap, identify where it is and the possible reasons for it.

- Who expresses confusion about responsibility for certain tasks or functions? List their areas of confusion.

- Where does your work come from? Where does it go?

Decision making and authority

- What kinds of decisions:
  - Get stalled, and why?
  - Should you be making?
  - Should your manager be making?
  - Should your employees be making?
  - Are you asked for your input on?

- To what extent do you have sufficient authority to carry out your responsibilities?

Organization structure

- What is your satisfaction level with the organization structure beneath you? What would you like to see changed?

- If you could change the structure of any part of your organization, how would you change it?

- To whom do you directly report? Do you report to anyone else in any capacity? What is your opinion of the effectiveness of this reporting structure?

- Does anyone who reports directly to you also report to anyone else in any capacity? If so, explain the situation and your opinion of its effectiveness.

- To whom do you go with your problems, clarification on procedures, and technical advice?

Span of control

- Do you feel that you supervise too many or too few people to be efficient and effective? If so, what could be done to remedy the situation?

- To what extent do you feel that your manager supervises too many or too few people to be efficient and effective? How could the situation be improved?

General

- Describe any other ways in which the present organization structure makes it difficult for you to do your job.

Improve the structure of your organization

An organization's structure needs to be dynamic. What once worked well may no longer serve the needs of the organization or its customers. Effective managers regularly review and adjust the structure of their organizations to meet shifting internal and external needs and the changing skills of employees.

The following suggestions can help you review and improve the structure of your own organization:

- Design your structure with empowerment in mind. Whenever possible, create a structure where people do the "whole job."

- Set up a team to evaluate the structure of the organization.

- Ensure that your organization's structure is current, especially if you have just experienced a reorganization, downsizing effort, or heavy growth. Reevaluate job descriptions, reporting relationships, and lateral structure to account for current reality. Make necessary changes in a timely and responsive fashion.

- Try out innovative structures to stay current. Analyze the feasibility of a new structure, and then develop a pilot to evaluate its effectiveness. If the pilot is successful, modify it as needed and implement it.

- When developing a new product or initiating an interdepartmental project, reach down into the organization to find promising talent and create a cross-functional task force. Look for participants at varying levels of the organization.

- When working on recurring problems, include representatives from groups not previously involved. Obtain customers' input; involve administrative employees; get new perspectives.

Use project teams and task forces effectively

Employees closest to the work are the people most likely to have sound suggestions for improvements in how the work gets done. It makes good sense, then, to include people from all levels of the organization on project teams and task forces.

To assemble and use project teams and task forces wisely, consider the following suggestions:

- Use project teams and task forces when you need input from others on a specific problem or focus. Keep in mind the problem or opportunity as you determine the composition of the team.

- Invite employees who raise issues or problems to participate on a task force that will generate the solutions. Involve employees in task forces that are set up to address issues raised through employee opinion surveys or other feedback instruments.

- Involve members at nonmanagement levels of the organization when developing new products or services. Draw on their experience with customers, manufacturing processes, and materials management. Include engineers and designers along with marketing and salespeople.

- Clearly define the purpose of the task force and its authority. The task force can then determine specific goals and objectives within this overall purpose, and work to achieve those objectives. Determine with the task force what it needs from you to get the job done.

- Provide task force training, including how to manage meetings, group process skills, problem-analysis strategies, and conflict resolution.

- When a project team or task force has completed its mission, recognize its work and dissolve the group. Modify and/or reunite successful task forces to work on related issues.

RESOURCES

The resources for this chapter begin on page 648.

15
MANAGE
CHANGE

PART 1: UNDERSTAND CHANGE MANAGEMENT
- *Understand how individuals react to change*
- *Identify your role in the change process*
- *Understand how organizations respond to change*
- *Understand resistance to change*
- *Address resistance to change*
- *View change as a way of life*

PART 2: SUCCESSFUL CHANGE MANAGEMENT
- *Communicate in ways that help people understand the scale and scope of change*
- *Be specific about the implementation process*
- *Increase awareness of the benefits of the new initiative*
- *Involve people in decisions that impact them*
- *Leverage the involvement of key stakeholders and opinion leaders*
- *Clarify the new behaviors, practices, and what successful implementation looks like*
- *Create opportunities to learn, practice, and experiment with new behaviors*
- *Establish structures and roles to support the change*
- *Allow opportunities for flexible implementation*
- *Establish and use feedback processes to monitor implementation of key events and their impact*
- *Reward and reinforce both progress and success*
- *Align the surrounding system to be consistent with desired new behaviors*

INTRODUCTION

From vision to reality… change management is the effective implementation of planned organizational change. Its hallmarks are planning and the execution of those plans to bring about a desired change.

The demands on modern organizations—competitive, global, technical, societal, and legislative—promote a constant stream of innovative ideas and challenges. Organizational leaders seldom lack the drive and inspiration to change. Where change usually fails is in its execution. The inability to effectively implement and sustain new initiatives is often cited as the reason for organizational stagnation and cynical attitudes about workplace change.

Successful managers provide their teams with insight, motivation, the opportunity to grow skills, real-world practice in those skills, and accountability as they manage the process of change—whether the change is within a single team or across a multinational corporation.

As the scope of change increases, involving greater numbers of people, crossing organizational and geographical boundaries, and impacting the basic culture of the corporation, the requirements for effective change management become more extensive. Such large-scale organizational change requires planning, coordination, governance, and even a set of temporary organizational structures to successfully carry out change of this scope.

In these situations, leaders do not just lead change; they must also influence the priorities of multiple stakeholders, align organizational resources, and build temporary change-management organizations within the organization to ensure deployment of the vision over time and across geographical and business functions.

This chapter presents techniques and procedures that can help ensure the successful management of short-term or large-scale change.

VALUABLE TIPS

- Be able to summarize the short- and long-term consequences of failing to implement the new initiative.

- Recognize that how and when changes are implemented are often as important as what is implemented. Solicit local involvement in the process of change even when the decision to change is not a shared one.

- Look for small wins to help maintain momentum and confidence in the viability of the new initiative.

- Anticipate other business priorities that might lead key stakeholders to shift attention from, or even withdraw their support of, the new initiative.

- Document ripple effects and unintended consequences of the change as it is being implemented. These may become as important as the primary change itself.

- Communicate the progress of change in a variety of ways, being efficient and capturing attention at the same time.

- Inform participants about the expected timing, impact, and support available to those who need to adapt to new processes.

- Create opportunities for people to provide feedback and comment on implementation progress.

- Establish a steering committee for large-scale or long-term change.

- Establish a site on the company intranet for employees to learn about implementation and to address frequently asked questions.

- Inform customers and suppliers of significant change initiatives, and ask how this may impact the support they receive from or provide to the organization.

- Create a formal communications plan to accompany phases and stages of change.

- Where possible, identify discrete phases or stages of change implementation.

- Create a change-management scorecard that summarizes progress against implementation goals, along with interim results and other consequences of change.

- Let team leaders and supervisors know how they can support others during the transition.

- Coach people on how they can coach others.

- Publicize stories of successful change and anecdotal experiences that humanize the process.

- Remember that when it comes to change, it is almost impossible to communicate too much. People hear things at different times. Therefore, it is necessary to communicate the same message or set of ideas many times and in many different ways for it to be heard and understood.

PART 1:
UNDERSTAND CHANGE MANAGEMENT

"It isn't the changes that do you in, it's the transitions....
Change is situational: the new site, the new boss, the new team roles, the new policy.
Transition is the psychological process people go through to come to terms
with the new situation. Change is external, transition is internal."

— William Bridges

Understand how individuals react to change

Think about significant transitions in your own life. What made some easier than others? Remember what it feels like to be in a period of transition—not yet fully in the new situation, not fully separated from the old.

Change typically requires some new behavior, a new way of thinking and responding, or a new set of practices to follow. Change also often involves some loss, whether it is a loss of habit, loss of relationships, or temporary loss of predictability. All of these can generate resistance to change even when you or others support the change, and the benefits of the new behaviors or initiatives are clear.

When people are in the midst of a transition, it is important that they be able to understand the change, make a choice to participate, learn new behaviors and skills, have opportunities to practice and experiment, and obtain feedback and reinforcement. In addition, people often need time to prepare for the change and to have opportunities to decide for themselves that the change has been effective.

Identify your role in the change process

How individuals respond to change is partly based on their role in the specific initiative. In any organization, there are typically three key stakeholder groups focused on change:

- Strategists

- Implementers

- Recipients

Strategists identify the need for change and create the alternative vision. They typically initiate change and display courageous change leadership. They focus on the overall outcome of change, how it impacts the core business and broader strategy of the firm or business unit.

Implementers translate the strategy into a workable plan and guide execution of that plan. They incorporate a broad range of people-leadership skills to accomplish broader change-management goals.

Recipients are the people expected to use, follow, and adapt to the change. They work through the transition to new practices, adapting the present focus to conform to the expected future. Or, they may reject the planned change, continuing more or less as they did before.

The following table, adapted from Kanter, Stein, and Jick, summarizes the differences among the three key stakeholders of planned change:

	ROLE AND MIND-SET	ORIENTATION TO CHANGE	ACTION FOCUS	TYPICAL ORGANIZATION LEVEL	DOMINANT STAGE OF INVOLVEMENT
STRATEGISTS	Visionary Instigator Corporate view	External environment	Ends Corporate values and business results	Top	"Unfreezing" current state of thinking
IMPLEMENTERS	Translator Division or department view	Internal coordination	Means Overcoming resistance "Project image"	Middle	Changing
RECIPIENTS	User and adapter Personal view	Impact on users and power distribution	Means-end congruence Personal benefits/loss	Bottom	"Refreezing" new behaviors

Each stakeholder group has a different mind-set and orientation. Each has a clear role in the degree to which new initiatives succeed or fail. In any transition, it is important that you identify your primary role. Often, managers are the change implementers, the ones who are given the task of converting vision to reality. They are also the ones who most need to balance the focus and interests of the other two groups.

Understand how organizations respond to change

Organizations, like individuals, respond to change in different ways, depending on a variety of factors, from the type of change itself to the "change hardiness" of the organization. Some organizations are overly cautious or change resistant. Others display a kind of change hardiness, in which adaptation to rapid change is the norm. In the former, effective change may require more formal approaches to get started; in the latter, the challenge may be to sustain or spread new practices once implemented, lest they be quickly replaced by other initiatives.

Successful managers understand how their organizations handle change so they are prepared when transitions occur. To help you better understand your own organization's response to change, consider the following suggestions:

- Examine your organization's "change hardiness." Ask yourself:
  - How often does change occur in my organization?
  - How readily do people in my organization accept change? Are they eager for change or overly cautious about any change?
  - How many people must approve an idea? Does it take more people to approve one than to kill one?
  - Does acceptance of the change vary according to the type of change? Is the response different when the change is small or removed from the key operations than when it is large or involves core processes?

- Talk with others about your organization's general response to change. Obtain as many perspectives as you can.

Most large organizations engage in multiple types of change simultaneously. Yet these changes are not necessarily in sync with each other and may also be limited by the capacity of people to adapt to multiple overlapping changes. The challenge may become one of sustained focus, allocation of limited resources, or competition to determine which of the initiatives will gain hold and maintain over time.

To better implement change in the midst of constant or overlapping changes, consider the following guidelines:

- Identify the perspectives of all those involved in the change. What is the business purpose of the change? How does it affect the various groups involved? What is the likely acceptance level of each group, and why?

- Identify the other changes affecting the people and teams involved in this change. Talk with people about their confidence to handle more change. Ask what they need in order to feel greater confidence of success.

- Find ways to combine initiatives so that people are not overwhelmed with the amount of change.

- Carefully gauge when to position the changes you want as big changes or small challenges. Some people are energized and excited about change, but others are not. At some point, most organizations and their people simply get tired of hearing that they need to get behind some big, revolutionary change because it is necessary to deal with competitive threats. It may be helpful at times to position the change as a necessary one, not a big deal, or an incremental change.

- Establish temporary transition teams when the change is an effort to make "lasting change to the character of an organization, significantly altering its overall performance" (Mohrman, et. al., in *Large Scale Organizational Change,* Jossey-Bass, 1989). An initiative of this scale and scope often alters the definition of the organization and requires the support of many key stakeholders. These teams will need to exist for a long time and incorporate other overlapping changes. They often outlast some of the initiators of change and provide needed stability during the change process.

Understand resistance to change

People grow throughout their lives, yet retain some degree of predictability, stability, and habitual behavior. They need both growth and stability to thrive. It is not surprising, therefore, that people may resist moving from a stable, comfortable state to one that is different and possibly unpredictable. Resistance is normal. Effective managers expect it and work with it. They see resistance as a sign that people care and are involved. It becomes a signal to delve more deeply into beliefs, ideas, and attitudes toward the proposed changes.

People *resist* change when:

- They believe it is unnecessary or will make the situation worse. Employees at lower levels in the organization often believe that upper-level managers don't know "what the real world is like."

- They fear that the change will mean personal loss—of security, money, status, friends, freedom, and so forth.

- They don't like the way the change was introduced or feel that past explanations of new initiatives were not consistent with what actually happened over time.

- They had no input into the decision. They may even feel manipulated if the changes were kept secret during the planning stage.

- They are not confident that the change will succeed, either because leader commitment will not be sustained or because needed resources will not be available.

- They lack confidence that they will be able to perform new practices effectively.

- The timing of the change is poor.

- They are satisfied with the status quo; they subscribe to the belief that "if it's not broken, don't fix it."

- They believe that prior initiatives were not properly implemented.

- They lack faith in those driving for the change to occur.

People *support* change when:

- They expect it to result in some personal gain.

- They can relate to the vision behind the drive for change. They believe the change makes sense and is the right thing to do.

- They are given an opportunity to provide input into the change.

- They respect the person who is championing the change.

- They believe it is the right time for the change.

- They believe that reward systems will reinforce the new initiative.

Address resistance to change

People vary in their reactions to change. Some naturally welcome the novelty and variety of change, while others fear change and resist letting go of the status quo. Ambivalence is also common; people can both welcome and resist the same change. A realistic assessment of resistance will help you design an implementation plan more likely to succeed.

To help work through resistance to change, consider taking the following steps:

1. Develop an attitude that resistance is neither good nor bad. In fact, signs of resistance can signal opportunities to improve the change effort or implementation process.

2. Encourage people to openly express their thoughts and feelings about the change.

3. When resistance occurs, listen carefully. Employees who are feeling resistant don't want to hear a lengthy explanation of why the change is necessary. Instead, work to understand the resistance by exploring their concerns and by taking their feelings and concerns seriously.

4. Recognize that it takes time to work through resistance to change. Try to view this time as an up-front investment in creating a smoother transition to the desired new state of performance.

For large-scale changes, it's important to assess organizational readiness. The following process can help you compare the degree and types of resistance to the level of support and resources available to successfully implement a change:

1. Prepare a balance sheet contrasting the pros and cons of implementing change, the apparent support and resistance, and the resources that have been committed to the change.

2. For each of the most significant constraining factors and sources of resistance ask, "What if we do nothing about this?" Then identify the possible consequences of implementing the change.

3. Identify the additional resources, time, events, and changes to the plan that would have to occur to turn around the constraints and resistance. Keep an open mind about when the costs would begin to outweigh the benefits.

4. Use the balance sheet to reassess the commitment to change and to explore what key resources and processes must be added to ensure successful implementation.

As you work through this process, involve the people affected by the change, a transition team if you have one, and key stakeholders. Determine what needs to be done to shift the balance in favor of change. Realize that not everyone must be on board; research indicates you need about 30 percent of the people to turn the tide in the direction of change.

View change as a way of life

Peter Vail uses the phrase *permanent whitewater* to describe the seemingly never-ending array of rough water and rapids organizations must go through. The phrase also captures the experience many people have of the change process. In some organizations, this experience promotes cynicism toward new initiatives. But constant change can also promote a level of change hardiness—both in developing an attitude of adaptability among individuals and in creating a more nimble organization that is capable of rapidly adjusting to new demands and opportunities. Organizations that become adaptive to change see themselves as nimble without losing focus on a core set of values and beliefs.

How change hardy are you? The following questions will help you make that assessment:

- Do you typically look at change as a nuisance or an opportunity?

- Do you find yourself more concerned about what will be lost as a consequence of change, or do you focus on the possibilities?

- Do you seek to incorporate new initiatives into your existing plans?

- Do you tend to view change as making it potentially easier or harder to achieve your goals?

- Do you ask others about early benefits of new practices? Do you experiment with new practices to see what you can do with them?

- Do you get frustrated that new initiatives don't seem to stop, or do you initially consider each as improvements over past and current practices?

Managers also need to consider whether the team they lead is ready to embrace change. How nimble is your organization?

- Do people treat change as an event to get past, or as a way of life?

- Do people quickly get down to asking questions such as, "How will we implement change?" rather than, "Why should we?"

- Do people ask about desired outcomes of change to ensure alignment with the big picture?

- Are resources (time, support, change-enabling roles, teams, etc.) identified and made available to help people learn?

- Do teams quickly propose contingency plans—how to concurrently address immediate commitments while preparing for new commitments?

- Do people get excited when planning how to accomplish new initiatives?

- Do people ask not only about the immediate change, but also about possible subsequent changes that might be necessary as a result?

Even in nimble organizations, however, as the pace of change quickens, managers must attend to key behaviors that enable others to adapt to and embrace new initiatives.

PART 2:
SUCCESSFUL CHANGE MANAGEMENT

Communicate in ways that help people understand the scale and scope of change

Communication is key to preparing others for change. First and foremost, you need to clarify exactly what change needs to occur. Is it a major transformation of work processes, or an adaptation to existing practices? Does it impact a sole division, or will it cut across multiple functions and operating units? Who is involved and who is not? Will customers be affected, and in what way? The clearer you are about the change and the expected behavior, the more likely it is that people will respond.

To ensure that your communication about a change is clear and thorough, use the following suggestions:

- Clearly explain the importance of the change to the organization and the rationale for the change. Be prepared to answer questions about the degree of importance.

- Communicate the consequences for the organization or team if the change is not made.

- Allow for personal communication about the change. Do not expect to manage a large-scale change through e-mail.

- Prepare regular updates so people know what is going on. Track the success of the change process so people can feel a sense of progress and accomplishment.

- Recognize that sometimes people begin to really understand the implications of change only when they are midway through the transition. Encourage leaders to be available to talk with people about their reactions.

- Communicate the visions and objectives frequently. It is important that people hear the new direction and the reasons for it repeated throughout the change process.

- Meet regularly and often with managers and others leading the change effort.

- In working with people who have issues about the change, allow them to describe what is happening in their own words and experiences. Let them work through how they feel and how they can handle the situation, instead of constantly trying to defend or sell the change. Sometimes people just need to talk and have someone listen.

- Recognize that initial reactions to change may reflect personal style. Some people prefer to talk, while others need to read and think about the change. Some people are comfortable knowing the big picture and that there will be opportunities for adapting as the plan is implemented. Others prefer to see a clear schedule of events. Be sensitive to the diversity of preferences while communicating the plan for change.

Be specific about the implementation process

More often it is the process of change, not the content, that evokes strong reactions. Lack of clarity may leave others feeling uncertain about how to conduct day-to-day business while the change is being implemented.
To ensure that your communication is as specific as it can be, consider the following suggestions:

- Prepare a flowchart of the change process. Show the starting and ending points and the logical sequence of steps.

- Where possible, estimate the overall time to accomplish the change and the length of any individual phases.

- Let people know if it will be necessary for different units to go through the same process at different times and, if possible, when and how this will occur. This is often the case in large-scale changes.

- If work processes need to stop temporarily during the change, indicate when and for how long.

- Consider communicating some things that will not be affected by the change, or practices that will not be interrupted. It is often helpful for people to know what will remain the same.

- Determine whether customers or suppliers need to know about the timing of the change so they can adjust their processes accordingly.

- Prepare a checklist of who needs to do what and by when. If possible, include a summary of communication events, training sessions, dates or times when phases are expected to begin and end, and when implementation should be having measurable impact.

Increase awareness of the benefits of the new initiative

The logic of a change may seem intuitive or obvious to those who first identified the need for change. Those charged with implementation may accept the change without much questioning. Those who are expected to carry out the new initiative must have a sufficient reason to change, particularly if they are satisfied with current practices.

To help you increase people's awareness of the benefits of a proposed change, consider the following suggestions:

- Communicate the limitations of current practices. What are the long-term consequences of the current state of behavior? What aspects of current practices are difficult, unpleasant, unsafe, or limit organizational performance? How might current practices be inconsistent with other goals that matter to the intended recipients of change?

- Communicate those events occurring beyond the immediate worksite that indicate a demand for change. What global, national, industry, or competitor trends might not be obvious during day-to-day activity?

- Communicate the vision behind the new initiative. Find out if the vision is attractive to those being asked to change and how important it is to them to realize the vision.

- Determine the tangible benefits of the new initiative. Where possible, provide measurable benefits or display expected benefits with pictures and graphs.

- Anticipate how you might answer questions such as "Why us?", "Why now?", and "Do we have a choice whether we do this?"

- Indicate who else in the organization is behind the initiative. It helps people to know the individuals and constituencies who support the change, such as key senior executives, bargaining groups, or customers.

Involve people in decisions that impact them

To maximize buy-in, minimize resistance, and make the change work, involve others in the process. When employees feel that they are valued participants in planning and implementing the change, they are more likely to be motivated toward successful completion. Even if employees do not have a choice about whether to implement the new initiative, they can still have an impact on how it is accomplished.

To ensure that others are involved, try the following suggestions:

- Examine how decisions will be made during the change process. Make sure that the decision-making process involves the appropriate people.

- Make a list of all individuals who should be involved. Recognize that the specific people will shift as you move through stages of the process. Identify which people on your list should be involved in shaping the choice of the initiative, and which should be involved in determining the best timing and process for implementing the initiative.

- Involve the people on the front lines early in the planning process. While the leader is responsible for providing the vision, or big picture, of where the organization is going, the way to get there is often best determined by those who are "in the trenches" day after day.

- Solicit and use input from your team, peers, and manager when planning your change effort. When you request input from a large and diverse group of people, it is not usually possible to follow all of their suggestions; therefore, indicate up front that you cannot guarantee that every suggestion will be implemented, but that you will genuinely try to include as many as possible.

- Ask employees from the areas affected by the change to serve as experts in determining the steps needed for change.

- If the change requires a new procedure, ask for volunteers to test the change. Solicit their feedback on what is working well, where the problems are, and how to work out any difficulties.

- For large-scale or long-term change, use e-mail, intranet sites, or surveys to allow large numbers of people to communicate and provide input into aspects of the change.

Leverage the involvement of key stakeholders and opinion leaders

"Only after a company's official leaders demonstrate their commitment to change will change leaders begin to emerge down the line," writes Jerome Want in *Managing Radical Change* (Oliver Wight Pub., 1995). Sometimes people take change seriously only because of who communicates the need to change. Many people also take their cues by watching what their leaders do, not just what they say.

Consider the following suggestions for using your leaders' involvement to support change efforts:

- Ask the most appropriate senior manager or executive to help communicate the need for change.

- Involve one or more of the senior or executive managers in kick-off meetings.

- If the change is one that has been carried out in another division or company, seek to involve participants from that change. Create an opportunity for them to provide a detailed description of what happened and what the benefits were. Ask them to present a realistic preview of the change process.

- Ask key leaders, both formal and informal, to participate in relevant kick-off and training sessions.

- Involve key leaders in reviewing feedback on the change, in providing ongoing messages to employees, and in rewarding people who help move the change process along and display desired behaviors.

Clarify the new behaviors, practices, and what successful implementation looks like

Sometimes the vision behind a new initiative is so obvious that everyone can support it. Yet even in these cases, the way to put ideas into practice may seem ambiguous and elusive. The more specific you can be in communicating the actions necessary for carrying out a new initiative, and the more you can contrast the new and old behaviors, the more successful others are likely to be in carrying out those actions.

To help people better understand the specific behaviors and practices involved in a change, try the following suggestions:

- Prepare a table contrasting old and new behaviors and practices.

- Obtain or create a video of others carrying out the new behaviors. This can be based on how practices are done elsewhere, or it can be a simulation of realistic situations and the new behaviors. Show the video in kick-off or training sessions and allow those present to describe the differences they see.

- At a group or organizational level, identify the types of metrics that would indicate progress toward successful implementation.

- In leadership or employee training programs, ask one group to handle the situation in the old way and another in the new way. This lets people see the difference.

- Be specific about what behaviors or practices need to be learned, modified, and discontinued.

- If the new initiative requires different decisions to be made, identify the types of situations likely to require different decisions. Construct a map of the current decision rules and process, and contrast that with the preferred process.

- When people begin to practice the new or changed behavior, talk about how it worked, what the person thought, what worked well, and where problems occurred.

Create opportunities to learn, practice, and experiment with new behaviors

New skills and practices take time to learn and develop. Even when people support the ideas behind a new initiative, resistance may surface if people don't believe they can successfully carry out the specific behaviors.

To support people in learning and practicing new behaviors, consider the following suggestions:

- Communicate the need to learn new behaviors. Create time and opportunities to practice. Identify and use technical experts as needed to help break down complex practices into smaller sets of behaviors.

- Obtain the active support of managers whose employees must learn new behaviors. Work with these managers to determine the best time for people to attend training.

- Create opportunities for people to learn together, to experiment with different ways of accomplishing tasks using the new practices, and to share what they discover to be best practices.

- Provide access to experts who can assist people as they try out new practices. Ways to do this include setting up a toll-free telephone number, establishing a hot-line for calls, designating an e-mail address for questions, and/or assigning floor walkers to assist with real-time support needs.

- Provide positive reinforcement for practicing new behaviors, learning key behaviors, and carrying out full sequences of complex changes.

- Reinforce people's confidence in their ability to successfully carry out new behaviors by publicizing best practices, the processes by which some groups experiment with change, and how other groups have worked through initial difficulties and failures to accomplish the desired change.

- To help employees feel like they have the time to learn and practice new behaviors, obtain additional temporary support for the work group. This can be done during the training period or just afterward, when people are experimenting with new practices. A manager's willingness to provide additional assistance sends a clear message regarding his or her sincerity in seeing the new behaviors properly implemented, as well as his or her respect for the amount of effort required to make the change.

Establish structures and roles to support the change

New behaviors and practices often require support, either in the form of technical expertise on how to carry out behaviors, advice on interpreting guidelines, or help in managing the details of implementation. Such support generally comes from the "change champion." For small changes, a manager may be the designated change champion; for large-scale changes, implementation teams are often established to guide the transition.

The following suggestions will help you create roles and structures to more effectively support a change:

- Assign the role of change champion to someone who will accept additional responsibility for others as well for him- or herself. Clarify the person's role in terms of communicating the purpose of the change, ensuring necessary support if available, and reporting progress.

- In situations where the change champion also provides the technical expertise and coaches others who must carry out new practices, provide additional training and feedback for the person, including supplementary training, if needed, on how to coach others.

- Create a communication network for change champions so that they also can exchange best practices, have their own questions answered in a timely way, and know that they are part of a special group making the change real.

- When a temporary team is created to manage large-scale changes throughout the organization, provide any additional training and support that the team may need. Consider the following steps:
  - Ask that the team participate in team development to fully understand its purpose, to develop internal practices and participation, and to create its own role structure and rules for guiding the change implementation.
  - Provide opportunities for the team to communicate regularly with key executives who initiated the overall change. This lets them raise new issues that have surfaced during implementation and ask for needed resources or guidance. It also helps ensure that the change remains a top priority over time.
  - Publicize the team's role and ways for employees to work with the team.

Allow opportunities for flexible implementation

Just as employees may expect some choice in how a new practice is initiated, they may also expect some latitude in adapting new practices. Consider the following ways to provide flexibility in the implementation process:

- As you examine the new initiative, consider whether there is only one right way to carry out the new practice, or if a variety of practices is possible as long as the same basic outcome is achieved. This will help you determine how flexible the implementation can be.

- Encourage people to experiment with implementing new practices so they are easier to carry out. Communicate variations in the implementation, or provide a location, such as an intranet site, where people can learn about different ways to implement the desired change.

- Identify internal or external resources that can help managers and teams with flexible implementation. These resources may include the designated change champions, members of the transition team, human resource development consultants, and internal or external technical experts.

- If employees seem stuck or resistant to change, ask what modifications might make the change work better. Find out about existing processes, commitments, or customer demands that might make the new change difficult to accomplish at this time. Help the group determine how they can both accomplish their other objectives and introduce the new practices. Alternatively, it may be necessary to delay a particular group's participation in new initiatives until other commitments are satisfied or renegotiated.

Establish and use feedback processes to monitor implementation of key events and their impact

The only thing worse than bad news is no news at a time when you know things are bad. It is important to have a steady flow of feedback about progress. Frequent feedback allows for modifications to planned approaches, provision of additional resources, and chances to see how well the change is progressing.

To ensure sufficient feedback processes for your change efforts, try the following steps:

- Create ways for people to communicate opinions, experiences, and reactions to change. This can be done through an e-mail site, a technical support group, focus groups, or a survey.

- Break down the change into key phases and behaviors. Use a checklist to assess how successfully each behavior is being implemented.

- Allow people to describe their successes, disappointments, and surprises during and after implementation. Encourage suggestions for how to improve implementation, both for groups that have yet to participate in the change and for future initiatives. This can promote organizational learning about successful change management.

- Publicize the results of periodic surveys. Use this as an opportunity to discuss honestly what is working well and what is not. Offer interim recommendations and accommodations to concerns. Also reinforce the vision behind the change and point out any benefits that may have been vague at the beginning of the initiative.

Reward and reinforce both progress and success

New behaviors must be rewarded and reinforced if they are to be sustained. Successful managers use a variety of ways to nurture and reward new behaviors. Consider the following suggestions for rewarding and reinforcing success:

- Identify specific accomplishments regarding the new initiative that should be rewarded. Consider rewarding the first individuals or groups to accomplish the change. This reinforces and celebrates efficiency at accomplishing change. Also consider rewarding all employees after the entire group has accomplished the change. This reinforces collaboration and collective success.

- Identify any current rewards that need to change. For example, organizations going toward a team-based approach often need to change their individual-based reward systems.

- Look for opportunities to use nonmonetary rewards to reinforce achievements. Examples include letters of appreciation, small celebrations, and congratulatory calls and messages from leaders. Be careful not to overdo the use of coffee mugs, t-shirts, buttons, or any single symbol, especially if large monetary rewards are being given to others for carrying out the change.

- Allow managers to distribute "spot bonuses" as a way for them to show active support for the change and reinforce their employees' behaviors.

Align the surrounding system to be consistent with desired new behaviors

For change to happen efficiently in both the short term and the long term, supporting structures and systems must be designed and implemented. Consider using the following approaches the next time you embark on a change effort:

- Try a zero-based approach, which essentially asks the question, "If we did not have any systems, structures, policies, and procedures in place, how would we create them from scratch to support the new vision?" This model requires you to look at the vision or goal of the change effort and build systems and structures from the ground up.

- Assess your current systems and structures by doing the following:
  1. List all of the current policies, procedures, and other formal and informal systems that could affect the change effort. Include reward systems, management style, cultural norms and values, performance management systems, and metrics commonly used to communicate departmental and organizational performance.
  2. Analyze the current structure of your organization and team. Look at the structure of your team and the way your team interacts (formally and informally) with other teams in the organization. Does the structure (job descriptions, compensation, geographic location, reporting relationships, etc.) support the change?
  3. Scrutinize each of these factors carefully in light of the new change. Ask yourself and your team, "Does this practice or procedure serve our new goal?" Eliminate unnecessary practices, modify those practices that are still helpful but out of date, and design new structures that will work for you.

     For example, change intended to promote team-based operations is more likely to succeed when the reward systems are not designed solely to reinforce individual accomplishment. Furthermore, when managers provide feedback and coaching to the team on its collective performance, members are more likely to focus on working as a team.

- Modify any systems that might lead people to perceive that they are penalized for being an active part of implementing large-scale change. Such change sometimes requires a team of people to temporarily give up their current roles and dedicate themselves full- or part-time to the new initiative. You may need to modify reward systems, succession management systems, and performance management systems to ensure that these individuals feel supported.

RESOURCES

The resources for this chapter begin on page 650.

MOTIVATION AND COURAGE FACTOR

A pessimist sees the difficulty in every opportunity;
an optimist sees the opportunity in every difficulty.
— Winston Churchill

A high level of motivation and the willingness to act courageously are necessary ingredients of managerial success in today's workplace.

A manager's level of motivation acts as the energy or fuel that enables him or her to achieve results and be successful. While it is important to have an adequate and consistent source of energy, or motivation, how you use those energy reserves is equally important.

A manager who effectively uses his or her energy sets high personal standards of motivation, focuses energy on the most critical issues, and works hard to achieve results and move beyond challenges and obstacles.

However, hard work alone is not enough. Managers must also be willing to take risks and step forward to address difficult issues. They need to challenge and encourage their people to do the same. Motivated and successful managers have a positive effect on others. They serve as role models for the drive, enthusiasm, and courage needed to be effective in their organizations.

The following chapters in this section contain development activities for both of these key skill areas:

Chapter 16 – Drive for Results: Sets challenging goals and puts a top priority on getting results; conveys a sense of urgency and drives issues to closure; persists in the face of obstacles; demonstrates initiative and sets high personal standards of performance; maintains a consistent, high level of productivity; is committed to the organization.

Chapter 17 – Lead Courageously: Makes decisions and acts in ways consistent with one's own principles; demonstrates the courage to do what is right, despite personal risk or discomfort; confronts problems promptly and encourages others to do the same; acts decisively.

16
DRIVE FOR RESULTS

- *Strengthen your personal sense of purpose*
- *Set challenging goals*
- *Put a top priority on getting results*
- *Drive hard on the right issues*
- *Convey a sense of urgency when appropriate*
- *Persist in the face of obstacles*
- *Bring issues to closure*
- *Maintain a high level of productivity*
- *Set high personal standards of performance*
- *Seek out new work challenges*
- *Make your job more interesting*
- *Readily put in extra effort to accomplish important tasks*
- *Commit to your organization*
- *Overcome procrastination*
- *Monitor your progress*

INTRODUCTION

Effective leaders focus on achieving results through and with others. They are concerned with accomplishments. Committed leaders set high standards of performance, pursue aggressive goals, and work hard to achieve them. They focus on what is important, rather than become overwhelmed by all that appears urgent. They persist in the face of obstacles and measure their success in terms of results achieved.

Yet most managers sometimes get bogged down by repetitive tasks and long hours, and find it difficult to maintain enthusiasm for and commitment to their jobs. Changing priorities, recurring problems, budget constraints, and lack of promotional opportunities can cause frustration and sap energy. Successful leaders, however, work through these difficulties by keeping their focus on what's most important.

This chapter presents suggestions on how you and your team can maintain that focus on attaining results, even in challenging situations.

VALUABLE TIPS

- Focus effort on what is important, not what is urgent.

- Measure results achieved, not hours worked or activities.

- Adopt a "can-do" attitude, and approach challenges from a problem-solving perspective. Look for alternative solutions, rather than focus on why things can't be done.

- Identify the critical path to your desired results and then remove the obstacles that get in the way.

- Be persistent, but not foolish. If what you are trying is not working, seek feedback and ideas from others.

- Review progress on your goals and objectives regularly and often. Reinforce yourself with rewards for achieving goals.

- Involve employees in setting departmental goals and objectives. Track results. Recognize and reward employees for their contribution to the success of your team.

- Show your enthusiasm for the organization through your commitments and actions.

- Undertake a daily exercise program to increase your energy level and endurance.

- Get involved in activities that make you feel excited and alive, both at work and in your personal life.

- Take calculated risks to demonstrate your orientation to action.

- Refrain from saying "it can't be done," and focus on how you can make it happen.

- Take the initiative to go beyond what is expected.

- To develop your work motivation, identify the outcomes you want from a job.

- Demonstrate your commitment to the organization in a tangible way by your willingness to "go the extra mile" when necessary.

- Discuss the satisfaction you expect from your career with company associates, your family, and friends.

- Write down your most important goals and keep them in front of you at all times—for example, on a mirror at home, in your desk drawer or on the wall in your office.

Strengthen your personal sense of purpose

Effective leaders persistently focus on what is important and work to achieve those goals. To drive for results in this way, and to develop the persistence sometimes needed, you must be sure of your purpose and goals. To strengthen your personal sense of purpose, consider these suggestions:

- Determine what is most important to you. What do you value? What is important for you to accomplish? What do you believe in?

- Next, identify the goals and results that your organization deems important.

- Examine the meaning and importance of achieving your group's vision for yourself and for your team. Look for alignment between your personal values and those of your team and your organization.

- Write your own personal statement of goals to which you are committed and in which you will invest your time and energy.

- Have each team member write his or her own personal statement. Discuss the alignment or lack of alignment with organization goals. Determine what can be done to create more alignment between personal and organizational goals.

Set challenging goals

"If you don't know where you are going, you will probably end up somewhere else," is an old adage. Setting appropriate goals is a necessary precursor to effectively driving for results. Consider the following suggestions:

- Make sure that your goals are clearly aligned with your organization's strategic objectives and business requirements.

- Determine that you have a high level of commitment to your goals. Otherwise, you are likely to get easily sidetracked.

- Translate broad, longer-term goals into specific milestones or subgoals. Then manage to these subgoals or milestones.

- Identify the constraints and obstacles that may stand in the way of your goals, and plan accordingly.

Put a top priority on getting results

Getting results is important for your organization's bottom line. You may be perceived as not putting a high priority on getting results because of the nature of your job (some staff work is seen as less results-oriented), because of work style differences between yourself and others, or because you are not clearly focused on the most important results. To be seen as driving for results, consider the following suggestions:

- Make sure you and your team have measurable goals and objectives. Then focus on results, not activity.

- With your team, develop a set of criteria for effective performance. Include a list of necessary accomplishments. Then make sure your reward system is aligned with the results you want to achieve.

- Ensure that you, supervisors or managers, or the team, monitors progress toward goals. Provide appropriate assistance when necessary.

- Challenge yourself and others to do better without minimizing what you or they have already accomplished.

- Keep others informed about what you and your group are doing.

- The priority you place on people, accuracy, quality, and so on, may be interpreted as not putting a priority on getting results. Ask for feedback about this. Ensure that all your priorities are compatible with achieving strong results.

- Recognize that you need quality processes to attain quality results.

- Show your employees how their efforts contribute to the bottom line and to organizational success. Discuss organizational results and what you and your team are or could be doing to impact those results.

Drive hard on the right issues

Remember the old adage "choose your battles carefully" when deciding how best to spend your energies. You can't possibly do everything, but it is especially critical for you to address the issues that get in the way of, or further hinder the development of, your most important goals. To ensure that you drive hard on these issues, consider the following suggestions:

- Assign responsibilities to resolve issues. Make sure everyone knows their roles, deadlines, and deliverables expected. Ensure that rewards are consistent with goals.

- Check on progress periodically to ensure that issues are being resolved appropriately. Provide additional guidelines and feedback, if necessary.

- Convey the importance of resolving issues promptly.

- When faced with a number of issues that need your attention, use the following criteria to decide which to handle first:
  - Will this issue have a direct impact on business performance?
  - Is this issue a roadblock in the critical path to the achievement of our team's or organization's goals?
  - Will this issue damage important relationships?
  - Is this issue important for now or for the future?

  Answering "yes" to any of these questions probably means you should address the issue.

- Develop a clearer understanding of the issue's importance by asking yourself:
  - What will happen if I don't address the issue?
  - For whom is the issue important?

- Ask your direct reports, peers, customers, and manager what they believe are critical issues on which you should focus.

- Determine the critical paths for your group. Address issues and problems that block or hinder the success of the group.

- Think ahead. What are the critical issues that must be addressed for success in the future?

- If you turn an issue over to someone else, follow up on it. Ask for updates, progress reports, and problems, and let others know you are on top of the issue.

Convey a sense of urgency when appropriate

Some people do not convey a sense of urgency at all, with the result that those around them may become nervous about not achieving deadlines. Still others may give the impression that everything is urgent and must be addressed immediately. Either approach is problematic.

The following suggestions will help you analyze the sense of urgency you convey and address areas you may wish to work on:

- Analyze the amount of urgency you've conveyed about the key projects and tasks you have been working on over the last three months.
  - Did you convey enough urgency?
  - Did you convey too much urgency on too many projects so that direction to your staff was unclear?
  - Did you convey a sense of urgency on your own projects but not on the projects of others?
  - Did you demonstrate a sense of urgency on only certain kinds of tasks or issues (for example, project process issues but not interpersonal issues)?

- Seek feedback from other people on how they view the degree of urgency you communicate on projects and tasks. Solicit specific information about when you have displayed appropriate urgency, when you have shown inappropriate urgency, and any patterns they have observed.

- Determine which of your projects are urgent and which are less urgent. Doing so will enable you and others to focus on a limited set of priorities. Communicating great urgency and importance on everything you're involved in creates unnecessary crises and resentment.

- When working on a key project, tell your employees that the project is a top priority so that they understand what counts for you. Also explain the importance of the project, why it is a top priority, and how missing deadlines will impact the organization or customer.

- Follow up on the progress of a key project and continue to convey the urgency appropriate to its priority.

- If you or your employees tend to wait until the last minute to complete a task, set checkpoints ahead of the actual deadline. This will give you and your employees time to ensure that the final product is of high quality and will avoid placing unnecessary pressure on others.

- Identify a role model. Look for a manager who shows an appropriate amount of urgency for important projects and tasks and less urgency on less important projects. Ask the manager how he or she prioritizes projects, how he or she specifically shows a sense of urgency (both verbally and nonverbally), and what strategies have worked well.

Persist in the face of obstacles

Some work is simply difficult to do. It takes time, is complex, is intellectually challenging, or is politically complicated. Yet successful people are persistent, even on tasks such as these.

Persistence does not mean banging one's head on an obstacle until one or the other gives way. It does mean finding and applying strategies that will move you forward. When you find that progress toward your objectives is impeded, consider the following suggestions:

- After working on a strategy for a while with no success, view that lack of success as an opportunity to find another approach. Acknowledge that you are stuck. Once you realize that your problem-solving processes are blocked, you can use a number of techniques to get past the block.

- If you cannot solve the problem yourself, determine who can help you to look at it objectively and brainstorm possible solutions. Seek ideas and suggestions from people with perspectives or backgrounds different from your own.

- Form a team to help identify the obstacles and brainstorm ways to overcome them. Try implementing one or two of the top solutions. Promise the team and/or yourself a reward for overcoming obstacles and achieving the desired results.

- Take a break from the project or problem. Sometimes a little incubating time will help you discover an obvious solution at a later date. Or sometimes an obstacle will disappear if you leave it for a while.

- Imagine how the most resourceful person you know would react to the same situation.

- Think positively. Instead of telling yourself the task is impossible, tell yourself that you have reached a momentary impasse and that a solution does exist and will eventually come to you. Adopt a "can-do" attitude. Remind yourself that if the task were easy to solve, it wouldn't be a challenge.

- Set reasonable expectations for the amount of effort and time things will take. In new areas, ask more experienced people for help in setting expectations. Know yourself—do you typically underestimate? Overestimate?

- Seek coaching. Find a coach to help you remain focused despite setbacks. He or she can offer advice, help you find alternatives, help you learn from his or her experiences, or link you with the support or resources you need.

Bring issues to closure

Nothing saps energy faster than constantly dealing with the same old problems. Don't let yourself be pulled down by these nagging issues. Resolve recurring issues by initiating action and encouraging others to get things done. The following suggestions can help you move toward closure:

- Communicate the urgency and importance of resolving the issue. Explain how it affects performance, productivity, morale, etc. Then challenge others to help resolve it.

- Get the people involved together in a room and set the expectation that a resolution must be found. Give all parties a chance to air their views. List the issues on a board or flip chart. Identify the areas of agreement, and then facilitate a discussion to resolve the areas of disagreement. If necessary, seek a neutral third party to intervene and negotiate or arbitrate a solution.

- Take time to investigate the issue and identify the real cause or underlying problems. Avoid making quick fixes. A solution that addresses only immediate, visible symptoms will not be sufficient to handle long-term repercussions.

- Create a plan, with specific dates, to tackle the issue and bring it to closure.

- Seek feedback from others on your ability to balance process with getting results. If you tend to be overly focused on how things get done, others may see you as not focused enough on achieving results.

Maintain a high level of productivity

Just as a monetary investment that yields a healthy return is valuable to its investor, a productive employee is certainly a valued asset to his or her employer. Consider the following suggestions to increase your productivity level:

- Use measurement tools to keep track of your accomplishments and evaluate how productive your work week, month, or quarter has been.

- Monitor your own efficiency and identify distracters or recurring problems that affect your productivity. Then brainstorm ways to reduce or eliminate these problems.

- Determine which activities you spend most of your time on—the important, the most easily done, or those that appear to be most urgent. Decide to focus on the most important first.

- If you see yourself as a productive and high-energy person, but others do not, seek to better understand the discrepancy between your view and that of others. Consider the following:
  - You may be a low-key person among hard-charging drivers. Talk to others about your priorities and your investment in your work. Doing so will show your commitment.
  - You may be accomplishing a lot without working 12 hours a day, but others may not see it. If so, share more of what you are accomplishing.
  - Others may conclude that you are not productive because you do not communicate energy through your voice and body language. Work to increase the level of enthusiasm and expressiveness in your speech.

- To help you more accurately predict the time required for various short-term tasks and show you which tasks are taking the majority of your time, complete this exercise:
  1. At the beginning of each day, plan—in detail—the work you expect to complete that day. List the tasks according to priority, and determine the amount of time you expect to spend on each. Make sure your priority tasks are linked to achieving your most important goals.
  2. At the end of the day, review your list to determine how much of the work you accomplished and how long it took to accomplish it.

  If your analysis reveals a considerable discrepancy between what you planned to accomplish and what you actually accomplished, look for causes. Too many interruptions? Procrastination? Lack of ability to estimate correctly? Plan and problem-solve accordingly.

- Take advantage of your natural body clock to work on your most critical assignments. Save the straightforward tasks that take less concentration for times when your biorhythms naturally dip, such as after lunch.

- If you find it difficult to maintain high energy on the job, you may want to assess your fitness level. Consider:
  - *Nutrition.* Examine your eating habits. If you typically rush out of the house without breakfast and eat lunch on the run, you may not be getting the balanced diet you need to sustain energy on the job.
  - *Exercise.* Regular physical exercise, whether it is a brisk evening walk or an intense workout, can go a long way toward making you feel energetic and alert all day.
  - *Sleep.* While individuals vary in the amount of sleep they need, you may need more or less than you're getting right now. Examine your sleeping patterns and determine the right amount for you.
  - *Stretch breaks.* Long periods of intense effort can create lethargy and drowsiness. Break up these sessions with short stretch breaks. Take a short walk outside, or do some simple calisthenics to relieve tension and relax stiff muscles.

- Develop a list of things you can do to rejuvenate yourself when your energy is low. Solicit ideas from others on what they do to revitalize themselves during times of low energy.

Set high personal standards of performance

Organizations look for individuals who are committed to excellence and are willing to invest themselves in their work. While high personal standards of performance can lead to recognition, increased status, and other rewards, your own satisfaction with your performance is the ultimate and longer-lasting reward. The following guidelines will help you set high standards for your performance:

- Analyze your work and set your own objectives using the following procedure:
  1. Write down your five most important responsibilities.
  2. Describe the characteristics of superior performance in each area.
  3. Describe the characteristics of performance that are not acceptable in each area.
  4. Using these extremes, set your own personal standards in each area. Make your standards challenging, yet attainable.

- On a regular basis, monitor your performance as it relates to your personal standards.

- Take time to congratulate and reward yourself when you accomplish a goal or meet a standard, and enjoy the feelings of personal accomplishment that go with these achievements.

- After six months, compare your own assessment of your work with the feedback and recognition you receive from others to see how accurate your self-assessment is.

Seek out new work challenges	Your initiative in seeking out new work challenges demonstrates your commitment to the organization and increases the variety and scope of your job. The following suggestions can get you started:

- Talk with your manager about your desire to broaden the range of your responsibilities. Indicate your interests and ideas. Make sure you have mastered all the duties of your job, not just the fun ones, before you ask for more.

- Identify issues critical to your organization's success in the future, and develop expertise in those areas. Talk about the knowledge and skills you have, and watch for opportunities to demonstrate their usefulness.

- Identify projects or assignments that are of interest to you, but for which you are not currently responsible. In particular, look for assignments that will stretch your strengths.

- Watch for opportunities to help out in other departments, as well as your own. This will give you greater exposure to other areas and will help to build your reputation as a team player.

- Identify opportunities for improvement and work to address these opportunities. Take the initiative to propose solutions to problems, and determine how to provide that input to those directly responsible without alienating them.

- Consider volunteering for special projects, task forces, or a lateral move in a different functional area of the organization to gain experience and add challenge to your work.

- Be realistic about what you can handle. Consider your strengths and weaknesses, and set your goals accordingly. Avoid taking on too much at one time.

- Consider being a coach. It's a great development opportunity.

Make your job more interesting	If you've held a job for so long that many of your assignments have become routine, you may have difficulty developing and maintaining enthusiasm for your work. Instead of looking at your work as an obligation, redefine your work activities into tasks that engage you, hold your attention, and leave you in a positive state of mind. Following is a method you can try for revitalizing your job and regaining your enthusiasm:

- Identify what you value and care about. Then, look to see what you can do in your current job that will allow you to focus on these values and goals.

- Review what you have done in your job during the past 6 to 12 months. What are you proud of? What do you feel good about? What brings you a sense of satisfaction? How can you do more of this kind of work?

- Discuss with your manager how you would like to change your role to make it more interesting and motivating.

- If you find yourself bogged down by responsibilities and work that is no longer interesting, investigate how you can delegate some of this work to others who may find it a learning experience.

- Consider a different way of looking at the less-interesting aspects of your job. When dealing with the unpleasant part of his job, one leader commented, "I just tell myself, 'This is what I get paid for. The rest of my job is fun.'" Many people enjoy much of their work, but have some things they find difficult or they do not like. Think about telling yourself that it is this part of your job for which you receive the paycheck.

Readily put in extra effort to accomplish important tasks

Undoubtedly you will experience times when you must make an extra effort to complete a project or get caught up on your routine responsibilities. When these times arise, it is important that you be responsible and tenacious. The following suggestions can help you deal with these situations effectively:

- When you are asked to work longer hours to deal with a specific crisis or meet an objective on time, do so willingly. If you cannot put in the extra time, clearly explain why, show your concern, and assist in finding someone who can help. With your manager, find a solution; with your peers, you may want to give suggestions.

- Putting in extra effort does not necessarily mean putting in extra time. You can also:
  - Identify a process that will ensure higher quality.
  - Include a feature or step that will meet an emerging need.
  - Include additional people to increase acceptance.

- If you are asked to stay late, but cannot, find out how you can nevertheless meet the commitment. It may mean borrowing help from others, working at home, redefining the project, or becoming more creative in freeing up your time.

- If some people have the perception that you do not put in extra time and effort, you may need to share your key accomplishments and help them see how productive you are during the hours you work. Some people pay more attention to the number of hours worked than to the results achieved.

I've enjoyed our discussion about going the extra mile... but you missed my turn back there.

- Look at the long-term consequences that working extended hours will bring. "Going the extra mile" shows others that you are willing to do whatever it takes to get the job done. As a consequence, you will likely find yourself involved in many interesting and challenging projects. On the other hand, working extended hours may be keeping you from other important goals and priorities you have set for yourself outside of work. You will need to decide which takes priority and accept the consequences of that decision.

- Track the hours you work beyond your optimal number (each person seems to have a range of hours he or she is comfortable working). If you frequently work beyond the optimal number for you, check to see how your experience fits with that of others in the organization. You may discover that you need to hire more people, reprioritize, eliminate work, delegate more, or become more comfortable with the number of extra hours.

- Be willing to make small sacrifices that yield much greater results.

Commit to your organization

People who are self-promoting and concerned only with what they and their group are doing are focused on the short term. On the other hand, managers who are committed to the entire organization often have a longer-term perspective. Being committed to your work and your organization is essential for your success on the job, for generating confidence and trust, and for developing cooperative work relationships with others. In the end, people are not impressed by and do not trust people who are merely out for themselves.

The following suggestions can help you strengthen and demonstrate your commitment to your organization:

- Pledge your commitment to your organization. This is a personal and private agreement with yourself that can help guide you through organizational life's ups and downs.

- Work to strengthen your commitment during both the good times and bad. It's easy to lose faith when the going gets tough. Your commitment is put to the test at these times. How strong will it be?

- In your formal and informal contacts with others inside and outside of your organization, speak up in support of the organization's mission, values, and goals.

- Make a commitment to yourself that you will do all you can to help your fellow employees, your customers, and your organization's leaders.

- Show honest, genuine concern about the people in the organization.

- Share credit for your accomplishments.

Overcome procrastination

People procrastinate in different ways, to different degrees, and for different reasons. Many people habitually put off things they know they should be doing. The following suggestions can help you chip away at procrastination:

- Determine the cause or reason for your procrastination. You may find that you're putting off a project because you lack confidence in completing it successfully, or you don't have the necessary skills to do it. Once you have identified the reason(s), take action to overcome it.

- Identify the types of tasks and activities you are prone to put off. Look for patterns. For example, do you tend to delay doing routine paperwork? Addressing interpersonal issues? Tackling ambiguous assignments?

- If you procrastinate on follow-up, block out time on your weekly schedule and dedicate it to following up.

- Make firm deadline commitments with your manager, employees, and customers, and note them on your calendar to force yourself to start the projects.

- If you put off projects that seem too difficult or overwhelming, make a list of the small, easy steps involved in the project and do these first. Their momentum may carry over into the more difficult work.

- Tell yourself you'll work on a project for a half-hour to see how it goes (knowing that you can handle it for a short period of time). By the end of the half-hour, you may have found the work isn't so difficult or distasteful after all.

- Establish ways to reward yourself along the way—for example, a coffee break after writing the introduction to a report or a change of pace after completing a major project.

- Think differently about undesirable work. Instead of focusing on your dislike, focus on the sense of accomplishment you'll feel after finishing.

- Simply do the undesirable first to get it out of the way.

- Ask your staff to give you feedback about how your procrastination affects them. If that input concerns you, write it down on a note card and keep it in sight on your desk as a reminder.

Monitor your progress

In both their personal and professional lives, people are motivated by their progress toward goals. By establishing and monitoring your goals, you will be better able to gauge your progress, thereby feeling an increased sense of achievement. Follow these guidelines for monitoring your progress toward goals:

- At the beginning of each day, month, quarter, or year, list the things you wish to accomplish and the dates by which you wish to accomplish them. Make sure these activities move you in the direction of your vision of your future. Then use this list as the basis for your daily activities.

- Compare your actual accomplishments with your scheduled accomplishments. Determine whether you are satisfied with your achievements during that time period.

- If you would like to accomplish more during a given time period, gradually increase the demands you make on yourself by slowly adding activities to your list. Establish a pace that will enable you to attain your goals, and set interim dates so that all activities will be completed by the end of your chosen time period.

- If you have difficulty achieving your goals, consider your use of time management techniques.

- Regularly evaluate your progress to determine whether your achievement level is satisfying your need to realize progress toward your goals.

- Conduct periodic checks to evaluate your progress. Set rewards for accomplishing major milestones. If you find that you're not progressing at the rate you should be, identify the causes for the delay. Then take the necessary actions to progress toward your goals.

RESOURCES

The resources for this chapter begin on page 652.

17
LEAD
COURAGEOUSLY

- *Clarify what is important to you*
- *Make decisions and act in ways consistent with your principles*
- *Demonstrate the courage to do what is right despite personal risk or discomfort*
- *Take stands to resolve important issues*
- *Confront problems promptly*
- *Address prejudice in yourself*
- *Address prejudice and intolerant behavior in others*
- *Act decisively*
- *Challenge others to make tough choices*

INTRODUCTION

Today's leaders constantly face tough situations and need to make difficult decisions—whether it's to initiate a CRM (Customer Relationship Management) software installation, outsource IT support, base their agribusiness company's future on genetic engineering, give money to government officials to seek favorable treatment, lobby for higher immigration quotas, invest in local education, or use inexpensive labor sources that would result in firing current employees. When facing these types of situations, effective leaders demonstrate principled leadership, personal courage, and decisiveness.

Effective leaders know what they stand for and follow their own values and ethics. They are willing to endure difficulty, take risks, and make themselves uncomfortable in order to live their values. People who work with these leaders typically respect them for their courage, decisiveness, and willingness to follow their values.

Courageous leaders confront problems and deal with issues, rather than ignore them. They do not look for problems or strive to be "tough," but they are able to be firm and decisive when necessary. They are willing to confront others, but they are also respectful, even with those with whom they disagree. In short, they live from their values.

This chapter presents suggestions on how you can clarify and act on your values, and lead with courage and respect.

VALUABLE TIPS

- Identify your most deeply held convictions. Use those convictions to guide your leadership.

- Create a clear vision of the kind of leader you want to be—and then live it.

- View yourself as a leader.

- Give people the feedback they need even when it may be difficult.

- Openly acknowledge it when your stand may be unpopular, and then explain why it is important for others to consider your point of view.

- Stand behind your employees and back their decisions.

- Attack problems, not people.

- Identify the people in your organization whose courage you most admire. Talk with them and learn how they act on their convictions.

- Talk with people directly about their prejudiced behavior or comments, but allow them a way to change without losing face.

- When you see a need or problem that you wish someone would address, ask yourself if you could be doing something about it.

- In meetings, verbalize your concerns so they can be openly discussed.

- Determine if one of your veteran staff members has a chronic performance problem that no one has really addressed. Then deal with it.

- Honestly determine if you tend to avoid passing negative information upward.

- Report on both your successes and failures with equal candor.

- Look at your staff and determine if you are spending more energy protecting them than holding them accountable.

- Step forward with a position of principle, even when there is ambiguity regarding the facts.

- After speaking up for what you believe is important, be gracious whether your ideas are accepted or rejected.

- Remember that management is not a popularity contest. You may not always be liked, but you should be respected.

- Show the courage to let your employees learn from their mistakes.

- Believe that you have the power to make a difference, and accept the responsibility of trying.

Clarify what is important to you

Championing something that you believe is right or important requires conviction. It's not always easy to go against the mainstream or to choose the more disruptive course of action. Therefore, knowing what is most important to you will strengthen your convictions and values. To clarify what is really important to you, use the following suggestions:

- Carefully consider the questions that follow. Then write down your answers and file them in a place where you can review and update them regularly.
  - What is most important to me?
  - What do I value the most?
  - What is worth fighting for or standing up for?

- Review presentations you have given. They will contain themes that can identify what you find most important.

- Develop a leadership creed that captures the essence of what leadership is to you. Share your creed with others. Periodically evaluate whether you are leading your team in a way that is consistent with your beliefs.

- Think about the legacy you want to leave your team and your organization. What things or qualities do you want to be remembered for? Evaluate what you are currently doing, and make whatever changes are feasible or most realistic.

- Ask your HR department for a values inventory, which may help you clarify your values.

Make decisions and act in ways consistent with your principles

Effective leaders are principled leaders. They know what they stand for and behave in ways consistent with their values. As a result, people often admire these leaders, even if they disagree with them. The willingness to take courageous stands for the sake of principles has a vibrant history in most societies. To more fully decide and act in alignment with your values, consider these suggestions:

- Periodically review your decisions and actions to ensure that they are consistent with your values. Some leaders have found that they had drifted farther than they realized. If your actions are not consistent with your values, decide whether you are comfortable with that, and change your behavior if you are not comfortable.

- As you make a decision, consider whether you would be comfortable appearing on national TV to justify it, or comfortable explaining the decision to your children, if you have them.

- When you encounter difficulties deciding a course of action, review the issues to see if they include any ethical issues. That may be why you are having a difficult time.

- When facing a difficult dilemma or decision, examine it in the light of your deeply held convictions and values. This will give you direction.

- Look for situations in which others may be overly concerned about taking a stand, but where you strongly believe in the correctness of your position based on your convictions. Make your rationale and position clear to others.

- Actively look for opportunities to stand up for what you believe. Visibly and openly push for the kind of involvement that supports your values.

Demonstrate the courage to do what is right despite personal risk or discomfort

Managers sometimes face situations and decisions in which the most appropriate action carries with it a backlash of negative reactions, concerns, complaints, problems, and even the possibility of personal risk. These decisions require courage. Sometimes these decisions risk one's career; other times the action may entail actual physical risk. Many times managers demonstrate their courage by tackling difficult problems, especially interpersonal ones.

When a decision requires you to go against what has been done before or differs from what others with higher authority or more power want, it can be difficult to do. The following suggestions can help you take the right actions despite risk or discomfort:

- Say "no" when necessary. Don't procrastinate or soften the blow by being tentative. When it's best for the organization to refuse a request, clearly explain to those involved why you cannot support them.

- Seek advice and counsel from others. They may see the situation in another way, identify more options, or provide important insight.

- When you want to do something different from other people, get a thorough understanding of their thinking and rationale before you make a final decision.

- When a decision entails risk, assess the risk carefully. Ask others to assist with this assessment so you have a broader base of knowledge and experience to draw from.

- Confront tough issues head on. In the long run, no one benefits by ignoring issues that must be addressed and resolved. You show respect and concern for people by confronting hard issues, not by ignoring them.

- Don't overlook the people aspect of making tough decisions. Be prepared to deal with other people's reactions and to direct people to resources that will help them deal with the impact of the decision.

- When facing a tough decision, such as trimming the budget or downsizing, carefully analyze various alternatives, get other people's input, and settle on the course of action that meets the criteria you deem important. Then, when you communicate your decision, you will have the background and data to support your actions.

- Support your employees when they make tough choices, particularly when people complain to you. Endorse your employees' decisions when appropriate.

- Don't be a "yes person" to upper management. Decide yourself what is best. Most upper-level managers are not impressed by people who will not stand up for what they believe is important.

- Identify one risk you are afraid to take. Carefully analyze its potential benefits and negative consequences. Figure out what you would do if the worst-case scenario occurred. Then reconsider whether you can take the risk.

- When you are reluctant to make a change, ask yourself what is behind your resistance. If you are afraid of change, push yourself to make the transition. Recognize that change is very difficult, but that being a willing champion of a new directive may be just what the organization needs.

Take stands to resolve important issues

Taking a stand and pushing to resolve important issues require clear communication, a strong emphasis on paying attention to and working with others, persistence, and the courage of your convictions. Use the following suggestions when you need to take a firm stand:

- Avoid using tentative language like "I might be persuaded to…" or "I'm not sure that it's the best way…" when stating your position. Instead, use firm, assertive language to state your position. Even if you are not ready to make a decision, explain this clearly to others (for example, "From the data I have, I am not comfortable making a decision at this time.").

- Listen carefully to reactions from others. Acknowledge their points of view and, when possible, incorporate them into your thinking or plans.

- Make an effort to help others see the issue from your point of view.

- Focus simultaneously on the stand you are taking and on trying to resolve the problem cooperatively whenever possible.

- Before you take a stand, decide how strongly and for how long you are willing to push or stand firm. What is your bottom line? How can you compromise? Then, pay attention to the impact of your behavior so you can accurately monitor its effect on others.

- Follow issues through to completion. Persisting at problem solving sends a strong message that you want issues resolved as quickly as possible and that you are willing to do what is necessary to bring problems to closure.

- Be gracious whether your ideas are accepted or rejected.

- When people ask you to be their advocate or to take a stand on a particular issue, listen carefully. Decide what you will do, and then get back to the person with the results. If you disagree with the request and cannot give your support, clearly explain your rationale.

Confront problems promptly

When important individual or team issues come to your attention, it is critical to respond quickly. Addressing problems keeps them from growing and conveys the message to your team that you are willing to tackle tough issues. To ensure that you confront problems in a timely way, try these suggestions:

- When you learn of an issue that has the potential to affect your group, take steps to look into it as quickly as possible. The steps may consist of informal meetings with others affected by the issue or a more formal investigation of the problem.

- If others come to you with a problem, let them know what you plan to do. If you say nothing, they may conclude that you are not concerned or are afraid to address the problem.

- Set goals for solving the problem. For example, set deadlines for investigating the issue and implementing the solution. Record these milestones on your calendar and adhere to them as closely as possible.

- Hold periodic update meetings as a way to catch problems before they get too big. Listen for information suggesting that people are having a hard time getting support and resources, and take steps to resolve these problems.

- If a problem recurs, it's likely that the root cause has not yet been addressed. If you find yourself dealing with the same problem over and over, take the time to determine what solutions have not worked in the past and why, and what could be done to solve the issue permanently.

- If you procrastinate on certain issues, identify the reasons for your reluctance to move more quickly. People procrastinate for a variety of reasons, including:
  - Lack of information
  - Unclear course of action
  - Lack of time to think through the issue
  - Fear of the negative consequences of acting on the problem

- Once you have identified your reasons for procrastinating, substitute decisive behaviors for indecisive ones. For example, if you lack information, quickly begin steps to get the information you need. If the course of action is unclear, get input from others on possible action steps and make a decision about how to proceed.

- Deal with people problems when they occur. Managers lose the respect of their peers and employees when they don't deal with people who are negatively affecting the team's success or morale.

Address prejudice in yourself

Prejudgments cause people to see others and interpret their behavior through a framework that does not allow them to get to know the individual. Such prejudging can inadvertently restrict the opportunities a manager gives someone.

For example, you might assume that a 55-year-old, long-term employee would not be interested in an overseas assignment that would uproot him or her at this point in his or her career. Or, you may view a male employee's request to leave work in time to pick up his children from daycare as a sign that he either is not career-minded or is an unusually caring parent.

Take the lead in examining your prejudgments while challenging others about theirs. The following steps can help you do this:

1. Identify your own prejudgments. You may believe you have none, but that is unlikely. Prejudgments are a shorthand way of thinking and can be based on cultural values, experiences, or stereotypes. They may include beliefs such as:
   - Men are less sensitive and less considerate than women.
   - Accountants are "bean counters" who can't see beyond numbers.
   - French people are arrogant.
   - System analysts can't communicate their work clearly to others.
   - Black people are good athletes.
   - Older workers have a hard time learning new technologies and don't want to.
   - Gay people are very neat.
   - Women are less committed to their business careers than men.
   - Japanese people aren't creative.
   - Immigrants rely on free benefits.

2. Become aware of your prejudgments by listening to feedback from others, through diversity training, or simply by questioning your own assumptions.

Notice the impact your behavior has on others. Do you:
- Have higher career aspirations for your male employees than for your female employees?
- Give less feedback to people of a different race for fear of being accused of racism or discrimination?
- Shy away from talking with employees who do not speak your language well?

3. Challenge your prejudgments. Take the time to get to know people. Work to eliminate the prejudgments that are hurtful and unfair to others.

4. Model behavior that is inclusive, respectful, and not prejudging. By including a wide variety of people in your world, you can more easily serve as a model to others.

Address prejudice and intolerant behavior in others

As a manager, you have the opportunity and responsibility to take the lead in defining what behavior is acceptable in the workplace. Your actions to discourage and refuse to accept racist, sexist, ethnocentric, and other insensitive comments and behaviors that attack the self-respect of others will strongly influence the conduct of your group. So challenge other people's prejudgments. Nurture respect and interpersonal sensitivity.

At times, it can be difficult for people to directly confront prejudicial behavior, particularly if they are part of the group being put down, for fear of being regarded as too sensitive. Others hope that if they ignore the behavior, it will go away. Such behavior usually does not go away, and people continue to be hurt, embarrassed, or alienated. Still others will agree with those who make the comments, not realizing the damage they do.

Recognize the difference between expressions of differing beliefs or opinions and deliberately hurtful comments or "humorous" sarcasm that is damaging to others. The following suggestions can help you address such behavior:

- When someone makes an offensive remark, simply say, "That comment is an insult to others. It's not appropriate," or "Comments like that are not welcome here." Then change the subject. This approach communicates that prejudiced or intolerant remarks are not welcome.

- If the person defends his or her behavior, simply reassert its inappropriateness. Your goal is not to humiliate the person, but to stop the comments.

- If the comments continue or form a consistent pattern of behavior, treat the behavior as an on-the-job performance issue. Follow your organization's disciplinary procedures.

- Realize that more controversial subjects will be more difficult (and more important) to speak out on. Demonstrate your leadership by clearly refusing to tolerate labeling and other prejudicial behavior.

Act decisively

Indecisiveness may result in the perception that you cannot make tough choices or take a stand on issues. Use the following process to help increase your decisiveness:

1. List the major areas in which you have decision-making responsibility (for instance, capital expenditures, staffing, delegating, and policy making).

2. Identify the areas in which you tend to divert responsibility for decision making.

3. Analyze your concerns about making the decision. Find common patterns. For example, you may be uncomfortable making decisions involving technical areas with which you are unfamiliar, or you may delay making decisions on issues important to your manager.

Would I characterize myself as decisive? I'm not sure...I'd like to think about it.

4. Consider whether any of the following indecisive behaviors applies to you. Then try the suggested action to become more decisive.
   - If you have difficulty determining which of several alternatives is best, don't go to others for a decision. Instead, force yourself to choose one of the options and develop a rationale for why that alternative is best. Only then should you seek input. Tell others the alternatives you've identified and your recommendation, and then ask for their opinions.
   - If you turn to others immediately, before you've formulated options, ask yourself why. Do you need more information? If so, gather the facts you need and formulate alternatives on your own.
   - If you tend to procrastinate on deadlines, commit to arrive at a major decision by a certain date. For minor decisions, make your judgments within a few minutes.
   - If you have a tendency to second-guess yourself, stand by your decision once you have made it. Avoid reopening the decision-making process unless new information strongly indicates a need for reconsideration.
   - If you tend to push your decision-making responsibilities upward, get into the habit of presenting recommendations, rather than problems, to your manager.
   - If others see you as indecisive because you use tentative language when describing your ideas, tape-record yourself as you state your decisions and/or get feedback from others on the style you use to communicate your ideas.

- If you have lost touch with what is important to you, ask yourself, "What is most important to me in this situation? What do I care about the most?" The answers may lead you to your decision.
- If you are concerned that taking a stand will cause others to dislike you, remind yourself that it is impossible for everyone to like you, and that even if people don't like you, they may like your ideas. Likewise, accept that when people reject your ideas, they are not rejecting you.
- If you look for approval before implementing your decisions, ask yourself whether this approval is really necessary. Constantly seeking approval can give others the impression that you lack confidence. If you are unclear about when you can make decisions independently, meet with your manager to discuss your span of control—where you can make decisions independently and where you need to seek approval.

Challenge others to make tough choices

As employees grow in capability and responsibility, they encounter situations in which they must make difficult decisions. Sometimes they turn to their manager to make these types of decisions for them. To help your employees develop confidence in their ability to make tough decisions, try the following suggestions:

- Resist taking responsibility for your employees' decisions. In areas that are clearly their domain, lend your expertise, but stop short of making the decision for them. By coaching people to take responsibility, you are building their skills and helping them to rely less on you.

- The amount of guidance you give your employees will depend on their individual expertise and experience. Gauge your coaching appropriately —provide more for less-experienced people, and less for those who have been on the job longer.

- Recognize your employees' independent decision making and initiative. Even when they make poor decisions, take time to applaud their initiative. Then talk through what went wrong and suggest ways to do it differently in the future.

- Model risk taking. When appropriate, talk through problems with your employees and describe how you arrived at your decision. Discuss the risks involved and the issues you considered in deciding to make the tough decision.

RESOURCES

The resources for this chapter begin on page 654.

LEADERSHIP FACTOR

Today's leaders are faced with an increasingly more complex workforce. In the past, leaders could simply demand performance. This is no longer the case. Matrixed organizations, sophisticated technology, a changing workforce, and stiff competition in the business environment and labor market now require leaders to quickly adapt their style and decisions to the situation at hand.

Consequently, successful managers now need a myriad of skills to lead effectively. They need to begin with a common vision, know when and how to assemble teams to solve problems, select and develop the right people for team and individual assignments, and influence others at all levels of the organization.

The chapters in this Leadership Section address the following five broad areas of leadership skills identified as essential to managerial success:

Chapter 18 – Influence Others: Understands the agendas and perspectives of others; presents a compelling case for proposals and ideas; wins support from others; is assertive and holds firm when necessary; negotiates persuasively.

Chapter 19 – Build Talent Pools: Recruits, attracts, and selects the right people, interviews effectively, provides effective orientation and training for new employees; builds a team with complementary strengths; grooms high-potential performers; anticipates long-term staffing problems.

Chapter 20 – Coach and Develop People: Creates an effective learning environment by creating coaching partnerships with employees; helps others understand their "skills portfolio"; creates joint development and coaching plans; orchestrates learning opportunities; provides relevant, high-impact feedback; is an effective role model for development.

Chapter 21 – Engage and Inspire People: Creates and communicates a vision aligned with the direction of the organization; clarifies others' roles and responsibilities; inspires a sense of personal ownership and commitment to work; creates a high-performance work environment; recognizes the achievements of others.

Chapter 22 – Foster Collaboration: Builds a team environment based on shared values; knows when and how to use a team approach for solving problems; effectively facilitates the group process; values the contributions of all team members; fosters give-and-take relationships; works to remove barriers to collaboration; shares credit with others.

18
INFLUENCE
OTHERS

PART 1: BE CLEAR ABOUT YOUR PURPOSE
- *Make your position known and ask for what you want*
- *Present a logical and compelling case for your position*
- *Get your ideas heard in a group*
- *Hold firm to your position when necessary*

PART 2: BE PROACTIVE AND ESTABLISH SUPPORT
FOR YOUR OBJECTIVE
- *Build a foundation for influence before you need it*
- *Generate enthusiasm for your ideas*
- *Win support from others*
- *Build coalitions or alliances to garner support for ideas*
- *Influence decisions of higher-level stakeholders*

PART 3: BE CLEAR ABOUT THE OTHER PERSON'S
PURPOSE AND VALUES
- *Anticipate reactions or positions of other interested people*
- *Understand the perspectives and agendas of others*

PART 4: FIND AN AGREEABLE EXCHANGE OR
WIN/WIN OUTCOME
- *Ensure that your own position addresses other people's needs and priorities*
- *Negotiate persuasively*

INTRODUCTION

Leadership has taken on new meaning and greater challenges in the last decades. Influencing is a critical skill in today's environment, one in which you must work with a multitude of people to do your job. No longer can you order things to be done; no longer are problems so simple that everyone agrees on one solution.

Looking further into the 21st century, it appears that leaders in business and industry will continue to encounter situations that will demand increasingly sophisticated skills to get other people to endorse their initiatives. Influencing skills, then, will continue to be critical management assets.

To influence effectively, it is most important to acknowledge your own purpose, clearly understand and recognize the values and purposes of others, and be determined to find an agreeable exchange or a "win/win" outcome. You will need to be proactive and skilled at winning support for your ideas.

This chapter presents suggestions for developing your influencing skills to meet leadership challenges now and in the future.

VALUABLE TIPS

- Use a variety of techniques to influence others. Consider as many ways as possible to influence a particular person and then tailor your approach specifically to him or her.

- Observe people in your organization who are highly influential and try out their techniques that best fit with your own style.

- Ask your peers for feedback on how persuasive and influential you are. Ask for suggestions on how you could become more influential.

- Seek assignments that require you to lead without formal authority. Staff assignments are particularly useful for this. This will especially help if you usually have line authority.

- Have regular, informal conversations with your staff, your peers, and your manager about their goals and concerns. Then seek ways to link your ideas to their needs.

- If you usually let others take the lead, be one of the first people to offer ideas in meetings.

- Ask yourself regularly how your goals and ideas fit into the broader goals of the organization, and communicate this to others.

- Be proactive. Show interest in the ideas, goals, and concerns of the people you work with before you need something from them.

- Don't back down quickly when challenged. Instead, restate your position clearly to ensure that others understand your perspective.

- Prepare for your next meeting by looking over the agenda and thinking about the contributions you want to make.

- Practice being more vocal and persuasive in situations such as community meetings where the costs, risks, and implications may not be as great as they are at work.

- When you think you may have to compromise on your agenda, classify your issues into "can drop," "nice to have," and "must have" categories. This will give you some flexibility for negotiation.

- To understand other people's perspectives, set aside your own agenda and listen to their ideas and rationales.

- When faced with possible resistance, consider preselling your agenda to a couple of key players.

- Analyze the costs of pushing your agenda to the exclusion of others' agendas: If you "win" this time, will you receive cooperation from the "losers" in the future?

- Learn to recognize when others are resisting your agenda by observing both their verbal and nonverbal behaviors.

- Be willing to discuss and accept the pros in the opposing viewpoint and the cons in yours.

- Think about your audience's needs, concerns, and perspectives. Consider how people are likely to react to your message and, whenever possible, position your message in a way that appeals to them and avoids strong negative reaction.

- Make a list of where key players stand on particular issues for future reference.

- Before presenting a new idea or action plan, list the people whose support you will need. Attempt to discover where each person stands in relation to your proposal—pro, con, or neutral—and formulate a plan to handle each.

PART 1:
BE CLEAR ABOUT YOUR PURPOSE

Make your position known and ask for what you want

The ability and confidence to present your point of view respectfully, even if you believe that others will disagree, is critical if you want to have impact. Often, getting your idea or request accepted is as simple as asserting yourself enough to ask for what you want. Effective managers are direct about what they need to do their jobs well. To be clear and direct about your purpose, try these suggestions:

- First, be clear about what it is you really want to ensure that you get the outcome you desire.

  For example, a manager tells two staff members to stop fighting with each other. He tells them to get along, and that he wants to see no more conflict. Now, even though they are interdependent coworkers, these two will never speak to each other. There is no more conflict. The manager got exactly what he asked for. He was successful in influencing their behavior, but he did not get what he really wanted.

- If you sometimes have a hard time speaking up because you aren't sure how to phrase your message, use the following technique to help you frame a strong, direct message:

  1. *State your observations first.* Observations are facts, things that can be seen, heard, or taken in through your senses. Observations differ from opinions in that opinions are your perspectives or beliefs. For example, "You were 15 minutes late for our meeting" is a fact. "You were inconsiderate in coming in late" is an opinion. Facts are objective, cannot be argued, and help the other person understand what you are saying.

  2. *Then, state your thoughts and feelings about the situation.* Begin each of these statements with "I" to indicate that they are your thoughts and your feelings. For example, "I was frustrated when you were late because it resulted in 15 minutes of unproductive time for the group members. It makes me wonder if our time and this project are important to you."

  3. *Finally, state what you want the other person to do.* Make statements about your needs, rather than solutions. Stating needs opens the door to generating alternative solutions. Stating solutions can close that door. For example, "I would like you to be on time for meetings" is a statement of needs. In contrast, "I will call you five minutes before meetings start to make sure you will be on time" states a solution. The first statement can naturally lead to a discussion of options for how to meet the need, while the second statement closes off discussion of other options and places the responsibility for the problem on you.

- When sharing your ideas or making a request, use the appropriate nonverbal communication to deliver an effective message. For example, maintain steady eye contact, a serious expression, firm voice, and moderate rate of speech. Avoid aggressive gestures or a rigid posture.

- Practice putting together clear, confident messages before delivering them to others. Role-play them in your mind or actively practice by saying them aloud to yourself or to a trusted colleague.

- Listen carefully to the other person's response to your message. He or she may not be pleased with what you have to say, and it is important for you to hear the other person out. Check Chapter 28: Listen to Others in this handbook for some good tips on how to do this more effectively.

- If you have been shaken or surprised about something, it may be better to remove yourself from the situation for a time. Calm down so you can express yourself more clearly with control of your intended message.

- Ask for feedback about when you are being appropriately persuasive versus pushy or aggressive. Some people are reluctant to ask for what they need or to attempt to influence a decision because they perceive their behavior as aggressive, when in fact others do not.

Present a logical and compelling case for your position

Different things persuade different people. Many people are impressed by a strong, logical argument, while others can be swayed by a vigorous, impassioned personal appeal. To be most compelling, adapt your persuasive style to suit the audience, whether your audience is one person or a large group. The following suggestions can help:

1. Before presenting your ideas, know the audience or the person.
   - What is important to your audience or the person? What are their main concerns about your message?
   - How will your message benefit them? What will they get out of accepting your ideas?
   - Speak with some of the people who will be key to getting your ideas accepted. Get their input on how to approach others from whom you need support.

2. Prepare beforehand. Jot down the three most important points you want to make. Assemble any data that support those points. Be sure to include information that addresses the concerns you uncovered during the investigation process.

3. Take time to think through each of the points you want to make and plan a logical progression of ideas that are easy for your audience to follow. In general, the simpler you can make the message, the better; you can always add in more detail as questions arise.

4. Give a brief synopsis of the information you will be discussing before you actually present your ideas. For example, "I've asked everyone to meet today to talk about next year's marketing strategy. I have three ideas I wish to share, and then I would be interested in getting your input."

5. When delivering your ideas, pay attention to the reaction of your audience. Do they appear engaged? Are they asking questions? Look for signs that they are interested in what you are saying and want to know more.

It's important not only to present the facts, but also to give your perspective on why you believe your ideas are valid. Refer to your beliefs, but also to the concerns of the audience; clearly relate the benefits of your proposal to their concerns.

Get your ideas heard in a group

Group situations are an excellent opportunity for you to get your best ideas heard and to have an impact on a large number of people. Take advantage of these opportunities by trying the following:

- Increase the level of your contributions in groups by making suggestions and asking clarifying questions more often.

- In addition to speaking up more often, demonstrate enthusiasm and confidence when stating your opinions. Don't hesitate to voice your thoughts or to label them as your own. Find ways to ensure that other group members take your contributions seriously and consider them when making decisions.

- Use effective eye contact and speak to all individuals in the group.

- Increase your impact by preparing for meetings beforehand. Having the information you need available, and taking time to consider the shared values of the group, will help you be more confident and persuasive when stating your opinions.

- Summarize positions frequently to build understanding.

- Look for opportunities to lead groups. Volunteer to lead a task force or project group, and try some new techniques to increase your impact. To get a feel for how effective your techniques are, ask people in the group for feedback.

Hold firm to your position when necessary

In order to be influential in your organization, you don't want to be seen either as a pushover or as stubborn and inflexible. It will always be important to pick your battles carefully. In some situations, you will need to maintain your position against the attempts to sway you.

When necessary, use the following suggestions to help you hold firm:

- When you run up against resistance, don't give in. Find out about the other person's concerns. To discover any potential misunderstandings, you may want to ask the other person to explain your viewpoint, while you offer to explain his or hers. Try restating your main points to check that you are being understood.

- After you have done all you can to understand any opposing viewpoints, you will likely want to hold firm when:
  - You believe that acquiescing would result in an action that is unethical, unsafe, illegal, or entirely inappropriate in the workplace.
  - You are convinced that any other decision would be harmful to the organization, your team, your customers, or the quality of your product.
  - You feel that all the essential facts or input needed to do otherwise are either not available or have not yet been presented.
  - You know that it would be unfair to any or all the stakeholders involved to not provide them equal representation or compensation.
  - You believe it would be too inconsistent with policy decisions made in the past.

  For example, Lucy has traditionally held her staff members accountable to a specified performance standard and believes in remaining consistent. One of the supervisors she manages believes Joe's situation has extenuating circumstance and he should not be held to the same standard. Lucy does not believe the situation with Joe warrants an exception. In fact, she believes it would serve to demotivate and disgruntle the others on the team.

When you have decided to stand your ground:

- If you are in the position of authority: Be clear in your message that this is your final decision on this matter. Do not leave others with the impression that you are still open to further discussion. Note also that you can lose integrity if you say this is your final decision and then back down later.

- If you are not the one with the authority to make the final decision: Be clear in your message that while you still disagree with this approach, you will do what you can to make it work; or in cases involving ethical or legal infractions, you may need to be clear that you will not go along, no matter what the consequence.

- If you reach an impasse with a peer, suggest that you bring in a third party to give input, add another perspective, and help mediate.

- Make sure your tone of voice and nonverbal messages match what you are saying.

- If the decision can wait, suggest that you table it for a time. The situation might change, more information may come to light, or alternatives may surface that none of you had thought of.

PART 2:
BE PROACTIVE AND ESTABLISH SUPPORT FOR YOUR OBJECTIVE

Build a foundation for influence before you need it

Having a good reputation with your coworkers can have endless advantages. It makes influencing others much easier. If you have a track record of being right, helping others when possible, and doing your fair share to give and take in conflict situations, it will improve your ability to influence others. To build such a foundation, consider the following suggestions:

- Be proactive. Don't wait until you need something from the people you work with to show an interest in their ideas, goals, and concerns. Take a genuine interest in them now.

- Make the effort to build all-around positive relationships with the people you work with. Start by reviewing Chapter 23: Build Relationships in this handbook.

- Do what you can to help out. If you are willing to pitch in and help when others need it, they will be more open to your ideas, needs, and requests in the future.

- Be respectful and supportive of other people's ideas and concerns. Don't be afraid to disagree, but when you do, disagree respectfully, and you will be much more likely to enjoy their respect and support in the future.

- While having someone "owe you big" could actually be detrimental to your relationship (because they may feel awkward and intentionally avoid you), doing small favors for peers, managers, and staff members can work in your favor during future decisions and negotiations.

- Act with integrity and work to earn the trust of your colleagues. For example, if you respect confidentiality and follow through on commitments, people will be more likely to take your word and trust that your initiatives will reflect their best interests as well as yours. Review Chapter 30: Inspire Trust in this handbook for more information on gaining trust at work.

Generate enthusiasm for your ideas

To generate enthusiasm for your idea, the first thing you need to do is to display enthusiasm yourself. If you are not obviously enthusiastic and energized, no one else will be either. To show your enthusiasm:

- Talk about your idea. Show your excitement by talking about all the benefits that will result from it now and in the future. Talk about how you see it connecting to other initiatives, both present and future.

- Think of yourself as painting a vision in people's minds of how great things will be when your idea becomes reality. Know and be able to describe what will be different when the results of your suggestion or request play out. What will it look like? What will be better?

- Don't get bogged down explaining too much detail. It is easy to lose the momentum and energy in your argument if you let that happen. Keep the conversation at a level that you find energizing and exciting. Use minute details of the plan only as needed to answer specific questions, and even then try to be creative and fresh at the detail level.

- Use nonverbal communication that is consistent with enthusiasm. Speak just a little faster and louder than your usual tone, smile more, and use more gestures as you talk about your idea. Let your genuine enthusiasm for the idea show through. This is not the time to try to hold back your passion in order to appear more cool, calm, and controlled.

- If you are not one who exudes enthusiasm naturally or easily, do so with the word choices you make. Say you are excited about the proposal. Use words that are more dramatic, powerful, or sensational than you would generally use, but that express your genuine enthusiasm for the idea.

Finding common ground among all interested parties and connecting shared values to your proposal can take you a long way toward gaining consensus.

To generate enthusiasm for your ideas by tapping into shared values, use the following process:

1. Before you present your position, ask yourself how your idea connects with your organization's stated values, purpose, mission, and vision. How does it fit with the values and purpose actually practiced, if these are different from what is officially stated?

2. Think specifically about your current audience. What do they value most as individuals or as a group? What do they see as their purpose? What excites them about their work?

   Is there a high value placed on developing their staff for purposes of retention and/or state-of-the-art expertise? Do they feel more strongly about delivering superior product quality and/or creating unprecedented customer satisfaction and loyalty? Is there a strong, shared value for connecting with the local community and/or becoming more global? How much do they value innovation, creativity, or perhaps crushing the competition?

3. Once you have identified these shared values, find ways to clearly make connections between them and your ideas or proposals.

Win support from others

Gaining support from others is a skill that can take time and practice to hone. Good ideas are often not enough to get others to accept your point of view.

If you find that you don't get support for your ideas as often as you'd like, try the following:

- Ask someone you trust in your organization to give you input on your ability to be persuasive. Have this person watch you in situations where you are attempting to gain others' support. Get feedback on how you came across and what you could have done differently.

- If you feel comfortable, ask for feedback from the people who did not give you their support. What were their concerns? What could you have done that would have swayed them?

- Observe a person in your organization who seems particularly skilled at gaining agreement from others. What techniques does this person use? What does this person do if he or she runs into roadblocks? How does this person state his or her argument? What in particular appeals to you when you listen to this person?

- Incorporate some of the most effective techniques you've observed into your influencing efforts and see how they work for you. Take care, however, not to choose a manner so far out of character for you that you won't be able to deliver it effectively. Not all techniques work for all people.

- Before presenting your idea, explain it to a few trusted colleagues. Get their input on its feasibility, and encourage them to challenge you on the various aspects of the idea. Use this information to analyze parts of the process you might not have considered.

- Be aware that your speaking style directly affects how convincing you can be. Record yourself as you practice presenting your idea and analyze how you sound. Ask yourself the following questions:
  - Are my tone of voice and inflection consistent with the meaning of my words and the intention of my message?
  - Does the pace of my speech facilitate understanding?
  - Is the level of my enthusiasm and liveliness appropriate for the topic and setting?
  - Do I express myself in language that is clear enough for others to easily understand what I'm saying?

- If you want others to support your efforts, reciprocate by supporting their ideas and objectives whenever possible.

Build coalitions or alliances to garner support for ideas

Depending on the scope of the issue being addressed and the variety of stakeholders involved, it may be beneficial or necessary to build alliances within or across workgroups or functional areas—even across organizations—to obtain the level of influence needed to win support for a particular proposal. Each member can have his or her own reason for supporting the common objective, but a demonstration of unity and numbers can be very persuasive.

While this approach can get quite complex, here is a process you can use to help create alliances:

1. Approach the people who are advocating for an idea that you also support and suggest to them that you join forces. Indicate ways you could contribute to their cause.

2. Together, brainstorm to think of others who could benefit from this proposal, and set up meetings with those individuals or groups. Think beyond your immediate work environment to the larger system in which your work takes place. How would this proposal affect people in other functional areas who contribute to the same core business processes you do? How would it affect your internal and external customers and suppliers? How would it affect sales processes?

3. Use your influencing skills to clearly present the proposal and specify the benefits in it for them. Ask them to be part of this joint effort, and together devise a plan for how each party can contribute. As each new member or group joins the alliance, ask for suggestions of others who may benefit and wish to be included.

4. Organize a way to jointly present your proposal to the audience you need to influence. You may choose to present as a group or send representatives from each faction in the coalition.

5. Be sure to clarify the benefits your idea would provide your audience and the organization as a whole. Also be prepared to address their concerns.

Influence decisions of higher-level stakeholders

For many managers, one of the most important areas in which to focus influencing efforts is higher-level management. The ability to win the interest and support of your manager and his or her peers is a critical skill to have. To do so, follow these guidelines:

- When you propose an action to upper management, be clear about how it will benefit the organization—for example, explain how your idea will help solve a problem, cut costs, increase return on investment (ROI), decrease turnover, and so forth.

- When you see that a decision from higher-level management might have a negative impact on your area, let your manager know. Clearly state the impact the decision will have by citing tangible consequences.

- Watch what is important to upper management. Look for ways to spot opportunities important to the company. Strategize with your manager.

- Meet with your manager periodically to let him or her know what you are doing, and to hear about issues that concern upper management.

- Use time wisely. Especially when you meet with higher-level managers who are or see themselves as quite busy, keep your explanations brief and focused. Don't burden them with details they do not need, decisions you can make, or problems you can solve. Instead, provide your manager periodic, condensed updates on your workgroups' activities.

- Find a mentor higher up in the organization who can help you think through your attempt to influence those with more authority than you. A mentor may have insights about norms or general techniques, as well as suggest tactics specific to certain individuals you will encounter. He or she may also connect you to networks that would be otherwise closed to you.

- Be willing to make concessions when appropriate. People's trust in you is enhanced when your motives are directed at benefiting the entire organization, not just your own area. Your manager will be more willing to give you what you want if he or she sees that you have a balanced perspective about what is best for your area and what is best for the company.

PART 3:
BE CLEAR ABOUT THE OTHER PERSON'S PURPOSE AND VALUES

Anticipate reactions or positions of other interested people

Knowing in advance how people are likely to respond to your proposal or idea is often key to influencing them successfully. Being prepared for reactions or resistance ensures a stronger presentation and defense of your position. For example, if you know that your manager feels strongly about a particular topic, you can present ideas in a way that shows their alignment with your manager's position.

Accurately anticipating other people's reactions shows your respect for them and allows you more flexibility. The following methods can help you anticipate other players' strongly held opinions or likely reactions:

- Regularly discuss general positions on work-related topics with your colleagues. Invite others to lunch or coffee break for this purpose.

- Keep a journal of what you learn so you can remember where others stand on particular issues, what their needs, goals, and agendas are, and so forth.

- Before presenting a new idea or action plan, make a list of the people to whom you will be submitting your proposal.

- Use a grid like the one below to determine where each person is likely to stand in relation to your proposal or agenda. For each person who you think is likely to block your objectives, briefly indicate why.

SUPPORT	BLOCK	NEUTRAL

- Determine whose support you absolutely need to have. Talk with others or review your past experience with these people to determine what you need to do to win them over.

- Identify peers or higher-level managers who seem knowledgeable about others' positions. Watch them closely, noting the methods they use to answer objections or questions. Incorporate these methods into your next presentation.

- Ask for feedback from the people you have chosen as models, as well as from the people involved.

Understand the perspectives and agendas of others

The meeting has already gone an hour over its scheduled time. The participants are restless, eager to close the discussion, make a decision, and leave. But John Smith refuses to end the discussion until he has restated his position at least five more times. By now, everyone else has identified the areas of agreement and disagreement and is ready to tackle the problems. If John had only taken a few minutes to really listen, instead of relentlessly promoting his own agenda, he might have realized an hour ago that no one was arguing his main points. The participants could have hammered out an agenda that everyone could at least live with.

Sound familiar? John Smiths abound in the corporate world, wasting time arguing moot points, obstructing processes, and alienating themselves from their colleagues. By taking time to understand other people's agendas and perspectives, John could have increased his effectiveness on the job and gained the respect of his peers and higher-level managers.

Demonstrating your willingness to look at all sides of an issue and to arrive at goals that are mutually beneficial can increase your chances of achieving personal, group, and organizational goals.

The following suggestions can help you learn to see others' viewpoints and establish mutually beneficial goals:

- Ask each interested person or stakeholder to list what he or she wants to accomplish during a given meeting, project, etc. Pool the lists, identify similar objectives, and commit to work on resolving areas of difference.

- Listen carefully to the other person's presentation and/or explanation of his or her position or agenda. Ask as many clarifying questions as needed to ensure understanding. Make sure you would be able to clearly explain the other person's position to an uninvolved third party before assuming that you completely understand his or her issues.

- Set aside your own agenda long enough to really listen to the other people's ideas and understand their rationales. You may discover that your positions aren't so far apart after all.

- For more tips on how to listen effectively, review Chapter 28: Listen to Others in this handbook.

- Be flexible. Realize that every situation is different, and every group has different dynamics.

- Commit to the substantial mental effort it will take to push your own opinions and goals aside in order to allow your interest and curiosity to be sparked by other perspectives.

- To air everyone's ideas, use a roundtable discussion in which:
  1. Someone first clearly explains the process and gets agreement from all others.
  2. Then one person shares his or her ideas and answers questions for clarification only; no criticisms or arguments are allowed.
  3. When all questions have been answered, the next person shares his or her ideas, and so on.
  4. Disagreements or modifications can be discussed only after everyone has shared ideas and answered clarifying questions.

  This process can be very effective in a two- or three-person conversation, as well as with a larger group.

- As you learn relevant information you had not considered, modify your position or proposal accordingly.

PART 4:
FIND AN AGREEABLE EXCHANGE OR WIN/WIN OUTCOME

Ensure that your own position addresses other people's needs and priorities

A win/win outcome for all stakeholders can be the goal of each influencing situation. Intentional influencing does not have to result in winners and losers, or be characterized as manipulation, conflict, or competition. Paying close attention to the needs and goals of current stakeholders is also the best way to build support for your future ideas and proposals, as well as foster consideration for your needs in future proposals by others.

To ensure that you are addressing other people's concerns in your proposals, use the following suggestions:

- Think of all the people your proposal would affect. Think beyond the most obvious people and about people in the larger system that your work is a part of.

- Consider the concerns these people might have if your idea were to be implemented or your request approved. Ask for their thoughts. Listen carefully to their responses, and answer their questions. Adjust your proposal accordingly as you hear things you had not considered.

- If what you are proposing will cause problems for others, consider asking these questions:
  - Why is it a problem? What could be done to alleviate that problem?
  - What would make the extra trouble worth it to them in the end? Is there something more important to them, even unrelated, that could be offered in exchange; something that would allow them to also walk away a "winner"?

- Offer something of value in exchange. Influence gained by exchange is a process of give and take that allows the act of influencing to be fully cooperative rather than adversarial. Once you have assessed your counterparts' interests and needs, examine your own resources to find something you can offer. What you offer should be of at least equal value to them as what you are asking of them. If your offer is agreeable to them, everyone wins.
  - Do a thorough assessment of your influencing capability in terms of exchange. What kinds of things can you legitimately offer that others may value? What can you offer to someone who values power, or someone who values recognition, or money, fame, opportunity, learning, inclusion, and so forth?

Examples of potential items for exchange can cover a large range. Some examples might be: the use of equipment or personnel to help with a particular project, access to information, active support for an idea or request, public praise, genuine appreciation, or the promise of returning the favor at some time in the future.

These kinds of exchanges can work successfully between people at different or equal levels in the organization.

For more information about using exchange as a method for influence, read Cohen & Bradford's classic book, *Influence Without Authority* (John Wiley & Sons, 1991).

Negotiate persuasively

Effective negotiation depends on a number of factors: preparation, knowledge of the other person's position and needs, and creativity in coming up with alternative solutions, to name just a few. One key to becoming a persuasive negotiator is to clearly specify how your objectives will benefit the other party or parties involved. The following techniques can help you improve your negotiation skills:

I'M NOT SURE IT'S A GOOD IDEA TO WAVE THAT DURING THE NEGOTIATING PROCESS.

- Before going into a session where you will be presenting your point of view, spend some time thinking about and investigating the other person's position and needs. What is important to them? What are their goals? What can you do for them? The answers to these kinds of questions will give you the information you need to frame your argument during the discussion.

- Before presenting your case, take the time to examine the pros and cons of both arguments. Too often in the attempt to persuade, a typical conversation involves one person arguing the advantages of their own position and the disadvantages of the alternative. The second person argues the merits of their own view and the flaws of the other. They inevitably get nowhere because they are simply not communicating. Be willing and prepared to discuss and accept both the pros of their argument and the cons of yours. Use the chart below to assist you in assessing all positions:

	POSITIVES (PROS)	NEGATIVES (CONS)
POSITION A	• •	• •
POSITION B	• •	• •
POSITION C	• •	• •
ETC.	• •	• •

- Talk with others who have dealt with the people with whom you will be negotiating. Find out what has and has not worked in the past.

- Identify someone in your organization who is skilled at getting others to go along with his or her initiatives. Observe this person and, if possible, meet to discuss how he or she approaches negotiation and what you can do to improve your techniques.

- Know what you want from three perspectives:
  - What is absolutely necessary
  - What is ideal
  - What you would be willing to give up

- Go in with the perspective that the other side is your ally rather than your enemy. Thinking about dealing with an ally can help you look for solutions that benefit both of you.

- While in the negotiation meeting, listen carefully to what the other person is saying. Try to discern the needs behind the requests they make. If you successfully identify their needs, you can better generate a number of alternatives from which you both can benefit.

  For example, if your colleague wants an extension on a deadline, work with him or her to figure out what needs would be served by extending the deadline (for instance, the need for more inspection of the product, the need to support other projects at the same time). Once you have identified the needs, generate alternative strategies for meeting the needs of both of you, and select the best one.

- Refrain from getting into a "win/lose" discussion where the only alternatives are for one of you to benefit and one of you to lose out. If the discussion reaches that point, note this fact to the others and communicate your desire for both or all of you to get something out of the agreement you reach.

- Be prepared to bargain, barter, and trade to find an agreeable exchange. Think about the resources you have to offer that would be of value to each person or group you want to persuade.

During a negotiation session, use the following guidelines to create the most beneficial outcome:

- Identify the issue or problem in terms of needs, not solutions.

- Maintain the perspective that your power, at a minimum, equals that of the other person. This will help you state your needs more confidently. If you begin to feel overpowered, ask yourself why, and do something to regain power.

- Draw out information from the other person using open-ended questions (questions that call for more than "yes" or "no") to facilitate dialogue.

- If you are presented with new facts, draw out the other person until you have a clear understanding of this information or, if appropriate, postpone the meeting and take time to get up to speed before you meet again.

- Seek common ground. Finding areas of agreement is often the critical first step in achieving win/win outcomes.

- Minimize time pressures. Decreasing the importance of a deadline can give you more power to hold out for what you believe you want/need.

- Avoid becoming overly emotional or defensive.

- Prepare for the possibility that no decision will be reached. Do this by creating a list of actions you can take if you fail to reach agreement.

- Don't be too committed to reaching an agreement quickly. Other alternatives may not be readily apparent.

- Deliver on your commitments.

Be careful not to "burn your bridges." Some people would say that the best outcome of a negotiation session is getting everything they wanted while giving up little or nothing to the other stakeholders. If you succeed at the expense of others, don't be surprised when any future attempts to influence these people fail, or when any of them take advantage of a future opportunity to benefit themselves at your expense.

RESOURCES

The resources for this chapter begin on page 656.

19
BUILD
TALENT POOLS

PART 1: ATTRACT THE RIGHT PEOPLE
- *Attract talented people*
- *Evaluate your recruiting efforts*

PART 2: SELECT THE RIGHT PEOPLE
- *Understand the job*
- *Improve the interviewing process*
- *Use multiple interviewers*
- *Increase your interviewing effectiveness*
- *Avoid common rating errors*

PART 3: STAFF EFFECTIVELY
- *Build a team with complementary strengths*
- *Match individuals to jobs*
- *Anticipate long-term staffing needs*
- *Identify, develop, and retain your high-potential employees*

PART 4: DEPLOY YOUR EMPLOYEES
- *Improve your employee orientation program*
- *Train new employees*

INTRODUCTION

Successful managers often have a knack for selecting and attracting talented individuals to their organization. Your success and the success of your group will depend greatly on the level of talent you are able to maintain within your organization.

You can attract a talented pool of job candidates by establishing your organization as a workplace in which individuals can maximize their skills and abilities with minimal bureaucratic interference. You can then increase your organization's talent level by selecting only individuals from your talent pool who have the knowledge, skills, abilities, and work experience to succeed in your organization.

Remember that staffing is an ongoing process. You must continually mold and groom your new and veteran team members to ensure that your team continues to function effectively over time.

This chapter presents guidelines and suggestions for ways to identify, attract, and select talented individuals for your organization.

VALUABLE TIPS

- Review the channels your organization uses for recruiting, and increase the number if it only uses one or two methods, such as campus recruiting or newspaper advertisements.

- Consider expanding your recruiting methods to include avenues such as Internet job sites, your company's Web site, search firms, and advertising in professional trade journals.

- Ask your employees what Web sites, magazines, radio stations, etc., they frequent to help determine where to expand your recruiting efforts.

- Conduct an informal survey of your top-performing new hires to find out how they heard about their positions. Focus your recruiting activities on those sources that have produced your best employees.

- Identify bottlenecks in your organization's staffing process by talking with some of your recent hires (or candidates who declined a job offer or lost interest in the opening). Learn about their experiences during the staffing process and discuss your findings with your human resources department to determine how you can improve the process.

- Monitor trends in your industry to determine which competencies and knowledge will become increasingly important. Make sure your organization has employees with these competencies by hiring from the outside or training your current employees.

- Clearly communicate the organization's vision and talk with new employees about how they fit into that vision.

- Use intranet technology to support effective recruitment and retention systems. For example, use on-line interview guides to speed up the collection and distribution of interview information to other interviewers or decision makers.

- Determine the composition and content of the workforce that will be required to manage ongoing industry changes.

- Use search firms to supplement your internal resources. Develop specific criteria for selecting a search firm to ensure that the firm's strengths match your needs. For example, one criterion might be the ability to supply the quantity of candidates you need.

- Provide realistic job previews in the form of videotapes, written information, and conversations with incumbents to reduce short-term turnover.

- Develop an employment-focused Web site to broadcast openings to a wider number and different set of potential employees. Include candidate profiling as part of the site to sift through the large numbers of candidates.

- Develop recruitment campaigns and incentives to mobilize the most effective source of recruits for your organization—its current employees. Research indicates that the largest source of recruits is referrals from current employees.

- Encourage, recognize, and reward employees who refer candidates.

- Establish the organization as the employer of choice in the community. Find out what will attract and retain local employees, and then work to provide this and to build community awareness of it.

- Participate in local career, recruitment, and open-house events to foster community identity.

- Create a workforce that is representative of the community in which the organization is located.

- Develop a strategic approach to campus recruiting to both increase the organization's visibility and build long-term relationships with institutions that are a source of candidates for the organization's key staffing needs.

PART 1:
ATTRACT THE RIGHT PEOPLE

Attract talented people

Remember the saying, "You can only be as good as your people." Attracting top-notch talent is essential for organizational success. The supply of and demand for employees vacillates, but successful managers are always scanning the talent landscape to identify individuals who can contribute to their organizations.

Recruiting is not a faucet that can be turned on and off depending on whether you have job openings. If you wait until you have vacancies before you begin to identify high-potential individuals, you may have difficulty finding strong candidates in a timely fashion.

Here are some tips on recruiting and attracting a quality candidate pool:

- Sponsor a conference in your field. Invite bright, effective people to contribute. Get to know them.

- Be proactive as you review unsolicited résumés. If you get résumés that look good, talk to the people that sent them even if you have no opening at the time. If they turn out to be good, keep in touch.

- Identify colleges and universities that produce quality graduates in your field. Build relationships with alumni groups and placement officers at the institutions.

- Actively participate in professional organizations that provide opportunities for you to meet talented professionals.

- Use multiple recruiting sources to help maximize your talent pool. Many employers and hiring managers use only one or two sources (e.g., campus recruiting, newspaper ads) for identifying potential employees.

- Recognize and/or reward your employees for identifying job candidates.

- Increase your organization's visibility as a top employer. People form impressions about companies based in part on their interactions with the organization's products, advertising, employees, and community involvement (e.g., sponsoring a local event). These interactions are an excellent way to demonstrate the organization's values and culture to potential employees.

Evaluate your recruiting efforts

Recruiting plays a significant role in the success of your staffing program. If you are in a position to evaluate the effectiveness of your program, conduct or, if appropriate, ask your human resources department to conduct, the following analysis:

1. Gather the following types of information about the effectiveness of your program:
   - What is the cost per hire? (Find this figure by dividing the cost of each recruiting source by the number of hires. Also, divide the total cost of your entire recruiting program by the total number of hires. This analysis will tell you whether a given source is cost effective.)
   - What is the time lapse from identifying the need for candidates to the hire date? (This analysis will tell you whether your recruiting process is efficient.)
   - How many hires are produced from each source? (This analysis, combined with cost information, will tell you whether a given recruiting source is productive.)

2. Analyze the data you've collected. Establish a rank order of recruiting sources based on each one's overall effectiveness.

3. As a general rule, concentrate your recruitment efforts on the sources that provide the best candidates at the lowest cost in the shortest time. However, for strategically important positions or jobs requiring a unique combination of background and skills, increased recruiting costs can be money well spent.

PART 2:
SELECT THE RIGHT PEOPLE

Understand the job

The key to successfully selecting employees is to understand the content of the job. As the saying goes, "If you don't know what you are looking for, you aren't likely to find it." When you are filling a vacancy, you must understand the knowledge, skills, and abilities required to perform the job. You must also understand industry-wide and organization-specific characteristics and trends that will affect how the job will be performed.

Here are some tips for developing this understanding:

- Obtain a copy of the job description from your human resources department. Job descriptions typically describe the job's basic duties and responsibilities; the knowledge, skills, and abilities required to perform the job; and suggested work experience. Review this description to make sure it accurately reflects the job.

- Review the contextual business factors affecting your work group. Are new technologies, products, and markets emerging in your industry? Will these changes require your employees to have different or more developed competencies in certain areas? Consider these future demands when staffing your work group.

- Know the kinds of employees who are successful in your organization. If you deliberately hire outside the profile of people who usually are successful, be prepared to support the person. Change agents cannot survive without support.

- Be wary of hiring in your own image. Managers tend to hire those who are similar to them, regardless of their qualifications. Do not be unduly influenced by similarities between you and a candidate that are not job-related (e.g., same interests, hobbies, hometown, etc.). For more work-related characteristics, such as education, training, experience, and working style, you may also wish to exercise caution in hiring people who are quite similar to you and your coworkers. A highly homogeneous work group may have limited perspectives and be less successful in dealing with change.

- Hire the best. It sounds obvious, but sometimes managers may, perhaps unconsciously, avoid hiring highly talented, intelligent, motivated employees. The managers may feel threatened that the employees will overshadow them or be difficult to manage.

- Consult with industrial psychologists to help you better understand your jobs. PDI's Strategic Performance Modeling services can help you identify the key competencies and industry factors related to success within your organization.

Improve the interviewing process

Although the interview is often the primary mechanism for obtaining information about applicants, many interviewers spend more time telling applicants about the job than finding out about the applicants. As a result, many interviewers make hiring decisions that are based more on "gut feeling" than on objective data.

The following process will help you obtain better information during the interviewing process:

1. Before you interview, determine the specific requirements of the job to be filled, including the knowledge, skills, and other competencies needed to perform the job effectively.

2. Prepare an interview guide containing questions that you will ask all candidates applying for a position. Research has shown that the use of a standard outline improves the reliability and validity of hiring decisions.

3. Emphasize questions that probe a candidate's past behavior in areas related to the job for which you are interviewing. The best predictor of future performance is past performance in similar positions. Also, recent and long-standing behavior has much greater validity than old and sporadic behavior.

I WANT TO BE OPEN MINDED ABOUT THIS INTERVIEW, SO TRY NOT TO CALL ME "DAD."

Avoid asking questions that are based on hypothetical circumstances, that inquire about the candidate's attitude, or that rely too heavily on the candidate's stated goals; these questions most often generate hypothetical "textbook" answers the candidates know you want to hear. Effective questions include:

- What is the most difficult decision you have made in the last six months?
- Tell me about your most challenging customer-service situation and how you handled it.
- Give me an illustration of the most successful team accomplishment your management team has had, and describe your role in its achievement.

4. Create a comfortable environment for your candidate by being on time, spending a few minutes chatting informally to put the candidate at ease, and avoiding interruptions.

5. Take notes during the interview to make sure you can evaluate the candidate based on facts (rather than unclear recall) when the time comes to make the hiring decision.

6. Try to get additional information about the candidate to confirm your conclusions. Reference checks and the conclusions of other interviewers can substantiate or contradict your own findings. If other interviewers disagree with your conclusions, consult with them and review the data they have collected. You may discover that you have obtained different information.

You may also discover areas in your own questioning that could be improved. PDI's partner ePredix can create customized interview kits or adapt elements from its standard interview kits that will help you select your employees.

Use multiple interviewers

Multiple interviewers help reduce individual biases and neutralize the impact of rating errors. It also makes more efficient use of interviewer time and permits the collection of in-depth information. The following guidelines can help make the multiple-interviewing process more effective:

1. Assign responsibility for coordinating the process to one individual. Typically, this is someone from the human resources department.

2. Give each interviewer a copy of the job description or a list of knowledge, skills, abilities, and other qualifications necessary to perform the job. This will ensure that interviewers know what to look for when they interview.

3. Assign each interviewer different dimensions of the job so that each can focus on a specific area. For example, one person could obtain information on technical skills, another could assess people skills, and a third could investigate project-management skills. Build in some overlap so there is more than one perspective on each skill area.

4. Have each interviewer use a standard outline containing questions that focus on the candidate's past behavior and accomplishments in the area being evaluated. Also, decide which interviewer will tell the applicant about various aspects of the job and organization so interviewers don't repeat or contradict one another.

5. After the interview, have each interviewer rate the candidate on the dimension he or she was assigned.

6. Compare the independent ratings and look for a consensus. If there is a discrepancy among ratings or if the position being filled is very important, have the interviewers get together to discuss the candidate and arrive at a consensus.

Increase your interviewing effectiveness

Interviewing is a skill that improves with practice. Consider the following suggestions to improve your interviewing effectiveness:

• Set a goal of having the applicant do 80 percent of the talking.

• Learn to differentiate good information from "sizzle." Good information usually contains specific behaviors that the candidate has engaged in, while sizzle information sounds good but means little, and serves to falsely inflate your evaluation of a candidate.

• Be comfortable with silence after you have asked a question. This will allow the candidate to think and take initiative.

- Display energy and show enthusiasm for the job for which you are interviewing candidates.

- Videotape yourself doing a practice interview. Watch the tape yourself and with others. Solicit feedback on how you can improve your skills.

Avoid the following ineffective types of questions:

- *Questions that can be answered with "yes" or "no."* These questions begin with "did," "should," "would," "are," "will," etc. Instead, use open-ended questions that start with "what," "how," "give me an example," "describe," etc.

- *Leading questions.* These questions tell candidates what they should have done and are highly prone to falsified responses. For example, a leading question is, "You must have had to put in a lot of extra hours to get everything done on time, huh?" To elicit a more meaningful response, change it to, "What did you do to handle the situation?"

- *Threatening questions.* These questions affix blame onto the candidate and imply that he or she did the wrong thing. For example, the question "Why didn't you just put in some overtime?" may be perceived as threatening. Such questions are likely to put candidates on the defensive, and may inhibit their responses during the rest of the interview.

- *Questions about philosophies, beliefs, and opinions.* An example of such a question is, "In your opinion, what qualities are essential to effective leadership?" Candidates tend to respond to these questions by giving "canned" answers designed to tell you just what you want to hear. This information tends to be misleading and may confound your perception and rating of the candidate. Asking the candidate to describe his or her behaviors in a leadership situation, on the other hand, will tell you more about that person.

- *Run-on or multiple-choice questions.* These questions tend to give the candidate hints about what to say and may be confusing to the person.

Avoid common rating errors

It is human nature to commit the following rating errors when evaluating candidates. Developing an awareness of common rating errors is the first step in avoiding them, and will result in more accurate selection decisions on your part.

- *First-impression effect.* This error occurs when the candidate is evaluated during the first four minutes of the interview. Such an evaluation is based on first impression data (smile, eye contact, handshake, and so forth). This first impression is weighted too heavily and carries into the entire interview.

- *Contrast effect.* This error occurs in comparing two or more candidates. If an interviewer sees a very weak person first, he or she might rate the second candidate, who may be average, higher than average due to the contrast between the first and second candidates.

- *Blind-spot effect.* In this case, an interviewer may not see certain types of deficits because they are just like his or her own. For example, the interviewer who prefers the big picture may not appreciate a detail-oriented person.

- *Halo effect.* The halo effect occurs when a candidate is strong in one dimension, and the interviewer then views him or her as being strong in all dimensions of the evaluation.

- *High-potential effect.* In this situation, the interviewer judges the candidate's credentials, rather than his or her past performance, experience, and other behaviors.

- *Dramatic-incident effect.* Here, the interviewer places too much emphasis on one specific behavior area. One problem may wipe out years of good work in the eyes of the interviewer.

PART 3:
STAFF EFFECTIVELY

Build a team with complementary strengths

Successful teams are made up of members whose strengths are complementary. Building your team requires a clear understanding of your staffing needs and talent gaps. To build a team with complementary skills:

- Define the team in terms of the knowledge, skills, and abilities required to accomplish team goals. Chart the current strengths and weaknesses of individuals in your group against the team's needs. Identify critical gaps in the team you may need to fill.

- Review your strategic plan and your understanding of the group's future challenges. Analyze the mix of people on your team and identify missing skills or perspectives.

- Once the needs are identified, develop your existing staff to meet those needs, and hire people who will add to the team as a whole, not just to the specific job.

- Each time you recruit a new team member, take a fresh look at your organizational structure and the key roles that must be staffed to achieve your business objectives. Outline the critical requirements for each role in terms of the specific skills and experience necessary for success.

Match individuals to jobs

The best performers are typically those employees with the skills and interests that closely match those required by the positions they hold. In addition, high-performing employees have the desire to learn more, work hard, and take on additional responsibility.

To improve your skills in matching individuals to jobs, try these steps:

1. Identify the signs of poor matches in your department. Examples of these signs include resignations, terminations, substandard performance, excessive absenteeism, and excessive interpersonal conflict.

2. Review each situation that signaled a poor match over the past year, and look for the reason for the mismatch. Were there skills an individual needed but did not have? Problematic personal styles? Skills the individual had but didn't use?

3. As you analyze these situations, look for a pattern. For example, are your employees' skills consistently underutilized or consistently lacking in particular areas?

4. Develop strategies for preventing employee/position mismatches by changing your selection or placement procedures. For example, if your past employees have been overqualified for their jobs, modify your selection standards.

5. If mismatches occur in the future, evaluate the reasons for them and, if possible, take steps to remedy them.

Anticipate long-term staffing needs

Staffing needs are constantly shifting, whether because employees leave or are promoted, department and team responsibilities change, or growth requires the addition of more staff members. Successful managers plan for these contingencies to ensure that job changes and the addition of new staff occur in a smooth, positive way.

To better anticipate and plan for your long-term staffing needs, consider the following suggestions:

- Draw an organizational chart of your division or department that includes all members of your team and shows all reporting relationships. Determine the likelihood of positions being opened as a result of promotions, lateral moves, resignations, and additions to staff.

- Examine strategic business objectives and identify staffing issues related to achieving these objectives. For example, suppose your work group, which has traditionally been responsible for new product development, has now been asked to assume more responsibility for increasing market share. What would this mean regarding whom you hire and promote? PDI's Strategic Performance Modeling can help you answer this question. This approach helps identify the competencies and level of proficiency required given the business strategy.

- Review business forecasts and strategic plans, and assess the current operating effectiveness of your work unit to identify staffing problems and to project staffing needs for the future.

- Once you have forecasted when, how much, and what type of talent is required in the future, determine how you can create the talent pipeline that will meet your staffing requirements. The types of options available include:
  - Retain and deploy the existing people in your organization who have the skills you require.
  - Develop existing staff who show the potential to become the type of talent you require.
  - Hire externally those who have the required talent.
  - Hire externally those who have the potential, with some development, to meet your talent requirements.

- Do scenario planning with your team, peers, and/or HR staff to explore different options and possible challenges.

  For example, suppose your focus is on reducing the turnover rate of existing capable staff and hiring on those with potential (who are less expensive than fully trained and ready external candidates).
  - Try to think what might happen in the event of unplanned changes, such as an increase in aggressive recruiting of your staff by key competitors.
  - Determine what scenario (or talent pipeline) would likely provide you with the best return on investment and carry acceptable risk.
  - Work with your internal HR and/or external consulting partners to create the talent pipeline you have decided upon.

Identify, develop, and retain your high-potential employees

The long-term success of an organization depends on identifying people who can become its future leaders. Furthermore, the process of identifying the right leaders is dynamic, because of an organization's growth, industry trends, and changes in its business strategy.

To help you get and keep the right people to support your long-term success, consider the following suggestions:

- Identify employees, within your department and in other parts of the organization, whom you believe have the potential or are ready to fill critical roles within the organization, including your own position.

  Evaluate each employee in terms of current performance, potential for promotability—both upward and laterally—and likelihood of leaving. For the most critical positions (often your own), you may need to identify back-ups who could immediately fill in if the position becomes open.

- Talk with knowledgeable human resource managers and other managers to get their perceptions of the performance of your team members and of the back-up candidates you have identified.

- Develop the skills of your back-up candidates. Coach them and give them on-the-job assignments that will help them prepare for future promotions.

- Keep your departmental succession-planning information current.

- Identify high-potential performers and poor performers.
  - Develop accelerated action plans for your high-potential people and link them into programs in the organization for high-potential employees.
  - Address the issues of your problem performers. Develop plans for improvement, and let them know the consequences if they don't improve.

- Identify and groom high-potential talent several levels below the targeted leadership role. When identifying candidates early on, look for those who have the basic building blocks required for leadership. These usually include the following basic abilities, personality traits, and values critical for leadership:
  - Strong analytical and visionary thinking abilities.
  - A drive for achievement.
  - Interpersonal effectiveness.
  - Adaptability.
  - Ability to effectively learn.
  - Superior focus and self-awareness.

  Also look for demonstrated past performance, which can be a good indicator of future performance related to these leadership building blocks.

- Identify specific experience requirements that are difficult to obtain or depend on timing of events. Challenge the need for these specific requirements (e.g., degree requirements, language proficiency, overseas assignment), knowing that some will be critical while others may unnecessarily limit potential candidates.

- Develop assessment processes and tools that clearly identify people who have the most important building blocks. These can include nomination forms, performance measures, and experience requirement checklists. PDI can assist in developing these measures and can also provide tests that assess leadership potential.

- After you've identified high potentials, target development experiences and activities that will ensure quick and high returns. Also determine how you will track the development of these individuals.

- Determine what you can do to retain this talent. Consider the value proposition your organization offers to its employees. Determine whether that value proposition is what employees truly value.

- Ask your HR staff for ideas on how you can align the value proposition you offer your best talent with what they truly value.

When identifying candidates who might be almost ready for the targeted leadership position, look for those with developed skills, not just talent. Typically, these individuals are one level below the targeted role and/or have been developed as high potentials. In identifying those who are ready or nearly ready, it is important to look beyond the basic building blocks and target specific capabilities as a leader. This would include the following evaluations:

- Does the person have strong business problem-solving, decision-making, leadership, and strategic-thinking skills?

- Does he or she have a history of leading? Of making things better or different?

- Does the person develop strong working relationships within the organization?

- Has his or her individual achievement drive broadened to enjoy achievement through and with others?

To help you identify high-potential performers at this level, carefully evaluate their work history, career aspirations, and strengths and weaknesses.

- Give job assignments that will challenge and further develop skills. In developing high-potential individuals, provide experiences that will focus on the management area for which they are best suited—for example, functional management or general management.

- For general managers, gear development efforts toward acquiring a breadth of general management experience, with versatility in business situations as the key. Provide experiences in managing a startup, fixing a business in trouble, downsizing a business, and so forth.

- For functional managers, focus on developing the individual's depth in his or her particular functional area.

- Develop high performers who may not have the potential or interest to be leaders, but who are critical contributors to the organization's success. If you are to retain and effectively deploy the high performers, the value proposition you offer them will need to be appropriate for them, and likely will be quite different from what you offer high-potential employees. For example, opportunities for development and challenge will focus on "development in place." Also, compensation may need to recognize the importance of a professional track for high performers.

PART 4:
DEPLOY YOUR EMPLOYEES

Improve your employee orientation program

New employees' formal and informal orientation to your organization and department will be one of their first and most powerful impressions of what they can expect. Hence, the quality of your orientation program has an impact on how well new employees perform on the job, how well they get along with their coworkers, their job satisfaction, and even their eventual career progress within the organization.

To develop an effective orientation program, follow these suggestions:

WELL, SIR, I'VE BEEN HERE FOR SIX MONTHS AND ... WELL ... JUST WHAT IS IT I DO HERE ?

- Evaluate your current program. The orientation program should provide employees with at least the following information:
  - A guide to the organization's policies, work rules, and employee benefits.
  - General information about the day-to-day routine (location of rest rooms and lunchrooms, how to use telephones and copy machines, obtaining supplies, and so forth).
  - A description of the organization's history, purpose, and products/services, and a discussion of how the employee's job contributes to the overall purpose.
  - The "musts" for survival and success (for example, mandatory attendance at financial planning meetings for all managers with budget responsibility and accountability).
  - Specific information about the work, people, and relationships in the new employee's area.

- Survey all employees to get suggestions for improving the organization's orientation program. Ask them what they think new employees need to function comfortably and effectively.

- Ask new hires to help you evaluate the effectiveness of your program by providing feedback at designated points—such as two weeks, one month, and two months—after their hire date.

- Assign an experienced employee as a sponsor for each new hire. Let the new employee know that this person will be available to answer any questions.

- Realize that it is your responsibility to see that new employees receive an effective orientation to their jobs, your department, and the organization. Decide which parts of the orientation you need to do and which parts would be appropriate to delegate to others.

- Conduct orientation for all levels of employees.

Train new employees

Too often, the training of new employees is forgotten in the day-to-day rush to get the job done. It's possible, however, to develop a program that takes minimal time to administer, yet effectively integrates new people into your department.

To develop such a program, build the following elements into your training program for new hires:

- Provide orientation. View orientation as the first step in the training program.

- Establish a support network. New employees should be introduced to more experienced employees who will provide general support and assistance during your absence. Inform the experienced employees of their responsibilities in this area.

- Establish an environment that is conducive to learning. Newcomers usually have a variety of concerns. Let them know that you don't expect them to absorb everything the first time around, that you realize mistakes will be made, and that you encourage their questions. To support learning:
  - Provide on-the-job training experiences. A mix of on-the-job and formal training experiences will help new employees integrate their new knowledge and enable them to feel that they are contributing to the goals of the department. The sooner you start them making a contribution to the group, the more excited and motivated they will be.
  - Encourage feedback from experienced employees. This will help you identify the areas in which the new employees require more training.
  - Create a manual of training materials. Keep a record of the training procedures used to train new hires. After several employees have been trained, identify the procedures that have proven most effective and include them in a training manual. As the manual becomes more specific and complete, you will be able to delegate more training-related tasks to your employees.

RESOURCES

The resources for this chapter begin on page 658.

20
COACH AND DEVELOP PEOPLE

PART 1: GET READY TO COACH
- *Define what coaching is and is not*
- *Review PDI's Leader as Coach strategies*
- *Assess your own coaching approach*

PART 2: FORGE A PARTNERSHIP
- *Build a foundation of trust*
- *Find out what is important to people*

PART 3: INSPIRE COMMITMENT
- *Cultivate insight about "GAPS" information*
- *Use "GAPS" to identify top-priority objectives*
- *Translate development objectives into an actionable plan*

PART 4: GROW SKILLS
- *Create an effective learning environment*
- *Vary your role in the learning process*
- *Create a coaching plan*
- *Work one-on-one with people*
- *Orchestrate learning opportunities*
- *Enhance self-reliance*
- *Recommend training programs, readings, and other resources*
- *Conduct debriefing sessions*

PART 5: PROMOTE PERSISTENCE THROUGH PRACTICE
AND FEEDBACK
- *Know the characteristics of high-impact feedback*
- *Discuss relevant feedback with others*
- *Equip people to obtain useful feedback from others*
- *Use 360-degree or multi-rater feedback tools*
- *Keep the momentum going*
- *Address ineffective performance*
- *Coach remote employees*

PART 6: SHAPE THE ENVIRONMENT
- *Be a powerful role model for development*
- *Coach in a team setting*
- *Enhance the learning environment of your area*

INTRODUCTION

Developing employees is not optional. It is a business necessity.

Just as technical research and development is essential for continued excellence and a competitive edge, so must coaching and development become the leader's focal point for leveraging the organization's human capital. Development is necessary to acquire the skills and learn the knowledge needed to achieve the business goals of today and the future. Development programs are also increasingly important to attract and retain good employees.

The leader's role in development is that of a coach. Coaches do not develop people; they equip people to develop themselves. Coaching is the process of equipping people with the tools, knowledge, and opportunities they need to develop themselves and become more effective.

Coaching others is no longer limited to your direct reports. In a learning organization, everyone must be prepared to learn from and coach anyone. Coaching depends not on hierarchy, but on who has the opportunity to create a learning experience. Nor is coaching a one-way street where you have all the answers; rather, it's a partnership where both people share responsibility.

Coaching doesn't need to take a great deal of your time. If you focus five percent of your energy and attention on those areas where people's development is likely to break down, you will yield healthy returns on your human capital investment. The following five coaching strategies from PDI's book *Leader as Coach* address the most common barriers to developing people:

- Forge a Partnership

- Inspire Commitment

- Grow Skills

- Promote Persistence

- Shape the Environment

The suggestions in this chapter describe a number of processes and tactics you can use to create a healthy return on investment for your coaching efforts.

VALUABLE TIPS

- Keep a running list of what is most important to your employees. Review it every quarter.

- Take time to listen carefully to other people's interests, opinions, concerns, and goals.

- Help employees clarify their personal goals and values.

- Meet individually with your employees to discuss their career goals and identify the skills they need to achieve these goals.

- Communicate current and future organizational needs and how they relate to the development priorities of individuals on your team.

- Make sure people get specific, relevant information about their performance.

- Help people formulate development goals that are consistent with organizational priorities.

- Encourage people to focus their development on areas where they can achieve the greatest leverage.

- Maximize your talent pool by making a concerted effort to develop the skills of your administrative staff.

- Maintain a development file on each of your employees. Keep track of their goals, abilities, perceptions of others, successes, failures, and how you have agreed to help.

- Use PDI's DevelopMentor® and *e*Advisor™ on-line tools to broaden your ideas and skills for developing and coaching others.

- Connect people with role models and mentors who possess the skills they are trying to develop.

- Remember that people master tasks in small steps. Help your employees become competent by gradually increasing their responsibilities.

- Be alert to articles and development tips that could be of help to others.

- Find ways to enrich the jobs of your employees by increasing their authority or span of control.

- Help people reflect and learn from their successes and failures.

- Find ways for people to capitalize on and further develop their areas of strength.

- Refresh people's commitment to development by periodically reviewing their goals and asking about their progress.

- Encourage employees to expand their comfort zone.

- Ask people what kind of feedback and support they would like from you.

- Focus your feedback on people's behavior. Be more descriptive and less evaluative in your feedback.

- Teach employees how to get feedback for themselves.

- Encourage people to treat feedback as a hypothesis to be tested.

- Recognize development efforts, not just results.

- Publicly recognize and reward people who develop themselves and others.

- Provide your employees with an opportunity to participate in a multi-rater, or 360-degree, feedback experience, such as PDI's renowned PROFILOR® products.

- Be a role model for development by openly pursuing learning and taking risks.

- Emphasize development in your department's business planning and performance-management practices.

- Establish processes that promote learning from each other, both within and across departments.

- Schedule time to talk about development as a part of regular one-on-one meetings, updates, team meetings, and so forth.

PART I:
GET READY TO COACH

Define what coaching is and is not

Coaching is the process of equipping people with the tools, knowledge, and opportunities they need to develop themselves. Effective coaches are catalysts who make development quicker and more effective. Consider the following:

- Coaches don't develop people—they equip people to develop themselves.

- Coaching isn't an occasional conversation—it's a continuous process.

- Coaching isn't something you do *to* people—it's something you do *with* people.

- Coaching doesn't center on fixing problem behaviors—it's about cultivating people's capabilities.

There is a payback for the coach, too. Not only will you build a strong team of highly capable people, but also you are likely to attract excellent talent—the best and the brightest want to work for leaders who will help them learn and grow.

Review PDI's *Leader as Coach* strategies

Even the people most committed to developing themselves face barriers to success. This is where your energy and attention as a coach can make a real difference. The following coaching strategies from PDI's book *Leader as Coach* target the most common barriers to development:

1. **Forge a Partnership:** Build trust and understanding so people want to work with you. With trust, people will be more willing to hear and act on what you have to say. With understanding, you will know what matters to each other. *Use this strategy when people don't believe you care about them or their development.*

2. **Inspire Commitment:** Build insight and motivation so people focus their energy on goals that matter. You cannot motivate people directly, but you can achieve commitment to development when people understand themselves and the personal payback from working toward organizational objectives. *Use this strategy when people don't understand their development needs or don't make their development a priority.*

3. **Grow Skills:** Build new competencies to ensure that people know how to do what is required. Once you know what the person needs to develop, your task is to help them find the best ways to acquire those new skills. *Use this strategy when people don't know how to learn the skills they need.*

4. **Promote Persistence:** Build stamina and discipline to make sure learning lasts on the job. People require daily effort to change old habits and put new behaviors into action. You can help people persist until their new behaviors become natural. *Use this strategy when people don't apply what they have learned to create real change on the job.*

5. **Shape the Environment:** Build organizational support to reward learning and remove barriers. Change is easier and the results last longer when the organization's values and rewards are aligned with coaching and development. *Use this strategy when people don't see organizational incentives for developing.*

Assess your own coaching approach

Effective coaches are developed, not born. They have, over time, acquired the skills and attitudes to create an environment that nurtures learning and development.

To become a more effective coach:

- First reflect on these questions:
  - How important is coaching to your success and the success of your organization?
  - What kind of coach do you want to be?
  - Think about your strongest coaching models. What have you learned from them?

- Next, complete the following evaluation to identify areas in which you are strong, as well as aspects of your coaching style that need improvement (you might also ask the people you coach to complete the evaluation).

- Based on the evaluation, determine which aspects of your coaching style you will develop more fully.

EVALUATE YOUR COACHING STYLE

5=Almost always
4=To a great extent
3=To some extent
2=To a little extent
1=Not at all

You:	5	4	3	2	1
Forge a Partnership					
Base your coaching relationships on trust, not similarity.					
Listen more than you talk.					
Approach resistance and reluctance to change with curiosity.					
Ask for feedback on how you can strengthen your coaching relationships with others.					
Inspire Commitment					
Have an understanding of the goals and values of the people you coach.					
Share information regarding expectations and success factors of the person's current and future responsibilities.					
Have an understanding of how the people you coach view their performance and capabilities.					
Help people understand others' perceptions of their capabilities.					
Help people identify development goals that are aligned with their personal priorities and the needs of the organization.					
Help people put together a solid plan for their growth and development.					
Grow Skills					
Create a safe and effective learning environment.					
Help people to find the best methods to learn new skills.					
Help people find readings, training programs, and other resources to supplement their development.					
Encourage people to take risks and learn from their mistakes.					
Help people learn the right lessons from their experiences.					
Promote Persistence					
Help people find assignments and other opportunities to practice their skills.					
Help people to identify daily reminders to stick with their development.					
Take advantage of "coachable moments" (e.g., times when people experience success, disappointment, or are trying a skill for the first time).					
Help people stay energized by revisiting their goals and recharging their development efforts.					
Regularly discuss feedback that is relevant to people's goals.					
Shape the Environment					
Know your own strengths and limitations.					
Act as a role model by sharing your development objectives, seeking feedback from others, and sharing what you have learned.					
Show your team that you value development through the rewards and opportunities that you directly influence.					
Work to align organizational policies and processes with coaching and development.					

PART 2:
FORGE A PARTNERSHIP

Build a foundation of trust

Trust is the foundation of any effective coaching relationship. In fact, it is trust (or lack thereof) that typically makes or breaks a coaching relationship. Use the suggestions below to get your coaching relationships started on the right foot:

- Show consistency between your words and actions by making realistic commitments and demonstrating followthrough to others.

- Be predictable by letting people know what to expect from you.

- Let people know how you are trying to balance individual and organizational interests and what decision-making process you will use.

- Demonstrate that you have their best interests in mind by genuinely promoting a win/win approach, showing compassion, and listening intently to their needs and concerns.

- Explain changes and apparent discrepancies in your actions.

- Demonstrate a strong awareness of the bounds of your own capabilities. That way, you will know what you can personally do for the person you are coaching and when you need to tap the expertise of others.

- Be willing to admit when you have made a mistake.

Consult Chapter 30: Inspire Trust in this handbook for additional strategies for developing trust with others.

Find out what is important to people

It is easy to fall into the coaching trap of wanting to solve others' problems. However, effective coaches master the art of listening and asking questions in a way that allows people to think for themselves and find their own solutions. Consider the following common pitfalls and suggestions for avoiding them:

- *Explaining instead of listening.* Set your mind on exploring, not fixing. Let go of your desire to help, motivate, or change people, and instead try to understand them. Assume that no two people are alike in their values, goals, motives, and experiences.

- *Repeating your views when you meet resistance.* Seek to see the world through the eyes of the person you are coaching. Ask questions to help the person clarify his or her own thinking. For your coaching to have an impact, people need to believe that you understand their issue or opinion.

- *Advising before understanding.* Suspend your agenda. Rather, set your mind on listening and concentrate on learning more about the person's goals and what matters to them. In particular, look for the following information:
  1. What excites them?
     - What do they find most meaningful and rewarding at work?
     - Where do you see their greatest energy and enthusiasm?
     - What are their goals and why?
  2. How do they view themselves?
     - How do they appraise their skills and abilities?
     - Do they have a tendency to either inflate or undervalue their abilities?
     - What are their current challenges?
  3. What do they believe about their ability to develop?
     - Are they confident they can change?
     - Are they willing to take risks to change?
     - Do they think their development will make a difference?

PART 3:
INSPIRE COMMITMENT

Cultivate insight about "GAPS" information

People are motivated to change and develop when they see a personal payoff. Yet individual development efforts must also be aligned with the needs of the organization. To create mutual commitment, development objectives need to be driven by a person's own goals while addressing organizational priorities.

Ongoing discussions of a person's GAPS—their Goals and Abilities as well as the Perceptions and Standards of others—is the starting point for creating this mutual commitment. Information about a person's abilities and how other people perceive him or her defines where the person is now; goals and standards define where the person and the organization are going.

Use the following information and GAPS grid when discussing and collecting GAPS information:

- *Goals and values* are the internal motives and values that drive behavior. To find out more about a person's goals and values, find out more about what matters to him or her. Possible questions to ask:
  - What do you value and care most about?
  - What is important to you in your work and career?
  - What are your career interests and aspirations?
  - What gives you the greatest sense of satisfaction and reward? The least? Why?

- *Standards and success factors* represent the expectations regarding the person's performance and behavior relative to current and future roles and responsibilities, organization and team objectives, and market and business challenges. Information you might share (and encourage the person to gather):
  - Clear expectations of performance for the person's current and possible future roles, including skill requirements, required experiences, and additional educational needs.
  - The mission and strategic plans of your organization.
  - The pressing issues and goals that face your organization, including. internal and external perspectives about industry trends and competition.
  - The capabilities in greatest demand in your organization, and which of them are expected of this person, now and in the future.

- *Abilities* information includes the person's view of their capabilities and performance, especially in relation to what is required of them and what they want to do. Possible questions to ask:
  - How do you view your performance and capabilities?
  - What skills are your strengths? In what areas are you most likely to offer your expertise to others?
  - Where do you need to improve? In what areas do you turn to others for assistance?

- *Perceptions* include how other people see the person's capabilities and performance, including interpretations and assumptions about what they observe. Information you might share (and encourage the person to gather):
  - Personal observations and what you have heard from others about the person's capabilities.
  - The person's reputation among people at different levels in the organization.
  - How the person performs in areas critical to success in their current and future roles.

GAPS GRID: CRITICAL INFORMATION FOR DEVELOPMENT

WHERE THE PERSON IS	WHERE THE PERSON IS GOING	
ABILITIES *How they see themselves* What I already know: What I need to learn:	**GOALS AND VALUES** *What matters to the person* What I already know: What I need to learn:	THE PERSON'S VIEW
PERCEPTIONS *How others see the person* What I already know: What I need to learn:	**STANDARDS AND SUCCESS FACTORS** *What matters to others* What I already know: What I need to learn:	OTHERS' VIEWS

Use "GAPS" to identify top-priority objectives

People make development a priority when it is linked to their goals and existing motivations. Hence, when people recognize gaps between their GAPS (goals, abilities, perceptions, and standards/success factors), they are usually energized to do something to resolve the difference. Once a person's GAPS have been identified, jointly work through the following process to identify the one or two most critical development objectives:

1. *Identify the person's top personal priorities.* People cannot work on everything at once, so ask them to identify what matters most to them at work, considering both short-term and long-term objectives.

2. *Match with organizational incentives.* Consider aspects of the person's performance that are most important to the organization now and in the future.

3. *Look for alignment.* Look for the personal priorities that are compatible with organizational interests. Consider creative ways for the person and the organization to both get what they want. Mutual commitment is achieved when people's goals and organizational standards are aligned.

4. *Determine return on investment (ROI).* Maximize the likely ROI by identifying development objectives that will yield the greatest payback for a given amount of effort.

5. *Pick one or two development goals* that make the most sense to begin working on now.

Revisit this process on a periodic basis, because a person's GAPS will change over time.

Translate development objectives into an actionable plan

One of the best ways to plan for development is to base the action steps on how people really develop, as referenced in PDI's book *Development FIRST*. The strategies outlined in this book define what people can do, in partnership with others, to drive their own development:

Focus on priorities: Identify critical issues and goals.

Implement something every day: Stretch your comfort zone.

Reflect on what happens: Extract maximum learning from your experiences.

Seek feedback and support: Learn from other people's ideas and perspectives.

Transfer learning to next steps: Adapt and plan for continued learning.

Ask the people you are coaching to create a development plan, or jointly prepare one with them. A sample development planning form can be found in Chapter 32: Practice Self-Development in this handbook. When jointly preparing or reviewing development plans, consider the following criteria based on PDI's proven Development FIRST™ strategies:

• *Focus on priorities.* Even when people are motivated to develop, they may stray off course because so many things vie for their attention. To focus on priorities, make sure the plan:
  – Focuses on one or two specific goals that have both a personal and an organizational payoff.
  – Helps the person put development in the forefront of his or her thinking.
  – Anticipates distractions that are likely to draw the person off course.

- *Incorporate daily action.* Successful development is evolutionary, not revolutionary. Hence, smaller, daily activities will yield better results than one big burst of activity. An effective development plan will:
  - Specify times, situations, and people that will trigger development action.
  - Emphasize on-the-job application and practice.
  - Stretch the person's comfort zone.

- *Reflect on new learning.* People who reflect on their development actions can make sure they are learning the right lessons. To ensure reflection, build the following into the plan:
  - Designate when and how the person will take time for reflection.
  - Provide a vehicle for tracking and summarizing what the person has learned.
  - Prompt the person to diagnose the barriers that might be impeding his or her progress.

- *Track and sustain progress.* People need to get accurate, current information on progress to persist toward their goals. An effective plan will:
  - Identify sources and processes for getting relevant feedback.
  - Identify people who can provide encouragement and support.
  - Indicate how the person will measure progress toward his or her goals.

- *Plan for next steps.* Plans need to be flexible so they can adjust to changes in the person's talent portfolio and changes in the organization. To allow for changes:
  - Indicate how the plan will adjust to changing circumstances.
  - Indicate how to adapt the plan to changing competency levels.
  - Indicate how and when the plan will be reviewed and updated.

PART 4:
GROW SKILLS

Create an effective learning environment

People learn more quickly when they have the right environment for learning. Use the following suggestions to create a safe atmosphere that is conducive to learning and development:

- Be genuine. Let your own personality, insights, observations, and self-disclosures add depth and richness to your coaching efforts.

- Promote active experimentation. When people try new things in different ways, they solidify their understanding of what really works and prepare themselves to use the skills effectively in a variety of circumstances.

- Give employees permission to make mistakes as long as they learn from them. Focus on what was learned rather than how the person performed. Encourage your team members to talk to each other about what they have learned from their mistakes. Back your words with a willingness to talk openly about your own mistakes.

- Tailor your coaching and support to each person's individual learning style.

- Emphasize small, reasonable steps. Because people learn in small steps, expecting too much too soon can discourage progress.

- Model your own commitment to development by sharing your development objectives and asking for regular feedback. In particular, ask others to give you feedback on your coaching efforts.

- Remember that your position as a manager may make some employees especially sensitive to what you say or do. Avoid offhand remarks or irrelevant criticisms.

Vary your role in the learning process

Individuals are unique. Consequently, you will need to vary your coaching process from person to person. While you will have a unique coaching plan for each person you are coaching, focus on the following three approaches to help others learn and apply new skills:

- *Working one-on-one.* This part of coaching is direct and personal and often the most time-consuming. It includes offering feedback, encouraging people to take appropriate risks, and encouraging others when they face setbacks and barriers.

- *Orchestrating resources and learning opportunities.* Part of your coaching involves finding other mentors and teachers for the person you are coaching, and opening doors to new experiences that could not be accessed without your help.

- *Enhancing self-reliance.* It's essential to teach others how to extract the right lessons from their experiences, how to find other people who can assist them, and how to obtain their own feedback and information. This will enable others to learn regardless of whether you are present.

Create a coaching plan

Research shows that development planning is more successful when the person's manager or coach is involved in the process. A coaching plan provides a vehicle for organizing what the person needs to learn, the best ways to learn and apply the skill, and the support and involvement you will provide the person.

The coaching and development processes work together. Just as your employees need to know when and how they can rely on you for guidance, you need to understand the specifics of their development plans. A two-way dialogue will enable the two of you to finalize your learning and coaching plans. A sample coaching plan appears below (and a sample learning plan appears in the About This Book section on page xxii).

Use the following guidelines when creating a coaching plan:

- Once a person's learning objective has been identified, help him or her create the criteria for success so he or she will recognize progress or achievement of the development objective. Make sure the success criteria delineate clear, observable, and quantifiable ways to measure progress.

- Determine your involvement by identifying specific ways you will work with the employee through his or her development process, including when and how you plan to coach the employee, specific areas of difficulty for the employee, and so forth.

- Investigate what learning style works best for the person. Does he or she learn best from first seeing something done, from doing, or from listening or reading?

- Next, determine your strategies for working one-on-one with the person, orchestrating resources and learning opportunities, and enhancing self-reliance.

- Identify reading, training programs, software, or other resources to supplement the person's development and ways you can help him or her apply learning to the job.

- Identify ways to help the employee overcome typical obstacles he or she is likely to encounter during the development process.

COACHING PLAN

Person's Name:	
The Person's LEARNING OBJECTIVE:	**MY INVOLVEMENT AS COACH:** (Specific ways you will work with the employee through his or her development process, including when and how you plan to coach the employee, specific areas of difficulty for the employee, etc.)
The Person's CRITERIA FOR SUCCESS: (Observable and measurable ways to measure progress)	

	Time Frame
Working One-on-one *What I will do to:* • Offer insight, observations, and feedback: • Share relevant stories and insights from my own experience: • Support and encourage the person's effort to learn: **Orchestrating Learning Opportunities** *What I will do to:* • Create meaningful challenges and identify appropriate opportunities: • Link him or her with people that he or she can learn from: **Enhancing Self-reliance** • People I can suggest he or she network with: • Ways I will encourage him or her to reflect and learn from success, mistakes, and other experiences: • Tactics to help the person take advantage of existing opportunities to develop him- or herself:	
RECOMMENDED RESOURCES: (Readings, training programs, software, and other resources to supplement the person's development)	
OVERCOMING OBSTACLES: (Coaching tactics to help the employee overcome typical obstacles he or she is likely encounter during the development process)	

Work one-on-one with people

If time is money, working individually with people is the most expensive approach to coaching. While working face-to-face is certainly worthwhile, it is important to ensure that you are making the best use of this time and integrating "coachable moments" into your daily activities. Consider the following:

- Jointly discuss and agree on ways you will work with the person you are coaching. For example, you might agree on the following:
  - Ways for the employee to practice or role-play new situations with you.
  - When you will observe the employee using the skill.
  - What feedback would be most useful for the person to receive from you?
  - How and when you will review progress.

- Learn to capitalize on coachable moments. Help others extract the right lessons from experiences, such as when they attempt a skill for the first time or experience success or failure. Use the following process:

  1. Diagnose the outcome. What did the person do that contributed to the quality of the outcome, such as preparation, attitude, etc.? What factors outside of their control contributed to the result?

  2. Identify the lesson. What should the person repeat, improve, and/or avoid at the next opportunity?

  3. Transfer the lesson to a new situation. Identify upcoming opportunities or similar situations where the lessons can be applied.

  People usually experience satisfaction when things go well, yet they often fail to review what happened so they can replicate their successes in the future. Help people realize the potency of learning from their successes.

- Be on the lookout for relevant stories and personal experiences you can share to supplement the person's learning process and further strengthen your relationship with the person.

Orchestrate learning opportunities

Most experts agree that the most powerful development happens on the job. Your role as a coach includes providing challenging on-the-job opportunities, both by being creative about the assignments you give others and by identifying opportunities for people to work with other people and in other functions. To be more creative and proactive about the assignments you give to others, consider the following ideas:

- Put your employees in charge of a cross-functional task force to give them exposure to other functions and an understanding of interrelationships.

- Identify situations your employees are currently in where you can optimize their level of challenge.

- Have your employees represent you at meetings, presentations, and conferences.

- Put people in situations where they have to perform a "fix-it" function to get experience managing change, analyzing business problems, and tackling tough assignments.

- Give employees a temporary lateral assignment that forces them to see the business from an alternative perspective.

- Assign projects that involve interaction with your manager to provide exposure and experience working with higher-level managers.

- Delegate complete responsibility for managing the execution of a complex project from start to finish.

- Assign employees to mentor a new or inexperienced employee, which will require them to learn how to coach, explain things, and support people.

- Challenge yourself to find ways for an employee to gain access to other people and functions. Ask yourself the following questions on a periodic basis:
  - What people can I help them network with to identify new places to practice and learn?
  - Who are the best people to learn from (e.g., role models, other coaches, experts) and how can I link my employee to them?
  - What are the best places to see this skill in action? How can I help them gain access to these opportunities?
  - What are the best resources (e.g., software, readings, courses) available and how can I help people access them?

- Find ways for people to learn from external sources, such as customers, suppliers, or contractors.

Enhance self-reliance

Responsibility for development belongs to the employee you are coaching. Therefore, a substantial part of your job as coach includes helping others to help themselves. Consider the following suggestions:

- Encourage the person to scan their daily schedule of activities to find the best situations to learn or practice something new. For example, a group meeting might provide an opportunity to observe facilitation skills.

- Help employees get learning tips from coworkers who have recently faced similar learning challenges.

- When others directly ask for your opinion, hold your comments in check and determine how to use the opportunity to help them find their own solutions.

- Help people take advantage of existing opportunities to stretch themselves.

- Encourage employees to network to find others who have the skills or knowledge they wish to learn. Discuss strategies for gaining access to mentors and role models.

- Help people identify and find additional coaches. Remind them that rarely can one person effectively provide everything that they need for their development. Have them identify people to play the following roles in their development process:
  - Sounding board for new ideas
  - Support person to celebrate success and provide encouragement
  - Accountability partner
  - Feedback partner
  - Confidant

Recommend training programs, readings, and other resources

The most powerful development opportunities occur on the job, but people may need to supplement that learning with other ideas, information, or background. Augment development efforts through training programs, readings, software, audio/videotapes, and other resources. To ensure the maximum benefit from this form of learning, consider the following suggestions:

- Discuss the specific learning objectives and intended results before the person invests his or her time in reading or attending a training program. With this preparation, the person will be more likely to be aware of and obtain the needed information.

- Identify resources that are current and timely. Check the recommended readings and suggested seminars listed in the Resources by Chapter section at the end of this handbook, and get recommendations from colleagues and human resources professionals.

- Having selected the appropriate program or reading, consider the optimum time for the employee to participate in the seminar or absorb the reading material. Timing the learning just before the person needs to apply the skill on the job will usually yield the greatest transfer of skills or knowledge to the job.

- When the person has completed the program or reading, take time to discuss what was learned and how he or she will apply the knowledge and skills to the job.

Conduct debriefing sessions

A debriefing session is a way to discuss an event or assignment after the fact. Debriefing is critically important when you are coaching someone to learn a new skill because it helps the person synthesize and solidify his or her learning. Keep these points in mind to conduct effective debriefing sessions:

- Before the event or assignment, jointly plan what the person hopes to learn or practice. This sets the stage for a good debriefing session.

- When debriefing, focus on both ends of the spectrum. Discuss what went well and what didn't.

- Make sure the debriefing session encourages open communication. The session should synthesize what was learned, not pass judgment.

- Use effective, open-ended questions to help the person fully realize what he or she learned from the experience.

- Discuss both what the person learned and the next steps in his or her development process. Use the session to reflect on what happened and to translate that learning into new situations or opportunities.

PART 5: PROMOTE PERSISTENCE THROUGH FEEDBACK AND PRACTICE

Know the characteristics of high-impact feedback

Traditional teachings on feedback are based on the notion that feedback should be "given" to people. High-impact feedback, however, is based on the following characteristics:

- *Discovery, not delivery.* View feedback as a process of joint discovery and discussion, rather than a declaration. The goal of feedback is to help employees gain relevant information to sustain their development.

- *Mutual understanding, not persuasion.* Feedback is most effective when you and the person you are coaching try to understand each other better. Work to find the linkages between both of your perspectives. That way, the feedback will be more relevant to what he or she cares about and is willing to act on.

- *Adaptive, not formulaic.* Feedback is most effective when it is sensitive to the person and the situation, rather than following a standard recipe. Effective feedback-givers individualize their approach and adapt it to different circumstances.

- *Nonjudgmental information, rather than "positive" or "negative" feedback.* Judgments about a person are likely to elicit defensiveness. Feedback that gives people information about where they stand relative to their goals is likely to be valuable.

- *Process, not an event.* Feedback is most effective when it is part of a regular process of inquiry rather than a single conversation. Through regular conversations about their performance, help people understand where they stand as well as the expectations of others.

Discuss relevant feedback with others

Consider the following definition of feedback:

Feedback is an exchange of information that helps people understand how others perceive them. Effective feedback increases insight and motivates action.

In essence, effective feedback gives people information about where they are in relation to their goals and the corresponding standards and success factors.

Use the following process to improve your feedback discussions:

1. As a starting point, make sure you understand the person's specific objectives, success factors, and standards. In turn, ensure that you have clearly conveyed your expectations of the person.

2. Begin with a discussion of where the person sees him- or herself. This will help you to appropriately position your feedback.

3. Share your feedback and observations in the context of the employee's goals and where you see them now. Make clear, direct statements about the behavior you have observed. Describe your feedback in terms of behaviors, potential impact, and likely consequences. For example:

Behavior: "You asked questions but then didn't wait for people to answer."

Potential impact: "They may conclude that you aren't really interested in their opinions."

Likely consequences: "As a result, they'll probably start to keep their opinions to themselves, which may cut you off from valuable information."

4. Engage in a dialogue and avoid any tendency to lecture. If appropriate, help the employee understand the difference between his or her intentions and other people's perceptions of the behavior.

5. Translate insight into actions and outcomes. Ask questions to help them explore applications of their new insights, such as "Where do you think you might apply this information?"

In addition, consider these additional tips when discussing feedback with others:

- Let go of the need to convince the person that you are right. If he or she becomes defensive or stops listening to you, check to see if you are pushing too hard on your point of view.

- Do not be afraid to allow periods of silence for the person to absorb the information and to respond.

- Don't dilute your message with unnecessary qualifiers like "maybe," "perhaps," and "a little."

- Avoid overwhelming the person with too much feedback all at once. Focus on relevant and important observations rather than making sure you cover every detail. Relevancy is more important than completeness.

- Read the person's nonverbal cues to get an indicator of whether you need to elaborate, provide support, or process his and her feelings and reactions.

Equip people to obtain useful feedback from others

Enhancing self-reliance is one goal of the coaching process. As a coach, you will certainly engage others in feedback discussions. Your more important coaching responsibility, however, involves equipping others to embark on their own search for feedback. By using this approach, the individual owns the responsibility for obtaining feedback.

To transfer the onus of the feedback process from you to the people you are coaching, discuss the following with them:

- Begin by determining the specific information they need in order to develop.

- Help them identify people who would be good sources of feedback. Suggest they consider a cross-section of people who have an opportunity to observe their behavior and who will be direct and honest with them. Have them consider peers, managers, customers, team members, and friends.

- Educate them on how to prepare their feedback-givers so they can provide helpful information. For example, a person who is working to improve his or her public speaking might ask a feedback-giver to pay particular attention to his or her use of visual aids.

- Coach them on how to create an environment that makes it safe for people to give them candid feedback. Teach them how to ask direct, specific questions, probe for additional information, avoid defensiveness, and show appreciation for the feedback.

- Suggest that they identify one or two people they can rely on for mutual feedback and support on a regular basis.

Use 360-degree or multi-rater feedback tools

Multi-rater feedback can be an effective tool for jump-starting the feedback process. The anonymity and confidentiality of these instruments often result in more candid feedback than face-to-face methods and can thus help a person gain a clearer sense of his or her abilities and others' perceptions. An effective multi-rater feedback process has the following characteristics:

- The objectives of the multi-rater feedback process are clearly defined.

- The roles and expectations of the participant, manager, and coach are clear.

- The competency model and instrumentation are well researched, reliable, and valid.

- Feedback reports and collateral materials are user-friendly.

- Clarification of the feedback results is built into the process.

- Development is the key emphasis of the process. The feedback is linked to development tools and processes.

PDI can provide you with state-of-the-art multi-rater feedback instruments and processes that meet all of these criteria.

Keep the momentum going

Only through practice and repeated application can people make new skills a solid part of their repertoire. New habits are forged through conscious effort and repeated practice. You can help ensure that learning is applied and lasts on the job by using the following suggestions:

- Walk the delicate line between pushing people so hard that they become discouraged, or easing up so much that they do not grow.

- Find opportunities for people to apply their new skills many times, in many places, and in many ways.

- Remind people of their goals and incentives.

- Set reasonable intermediate goals to prevent discouragement.

- Help people identify cues that signal when they are slipping into old habits. Then, whenever they notice the signal, they can replace old habits with new behaviors. Have them identify:
  - Internal emotional cues that the old habit might be clicking in.
  - External cues that signal an opportunity to apply a new skill.

- Encourage people to establish a continuous loop of feedback and information.

- Encourage employees to keep a log of their most successful learning experiences so they can institutionalize their best practices in their day-to-day activities.

- Reinforce people when they try something new or take intelligent risks.

- Celebrate successes.

Address ineffective performance

Most people want to be successful in their job. Ineffective performance is often a sign that the coaching and development process needs to be adjusted. Consider the following process when you observe performance that is not meeting expectations:

- Make sure you and the employee have adequately discussed his or her GAPS (goals and values, abilities, perceptions of others, and standards/success factors for goal achievement). A mutual understanding of a person's GAPS plays an important part in the performance-management process. In fact, effective performance is defined through this mutual understanding. (See the section earlier in this chapter that explains the GAPS process in detail.)

- Find a time to have a conversation with the person when you will not be rushed.

- Begin by ensuring that you both have an up-to-date, mutual understanding of the person's GAPS.
  - Find out what they are trying to do (their Goals and values) and how they see their own performance (their Abilities).
  - Share your expectations (Standards and success factors) and Perceptions.

- Discuss the discrepancies. Probe to understand the underlying reasons for the discrepancy.

- Listen thoughtfully to the person's view of the situation. Paraphrase what you have heard to ensure understanding.

- Keep the conversation focused on the future rather than the past.

- Once you have come to a mutual understanding of the situation, solicit from the person ideas and solutions for closing the gap. Mutually agree on the steps to be taken and the time frames for each step.

- Follow up on employee performance. When monitoring the employee's actions, be sure to recognize and reinforce any improvements in behavior—especially in the beginning—until the employee has incorporated these new behaviors into his or her routine.

Coach remote employees

Coaching from a distance is becoming common in today's workforce. When you coach remotely, the need for a strong bond of trust and candor is especially critical. You will often need to use indirect sources to coach, so employees must trust your intentions. Consider the following ideas:

- When visiting remote sites, build in time to solidify the coaching relationship. For example, arrive the evening before and schedule a dinner. Avoid being overly task-focused during early meetings. Time spent now will pay off later.

- Together create ground rules for the relationship. For example, make a pact that you will not act on things you have heard without talking to each other first. Periodically revisit the ground rules you've established and make appropriate adjustments.

- Be accessible when you are not available. Create a confidential way to be reached.

- Adjust your work schedule to overlap the time zones of your remote employees.

- Create an electronic forum to keep the communication flow going.

- Establish peer support groups geographically.

- Act as a broker to find mentors in local areas.

- Line up local advocates who can use the skills your employee is developing.

PART 6:
SHAPE THE ENVIRONMENT

Be a powerful role model for development

Your level of commitment to your own development demonstrates just how much you really care about development. If you back what you say with an investment in your own growth, others are more likely to believe that you mean business.

Here are suggestions for increasing your personal impact as a role model for development:

- Regularly outline the areas you are working on.

- Push yourself out of your comfort zone by taking risks and experimenting with new approaches

- Get a coach for yourself.

- Invite feedback and coaching from others. Make it easy for others to talk with you about how you are doing.

- Share what you have learned from both your successes and mistakes.

- Celebrate your achievements.

Coach in a team setting

A team setting provides an opportunity for team members to learn from one another. Consider the following ideas to take advantage of team learning:

- Establish team ground rules that promote candor and openness.

- Match team members who have specific skills with those who need to develop those skills.

- Create loops of learning. Make it routine for team members to bring what they learn back to the team.

- Encourage team members to create opportunities for each other to practice new skills (e.g., use the team setting to do dry runs around new skills). Then have members debrief with the team after trying new skills.

- Make it routine for members to make development goals public. Then establish a system for extending support and holding each other accountable for achieving development goals.

- Focus more on "how" than on "what." Encourage people to describe new things they tried, their struggles, and what they learned, rather than just the final results.

- Use project milestones, quarterly planning sessions, and other natural junctures for reflection on group learning.

- Spend two or three minutes at the end of each meeting evaluating what worked well and what didn't.

Enhance the learning environment of your area

Change is easier and longer lasting when the environment reinforces the learning process. Periodically audit your environment to identify ways to further enhance learning and development. Consider the following questions:

- How can you further integrate development into your department's business-planning and performance-management practices?

- What can you do to make development activities, including sharing information and taking risks, safer for everyone in the group?

- What additional resources can you deploy to support development (including people's time, money, and new opportunities)?

- How will you continue to reinforce the importance of development for everyone?

- What other ways can you publicly recognize and reward employees who develop themselves and others?

- What processes can you establish that will promote learning from each other, both within and across departments?

- What are the development barriers that people mention most frequently? How can you influence the removal of those barriers?

- In what ways can you be a champion or spokesperson for development throughout the organization?

- How can you form a coalition of those who share your focus on development to influence organizational policies and practices?

- How will you hold others accountable for developing their employees?

RESOURCES

The resources for this chapter begin on page 660.

21
ENGAGE AND INSPIRE PEOPLE

- *Create a vision aligned with the organization's mission, strategy, and direction*
- *Communicate a clear vision and direction*
- *Clarify other people's roles and responsibilities in attaining the vision*
- *Encourage high standards of performance*
- *Impart to others a sense of energy, ownership, and personal commitment to work*
- *Inspire action without relying solely on authority*
- *Inspire others to define new opportunities and continuously improve the organization*
- *Trust other people's judgment, recognizing that the best decisions are not always made at the top*
- *Celebrate and reward significant achievements of others*
- *Create an environment that encourages others to do their best*
- *Positively address work environment and balance issues*

INTRODUCTION

A vision is only a dream if it does not have the commitment and support from the people involved.

— David Lee and Lou Quast,
Senior Consultant and Vice President (respectively),
Personnel Decisions International

One of the hallmarks of effective leaders is their ability to both get results and generate a high level of morale among employees. Leaders do this in different ways. Transformational leaders paint a compelling vision of the future, exhibit high levels of self-confidence, model the way, instill trust in others, and form strong emotional attachments with their employees. Transactional leaders, on the other hand, get results by setting clear roles and goals, providing regular feedback, and obtaining necessary resources for their team.

Transformational leadership comes into play when leaders:

- Create a clear vision of where their team or organization is going.

- Ensure this vision is aligned with that of the larger organization.

- Use this vision to inspire their employees and their organization.

Some leaders generate this vision and direction from within themselves and then develop support for it in their organization. Others work with their teams to create a vision together. In either case, it is this clear vision and focused direction that allows leaders to align and direct the energy and resources of the organization to achieve desired goals.

Transactional leadership comes into play when leaders:

- First identify the mission and goals of the team and then the roles and responsibilities of each individual.

- Set high standards of performance and tailor rewards for each person on the team.

This process helps ensure that each individual's objectives, decisions, and behaviors are aligned with the organizational goals and eliminates potentially counterproductive activities.

Research has consistently shown that leaders who successfully employ both transformational and transactional leadership techniques often have higher levels of productivity and morale than leaders who use only one or neither of these leadership approaches.

This chapter provides suggestions on how to create and communicate a compelling vision for your area and clarify each person's responsibilities in attaining that vision—in other words, to adopt both transformational and transactional leadership methods.

VALUABLE TIPS

- Use your employees or management team to help create and update the team's vision, objectives, and strategies.

- Communicate the vision, mission, and strategies—and the rationale behind them.

- Clearly communicate departmental objectives and solicit input from your employees on what they can do to help achieve them.

- Be willing to set priorities.

- Show employees how their contributions support organizational goals.

- Provide new employees with a copy of the department's vision statement and objectives and make sure their role in meeting these is clear.

- Meet with people who are skilled in translating broad strategies into day-to-day activities; ask for their ideas on how to provide good direction to your employees.

- Use annual off-site meetings with your entire department to discuss performance in the past year and goals for the upcoming year.

- Encourage employees to set ambitious goals. Reward effort and achievement.

- Serve as a positive example to others.

- Communicate the achievements of your unit and your employees to higher-level management in a visible and positive way, showing pride in, and support for, your people.

- Ask employees for advice in areas where they have expertise.

- Know what aspects of the job interest and excite your employees, and then provide them with opportunities to pursue these.

- Identify the behaviors that you feel are critical to success in your team, and then lead by example.

- Learn what rewards your employees value that you can provide.

- Establish a "team identity" and work at building pride in group membership—"esprit de corps."

- Give recognition to people who strive for excellence.

Create a vision aligned with the organization's mission, strategy, and direction

Visions are future oriented and help the team focus energy, clarify goals, and set priorities. Good vision statements bridge the gap between the organization's vision and mission and the team's or department's accountabilities. Therefore, leaders need to clearly understand where their organization is going and how their department contributes to the overall success of their organization before they create their own vision statements.

The following suggestions will help you create a vision in alignment with the larger organization's goals:

- Before creating a team vision statement, fully understand the organizational mission and vision. Focus on the present state and answer these questions:
  - What is the mission and vision?
  - What are the business goals and strategies to achieve them?
  - What is the strategy for sustained competitive advantage?
  - Which markets are served?
  - What products and/or services are provided?

- Have a clear understanding of the objectives and accountabilities for your unit. Some key questions that need to be answered include:
  - Why does our unit exist?
  - Who are our customers?
  - What does my manager or the team sponsor expect from my team?
  - What are our goals or objectives?
  - How is department or team success measured?

- Create a vision statement that is future oriented and describes an ideal state. For example, an organization's vision may be "to be the market leader in computer peripherals in the next five years." While it's true that many organizations never achieve the ideal state of their vision, well-designed mission and vision statements provide a sense of direction for the organization and help people better understand how their jobs contribute to organizational success.

- Take responsibility for initiating the creation or refinement of your team's vision, but capitalize on the synergies of the team. This improves the odds of creating a vision statement that provides a compelling picture of the future and has a high level of team buy-in.

- Set aside time for you and your unit to meet and create a vision statement. Off-site meetings are commonly used for this purpose. Begin with a discussion of the organization's mission and vision, the team's objectives and accountabilities, the history of the team, and what people hope to accomplish by being on the team. Then discuss those factors listed below that have the most impact on the team now and will in the future, and whether these factors are within or outside the immediate control of the team.

External to Team	*Internal to Team*
Competition	Strengths and weaknesses
Resources	Financial/operational history
Market	Talent pool
Vendors and suppliers	Quality processes
Customers	Organizational culture
Legislation/regulation	Management style
Global issues	Sources of dissatisfaction
Technology	Sources of potential resistance
Industry trends	Geographical dispersion

- Have employees create individual vision statements for the team. The best team visions are often a synthesis of individual ideas, so encourage their visions by having them:
  - Predict where the organization will be in the next one to three years.
  - Identify how the team would ideally contribute to the organization's success. What is possible, given the factors under the team's control?
  - Consider who the team's customers would be, what the team would look like, and how and where it would get its work done.
  - Describe how they would personally benefit by being on this team. What would give them a sense of pride, ownership, and accomplishment as a team member?

- Post and describe team members' individual vision statements to the rest of the team. Then review all vision statements without judgment, identify common themes, and obtain agreement on a final statement.

- Check with the group to ensure the vision meets the following criteria:
  - Is future oriented.
  - Bridges the gap between the organization's vision and the team's objectives.
  - Stretches the team but is within the realm of possibility.
  - Provides each person with a personal sense of pride and ownership.
  - Generates excitement and enthusiasm among team members.

Communicate a clear vision and direction

After your team has created a vision statement, the next step is to develop a communication plan to convey the vision to the rest of the department, internal customers, and other teams. Many teams make the mistake of formulating a vision, making a single pronouncement, and then wonder why everyone else doesn't fully comprehend or buy into the new team vision. To avoid this mistake, the plan should use multiple modes of communication, as well as repeated messages.

Consider the following components for your communication plan:

- Post your vision so that people who enter your work area can see it.

- Use staff meetings to keep people focused on the vision.

- Keep your manager abreast of your group's progress in fulfilling your mission. If you turn in status reports, include a section on how well your group is doing relative to the vision. Include hard data (for example, dollar figures, specific feedback, production numbers) to support your comments.

- Create an "elevator message" as part of the communication plan. An elevator message is a colorful story, metaphor, or saying that captures the essence of the team's vision and can be conveyed in less than 30 seconds (i.e., the length of a typical ride in an elevator).

- Groom some employees as spokespersons to represent your area at company-wide meetings. Rotate this assignment if possible. Giving employees a chance to talk about their area's work and hear from others is an excellent way for staff members to see how their work fits into the overall picture.

- Remember that making your team's vision clear to others is a process, not an event. Constantly watch for opportunities to tell success stories about the team's vision. This helps keep the vision alive and builds momentum for further team successes.

Clarify other people's roles and responsibilities in attaining the vision

A team or department's vision will become reality only when people have a clear idea of what is expected of them, both on a daily basis and over the longer term. Effective leaders link and clarify the connections between individual efforts and team objectives; they ensure that individual efforts are aligned with the team's vision of the future. They also clarify responsibilities to increase ownership, alleviate conflicts, and eliminate unnecessary ambiguity.

In addition, letting other departments know who is responsible for what function allows your department to be more responsive to customer needs and keep things from "falling through the cracks." Role clarification is an ongoing process. The following tips, adapted from P.M. Senge's *The Fifth Discipline* (Doubleday, 1994), can help your team members clarify their roles and responsibilities:

Performance reviews make me uncomfortable. Can I wait outside?

- Ensure that each employee has a clear set of objectives/expectations that clarifies the role he or she plays in achieving team goals. It usually works best for employees to identify their perceptions of their role and set their goals. You as the leader can then review these and modify or add to them only when necessary. This approach gives employees more accountability and personal ownership. In addition, it promotes learning and commitment. Annual or periodic goals should supplement the role or job description.

- Periodically meet with team members to hear their perceptions of their roles and job expectations. Discuss similarities with and differences from your expectations.

- Work with your unit to identify voids in responsibilities and find ways to fill them. When consensus is not possible or appropriate, make a decision and let the group know the rationale for your decision.

- Clarify each team member's role and contribution to attaining the vision. Help them understand how their efforts and performance affect the overall results.

- When your team members differ about role expectations, work with them to resolve the differences. To negotiate team roles:
  - Find uninterrupted time for your team to meet.
  - Have an objective person facilitate the meeting if emotions are heightened.
  - Have each team member share specific expectations of other team members. If helpful, structure the sharing of expectations by having people describe what they'd like the others to do more of, less of, or the same as they currently are doing. The resulting discussion can be an effective catalyst to clear the air and build a commitment to the team's vision.

- Capitalize on opportunities to regularly communicate priorities and responsibilities to the team.

- During department meetings, take time to review progress toward the team's objectives and vision and determine whether a change in direction is necessary.

- Take time to orient new team members to the environment. Clearly explain team relationships, what to expect, and who is responsible for what.

**Encourage
high standards
of performance**

Once roles and responsibilities have been clearly outlined, it's important to set individual goals and performance standards that will lead toward the achievement of the team's vision and objectives. This will help team members understand how their efforts contribute to and are aligned with team success. Leaders need to ensure that employees know what performance level is expected, what performance is below standards, and what it takes to achieve high standards of performance.

The following guidelines can help:

- When setting new objectives, help your employees see how they contribute to the group and to the organization as a whole. For example, explain how the group's tasks contribute to profitability.

- Identify "stretch objectives" for each person—that is, the goals for performance that exceed the job requirements and are challenging yet attainable. Examples may include giving the team member more decision-making authority, adding responsibilities, assigning a supervisory role, or increasing productivity goals.

- Define the requirements for satisfactory performance relative to the team member's tenure, experience, and expertise. Make these standards clear to your team.

- Discuss your expectations with each person, taking into account his or her perspective and any information you may have overlooked that would affect standards of performance. The more input people have in setting performance expectations, the more likely they will be to agree with the standards.

- With each team member, come to consensus on goal prioritization and performance standards that meet and exceed expectations. Be sure to document your decisions.

- Clarify with each person the rewards for performance.

- Meet periodically to discuss progress. If appropriate, revise expectations while keeping goals challenging and reward people for their contributions to the success of the group.

Impart to others a sense of energy, ownership, and personal commitment to work

Today's leaders need to be exceptionally good at inspiring others to achieve team goals. Leaders who are effective at this present a compelling vision of the future, and outline what needs to be done to achieve the vision. They then model the way for others—demonstrating how team members should interact, behave, and react as they proceed toward team objectives. These leaders are also adept at heightening emotional levels of team members by developing strong, personal relationships with team members, and pointing out how each team member will personally benefit if the team's vision is achieved. If leveraged properly, these heightened emotional levels can fuel team members' efforts to achieve more than they thought possible.

The next two sections of this chapter include steps for imparting a sense of energy and personal commitment to a team vision. But leaders also need to model the way. They do this first by looking inside themselves to determine their own level of commitment to the team and its vision. If you are not personally inspired by the team's vision, you can hardly expect others to be enthusiastic about it. Don't think you can successfully deceive team members by acting enthusiastic, but secretly harboring serious doubts about the team and where it is headed.

To create energy, enthusiasm, and commitment, by modeling the way, consider the following suggestions:

- Assess your true feelings about the team and where it is headed. If you are not completely on board, you may want to consider stepping aside as the leader or modifying the team's vision to raise your commitment level.

- Emphasize the importance of the team's vision. The more excited and energetic you are about the team's vision, the more committed others are likely to be in supporting you. Display your enthusiasm by conveying how important the team's goals and vision are to you and how pleased you are that people are willing to pitch in and work with you. Continue to link people's efforts to the overall objective.

- Behave in a manner consistent with the team's vision by modeling excellence and enthusiasm in everything you do. Remember that your actions speak louder than your words.

- Look for opportunities to contribute to team success through individual efforts. In other words, help the team by periodically covering the phones, photocopying, running errands, filling orders, getting coffee, maintaining equipment, and so on. Performing these small and often mundane tasks demonstrates to the team that everyone's work is important and that you are willing to sacrifice your time and effort to help the team succeed.

- Look for and reward progress whenever you can. Be sure to also recognize and reward attempts to increase the team's effectiveness.

- Empathize with the perspective that it may be difficult to make things better, but refrain from making statements like, "Things will never change."

- Develop strong, trusting relationships with your team members. Try to understand each member's personal and professional goals, why they come to work, why they chose to be a member of this team, and what they hope to personally accomplish if the team achieves its goals and vision.

- Make explicit connections between the team's goal and vision and each person's needs, motives, and personal and professional goals. Be vigilant for opportunities to point out how the team's success will help each team member to succeed.

- Capitalize on people's competitive spirit and sense of pride. Provide benchmarking information about your external competitors or other teams within your organization. Help the team understand how it stacks up against others and what members need to do to improve.

- When assigning new projects to team members, take time to explain how the project fits in with the team's overall objectives and vision. When people understand how their work contributes to the whole, their commitment to it increases.

- Expect your people to excel. Research shows that conveying positive expectations about what others can achieve can lead to better performance than when negative expectations are communicated—what is commonly called the "self-fulfilling prophecy."

- Build on small wins by regularly telling stories about progress toward the team's goals and vision. Recognizing small wins builds momentum and confidence in the team.

- When negative feelings or attitudes come to your attention, bring them into the open. Discuss the issues and what can be done to improve the situation. Express optimism that things can be different.

- Provide rewards. People are typically more willing to cooperate when they perceive that they will benefit from the effort they put in. As a manager, you can offer tangible rewards (bonuses, salary increases, promotions, etc.) to your team members. When these rewards are not appropriate or when you do not have the authority to offer them, use your creativity to come up with other ways people will benefit from helping you out.

- Heighten the exposure of people who perform low-visibility responsibilities. For example, when recounting a successful project, explain how the accuracy and timeliness of the typist contributed to efficiency and quality.

- Discourage actions that minimize the contributions of others. For example, when coordinating project-planning meetings, include the staff responsible for typing, collating, and proofing, etc., to help them see how their work will affect the overall project.

- Openly recognize attempts to go beyond what is expected. In particular, reward people who overcome difficult obstacles and achieve strong results. Acknowledge what these individuals did and how they did it.

- Make it a point to regularly reinforce the importance of each individual's contributions and his or her value to the team's vision and objectives.

- Understand that peer pressure can play a positive role in inspiring work commitment in less enthusiastic team members. Often those who have been identified, been rewarded, or gained visibility for their positive contributions to team success will put pressure on others to get on board.

- Remind your people often that the success of the department or team is key to the success of the organization.

Inspire action without relying solely on authority

Effective leaders use a variety of levers to inspire their team members to action without relying on authority. One lever is creating a team vision. Other levers depend on the leader's own talents and skills, the team members' talents and skills, and situational factors. The potential to inspire others to take action depends on what type of and how much power or influence both the leader and team members possess.

Leaders have more influence when their sources of power are more variable. Versatile leaders understand their sources of power or influence, know how to use this influence, and work to broaden it. The five bases of power are listed below. The most effective leaders work to improve and are adept at using all five of these bases.

- *Expert power* is the ability to influence others based on one's skills, knowledge, experience, or expertise. It is a function of the amount of knowledge one possesses relative to the rest of the members in the group.

- *Referent power* is the ability to influence others based on interpersonal relationships. The more and stronger the relationships, the more referent power you have. Referent power takes time to develop, places a premium on interpersonal skills, and becomes more difficult with organizational flattening initiatives. To increase referent power, you have to be willing to spend time honing interpersonal skills and building relationships with others.

- *Legitimate power* is the ability to influence others based on the authority vested in one's position. Legitimate power allows you to make decisions and take action relatively quickly. The farther you move up the corporate ladder, the more legitimate power you have.

- *Reward power* is the ability to influence others based on control over desired resources. One key to using reward power is determining what type of rewards team members want. Too often, leaders mistakenly assume that the rewards they appreciate are the same rewards their team members would appreciate. Spending time building relationships with team members not only builds referent power, but can also give you clues as to the types of rewards that will best motivate individual team members.

  Another key to using reward power is to not limit yourself to using only organizationally sanctioned rewards. Leaders who are adept at using reward power are often quite innovative with the kinds of rewards they administer. Unskilled use of rewards, however, can lead to perceptions of inequity, and may lead to compliance rather than commitment.

- *Coercive power* is the ability to influence others through the administration of negative sanctions or the removal of positive events. Several myths surround the use of coercive power or punishment. None of these myths have stood up to scientific research. When used skillfully, coercive power can actually increase the overall job satisfaction and performance of the team. For example, some people need to know that negative consequences will result if they harass others. To use punishment or coercive power correctly, it should:
  - Be consistent across people and behaviors.
  - Be immediate.
  - Emphasize the behavior, not the person.
  - Get the attention of the person being punished.

The more expert, referent, and reward power you have, the more likely you will be able to inspire action without relying solely on authority. Leaders with little expert, referent, or reward power are likely to gain team members' compliance, but not their commitment to the team's vision and objectives.

To determine which power bases are currently available to you to inspire action among team members, answer and score the questions below:

Use the following scale to respond to the items:

1 —————— 2 —————— 3 —————— 4 —————— 5
Strongly   Disagree   So-So   Agree   Agree
Disagree   Strongly

1. I have the education and training needed to be successful in my job. _____

2. I have relevant knowledge, experience, and skills for my job. _____

3. My coworkers see me as a subject-matter expert. _____

4. I easily build relationships with others. _____

5. I have an extensive network of friends within the organization. _____

6. I can leverage relationships to get others to take action. _____

7. I have a lot of latitude in deciding how or when work gets done. _____

8. I have a lot of formal authority in my current position. _____

9. I control a budget. _____

10. I can provide others with monetary rewards when they do a good job. _____

11. I use different rewards to motivate different people. _____

12. I control a large number of potential rewards or benefits to give to others. _____

13. I can withhold perks and privileges if others are not doing a good job. _____

14. I have the authority to terminate direct reports if they do not perform. _____

15. I can use formal sanctions to influence others. _____

Total of Items 1–3: _____ Total Expert Power Score

- 12–15   You can exert considerable influence based on what you know.
- 9–11   A solid score, but you could do more to develop your knowledge base.
- Less than 8   You need to spend time building your expertise if you want to influence others based on what you know.

Total of Items 4–6: _____ Total Referent Power Score

- 12–15   You can exert considerable influence based on who you know.
- 9–11   A solid score, but you could do more to develop your network.
- Less than 8   Spend more time building relationships with others if you want to exert more influence.

Total of Items 7–9: _____ Total Legitimate Power Score

- 12–15   You can exert considerable influence based on your position.
- 9–11   You have some ability to influence others based on your position.
- Less than 8   You have limited ability to influence others based solely on your position in the organization.

Total of Items 10–12: _____ Total Reward Power Score

- 12–15   You can influence others via the rewards you control.
- 9–11   You can exert some influence, but you may need to expand the types of rewards you can administer or better match rewards to employees' needs.
- Less than 8   To increase your reward power, ensure that rewards meet team members' needs and reward performance more frequently.

Total of Items 13–15: _____ Total Coercive Power Score

- 12–15   You can influence others using punishment or threats.
- 9–11   A solid score, but you may not be able to get others to do what you need them to do using threats or sanctions.
- Less than 8   You may not be able to exert much influence using threats or punishment.

Inspire others to define new opportunities and continuously improve the organization

Effective leaders are highly skilled in modeling the way for team members. They personally demonstrate what needs to be done if the team wants to achieve its vision and objectives. These leaders are also very good at intellectual stimulation; they constantly question the current status quo, challenge the way it has always been done, and get team members to look at old problems in new ways. Part of this intellectual stimulation is designed to get team members to identify what is working well and not so well, and to develop ideas to improve team or organizational functioning and performance.

The following suggestions can help you inspire your team to continuously improve its performance:

- Ensure that the team's vision is aligned with that of the organization. This will improve the likelihood that new ideas and solutions to problems are aligned with the direction the organization is trying to go.

- Build strong, trusting relationships with team members. If team members do not trust you, they are very unlikely to offer suggestions on how to improve the team or organization.

- Model the way; lead discussions with team members on how the team or organization can improve. Challenge assumptions, get team members to identify root causes rather than symptoms of problems, and get them to think through all the implications of the solutions they propose.

- Reward those who look for opportunities to continuously improve team or organizational functioning.

- Conduct an audit to determine the types of people who make up your team. Some people are more challenging and skeptical by nature, whereas others are more likely to accept things just as they are, and are less willing to question the status quo. Your ability to get team members to generate new solutions to team and organizational problems will depend to some extent on the nature of your team members.

Trust other people's judgment, recognizing that the best decisions are not always made at the top

Leaders cannot accomplish the team's vision by themselves. A key to success for many teams is bench strength—the stronger the individual team members, the stronger the team is likely to be. Leaders who focus on building the technical and decision-making skills of all team members systematically empower the team to accomplish results.

Effective leaders understand that trust is a two-way street and that people closest to the problem often make the best decisions about the issue. Nevertheless, people are likely to make poor decisions if they lack pertinent knowledge and skills.

The following process will help you move toward trusting your team's decision making:

- Begin by building trusting relationships with team members and making sure that everyone understands and buys into the team's vision and their individual roles and goals.

- Once everyone understands the team's direction and how their roles and responsibilities fit into team success, focus on empowering individuals by giving them decision-making autonomy and backing up the decisions they make.

- Support their decisions as much as you can. This helps to build even more trust and momentum toward the accomplishment of the team's vision and objectives.

For team members who lack confidence and competence, effective leaders begin the empowerment process by systematically identifying development needs and then building key knowledge and skills. As their skills and self-confidence grow, the team members are allowed to make more decisions in their area. Eventually they should have all of the skills and confidence they need to make almost all of the decisions within their role. To empower less-talented team members, use the following process:

1. Identify the standards of performance for the task. Consider which outcomes are acceptable, which are unacceptable, and which reflect outstanding performance. Explicitly convey to the person what is necessary to accomplish the task. The more explicitly task goals and criteria are presented, the more likely they are to be met.

2. Allow time for the team member to respond to what you have said. Ask for the employee's perspective and ideas on how to accomplish the job. Express your confidence in the person's ability to do the job.

3. Decide on a course of action with the team member and, depending on the team member's expertise and the task complexity, follow up as he or she performs the task. (For example, follow up more closely for less experienced team members, less closely for more experienced team members.)

4. As the team member gains experience, add additional decision-making authority. Resist taking over when things go wrong; instead, coach him or her on how to correct the mistake.

5. Identify the areas of the job where the team member is particularly skilled. Then fully delegate to the team member in those areas.

Celebrate and reward significant achievements of others

Many managers believe they have no impact on the motivation of others because motivation occurs within an individual, or because they have no control over some of the factors that affect employee satisfaction, such as working conditions and benefits. However, managers play a major role in distributing many of the rewards team members seek. Two keys to motivating team members are to first understand what they find rewarding, and then to administer the desired rewards for behaviors that are aligned with team success.

GREAT JOB, JENKINS! AS A REWARD, I'D LIKE YOU TO PREPARE THE OTHER 65 REPORTS.

Individuals vary dramatically in the motives that drive their behavior. Some people are at their motivational best when they are given autonomy to decide how to accomplish tasks. Other people find it more energizing to work with others than by themselves, while some will put in the most effort when given high-risk, high-visibility assignments. Good leaders understand how to motivate individuals. Likewise, they also know that the rewards that motivate some team members could potentially *demotivate* others.

Following are some of the more important types of motives people have:

Achievement Motive
Drives to personally accomplish significant goals:

- Takes risks

- Pushes oneself

- Achieves challenging goals

- Subjects others to stress

- Seeks visible results

Balance Motive
Drives to seek work environments that place equal emphasis on nonwork activities:

- Wants flexible hours

- Enjoys nonwork activities

- Dislikes overtime

- Likes time off

- May like to telecommute

Autonomy Motive

Drives to act independently and to express creativity:

- Prefers to do his/her own thing

- Wants independence

- Takes initiative

- Contributes to and enjoys the beauty in the world

- Develops new ideas, materials, and methods

Job Security Motive

Drives to seek work environments that provide security and stability:

- Prefers stability

- Prefers job security

- Prefers predictability

- Seeks comfortable, clean, and safe working conditions

- Prefers a regular income

Power Motive

Drives to seek out opportunities for recognition, prestige, authority, and/or control:

- Seeks visible signs of success in others' eyes

- Seeks to lead and set direction for others

- Prefers visible signs of recognition

- Focuses on getting ahead and advancing his or her career

- Wants visible signs of prestige

Relationship Motive

Drives to seek out opportunities to build strong relationships and/or to be of service to others:

- Seeks to relate to and help others

- Fosters harmony

- Provides service to others

- Emphasizes giving to others

- Works with and lives by strong values of religious, racial, social, ethnic, or cultural groups

To celebrate and reward your team members appropriately, consider the following suggestions:

- Identify the consequences that need to be changed to improve desired behaviors. Do this by determining how to remove the positive consequences of undesirable behaviors, and create positive consequences for desirable behaviors.

- Discuss the desired goals with the team member, phrasing the goals in behavioral, observable terms.

- Catch team members doing something right. Then make sure you give them positive feedback.

- Once the desired behavior is performed, reward it immediately. Positive consequences increase the probability that the behavior will occur again. Your rewards should match up with the team member's personal motives as much as possible.

- As desired behaviors become more frequent, observe team members to determine the optimum timing for rewards. For example, some people may appreciate frequent encouragement and recognition throughout a project, while others may prefer to receive these rewards upon project completion.

- Develop and implement an expanded list of the rewards you can provide team members to positively influence their individual motivation levels.

- Hold special recognition or celebration lunches to acknowledge team member accomplishments or successful completion of projects.

Create an environment that encourages others to do their best

A high-performance environment is one of the hallmarks of a successful leader. These leaders are able to achieve more than anyone thought possible by creating work environments where:

- The focus is clear—because the team vision is understood by all.

- The work is challenging—a result of high performance expectations.

- People feel appreciated—an outgrowth of building strong, trusting relationships.

- Barriers to accomplishing work are at a minimum.

- Resources are available.

- People help and support one another—because transformational leaders point out how everyone benefits by being on the team.

The first step in creating a high-performance environment is to identify your team members' perception of "what exists today" and "what is needed." To gain a clearer understanding of your current environment and what action is needed to develop it into a high-performance environment, ask your team members the following questions:

- What have you done in the last six months that makes you most proud?

- What is challenging about your work? What challenges do you like?

- What sources provide you with a sense of job satisfaction?

- Who appreciates the job you do? Where do you get your recognition?

- What has motivated you in the past to work harder?

- What obstacles exist to doing your work?

- What resources are or are not available for you to do your job?

- Who can you count on when faced with difficulties and constraints?

- Where do you get support?

Creating a work environment where people enjoy what they do is critical to maintaining an energized and creative work team. People are more motivated in situations where they can combine hard work with fun. Consider the following suggestions for creating a more enjoyable work environment:

- Examine your own attitude about work and fun. Do you believe that work should be fun? If not, it will be very difficult to create an environment where others can have fun. Remember that the more enjoyable and rewarding the work is, the more satisfied people will be.

- Try the following suggestions to help make work more fun for your team:
  - Create situations where people can get to know each other (for example, interdepartmental meetings, parties, brainstorming sessions, celebrations).
  - Smile more.
  - Organize company-sponsored events such as volunteer opportunities in the community or sports activities.
  - Be a model of how to laugh at oneself. Be willing to admit to and see the humor in your mistakes.
  - Focus on small wins in addition to the big ones.
  - Talk about and celebrate successes.
  - Give people recognition for their efforts.

Positively address work environment and balance issues

In high-performance work teams, team members completely buy into the team's vision and identify with the team and the team leader. They can get so emotionally involved with their team that they end up working more hours a week to accomplish the team goals.

While these long hours of focused effort often result in team success, they can also lead to team-member burnout. This is particularly true for people who have strong achievement and balance motives. People who spend long hours achieving goals (i.e., have a strong achievement motive) often do not have much work/life balance. This may not be a problem for them unless they also have a strong balance motive.

Effective leaders understand that individual motivation is complicated. Sometimes the motivation works well for people; other times an individual's motives are in opposition to one another.

To more effectively address such issues, learn some common ways in which personal motives can be difficult to manage for individuals:

- People with strong power and relationship motives will often struggle with promotion opportunities. On the one hand, a promotion is likely to result in recognition, status, and influence. On the other hand, it may mean moving to another job, location, or company and disrupting all the relationships they have built in their current position.

- Team members with high autonomy and job security motives will struggle with opportunities to create new positions for themselves—they might enjoy the latitude of the new position, but worry about their long-term future with the company.

- People who are achievement oriented may find that motive conflicts with their desire for life balance.

To help people cope with work environment and balance issues, consider the following questions:

- Have you successfully created a high-performing work environment? If so, what are the norms and expectations around work hours? You may find that people are expected to work 50-80 hours if they want to be seen as a valued member of the team. Is this what you want? What are the morale and retention risks if team members maintain this work pace?

- Have you told team members that work/life balance is important? Are you modeling an overactive achievement motive or a strong balance motive?

- Do team members expect everyone to work long hours? How do other people treat those who don't put in these hours?

- Do you have any team members with strong achievement and balance motives? What are you doing to help them cope with these conflicting motives?

In addition, use the following suggestions to help with work/life balance:

- Be available to help team members work through conflicts about their values.

- Remember that leaders set the tone for their teams. Leaders who are exclusively task focused are likely to have teams that concentrate on getting results at the exclusion of anything else. This may help the team to accomplish its objectives, but it can also lead to unnecessarily high levels of dissatisfaction, stress, and turnover.

- Periodically take time to assess whether the team you created is what you intended it to be. You should review team results, employee opinion survey results, turnover rates, and exit interviews as part of this assessment process.

RESOURCES

The resources for this chapter begin on page 662.

22
FOSTER
COLLABORATION

———

PART 1: SPONSOR TEAMWORK IN YOUR ORGANIZATION
- *Build a team environment*
- *Work to remove barriers to collaboration*
- *Value the contributions of all team members*
- *Sponsor teams in your organization*
- *Discourage "we versus they" thinking*
- *Acknowledge and celebrate team accomplishments*
- *Share credit with others*
- *Foster effective give-and-take relationships*
- *Support teams through stages of team growth and maturity*

PART 2: BUILD YOUR TEAM
- *Build a shared vision and shared goals*
- *Build shared values and team norms*
- *Evaluate your effectiveness as a team member*
- *Facilitate effective interactions among group members*

PART 3: DEVELOP TEAM PROBLEM-SOLVING AND DECISION-MAKING SKILLS
- *Decide when to use a team approach for problem solving*
- *Improve your team decision-making process*
- *Seek involvement of others in decision making*

INTRODUCTION

The complexities of today's business challenges more than ever require collaboration across the organization and among management team members. Just as "the whole is greater than the sum of the parts," people achieve more by working together than through individual efforts. To realize this synergy, however, managers must be actively involved in fostering teamwork.

Effective leaders in team-based organizations work with others to create the conditions for team effectiveness. They know when and how to use teams; they know that sometimes a team approach is not the best choice. They also provide the tools, systems, and resources that create a supportive environment for collaboration.

To increase the benefits of using teams, leaders need to increase participation and commitment to teaming, appropriately leverage team involvement, and increase trust among teams—and not just among team members, but also trust between cross-functional teams, cross-business teams, and internal and external teams. In addition, leaders need to increase the commitment of teams and team members to organizational goals.

This three-part chapter provides suggestions to help managers foster successful teamwork. It includes recommendations for developing skills with a variety of team-based approaches, including problem-solving groups, high-performance teams, self-directed work teams, task forces, and so forth.

VALUABLE TIPS

- Provide a clear charter and purpose for the teams you sponsor. Also state your expectations up front.

- Encourage others to form teams made up of diverse individuals who represent different functional or business areas. This provides the team with a broader perspective on issues.

- Assess your decision-making style and pay attention to the extent to which you solicit others' ideas. Look for opportunities to use a more participative approach.

- Ensure that teams have defined their purpose, goals, and vision. To be a team, team members must share goals, and their work needs to be interdependent.

- Make a list of the key strengths and limitations of each person on your team. Find ways to utilize the strengths and to build understanding of one another's styles and interests among your team members.

- Find ways to involve quiet team members without embarrassing them. Use open-ended questions to draw out quieter members of your team, and then listen carefully.

- Acknowledge, summarize, and reinforce the contributions of your team members.

- Identify ways to build ongoing relationships with stakeholders outside the team and to create opportunities for team members to interact with them.

- Solve problems with the people who will be most affected by the decision.

- Reward team accomplishments and celebrate successes. Find creative ways to recognize individual contributions to the team.

- Create opportunities for people to generate and implement their own best ideas.

- Encourage cooperation, rather than competition, between different work units. Make sure groups set their goals in harmony with one another and that the goals are mutually supportive.

- Include an appraisal of team performance, in addition to individual performance, as a part of your performance-management system.

- Help team members understand one another better. Share information about how work is being done. Discuss work histories, specific skills, successes, and talents.

- Help team members to understand, appreciate, and use differences among themselves to arrive at better solutions and to do better work.

- Encourage everyone involved to speak a common language. To avoid alienating outside groups, educate them and help them to understand the "lingo" of the team.

- Foster an environment of trust by ensuring that all criticism is constructive and is focused on individuals' behaviors, not personalities.

- Establish meeting practices that enforce collaboration and include the full participation of everyone.

- Share success with team members. Give others credit for their contributions to the success.

- Have fun while working.

PART 1:
SPONSOR TEAMWORK IN YOUR ORGANIZATION

Build a team environment

An organization's success at working in teams depends largely on the attitudes, directives, and policies that come from the management team. These policies and organizational systems can either discourage team practices or help build a team environment.

Building a team environment is not an overnight process. It takes more than the manager's efforts to create a culture where trust and teamwork are evident. It requires systems (e.g., performance management, communication, technology) that support people working together and leadership that models the behaviors of teamwork.

The following suggestions can help you build a team environment in your workplace:

- Consider the following questions to determine the extent to which your organization represents a team environment. Your answers may reveal areas of opportunity for you to improve your present team environment.
  - Do people in our organization act as if they care about one another's success?
  - Are people's actions consistent with what they say?
  - Do we share information with one another openly?
  - Do we keep our commitments to one another?
  - Do we solve problems together?
  - Do we surface conflict and productively resolve it?
  - Do we value differences (for instance, do we value introverted members to the same degree as extroverted members)?
  - Is the work environment inclusive of others?
  - Do we foster cooperation and information sharing with other departments?
  - Do people enjoy working together?

  Ask your team members the same questions, and then discuss their responses.

- Provide a structure conducive to teamwork. Too much hierarchy, whether formal or informal, can impede teamwork.

- Encourage cooperation, rather than competition, between different work units. Make sure groups set their goals in harmony with one another and that the goals are mutually supportive.

- Provide the necessary resources for team success (for example, proper staffing, up-to-date information, and so forth).

- Give work teams the authority to act upon their team decisions.

- Include an appraisal of team performance, in addition to individual performance, as a part of your performance-management system.

- Reward successful team contributions, as well as individual contributions.

- Show by example how to be both an effective team leader and team member.

Work to remove barriers to collaboration

You and your management team play a key role in building collaboration in your organization. Management needs to be actively involved in removing barriers that could stand in the way of effective teamwork in the organization.

Barriers to collaboration are typically related to team processes, performance measures, lack of communication, and lack of clarity and alignment among functions. Following are ideas for how to address the more common barriers:

- Establish clear agendas, ground rules, and team decisions/actions as part of an effective meeting approach. Productive meetings are critical to teamwork.

- Be sure that the goals of all teams are in alignment with the organization's goals.

- Clarify the decision-making boundaries for all teams in your organization.

- Clearly communicate the team's purpose and goals. Then make sure you have buy-in from every team member.

- Clarify each team member's roles and responsibilities in the team effort. Whenever possible, divide the workload equally.

- Clearly define team performance expectations and hold members accountable for results and behavior.

- Establish measures that support teamwork.

- Develop relationships with key customers and stakeholders to provide support for your teams.

- Provide key information to your teams. Managers often err by under-communicating and by making assumptions about what people in their organization know.

Value the contributions of all team members

All team members—those who have more complex jobs as well as those whose responsibilities are more straightforward—are important to the success of the organization. For all members to feel valued and worthwhile, there must be a pervasive attitude that everyone's work is important. Following are ways to foster that attitude:

- Value the work that everyone does. Some people believe particular functions are more important to business success, and others value work only if it is intellectually complex. Your team will function more smoothly if no one is considered better or more important than anyone else. Eliminate the symbols that distinguish some as more important than others.

- Provide verbal recognition for everyone's contributions.

- Include team members at all levels in as much planning, decision making, and problem solving as possible. If direct involvement is not appropriate, at least discuss the impact the decision will have on workload.

- When you want input from the team, ask for comments and suggestions from everyone. Don't treat your administrative staff differently than you treat other employees.

- Give your staff feedback if you see any of them devaluing members of the team.

- Reinforce and recognize the attainment of goals. Praise the accomplishments of less visible employees as often as those of employees who are more in the spotlight.

- Take time to listen to all team members' ideas and opinions. Then thank them for their input, even if you disagree with their point of view.

- Be especially attentive to comments from less assertive individuals who may not feel comfortable or experienced in contributing ideas and opinions in a group.

- Tie individual team members' roles and responsibilities to the overall goal of the team. Make sure they understand how they affect team goals and can contribute to achieving them.

Sponsor teams in your organization

To maximize the ultimate success of your team, it's important that everyone in your unit, division, and functional area work together. Teamwork takes time to build, and requires practice and effort on the part of both manager and employees. In addition, members of all teams in the organization, including your management team, need to understand why they will approach work as a team rather than as a group of individuals. They must also agree about how to work together as a team.

Management's role in building organizational teams is to provide clarity about purpose, expectations, and decision-making authority. Managers must also support organizational initiatives that provide a foundation and reward system for teamwork.

The following suggestions can help you more effectively sponsor teams in your organization:

- Ensure that teams have defined their purpose, goals, and vision. To be a team, team members must share goals, and their work needs to be interdependent.

- Help teams clarify roles and responsibilities. Provide opportunities for team members to clarify and negotiate roles and relationships with one another. To empower teams, allow team members to work out responsibilities and roles among themselves, and report their recommendations to you.

- Provide the team with an appropriate level of authority and decision-making power. Encourage the team to make collaborative decisions and to implement their solutions.

- Set performance goals based on team accomplishments and how well members work together as a team.

- Help team members understand one another better. Share information about how work is being done. Discuss work histories, specific skills, successes, and talents. Help team members to understand, appreciate, and use differences among themselves to arrive at better solutions and to do better work.

- Find opportunities for team members to work across functions and to find integrative solutions to problems.

- Encourage teams to meet regularly. Establish shared decision-making opportunities when the team meets.

Discourage "we versus they" thinking

Promoting teamwork among groups across an organization is essential for creating an environment where people pursue common goals. To discourage "we versus they" thinking and increase efficient communication and collaboration across groups, consider the following ideas:

- Build teamwork among different groups by identifying a common problem or issue that a cross-functional task force or committee could solve.

- When making decisions using people from a variety of teams, avoid voting for decisions. Instead, strive for consensus. Voting is not likely to produce a true team decision.

- Avoid labeling and stereotyping (for instance, referring to accountants as "bean counters"). Respect for other groups and professions is critical to promoting teamwork among different groups.

- Encourage everyone involved to speak a common language. To avoid alienating outside groups, educate them and help them to understand the lingo of the team. Language that leaves others in the dark results in blocked communication, confusion, and disinterest.

- Evaluate your employees on their willingness and ability to work as part of a team. Encourage them to develop relationships throughout the organization, not just within their own functional area.

- Gather data from stakeholders, customers (internal and external), and other functions to gain a better understanding of how your teams are meeting the needs of team stakeholder groups. Ask the teams to create a plan to better address those needs, and to create integrated strategies or approaches to solve problems.

Acknowledge and celebrate team accomplishments

Acknowledging and celebrating team accomplishments is a powerful way to recognize your team efforts and to keep motivation and momentum going. Following are some suggestions for celebrating team accomplishments:

- Make it a point to tell your team in staff meetings that you appreciate their contributions. Be specific about what they have done well.

- Publicly acknowledge good team performance in meetings and other company communication vehicles such as company newsletters.

- Keep in mind that different things motivate people. Use a variety of nonmonetary recognition and rewards that are consistent with people's aspirations and values.

- Incorporate into the performance-appraisal process objectives that evaluate effective team involvement and behaviors.

- Keep team members informed about the team's performance (for example, share sales figures).

- Organize special get-togethers such as team lunches, barbecues, breakfasts, or coffee and rolls, upon successful completion of projects.

- Consider instituting a formal awards program with certificates, plaques, a traveling trophy, or other awards to honor teams for their work. When presenting the award, explain the specific efforts of the team and how they worked together to achieve an objective or complete a successful project.

- Ask a team that recently completed a successful project or initiative to share their learnings and experience with other teams or departments. This is a good way to acknowledge their success as well as help others learn from it.

Share credit with others

Extraordinary achievement cannot be accomplished without the involvement, effort, and support of many people. In collaborative organizations, everyone is important, not just the leader. Effective leadership focuses on how to enable others to act, not just on one's own effectiveness. Managers work from the basic assumption that results cannot be attained solely through their own efforts.

If you tend to be competitive to the point where your success comes at the expense of others, you may be impeding the opportunities for collaboration with others. Being a team player means that you share credit with others involved and look for opportunities to make the success of others more visible. Following are some suggestions to help you do that:

- Say "we," not "I." Monitor your language in meetings with peers, direct reports, and other company leadership. How often do you use the word "I" compared with your use of the word "we"? How often do you give credit to others when you are recognized for individual success?

- When you acknowledge the success of a project, make sure you recognize the efforts of all team members involved, no matter how small their role or contributions are.

- When presenting publicly, find a way to recognize those who contributed to the ideas and the work behind your presentation.

- Look for opportunities to make other people's leadership or contribution more visible than your own.

- Ask your team to give you feedback about the extent to which you give credit to peers and others when speaking publicly.

Foster effective give-and-take relationships

Projects often require more resources than a single manager possesses. Sometimes the only way to complete a project successfully is to work with other managers to "borrow" or "lend" personnel, expertise, or financial resources.

The ability to work cooperatively with other managers who have different skills and objectives—to avoid, whenever possible, the unproductive rivalries that are common in many organizations—is a skill that helps savvy managers hurdle seemingly insurmountable obstacles with apparent ease. Building give-and-take relationships requires both compromise and responsiveness

Relax, Bob, I'm not about to fight you on this one.

on your part. By conceding relatively unimportant points and offering your own resources to others when feasible, you can create and maintain "quid pro quo" relationships that will serve you well.

Use the following guidelines to help build effective give-and-take relationships:

- Identify the resources you can offer to others. Then, when someone approaches you for help, state your resources up front. This demonstrates your willingness to be helpful.

- Make sure you understand exactly what the other person is requesting by asking questions and investigating the issues before agreeing to help. If possible, write down and agree upon the resources you will contribute.

- When you think compromise may be required, classify your issues into these three categories:
  - Issues that can definitely be dropped or tabled without penalty to you. When negotiating, use these issues first as conciliatory gestures.
  - Issues that are nice to have, but not essential. These are the next offerings you can make.
  - Must-have issues. Hold out the longest for these.

- Keep in touch with people, so you can volunteer to help when needed. This proactive approach shows real awareness and concern for others. It builds solid relationships.

- Resist the urge to forward your request to a higher level in the organization when someone cannot help you. This tactic will alienate the person whose support you will need in the future. Instead:
  - Believe he or she does want to help, but really does not have the time or resources.
  - Make your request again, emphasizing your common goals or the importance of the need.
  - Give the person direct feedback about the impact of his or her refusal.

- When you can't offer assistance directly, advise the person making the request how he or she can get help. Sometimes you will not have the time or resources to help. Giving suggestions about other possible resources at least shows you are concerned.

- Don't be too busy to listen to another person's requests; this can brand you as a manager who uses others, a reputation that can hurt you. Other managers may not want to work with or promote individuals who do not know how to give as well as take.

- If you truly are too busy to help, the following tips can help you say "no" without jeopardizing the relationship or future support:
  - Consider the importance of the task you are being asked to perform. Is it an integral part of your organization's major goals? Do you have the capability and resources to help?
  - If the task is not integral, suggest someone else who could help.
  - If it is, before you decline, make sure there is no possible way you can take it on. Look for ways to rearrange your current priorities to allow you to accommodate the request. Or try to identify a peer or team member who could temporarily or permanently assume one of your other responsibilities.

Support teams through stages of team growth and maturity

Leaders play an important role in supporting their teams through stages of growth. Knowing where a team is in its life cycle can help you manage expectations about the team's performance and deepen your understanding of team behavior.

Following are ideas to support the team's development through its stages of growth:

Formation of the team

In this phase, the organization has recognized an opportunity where forming a team would be a useful approach. Your role will be to:

- Ensure that the team has a clear charter that outlines its purpose, scope of responsibilities, goals, and boundaries of authority. Assist the team in selecting its members and assigning roles and responsibilities.

- Create opportunities for team members to get better acquainted and build initial rapport. This can be achieved through a kick-off session or a team lunch.

Establishing norms and operating practices

In this phase, a team undergoes a period of questioning and "testing" of one another to determine commitments, roles and responsibilities, and acceptable team behavior. This phase may include periods of "storming" as team members sort out decision making, individual contributions, and issues that may keep them from coming together as a coherent, high-performing team.

In this phase, you can help the team in the following ways:

- Identify the conflicts and facilitate discussions to reach productive solutions.

- Further clarify roles and responsibilities and provide more time for team members to work out differences in perspectives and approaches.

- Provide opportunities for team members to have fun together and build camaraderie.

- Work together collaboratively to resolve any conflicts that may arise.

- Manage the tendency toward competition and coalition forming among subgroups.

Focused, productive team performance

In this stage, team members share a clear idea of their shared goals, roles and responsibilities, and accountabilities for the team's success. The team meets regularly, demonstrates progress, and makes decisions together. Team members are optimistic about the team's success, and are comfortable with one another.

In this phase, you can build on the team's success in the following ways:

- Recognize positive outcomes, and reward team spirit and progress on goals.

- Convey appreciation for each member's contribution.

- Seek new ways to raise the bar of team performance.

- Foster creativity, innovation, and new ways of thinking.

Team renewal

In this phase, an aspect of the team changes, requiring the team to form itself anew and rebuild its collaboration. This process can include a change in membership or leadership, or a change in the team's purpose or overall goals. When this happens, the team must spend time together to revisit goals, roles and responsibilities, and plans. Many of the activities in the forming stage can be helpful in this stage (e.g., social activities, meetings focused on clarifying charter and goals).

Your role in this phase may include these actions:

- Refine/redefine the team's mission.

- Facilitate the team in reestablishing its goals and its agreements regarding team behavior, especially when team membership has changed significantly.

- Encourage the mutual support and involvement of all members in renewing the team and exploring alternatives.

PART 2:
BUILD YOUR TEAM

Build a shared vision and shared goals

An effective leadership team has a clear vision for the organization and a shared understanding among its members about how the team will work together to achieve this future state. It is important that the management team believes in the vision and can articulate its meaning to people from all levels of the organization.

To develop shared vision and goals, consider the following suggestions:

- Involve key stakeholders in building the vision and goals. Invite others to share their ideas or provide input. This will increase commitment and buy-in to the vision and goals.

- Translate the vision into concrete goals and plans to execute.

- Identify initiatives or projects that require members to work together collaboratively to achieve the desired results.

- Establish accountabilities for achieving shared goals. Link people's responsibilities to the impact on the goal.

- Communicate the vision and goals clearly and frequently.

Build shared values and team norms

Behaviors that build trust, openness, and a sense of give-and-take among members are critical to a team's success or failure. After the team reaches agreement about its shared values and team norms, the manager plays an important role in holding people accountable for those agreed-upon behaviors.

Even though you can't control how team members feel about one another, you can reinforce positive behavior and address what is unacceptable. To ignore negative behavior will undermine the team and your own credibility.

To build and reinforce shared values and team norms, consider the following suggestions:

- If the team has not reached agreement about guiding values and team norms, set aside time to reach agreement. Ensure that team members have a shared understanding of what the values and norms mean before they begin the work of the team.

- Ensure that the team mutually agrees on a set of behaviors that serve as guidelines for how to perform, interact with each other, make decisions, and accomplish the team goals.

- Create opportunities to facilitate team discussions about the ways in which the team's behavior has exemplified or disregarded team values and norms. Recognize and champion the positive behavior you are seeing. Reinforce your expectations for team members' behavior. You can do this as a debriefing at the end of team meetings. Team members need to realize their responses have consequences and impact.

- Make sure that any agreements about the team's values and norms are written down and distributed among team members. You can even post the values and your team's "code of conduct" on the wall of your meeting room.

- Meet one-on-one with anyone whose behavior is hurting the group dynamic. Be clear about the behavior and explain how it is affecting the team. Give specific feedback and set clear expectations for how his or her behavior needs to change. Expect your management team members to hold people accountable for behavior that may hurt effective teamwork.

- When the team faces a challenging situation or problem, ask: "In this situation, how can we respond in ways that are consistent with our values? How could we respond that would build trust and openness among ourselves?"

- Create a "Team Spirit" award that is given to a team member each quarter. Ask team members to vote for the best candidate. Find creative ways to recognize the winner.

- Conduct a "Compliment Session" where team members comment on the strengths and contributions of one another. ("What I appreciate about you is…"; "You contribute to our team by…"; "What I wish you would do more of is…")

- Encourage behaviors that provide constructive, open communication among team members.

- Model appropriate conflict-management behaviors that the team can learn from. Conflict is inevitable for teams. To help teams learn to handle tension constructively and creatively, you and your management team set the example for how to address tough issues in productive ways. Behave in ways you expect of others.

- Keep team members focused on their shared purpose and their accountabilities to one another.

Evaluate your effectiveness as a team member

Part of being an effective team leader involves being an effective team member. How effective are you in team situations? Do you contribute too much? Too little? Does the impact you have on a team depend on the circumstances? In developing a plan for improving your team skills, sharpen your awareness of how you currently function as a team member.

The following process can help you develop this insight:

- For the next several months, keep a record of your contributions in committees, meetings, informal team gatherings, and other team settings. Also keep track of ideas, plans, and solutions that you could have contributed but did not.

- Determine your overall impact in each situation. Did you contribute a great deal? Very little? Was the effect of your participation positive, negative, or neutral?

- Evaluate and determine the reasons for your performance. These may include:
  - The amount of preparation you've put in.
  - Knowledge of the area.
  - Interest in the topic.
  - Comfort level with other team members (other members expected and/or welcomed contributions, the opinions of other members warranted responses/rebuttals, other members were quiet, and so forth).
  - Willingness to listen to others.

- Closely scrutinize your attitudes and behavior in team situations. Add to the list above to gain a clearer understanding of your level of effectiveness in team situations.

- Ask a trusted coworker or manager to observe and critique your performance in team settings. Analyze that person's feedback to determine patterns or tendencies that impede effective team performance. Realize that the first step of making a change is to understand the reasons behind your effectiveness and ineffectiveness in team situations.

- Develop an action plan for positive change. Seek ongoing feedback to gauge changes and improvements made.

Facilitate effective interactions among group members

To maximize the resources and capabilities of group members, managers need to draw from the participation of others in group discussions. Interactions in group meetings typically take one of three forms:

- The group is largely silent, with the leader doing most of the talking.

- Group members interact with the leader.

- Group members interact with one another.

The third form represents the most effective type of interaction. When group members interact, the resources of all members are used most fully and problem solving is promoted.

Leaders who effectively facilitate the interaction of others ask questions that spark lively discussions, listen well, invite reactions, build on other people's ideas, and navigate the group discussion to agreement and shared decisions.

Following are ways to encourage group interaction:

- Send out an agenda in advance of the meeting. Indicate what topics team members should be prepared to discuss.

- Assign team members to lead the discussion of appropriate topics. Having others lead the discussion can help you facilitate interactions more effectively.

- Establish the norm of group interaction immediately upon formation of the team. Have the team agree on a set of meeting and communication ground rules.

- Redirect comments that are inappropriately directed to you. For example, a team member responding to a comment made by another team member might look to you for your reaction. Avoid reacting. Instead, ask the team member who made the original comment, "What do you think?"

- Encourage participation by not always doing work as an entire team. Some tasks are more conducive for small groups, pairs, or even individual members. If necessary, divide into smaller groups. Ensure that the groups have clear directions, and summarize their work for the rest of the team.

- When someone proposes an idea, explore its possibilities. Ask the team questions such as:
  - How could we build on that?
  - How could we work together collaboratively to make it possible?
  - What could be the value of that idea?

- Listen for full understanding when team members are speaking. After an important exchange of ideas, summarize what you have heard, or invite other team members to paraphrase what has been said.

- Encourage the involvement of everyone. For example, say, "Let's go around the room and get everyone's opinion about that." Be especially attentive to comments from less-assertive individuals who may not feel comfortable or experienced in contributing ideas and opinions in a group.

- Monitor yourself when you are in front of the group. Do you tend to look at one or two members more than others? Establish eye contact with everyone. It makes people feel more engaged in the discussion.

- Check yourself for how long you take up the "floor time" during discussions. Are you dominating the discussion? Are you allowing certain members to dominate the discussion?

- Protect minority opinion. Reserve your judgment and provide ample opportunity for others to share their ideas and opinions. To ensure that all suggestions are given full consideration, provide those who propose minority solutions with an environment in which they feel comfortable voicing their ideas.

- Arrange the meeting room in a way that facilitates interaction. Tables arranged in a U-shape are more conducive to discussion than those in straight lines. Seating arrangements are also important. Choose a place that deemphasizes your leadership role. For example, sit at the side of a table instead of at the end.

- Be sure to have someone scribe the key comments, actions, and decisions from your team meetings. Writing notes on a white board or on flip-chart paper during the meeting keeps everyone's attention and also maintains an ongoing record of what people are saying as the meeting progresses. Distribute the minutes and key information after each meeting.

PART 3:
DEVELOP TEAM PROBLEM-SOLVING AND DECISION-MAKING SKILLS

Decide when to use a team approach for problem solving

Team leaders need to decide when and to what degree to use a team approach for decision making and problem solving. In general, the higher the level of commitment and buy-in your team members show, and the more creative, varied, and informative the input and opinions they offer, the more important a team approach for solving problems becomes.

When team members are involved in problem solving and decision making, they are more likely to accept the final decision, and to feel ownership and shared responsibility for the success of the overall goal. Furthermore, the quality of decisions and problem solutions is greater because the group process generates a variety of perspectives and opinions that lead to more creative, effective results.

A team approach to problem solving and decision making tends to work best when:

- Full acceptance of the decision is necessary for effective implementation.

- Information from more than one person is required to make the decision.

- A high-quality result is desired.

- A creative solution is needed.

- The decision does not need to be made quickly.

Consider the following suggestions to increase your use of team problem solving:

- Write down all the decisions you have made in the last month. Assess the quality and the acceptance of your decisions. Analyze whether your final outcome would have benefited from some type of team approach. Look for trends, such as avoiding team involvement on certain kinds of problems or decisions.

- Think about the meetings you have conducted in the last month. Looking at the decision-making and problem-solving processes involved, what is the ratio of the number of times you directed them to the number of times you facilitated them? If you tend to underutilize the facilitation process, increase your use of it by allowing others more input into problem solutions. Learn additional skills on how to be an effective facilitator.

On occasion, turn over facilitation of a problem-solving or decision-making effort to one of your team members.

- Seek feedback from your employees, manager, and peers. Ask for their perceptions of when you have effectively used a team approach to solve problems and when you have missed opportunities to do so.

- Identify other managers who effectively use a team approach to solve problems. Use them as role models. Observe what they do that makes them effective, and ask them for tips on how you might improve your own approach.

Improve your team decision-making process

When a group has problems making decisions, it is usually because its members are confused or disagree about one or more of the following:

- What decision they are trying to make.

- Who should be involved in making the decision.

- How individuals should be involved (as information sources or decision makers, for instance).

- When the decision must be made.

- What the best solution/decision is.

You can increase the effectiveness of group problem solving by asking the following questions before each session:

1. What is the problem we are trying to solve? What are the underlying causes? Before the team attempts to generate ideas, it is important that members fully understand the problem to be solved.

2. Who should be involved in this decision? Consider the following:
   - Who possesses the knowledge to ensure that the decision is logical and sound?
   - Who will be involved in implementing the decision?
   - Who must approve the decision? Approval may be easier to obtain if those in authority are invited to participate in the decision-making process.

3. How should each person be involved? Group members may be involved directly (actually make the decisions) or consulted (provide information or opinions). Clarify in advance the roles your group members will play in the process.

4. When will the decision need to be made? Set a time frame so people know when the decision is due.

5. What are the steps you will take to improve group problem solving and your reasons for taking these steps? Let the team know.

For example, you might start the session by saying, "Today, I'm going to help the discussion along but not participate in or direct it. I'll try to protect minority opinion so that the full range of alternatives will be presented, and encourage group interaction to ensure that we all benefit from each individual's experience."

Then provide a structure for the team to guide their decision-making or problem-solving efforts. A typical problem-solving process involves five parts:
- Defining the problem
- Generating alternatives
- Selecting an alternative
- Implementing a plan
- Evaluating the plan

Seek involvement of others in decision making

Rarely can important decisions be made without input from others. When plans impact people, it is critical that they have the opportunity to share their opinions and be involved in the decision-making process. Managers need to solicit input before making decisions for a variety of reasons: to obtain critical input, to build commitment in others, to develop others, to show respect for others' opinions, and to foster open communication and problem sharing.

Knowing whom to involve—and when—maximizes your opportunities for success and positive recognition. The following guidelines suggest ways to solicit input for the decision-making process:

• When you first learn that you must make a decision, determine who has the information you need to make a good decision, who you need to involve to get buy-in, and who you think should be involved.

• When putting together a task force or project team, ask members who else should be included. Invite others to sit in on meetings when you are discussing a topic that affects them, even if they aren't regular members of the committee. Send minutes of action items to interested parties for their information.

• Consider when to involve people. You may involve everyone in every phase or engage different people in each one, depending on the decisions and input needed for that phase—defining the problem or opportunity, identifying other ways of looking at the problem, generating optional approaches, selecting criteria for making a final decision, making the final call, or planning implementation.

- Use a variety of ways to solicit input. Options include:
  - One-to-one conversations
  - Group discussions
  - Memos requesting input
  - Electronic mail discussion
  - Internal computer bulletin boards/discussion areas

- When interviewing others to gain information for problem solving, use open-ended questions and active listening. (See Chapter 28: Listen to Others in this handbook.) Take care not to judge others' suggestions or to convey, verbally or nonverbally, that you disapprove of their ideas. When appropriate, pull people together as a group so that individuals can work together to define the opportunities, goals, and best course of action.

- Develop supporters in the group who will help you keep it focused and working constructively. Be clear about what you want, particularly with those you rely upon as supporters.

- If people have difficulty working together, talk to them individually first. Ask for their cooperation and deal with their concerns respectfully. If a particular person's involvement is seriously disruptive to the team:
  - Offer to keep the person informed, and identify ways to get the necessary support without involving him or her as a member of the team.
  - Involve the person on a one-to-one basis by asking him or her to be your advisor.
  - Assign the person to another project requiring his or her expertise to minimize involvement in this team.
  - Don't be afraid to exclude the person from the team.

- Identify a peer or higher-level manager who is effective at involving others.
  - Observe how this person determines who should be involved in what situations, as well as how he or she involves those people.
  - Write down the methods you observe.
  - Arrange a time to discuss these methods with the "expert."
  - Ask this person to give you feedback and suggestions on the people you involve in your next project.

RESOURCES

The resources for this chapter begin on page 664.

INTERPERSONAL FACTOR

Leadership is a reciprocal relationship between those who
choose to lead and those who decide to follow....
If there is no underlying need for the relationship, then there is no need for leaders.
— James Kouzes & Barry Posner in *Credibility*

The "people" skills of management have never been more important. Yet with all the organizational changes in recent years (including downsizing, rightsizing, delayering, mergers, acquisitions, and so on), the relationships between leaders and the people that work for them are continually challenged.

Building and maintaining understanding, mutual trust and respect, and meaningful cooperation requires dedication, sensitivity to others, flexibility, and continual effort. Your efforts in this area are critical to creating a vibrant climate, a healthy work environment, and a high level of productivity.

When ruptures occur in the relationship fabric of the organization, as happens with downsizing or losing good people to the competition, you may have to work harder than ever to build a high degree of understanding and rapport with those who work for and with you. It's important work that needs to be done.

Other times, when time is your most limited organizational resource, you may find yourself driven to pay attention only to execution. Guard against making this common mistake. Your success really does depend on whether you have the people with the skills to execute your strategy. They are hard to find, costly to get, and require ongoing effort to keep. You may find that you need to develop and sustain more and better working relationships than ever before.

The following chapters of this section present suggestions and development activities for improving your interpersonal skills in key skill areas:

Chapter 23 – Build Relationships: Relates to others in an open, friendly, accepting, and respectful manner; viewed as approachable and shows interest in others; develops and maintains high-quality relationships with manager, peers, and direct reports; demonstrates style flexibility when relating to a variety of people and situations; uses formal and informal networks to get things done; identifies and cultivates relationships with key colleagues and stakeholders in other parts of the organization; builds and maintains appropriate contacts and networks with people in the industry or profession.

Chapter 24 – Manage Conflict: Seeks to analyze the underlying causes of conflicts; knows when to encourage disagreement and when to minimize or resolve it; deals with disagreements and conflicts in a respectful and tactful manner; knows how to deal with conflict situations constructively; brings substantive conflicts into the open and attempts to deal with them collaboratively.

Chapter 25 – Leverage Individual and Cultural Diversity: Shows and fosters respect for each person and his/her background, culture, values, perspective, or approach; works to understand the background and worldview of others; assists people from diverse backgrounds and cultures to effectively contribute and succeed in the organization; seeks to utilize the different personalities and backgrounds of people for the betterment of the enterprise; pursues ways to accommodate the differing needs, work patterns, and preferences of a diverse workforce.

23
BUILD
RELATIONSHIPS

PART 1: BUILD RELATIONSHIPS
- *Obtain feedback on your interpersonal style*
- *Be approachable: project warmth, sincerity, and openness*
- *Adjust your interpersonal style to cues from others*
- *Relate well to people regardless of their personality or background*
- *Treat people with respect*
- *Maintain positive relationships even under difficult or heated circumstances*
- *Develop good timing*
- *Consider people's feelings when you make decisions*

PART 2: FOSTER RELATIONSHIPS WITH YOUR COLLEAGUES
- *Develop effective working relationships with your employees*
- *Solicit feedback from your direct reports*
- *Help others have fun on the job*
- *Develop effective working relationships with your peers*
- *Develop an effective working relationship with your manager*
- *Give feedback to your manager*
- *Develop effective working relationships with higher management*

PART 3: BUILD AND LEVERAGE NETWORKS
- *Cultivate networks with people across a variety of functions and locations within the organization*
- *Establish networks with people in the industry or profession*
- *Develop your network*
- *Strengthen your network by giving information and support*
- *Build support for your own ideas through contacts with others*
- *Leverage networks to get things done*

INTRODUCTION

No leaders are totally self-sufficient; they need the support, cooperation, and goodwill of their managers, peers, and employees to accomplish their goals. In most organizations, effective leaders at all levels are adept at working both the streets and the alleys. The streets are the formal procedures through which work is accomplished—in other words, the organization's formal chain of command and its written policies. The alleys are the informal networks that enable managers to marshal the resources they need to get things done.

Leaders who operate only through informal channels will find themselves challenged when they work in or with organizations that are more formal. Leaders who are comfortable working only through formal channels will be much less effective in informal organizations and can get bogged down in time-consuming procedures in formal ones. Their colleagues may see them as roadblocks that prevent work from getting done quickly.

Finding the right balance between the two ways of operating is essential to your success. This balance will vary depending on a number of factors, including the organizational culture, your functional area, and your position. Whatever your situation is, the suggestions presented in this chapter can help you to build all of the kinds of relationships you need to be a successful manager.

VALUABLE TIPS

- Extend common courtesies to others; for example, greet people in the morning, say "hello" in the halls, and say "thank you" when someone does something on your behalf.

- Seek feedback about your personal impact from people you trust.

- Apologize to people when you have hurt or ignored them.

- Focus on people's good qualities rather than on their deficiencies.

- Be aware of times when coworkers are hurting in their personal lives—death, illness, divorce, and so forth—and express your interest and concern in words, by a visit, with an appropriate card, or with a gift of flowers.

- Learn about others by asking them about their interests.

- Confront issues, not people.

- Make sure you are not manipulating people or creating a climate of mistrust around you. In particular, don't use information unfairly to gain advantage.

- "Manage by walking around." Frequently go into the work area and talk to your employees about their concerns.

- Show respect for employees' ideas and experience by asking for their input, advice, and involvement.

- Convey respect for all people, even those you disagree with or do not understand.

- Recognize your employees' contributions.

- Seek feedback regarding instances when you may have reacted without considering others' feelings.

- Offer to help colleagues who need assistance on projects or assignments.

- Remember, "The right message at the wrong time is the wrong message."

- Make sure your network is reciprocal; share information, ideas, resources, or influence; don't just take from the network.

- Develop a systematic approach to networking. Analyze what you need in a network and what you can offer other members.

- Ask a knowledgeable and well-connected person in your part of the organization to act as your mentor.

PART 1:
BUILD RELATIONSHIPS

Obtain feedback on your interpersonal style

To improve your relationships with other people, you must see yourself as they see you. Unfortunately, you may get little feedback about how others see you. As people move higher in organizations, they often receive less feedback. As a result, high-level managers may not have a clear idea at all of how they are seen. In addition, people who are defensive and who get upset, angry, or hurt when given feedback will find they hear less feedback.

To ensure that you get feedback from others on how they see you, use the following suggestions:

- Ask a respected colleague or manager with whom you regularly interact in one-to-one and group situations to serve as a feedback source. Ask for the person's impressions of your style and impact in a variety of situations.

- Determine what type of first impression you give. Ask others for feedback. Based on this feedback, consider how others will react when they first meet you. Determine whether you want to make a different first impression.

- If employees currently view you as unapproachable, determine what you do to give this impression. Do they see you regularly? Do you appear uninterested in their problems? Do you become angry when people tell you about problems? Try to see yourself as your employees see you and decide what you want to change.

- Seek feedback from others on the behaviors you are trying to change. If possible, tape several discussions and review them with someone in a position to give you objective feedback. That person's feedback can help you determine which areas need improvement. An alternative is to obtain feedback using a 360-degree feedback instrument such as The PROFILOR® Family available through Personnel Decisions International.

Be approachable: project warmth, sincerity, and openness

Research shows that people are able to develop relationships more rapidly when they are seen as approachable and likeable. People will respond more favorably to you if they see you as personable and professional. To appear approachable and project openness, try the following suggestions:

- When you meet someone, be quick to greet him or her. Stand up and shake hands, or greet the person with whatever gestures and protocol are appropriate in the culture to communicate welcome, respect, and interest. Help the person feel at ease by initiating conversation with him or her. When appropriate for the culture, make small talk and use light humor in your initial conversation.

- Show interest in the other person by asking questions about him or her and what he or she does. For example, when you are handed a business card, look at it, and make a comment about the person's role.

- Listen for "free" information to stimulate conversation. As people talk, listen for hints they give about their interests, likes, and dislikes. For example, in a casual conversation about the weather, people might mention that they can't wait to get home to the garden or out on the lake. You've learned two topics of interest to those people—gardening and boating.
  - Over the next week, listen to a variety of conversations and note the information people give that could be used as a lead-in to conversations.
  - Use this information to formulate questions. For example, if a person mentioned that it's a great day for golf, you could find out about his or her interest in the game by asking such questions as, "How long have you played?" and "Do you play often?" You may want to practice this skill with a friend. Ask the friend to make a comment and then respond with a question.
  - Take care not to ask too many questions in rapid succession. Once you have asked some questions, reveal some information about yourself. Mention how you feel about the subject or offer some information about your own interests.

- Remember that small talk does not have to be about personal interests. It can be about business as well. Look for opportunities to engage in business-related small talk with people with whom you want a relationship.

Adjust your interpersonal style to cues from others

Effective communicators are versatile and adaptive. They can be enthusiastic, tentative, inquisitive, self-disclosing, confident, and/or humorous—and know when each quality is appropriate. No one style of interaction will fit every person or situation. Anyone who is a parent of several children understands this to some degree because, in some ways, you parent different children differently. The emphasis is on what will be effective and what will work in a particular situation.

Use the following suggestions to enhance your skill in adjusting your interpersonal style to adapt to other people:

- If you have picked up some subtle, or not-so-subtle, feedback that you seem oblivious to the reactions of others in some situations, have a heart-to-heart discussion with a trusted colleague and friend. Ask for feedback and suggestions he or she might have for you.

- Look for cues from other people. Does the nature of their comments or questions give you any signals? Who seems to be doing most of the talking? Do you regularly ask questions of others?

- Look for nonverbal cues from people, including:
  - Facial expression
  - Eye contact
  - Voice expression
  - Body language and position
  - Gestures

- If people are giving you negative nonverbal responses, make adjustments by:
  - Asking about their experiences, preferences, and so forth.
  - Asking for feedback about some topic or issue you share.
  - Adopting a listening and learning role for a while.

Relate well to people regardless of their personality or background

People in organizations find themselves meeting and working with all kinds of people. Some are easy to work with; others are more challenging. Some you like; others you may not particularly like. Make the choice to accept people as they are, not as you would like them to be. Try to understand all people on their own terms and find things that you can appreciate and learn from each one. To focus on relating well to people, consider these suggestions:

- When you meet people, concentrate on developing effective working relationships. Focus on what you need to do to make the relationship work. Communicate openly about what you need.

- Suspend judgment based on the background or experience of people, or on other people's experiences with them. Instead, learn about each individual and how you can work together.

- Identify two or three people with whom you find it difficult to work. Over the next few weeks, concentrate on the positive aspects of working with them.
  - List at least five positive characteristics of each individual.
  - Identify the qualities that make that person likeable to his or her associates and friends.
  - Whenever you work with these individuals, concentrate on their strengths. Give compliments on their strong points when appropriate.

- Continue to focus on and appreciate people's strengths. This will help you be more tolerant of the qualities that bother you. Sustained effort and concentration will help you improve your working relationship with each person.

Treat people with respect

Consistently showing respect for others is an essential ingredient for creating and sustaining an environment of high morale and productivity. Here are some guidelines to consider:

- Treat other people as they want to be treated, not as you want to be treated.

- Give people the benefit of the doubt.

- Be objective and nonevaluative in your day-to-day dealings with people.

- Confront issues, not people.

- Foster an environment of openness and trust.

- Allow people to save face.

- Be aware of instances in which you might be perceived as insensitive.

- Minimize sarcasm. Remind yourself that your goal is to retain your sense of humor while avoiding any tendencies to insult or hurt others. If you offend people, analyze the way in which you misused your wit.

- Treat those you are close to with the same courteous attention that you extend to strangers and acquaintances.

Maintain positive relationships even under difficult or heated circumstances

In difficult circumstances, relationships can get strained. It is tempting to vent or say some sharp words when something has gone wrong. Successful managers don't. Instead, they concentrate on solving problems and dealing with issues in such a way that their relationships remain positive and constructive. They confront problems, not people. They remain calm.

Use the following guidelines in difficult situations:

- Focus on the problem or issue, not on the personalities involved. Do not accuse people or put them down verbally. There is no place for comments such as "You were stupid to do that," or "Why in the world didn't you pay attention to the problem?" Such comments take the focus off the problem and generate hard feelings and resentment, which are counterproductive.

- When you are angry with a person, do not start a sentence with "you." When you say "you" when you are angry and trying to talk about a problem, most of the time the next words will be something that the other person will hear as blaming or accusatory. Instead, start the sentence with "I." For example, rather than saying, "You made me angry when you verbally attacked me in the meeting," say, "I am angry because I heard you attack and criticize me in the meeting." The latter statement will make the person less defensive.

- Focus on asking open-ended questions that encourage others to give their points of view more fully.

- Ask other people to speak in a discussion before you give your opinion.

- Allow people to vent to some extent—you will learn how strongly they feel about the matter.

- Do not become defensive or adversarial in your own remarks.

- Refrain from immediate judgment and criticism of others' ideas. If criticism is required, deliver it in a way that demonstrates respect for and sensitivity to the feelings of the other person.

- Present your viewpoints in a less dogmatic or vehement manner. Use "I think" or "in my opinion," rather than global pronouncements, such as "obviously…" or "everyone knows…."

- Ask how, if, when, and with whom the issue can be resolved.

- Review Chapter 24: Manage Conflicts in this handbook for suggestions on dealing with serious conflicts.

Develop good timing

Requesting resources during budget cuts, criticizing someone's work after he or she stayed up all night to finish a project, and pointing out that you had warned someone of a consequence that just occurred are all examples of poor timing.

Some people are so concerned with demonstrating that they were right, or so sure they know the best way, or simply oblivious to what others think and feel, that they harm themselves by using poor timing. These people are often labeled as abrasive or insensitive.

To develop the ability to time actions well, try the following suggestions:

- Recognize that timing is important. Your message may be the right one, but it won't be well received if it is delivered at the wrong time.

- Before delivering your message, ask yourself: "How will others feel if I say that?" or "What will others think of me if I say this?"

- View your comments or requests in the context of the situation. For example:
  - Commenting to a leader committed to the organization's quality effort that the quality program is just a new fad is not sensitive.
  - Commenting that the organization is not really committed to diversity at a meeting announcing a new diversity program will not be well received.
  - Disagreeing with an idea just to generate discussion or analysis is not useful when the decision has already been made and no amount of discussion will change it.

- Realize that it is better to praise people publicly and criticize them in private. If you criticize someone in a large meeting, a lot of ego is at stake for everyone involved. A private conversation makes it easier for either party to modify their position. Also pay attention to the cultural aspects of positive and negative feedback. In some cultures, it is rude to compliment others in public.

Consider people's feelings when you make decisions

Decisions are not implemented in a vacuum; they impact people. When you make a decision, get into the habit of considering the impact it will have on the people affected by it. Sometimes you may determine that a decision has a higher cost than it is worth, in terms of its impact on people. Other times, you may make the same decision, but you will be able to reduce the negative impact on people.

While you may not be able to accommodate everyone's needs, consulting others will help you demonstrate concern and enhance others' commitment to your decisions. The following suggestions can help you do this:

- Allow enough time to gather input from those affected by the decision.

- As much as possible, incorporate reasonable solutions into your final decision.

- If you can't accommodate some needs, let people know why and be prepared to use active listening to deal with their reactions. Refer to Chapter 28: Listen to Others in this handbook for suggestions on developing your active-listening skills.

- Minimize the impact on people as much as possible. For example, involve people in the decision, prepare people for the decision, provide transition, provide support, and so forth.

- Offer to further discuss people's reactions to your final decision.

PART 2:
FOSTER RELATIONSHIPS WITH YOUR COLLEAGUES

Develop effective working relationships with your employees

Gone are the days of distant bosses. Employees want managers who are involved, are helpful, and provide coaching. They want leaders they can respect. In many parts of the world, many employees are at their jobs by their choice, not yours; they have plenty of other options. It becomes critical, then, to strengthen the relationship between you and your staff. The following guidelines will help you do so:

- Be accessible. Consider moving your office closer to your employees' work area to appear less remote and show your interest in day-to-day operations.

- Establish an open-door policy. Set aside regular blocks of time for discussing employee concerns. Make sure that employees are informed of this schedule.

- Stick with your policy once you start it. Insincere attempts to appear approachable may worsen communication instead of improving it. For example, if you establish times when you will be available and then consistently schedule other events at these times, your employees may decide that you are not really interested in communicating with them and may view your efforts as a half-hearted experiment.

- Set aside one transition time during the day to informally chat with your people. The transition times are the first and last hours of work each morning and afternoon.

- Gradually increase the frequency of your informal, drop-in visits with employees. (A drastic change may cause them to think you are unhappy with their work and want to check up on them.)

- Take time for informal chats with employees in hallways or during brief, unscheduled visits. Ask about their personal interests—family, hobbies, and goals. Follow up by occasionally inquiring about their current concerns.

- Share some of your personal interests. Employees will feel more comfortable sharing their interests with you if they see that you are willing to reveal information about yourself.

Solicit feedback from your direct reports

Because your relationship with your employees and their commitment to the organization are so important, it's essential that you regularly ask for feedback. You can do this informally or through formal feedback processes. To obtain feedback informally from your employees, use the following suggestions:

- Arrange an individual, informal meeting with each employee to discuss your working relationship. Provide as nonthreatening an environment as possible for this meeting. Hold it in neutral territory—a conference room, the cafeteria—not in your office.

- Ask for feedback in an informal, nonthreatening manner. Let employees know that your reason for requesting such information is to improve your working relationships with them.

- Ask the employee for comments on things you do that help the working relationship and for suggestions on how you might improve it. Be careful not to dominate the conversation, and try to respond to the employee's remarks in a nondefensive, honest way.

- Explore additional ways to solicit employee feedback on your working relationships with them. For example, find a way for employees to give anonymous feedback, or ask for feedback from a trusted peer who has observed your relationships with your employees.

- Use the feedback to generate goals for improving your working relationships with your employees. You may want to share your goals with them. After working toward your goals for a while, go through this feedback process again to get their impressions of how your relationships with them have changed.

- Don't promise more than you can deliver; remember, your follow-through will be the key to improving the relationship.

- If you invite employees to discuss problems, be prepared to respond nondefensively. Be a problem solver rather than a problem reactor. Let people know you value good information, whether the news is favorable or unfavorable. A "shoot the messenger" reaction will put you right back where you started, regardless of how much time you set aside for discussions.

- If employees wish to discuss personal problems, be willing to listen. Take care, however, not to take on roles for which you are not professionally trained, such as that of financial or family counselor.

- Respect the confidentiality of employees' personal concerns. Avoid using shared personal information in a way that employees may see as using their openness against them. For example, you may say, "I know you have small children you must take care of in the morning, but it's essential that you get to work on time." This can make the employee regret that he or she opened up to you and be reluctant to share personal information in the future.

Help others have fun on the job

Research that PDI has conducted in some organizations indicates that one of the differences between good managers and excellent ones is that excellent managers make work fun and enjoyable. They show their passion for the work they do, but also deliberately cultivate a culture of enjoying one's work and work relationships. Certainly all of work is not fun, but parts of it can be.

To build more fun into your work environment, consider the following suggestions:

- Examine your views toward fun at work. Does it seem like a contradiction in terms? Do you have fun at work? Why or why not?

- Think of fun as an ongoing goal, not an occasional task.

- Ask people to contribute ideas for making work fun. Give a small prize every month for the best idea.

- Designate a person or team to create fun situations or events.

- Share your sense of humor. Humor can help people cope more effectively with work stress.

- Show your team that it is acceptable to laugh at yourselves. Take your work seriously, but do not take yourself too seriously.

- Look for opportunities to celebrate. Keep a calendar of birthdays, hire dates, and so forth, and recognize people on significant dates.

- Build in time to be creative.

- Recognize people who make work fun.

Develop effective working relationships with your peers

There is an old adage, "Friends come and go, but enemies accumulate." In organizations, people have to depend on others in the value chain to accomplish their part for the business model to work. Peers and colleagues are important to the success of your group and the organization. Peers rely on each other. It's important to spend time nurturing or working on these relationships.

The following suggestions can help you make these relationships more effective:

- Be a team member, not a competitor. Spend time on the relationship itself, not just on the work to be done.

- Prepare a list of the peers with whom you work on a regular basis. Rate the quality of your working relationship with each person on your list, using the following scale:
    1 = Work poorly together
    2 = Have an adequate working relationship
    3 = Work reasonably well together (room for improvement)
    4 = Work very well together

- Identify the barriers or problems in the relationships. Determine what you can do to resolve these issues. Set a date (such as within three to six months) by which you can reasonably accomplish your goal of improving your working relationships with peers. After this date, reevaluate each relationship.

- As you work with your peers, ask yourself if you're emphasizing your tasks and opinions at the expense of team relationships. Take notes on your behavior and write a goal for improvement based on your assessment.

- As you become more relaxed, less intense, and more attentive to your peers, monitor whether they are more willing to volunteer information, provide feedback on your ideas, and discuss issues with you. You'll know you're making progress when you start getting feedback from peers who have never offered it in the past.

Develop an effective working relationship with your manager

All relationships are two-way. Each needs to do his or her part to make the relationship work. While you may have beliefs about how your manager should and should not treat you, you also have a responsibility to make the relationship as positive as possible.

Remember that managers are people, too. They prefer positive feedback, they prefer when people do not argue about everything, they prefer for people to like them. Managers view employees who are responsible and follow through, who treat others respectfully, demonstrate integrity, and are open to coaching and development, as people with whom they want to work.

To enhance your working relationship with your manager, try the following suggestions:

- Talk with your manager about what he or she expects from you in your role. Share your opinions and perspectives, including where they are similar and dissimilar. Remember that part of being effective in a managerial role is helping to negotiate your manager's expectations of you.

- Learn about your manager's professional and personal goals, and determine how you can help him or her achieve them.

- Identify your manager's strengths and weaknesses, and use your skills to complement or compensate for them.

- Be aware of style issues, such as the following, and work with them:
  - Does your manager want to hear about ideas first in writing or in person?
  - When is your manager most likely to be open to informal conversation? Before 8:00 a.m.? After 5:00 p.m.? At lunchtime?
  - What does your manager want to know about?
  - How open does he or she want dialogue to be?
  - What will get you into trouble?

- If your manager is a big-picture person, present an overview of the problem rather than stating its small details.

- If your manager sees limited options, give specific alternatives and the business rationale behind them.

- Do not let your manager be surprised—let him or her know what is coming.

- Be open, direct, and respectful.

Give feedback to your manager

Relationships work better, when there is open dialogue. This is as true for manager/employee relationships as for others. Open dialogue includes the willingness to give and receive feedback from one another. In some relationships, this kind of dialogue happens easily and naturally. In others, it seems more difficult and requires more deliberate work.

These suggestions will help you establish two-way feedback with your manager:

- Establish an agreement with your manager that you want feedback from him or her. You can say, "It is helpful to me to get regular feedback, so I know when I am on track and when I am not. I would appreciate your letting me know when you are concerned about what I am doing. Of course, it would be nice to have some positive feedback, too, if you view that what I have done is particularly valuable or helpful."

- When you receive feedback, listen, summarize, and take it seriously. Recognize that feedback is a gift; it is an investment that other people are making in you. They are most often trying to help you and make things go well for you and for them.

- Ask your manager if he or she wants feedback from you. When asked, most managers are open to this. At the point you want to give feedback, ask permission by saying, "I have some feedback or a few ideas if you are interested in hearing."

- Give your manager positive feedback. Let your manager know what you appreciate, what you are learning from him or her, or what he or she has done that you like or respect. Managers are people first; they like to be appreciated, too.

- Whenever possible, state the feedback in positive, objective terms. Describe the situation, your manager's behavior or action, and the impact the behavior or action had on you, on others, or on the task. Avoid using inflammatory language or assigning motives.

- If you feel a good deal of discomfort with giving your manager feedback, find someone who has or has had good rapport working with your manager. Ask that person what your manager values and appreciates from others. Ask the person about any "do's and don'ts" with your manager.

- Frame your message appropriately. Consider the type of feedback that was effective in the past, and learn from your successes and mistakes.

- When you are giving feedback, assume your manager's intentions were good. For example, "You may not have been aware of it, but when you gave me the negative feedback in the team meeting, I felt badly and somewhat humiliated in front of my peers. I would appreciate it that when you want to give me feedback again, you do it in private."

- Actively listen to your manager's response and thank him or her for listening to the feedback.

Develop effective working relationships with higher management

To obtain the support you need for your area, to help to advance your career, and to gain more information about the direction of the organization and concerns of senior management, it's important to develop relationships with higher-level managers.

To develop your working relationships with higher management, consider the following suggestions:

- When you find yourself working and associating with higher-level managers, take the opportunity to get to know them and for them to get to know you. Establish rapport by commenting on a presentation they made, inquiring about something you know they are interested in, or providing information they are probably interested in. For example, if an executive has sponsored an initiative to get closer to the customer, tell him or her about something that happened in your business unit regarding that initiative. Think less in terms of providing self-serving information and more in terms of information that will reinforce the executive's point. For example, you may have learned about a new customer direction, which would be important information for the executive to know.

- Identify two or three managers above you whose areas interact and intersect with yours. Discuss your common goals and ways you can work with each other to achieve them. If appropriate, volunteer to act as a resource to the manager and/or the team.

- Serve on a committee or work on a special project with higher-level managers. This will give you a chance to get to know them better, and they will experience your skills, reliability, and enthusiasm firsthand. Then look for opportunities to maintain the relationships after the committee or project work is done.

PART 3:
BUILD AND LEVERAGE NETWORKS

Cultivate networks with people across a variety of functions and locations within the organization

Organizations have both formal and informal channels. Some organizations work almost entirely through informal channels—written rules don't exist; there is not much of a formal structure; people are encouraged to get things done and not be concerned about protocol or following organizational structure. Start-ups are often like this.

Even in organizations that have both formal and informal structures, it is the informal relationships that provide the lubricant to make the organization work smoothly.

To develop your networks and become effective at working through formal and informal channels, use the following suggestions:

- When you first come to an organization, figure out how things are done—informally or by following more formal channels. You probably want to make this one of your criteria for deciding what organization to join. Some people much prefer formal to informal structures; others prefer the opposite.

- If the structure is formal, learn about it and understand the protocol. Develop the habit of checking with a more experienced colleague before plunging ahead to do something.

- If the structure is informal, find a mentor to help you navigate the organization and figure out whom you need in your network.

- When you have a new assignment or responsibility, ask other people whom you need to know to get the job done.

- Draw a map of your potential network. Include both lateral individuals (your peers in other departments) and vertical individuals (peers and upper- and lower-level managers in your own department). List their names, their functional responsibilities, the ways in which they can support you, and the support you can offer them.

- Serve on cross-functional committees to work with managers in other areas. Make an effort to stay in contact with these people once your involvement with the committee has ended.

- Become acquainted with key managers and professionals at levels below yours. These people may be closer to the day-to-day functioning of the organization and can offer a different perspective on how things get done most efficiently. In addition, their cooperation may be essential for accomplishing your unit's goals.

- Attend company social events to meet managers and peers from other functional areas. Company picnics, award banquets, open houses, and company-sponsored charity events are excellent ways to informally meet people from other areas.

Establish networks with people in the industry or profession

Effective leaders ensure that they have information and relationships outside their own organizations. This is one highly effective way to have access to a continual source of information with perspectives different from those of your own organization. If you have been in the same organization for a long time and do not have relationships with other people in your industry or profession or that of your customers, you probably have too much of an internal focus or point of view.

Some leaders gain their reputations by knowing things others do not. Involvement in industry or professional groups gives you access to this kind of information.

To build valuable networks outside your organization, try the following suggestions:

- Determine the groups or people with whom you want to have a stronger relationship. Think in terms of who may know things that you want to know. Consider professional groups, industry groups, continuing educational networks, customer groups, etc.

- Join one or more industry or professional associations. Attend meetings, conferences, and seminars. Work on program committees. Actively involve yourself in the group so you can get to know people. Spend time with those with whom you have interests in common and begin to develop a personal relationship beyond the professional association.

- Call several key people in your field to ask for information, discuss an idea, or ask for advice. Most people like to help out and share ideas.

- Read professional newsletters and trade journals. These publications can keep you up-to-date on new developments in your field, and they often provide the names of people you may want to contact.

- Join (or form) a group of professionals from other organizations that gets together informally to exchange information on technical advances and discuss issues of common interest.

Develop your network

Relationships with people need to be nurtured, not taken for granted. Networks are the same way. Although you do not need to be in frequent contact with each person in your network, you should touch base with them on a regular basis—every month or so. It is important that the time you call for support is not the only time someone hears from you. Networks are strong when they are based on mutual respect and interest.

To develop your network, try the following suggestions:

- Identify your needs. Whose support, advice, or cooperation do you need or want? Who do you particularly want to help?

- Determine what you have to offer a network.
  - Do you have special knowledge or expertise needed by others in a network?
  - Can you help get an idea accepted by key people in the organization?
  - Do you have personnel or other resources that you can lend to another department temporarily?
  - Do you personally have time to help?
  - Can you access other resources for network members?

- Compile a list of employees from other units/departments that you work with now or will in the future. Identify the individuals on that list whom you don't know well.

- Arrange an introductory meeting with each person. Choose a relaxed, informal atmosphere, such as going for coffee or lunch. After you meet, maintain contact with each person. Pursue joint interests with them or simply call them periodically to stay in touch.

- Update your list of contacts on a regular basis—e.g., every few months. As time permits, arrange informal get-togethers with new colleagues, as well as with those whom you have already met.

- Broaden your circle of acquaintances. Introduce yourself to people you have wanted to meet but were too busy or shy to talk to. Consider setting a goal to become acquainted with a certain number of people per week.

- Identify a well-connected person who would be willing to act as your mentor. This person can provide valuable information about key people in other functional areas: who has the authority or influence to get things done, who can provide advice or political support, who has experience or skills in an area relevant to yours. This person may also be willing to personally introduce you to these people.

Strengthen your network by giving information and support

Networks work because they benefit the people involved. Sometimes networks are based solely on personal relationships, but often they are based on mutual needs. Be sure to make your contribution to the network, so that your relationship with people is not one-way.

Some ideas for strengthening your network are as follows:

- When a colleague asks you to support an idea or plan, consider it carefully. If you think the idea or plan is feasible, actively support it. If you sense problem areas, explain what they are and recommend changes.

- Recognize the give and take nature of networks. Determine whether your requests for and sharing of ideas, time, resources, and so forth, are balanced.

- Establish trust by speaking highly of your colleagues to others and by maintaining confidentiality regarding sensitive information.

- Show concern and provide help without being asked when you know that a colleague is swamped or is facing unexpected difficulties.

- Develop an information exchange among network members, if one does not already exist. Arrange for periodic meetings during which network members can discuss new ideas, express their perspectives about particular issues, and seek input.

- Meet with a colleague and outline several of the issues you are currently facing and how you are handling them. Ask the person for suggestions. Your objective is to create an open dialogue in which you both feel comfortable discussing common experiences and problems.

Build support for your own ideas through contacts with others

It is not reasonable to just assume that if you explain your idea well, others will support it. Support for ideas, changes, and new ventures needs to be gathered and earned. Many decisions are already made before the meeting to make the decision. When you want support, here are some strategies:

- Be able to explain how other people will benefit from your ideas. What is in it for them? Tying your idea to an already acknowledged problem can help you sell the solution.

- Create and use opportunities to share your position with individuals and groups. Focus on the positive aspects of the idea and be persistent when necessary.

- Express your enthusiasm when you are trying to influence people. They will remember your commitment and excitement for your ideas.

- Match your words and nonverbal actions. Display your enthusiasm through your voice, facial animation, and gestures.

- Remember where people stand on issues. If necessary, keep notes. When you need to garner support, you will have a better idea of who will support your idea and who will need more convincing.

Leverage networks to get things done

Effective leaders use their relationships with people inside and outside the organization to get things done. They know how and when to involve others, gain support, and mobilize support. Research on influence indicates that the most frequently used influence style is that of logical persuasion. Yet it is not the most effective. One of the more effective means of influencing others is by calling on one's network for support. To leverage your network, use the following suggestions:

- Ask for assistance from your network when you need it. Networks are based on reciprocal relationships: "I'll help you now—you can help me in the future."

- Vary your approach depending on the individual. Effective managers use an array of interpersonal skills to gain the support or assistance of others: direct requests, motivation, recognition, diplomacy, encouragement, influence, and praise. What works well with one person may not work with another.

- If you need practical assistance—such as, advice or input on a proposal, another person's time, or priority for your project—state your needs in person instead of calling or sending an e-mail. Be prepared to negotiate if the other person cannot provide the assistance that you need.

- If you need support or backing from several people, think about the best way to present your position so others will view it as mutually beneficial.

- Treat other network members with respect. Always ask for people's help; never demand it. Keep in mind that strong networks are built on mutual respect and common goals.

- Realize that asking for help after having no contact for a long time may feel manipulative to some people. A colleague who hasn't heard from you in several years may not be responsive to your request for support. Although it takes time and effort to maintain regular contact, the benefits of doing so are well worth the investment.

- Identify the people in your organization who successfully achieve results and influence others. How well do you know and relate to these people? Find out how they leverage their networks.

RESOURCES

The resources for this chapter begin on page 666.

24
MANAGE
CONFLICT

PART 1: ANALYZE AND DIAGNOSE CONFLICT SITUATIONS
- *Analyze your conflict-management style*
- *Discuss the real reasons underlying the problem*
- *Know which battles are worth fighting*

PART 2: COMMUNICATE CONSTRUCTIVELY DURING CONFLICT
- *Use active listening to reduce conflict*
- *Address conflict directly and constructively*
- *Address your reluctance to manage conflict*
- *Express disagreements tactfully*
- *Voice disagreement with your manager*

PART 3: COLLABORATE WITH OTHERS TO HANDLE CONFLICTS
- *Facilitate conflict discussion and resolution*
- *Work toward win/win solutions*
- *Minimize recurrent conflict*
- *Resolve conflict among your employees*

MANAGE CONFLICT

INTRODUCTION

Disagreements and conflicts are part of any dynamic business organization. They arise because people have different experiences, backgrounds, and perspectives. They often surface because people care and want to do their jobs well.

The implication of the phrase "conflict management" is that there are different ways of handling conflict. Clearly, conflict often needs to be resolved. Other times it should be encouraged. For instance, it should be encouraged when discussion and debate can generate creative, innovative approaches to an issue or decision. Conflict is beneficial when the focus is on finding the best solution. It becomes destructive when the focus is on personal tensions, personalities, or egos (simply winning).

Conflict arises for a variety of reasons. Sometimes it's due to limited resources. Other times it surfaces out of differing goals, priorities, responsibilities, or methods. Or it may arise from differing information, ideas, interpretations, or values. Conflict is especially difficult when it fails to produce mutually satisfying solutions or when it becomes personal in nature.

As a leader, your goal should be to avoid win/lose situations and to ensure productive and effective handling of conflict. Effectively working through conflict can result in stronger working relationships and encourage creative solutions. Handling conflict badly results in damaged relationships and inhibits the expression of valuable differences in perspectives.

This chapter suggests ways to develop conflict-management skills that will enable you and your team to encourage beneficial differences and minimize hurtful conflict.

VALUABLE TIPS

- Seek to understand the other person's point of view before you explain yours. Summarize what you hear until the other person agrees that you understand what he or she thinks and feels.

- Try to arrive at a common goal around which everyone involved can focus, and agree to work through areas of disagreement.

- Build on areas of agreement, before you address areas of difference.

- At the beginning of resolving differences or a conflict, clearly state your desire to find a solution that will work for all involved.

- Depersonalize the conflict. Catch yourself when you fall into the trap of believing the other person is deliberately trying to make the situation difficult for you.

- Avoid blaming, accusatory, pejorative, and inflammatory comments unless you want to escalate the disagreement.

- Ask yourself if this is the time and place to pursue an issue of conflict.

- See conflict as a disagreement about goals, ideas, or methods, rather than a personality or style conflict. Disagreements that are seen as personality or style conflicts become more difficult to resolve.

- Recognize that it takes at least two people to have a conflict. It is an example of highly cooperative behavior. Identify what you are doing to contribute to the conflict.

- Use a third-party negotiator when you are unable to practice cooperative problem solving. An objective person is often helpful to resolution.

- Define the conflict in terms of needs, not solutions. People may disagree about the right solution, but they can agree on needs and thus focus on creative problem solving and looking at alternatives.

- Listen to other people's concerns. Do not defend or explain yourself.

- Ask others for feedback on how you handle conflict.

- Before meeting about a conflict, visualize the conflict resolved in the best way for all parties.

- Provide motivation for people involved in ongoing or recurring conflict to resolve their differences.

- Always focus on reaching win/win solutions.

PART I:
ANALYZE AND DIAGNOSE CONFLICT SITUATIONS

Analyze your conflict-management style

Some people approach conflict situations differently, depending on the conflict, the people involved, the issues, and so on. Other people tend to respond to all conflict in a similar way. It can help you to know how you approach conflicts.

To analyze your style of conflict management, use these suggestions:

- Recall feedback from others or look at 360-degree feedback you may have received about whether you work toward win/win solutions or approach conflict from a win/lose perspective. If you have been given feedback that you tend to approach conflict more from a win/lose perspective, talk with a coach or trusted peers about the impact of this behavior on your work and the people you care about.

- Ask your Human Resources consultant for a conflict-style instrument or test that can help you understand your approach to conflict.

- Keep a journal or log, charting the disagreements and conflicts you have with others. Note the issues, your response, your perception of the other person's issues, concerns, and response. Observe whether your response is:
  - Withdrawal: Avoiding or withdrawing from conflict situations as much as possible.
  - Agreeable: Deferring to the other person's point of view.
  - Aggressive: Trying to convince the other person you are right, insisting on your own way, winning the point.
  - Collaborative: Working through issues to arrive at a mutually satisfactory agreement.

- Identify the people and situations that are a challenge for you to approach collaboratively. Analyze what it is about the situation or the person that causes you to get caught in less-than-cooperative behavior.

Discuss the real reasons underlying the problem

Many disagreements and conflicts have multiple sources. It is difficult to arrive at a meaningful solution, however, unless you deal with the real causes of the problem. Part of the challenge in conflict resolution is that people often do not clearly or adequately know what the issues are. They may not even be aware of all of their own concerns.

The following suggestions can help you uncover the real reasons underlying a conflict:

- Listen first, and then talk about your point of view.

- Try to determine the root cause or causes of the conflict. Does it appear to be a conflict of facts (lack of information), goals or priorities, resource allocation, methods or procedures, or values? The values conflict is most difficult to resolve. In any case, pinpoint where the most important conflict seems to be. Be aware that a specific conflict may involve several issues.

- Express your views in terms of your needs and goals, not solutions.

- Emphasize the importance of honesty, openness, and mutual respect during the discussion.

- Listen carefully during a conflict discussion. If you hear hints of underlying issues, ask about them. For example, you might say, "I wonder if you are angry because someone else got the assignment, and it was something you wanted?" Or you can observe, "It seems that there might be something else bothering you." These types of questions or observations, quietly stated, can open the door for additional information.

- When you think you know the issues, summarize your understanding of them and ask if that accurately and adequately summarizes the other person's concerns.

- During a conflict discussion, spend sufficient time on conflict definition and related analysis and diagnosis before moving to a discussion of possible solutions.

- Periodically summarize areas of agreement that have come up, as well as areas of continuing disagreement.

- When you are having difficulty reaching agreement on a problem, suggest to the other person, "I wonder if we have all of the issues out on the table." Then both of you can rethink and discuss any additional issues that are uncovered.

Know which battles are worth fighting

Managers who have to win every argument, even at the expense of other people, reduce their overall effectiveness, as well as diminish their influence in the organization. Because they are so busy championing their own agendas, they may not be sufficiently aware of the needs or concerns of others. Or, if they are aware of them, these managers tend to ignore the agendas that are contrary to or out of alignment with their own. These managers are sometimes avoided because they are often perceived as contrary to others and, therefore, difficult to work with.

You can increase your influence and foster greater cooperation by learning when it is appropriate to assert your agenda and when to set it aside for more collaboration and negotiation. The following guidelines can help:

- Ask others if you are currently involved in any conflicts in which they believe you are unwisely invested. Talk with your peers about the price you are paying for this involvement.

- Solicit feedback about whether you frequently get into conflicts that others believe are unimportant or costly to your or your team's performance or relationships with others.

- Learn to catch yourself before you get locked into a conflict. Observe whether:
  - Your voice is getting louder and louder.
  - You feel angry or hurt.
  - You are talking a long time or explaining your point of view over and over again.
  - You feel challenged or judged by the other person.
  - You feel frustrated, irritated, or fed up with the other person.
  - You find yourself saying hurtful or judgmental things to others, such as, "I'm sorry that you just do not seem to be able to understand this situation."

  These are signs that you are emotionally involved in the conflict. Emotional involvement is an indication that the issue or situation is important to you. This is good information. But it also is a warning that you may find it difficult to approach this situation collaboratively. Rather than getting immersed in a conflict, refocus your goal to find a mutually satisfactory solution to the issue.

- Look for a role model for yourself—someone who has accomplished a lot and is able to work through disagreements with others. Observe the person carefully. Identify things the person does that you may be able to adopt yourself.

PART 2:
COMMUNICATE CONSTRUCTIVELY DURING CONFLICT

Use active listening to reduce conflict

Too often, the parties involved in an argument spend most of their time talking instead of listening. When one person is speaking, the other is busy preparing a rebuttal or thinking of additional ways to support his or her viewpoint, rather than listening to what is being said. In addition, most people immediately judge the statements of others—either to agree or to disagree. Frequently, the listener judges a statement from his or her point of view without considering the other person's perspective.

In those cases, true listening does not occur; people hear what they expect or want to hear, rather than what the speaker intends to communicate. Both of these behaviors can cause disagreements to escalate into arguments. When neither person stops to listen, there is a good chance that agreement will be delayed or prevented altogether. In addition, when emotions run high, people may say or do things they later regret.

Over the next month, each time you sense an argument is about to begin, switch from a defensive position to the listening mode. To accomplish this switch, use a technique called active listening:

- Listen carefully to what the speaker is saying. Give the speaker your full attention, without thinking about how you are going to respond, and without judging the speaker's statements. Show that you are really listening by using nonverbal behavior such as leaning forward, raising your eyebrows, nodding your head, and so forth.

- Get the speaker to clarify his or her position by asking open-ended questions that start with phrases such as:
  - Tell me about…
  - Explain…
  - How do you feel about…
  - Describe…
  - What…

- Avoid closed questions that can be answered "yes" or "no"—questions that start with words such as "is," "are," "could," "would," "do," "did," and "should."

- Periodically paraphrase what the speaker has said to ensure that you understand what was meant and to let the speaker know that you are really listening. In doing so, reflect the feeling as well as the content of the message. Use phrases like, "As I understand it, your position is..." or "You seem to be concerned about...." If the speaker disagrees with your paraphrase, ask him or her to clarify the statement.

- Determine whether your interpretations are becoming more accurate as the discussion progresses. If you are listening well, you will probably hear comments like, "That's exactly what I meant," and "That's right! I think you understand my problem."

- Resist interrupting the speaker. Mentally tally the number of times you interrupt a speaker, and eliminate such interruptions by the end of the month.

If you effectively apply active-listening skills, your conflict situations will become less intense, and people will likely become more open to listening to your point of view and compromising. You will find that you are involved in more constructive debates and fewer destructive arguments.

Address conflict directly and constructively

Disagreements and conflicts are a part of normal organizational life. They are inevitable. A key challenge is finding direct and constructive ways to handle conflicts. In most cases, conflicts do not easily go away or dissipate. If you tend to avoid or ignore conflict situations in which you are involved, it may simply be because you don't have a process for dealing with conflict collaboratively.

To structure the way you deal with a conflict, try the following process:

1. Ask to meet with the other person or persons in a nonthreatening place, such as a conference room.

2. Begin the session with a statement defining the purpose of the meeting—something like, "Kim, I asked to meet with you today to discuss the disagreement you and I are having over the Fox contract. I want to work something out with you that we can both be satisfied with."

3. Use active-listening skills to draw out information from the other person and to help pinpoint the real source of the disagreement.

4. Treat the other person in a respectful manner. It often takes willpower to avoid disrespect and negative emotional reactions when you disagree.

5. When you have pinpointed the problem, investigate alternative solutions together. Remain nonjudgmental and search for at least three possibilities.

6. Together, evaluate the possibilities you've both generated, listing pros and cons. Remember that the goal is to work with the other party to find the best solution for you both.

7. Once you have evaluated the alternatives, commit to a solution with the other person.

8. At this point, clearly state the solution and develop a plan to execute it. List the specific action steps, assign responsibility, and set specific completion dates for each step. It's important that the plan be specific and that each step be measurable and attainable.

9. Develop a plan for future follow-up meetings or discussions to evaluate how things are going. Provide positive feedback when things are working well.

Address your reluctance to manage conflict

Effectively working through conflict results in stronger working relationships and encourages creative solutions, while avoiding or ignoring conflict results in damaged relationships and inhibits the expression of valuable opinions.

To address conflict more frequently:

- Ask yourself, "What am I concerned about?" "What prevents me from approaching this head-on?" "What am I afraid of?" As Franklin D. Roosevelt said, "We have nothing to fear but fear itself." Once you know the barriers, you can evaluate the probabilities and risks more accurately.

- After you have identified your fears, use your problem-solving skills to determine what you need to do to reduce the probability of the fears being realized.

- When you are reluctant to approach a conflict, determine what the consequence will be if the situation continues. This technique will let you identify situations that are serious and that you expect will worsen if you try to ignore them. Use this approach to help motivate you to take action.

- Ask others to give you feedback on what you are doing and for ideas on how to approach conflict. It is very easy to get locked into behavior or approaches that are not working. Consult with your manager, peers, and others for new ideas and insights.

Express disagreements tactfully

In voicing disagreement, work to avoid emotional reactions and to communicate clearly. The effectiveness of the interaction will be greatly increased if each party clearly understands the other party's point of view. Put yourself in the other person's situation and imagine how you would feel and react. Look at the other side before defending your own. A useful guideline, and one of Stephen Covey's *7 Habits of Highly Effective People: Powerful Lessons in Personal Change* (Simon and Schuster, 1993), is to seek first to understand and then to be understood.

To practice expressing disagreement, try these suggestions:

- Treat the other person with respect. In other words, respectfully disagree.

- Depersonalize the conflict; look at it as a conflict of ideas, priorities, or approaches, rather than of personalities or egos.

- At the beginning of a conflict discussion, express your desire for a resolution that is acceptable to both or all of you and that serves the organization well.

- Listen for meaning. Use active listening to understand the other person's point of view.

- Once the other person knows you have understood his or her point of view, communicate your point(s) of disagreement.
  - First, share your areas of agreement.
  - Then, share why you disagree or see it differently and explain your view.
  - Avoid using loaded words that may insult or attack the other person.
  - Say what you mean and mean what you say. Be direct, stating your position forthrightly and concisely. Give reasons and share experiences that clarify your position.
  - Don't lecture about why you are right. Simply state your point of view and what led to your position.

Voice disagreement with your manager

Many people find disagreeing with their manager to be an unpleasant and difficult part of their jobs, yet there are times when it is necessary. If you are hesitant to express disagreement with your manager or to deliver bad news, follow these guidelines for developing a plan to voice disagreement in a confident, straightforward manner:

1. Talk with your manager about how, in general, disagreement between the two of you can best be handled. Ask your manager how, where, and when he or she would like you to express disagreement when it is necessary to do so.

2. Before approaching your manager with a topic that may produce disagreement, think through the reasons for your position. Be prepared to state them clearly, concisely, and calmly during the discussion. Think of ways to resist either becoming defensive about your position or quickly deferring to your manager's position. Vividly picture the scene in your mind, imagining both your manager's expression of opinion and your statement of your case. Doing this can help you take a more positive and firm stand during the actual discussion.

3. Acknowledge your understanding of your manager's point of view.

4. Instead of criticizing your manager's point of view, state your own.

5. Work out the differences collaboratively when possible.

6. If your manager does not agree with your point of view, recognize when to stop trying to convince him or her. A graceful withdrawal is helpful. If you are right, it will likely become obvious over time.

PART 3:
COLLABORATE WITH OTHERS TO HANDLE CONFLICT

Facilitate conflict discussion and resolution

Handling disagreement among group members is a sensitive issue. While it's important not to interfere too much, your intervention may be helpful and even essential at times. When you sense disagreement among members of a group, help them express their different points of view and listen to each other. Use the following process:

1. Communicate your perception that there are differing positions and suggest that it would be helpful to explore those differences.

2. Help the individuals involved define the problem or issue where the conflict appears to be. Ask people to express their positions in specific terms rather than in generalities.

3. Ensure that each person listens to the others. Check to see if the listener paraphrases the speaker—that is, repeats in his or her own terms the statement(s) of the speaker. If not, request that he or she do so. Paraphrasing enables both individuals to share their points of view and have them heard by the other person.

4. Once both sides have stated their problems, move into the problem-solving mode to determine ways to work together to minimize conflict in the future. In this phase, it is important that both sides remain open to compromise.

5. Help them identify areas of agreement. Pinpoint areas of agreement you see and ask them to do the same. You may need to emphasize an overriding priority or objective toward which everyone is working. Point out the elements of the issue that could draw them together.

6. As they reach an agreement, make sure that each person is satisfied with the solution. Ask if they both (or all) feel comfortable with the resolution.

7. Encourage them to set up a meeting to discuss how things are progressing, and to verify that the chosen approach is working.

Work toward win/win solutions

Successful negotiation engages people in seeking and identifying a solution satisfactory to all. When both sides are open to winning on some points and compromising or losing on others, they are more likely to arrive at a solution they can accept and support. When a clear winner and a clear loser emerge from a negotiation session, hard feelings are likely to result. The "loser" may undermine the solution, and it is possible that no one will "win" in the long run.

To develop a win/win style, use the following process:

1. Carefully monitor your tendencies to want to win. Look for positions proposed by the other person that you could live with. Seek an outcome that meets the needs of both.

2. During a disagreement, find a common goal on which you both agree and keep focusing on that goal. Tackle the disagreement after identifying areas of agreement. Remember to attack the problem, not the person.

3. After a disagreement, write down your analysis of what took place. Recall both of the initial positions, and compare them with the outcome. Note the extent to which both sides compromised and the extent to which both sides "won."

While you may want to work toward a win/win outcome, you could find yourself in a conflict with someone who approaches situations from a win/lose perspective. In these cases, you may feel that you have to protect yourself. The result of such defensiveness, though, is that you can fall into win/lose behavior yourself.

To better deal with such situations, use the following suggestions:

• Be aware of when you're falling into a win/lose mode. Stop yourself.

- Challenge the other person on your perception of his or her behavior. For example, you might say, "It seems to me that you want to resolve this in a way that benefits your group and that you don't care about the impact on my people." By checking out this perception and confronting it directly, you may find that you were wrong, or that after the clarification, the person stops the behavior. If you confirm your initial feeling on the matter, resist the temptation to retaliate against the other person.

- Continue to strive to resolve the conflict in a win/win style, but also be prepared to find another solution that doesn't require the cooperation of the other person.

Minimize recurrent conflict

Recurring conflict decreases productivity and harms working relationships. Most of the time, recurring conflict occurs because a root-cause issue has not been addressed. The conflict recurs because there is a real problem that must be addressed. Other times, conflict recurs, because individual people or groups of people continue to have difficulty getting along. To minimize recurring conflict, take the following steps:

- Avoid labeling a recurring conflict as a personality conflict, even if it appears to be one. It is much harder to resolve a personality conflict than other kinds of conflicts. Instead, focus on the goals and issues of each party. Solve what appears to be a personality conflict as a problem. What is each person trying to accomplish? What is the underlying issue?

- If efforts at problem solving in the past have not worked, do something different. Most often the reason for the failure is that the root cause has not been addressed, or the motivation to stop the behavior or to resolve the conflict is not strong enough.
    - If the root cause has not been addressed, use a problem-analysis tool to get at the root cause. Involve more people in identifying the underlying issues. Interview people separately to gather information about the problems. Involve a facilitator in the process.
    - If the root cause is lack of motivation to do what needs to be done to resolve the conflict, increase the motivation to deal with the issues. You can increase motivation by finding out why it is in the interest of each party to address the conflict. You can literally ask, "Why is it important to you that these conflicts be resolved?" or "What would cause you to be more interested in resolving these conflicts?"
    - Occasionally, you may need to increase the motivation to resolve the conflict by setting some limits as the manager, such as making it clear that it cannot continue, that it is causing too much negative impact, that you see the lack of resolution as a performance issue for the parties involved.

- Recognize that most conflicts can be reduced to the underlying issues of status and control. If two teams are disagreeing over how to solve a problem, each team is saying they know the one right way. When someone is harassing someone, the issue is status. The harasser is saying, "I am better than you are and I can do what I want even if you do not want me to."

  Whenever the issue is status, the conflict will not get resolved until that issue has been addressed. Therefore, the harasser needs to know that he or she cannot continue to harass the other person and make the work environment noxious. When people are disagreeing about who will decide a course of action, they both need to agree that they each have a role in deciding the course of action.

Resolve conflict among your employees

Handling conflict between employees is a sensitive issue. While it's important not to interfere too much, your intervention may be necessary at times. The following guidelines will help you choose an appropriate and productive level of involvement:

- Whenever possible, encourage your employees to resolve their conflicts themselves and not come to you for resolution. If an employee is reluctant to do so, coach him or her on how to deal with the other person to resolve the conflict. If necessary, role-play a conflict-resolution situation with the employee to allow him or her to practice.

- Get feedback from your employees on your current level of involvement in their conflicts. Are you involved too much, or not enough?

- When conflict arises that does require your intervention (such that the employees cannot resolve it themselves), follow this procedure:
  - Help the individuals involved define the problem in specific, observable terms.
  - Ensure that each person listens to the other.
  - Help them identify areas of agreement.
  - Have them brainstorm alternative approaches and determine viable solutions.
  - Create a problem-resolution plan. If they are unable to do this cooperatively, it may be necessary for you to step in and determine the best course of action.
  - Set up future meetings during which they can discuss how things are going and whether the chosen approach is working.

RESOURCES

The resources for this chapter begin on page 668.

25
LEVERAGE INDIVIDUAL AND CULTURAL DIVERSITY

PART 1: UNDERSTAND AND VALUE DIVERSITY
- *Assess your beliefs about valuing diversity*
- *Increase your sensitivity to issues of diversity*

PART 2: MANAGE DIVERSITY
- *Create an environment of respect for differences*
- *Utilize the diversity and potential of employees*
- *Recruit and promote for workforce diversity*
- *Assist people from diverse backgrounds to succeed*

PART 3: ORGANIZATIONAL EFFORTS—EFFECT SYSTEMIC CHANGE
- *Assess organizational readiness*
- *Accommodate the needs of a diverse workforce*
- *Make it happen*
- *Focus on the goal of valuing the individual*
- *Evaluate progress toward systemic change*

INTRODUCTION

Managers are constantly confronted with new, varied, and complex challenges and opportunities as they try to balance the wants and needs of a highly diverse workforce. In many organizations, today's workers don't look, think, or act like workers of the past. Workers don't hold the same values, have the same education or experiences, or pursue the same needs and desires. It is increasingly common for people of different ages, cultures, first languages, and educational backgrounds to be working side by side.

On the broadest level as the global workforce continues to connect more regularly and more closely through mega-mergers and acquisitions on an international scale, the issue of individual and cultural diversity—knowing how to both value it and leverage it in appropriate ways—is increasingly key to organizational success.

People can think of diversity in different ways. For our purposes in this chapter, the continuum below illustrates the range of issues that can be included in diversity considerations.

CULTURAL	SUB-CULTURAL	INDIVIDUAL
(Ethnicity, nationality, religion, language, etc.)	(Age, gender, community, etc.)	(Personality traits, learning styles, etc.)

The first step for some managers is to more fully notice, appreciate, and value the differences between and among people in the organization; to view differences as assets rather than sources of confusion and misunderstanding.

An important next step for many managers is to view the differences as assets that can offer new insight and advantage and then use them in constructive ways to produce results. It's easier said than done; yet the challenge is clear: Organizations that value and leverage their diverse workforces in proactive and planful ways will more easily gain and maintain competitive advantage in the marketplace.

The issues and implications related to leveraging individual and cultural diversity vary from culture to culture, country to country, and organization to organization. Several assumptions this chapter makes are:

- Individuals are different in ways that matter in the workplace.

- More perspectives are better and can result in more engagement and better solutions.

- Work decisions should be based on job-related characteristics, not extraneous ones; that is, organizations cannot be infinitely flexible in responding to individual backgrounds and preferences.

Effectively leveraging diversity means utilizing the differences in workforce members to accomplish organizational goals, finding the balance between developing shared organizational values and respecting diversity, and challenging assumptions and practices that limit opportunities. This chapter provides suggestions, insights, and guidelines that managers can use to effectively leverage individual and cultural diversity in their workplace.

VALUABLE TIPS

- Actively solicit input from a wide variety of people and functions.

- Get to know your employees. Ask them about their backgrounds, experiences, education, and so on.

- Educate yourself about your own cultural values, assumptions, and background.

- Challenge assumptions that limit opportunities.

- When asking someone to explain a point of view different from your own, be sure to say that your intention is to understand that person's viewpoint, not to have him or her justify it.

- Look at issues and opportunities from other people's viewpoints before making decisions.

- Make a point of drawing together diverse groups when discussing issues, solving problems, and developing opportunities.

- Consider the variety of time zones or office locations of those you are contacting and rotate locations and/or start times for meetings.

- Slow down or use easier vocabulary when communicating with nonnative speakers so they can more easily follow and offer their own thoughts.

- Seek to understand diversity from a global, not just a national, perspective, if appropriate to your business and location.

- Speak out when others are not valued or their ideas or views are not taken into account.

- Learn about and work to align your organization's strategies, practices, and values with those of your target clients so a better fit can be created.

- Remember that some people want their national, philosophical, or other differences to be recognized openly, while others do not.

- Avoid the tendency to joke about differences in ways that may be seen as hurtful or inappropriate.

- Recognize the tension between the need to value and accept others and the desire for shared organizational values.

- Let people know when their behaviors or values negatively affect their credibility and effectiveness.

- Partner with an individual whose background and experiences are different from your own and contract to both learn and teach one or two skills that will improve your performance in some way.

- Broaden your view of diversity to include any significant individual or cultural differences and how they may affect work practices, strategy, or style.

- Question and learn more about your own cultural values and background to gain a better appreciation for how they may impact your decision-making style, values, and reactions to different views.

- Challenge organizational policies and practices that may exclude people or groups.

- Recognize that people who are a minority in one group may be the majority elsewhere.

- Build a support network with colleagues who are interested in more effectively leveraging diversity. Explore ideas with each other and implement them.

- Use personality tools such as the Myers-Briggs Type Indicator® (MBTI®) to learn ways of understanding individual differences among people.

- Monitor yourself to detect any incorrect, inappropriate assumptions you unconsciously make about or stereotypical ways you respond to other people.

- Review suggestions in Chapter 24: Manage Conflict in this handbook to learn ways of handling conflict that may arise out of interactions among people with diverse backgrounds.

- Learn more about other cultures and their values through travel, books, films, and conversations with those who have experienced other cultures, and by attending local cultural events and celebrations.

PART 1:
UNDERSTAND AND VALUE DIVERSITY

Assess your beliefs about valuing diversity

A helpful step in learning to value the diversity of people around you is to understand your own values and beliefs. It is important to see how beliefs contribute to making you who you are, and to recognize that other people often may not agree with your beliefs or understand them. You will also find out that people from other countries and cultures believe different things than do those from your own background.

The suggestions that follow will help you assess your own attitudes, assumptions, and feelings about people who are different from you. These attitudes, assumptions, and feelings can affect your managerial effectiveness.

- Complete some testing that can assess such things as your personality (e.g., the Myers-Briggs Type Indicator®), learning style, cognitive approach, interests, personal and work values, and so forth. You may have done this previously. If so, review the results.

- Connect with and value your own culture, background, and heritage. Expand your definition of culture to include educational background and values, economic status, religious beliefs and affiliation, rural versus urban focus, and so on. Think of culture as a software program written over an extended time period, even centuries, that greatly influences the way you think and behave. This software program shapes areas such as:
  - Belief systems: anything you think of as an original truth; assumptions you make about others.
  - Norms: what are the right or appropriate behaviors and the inappropriate behaviors.
  - Values: what is important to have, know, and be.

- Think through what your background says about the above areas, and how the answers translate into your lifestyle, values, and view of the world.

- Examine the language you use. For example, recognize that the word "minority" is a relative term that can be devaluing as well as inaccurate.

- Think about how it feels to be different by remembering times when you felt you were in the minority. For example, you may have been in a situation where you were the only male, the only monolingual person, the only German, or the only older person. Examine how you felt and the impact it had on your behavior, or even how you thought about yourself in that situation.

- Over the next few weeks, examine the assumptions you make about others. Such assumptions are based on both external, easily identifiable differences, as well as more subtle, invisible differences. Some people find it difficult to acknowledge that their assumptions and cultural beliefs significantly affect how they view, develop perceptions of, and make judgments about other people.

- Spend time with someone you respect who comes from a very different background than you do. Ask the person how he or she thinks about culture, relationships, work, values, and so forth. Ask his or her perceptions of you.

- Use an exercise based on Taylor Cox, Jr.'s concept of "culture identity structure."
  1. Begin by thinking of all the groups with which you identify. Use the broad definition mentioned above. Weigh each group identity, considering how important it is to your self-identity.
  2. Draw a circle.
  3. Divide the circle into pie-shaped slices. Assign each slice to a group identity you value. Give more important identities larger slices; give less important ones smaller slices. For example, a person may strongly identify with both a profession and an age group, but not equally. By increasing the size of either slice, he or she indicates that it is more important than the other.
  4. Have others perform the same exercise.
  5. Compare your identity pie with theirs. Note the similarities and differences. Note how the same group identity can be of different size and importance from person to person. Think about and discuss with coworkers the implications of your similarities and differences. What are the advantages and the challenges?

- Balance your discussion of background with attention to individuality. Background is important to understanding a person, but individuals are more than just members of a group. Recognize that it's just as possible to alienate by accentuating differences as by discrediting them.

- Evaluate how you view people who disagree with you. Do you try to understand the basis for their views? Do you ask questions respectfully? Do you work toward mutual understanding, or simply try to convince them that you are right?

Increase your sensitivity to issues of diversity

It is important for managers to push themselves beyond their current environment and interactions to develop their knowledge of and sensitivity to issues of diversity. Doing so can help you more fully understand, appreciate, and maximize the talents of others. It can also help you find ways to change the environment to encourage the full participation of all employees.

The more you understand others' assumptions and backgrounds, the more you will know about their motivators. Consider these suggestions:

- Establish relationships with people who are different from you. Although it is a natural tendency for people to surround themselves with others similar to them, connecting with people of different backgrounds will help you learn about the unique perspectives and contributions others have to offer.

- Ask people from a variety of backgrounds for help in understanding their experiences, perspectives, and culture. Seek to understand the individual rather than seeing the person as a representative of a group. Looking at the person either as an individual only or as a representative of a group only could lead to wrong assumptions.

- Some people won't want their differences recognized at all. Others may see your overtures to support underrepresented groups as threatening. Make sure your message always returns to the central issue—how to recognize and enable each person's unique talents.

- Over the next few weeks, monitor the assumptions you make about people and ideas. Such assumptions are based on both external, easily identifiable differences, as well as more subtle, invisible differences. Some people find it difficult to acknowledge that their assumptions and cultural beliefs significantly affect how they see others.

  Consider the following example:

  In a U.S. company, a white, male manager walks past the office reception area and sees two black men laughing. He concludes that they do not take their jobs as managers seriously. Next, he passes two women talking to each other at the mail station and assumes they are gossiping. Just before he reaches his office, he passes two white men talking and chuckling, and thinks nothing of it.

  This manager has made assumptions without listening to the actual conversations. Instead, he has used external differences to draw conclusions.

  Making assumptions such as those in the example is often an unconscious process, not a deliberate one—which is why assumptions can be so difficult to catch.

- Make a list of your heroes and heroines, people you admire, in sports, entertainment, business, politics, etc. Examine your list for its diversity. In conversations with others, ask about people they admire and what it is they admire about them. The answers will help you find out more about your own values, as well as the values of others.

- Consider your actions or your group's work processes from the viewpoint of a different function or a person with a different background. In some cultures for instance, it is not common to ask for help. It may be an indication of deficiency, a form of losing face. Pay attention to the environment, to how people ask for help. You may need to rely on a third person, someone closer to the employee, to provide insight and assistance.

- Participate in company or community programs that focus on learning about and valuing different cultures, races, religions, ethnic backgrounds, and so on. Learn about the beliefs and assumptions of people with backgrounds different from your own.

- Volunteer for an organization where you are in the minority. Reflect on your assumptions and behavior.

PART 2: MANAGE DIVERSITY

Create an environment of respect for differences

Creating an environment of respect, appreciation, and acceptance for everyone goes beyond simply tolerating people who are different. You must actively welcome and involve them so they gain a sense of belonging, loyalty, and significance to the operation. People take cues from the environment about how well they are accepted. For example, actively enlisting and involving people, versus merely responding if they ask to be involved, convey two very different messages.

The following suggestions can help create a more accepting and respectful environment:

- Support an atmosphere in which it is safe for all employees to ask for support or information. In this environment, a person is not seen as weak if he or she requests assistance. You may need to emphasize that requesting assistance is an appropriate and valued practice in your organization's work culture.

- Actively seek information and input from people with varying backgrounds and include them in decision making and problem solving.

- Include coworkers who are different from you in informal gatherings; invite them to lunch or to attend organizational social events.

- Establish relationships with people from other backgrounds and cultures. Although people have a natural tendency to surround themselves with others like them, connecting with people of different backgrounds will help you learn about the unique contributions others have to offer.

- Challenge displays of intolerance from others. Usually this should be done privately, but in all cases, intolerant behavior should be addressed.

Utilize the diversity and potential of employees

Some managers assume that being different is a source of confusion and difficulty. They may show their discomfort and judgmental attitudes by their actions and body language. Others may ignore differences in personality, ethnicity, culture, and background, and treat everyone in exactly the same way. An effective manager, however, recognizes the value of maximizing the full potential of all employees through building on their different but complementary skills, backgrounds, and cultural knowledge.

The following suggestions can help you optimize your employees' talents in this way:

- Recognize different learning and work styles, and explore with your team or work group ways to use these styles advantageously. A mixture of styles and approaches usually yields a richer, more innovative outcome. Examples of such differences include:
  - A preference for a structured, time-efficient approach to projects, versus a less-structured approach that may yield more creativity.
  - A preference for a focus on details, versus a focus on general principles or patterns that generate a big-picture perspective.
  - A preference for bouncing ideas and strategies off others, versus a desire to work in solitude.
  - A preference for individual projects, versus a preference for group involvement.
  - A preference for a set of general rules regarding the functioning of the work process, project, or system, versus dealing with each situation differently.
  - A preference to build on already-known facts, experiences, and success, versus a preference to work with ambiguous situations where creativity and innovation are required.

- Focus on, read about, and speak to the value of diversity in your organization. Support the mind-set that the involvement of employees representing a broad base of experience more effectively helps the organization understand its partners, customers, and clients.

WE WORK SO WELL TOGETHER, YET WE HAVE SUCH DIFFERENT BACKGROUNDS.

- Create awareness that the same goal can be approached in different ways. Encourage people to work on different types of problems, issues, and methods, and then determine the most effective approach.

- Include employees from a variety of backgrounds and experience in your problem-solving and decision-making processes. Use differences as a way of gaining a broader range of ideas and perspectives. Research shows that heterogeneous groups are significantly more effective problem-solvers than are homogeneous groups. (Homogeneous groups usually feel more comfortable, but are often less creative and productive.)

- Use cross-functional and multilevel groups to solve problems, spot opportunities, and go beyond conventional ideas and solutions. Make a point of including two or more people who bring unique backgrounds and perspectives.

- Challenge your own assumptions about others. For example, do not assume that an employee who uses a wheelchair cannot do a particular job where mobility is an essential element. Ask the employee if he or she can handle the job requirements and, if not, ask if there is a reasonable accommodation that the organization can make to assist him or her. (Note: In the United States, the Americans with Disabilities Act prohibits a manager from discussing an applicant's disability before a job offer is made.)

- Ask people how you can most effectively manage their work. This may include:
  - Finding out if a person needs more definition, information, and guidance to perform at his or her best, or if a person works better independently.
  - Understanding if too many instructions cause a person to lose face, or being supervised too attentively is viewed as a lack of trust.
  - Learning what motivates a person. For example, in some cultures where a personal relationship with the manager is especially highly valued, employees often tend to work in order to receive praise from their manager. Lack of recognition and appreciation by the manager is a sign that they are failing.

- Take risks. For example, suppose a particular person such as a foreign national is the most qualified person for a job, but you are concerned about the negative reaction of some customers or clients. Instead of selecting someone else, determine how you can address the discomfort of those customers and help the person be successful.

Recruit and promote for workforce diversity

Successfully recruiting people from diverse backgrounds involves long-term, concerted efforts with others throughout your organization. To help you with this process, try some of the following ideas:

- Develop specific strategies to increase your flow of applicants from a variety of backgrounds. For example, ensure that the recruiting pool represents a diversity of backgrounds. Consider drawing on other target populations by advertising in different magazines, on the Internet, or through international job fairs. If you commonly recruit students from certain colleges or universities, ensure that the student population represents a diversity of backgrounds.

- Use internships to bring more diverse people into your organization or work group and help them gain on-the-job experience and skills.

- Be willing to hire employees with nontraditional backgrounds and skills and implement support systems to get them up to speed quickly so they feel like part of the group.

- Use referrals from employees within your organization to help identify promising candidates for recruitment. Pay attention to the diversity of this informal network.

- Always try to bring in more than one person of any particular group so they can act as a support for each other.

- Study other companies or even other units within your company. What are they doing that can be brought into your organization?

Hiring is the first step, but retaining, developing, and promoting the employees you hire is a critical step as well. The following suggestions can help you with this effort:

- Look for opportunities to develop employees from diverse backgrounds and to prepare them for positions of responsibility in your organization. Tell them about the options in their present careers, as well as other career opportunities within the organization.

- Look at career paths and opportunities in your area with a fresh mind-set. Aggressively attempt to eliminate intentional or unintentional discrimination or favoritism based on language skill, academic achievement, or indirect measures of past performance.

- Publicize available career paths and the skills required for people to get there.

- Form an officially recognized and supported steering committee to address issues of diversity. Invite team members who represent a diversity of backgrounds to join the committee.

Assist people from diverse backgrounds to succeed

Proactive managers understand the business case for investing in the talent of people from diverse backgrounds. They recognize and seek to develop the skills of all employees; not just those who they think fit the traditional, familiar, or dominant culture of the organization. They are willing to take risks in hiring, training, and coaching.

Evaluate what you can do to help employees from different backgrounds succeed in the organization. Consider these suggestions:

- Most organizations have informal networks that utilize "tried and true" employees for new projects or work opportunities. The work of these employees is known, and they are regularly called upon when such opportunities arise. Help propel nontraditional employees into these informal networks by actively promoting their talents and their potential.

- Implement an informal mentor or buddy system, especially for employees who are less proportionately represented. Pair each new employee with a more experienced person who can help the new employee adjust to the organization and the work group. In some cultures this should be handled with great care. For some persons from a very individualistic culture, the person may be eager to show his or her capabilities and performance. A mentor relationship, in this case, may be perceived as condescending.

- Make sure employees understand the unwritten as well as the written rules of the organization and how to work with them or around them where necessary.

- Be flexible, and recognize that each employee's development needs and preferred styles may also be unique.

- Assign diverse employees to cross-organizational teams and task forces, thus increasing their exposure to employees in other divisions and departments in the organization. Let them know you will support them when they need help.

- Give people feedback to help them succeed in the organization. Coach people to use their differences effectively and not alienate others.

- Be aware that giving feedback is done differently in different cultures. In some cultures, people feel uncomfortable getting direct feedback. You may want to ask someone how they prefer getting feedback, both compliments and constructive suggestions. Also, consider the time and place for feedback. In some cultures, feedback is not given in a working context but rather in a more informal situation and only indirectly. One possibility in such situations is to tell a story that illustrates the content of your feedback.

- Reexamine how you have traditionally judged the characteristics or qualities you look for in high-potential employees.

- Help employees deal with frustrations caused by their perception of slow change in the system or slow progress toward acceptance. Listen.

- Recognize and confront aspects of your organizational culture that prevent capable employees from being fully included and successful within your organization.

PART 3: ORGANIZATIONAL EFFORTS— EFFECT SYSTEMIC CHANGE

Assess organizational readiness

Before you embark on a plan to significantly change your organization's approach to diversity, it is wise to assess the organization's readiness. Assessing readiness for a "valuing diversity initiative" allows you to determine the best timing and level of change you want to pursue.

To examine your organization's readiness, use the following suggestions:

- Determine your organization's readiness by answering these questions:
  - Do employees and top management see a connection between efforts to value differences and the success of the business?
  - Are your operating officers and managers on board?
  - Is the organization already very diverse?
  - Does the organization's power structure include a mix of people from diverse backgrounds? Countries?
  - Is acceptance of differences part of the corporate language and culture?
  - Do the policies and procedures of the organization permit a great deal of personal choice, freedom, and flexibility?
  - Do reward and recognition systems and practices include options?
  - Does the organization permit flexibility for employees in their "psychological employment contract" as people try to integrate work with the rest of their lives?

- Recognize that in some organizations, tradition is highly valued. This is especially true in many Japanese and European companies, among others. So, if you are working with companies such as these, ask yourself and others:
  - What impact does tradition seem to have in this organization?
  - To which traditional value can diversity be related?

- Use your answers to these questions to guide your pursuit of systemic changes. Initiatives that promote valuing diversity are more successful when they are seen as a business necessity. Therefore, it is important to establish this belief.

Accommodate the needs of a diverse workforce

To seriously address the needs of a diverse workforce, an organization must have systems and policies that are sensitive to and accommodate those needs. Following are some ideas and issues to consider:

- Explore the possibilities of flexible working hours, compressed work weeks, part-time hours, job sharing, and working from home.

- Develop a process for deciding which language should be used during particular meetings.

- If English is the standard language of the organization, support learning and development of the language mastery required.

- Expand options for childcare programs and other family-oriented benefits.

- Offer flexible benefits packages that readily allow for individual preferences.

- Promote programs designed to actively recruit and retain older workers (for example, opportunities for upward and lateral mobility, close monitoring of hours to avoid adverse Social Security ramifications, etc.). In some cases it may result in permitting older workers to work part-time.

- Eliminate unnecessary job requirements (for instance, too high a level of formal education).

- Evaluate the holidays your organization officially recognizes and celebrates; do they accommodate a diverse workforce? If not, explore how they could be made more flexible.

- Show sensitivity in your physical work environment (for example, display artwork representing a variety of cultures).

Make it happen

Systemic change does not happen overnight, although you can influence its direction and provide a model in your department or area.

To increase the likelihood of systemic change in your organization, consider the following steps:

- Clarify your organization's operating image and philosophy. For example, assess your customer base, both current and potential.
  - Do your products and services communicate an awareness of and commitment to all segments of the market that could benefit from them?
  - Do your marketing and advertising materials represent your philosophy of valuing diversity?

- Clearly impart your vision for a diverse workplace to others through organizational meetings and forums.

- Study other companies. What strategies do they employ that can be brought into your organization?

- Promote and value diversity by involving all team members in your organization's surveys, task forces, steering committees, and specific training programs.

- Recognize that strong emotions may be generated by the organization's move toward a more inclusive environment. Emphasize that learning about, understanding, and respecting someone else's values, background, and preferences does not mean accepting them as your own.

- Be alert to details especially when working in an international context. For instance, colors, numbers, and symbols often have different meanings in different cultures.

- Implement training programs that focus on the organization's commitment to promoting diversity in the workplace (programs designed to develop a greater awareness of and sensitivity to differences). When delivering workshops and other training, pace the delivery of new information and allow time for discussion and debriefing.

- Celebrate differences through team-building activities.

- Hold managers accountable for making the necessary changes through formal channels such as performance reviews and departmental goals.

- Model the respect for and use of differences to address issues. For example, be aware that people from different cultures practice different degrees of openness and directness. In some places, directness would be considered rude and offensive. As a manager, learn about those differences and adjust your approach accordingly.

Focus on the goal of valuing the individual

Your efforts to manage diversity can easily stir powerful frustrations and other emotions within your organization. Those who have stifled feelings of frustration for years may suddenly voice their anger. Some may see the diversity program as a "quota" plan that will advance others' careers at the expense of their own.

To be effective, you need to keep sight of the overall goal—to value the individual—and communicate the purpose clearly and repeatedly. Valuing diversity is a means of valuing everyone. Leveraging individual and cultural diversity is essential to managing effectively; that is, appreciating each individual for his or her unique strengths and developing and using them for the benefit of the enterprise. Consider the following suggestions:

- Clearly communicate that diversity refers to everyone. Use a broad definition of diversity in your discussions: personality, age, profession, family status, country of origin, culture, urban/rural, and so forth. People who might otherwise consider themselves irrelevant to the discussion can feel they are full participants, while those who consider themselves overlooked can have their voices heard.

- Emphasize the importance of understanding and respecting each other's view of the world. Encourage people to share their worldview. Draw on people's travel experiences as a way of illustrating differing worldviews.

- Be clear about your intent. Some people don't want their differences recognized or emphasized. Others may see your overtures to underrepresented groups as threatening. Make sure your message always returns to the central issue—how to recognize and enable the organization to effectively use each person's talents.

- Avoid blaming. Some people have suffered through poorly designed or conducted diversity programs or sensitivity sessions and may already be defensive and skeptical. Accent the positive. And accent the benefits to the business.

Evaluate progress toward systemic change

The success of any plan requires continuous improvement. To ensure the effectiveness of your efforts to value, promote, and maximize diversity, establish baseline measures or benchmarks to evaluate your progress. Then monitor the progress toward your goals on an ongoing basis. Keep in mind that this is often a long-term change effort. Consider using the following evaluation measures:

- Develop a greater understanding of diversity in your organization by asking about the current attitudes and experiences of your employees through focus groups, questionnaires, and exit interviews. Share feedback on results with all employees. Note that with people who have experienced authoritative regimes, you need to build a solid base of trust before you talk about attitudes and values. They may not open up because information like that was used against them in previous situations.

- Research the demographics of your organization as a whole and its individual departments. Determine what level of diversity already exists in your work group and your organization.

- Examine personnel records to compare your organization's current level of diversity with what you would like it to be in the future.
    - Review who gets hired at different levels in your organization.
    - Look into whether promotion and advancement opportunities are equal for all employees.
    - Ask why people leave the organization. Do people from a diversity of backgrounds stay with your organization? Are there certain work groups that tend to have unusually high or low retention rates?

- Assess the organization's publications, such as employee newsletters. Do they reflect a diversity of ideas, cultures, and perspectives?

- Scrutinize organizational policies and programs to uncover any possible unfairness or barriers that may exist.

- Develop other organization-specific measures to monitor progress toward your goal of valuing and maximizing diversity.

- Ask for feedback on your ability to develop strong shared values and your acceptance of diversity among the staff. Listen to and act on it appropriately and in a timely manner.

- Strive to continuously improve your ability to leverage individual and cultural diversity.

RESOURCES

The resources for this chapter begin on page 670.

COMMUNICATION FACTOR

It used to be easier to be a poor communicator. Life was slower and communication options were limited. Hierarchical management encouraged issuing orders rather than building consensus. Now, with e-mail and the Internet, fax machines and mobile phones, you can be interacting with others nearly around the clock. Business requirements demand that you communicate quickly, clearly, concisely, appropriately, and intelligently.

No matter what your organization creates or provides, from industrial equipment to consulting services, effective communication will give you a competitive edge. Better, smarter, faster—they are possible only through frequent, useful, dynamic communication.

The chapters in this section will help you develop your skills in the following areas:

Chapter 26 - Foster Open Communication: Establishes communication vehicles, structures, and processes; interacts with people openly and directly; seeks honest viewpoints; and proactively shares timely information.

Chapter 27 - Speak with Impact: Expresses oneself clearly, concisely, and effectively; adapts content and level of detail to the situation; prepares and delivers clear, well-organized presentations; develops a smooth, polished delivery style; and creates high-impact visual aids.

Chapter 28 - Listen to Others: Demonstrates genuine interest and empathy; listens patiently and carefully to input; correctly interprets nonverbal behaviors; clarifies others' points of view; and listens well in a group.

Chapter 29 - Write Effectively: Develops a professional, clear style; uses correct grammar; productively edits one's own work and that of others; adapts the level of content to the readers; overcomes procrastination; and chooses the correct format for the message.

26
FOSTER OPEN
COMMUNICATION

- *Establish vehicles, structures, and processes for open exchange of information and viewpoints*
- *Communicate the message that every idea is worthy of consideration*
- *Structure creative ways to obtain input from others*
- *Interact with people openly and directly*
- *Use PDI's talk/listen process in your conversations*
- *Express reactions and opinions without intimidating others*
- *Encourage others to express their honest views, even contrary ones*
- *Facilitate discussions to ensure that everyone's viewpoint is heard*
- *Proactively share timely updates and information with relevant parties*
- *Make sure people have no "surprises"*
- *Choose the appropriate communication vehicle for the situation*

INTRODUCTION

Information is power, but it is pointless power if hoarded.
Power must be shared for an organization or a relationship to work.

— Max DePree, in *Leadership Is an Art*

In this era when information rules, no organization is exempt from the need to create an environment of communication that, as Max DePree says, "liberates us to do our jobs better." Without sufficient, timely information, most people are handicapped in their ability to excel. Successful managers know this and seek to create an environment where communication is open, encouraged, rewarded, frequent, and relevant.

Sometimes the very idea of open communication seems too utopian. Some people don't know what information to share, who would be interested in it, or how to communicate so others will pay attention to their message. Others don't want to get involved in the politics of communication. Still others hold onto what's always been done because it takes less time and is predictable.

Creating a culture of open communication is not easy. It takes time, effort, and courage. It is occasionally risky, and it sometimes upsets the power structure. Yet open communication is absolutely necessary. Your organization cannot survive in an atmosphere of secrecy, stagnation, and recycled ideas. If you want to charge up your employees, shake up your competitors, and excite your customers, you have to invite and expect people to communicate, and listen carefully to the messages they convey.

This chapter presents suggestions for ways you can foster an environment of open, successful communication in your organization.

VALUABLE TIPS

- Ask your employees what information they would like to receive regularly from you, and then tell them what you'd like to hear from them.

- Communicate the "why" behind the "what."

- Encourage members of your staff to share information with each other.

- Establish a site on your intranet where people can find current information on strategic initiatives, projects, new clients, and other important topics.

- Train telecommuters and in-house personnel how to use communication technology so both groups will be able to use the systems efficiently.

- Discuss with your staff recent developments in the organization.

- Realize that true communication takes time.

- List the key organizational people upon whom your success depends, and make a special effort to keep them informed.

- Don't punish people who give you negative news.

- Make a point of listening attentively when people express differing or contradictory views on an issue.

- Respond nondefensively when people express contrary viewpoints.

- Alert your manager to possible implications of events occurring inside or outside the organization.

- Don't ignore or downplay negative issues or situations in your area. Report the situation as accurately as possible.

- Ask people in your group to serve as resident experts on specific topics. Publicize this information throughout the organization so people will know whom to contact with questions.

- Design your staff meetings so you are not the sole source of information. Ask other people to give updates and share relevant information.

- Distribute notes outlining action steps and decisions from your meetings.

- At the end of every week, have your group share status reports on important projects and initiatives.

- Don't rely only on written communication to inform people; you can't guarantee they will read it.

- Use at least two communication vehicles to send important organizational messages.

Establish vehicles, structures, and processes for open exchange of information and viewpoints

Open communication results from an environment in which people know their ideas are respected and wanted. To foster such an environment, successful managers make conscious efforts to establish vehicles, methods, and processes for communication. This is especially necessary when team members and those with whom they work are not geographically in the same place. To foster open communication in your area, consider the following suggestions:

- Make sure your communication strategy supports your overall organizational strategy and structure. For example, if you have participatory management, information needs to flow easily and quickly to the decision makers.

- Build communication strategies into your business plans. What type of information sharing and feedback do you need to accomplish your goals?

- Analyze how your area currently communicates. Is it like a web, where there are many communication points? Or is it like a downspout, where it is dry most of the time, then a flood of information comes from the top down?

- Talk about communication with your group. Ask people how communication helps them perform their roles. Discuss your current communication culture and whether or how you want to change it. Strive to get below the surface, to get past merely saying, "We need to communicate more."

- With your group, develop a communication philosophy for your area. Every person should understand and be able to explain your group's communication mission and goals.

- Measure your communication efforts. Set goals and expectations, and specify how people will be evaluated.

- Make sure people across your organization know how to get in touch with each other. For example, do people in the traditional office know how to reach telecommuters or contract employees?

- Create places for people to have conversations. Examine your office layout. Are there common areas where people gather and talk? If not, where could you put them?

- Regularly ask people what they have learned from others in their group or in another area of the organization. Encourage everyone to learn at least one thing each week from another person.

- Make teleconferencing more effective by establishing standard protocols of introducing all people on conference calls and having them state their names before speaking.

- Determine times when people who work remotely can contact others in the organization. These times may include staff meetings, project update meetings, etc.

- Avoid building your communication structures around one person's personality or skill. For example, you may have a CEO who is very charismatic and eager to give speeches that inspire employees. He or she may decide that all senior managers should give rousing speeches to their groups. The odds are low that this will be effective over the long term.

- Consider whether your communication vehicles will work as well during stressful, adverse times as they do during good times.

Communicate the message that every idea is worthy of consideration

Valuing the ideas of others is an important prerequisite to fostering open communication. You can set the tone for your part of the organization by deliberately and consciously sending the message that ideas and contributions are valued. The following suggestions can help you communicate this message:

- Be an advocate for the view that contributing ideas and knowledge is a part of everyone's job, regardless of function or level of responsibility.

- Specify the types of ideas you're looking for. If you are brainstorming, stress that all ideas are welcome. If you are refining ideas or planning the execution, specify that you are looking for ideas in those areas. It can be frustrating if you're looking for specific types of ideas during the planning stage and someone wants to brainstorm.

- Actively solicit ideas from every level, from the CEO to the parking lot attendant. Valuable ideas can and do come from people in every role.

- Communicate examples of new products and services that resulted from ideas from interesting sources.

- Be receptive to the ideas you hear. Part of open communication is being willing to listen to a wide range of ideas. Even if you think an idea has no merit, show your willingness to hear about it so you don't shut off the flow of ideas.

Structure creative ways to obtain input from others

Effective leaders work to establish a culture in which people openly contribute their ideas and thoughts. This does not happen automatically. Leaders and team members need to take deliberate steps to create such an environment. In addition, sometimes a particular problem or issue requires especially creative ideas to find a solution. At these times, it helps to have strategies that will generate different ideas and approaches. To establish creative ways to gain input, consider the following suggestions:

- Identify how you currently obtain input from people within and outside of your group. Do you count on people to be proactive, or do you ask for specific pieces of information? Do you typically rely on traditional vehicles such as face-to-face meetings and memos?

- Identify all vehicles available for soliciting and receiving input, and think of at least one new way to use each vehicle. For example, you could ask people to leave you voice-mail messages about a certain topic on a particular day. Or you could send a structured, survey-like form via e-mail or interoffice mail to make it easy for people to respond to specific questions.

- Be patient when you solicit input. People communicate in many different styles, especially if they are from another culture. They may need time to develop their ideas more fully, or they may need to establish a relationship before they discuss business. Don't expect (or demand) everyone to communicate the way you do.

- Look for and reinforce behaviors that facilitate information sharing, such as debriefing sessions following a project, sharing information about a competitor, documenting best practices, and sharing newly acquired skills.

- If you have people in your group at other geographic locations, identify your options for collecting their input. Ask them how they would like to participate, then determine ways to make it happen.

- Recognize people who find creative ways to collect and share ideas and knowledge. Be sure to explain the positive impact of their actions on the group, department, and organization.

- Choose a theme or topic each month on which you solicit ideas. Select winners in a number of categories, such as:
  - Most ideas
  - Most creative idea
  - Most practical idea
  - Easiest idea to implement
  - Best idea for the future

Interact with people openly and directly

Warren Bennis from the University of Southern California discovered in his research that effective leaders are consistent and predictable. Interacting with others openly and directly helps to communicate predictability, as well as build stronger relationships. Effective managers also combine this open and direct style of interaction with obvious and consistent respect for others. The following suggestions can help you interact openly, directly, and respectfully:

- Ask trusted colleagues for feedback on your ability to communicate your ideas, intentions, and feelings openly. What is your reputation? Do people trust the information they receive from you?

- Be open and direct about both positive and negative news. This will build your credibility as a candid, reliable source of information.

- Realize that your nonverbal actions convey your attitudes about open communication. Check your posture, gestures, facial expressions, and vocal variety. Make sure they convey your willingness to share and discuss issues.

- Consider whether you give inconsistent details to people. For example, do people feel like they get a different story every time they talk to you? Do you withhold details from certain groups of people? Such behaviors can make people skeptical about your ability to interact openly and directly.

- When you need to send tough messages, focus on the issue and the person's part in the situation, not the person's personality or past incidents. Be direct with your message, then give the person time to react. Don't expect a quick resolution.

Use PDI's talk/listen process in your conversations

Communication is at the heart of working with people, whether you are leading, coaching, managing, influencing, resolving conflict, solving problems, building relationships, or strategizing. The talk/listen process is a simple framework that can help you communicate effectively and create better working relationships. It begins with two key questions:

- Are you talking or listening?

- Are you exploring or solving?

Talking, listening, exploring, and solving are all critical for effective communication. Most communication difficulties result from short-circuiting one of these elements. People frequently do not allow enough time for listening or they move too fast from exploring to solving. They make these errors because they want to get to a solution quickly. What surprises most people is that spending sufficient time listening and exploring actually makes the entire process more efficient because it:

- Addresses the root cause(s).

- Identifies and deals with important concerns and barriers.

- Finds a solution that people are committed to, so the topic doesn't need to be revisited.

Following are some key features of each element:

Talking:

- Present your ideas, views, goals, or feelings.

- Explain your position.

- Sell your view and rationale.

- Make sure you are thoroughly understood.

- Use nonverbal behaviors that show your reactions to what others are saying (e.g., nodding your head).

- Ask leading questions.

- Ask questions when you already know the answer.

Listening:

- Work to understand other people's ideas, views, goals, and feelings.

- Summarize their position.

- Try to understand other people's views and rationale.

- Show that you understand all their main points.

- Read their body language and nonverbal messages.

- Ask questions that encourage people to say more about what is really on their minds.

- Demonstrate curiosity about other people's views.

Exploring:

- Attempt to understand the nature and scope of the problem.
- Figure out what really matters to people, including yourself.
- Suspend your judgment until the picture is clear.
- Search for the root cause.
- Check underlying assumptions.
- Try to understand the real needs of all stakeholders.
- Clarify the requirements for a mutually acceptable solution.

Solving:

- Find potential answers to the problem.
- Make decisions about what to do next.
- Choose a course of action.
- Search for the best options to accomplish the task you've identified.
- Propose action steps.
- Search for a solution that addresses the needs of all stakeholders.
- Evaluate how well different recommendations meet the specified requirements.

To apply the talk/listen process in your work, consider the following suggestions:

- For one week, note the talk, listen, explore, and solve ratios in your conversations. How much time do you typically spend on each? Do you focus on one or two much more than the others? When you need the input and involvement of others, focus more on listening and exploring.
- Observe effective problem solvers. What ratio of talk, listen, explore, and solve do they use?
- When you are problem solving and need information and the commitment of other people to execute the decision, spend more time listening and exploring. The others should spend more time talking and solving.
- When you are coaching a person, focus on listening and exploring far more than on talking and solving.

• When dealing with performance problems, make sure the employee talks more than you do. In such situations, managers often talk far more than the employee. That approach does not work, however, because the manager, not the employee, then becomes the problem's owner. When the employee takes responsibility for the problem, he or she works harder than the manager to figure out what he or she will do differently.

Express reactions and opinions without intimidating others

The confidence and conviction many leaders display is one of the reasons they are seen as leaders and placed in leadership positions. Yet, these same characteristics may cause difficulty later because these leaders may be seen as somewhat intimidating.

Effective leaders have learned the importance of monitoring their reactions to other people to ensure they do not unintentionally intimidate them. They have also learned that they may need to adapt their normal behavior when working with people from different national or corporate cultures. For example, if a free-wheeling, fast-paced organization that assigns little meaning to levels in the organization takes over a more conservative organization in which levels are important, leaders will need to recognize the differences in expectations.

To develop your ability to express your opinions without intentionally or unintentionally intimidating other people, try the following suggestions:

• Think of how you typically state your views. Do you state them as if they are final decisions? For example, do you say, "That will never work," "We can't possibly do that," or "You haven't thought that through"? Such phrases can intimidate others.

• Determine whether you are sharing your opinion or trying to convince people that you're right. If you are trying to convince people, you may be tempted to intimidate them to make them agree with you.

• Ask your colleagues at a number of levels in the organization for their feedback on whether you come across as intimidating when you express your opinions. People with power can intimidate others through their tone of voice, the certainty of the expression, their physical posture, etc. If you receive feedback that you are seen as intimidating, identify which behaviors give this impression and work to change them.

• Recognize that others may see you as intimidating even if you don't have that intention or self-perception. When you receive feedback about it, listen carefully and determine what you do that is considered intimidating. Do not argue or just say, "I don't mean to." Instead, change your behavior—your tone of voice, your body posture—when you ask for others' opinions, etc.

- If you see the ability to intimidate as a positive attribute, analyze its effectiveness. When did you use intimidation? What did it accomplish in the short term and long term? Look at examples of intimidating leaders. How effective are they over the long term? Find other, more effective ways to accomplish your goals.

- When you share a reaction, point out that it is a reaction, not a decision. Sometimes it can be helpful to explain your behavior.

- Before you share your opinion, ask other people for their views. Listen intently and try to find some areas of agreement to which you can refer as you express your reaction or opinion.

- When you need to make a strong point, be direct but nonaggressive. Simply say what you think and feel without putting other people down.

- Use "I" statements and "whole messages" when you express your opinions. "I am not sure we have fully explored the alternatives on this issue" sounds less intimidating than "You have not investigated this issue fully." Whole messages, which include observations, thoughts, feelings, and goals, provide the context for an "I" message.

Encourage others to express their honest views, even contrary ones

In an environment of open communication, people feel reasonably comfortable sharing any and all information, whether it is good news or bad, agreement or disagreement. To have the most flexible culture, most effective problem solving, and most adaptable workforce, the open sharing of ideas and thoughts is necessary. Without this openness, people will monitor their communication, judge whether it is safe to say something, and perhaps withhold contrary or different ideas when these very ideas and unusual approaches may be exactly what is needed. To encourage others to express their ideas, use the following suggestions:

- Tell people that you want to hear their opinions, and then support your statements with behaviors such as listening, considering the idea seriously, thanking people for their ideas, incorporating ideas into plans, and giving credit to others for their ideas.

- Analyze your typical reaction to outspoken people. Do you look forward to hearing their views? Or do you dread their presence at a meeting because you think they will slow things down or create conflict?

- Ask for the opinions of others before you have made up your own mind, so that you are open to influence. If you ask for others' opinions after you've already made up your mind, you may sabotage your willingness to listen to honest opinions, especially if they contradict your decision.

- Learn to value diverse or different views. When you hear an idea that does not seem to make sense or be useful, look at it carefully, rather than dismissing it quickly. At first, the approach may seem confusing and time-consuming, but as you ask for and foster this feedback, you will see that some of these ideas have real value. For example, the first time someone had the idea to include customer training in the organization's corporate university, the suggestion probably seemed quite strange. Or the first time someone suggested collaborating with a competitor to get a particular contract, the idea probably appeared ludicrous. Both of these practices are common now.

Please, feel free to voice any disagreements you might have with management.

- Give people options for expressing their views. Don't force everyone to tell you his or her views face-to-face. Ask people to convey their ideas and opinions in a way that is comfortable for them, with the understanding that you may wish to contact them later with clarifying questions.

- Monitor your reactions to situations in which people from different levels, functions, or cultures express contrary views. Do you respond differently in some way? Is that appropriate? Ensure that you are willing to listen to ideas expressed by different levels, functions, groups of people, and individuals. It is not helpful to be open to some and not to others.

- When people express a point of view with which you strongly disagree, wait until they have finished speaking. Restate the main points of their argument and ask them to verify your accuracy. Indicate points of agreement if you can do so honestly and sincerely. Then, and only then, specifically state which points you disagree with and why.

- When you disagree with someone, avoid labeling his or her opinions as right or wrong. Instead, use words such as "concerns," "doubts," and "questions." If people feel that their opinions will be judged, they will hesitate to speak up.

- Whenever possible, incorporate the ideas of others into the solution. Unless people believe you will use their ideas, they will cease to provide them.

- Guard against viewing dissension, differences of opinion, or disagreement as obstacles. Showing frustration, even in subtle ways, with people who express contrary views will inhibit them from offering their views in the future.

Facilitate discussions to ensure that everyone's viewpoint is heard

As leader of a team, it is your responsibility to ensure that all team members contribute their ideas. One way of accomplishing this is to facilitate discussions such that other people share their views. In addition, expect your direct reports to share this same responsibility with their own teams. The following suggestions can help you facilitate discussions:

- Be a good listener. Watch your tendency to immediately evaluate and critique what others have to say. Nothing will shut down participation more quickly than a rebuttal, a "yes but," immediate criticism, or an interruption.

- Make it easy for people to participate. Check any tendency you have to dominate the conversation. Invite others to share their ideas.

- Ask questions. Questions are excellent tools for monitoring and facilitating discussions. Asking the right questions can be more important than knowing the answers.

- Integrate contributions. Link various points of view and identify areas of understanding, agreement, and disagreement.

- Summarize key ideas or major points to keep the group focused.

- Draw out quiet or reticent team members. They may never speak up unless you deliberately solicit their ideas, and you might miss valuable information and perspectives. Use open-ended questions and listen carefully to what they have to say.

- Protect minority opinion. Support people who present a new view, raise a concern, or challenge conventional wisdom. Make sure they have a chance to be heard.

- Periodically ask people for feedback about your facilitation skills.

- Attend a workshop that will help you develop facilitation skills.

- Periodically attend meetings led by your direct reports and observe their facilitation skills. Provide feedback on what you saw.

Proactively share timely updates and information with relevant parties

Information sharing is critical to many, if not most, work situations. Work processes rely on the smooth flow of information among people internal and external to the organization. Without information sharing, teamwork disappears and customers are ill-served. In times of change, it's even more important to put tremendous effort into establishing a communication plan and continually updating and implementing it. The following suggestions can help you ensure information is effectively shared, in times of both change and stability:

- Identify the type and amount of communication that needs to occur on a daily, weekly, or monthly basis. What kinds of decisions do people make? Do they have what they need to make those decisions?

- Use a three-month calendar and mark dates of major projects and initiatives. Plot out a communication schedule for updating people on milestones, such as the beginning of a project, the midpoint, or the completion of a crucial phase.

- Designate a communication contact person for each project. Funnel all memos and messages through that person.

- Identify your typical obstacles to sending timely information. For example, projects may move fast, you may be traveling, you might not have time to follow through on all the details. Next, determine what you will do to counteract each obstacle—for example, delegate specific responsibilities while you're traveling.

- Ensure that any major change has a communication plan. Check that the plan is not merely a paper document, but is followed and updated.

- List everyone who should receive information during a project or initiative. Make sure they receive all updates and have opportunities to give you feedback.

- Ask your manager to identify the kinds of information he or she is most interested in receiving from you. Regularly check to see if you are providing the desired amount of information—neither too much nor too little—in each critical area.

- When you get an informational memo directed specifically to you, consider whether the information would be useful to your employees. If so, route the memo as is, or modify it first to fit the circumstances and their needs. People need to know what is going on in other functions in order to understand how their work affects the broader organization.

Make sure people have no "surprises"

People do not like surprises, especially negative ones. Therefore, it is critical that you do not keep from others information that may result in their being surprised or caught off-guard and ill-prepared. Even when you know the other person will be angry or displeased, it is far better to say something yourself, before the person learns the information from someone else. The following suggestions can help you avoid unnecessary surprises:

- Give your manager any information that may have negative implications for your work unit. Make sure your manager hears the news from you.

- When you get information that affects your direct reports or their teams, make sure you share it with those involved as soon as possible. People expect that their managers will share information with them. Your actions to share information will also encourage them to share news—especially bad news—with you.

- Share potentially surprising information with people in your department before they hear rumors. Let them know what the issue is and how it will affect your department. Encourage them to come to you with their questions and concerns.

- When there is a crisis, tell people as much as you can about the situation, even if you don't have all the details. Explain that you will share details as they become available. If you wait until you know every detail, you will lose the opportunity to deliver and shape the message.

- Present surprising or bad news calmly, especially if it is stressful, charged, or potentially job-altering information.

- Meet regularly (at least monthly) with your peers in other areas of the organization to share information with each other and thus prevent surprises.

- Realize that you will likely face some strong emotional reactions to certain information, whether it is positive or negative. Recognize and empathize with people's emotions, and give them time to process what the information means.

- Make yourself available while the situation unfolds so people can talk with you and ask questions.

Choose the appropriate communication vehicle for the situation

How you communicate is as important as what you communicate. Managers today have a myriad of communication vehicles available to them. They can meet in person with an individual or a group; they can meet in the other person's area or their own; they can use telephone, voice mail, fax, or e-mail; they can use formal or informal written communication, etc. Whenever you communicate, decide the method that will work best for the message, the person, and the goal. The following suggestions can help you choose the best form of communication:

- Discuss personally sensitive information in person. If the message is new, difficult to understand, needs elaboration, or is sensitive, you should deliver it in person.

- Choose face-to-face communication when you need to have a conversation or a dialogue, not just deliver information. This will allow you to present a message and get immediate feedback through verbal and nonverbal responses.

- When a dialogue is needed and a face-to-face meeting is not possible, use the telephone or groupware that allows for real-time conversation on-line.

- Routine messages or follow-up communication often can be delivered through e-mail or voice mail.

- Use more than one vehicle when you have an important message to deliver; this will help you capture the attention of more people. Different people respond to different vehicles.

- Watch how people in your organization use communication vehicles. Identify which ones work well and use them to your advantage. If nothing is working well, consult with an internal or external communication group to learn new techniques.

- Choose voice mail when the message doesn't need to be delivered in person, when it is after hours, or when the person is out of the office. Organize your thoughts before you leave a voice mail so you can make the message clear and concise.

- Use e-mail when you want to document your message or send attachments. E-mail allows you to send a single message to a large number of users and is of great use in communicating across geographical areas with a number of time zones. However, recognize that the effectiveness of e-mail depends on your writing skills and the reader's willingness to read it thoroughly.

- Use videoconferences when you need to see the participants but, because of costs or lack of time, cannot be in the same location.

RESOURCES

The resources for this chapter begin on page 672.

27
SPEAK
WITH IMPACT

PART 1: EXPAND YOUR SPEAKING SKILLS
- *Speak with enthusiasm and expressiveness*
- *Speak clearly and concisely*
- *Get your point across when talking*
- *Express yourself effectively in one-on-one conversations and small groups*
- *Adapt content and level of detail to meet other people's needs*
- *Use humor effectively in group discussions and presentations*

PART 2: SPEAK WITH IMPACT DURING PRESENTATIONS
- *Prepare clear, well-organized presentations*
- *Use a smooth, polished delivery style*
- *Manage anxiety effectively*
- *Use nonverbal behavior appropriately to emphasize key points*
- *Actively engage the audience during presentations*
- *Gauge audience reactions and make appropriate adjustments*
- *Prepare effective visual aids*
- *Use handouts, flip charts, and slides effectively*
- *Use visual aids smoothly*
- *Answer questions clearly and concisely*

INTRODUCTION

Imagine if every time you spoke, your speech was clear and compelling. People hung on every word, eager to hear what you would say next. They crowded into your meetings, recorded your speeches, and recalled your stories like sports fans describe championship matches.

Sound impossible? Perhaps, but speaking well and engaging your listeners are not impossibilities. You have a great deal of control over your content, your manner, your diction, your gestures, and your timing. When you don't like something, you can change it. Furthermore, as a manager, you most likely have frequent opportunities to practice.

You may or may not become a world-class speaker, but you can adopt habits and practices that will result in reduced anxiety, well-prepared speeches, and effective conversations.

This chapter presents targeted suggestions to develop or fine-tune your speaking skills and help you to become a more effective communicator in all situations, from one-on-one meetings to large, formal presentations.

VALUABLE TIPS

- Know the main points you want and need to make.

- State key messages in concise, simple, declarative sentences.

- Determine what you want people to remember. State it at the beginning and end of your conversation or presentation.

- Ask a colleague to signal you whenever you go off the topic at a meeting.

- Distill your message to key points, then only include supporting material relevant to those points.

- Build your vocabulary; deliberately use a new word every day.

- Use appropriate gestures to animate your discussions.

- Vary your volume, pitch, and pace to emphasize major points in discussions. Avoid speaking in a monotone voice.

- Address individuals, not a collective group called the audience.

- Change your perception of giving a presentation; anticipation is usually worse than the actual event. Anticipate what will go well instead of what might go wrong.

- Choose and practice a stress-management technique. Use it whenever you feel anxiety about speaking to individuals or groups.

- If you are nervous, concentrate on getting your message across, not on your abilities as a speaker.

- Learn as much as possible about the audience, the room, other speakers, why you were invited to speak, and what people hope to learn from you.

- Seek feedback on your gestures, grammar, vocal expressiveness, general delivery style, and visual aids after you give a presentation.

- Keep in mind that visual aids should complement, not substitute for, your presentation. Don't simply recite your overheads or slides.

- Anticipate questions, especially tough ones, and prepare strong answers.

- Pause for a moment before you answer a tough question. Don't say the first thought that comes into your mind.

- Practice giving presentations; give speeches at community or service organizations or take classes in which you have to make regular presentations.

- Videotape your presentation and review it critically with an experienced presenter or professional speech coach.

PART I:
EXPAND YOUR SPEAKING SKILLS

Speak with enthusiasm and expressiveness

No one likes to listen to a speaker who drones. If you want to engage, motivate, inspire, captivate, energize, or wake up people, you need to be enthusiastic and expressive. Your ideas deserve the best delivery you can give them. To speak with appropriate expressiveness, consider these suggestions:

- Don't confuse enthusiasm with cheerleading. You don't have to jump up and down and wave your arms to show you're excited about an idea. Relax and let your natural enthusiasm and commitment to your message show.

- Listen to different leaders speak. How do they communicate their enthusiasm? Identify things these leaders do that would be appropriate ways for you to demonstrate your enthusiasm. Experiment with these ideas.

- Watch people as they listen to enthusiastic speakers. What is their reaction? How do you know that the audience is reacting positively to the enthusiasm and commitment from the speaker? Next time you are presenting or discussing, watch for positive reactions from your audience.

- Videotape yourself giving a presentation in which you need to be enthusiastic about your topic. As you review the tape, consider the following questions:
  - Do your tone of voice and inflection accurately reflect the meaning and importance of your words?
  - Do you speak at the right pace and with varied intonation?
  - Is your level of enthusiasm appropriate for the topic, the audience, and the setting?
  - Do you use lively, engaging language that makes your message memorable?

- If you were dissatisfied with what you saw on the tape, decide what you want to change. Be specific. For example, you may decide that you need to speak more rapidly or use different gestures. Videotape yourself again after making these changes. Continue to experiment and fine-tune until you are comfortable with your presentation.

- Develop your expressive skills outside of work.
  - Read children's books, novels, or plays aloud. Act out all the parts. Use a different voice for each character. Make sound effects.
  - Take an acting class. Learn about movement, conveying a message, projecting your voice, matching body language to words, and dealing with stage fright.

Speak clearly and concisely

One hallmark of effective speakers is that they speak clearly and concisely. People easily understand the content and the message they are communicating. To speak clearly, it's essential to know your content, the messages you want to deliver, and the points you want to make, and then tailor the content and delivery to the audience. The following suggestions can help you develop clear, concise speaking skills:

- Use short, simple sentences. Compound, complex sentences may work well in documents, but they can be confusing and difficult to follow when spoken.

- Think of how you react to someone who is unclear. How receptive are you to the person's information? It's easy to become impatient with people who can't deliver a message clearly.

- Watch your use of "business speak." People are more interested in your ideas than whether you know the latest jargon. If you use too much jargon, they may wonder if you're hiding behind it.

- Ask a trusted coworker or your manager to describe instances when you rambled, were difficult to understand, or were imprecise. If they cannot think of any, ask them to observe you for the next two weeks and point out specific examples.

- Pay attention to how people react to you during discussions and meetings. If they lose eye contact with you or get restless, you may be straying from the topic or giving excessive or irrelevant detail.

- If you sense that you are on a tangent, quickly segue back to your main point. Acknowledge that you were off-track and reiterate your main point.

- Use clear, concise language, even in casual conversation. This will help you be aware of the need to speak clearly and will give you more chances to practice.

Get your point across when talking

Whenever you talk, focus on the point you want to make or the message you want to convey so that your communication is purposeful and direct. People are bombarded with information. They are more likely to remember a message that is told simply. The following suggestions will help you get your point across clearly and directly:

- Distill your message to its main points. Before speaking, write a sentence of only five to eight words that presents each point, and then explain each point in three sentences or fewer. This will ensure that you know exactly which points you want and need to make when you are speaking.

- Assume that people will only remember one thing you said. What do you want it to be? Emphasize that point while you speak.

- Make your message memorable. Use examples and anecdotes to illustrate your points. Stories give people something to relate to and remember.

- When you are expanding a point, begin with an example (concrete), and then move to an explanation (more abstract).

- Avoid clouding your message with extraneous detail. Give people a chance to ask questions if they want more details.

- Once you have made your point, ask the listeners for their reactions. Can they identify your main point? Was it clear? This will give you an opportunity to restate your point more clearly if necessary.

Express yourself effectively in one-on-one conversations and small groups

Communicating effectively is a key foundational skill for all leaders. It is a prerequisite for many complex skills, such as persuasion, building high-performance teams, and managing change. Communicating effectively one-on-one and in small groups actually involves both listening and speaking. Without listening to others first, you will be a less effective communicator.

To learn more about listening skills, see Chapter 28: Listen to Others in this handbook. To develop your ability to express yourself effectively, consider the following suggestions:

- Ask your coworkers, manager, friends, and family for feedback on your skills in expressing yourself. Compare their perceptions to your assessment. Where are the gaps? What are your strengths? Your development needs?

- Determine what you need to do differently to express yourself more effectively. This may include:
  - Knowing your audience and speaking to them.
  - Being more clear and concise.
  - Showing more enthusiasm and commitment.
  - Speaking faster, more slowly, or in a more interesting manner.
  - Speaking more frequently or less frequently.

- Pinpoint the obstacles that keep you from expressing yourself effectively. Are you unprepared? Are you caught off-guard? Do people in the group intimidate you? List your personal obstacles, then talk with an experienced colleague or your mentor on how you can overcome them.

- Observe people who express themselves effectively. What do they do? How does it differ from what you do? Choose one or two effective behaviors to emulate.

- Identify the message you give yourself through your "inner critic." For example, you might believe that you are an introvert who will never be comfortable talking to groups or that you can't talk about technical subjects. Become aware of your inner dialogue and substitute a positive message each time you criticize yourself.

- If you are an effective speaker, check to see if you are overusing this strength. For example, you may not give others a chance to talk, you may try to overpower people through forceful arguments, or you may rely so heavily on your eloquence or glibness that you neglect to do adequate research to support your claims.

Adapt content and level of detail to meet other people's needs

How many times have you been trapped in a conversation with someone who loves the sound of his or her voice? Perhaps you have talked to people who assumed you were equally as interested in the topic as they were, despite progressively less subtle hints from you. If so, you know how important it is to adapt content and detail to the listener and the situation. Consider the following suggestions for more effectively meeting other people's needs when speaking to them:

- Learn why people want or need the information. Do they need to make a decision? Do they simply need more background? Do they need more information to implement decisions? Use this information to guide what you say and how you say it.

- Recall other conversations or meetings with this individual or group. What worked well? What did they respond to?

- Observe people during casual conversations. Do they tend to hold back and let other people talk? Do they ask for more data? Do they push for the bottom line? Knowing how specific individuals generally act will give you hints on how you should tailor your style and approach when speaking to them.

- Identify people who are skilled at adapting content to meet others' needs. Ask them how they developed this skill and if they have any advice for you.

- Use the appropriate level of formality for the situation. If you are unsure of how formal to be, err on the side of more formality.

- If you decide to shift your style or approach, be careful that you don't shift too abruptly or drastically. It may confuse your listeners, and they will focus more on your shift than on the content.

Use humor effectively in group discussions and presentations

Used well, humor is a wonderful aid to communication, diffusing emotion, making work fun, and building relationships. Used poorly, however, humor can hurt people, create distance, and make the workplace hostile. Those who use humor effectively pay close attention to how others react to their humor. They pick up the subtle and not-so-subtle cues about the appropriateness of humor. They also pay attention to humor used by others and the reaction to it. They are willing to confront inappropriate uses of humor so others are not offended or made uncomfortable.

To use humor more effectively, try the following suggestions:

- Seek feedback from a trusted colleague or team member on your current use of humor. You may think you are always using appropriate humor and may be surprised to find out that people view it differently. Or you may find that you are using humor well and people would like to see you use it more frequently.

- Humor is highly personal. When you use humor, consider what effect your words will have on all members of your audience. Be especially sensitive to issues of diversity.

- Do not use sarcasm. Sarcasm is not funny. It may seem funny unless you are its target. Even when people are laughing, at some level they are concerned about when the sarcastic wit will be turned in their direction.

- If you feel uneasy about a joke or an image, don't use it.

- Choose humor that will be understood by the general population. If you have to explain why something is funny, don't include it.

- Watch how others use humor in business settings and incorporate effective methods they use into your work.

- Spend time with friends and colleagues who display a good sense of humor. Note what they do and how they use humor.

- When appropriate, use cartoons projected on overhead slides to start meetings or presentations. This will help establish a more relaxed tone.

- Collect a few humorous books, tapes, and videos. Stay up-to-date on which comics are popular with your team and colleagues.

PART 2:
SPEAK WITH IMPACT
DURING PRESENTATIONS

**Prepare clear,
well-organized
presentations**

Giving presentations is a common activity for many managers. As a manager, you may make presentations in staff meetings, to your peers and manager, to an investor group, to a large employee group, or to the media. Whatever the purpose of the presentation, it's essential to know your objectives, your content and key points, and your audience. To prepare well-organized presentations, try the following suggestions:

- Know why you're making a presentation. Answer the following questions:
  - What is the specific purpose of this presentation?
  - What type of response or outcome do I expect or want?
  - What is important to the audience?
  - What do they want, need, or expect to take away from the presentation?

- Determine your key messages. Choose no more than five.
  - State your key messages in simple, declarative sentences.
  - Express them as precisely and vividly as possible.
  - Include only one idea in each key message.
  - State all main ideas positively, if possible.

- Choose supporting material that adds interest, clarity, persuasion, and impact. Vary the types of supporting data for each main idea. Select from examples, anecdotes, statistics, comparisons, explanations, and quotations.

- Organize your material. Choose a structure that best accomplishes your objective. Common structures include:
  - *Problem-solution:* Present a problem, suggest a solution, and indicate likely benefits if the proposed solution is put into effect.
  - *Classification:* List the important items and make them the major points in your presentation.
  - *Chronology:* Arrange events in sequential order.
  - *Climax:* Present the main points in order of increasing importance.
  - *Simple to complex:* Arrange the main points from simplest to most complex.
  - *Proposition-support:* State the key messages and support them with evidence.

- Create an introduction. The introduction needs to do three things: capture the audience's attention, provide appropriate background information, and introduce your key messages. The introduction is your opportunity to set the stage; use it to your advantage. If you waste this chance and deliver a static, boring introduction, the audience will dread, and possibly ignore, the rest of your presentation.

- Develop the conclusion. Summarize your key messages and tell the audience what you want them to do and why (in others words, answer the "so what?" and the "what's in it for me?" questions).

Use a smooth, polished delivery style

You have no doubt seen and heard speakers with a smooth, polished style who were easy to follow and understand. Effective presenters make it look effortless. Most of the time, however, it is far from effortless. Typically the person has put a great deal of work into developing a polished presentation style. To polish your delivery, try the following suggestions:

- Concentrate on the audience, not on yourself and your performance.

- Enjoy yourself and the speaking process. Your listeners will detect your confidence and also enjoy themselves more.

- Be genuine. You will be convincing because you believe in what you are saying.

- Use large print for your speaker notes. You don't want to squint or lose your place because you can't read your notes.

- Pause for a moment before you begin to speak. Let the audience's expectation build.

- Grab the audience's attention at the beginning of your introduction. For example:
  - Use a dramatic statement.
  - Ask a question that requires a response from the audience.
  - Refer to a recent or well-known event.
  - Tell a story from your own experience.
  - Cite a quotation from an authoritative source.

- Find opportunities to smile. Smiles indicate humor, warmth, irony, or empathy. A smile will convey your personable side. The best presenters come across as both personable and professional.

- Avoid distracting mannerisms, such as speaking in a monotonous voice, mumbling, repeating too much, saying you're sorry, appearing unprepared, being vague, jingling change in your pocket, or using vocalized pauses such as "ah," "um," "like," and "you know."

- If you want to change a mannerism, focus on changing one at a time. If you try to change them all at once, you will not be able to focus on your message.

Manage anxiety effectively

Even the most polished, competent presenters experience nervousness in at least some situations. While you may never eliminate your anxiety, you can take steps to manage it and make it work for you. Consider the following suggestions for doing so:

- Practice positive self-talk. As the adage suggests, whether you think you can or you think you can't, you're probably right. Believe that you can stay calm and focused during your presentation.

- Prepare as much as you need to, not as much as your colleagues need to. Other people may only need to glance at their notes a few minutes before speaking in front of 500 people. You, on the other hand, may need to go through your presentation seven or eight times before you feel comfortable. Do what you need to do to feel prepared.

- Dispel the notion that you need to eliminate all anxiety before you can give a successful presentation. Most experienced speakers have some anxiety. Channel this energy into improved concentration and expressiveness.

- Realize that anxiety decreases (but doesn't disappear) with experience, and that anxiety is not nearly as noticeable to your listeners as it is to you.

- Visualize yourself giving an effective speech. Imagine the room, the audience, and your position in the room. Mentally go through each step—your walk to the podium, your opening line, each key point, your conclusion, and your walk back to your seat amid thunderous applause.

- Come to grips with your fear of making a mistake. The belief that a good presenter never makes a mistake is both untrue and unhealthy. The key is to regain control after the error occurs. If you pick up and go on, so will the audience.

- If you stutter or stumble, stop, take one or two deep breaths, and continue. If that does not work, say something about the mistake, such as, "Obviously, this point is important to me." By making a statement like that, you are changing your focus so that when you go back to make the comment you will be able to do so. In addition, you are engaging the audience in helping you, and they will. They want you to be able to say what you want; they will be supportive.

- Remember that most people are not looking for perfection, just information. They want to be reasonably engaged in your speech and will forgive some mistakes as long as you are obviously prepared.

Use nonverbal behavior appropriately to emphasize key points

Nonverbal behavior tells the story behind the story; it can verify your words or undermine them. It's important to be aware of and choose your nonverbal messages to enhance your words. Check the following areas:

- *Facial animation.* Your face displays your attitudes and emotions, so make sure your expressions match your content.

- *Eye contact.* Eye contact conveys your confidence and interest in the audience. Make eye contact with many members of the audience; avoid gazing exclusively at one person or at a spot above people's heads.

- *Vocal variety.* Develop a good speaking voice that varies in pace, pitch, volume, and tone. While many people are not naturally endowed with melodious voices, most have the potential for a wide range of pitch and tone.

- *Gestures.* Use gestures to emphasize and reinforce statements. Allow gestures to flow naturally from your message. For example, if you are excited and enthusiastic about your message, use more frequent and prominent gestures.

- *Stance.* Adopt a relaxed stance, and move in ways that complement and support your message. A rigid posture usually conveys nervousness, and random walking or other movements tend to be distracting.

- *Dress and appearance.* Dress appropriately for the audience and the situation. First impressions often begin with how someone is dressed. If people are preoccupied with your clothes, they won't listen as intently to your message.

Actively engage the audience during presentations

Effective presentations involve the audience as well as the presenter. The more you can engage your audience before and during a presentation, the more likely the audience will be to hear and accept what you have to say. To engage your audience, consider these suggestions:

- If you are presenting to an audience that does not know you, walk around and talk to people before you speak. Ask about their interest in your topic and tell them some background information about yourself. Incorporate what you learned into your presentation. For example, share an anecdote or quote (with the person's permission).

- Engage the listeners by asking rhetorical or actual questions. This will prompt them to think about your topic.

- If you are giving a speech in another country, greet the audience in their own language. Also make sure you follow local customs and protocol.

- Clearly indicate what impact your ideas will have on the audience. They will be more interested in your presentation if they know how it affects their daily lives.

- If your audience contains people with varying degrees of expertise in the topic, gear your material toward those with less knowledge. For example, say, "Some of you are already familiar with _____ ; please bear with me for a moment while I elaborate for those less familiar with this concept."

Gauge audience reactions and make appropriate adjustments

Successful presenters know the importance of watching their audience's reactions to ensure their presentation is on target. They look for indications that the audience either does not understand their message or finds it simplistic and boring. When this happens, they immediately take steps to get everyone back on track. Consider the following suggestions for improving your ability to gauge your audience and adjust your presentation:

- Watch your audience's reactions as you speak. Do they look restless or puzzled?

- If you sense your audience is lost, pause after you finish your point. Briefly recap what you have said so far, using simpler language or less detail.

- Invite questions from your audience. Their questions will help you pinpoint anything that is unclear. If you need to restate or clarify a point further, use a concrete example, then move on to the next question.

- Don't assume that people will eventually catch up. They may simply tune out and ignore the rest of your speech.

- Watch more experienced colleagues during situations when the audience loses interest. How do they acknowledge it? How do they get people back on track?

- Role-play situations with your colleagues in which audience members get lost, restless, or otherwise disengaged. Give each other specific feedback on what works well and what is ineffective.

- If you sense that some members of the audience are drifting during a presentation, try these techniques:
  - Vary your vocal projection, pitch, and pace.
  - Make eye contact with these individuals.
  - Ask a question.
  - Use a visual aid.
  - Tell an anecdote or a first-hand story.
  - Use some humor, even to make or emphasize a serious point.

Prepare effective visual aids

Many people believe that if they use enough overheads or presentation slides, they won't have to look at the audience, they'll never lose their place, and they won't have to prepare anything formal. They forget one important fact: slides are rarely as interesting as the person presenting them. People don't want to watch you read, they want to hear you talk. To prepare visual aids that will enhance your presentations, consider the following suggestions:

- Use a visual aid only when it is necessary, such as when you want to portray something that would be difficult to explain—in other words, when a picture is worth a thousand words.

- Avoid using too many visual aids during your presentation; too many are worse than too few. Think of them as the seasoning, not a main ingredient.

- Find out what options for visual aids are available at the location of the speech or presentation. Will you have flip charts, white boards, overhead projectors, or computer projectors?

- Learn about types of visual aids and the advantages and disadvantages of each. For example, PowerPoint® slides look very professional, but your computer might crash.

- Choose a visual aid based on your purpose, the audience, and the physical setting. If you are presenting in another country, make sure you have an adapter for your equipment.

- Avoid complex and highly detailed visual aids. When you need to explain a subject in detail, use a series of simple visuals rather than a single complex visual, or use a series of visuals that build on each other.

- Proofread your visual aids. Correct errors in spelling and grammar; make them visually consistent; and verify the accuracy and precision of charts, diagrams, and drawings.

- Look at your visual aids from the back of the room where you will be presenting. Can you see them clearly? Make any necessary adjustments before you present.

- Do not put large tables of data on an overhead transparency or presentation slide. Your audience will be unable to read it unless the group is very small. Instead, include only your key data on a graph or picture, or summarize your conclusions.

Use handouts, flip charts, and slides effectively	Most audiences expect to have written or e-mailed material to follow along with or support a presentation. If your presentation will include a lot of data or findings, the audience will want to see charts and graphs to help them grasp the information. To incorporate handouts, flip charts, and slides most effectively into your presentations, try the following suggestions:

- Find out the expectations for support material in your workplace. The use of flip charts, PowerPoint® presentations, etc., is specific to the organization and the culture.

- If you copy overheads and use them as handouts, include only the most important pages. People pay more attention to a smaller selection of handouts because they assume you have included only vital information. To enhance the usefulness of your handouts, add any interpretive comments during your presentation.

- Provide handouts in advance only if people need to see them during the presentation. If they do not, distribute them after your presentation. Otherwise the audience will read your handouts instead of listen to you.

- Use flip charts only if your audience consists of 50 or fewer people. If your audience is larger, an overhead projector will more clearly present your material.

- Write in dark colors on flip charts for better visibility. Try alternating between two or more colors when you are writing lists. This will help people track the content.

- Practice drawing simple images and graphs that you can use on flip charts and white boards. Take advantage of the fact that people remember images longer than they do words.

- When you create overheads or slides, follow these guidelines:
  - Use a large font, at least 28-point for text and 32-point for titles.
  - Use key words, not sentences.
  - Use the 1x5x5 rule: no more than five words per line, no more than five lines per transparency or slide.
  - Be consistent in the fonts, style, color, and position of words and images.

Use visual aids smoothly	Visual aids can greatly enhance your presentation—or they can seriously detract from it. It all depends on how prepared you are and how effectively you incorporate them into your presentation. To ensure that your use of visual aids is smooth and effective, consider the following suggestions:

- Before the presentation, make sure the visuals and equipment are in place, the equipment works properly, and you know how to operate it.

- Bring extra copies of your presentation, both printed and on disk.

- Be prepared to give your presentation even if there is an equipment problem.

- Practice giving your presentation with your visual aids. Introduce the aid, display it, describe it, show why it's relevant, and transition to your next point.

- Display the visual aid only when it relates to the point you are making.

- Speak to your audience, not to your visual aid.

- Avoid standing between the visual aid and your audience.

- Maintain maximum eye contact with the audience.

- Resist the tendency to lower your voice while you use a visual aid.

Answer questions clearly and concisely

Whether you are giving a formal presentation, addressing a news conference, or speaking informally, questions arise. Since the purpose of your presentation is to communicate something, these questions are helpful to you and to the audience. Questions help you determine how well your message is understood and agreed with, what you need to be clearer about, and what you need to be persuasive about. Questions also let you know what the audience is interested in. From the audience's perspective, questions provide an opportunity to clarify ideas and messages, point out areas of disagreement and challenge, and get the point across.

To handle questions effectively, try the following suggestions:

- Determine the intent of the question asked. Otherwise, you may give an answer that is literally correct but ignores the larger issue of concern to the questioner.

- Speak to the entire audience when you answer questions. This will focus your audience's attention on you rather than on the questioner. If you are in a large group, repeat the question before you answer it.

- Before the presentation, think of as many potential questions as possible, especially difficult or hostile ones. Prepare strong answers that relate to your key points. You may still be surprised by a question, but this will take away much of the "what if" anxiety.

- Decide whether you want questions while you speak or afterward; then tell the audience. If your purpose is to create a dialogue, definitely allow for questions while you speak or you will be negating the purpose of your presentation.

- If you want an interactive session, ask questions of the audience within the first five to ten minutes of your presentation. As you speak, if you are not getting questions and comments, continue to ask questions about their point of view.

- If you've requested that questions be held until after you present and someone asks a question during your presentation, offer to answer it at the conclusion of your remarks (if possible and appropriate). Don't get sidetracked into areas that are not relevant to your key points.

- When you answer lengthy or multifaceted questions, first restate the question more concisely. Then give a brief synopsis of your answer before going into details.

- Answer concisely. Research shows that answers that are 10 to 40 seconds long work the best. Shorter answers can seem too abrupt and longer answers too elaborate.

- Whenever possible, relate your answers to one or more key points in the presentation to reinforce your most important messages.

- Be honest. If you don't know, say so. Answering honestly will give you and your message more credibility. If someone else can better answer a question, invite that person to respond.

- If you receive an aggressive or hostile question, first empathize with the emotion. Then paraphrase the question in neutral terms. Answer by addressing the negative and/or emotional issues, then adding neutral or positive information. Always try to respond to the substantive issues raised by the question.

- Provide a recap after a question-and-answer session. The questions can distract from your key points, especially if the last one is about an unrelated or peripheral topic. Avoid ending with an answer to a question. Instead, take the last few moments to restate your key points.

RESOURCES

The resources for this chapter begin on page 674.

28
LISTEN
TO OTHERS

- *Evaluate your current skills*
- *Demonstrate genuine interest and empathy when listening to others*
- *Listen willingly to other people's concerns*
- *Listen carefully to input*
- *Exhibit appropriate nonverbal behavior to show receptivity*
- *Interpret nonverbal messages*
- *Improve communication through paraphrasing, reflecting, and summarizing*
- *Ask questions to clarify other people's points of view*
- *Listen patiently to others without interrupting*
- *Listen well in a group*
- *Practice strategic listening*

INTRODUCTION

Listening is not the absence of talking, but the presence of attention. Listening is not simply hearing, it is understanding. It requires participation, action, and effort. Listening is the glue that holds conversations together. It is the foundation of understanding. And it is absolutely essential for effective leadership.

Listening to employees, managers, peers, coworkers, and customers is a core, foundational skill for successful managers. The ability to listen is key to developing and maintaining relationships, making decisions, and solving problems. Without it, leaders can't create adaptable, quick-response cultures capable of facing today's business challenges.

Effective listening presents many challenges. People can be oblique, inarticulate, and imprecise. They can use words in unusual ways and define them differently. Body language sometimes contradicts the accompanying words. Listeners often hear what they want to hear. With these barriers, it's not surprising that listening seems difficult, if not impossible, in some situations.

Like all communication skills, listening improves quickly with practice and technique. This chapter presents suggestions on how you can develop the listening skills required of successful managers.

VALUABLE TIPS

- Follow this sequence when you are listening: 1) hear, 2) understand, 3) interpret, and 4) respond.

- Focus on understanding the speaker's meaning instead of preparing your response.

- Listen for the speaker's ideas, thoughts, and feelings. It is important that you understand what the person thinks and how he or she feels.

- When you are listening, the other person is most important. Concentrate on him or her, not on you.

- Identify your biggest obstacle to listening, such as lack of time. List three things you can do to overcome that obstacle.

- Pay attention to the feelings being communicated. They convey critical information, such as importance, sense of urgency, desperation, hope, etc.

- When you are on the phone, pay attention to the other person. Avoid reading your e-mail or doing other work. Close your eyes while you listen if you are easily distracted.

- Use a speaker phone only for conference calls. Many people dislike the public nature of a speaker phone and assume you are not giving them your full attention. It also inhibits them from bringing up sensitive issues or concerns.

- Reschedule a conversation if you cannot give the other person your undivided attention.

- Check your listen-talk ratio. If you want to be listening, observe the amount of time you are talking; it should be very little. Learn to catch yourself when you are talking but should be listening.

- Watch a person's nonverbal behavior to assess how he or she is feeling. Also be aware of your own nonverbal actions, for example, do you look receptive?

- Paraphrase what others say to check and communicate that you understand.

- If someone rambles, summarize more frequently. This will communicate that you understand and help the person clarify his or her thoughts.

- When you disagree with someone, summarize his or her position before you share your point of view.

- Ask open-ended questions to draw out people's thoughts and feelings—questions that begin with "what," "how," "describe," "explain," and so forth.

- Limit your use of closed questions—those that can be answered with a "yes" or a "no."

- Adapt your listening behaviors to reflect cultural differences.

- Avoid interrupting people; wait until they have finished.

- Don't bring extra work to meetings. Focus on the issues and the other people at the meeting.

Evaluate your current skills

Before you can effectively improve your listening skills, you need to evaluate them. For example, you may find that you are highly skilled in listening, but whether you listen depends on who is talking and what they are talking about. To assess your listening skills honestly, use the following suggestions:

- Solicit feedback on your listening skills from a number of people within and outside your organization. Find people who can give you information on how you listen to individuals and in groups. Ask people to help you identify when you do and do not listen well. Once you have this information, decide what you will do differently.

- Consider your typical behavior when you listen to individuals and in groups. Do you frequently:
  - Interrupt?
  - Show impatience?
  - Suggest solutions before the problem is fully explained?
  - Misinterpret what the person said, causing him or her to correct your interpretation?
  - Spend more time talking than listening?
  - Let your mind wander and miss what was said?
  - Think about your response instead of listening to the speaker?

  Establish the goal of eliminating one of these behaviors from your usual responses. Learn to catch yourself before you do the behavior and continue to listen instead.

- List some of the reasons you don't listen to people. For example, perhaps you:
  - Don't have enough time for the conversation.
  - Don't feel like making the effort.
  - Think you know what the person will say.
  - Don't respect the person.
  - Don't like the person.
  - Believe the person's opinions are irrelevant.
  - Think the person is boring.

  When you encounter one of these situations, determine what you will do differently so that you listen to the person.

- Identify why listening is important in your role. For example, you need to work through others to accomplish your goals, building relationships is necessary for working with people, and listening helps you create and sustain those relationships.

Demonstrate genuine interest and empathy when listening to others

Listening to others is not a passive activity; nor is it a series of mechanical skills you learned in a communication or listening class. Listening is active, characterized by your engagement in understanding what the other person is saying. To listen to others, you do not have to like, agree with, or have a relationship with them. All you need to do is try to understand. With this as your motivation, you will come across as genuine.

Whether you have real empathy, however, depends on whether you decide to understand the situation, thoughts, or feelings from the other person's point of view. When the relationship between you and the other person is important, learn the skill of understanding from his or her point of view. This requires that you suspend your own view temporarily.

Empathy is critical to the resolution of difficult disagreements, managing change, and coaching others. The following suggestions can help you develop the skill of demonstrating empathy:

- Decide that understanding the other person is important.

- Listen carefully and ask questions until what the person is saying makes sense, at least from his or her point of view.

- Remember that listening well does not mean you agree; it simply means you are trying to understand.

- Use active listening skills such as asking open-ended questions, paraphrasing, and reflecting. Besides checking that you understand and communicating that you do, these actions give you something specific to do while the person is talking, instead of formulating your own ideas and response.

- Identify people to whom, and situations in which, you find it difficult to listen. Determine why and what you can do to get yourself to listen more effectively.

- Allow yourself to understand the other person's feelings. It will help you work with them more effectively.

- Identify people who are considered skilled listeners, such as interviewers on television, and watch them in action. How do they convey interest and empathy? What nonverbal actions do they display? What questions do they ask? How do people respond to them?

- Watch and listen to your colleagues. Who displays interest and empathy? How does that affect their reputation and skill as a leader?

- Focus on the moment. You may have several things you would prefer to do other than listen, but your priority is to be present and pay attention to the person speaking.

Listen willingly to other people's concerns

Do you often find out about work concerns through a third party? Do you wish people would tell you directly about their concerns? If people don't communicate directly with you, perhaps it is because they don't perceive you as being willing to listen. To develop your ability to listen to other people's concerns, try the following suggestions:

- Realize that part of your role is listening to concerns and problems. You need to know what people are thinking and feeling in your area and across the organization.

- Consider how much achieving your area's goals depends on knowing people's concerns. Whether you are trying to change a process, a system, or culture, you need to hear concerns so you can address them directly and effectively.

- Offer to serve as a sounding board. People simply need to express their concerns or frustrations.

- Make yourself available formally and informally to listen.

- Ask people what they think. Then listen.

- Listen to people even when you don't feel like it. Your effort will improve or sustain your relationships.

- If you are unwillingly to listen to people, identify the reasons. For example, you may expect the worst, be uncertain of your ability to solve the problem, or be afraid that people will get emotional. Once you know why, work to change the reason, or listen despite your fears or concerns.

- When people need to express their concerns and you're doing work that can't be interrupted, set an appointment with them for later in the day. It is important that you find a time when you can listen wholeheartedly.

Listen carefully to input

Effective leaders listen to others and value their ideas. They rely on others not as a leadership gimmick, but because they need those people and their ideas. Successful leaders listen to input that is volunteered and seek input when it is not. They know that they will not be effective and the work will not be done well unless others contribute and do their part. The following suggestions can enhance your ability to listen to input from others:

- Listen to the ideas, thoughts, and feelings of others. If they do not volunteer them, ask to hear them.

- Learn the context for the speaker's message. What background information will help you understand his or her viewpoint?

- Accept silence as part of a conversation. Even though it may make you uncomfortable, don't rush in to fill every moment with words. Use the time to think about what the person said.

- When someone is talking, identify the content. What is the main idea? What are the facts? What is opinion?

- Ask clarifying questions to confirm the main thoughts or ideas. This is especially useful when you are listening to people who include a lot of detail in their messages or who tend to ramble.

- Recognize that the higher up on the organizational ladder you are, the more important it is for you to ask others for their opinions and to just listen when they talk. Do not dialogue until the person has fully expressed his or her own opinion. Some people are reluctant to talk with those higher in the organization. With those people, it is important that you actively seek their ideas and contributions.

- If you are in a meeting with people who are less likely to be open if you share your ideas first, wait until the others have spoken and you have communicated your understanding of them.

- Compare the amount of time you spend talking and listening during a typical conversation. Who does most of the talking? Make sure you are listening more than 50 percent of the time.

- Be aware of any tendencies you have to tune out or daydream while the person is talking.

- Recognize that some people may equate listening with agreeing. They may not feel heard if you don't do what they say. State up front what you intend to do as a result of the conversation, even if it is to reject the person's idea.

- Keep in mind that miscommunication occurs because of miscues from both the speaker and the listener. Work to remain nonjudgmental when you face communication problems.

Exhibit appropriate nonverbal behavior to show receptivity

Your nonverbal actions establish the atmosphere for the conversation. Just as you look for nonverbal signals when you are listening, speakers look for nonverbal signals from you. They can tell if you are interested, engaged, in the right mood, patient, bored, annoyed, dismissive, etc. To show appropriate nonverbal behavior, use the following suggestions:

- Don't sit behind your desk. Move your chair so there are no barriers between you and the speaker.

- Check your posture. Lean slightly toward the speaker and face him or her.

- Nod to indicate that you understand or agree.

- Maintain eye contact, but don't make the other person uncomfortable.

- Smile when the speaker uses humor.

- Cut down on distractions. Don't constantly look out in the hallway, greet people, or answer the phone.

Interpret nonverbal messages

Research shows that we get more than 65 percent of our information from nonverbal communication. We take cues from people's behavior about whether they agree, are comfortable, like us, etc. Nonverbal behavior is important to understanding others as well as communicating with them. At the same time, nonverbal behavior can be difficult to interpret. Our interpretation may or may not be accurate. To develop your skill in interpreting nonverbal messages, consider the following suggestions:

- Notice nonverbal behavior and comment on it when it will contribute to your mutual understanding. For example, if someone looks tense but is talking calmly, coolly, and objectively about a situation, it might help to say, "It looks like you're tense or concerned about this situation." That comment will encourage the person to tell you what he or she is concerned about.

- When commenting on nonverbal behavior, do it quietly, without judgment, and in a tone of voice that indicates you are checking out your understanding. This approach will allow the person to tell you that you are wrong or interpreted the behavior incorrectly.

- Identify the underlying emotion in the message. Notice the speaker's vocal pitch, intensity, and pace, and how it may differ from the person's usual way of speaking. The words may be neutral, but how they are stated will give you additional clues. This will help you to understand how important something is to the person.

- Look for discrepancies between the speaker's words and his or her nonverbal messages, and check your interpretation. Be willing to accept that you are wrong in your interpretation.

- Practice observing nonverbal messages by watching a video with the sound off. Focus on people's nonverbal actions. How much can you understand through posture, gestures, and facial expressions?

- Be aware that nonverbal behaviors vary among cultures. Learn about the differences before you speak with a person from a different country or culture.

Improve communication through paraphrasing, reflecting, and summarizing

Paraphrasing, reflecting, and summarizing are three active-listening skills that can significantly improve your communication. These skills not only let the speaker know that you are listening, they also help ensure that you hear what is being said.

Paraphrasing

A paraphrase is a brief restatement of what another person has said. It focuses on content—i.e., information, ideas, facts, and opinions. Paraphrasing shows that you are listening and that you understand what the speaker is saying. Here is an example:

> *Manager:* I can't figure out what to do with Sarah. She wants to be more involved with planning, but she doesn't understand the business context. Her ideas are interesting, but they require changes that we don't have the time or money to explore.
>
> *Peer:* You think her ideas are intriguing but they would be difficult to implement.

To develop your skill in paraphrasing, try the following suggestions:

- Make sure your paraphrase is shorter than the original statement. When people first use this skill, they often overdo the paraphrase.

- Practice paraphrasing with a colleague who can give you informed feedback.

Reflecting

Reflective statements are short, declarative statements that repeat the speaker's emotions or feelings. They help you create rapport, give the speaker a chance to vent his or her emotions, and allow the speaker to feel understood. Here is an example:

> *Manager:* Since I've become a unit manager, I'm not sure how I'm doing. I don't know if I'm really in control. Sometimes I think I made the wrong decision in accepting this promotion.
>
> *Peer:* You're worried about succeeding in your new position.

To create reflective statements:

- Listen for words that indicate feelings, such as being happy, sad, worried, upset, annoyed, etc.

- Watch for nonverbal clues to the speaker's mood.

Summarizing

A summary statement briefly restates both content and feelings. It helps the speaker identify the key elements of his or her situation, shows that you are making an effort to understand the speaker's point of view, and promotes further discussion of the issue. Here is an example:

> "As I understand it, Charlie, you think the problem with the first-line supervisors is their perception that they do not have enough responsibility and authority."

To practice creating summary statements:

- Create summary statements during meetings and note them on your copy of the agenda. (This has the added benefit of helping you remember what was said during the meeting.)

- Write summary statements of news stories from radio or television.

Ask questions to clarify other people's points of view

Asking good questions takes skill. Effective questioning can help you understand customer needs, the point of view of people engaged in a conflict, or the development needs of employees. Effective questioning can help in employee retention and customer loyalty. To build your skill in asking questions, consider the following suggestions:

- Ask more open-ended questions. These are questions that begin with statements such as "tell me about," "describe," and "what happened next." Closed questions can be answered with a "yes" or "no." Open-ended questions give the speaker a chance to expand on his or her answers; closed questions cut the speaker off.

- When you ask open-ended questions, listen carefully to the answers. Don't move on to the next question without showing that you heard and processed the information from the first question. Otherwise the speaker will believe you are more interested in asking your questions than in hearing and understanding the answers.

- Encourage the speaker to ask you open-ended questions. This will help you create a dialogue.

- Listen for examples of open-ended questions during meetings. When someone asks one, what is the result?

- Guard against asking too many questions at one time. If you simply ask a series of questions, the speaker may feel like you're fishing or that you don't really have a purpose. Use questions wisely, and they will lead you to a wealth of information.

Listen patiently to others without interrupting

Interrupting is a common barrier to communication. It shifts the focus to the interrupter and often stifles the flow of ideas from the other person. Therefore, it is best to limit the interrupting you do, especially of those less powerful than you in the organization and who may be intimidated by the interruption. The following suggestions can help you develop your skill in this area:

- Over the next month, ask people to point out every time you interrupt them. Analyze each incident, asking yourself the following questions:
  - Whom did I interrupt?
  - What was the situation?
  - What was the topic?

- Look for patterns. Do you tend to interrupt only in certain situations, such as when you talk to a specific individual or about a certain issue? Raising your awareness level will help you act more appropriately next time.

- Tell people you are aware of your frequent interruptions and want to improve. Ask them to give you feedback as you work on this area.

- Set small goals for improving this skill. Instead of saying, "I will never interrupt again," say, "I will not interrupt during this meeting."

- Since the barrier to communication that interruption causes is somewhat culturally determined, pay attention to what happens when you interrupt. Does it add to the conversation by stimulating the other person to continue to talk, or does it shift the attention to you? If it seems to contribute, it may not be as important that you stop. Ask others if they see your interruption as disruptive.

Listen well in a group

Effective group and team participation requires that all members listen to one another. Listening sends a message of respect, interest, and concern. When you're in a group and do other work, you are sending the message that you are not interested in the topic or issue and that you do not want to hear what the person has to say. Further, you send a message that you will pay attention only to topics that you personally find relevant and interesting.

Although it is possible to multitask, it's very difficult to listen effectively and do something else at the same time. The downfall of multitasking comes when people ask you about the information that was discussed at the meeting.

To be more effective at listening in groups, try the following ideas:

- Look at the speaker.

- Ask relevant questions.

- Sit where people can see you. Don't automatically head for the back or side of the room where you can ignore the main activity.

- Challenge yourself to learn something from the speaker, even if the discussion does not pertain to you or your area of responsibility. For example, watch how the speaker tries to influence others, the way a group member builds support for his or her position, or the way in which he or she uses visual aids.

- When you are leading a meeting, note your reactions to people who have side conversations or do paperwork while you are talking. This will sensitize you to the impact of your behaviors.

Practice strategic listening

Strategic listening can help you proactively seek the information you need to accomplish your goals. There are five components of strategic listening:

1. *Open attitude:* Find your own reason to understand another person's point of view. Accept others' views as valid for them and show them that you understand. Be willing to set your agenda aside temporarily in order to understand their views.

2. *Open-ended questions:* Ask questions that explore other people's views rather than aim to gather specific information or lead them to a predetermined conclusion.

3. *Identification of emotions:* Name the other person's emotions. Directly acknowledge his or her emotions to demonstrate your understanding of them and make it easier to deal with them.

4. *Nonverbal actions:* Demonstrate an open attitude through your nonverbal actions (eye contact, facial expression, posture, vocal tone, inflection, etc.), and accurately read the other person's nonverbal behaviors.

5. *Silence:* Allow people sufficient time to let their ideas percolate and take shape in words. Waiting for them to speak will foster trust, communicate your interest in what they have to say, and allow them to discover deeper insights.

Resources

The resources for this chapter begin on page 676.

29
WRITE EFFECTIVELY

PART 1: BUILD BASIC WRITING SKILLS
- *Follow the basic rules of grammar*
- *Avoid common mistakes in writing*
- *Edit your written work*
- *Review and edit the written work of others constructively*

PART 2: ADVANCE YOUR WRITING SKILLS
- *Communicate clearly in writing*
- *Write in a professional manner*
- *Prepare written materials in a timely and efficient way*
- *Adapt written communication to the audience*
- *Prepare persuasive written materials*
- *Use style and voice effectively*

PART 3: WRITE FOR SPECIFIC COMMUNICATION VEHICLES
- *Choose the correct format for your message*
- *Make effective use of e-mail*
- *Prepare written reports*
- *Enhance your written work with graphics*
- *Adapt your writing for Web pages*

INTRODUCTION

The crush of tasks and responsibilities in most people's work lives makes it hard to find time to craft well-written documents and polish all written communication. At the same time, the expansion of the Internet has generated more ways than ever for people to communicate in writing. Web sites and e-mail are giving people unprecedented opportunities to express themselves. Written information is an essential component of nearly every business process.

Successful managers have mastered basic writing skills and make effective use of all the communication vehicles available to them. They have taken the time to learn correct rules of grammar and how to write in the clearest way possible for the specific audience. Effective managers know they must lead through the written word, as well as the spoken word.

Fortunately, effective writing is a skill that everyone can develop, even those who don't believe they are gifted writers. Learning to write is like learning to play a sport: There are fundamental rules of the game, coaching tips that can turn you into a better player, and tools that can help your performance. And like any sport, it takes practice.

This chapter presents tips and suggestions for how you can create written documents in the most effective way possible, no matter what your current skill level is.

VALUABLE TIPS

- Edit and proofread your correspondence.

- Don't mix metaphors.

- Keep a dictionary and thesaurus on hand to check spelling and word usage.

- Bookmark an online dictionary and thesaurus.

- Make a list of words you commonly misspell or misuse and refer to it every time you write.

- Ask your organization's communication group for a style guide. If there is an electronic version, create a shortcut to it on your computer desktop.

- Circle all technical jargon in a document meant for a nontechnical audience. Then eliminate it or include a glossary.

- Use spell- and grammar-checking software.

- Whenever appropriate, replace passive verbs with active verbs.

- Use a variety of sentence structures—simple, complex, and compound—to add interest to your writing.

- Restrict your use of adjectives and adverbs; too many of these can weaken your writing. Instead, let nouns and verbs carry the weight of your message.

- Set deadlines for writing a draft, editing, and finishing your documents.

- Don't use lack of time as an excuse to procrastinate. You can get a great deal done in several 30-minute blocks.

- Consider your audience. What do they know already? What do you want them to do?

- Outline your documents before you begin to write.

- Make sure the content of a paragraph supports the topic sentence.

- When you write reports, summarize your key points and conclusions on the first page.

- Seek immediate and specific feedback on your reports.

- Take a second look at your e-mails before you send them.

- Use charts, tables, and graphs to present numerical information.

- Use short paragraphs and bulleted and numbered lists to break up text and make it easier to read.

PART 1:
BUILD BASIC WRITING SKILLS

Follow the basic rules of grammar

In some places, grammar has become a much-maligned concept. Some people see the rules of grammar as too old-fashioned in this era of instantaneous electronic connection to nearly all points on the globe. Successful leaders, however, understand that the power of their written words can often fall or rise on their use of basic rules of grammar. They don't view grammar as a straitjacket, but as a tool to help them create powerful, effective communication. If you need brushing up on these basic rules, review the following guidelines:

- Make sure the subject of your sentence (the person or thing doing the action) agrees with the verb (the action). Singular subjects need singular verbs; plural subjects need plural verbs. In complex sentences, watch to see that the verb agrees with the main subject, not just with the noun that is closest to the verb.

- Put adjectives and adverbs by the words they modify. Otherwise they may give your sentence an unintended meaning. For example, "a hot cup of coffee" has a different meaning than "a cup of hot coffee."

- When you use pronouns, make it clear who or what they are referring to.

- Use correct sentence structures to ensure your writing is understood. Watch out for run-on sentences and comma splices.
    - Run-on sentences are those that should end before they do. They combine two or more sentences into one, and they can often be difficult to understand. Consider, for example, this run-on sentence: "My findings show that merger is the only solution we need to take action on the plan now." Using proper grammar makes it much clearer: "My findings show that merger is the only solution. We need to take action on the plan now."
    - Comma splices are similar, but use a comma to separate the two independent clauses. Using the example above, the comma-splice version would be, "My findings show that merger is the only solution, we need to take action on the plan now." While this isn't as confusing as a run-on sentence, it doesn't provide a structure that allows you to make your important points clearly and concisely.

To avoid these errors, end every complete sentence with a period, or separate two or more sentences with a conjunction (and, or, but, yet, etc.), semicolon, dash, or colon as appropriate.

- Avoid excessive use of sentence fragments—i.e., sentences lacking either a noun or a verb—the two essential components of a sentence. For example, "in my examination of this problem" is a sentence fragment; it has no verb. Skilled writers use sentence fragments to create a special effect or emphasis. When they are overused, however, they make the writing difficult to understand.

- Avoid the use of dangling modifiers. A dangling modifier is a phrase that modifies a word that isn't in the actual sentence, but rather is implied. For example, in the sentence, "Having reviewed the report, your conclusions appear incorrect," "having reviewed the report" is a dangling modifier because it refers to a person who isn't mentioned in the sentence. A better way of phrasing that sentence would be: "Having reviewed the report, I find your conclusions to be incorrect." The phrase actually modifies "I."

- Relax about splitting infinitives and ending sentences with prepositions. Both are now considered acceptable usage.

- When you create bulleted lists, use parallel structure. In other words, each item in the list needs to follow the same format. For example, begin every item with a verb or make every item a question.

- Buy a grammar/style book—such as *Woe is I: The Grammarphobe's Guide to Better English in Plain English* by Patricia T. O'Conner (Putnam Publishing Group, 1996)—and look up questions you have about grammar. Every time you look something up it will solidify your knowledge.

Avoid common mistakes in writing

Writers make typical mistakes no matter what their native language is. It helps to be aware of these common mistakes, so you can look out for them in your writing. Following are some tips for avoiding common mistakes English writers make:

- Don't use "myself" to replace "I" or "me." Myself is a reflexive pronoun, which means the doer and the receiver of the action are the same person. For example, "I burned myself on the stove."

  When "I" is the subject, or the one doing the action in the sentence:

  - *Incorrect:* Miranda or myself will contact the customer about the refund.

  - *Correct:* Miranda or I will contact the customer about the refund.

  When "Me" is the object, or the one receiving the action:

  - *Incorrect:* Send your completed forms to Alma or myself.

  - *Correct:* Send your completed forms to Alma or me.

- Watch out for words like someone, anyone, anybody—they are singular and take the singular form of verbs. These words also require the use of singular pronouns. For example, the correct usage is, "If anyone wishes to go, he or she..." rather than, "If anyone wishes to go, they..."

- Avoid making up words. Business people are notorious for making up new words by adding suffixes, such as "ful" or "ity" or "ization," or turning nouns into verbs. While part of the charm of English is its flexibility, stretching it too far will reflect poorly on you.

- Differentiate between it's (it is) and its (possessive); you're (you are) and your (possessive); who's (who is or who has) and whose (possessive); and they're (they are), their (possessive), and there.

- Use "i.e." and "e.g." appropriately. The expression "i.e." means "in other words" or "that is to say," while "e.g." means "for example."

Edit your written work

All written work needs to be edited and proofed. It is not reasonable to expect that your writing is always as clear and accurate as you need it to be. Often you will be able to ask others to edit and proof your work. This is particularly helpful for lengthy written work that you have spent considerable time on; in such cases you can become too close to the work to see its problems.

It is unlikely, however, that someone will be available to check all of your written work, including e-mail. If you get into the habit of editing your own work carefully, you will ensure that the piece is well-written, clear, and meets the need for which it is intended.

To improve your editing abilities and habits, consider the following suggestions:

- Ask an experienced editor to read your documents for a while. Compile a list of your most common mistakes and learn how to correct them.

- Analyze the tone of your writing. What tone do you want to convey? Are you using the proper words to do so? For example, if you are trying to be informal, avoid using phrases that you don't hear in conversations.

- Look for sentences that seem out of place. For example, does any of the language sound inappropriate or unnecessarily forceful, compared with the rest of the document?

- Determine whether your content passes the following test: Everything in the document needs to be there for a reason, and that reason must be clear to the reader.

- Focus on the action in each sentence and state it succinctly. For example, use "investigate" instead of "conduct an investigation," and "decide" instead of "make a decision."

- Circle the passive verbs in your document, and then turn them into active verbs by moving the subject in front of the verb and removing the form of "to be" (am, are, is, was, and were) that you had used. Too many passive verbs create flat, tepid writing. For example:
  - Managers are motivated by the idea of quality. (passive)
  - The idea of quality motivates managers. (active)

- Remove redundancies from expressions like *duration of* time, *red in* color, *advance* planning, *small in* size, and *past* history.

- If you repeat a phrase or sentence to make a point, make it clear that you are doing it deliberately, not mindlessly repeating yourself.

- If you have difficulty cutting text, try the following tips.
  - Cross out all unnecessary adjectives, adverbs, and descriptive clauses.
  - Change passive verbs to active verbs.
  - Address only one idea per sentence.

- Use your word processor's spell-check utility, but be aware of its shortcomings. It only looks for whether the existing word is spelled correctly. For example, if you accidentally typed the word *manger* instead of *manager*, the spell-checker would not pick up anything wrong.

- Refer to men and women in the same way. For example, don't refer to women by their first name if you are referring to men by their full name. Don't describe how women look unless you are also going to mention the men's appearance.

Review and edit the written work of others constructively

Managers frequently need to review the work of others. When you are reviewing work, you may review for content, writing, and style, or any combination of these. The following suggestions will help you review and edit text constructively:

- Remember that writing is difficult for many people and the editing process can be painful. Your role as editor is to help the writer make the document as clear as possible, not to rewrite it in your own words.

- Find out how thoroughly the person wants you to edit his or her work. Are they looking for feedback on the tone and content, or do they want you to look for inconsistencies and typos, or both? Come to an agreement before you begin about the kind of review you will do.

- Read the entire document before you start to edit.

- Check your content questions with the writer before you modify the document. You may be making unnecessary or incorrect changes.

- Analyze whether the tone or style conflicts with the message. If it does, help the writer identify a tone that would be more appropriate for the document.

- Tell the person why you think significant changes will make the document stronger. However, you don't need to explain every typo correction.

- Share your edits in a positive way. Consider how you would feel receiving this feedback.

PART 2:
ADVANCE YOUR WRITING SKILLS

Communicate clearly in writing

Managers write to communicate information to others. The most effective way to do that is to write as clearly as possible. The most elegant, sophisticated language will fail to achieve its purpose if it is not presented clearly. To ensure that your writing communicates clearly to its audience, try the following suggestions:

- Before you begin to write, clarify the purpose of the communication. Determine if it is to inform, persuade, begin a dialogue, etc. Then, decide the messages that are critical to communicate.

- Ask several experienced writers and editors for feedback on how clearly you write. Are you wordy? Do you include unnecessary information? Does your writing lack structure?

BUT THIS IS THE SUMMARY!

- Remember that your job is to convey a message, not display your vocabulary.

- Distill your key message down to one declarative sentence. If you can't do this, your message is not clear enough. For example, your message may be, "I want people to understand the new procedure for entering customer orders into the software."

- Don't include every detail you know about the topic. Choose the details that most effectively support your point.

- Recognize that it is your responsibility to sort the material for the reader, not the reader's responsibility to sift through irrelevant details.

- When you write your first draft, keep it simple. Write your topic sentence and supporting sentences. Don't use any adjectives, adverbs, or clauses. Just write short, simple sentences.

- Make sure every sentence in a paragraph relates to the main topic.

- Reduce the number of words you use. For example, "We need to sit in the same room and talk about the issues that we face in trying to expedite the process necessary to get the work done" could simply be, "We need to meet and discuss the process we use."

Write in a professional manner

Many people will first get to know you and your point of view through your writing. They will form their impressions of you from the reports, policy statements, papers, e-mails, and other documents that you write. Some may never be in personal contact with you. It is essential, therefore, that you develop the ability to write in a professional manner. Use the following suggestions to fine-tune this skill:

- Review the e-mails you send for one week. Think about what people are learning about you from them. Are you communicating the information you want known about you? If your e-mails were the only thing people saw from you, what would they conclude about you?

- Think of every communication as an opportunity to represent you and your organization. Would you be comfortable sharing your document with people outside the organization? If you were reading the document, what opinion would you have of the writer?

- Check your level of formality. If you are too informal, readers may think you are not serious about the information or the situation. If you are overly formal, it may look like you are trying to distance yourself from the material and your readers.

- Be concise and address the issue. Most likely your audience has limited time to read the document and won't appreciate rambling.

- Gauge the appropriateness of using humor. Your audience may misunderstand the joke—is it worth the risk?

- If you are writing for an international audience, watch your use of jargon, slang, and idioms. They may not be commonly understood around the globe.

- If you are writing an article for publication, get a copy of the submission guidelines. Make sure you follow the guidelines exactly.

Prepare written materials in a timely and efficient way

Many people dread writing, especially when they need to write something that is considered important. Some start and stop over and over again. Others find ways to put off writing to the last possible moment, which means they rarely leave enough time to write and edit the work thoroughly. Then, their worst fear is realized; the work is not written or received well. To avoid procrastination and to write efficiently, try these suggestions:

- Set aside 30-minute blocks for writing. This is a manageable amount of time to write if you dread the process, and it's a small enough chunk to carve out of a busy schedule.

- Set small goals that you can achieve in 30 minutes. For example, write an outline or one paragraph.

- Shut your office door so you won't be interrupted. Writing takes concentration; give yourself the space and time to do it well.

- Begin writing the section you are most familiar with or the one you like the most. The key is to get started.

- Focus on capturing your ideas. Don't worry about elegance; just put your ideas on paper. You can edit them later.

- If you have trouble getting started, write for five minutes without stopping. If you can't think of enough to write about the topic, write about something else. Just keep writing. Don't get stuck trying to think of the perfect word. This kind of writing is like priming the pump; eventually the words will flow out.

- Don't wait for inspiration to strike. Usually the act of writing itself will trigger your thoughts to flow.

Adapt written communication to the audience

The purpose of writing is to communicate something to someone. Effective writers determine what they want to communicate and to whom before they put a single word on paper. They find out about their audience and write for that audience. The following suggestions can help you adapt your writing to its audience:

- Match your writing to the situation. For example, use a different style and tone for a technical report than for an informal memo that thanks employees for their hard work.

- Learn as much as you can about your target audience.
  - Are they familiar with the topic?
  - What are their expectations?
  - Do they all work in the same location?
  - Do they all speak the same language?

- Focus on what your readers need to know. For example, if you are writing a memo about policy changes, you may be tempted to include extensive background material on why the decision was made. The readers, however, may simply want to know the final decision and how they should proceed.

- Anticipate your readers' questions on the topic and address them in your document.

- Ask a member of the audience to give you feedback on your document before you send it to the entire group.
  - Did you address all the questions and issues?
  - Is your message clear?
  - What would make it more effective?

Prepare persuasive written materials

Leaders often need to write to persuade others to their point of view. In those cases, the writing becomes much more than simply communicating a message; it needs to be convincing and engaging, and to capture the minds and hearts of its readers. Try the following suggestions to help you write more persuasively:

- Determine what you want your audience to think or do after reading your document. If it is not absolutely clear to you, it will not be clear to your readers.

- Clearly state in the document what you want people to think or do. Don't leave this to your readers' imagination; they might reach the wrong conclusion.

- Show how your proposal will bring value or benefit to the reader, such as save money, increase productivity, solve a problem, avert trouble, or improve job satisfaction. Paint a vivid picture of how their lives will change if they think or do what you recommend.

- Link your proposal to acknowledged problems and opportunities. Then you can focus on selling the solution.

- Only include relevant facts and supporting material. If you lead your readers down a pointless path, it will weaken your argument. However, don't exclude conflicting or contradictory facts. Address these facts directly and show how they fit into the broader picture that leads to your conclusion.

Use style and voice effectively

Think of authors you admire, whose books and articles you always read. Why do you like to read them? What makes their writing compelling? It has to do with style. Style turns reading into an experience. Style draws readers in, assures them they are in capable hands, and informs or entertains them. Whether or not you recognize it, you already have a style. People have an expectation of your writing—they already know whether it will be an enjoyable experience or an ordeal.

To enhance your style and make your writing more inviting to others, consider these suggestions:

- Ask for feedback about your writing style, and then decide if you are satisfied with it.

- Be aware of style when you read articles, books, Web sites, letters, e-mails, etc. What general impression do you have of the piece? For example, is it formal, informal, academic, brisk, plodding, or lively? What makes it that way? Look at word choice, sentence length, the amount of detail and explanations, whether it is in first, second, or third person—they all affect the style.

- Raise your standards by reading excellent writing—well-written novels, essays, articles, biographies, reports, etc.

- Remember that writing is not speaking. Writing gives you time and space to choose the right word, use the right tone, and strike the right note. Viewed this way, writing is a luxury, not a chore. You can literally think before you speak.

- Consider working with a writing coach to develop or alter your style. Individual feedback will be especially valuable if you dread the experience of reading your work aloud to a class.

PART 3:
WRITE FOR SPECIFIC COMMUNICATION VEHICLES

Choose the correct format for your message

Written communication is often viewed as a one-way exchange. You put out a message and hope people will take the time to read it. Choosing the right delivery method can help ensure that the right people will read it at the right time. Use the following suggestions to help you select the best method for your message:

- Ask people throughout the organization which communication vehicles they prefer. This will give you a better idea of what people ignore and what they actually read.

- Assess your organization's technology habits. Do people use their e-mail? Are people more likely to read something that arrives in their traditional mailbox? Will they read e-mails, but not attachments?

- Determine how soon people need the information. Can you send a short memo with the main message and follow up later with a more detailed explanation?

- Determine your core message. Does it require a great deal of background information or can it be conveyed in one paragraph?

- Learn how to use each delivery method effectively. For example, the type of language and length of sentences in a memo differ from those in a report, and e-mail has its own etiquette. Use the correct style for your method.

- Ask your internal communication group for a style manual and appropriate templates.

- Periodically ask a cross-section of your audience for feedback on your choice of vehicles. Do they read what you write? Would a different communication vehicle serve them better?

Make effective use of e-mail

More and more communication is done through e-mail or other on-line communication tools. E-mail has become an important vehicle for leaders who know how to use it well. It is also the source of frustration and overload when used poorly. To make the most effective use of e-mail, consider the following suggestions:

- Think about what you put into e-mails, especially when it involves sensitive company information. E-mails can be stored permanently. You may think you're deleting them, but a skilled person can retrieve them weeks, months, and even years later. Before you write, consider how it would sound being read aloud in court.

- Write for a wide audience, even when you think it will only go to your intended recipient. E-mails can be forwarded on to other people without your knowledge.

- Make your subject line count. Some people won't open an e-mail unless the subject line clearly indicates that it is important for them to read.

- Put the most vital information at the beginning of the e-mail. You can't be sure that someone will read the entire message.

- If you address an e-mail to a wide audience, such as the entire company, begin with a line stating what the e-mail is about. Then people can delete it if it is not relevant for them.

- Check the spelling and grammar in your e-mails. Part of the usefulness of e-mail is its immediacy, but poor writing can negate that quality.

- Format your e-mails using bullets, numbered lists, bold, italics, or color. Just don't use them all in the same message.

- Break up the text into paragraphs to make it easier to read.

- Be aware that using ALL CAPS in e-mail indicates you are shouting.

- When you send e-mails to colleagues in other countries, avoid jargon. Your terminology may be unfamiliar and colloquialisms literally may not translate. Also gauge the level of familiarity you adopt; some cultures require a more formal tone than others.

- Find out how your IT department wants to handle attachments. For example, they may discourage sending attachments to large groups of people. Or they may prefer that you attach shortcuts or links instead of the entire document.

Prepare written reports

Some jobs require much more report writing than others do. In some organizations, long reports and white papers are common, while in others, reports may be simply a couple of pages of text or PowerPoint® slides. Whatever the requirements of your job, it's important to be able to write the appropriate reports well. The following suggestions can help you:

- If you are new to the organization or role, find out if there is an expected format for a report. When you have a new manager, learn his or her expectations for reporting.

- Follow the style guide for your profession or organization.

- Choose a topic sequence that most effectively organizes your information. Examples of sequences include: general to specific, most important to least important, chronological, compare and contrast, classifications, and cause and effect.

- Use headings and subheadings to indicate new sections. Examples of headings include "Background Information," "Conclusions," and "Recommendations."

- Include a table of contents for reports that exceed ten pages.

- Include an executive summary so you can be more confident that the main points of the paper are read.

- If your report is meant for a technical audience, use appropriate technical terms and concepts. If it is meant for a broad, more diverse group, limit the number of technical terms.

Enhance your written work with graphics

The written word is not always the most effective way to communicate a message. Graphics can often convey the information with far greater impact. Many leaders rely on their administrative support people to incorporate graphics into their documents. Many managers, however, have discovered the value of having these basic skills themselves. Knowing how to use graphics allows you to change or add to reports when no staff members are available to help. The following suggestions can help you make more effective use of graphics in reports:

- Ask your administrative assistant, a peer, a direct report, or an IT trainer to teach you the basics of creating and adding graphics in programs you use frequently, such as Microsoft Word®, PowerPoint®, etc.

- Insert the graphic into the correct place in your document. Lay out the document so your explanations or interpretations of the graphic are adjacent to it.

- Clearly label the data in graphics. Readers should know exactly what is represented and why.

- Make the font on the graphic large enough for people to read. Don't use a small font size to save room on the page.

- Check your graphic for typos.

- Solicit feedback on your graphic and ask for suggestions on how you might improve it.

- If you use cartoons, be sure to get permission from the illustrator. Also make sure the cartoon is appropriate for the tone and style of your document.

- When necessary, work with a graphic designer to create the most effective representation of your idea.

Adapt your writing for Web pages

People read differently on the Web than they do on the printed page. They scan, looking for key words. They jump around if or when they get bored. They pursue hyperlinks and enter documents at any point, not just at the beginning. Your writing for Web sites needs to be even more clear, relevant, and specific than usual. To make the most of writing for Web pages, try the following suggestions:

- Think about your browsing experiences. How willing are you to wade through thick, dense text on the computer screen?

- Take your text and cut it in half. Then edit it down some more.

- Avoid hype; it affects your credibility. Stick to the facts and be objective. People can quickly go to another site to see if you are telling the truth.

- Include key words that can be found by a search engine.

- Display information in bulleted lists.

- Include links to relevant pages on your corporate site or other sites.

- Write for an international audience. Avoid country-specific vernacular and sports cliches.

- Consider how long it will take to load your page. You don't want people to leave your site because they have a slower modem. Reconsider adding the graphic that requires the latest version of a browser.

RESOURCES

The resources for this chapter begin on page 678.

Self-Management Factor

I am not afraid of storms for I am learning how to sail my ship.
— Louisa May Alcott

Effective leaders are people whom others want to work with, be inspired by, and are willing to follow. They are principled, values-driven, and trustworthy. Their behavior is consistent and ethical; they follow through and deliver on commitments. They are able to balance the needs of individuals and those of the organization, so that people can trust them to lead, as well as trust them as human beings.

Effective leaders also need to excel at self-management and pursue continuous learning. Leaders who are able to balance self-acceptance with the desire to be the best are more equipped than others to be successful. Effective leaders seek feedback from others. They learn from their mistakes. They actively seek out new information and ways of doing things. They thrive on challenge.

Effective leaders know that change is continual. They are masters at dealing with stress and change. They are flexible and adaptable.

This section of the handbook covers the self-management skills that effective leaders need to thrive.

Chapter 30 – Inspire Trust: Demonstrates principled leadership and sound business ethics; shows consistency among principles, values, and behavior; gains the confidence and trust of others through their own authenticity and follow-through on commitments; works to establish an environment where uncompromising integrity is the norm.

Chapter 31 – Demonstrate Adaptability: Works effectively in situations involving ambiguity, shifting priorities, and rapid change; demonstrates resilience and composure in trying circumstances; deals constructively with mistakes and setbacks; copes effectively with stress and pressure.

Chapter 32 – Practice Self-Development: Engages in a continuous learning process by focusing on top-priority learning objectives; spends time each day on learning and development; reflects on both successful and unsuccessful experiences; learns from others' feedback and ideas and transfers learning into next steps.

30
INSPIRE
TRUST

PART 1: ESTABLISH TRUST
- *Gain the confidence and trust of others*
- *Express your own views openly*
- *Treat people fairly*
- *Build trust with remote employees*
- *Handle different cultural expectations of trustworthy behavior*

PART 2: INCREASE AND REGAIN TRUST
- *Evaluate others' perceptions of your integrity*
- *Demonstrate consistency between words and actions*
- *Live up to commitments*
- *Do not undermine others for your own gain*
- *Do not distort the facts with your own biases or agendas*
- *Accept responsibility for your own mistakes*
- *Recover from violating trust*

PART 3: DEVELOP AN ETHICAL ORGANIZATION
- *Model ethical behavior for the organization*
- *Actively consider ethical issues before making decisions*
- *Protect confidential information*
- *Confront actions that are or border on unethical*
- *Encourage discussion of ethical standards*
- *Align the organization's systems and processes with its ethical standards*

INTRODUCTION

With global expansion and changes in the marketplace and workforce, organizations have moved away from hierarchical structures and position-based power. One result of the new economic realities is that teamwork, joint accountabilities, remote decision making, and a reliance on networks are replacing compliance as the cornerstone of organizational behavior. Such changes require trust-based relationships among coworkers at all levels. Without trust, decisions are questioned or sabotaged, important information is covered up, loyalty crumbles, and turnover skyrockets.

At a time when trust has become more important, changes in the organizational climate have made building trust even harder. People are in locations remote from each other, reducing the opportunity for face-to-face interaction. Workers are dealing with other cultures that may define trust differently. Acquisitions are requiring employees from different companies—and often former competitors—to work together. The ever-increasing need for rapid change leaves even less time and energy for developing solid relationships. The emphasis on short-term profit causes some organizations to adopt a "what have you done for me lately" perspective on employee performance, damaging loyalty between workers and their organizations.

Successful managers continue to inspire trust despite the forces that undermine it. They demonstrate trust in the way they behave, follow through on commitments, conduct business, and treat people. Generally, people who inspire trust are those whose actions are consistent with their words; who have high ethical standards; who respect others; and who behave in a truthful, principle-based way. Leaders who are trusted create an atmosphere of integrity, marked by respectful behavior.

This chapter will help you build trust with others. It describes how you can create a more trusting environment in your workgroup, and it will help you understand why others may not trust you and what you can do about that.

VALUABLE TIPS

- Do not promise or commit (including to deadlines) unless you will honor the commitment. Consistently follow through on commitments.

- Avoid doing things you would be uncomfortable hearing about on national news programs.

- If you change your mind about an issue, explain why your opinion changed.

- Behave in a way that is consistent with what you say.

- Share the credit and acknowledge the contributions of others.

- Don't promise confidentiality if you aren't certain you can or should keep the information private.

- Model behavior consistent with high ethical standards.

- If you have lost trust and do not know what you did, ask.

- Recognize that regaining trust is a long-term process that requires genuine remorse and often penance.

- Give as complete an answer to a question as possible. Avoid the appearance of hiding information.

- If you don't know the answer, say so. Don't try to fake it.

- If you make a mistake, admit it.

- Learn what behaviors build or erode trust in cultures other than your own. Use this information while building relationships with coworkers and customers from other cultures.

- Stay in touch with people in remote locations by setting up regular phone conversations.

- Don't give tough messages or express negative emotions via e-mail or voice mail.

- Stand up for others, especially your staff, when they need your support.

- Acknowledge courageous employees who have demonstrated high ethical standards.

- Be proactive. If you sense mistrust or discomfort, ask about it quietly, nonjudgmentally, and with real concern.

- Make sure your message is consistent. Avoid saying different things to different audiences.

- If you are biased on an issue, explain your bias openly.

PART 1:
ESTABLISH TRUST

Gain the confidence and trust of others

Establishing trust takes time. The first step is to form relationships with people so that you can understand what motivates them, who they are, what they care about, what their ideas and concerns are, and what they need from you. To the extent that you actively demonstrate acceptance and understanding of people, you will establish the basis for trust.

To gain the trust and confidence of others, try the following suggestions:

- Set aside time for an initial face-to-face meeting with new employees, peers, and managers—even if they are in remote locations.

- Ask open-ended questions about people's work—what they enjoy the most, what gives them the most satisfaction, what their biggest challenges are. Ask what they want from you. Listen. Show genuine interest.

- Regularly follow up with telephone calls, meetings, or informal chats. Try to touch base with your employees at least once a week.

- Schedule times for follow-up if regular contact does not happen spontaneously.

- For remote employees, schedule time so that you share the burden of different time zones.

- Trust your staff to do what they say and to keep confidences. Trust builds trust. When you are open with others about information, ideas, and feelings, they are more likely to develop trust in you.

Express your own views openly

An important element in building trust is being open about your own views and motives. People more readily trust those who trust them with their opinions. To enhance your ability to express your own views, consider these suggestions:

- Share with people what you think and why.

- State your position on ethical issues when there is an opportunity and it is needed, but not obvious.

- When you state your own opinion, say "*I* think…," not "*We* think…."

- Decide whether it is better to express your opinion first or second. If you are gathering ideas, wait to express your ideas so people will feel free to share their own. Then let people know your current thinking, but express it in a way that makes it clear you are open to changing it, if appropriate.

- Give honest answers to questions and challenges. The perception that you waffle or are evasive can damage your integrity. If you're not able to answer a specific question, say so and explain why whenever you can. Try to address the underlying concerns raised by the questioner. For instance, you may not be able to indicate the level of the bonus this year, but you could say a bonus is planned that will be based on profits against goal.

Treat people fairly

Treating people fairly involves a wide range of behaviors. Perceptions of unfair treatment or favoritism can arise in many situations. For example, the amount of work and types of opportunities given could be perceived as favoritism; attempts to assist people could be perceived as discrimination; and decisions for which people haven't been informed of the rationale could be interpreted as unfair.

To ensure that your behaviors support your intention to treat people fairly, use the following guidelines:

- Pay attention to any feedback you receive that you show favoritism or treat some people differently from others. When receiving feedback, keep the following in mind:
  - Listen carefully. Understand the example. Take care to not argue with the person or defend yourself.
  - Summarize the person's concerns and how he or she feels.
  - Say you are sorry the person feels that way.
  - If the point of view makes sense to you, figure out what you can do differently, and then do it.
  - You may want to ask the person what he or she thinks you should do.
  - If you do not understand or know what to do, or if you feel angry or hurt, let the person know you heard what he or she said, say you want to think about the situation, and then find someone, such as your manager, coach, or HR representative, to help you.

- Give recognition to all involved in a project—not just the visible star.

- Examine how you assign work:
  - Look at the assignments given to each team member and analyze that person's interests and abilities, the visibility and complexity of the assignments, and the person's interest in the assignments.
  - Determine whether the assignments are equitable, given the skills of each individual.

- Check that you have not unintentionally given specific kinds of assignments to particular people or groups of people. For example, you may find that you give assignments based on your perception of how willing people are to travel, to work long hours, or to work on special action teams, or on their gender or national origin.
- Ask your employees for their opinions of the current distribution of responsibilities. If there are concerns, address them.
- If people believe they should have more challenging assignments, tell them what they must do to get them.

- Avoid taking sides in disagreements between or among employees.

- Explain the reasons for your decisions. When people understand the rationale behind a decision and feel as if they have been a part of the process, they are more likely to perceive you as being fair.

Build trust with remote employees

The biggest hurdles to building trust with people in distant locations are logistical: different time zones, lack of opportunity to meet face-to-face, and reliance on e-mail and voice mail as the main communication vehicles. To overcome these obstacles and build trust with your remote employees, consider the following suggestions:

- Find ways to have regular contact.

- Meet in person periodically.

- Include all employees in communications and decisions, and schedule staff meetings so remote workers can join in, even if it's by telephone. Fax or e-mail documents to them before the meetings.

- Do not expect employees to always travel to you.

- Use e-mail to stay in touch, especially with those in different time zones. Use e-mail for the kind of friendly chat you might have with someone walking down the hall (e.g., "How are you?" "What did you do this weekend?" "What did you think of our CEO's message?").

- When setting deadlines, take into account time zones and varying mail schedules.

- Schedule regular voice-to-voice conversations, no matter how difficult this is to do. Because e-mail can be easily misinterpreted and is inappropriate for many kinds of messages, you'll need the opportunity for dialogue.

Handle different cultural expectations of trustworthy behavior

When you have employees from cultures different from your own, you'll need to work actively to establish trust. Consider the following ways to help build trust with someone from a different culture:

- Learn about the customs and values of the person.

- Ask the person directly what he or she considers to be the behaviors of a good manager.

- Talk with the person about the fact that cultural differences exist. Express your interest in learning to work together.

- Find out about the person's culture from others in the organization or community.

PART 2: INCREASE AND REGAIN TRUST

Evaluate others' perceptions of your integrity

Trust is lost through broken promises, inconsistency, failure to support others, unethical behavior, insensitivity, distortion of facts, self-promoting behavior, and dishonesty. Regaining trust takes time and much effort. Your effectiveness as a manager and leader is severely compromised if people distrust you.

A first step is to evaluate how others think about your integrity. Use the following checklist.

Do you consistently:

1. Keep promises and agreements?	Yes	No
2. Give honest and complete answers to questions and challenges?	Yes	No
3. Protect confidential or sensitive information?	Yes	No
4. Admit when you've made a mistake?	Yes	No
5. Consider the trust and confidence of your coworkers to be important?	Yes	No
6. Make an effort to foster open, honest, and sincere communication?	Yes	No
7. Encourage others to question practices they cannot support?	Yes	No
8. Make use of your company's written code of ethics to guide you when making ethical decisions?	Yes	No
9. Demonstrate consistency between your words and actions?	Yes	No
10. Allow time for others to ask questions?	Yes	No

If you couldn't answer yes to most of these questions, you will find this section useful in helping you to establish and maintain an open and trusting environment. The suggestions offered here can assist you in further leveraging this strength.

If you have received feedback that you are not trusted, determine why. Ask people you trust to tell you what you do or do not do that results in a lack of trust. Be sure to remain nondefensive—just listen, don't explain yourself. It is very hard for most people to hear that they are not trusted. Yet the only way to improve the situation is to listen and hear what others think and feel without arguing or defending yourself.

Demonstrate consistency between words and actions

You are judged by your actions, not your statements of intent. Consistency between what you say and what you do builds trust. This predictability is a cornerstone for trust. People need to know that they can count on you. To ensure your words and actions are consistent, consider the following suggestions:

- Keep both implicit and explicit promises. Broken promises do considerable damage to relationships.

- Ensure that your nonverbal actions convey your thoughts and feelings accurately. Actions speak louder than words. For example, if you say you want to listen to employees' concerns and then avoid eye contact when an employee is talking to you, your verbal message to the employee is inconsistent with the nonverbal message you are sending.

- Be aware of any internal conflicts you have and recognize that you may telegraph mixed messages to others. This is confusing and, if frequent, can erode feelings of trust.

- Go beyond merely expressing verbal concern for others. Back up your concern with your behavior. Be available and approachable, and help out whenever possible.

- Freely admit your mistakes. Use them as examples for all to learn from. Encourage others to do the same.

- Communicate your values and then stand up for what you believe is right. Don't allow yourself to be swayed by what others would like you to say.

- Give full and honest answers to tough questions. Withholding pertinent information may be construed as lying, as trying to hide things, or as lacking courage or integrity.

- Be aware of your own motives. Sometimes people can be inconsistent when they are not being honest with themselves about what they really want or need.

- Deliver consistent messages to different audiences. While you need to consider your audience when formulating the tone and wording of your messages, be sure that the underlying idea or opinion remains the same. Stating a strong opinion to your peers and then watering it down when you're in front of your manager will only serve to raise questions about your integrity.

Live up to commitments

Trust is built on fulfilled promises. When promises are not made in earnest but simply to buy time or escape pressure, hard feelings and tarnished relationships result. Failure to keep a promise without advance warning, follow-up, or apology can harm your credibility and may lead to serious loss of trust.

Follow-through on commitments is an essential component of building trust and integrity. Attending meetings on time and completing assignments on schedule may seem like good organizational skills or time management, but they are also measures of your integrity, reflecting your ability to make and keep promises. To ensure that you live up to your commitments, consider the following suggestions:

- Use a good time-organization system or have your assistant keep one for you.

- Do not make commitments you cannot keep. Make realistic time and resource estimates based on your previous experience. If you have not had experience in an area, ask someone who has such experience to give you estimates, and then add time for the initial learning curve.

- Attend meetings and appointments you've agreed to.

- Avoid making statements that others may misinterpret as promises. For example, someone hearing you say, "I'll try to read your report by Monday," might believe that you will be ready to discuss the report on Monday. Using clear and unambiguous statements will eliminate any confusion—e.g., "I will read your report by Wednesday for sure; if I get to it earlier I will call you."

- If you are not going to make a deadline, let those affected know ahead of time and tell them when you will be ready. Make certain this is rare behavior for you.

- Keep a tally of your implied or direct promises. Check whether you have followed through on each of these promises in a timely way. Examine the extent to which you deliver on your commitments. If appropriate, develop an action plan to improve your behavior.

- Take steps to overcome problems that get in the way of your keeping commitments. Many people who are prone to procrastination or perfectionism have difficulty meeting commitments. If you have trouble with these problems, take action to rid yourself of these behaviors.

- Tell your coworkers you are working on these behaviors and ask for their help. This may allow you the fresh start you need to make the necessary changes and help you stay focused on the goal.

Do not undermine others for your own gain

Sometimes people deliberately undermine others to make themselves more successful. You may believe that the only way to stand out in your organization is to make sure you are seen as better than everyone else. Or, you may find that people see you as undermining others to get ahead. To avoid undermining others, use the following suggestions:

- Listen to yourself. Do you make sarcastic remarks about others? Sarcasm is not funny. Although people may laugh, sarcasm subtly undermines trust. People wonder when your rapier wit will be turned on them.

- Listen for critical and undermining comments you may make about others. In your effort to win a point or a decision, you may speak judgmentally of others, not merely disagree with their ideas.

- State your disagreement respectfully, without evaluative comments (e.g., "that's stupid"). Base your opposition on facts, and state all your reasons openly.

- If disagreeing with someone in public will cause them to lose face, state your difference privately to them beforehand, if possible. If not, pull them aside during or after the meeting to voice your concerns.

- Be honest with yourself about whether you believe it is important to win or to be seen as better than others, no matter what the consequences. If you believe this:
  - Concentrate on achieving success without hurting others. If you are good, take the challenge to be a star without putting others down.
  - Ask someone you trust for feedback on the impact of your way of operating. (You may find you have a hard time trusting others, since you cannot be trusted to not hurt others.)
  - Consider that your way of operating—win no matter what the cost— usually breeds increasing distrust and similar behavior from others.

- Speak honestly about how you or your organization might gain if a decision goes your way, even if that is not the primary reason you are advocating it. In this way you will avoid being seen as sneaky.

- Listen carefully and attentively to others' ideas, especially if you initially disagree.

- Don't talk disparagingly to people about someone else's idea. Talk to the person directly and be straightforward about your concerns.

- Do not try to win an argument by lining up opposition or people on your side without having first tried to work through the issue with the person. It may appear to be an ambush and could damage the trust you receive from those on both sides.

Do not distort the facts with your own biases or agendas

People are wary of those who appear to twist or distort arguments in order to win them. You will appear biased in situations where you don't see the different sides to an issue, where you use facts selectively, or where you argue an idea that will benefit only you. To avoid appearing biased, consider the following suggestions:

- Take into account all the facts when you build your argument, not just the ones that support your view. Ask someone to review your suggestions critically and to indicate how biased he or she feels they are.

- Use accurate facts.

- Ask for other views on the issue. Invite people to air their concerns.

- Acknowledge those facts and concerns that seem to support a viewpoint different from your own.

- Summarize the points someone has made by using the facts they used. For example, "So, based on your people having greatly exceeded their targets on four out of six projects, you'd like them to get a bonus." Then ask for confirmation that you've expressed what the person meant.

- If you have a bias that leads you to feel strongly about an issue, state your concern openly so people can deal with the underlying issue.

- If you have a personal agenda on an issue, state it openly as a goal you have. Be flexible in finding ways to meet both your goals and those of others.

Accept responsibility for your own mistakes

Few actions can erode trust faster than blaming others for your mistakes. At the same time, fewer, more powerful opportunities exist to build trust and establish credibility than to openly take responsibility for a mistake or failure. Mistakes can also prompt leaders to look inward and evaluate their limitations and shortcomings, learning more about themselves and, in the process, developing more trusting relationships and environments.

The following suggestions can help you accept responsibility for your mistakes and use them to increase your self-awareness:

- When you fail or do not achieve what you want, ask yourself what you learned from the situation. You may want to write down your learning.

- Consider sharing your mistake. Talking through a mistake with others will increase your understanding of the situation. Ask for their suggestions and ideas on what you might do differently in the future. When you can openly share your mistakes with others, they will become more comfortable sharing their mistakes with you.

- In the failure, focus on your role rather than looking at what others did or didn't do. Avoid any temptation to blame others. Instead, examine what you did or failed to do so that you can learn from your actions to create more success in the future.

- When you make a mistake, ask yourself and others, if appropriate, if you have made a similar mistake in the past. You can gain powerful insights by studying patterns of behavior that have resulted in repeated mistakes, miscalculations, or misreading of situations.

- When you make a mistake and are confronted by others, listen to their concerns and feelings first. Do not explain yourself, your behavior, or your intentions until they feel you have heard and understood them.

Recover from violating trust

If you have lost trust or are seen as lacking integrity, you will need to work to repair your reputation. Nothing is as damaging to a person in an organization as an integrity problem. Therefore, it is critical that you take remedial action quickly rather than get mired in your personal frustration, guilt, or defensiveness. The following suggestions can help you regain lost trust:

- If you know what you did to damage the trust, stop doing it. That may sound obvious, but some people think they can continue behavior without others knowing.

- If you do not know what you did to damage trust, find out. Ask others. Listen. Do not defend yourself.

- Expect to disagree initially that what you said or did showed lack of integrity or violated trust; people usually behave in ways they can justify or decide are all right. It is critically important, however, that you really hear how the other person was affected. To rebuild trust, you need to hear and understand what you did from the other person's point of view.

- Be aware that you may need to do penance for the offense. For example, you may need to listen repeatedly to the person expressing his or her anger or disappointment. If you are important to the person and you have seriously violated his or her trust, the person will not get over it quickly; it will take time.

- Ask what the person will need from you to begin considering trusting you again.

- Continue to behave in a trustworthy way even when the situation does not seem to improve. It won't get any better if you return to the old behavior.

PART 3:
DEVELOP AN ETHICAL ORGANIZATION

Model ethical behavior for the organization

An ethical organization is one that adheres to ethical rules and principles in all its actions, whether the actions are internal or external, written or spoken, at high levels or low, regarding strategic issues or the smallest details. Ethical organizations often have a written code of conduct, but more generally have well-grounded and widely understood principles and values that guide even the smallest decisions or actions.

Modeling is the best way to teach about your organization's ethical principles and to foster an environment of sound business ethics. The following suggestions can help you model ethical behavior:

- Actions speak louder than words. Set a good example for others throughout your organization by consistently engaging in solid ethical behavior and confronting any unethical practices.

- Relay stories of past and present leaders within your organization who implemented or abided by the company's guiding principles and values.

- Consistently be the one to initiate discussions of ethical considerations before decisions are made.

- Know who developed your organization's guiding principles and how they were adopted. Share this story with others.

AS A MATTER OF ETHICS, I THINK WE SHOULD ENLARGE THE SMALL PRINT AT THE BOTTOM OF ALL OF OUR CONTRACTS.

- Freely admit your mistakes to your manager, as you encourage your staff to do with you.

- Stand up for what you believe is right with those above you and outside your functional area, as well as with your own staff.

- Reward behavior that upholds high ethical standards for your work group by recognizing it in a setting that goes above and beyond your own group.

- Make sure the processes, measures, and rewards in your area do not promote unethical behavior.

- Share the ethical dilemmas you have. Ask for input and help from your manager, your peers, and your own staff in determining how to handle them.

Actively consider ethical issues before making decisions

As a leader, you undoubtedly will be faced with ethical dilemmas when making decisions. Making ethical decisions and confronting practices you cannot support can be a challenging, yet strengthening, process. When faced with such situations and decisions, asking yourself the following questions can help you examine the ethical considerations and take an appropriate stand:

- What is the issue? How important are the consequences in the short term? In the long term?

- How would my organization's code of ethics apply in this situation?

- Are my needs, or the needs of those I report to or advise, keeping me from seeing the full reality of the problem?

- Is this situation harmful or dangerous to others? Is this information necessary to prevent something from happening that could damage the reputation of the company, my clients, or myself?

- If someone else came to me with this problem, how would I advise him or her to handle it?

- Will my action stand the test of time? A year from now, will I be glad I ignored the problem or took the action I did?

- If this knowledge were taken to a higher level in the organization, would upper management approve of my actions?

- Would I be comfortable with my decision if it were broadcast on national television?

- Am I willing to be patient and not take immediate action? Do I act carefully, considering both the results I want to achieve and the actions required to achieve them?

- When I find myself in a situation in which I don't ethically know what to do, do I seek help? Do I inform and involve my manager?

Others in your organization probably have some of the same concerns that you do. Seek them out and support one another in your dilemmas. There is both strength and greater wisdom in numbers.

Protect confidential information

Leaders are caretakers of sensitive information, such as personnel records, compensation figures, proprietary technical information, and corporate secrets. How you handle this information and to whom you choose to impart it reflects on your integrity. These suggestions can help you deal ethically with confidential information:

- Know what kinds of information you cannot keep confidential, and communicate that before agreeing to keep any information or conversation private.

- Read your corporate code of ethics for guidelines on handling sensitive information. Or see if there is a handbook that details common ethical concerns for your field. When working in sensitive areas, these documents can be a good source of guidance.

- Read Barbara Toffler's *Managers Talk Ethics: Tough Choices in a Competitive Business World* (John Wiley & Sons, 1986). Talk with other managers to see if the ideas presented could be relevant to your company.

- When faced with a situation where the appropriate response is not obvious, ask for advice from your manager, coach, or peers.

- Consult with your legal staff.

- Understand that your organization's culture determines the way in which confidentiality is addressed and maintained. If a situation demands an exception to these rules, use your best judgment to resolve the issue. Can you, in good conscience, say you are comfortable with your knowledge and the actions you took on it?

- Ask yourself the following questions to determine whether you protect confidential information:
  - Do I protect employees who are willing to take the risk of revealing concerns?
  - Do I encourage an open-door policy wherein employees can talk with supervisors about issues without their names being revealed?

- Do I keep my door shut or go to a private office when discussing confidential information with others?
- Do I keep sensitive files, documents, correspondence, etc., locked away when I am not in my office?

Confront actions that are or border on unethical

Leaders are responsible not only for modeling ethical behavior themselves, but also for pointing out when others are behaving in inappropriate ways. To respond appropriately to actions that are or may be unethical, use the following suggestions:

- Be sure all employees understand the standards and principles to which they are being held by distributing them in writing and talking about them often.

- When you are aware of behavior that you consider to be unethical, first talk to the person to understand his or her motives and intentions. Phrase your concerns in terms of the principle involved as you indicate your personal discomfort with his or her actions. For example: "I'm uncomfortable with your using the money in this budget for another project without alerting the manager, who has asked us to give up unused budget dollars."

- When someone violates social rules, such as talking offensively about someone's racial or ethnic background, remember that silence means consent. Politely but firmly objecting to the offensive comment is critical to establishing standards of behavior.

- When someone's behavior blatantly contradicts ethical standards or corporate policies, swift action is necessary to signal to the individual and the organization that certain behaviors won't be tolerated. Your actions could take either or both of the following forms:
  - Talk to the employee about what you have observed or heard. Be very specific about the principle or policy that seems to have been violated and the behavior that violated it. Probe for the reasons why the employee acted in this manner.
  - Call in Human Resources, Legal, or other appropriate internal resources to investigate the issue and clarify the extent of the problem.

Encourage discussion of ethical standards

One reason employees behave inconsistently when confronted with ethical dilemmas is the lack of a shared understanding of what behavior is expected. If your organization has no written statements on ethics or principles, consider constructing a code of ethics.

An effective written policy:

- Incorporates business ethics with corporate strategy.

- Uses clear and specific wording.

- Spells out the rules by detailing standards, thus keeping misinterpretation to a minimum.

- Provides guidelines for dealing with vendors, competitors, and customers, as well as coworkers.

- Changes company rules and policies that do not support strong business and personal ethics.

It is up to top management to send a clear message to employees that ethical behavior is the foundation of good business. It is up to each manager to send this message (through both words and actions) to his or her employees. The following suggestions can help you integrate ethical behaviors into your organization's standard operating procedures:

- Have each department discuss how its members can influence opinion about approaches to policy in your organization.

- Emphasize integrity, concern for people, and orientation to company values and policies in documents such as handbooks, policy statements, and job descriptions.

- Encourage and support firm action to be taken with employees at any level in response to wrongdoing.

- Unite your professional staff to develop and promote a code of ethics. Ask for these issues to be addressed in official individual and team goals.

- Provide training courses on dealing with ethical issues.

- Recruit people who share the company's values.

- Post your written code of ethics (or a summary of it) on bulletin boards.

- Create an ombudsperson or a telephone hotline where employees can confidentially discuss ethical concerns and get answers and actions.

Align the organization's systems and processes with its ethical standards

It has been said that a "bad" system will beat a well-intentioned person every time. For example, discrimination in hiring or promotion generally has a great deal more to do with a faulty or unclear selection system than any prejudicial intent by individual decision makers. Therefore, it is important to examine all current and proposed processes in light of the organization's guiding principles and values.

To help align systems and processes with ethical standards, consider the following guidelines:

- Explicitly connect goals for ethical behavior to things that are highly valued by your staff (promotions, more interesting or important work assignments, etc.).

- When unethical behavior is discovered, thoroughly review the surrounding systems and processes to determine how these may have played a role. Solicit suggestions for solutions, and make the necessary changes.

- Include measures of ethical behavior in performance appraisals. You get what you measure and reward. In addition to trustworthiness, accountability can be a measure of ethical behavior. For example, salespeople who make unrealistic claims regarding their product in order to make a sale are often only measured on their total sales in dollars and are unaffected by any negative consequences. A possible ethical measure in this case might be the number of customer complaints from the clients to whom they have sold.

RESOURCES

The resources for this chapter begin on page 680.

31
DEMONSTRATE ADAPTABILITY

PART 1: INCREASE YOUR ADAPTABILITY AND RESILIENCY
- *Increase your flexibility when interacting with others*
- *Use a flexible problem-solving approach*
- *Work effectively in ambiguous situations*
- *Readily adapt to change and shifting priorities*
- *Keep your composure in trying situations*
- *Display an appropriate level of patience*
- *Deal constructively with mistakes and setbacks*
- *Maintain a positive outlook by using affirming self-talk*
- *Use humor to increase your resiliency*

PART 2: COPE EFFECTIVELY WITH STRESS AND PRESSURE
- *Emphasize focus, not life balance*
- *Identify your stressors*
- *Use a support network to cope with life's challenges*
- *Use physical coping strategies to reduce stress*
- *Relax through mental imagery*

INTRODUCTION

Talent is nurtured in solitude;
character is formed in the stormy billows of the world.

— Johann Wolfgang von Goethe

The rapidly changing world requires leaders to be adaptable. Constant change drives the need to move quickly, deal with ambiguity, accept change, and handle stress.

In addition to developing comfort with ambiguity and a fast pace, successful managers must juggle the demands of personal and work-related activities and find an appropriate balance among the needs of the organization, others, and self. Doing all of this with some grace, while maintaining a sense of humor and a reasonable level of patience and perspective, are hallmarks of the best managers.

This chapter contains activities to help you develop your flexibility and adaptability while coping with the natural stress of a challenging business environment.

VALUABLE TIPS

- Expect change, ambiguity, and frustration at least part of the time.

- Develop your sense of humor. Learn not to take yourself too seriously.

- Look for two or three quick and simple ways to relax and escape daily tensions.

- Learn to share your concerns and challenges with others. Talking about issues provides you with thinking time, good alternatives, different ways of seeing things, and support.

- Have your manager put you in ambiguous situations and coach you on how to cope with them.

- When feeling negative, force yourself to "count your blessings." Make a list of all the things you have to be thankful for, and add to it whenever you are focusing on the negative.

- Review successes, especially when you are going through a challenging time.

- Build in the discipline of thinking before responding in pressured situations. This gives you time to calm down, think of alternatives, and see things in other ways.

- If you tend to be a quick decision maker, force yourself to set aside immediate reactions and consider alternatives.

- Be alert for times when you hold on to a solution or procedure because "that's the way it has always been done," instead of considering other viable alternatives.

- Watch for habits of negative or self-defeating inner conversations, or self-talk. Work at replacing them with positive inner dialogue.

- Live in the present. Avoid fueling stress fires by bemoaning the past or spinning your wheels about the future.

- Set aside time for vigorous physical activity, and then do it.

- If you are overcommitted and expect to be great at everything, focus your energy on the most important areas and allow yourself to be average in less important matters.

- Finish what you start. Anxiety can result from a lot of loose ends.

- Use the Serenity Prayer from Alcoholics Anonymous: "God grant me the serenity to accept the things I cannot change, the courage to change the things I can, and the wisdom to know the difference."

- Hold to simple truths.

- Establish and deepen nonwork friendships. Be yourself, and talk about sensitive areas without being afraid.

- Decontaminate your leisure time. Set aside time to have fun, and don't let work—or thoughts about it—intrude.

- Broaden your family activities.

- Set aside time for attending to the spiritual side of your life, and then do it.

- To control your temper, take ten slow, deep breaths through your nose before responding.

- To help reduce stress, get organized and manage your time better.

- Pay attention to your diet. Learn more about good nutrition and about drugs that can affect your stress level or sleep patterns.

- Don't "catastrophize" events at work. Problems are to be expected and are rarely catastrophic.

- Get involved in enough other areas of your life to enhance your feelings of competence even when one area is going wrong.

PART 1:
INCREASE YOUR ADAPTABILITY AND RESILIENCY

Increase your flexibility when interacting with others

If you are strongly opinionated, you may not spend enough time listening to what others are saying. Rather than listening to alternate approaches, you may tend to prepare rebuttals to argue your own case. This can cause others to see you as rigid and inflexible. Use the following exercises to increase your flexibility in this area:

- To ensure that you are listening for understanding (rather than to strengthen your own position), concentrate on paraphrasing or summarizing the speaker's message. This will help focus your attention on the speaker and let the speaker know that you are tuned in to his or her message.

- If you have difficulty seeing the value of another person's viewpoint, mentally reverse sides to see if you can come up with ideas that support that person's position. While your goal is not necessarily to accept the opposite view as your final opinion, understanding another person's thinking may enhance your own ideas and make you appear less rigid.

- Ask trusted coworkers to provide feedback on situations in which others think you tend to be overly opinionated or rigid in your thinking. Most people have specific problem areas. Recognizing the fact that you are becoming inflexible is the first step in changing.

- If you are seen as strong-minded, ask others for their opinions before you state yours. When sharing your opinion, preface your statements with words such as, "In my opinion…" or "I think…."

- Show a willingness to adapt to the working styles and schedules of others. For example, conduct conference calls with colleagues in different time zones during a time that is convenient for them, rather than convenient for you.

Use a flexible problem-solving approach

If your typical response to a problem is to immediately generate a specific solution or to hold on to a solution or procedure because "that's the way it's always been done," you may find it difficult to consider other possibilities. This tendency can decrease the quality of your decisions. To ensure you use a flexible approach to problem solving, follow these guidelines:

- When you approach a problem, remind yourself that there are many possible solutions to any given problem and that you must be willing to consider the unique facts about the situation before making a final decision.

- Watch for snap reactions. Rather than assuming that the first alternative that enters your mind is the best solution, consider other options.

- If you tend to make decisions too quickly, consciously delay making a final decision. Gather more information so you can gain a thorough understanding of several possible solutions and their unique benefits and drawbacks. Once you understand the solutions, weed out those that are least appropriate, using facts to substantiate your decisions.

- If you tend to treat all problems as crises, create a log of the crises you encounter each day and give each one a rating from 1 (can wait) to 10 (urgent, immediate attention required). Periodically examine the list to identify the situations you tend to erroneously define as crises.

- Look for ways to combine the best features of several solutions to improve the quality of your final decision.

- Adopt the philosophy, "If it works, make it better."

Work effectively in ambiguous situations

Ambiguity is inevitable in positions of increasing responsibility. If you are uncomfortable with ambiguity, consider the following:

1. Identify key past and current ambiguous situations. How did you behave? Did you:
   - Try to get control of what was happening?
   - Wait for others to make clear what was expected?
   - Worry about whether the decision was right?
   - Wonder when things would become clear?

2. Examine how you felt about these situations. Did you feel:
   - Angry about a lack of direction?
   - Hurt or angry about not being involved in the decision?
   - Anxious that the course of action may not work?

3. Adopt more useful approaches in future ambiguous situations. Some ways to do this include the following:

- Rather than avoiding unstructured situations, seek them out. Ask people you trust to give you feedback and suggestions for how you could be more effective.
- Change your own expectations; don't expect to have all the information when you make a decision.
- Expect that things will change.
- Recall how you have weathered ambiguous situations well in the past, and use those strategies.
- Ask others what they do to cope.
- Volunteer for projects and activities that will give you practice working under ambiguous conditions.
- Watch and talk with people you believe handle ambiguity well. Identify things they do that fit for you.

Readily adapt to change and shifting priorities

It has been said that change is the only constant in the universe. Change demands that we learn new skills, continually push beyond our comfort zone, and respond with flexibility. Use the following suggestions to increase your comfort in dealing with shifting priorities and rapid change:

- Expect that your work environment is dynamic and chaotic, not consistent and stable. With this expectation, you can:
  - Scan the horizon for possible changes, identify them early, and reduce surprise.
  - Take a proactive stance toward expected changes.

- If you dislike change because you feel a loss of control:
  - Acknowledge that you are not in control, nor do you need to be in all situations.
  - Consider a past change that you effectively managed and identify steps you took in that situation that you can also try here.
  - Look long term to see what you can start doing to gain some sense of control in the situation.
  - Realize that the feeling of being in control may have changed from what it once was. Maintaining control in a static situation is very different from maintaining control in an environment of rapid change. Alter your definition and expectation of being in control so that it will fit with a changing environment.

- When you first encounter shifting priorities and change, don't react. Gain more information before you express your reaction. Internalizing the change may make it easier for you to accept.

- View shifting priorities and other changes as new challenges or opportunities to think creatively. Be confident that you will be able to brainstorm ways to get around any obstacles that the change presents.

Keep your composure in trying situations

You may discover times when you become too emotionally involved in trying situations. The following suggestions will help you gain better control of your emotions during difficult situations so you can view them objectively and reduce unnecessary stress:

1. Learn to recognize your symptoms of excessive emotional involvement. Because it's difficult to be objective about one's own behavior, you may need help with this step.
   - Ask a colleague to observe your behavior the next time you're involved in a difficult situation and to watch for signs of stress, such as clenched fists, irritability, and so forth.
   - Afterward, ask your colleague to describe your behavior. As you listen to the description, take note of the behaviors that indicate increasing emotional involvement. Try to remember how you were feeling when you exhibited these behaviors.

2. Watch for any inner signs or signals that you are starting to lose your composure. Make it a habit to note your inner progression of signals as you lose your composure.

   For example, you may find yourself holding your breath, breathing shallowly, clenching your teeth, flexing your muscles, feeling like you want to cry, etc. Use these symptoms as a signal for yourself. Find a way to either regain your composure there or get away for a short time to regain it—for example, excuse yourself to go to the restroom.

3. The next time you're involved in a similar situation, monitor your behavior. Remember that it is easier to regain composure sooner rather than later in the progression of increasing emotional involvement.
   - In situations involving only one or two people, be flexible in scheduling your time to help alleviate stress. At the first sign you are becoming too emotionally involved, pull back if possible and set the problem aside for a time. When you feel ready to review the problem objectively, return to it.
   - In situations where you can't set the problem aside, such as in a group meeting, monitor your behavior while you work on the problem as if you were an objective third party. When you see yourself becoming too involved, talk yourself into calming down and becoming more objective. For example, if you find yourself getting angry, you might say to yourself: "I'm getting angry about this. I don't need to take it personally; I'll just step back a little and calm down."

Display an appropriate level of patience	Patience with others may require active effort on your part to accept and understand their experiences and points of view. To become more patient with people:

- Seek feedback from others regarding recent occasions in which you did not demonstrate an appropriate level of patience.
  - Don't try to justify or explain your behavior. Listen intently and take notes about what they observed.
  - Later, analyze the circumstances and try to identify themes in your impatience.
  - Attempt to identify situations in which you tend to lose your patience. For example, do you lose patience when you are overwhelmed, or when working with slower learners?

- To control your impatience, change your perspective by thinking more accepting thoughts (for example, "I have the time," "If I wait, I'll understand," or "This will pass"). Temporarily leave the situation if you cannot refrain from saying something inappropriate.

- Look carefully at the strengths and development needs of others to gain insight into their behavior and to increase your tolerance of it. Be attentive to the qualities that make a particular person likable and valuable; then concentrate on his or her strengths. As you learn to focus on and appreciate the strengths of others, you will find yourself more tolerant of their weaknesses.

- Avoid interrupting others when they are talking.

- Consciously refrain from immediate judgment or criticism of others' ideas and concerns. Instead, ask open-ended questions to understand their issues more fully. Recognize that what may not be an issue to you may be a valid concern to others.

Deal constructively with mistakes and setbacks	Successful people experience failures and setbacks. Sometimes they make poor judgment calls. Successful people differ from unsuccessful people, however, in that they learn from these experiences. To make the most of a situation in which you find your personal or business plans thwarted, look at your setbacks and mistakes as development opportunities. The following guidelines will help you deal constructively with your setbacks:

- Consider a setback or rejection a learning experience. Review the events that led up to it, and assess your attitude and behavior at the time. Did you neglect to get buy-in from employees? Did you take a high-handed approach with others? Did you fail to do your homework? After you have assessed the situation, decide how you can change your attitude or behavior to achieve a more favorable outcome the next time.

- Focus on the process rather than the outcome. Thwarted plans may mean you have neglected to build relationships with internal or external sources who are important to organizational goals. Focus not on the failed outcome, but on the conditions and causes of the setback. Consider in particular your relationship with individuals and groups that were an integral part of the situation.
  - Do you have a viable relationship with those involved?
  - Have you shown your trustworthiness?
  - Have you "walked your talk" and "lived your values"?

  Seek feedback from people who can comment on these questions to check the validity of your assumptions. Resolve to build or strengthen crucial relationships with others.

- Consider the situation a challenge. Look at it not as a failure or rejection, but as an opportunity to think creatively. Brainstorm ways you can get around whatever obstacles it presents.

- Confront errors. When you attempt something and fail, ask yourself, "What have I learned?" rather than kicking yourself or blaming someone else. Discovering the value in your mistakes will make you a better, smarter manager.

If you have not weathered setbacks, mistakes, or rejection in your organizational life, you probably have not taken many risks or stretched yourself by taking on tough and difficult goals. The key to organizational success over the long run is to take some calculated risks and use failures as opportunities to learn.

Maintain a positive outlook by using affirming self-talk

What we say to ourselves—our self-talk—about the situations, trials, and challenges that confront us affects how we feel and behave. Positive attitudes and affirming ways of approaching situations will likely increase your resiliency and reduce your stress level. To increase your positive mind-set, try the following suggestions:

- Allow performance to be acceptable instead of needing it to be perfect. This may mean being comfortable with a job performed by one of your employees or learning when to let go of a project and declare it done.

- Avoid black-and-white thinking. This type of thinking often results in viewing performance as either a total success or a total failure. In reality, most performance falls somewhere in between.

- Focus on the positive things you do. Dwelling on the negative and downplaying the positive will only increase stress and decrease self-esteem. Give yourself credit for positive experiences, and avoid magnifying negative events.

- Watch the extent to which you personalize the outcome of situations. Personalizing involves seeing yourself as the primary cause of some negative external outcome for which, in reality, you were not primarily responsible.

- Think optimistically. Assuming that things will not work out well can turn into a self-fulfilling prophecy. Anticipating a positive outcome will increase your chances of success, as well as your sense of well-being.

- Listen to how you talk to yourself out loud and in your head. Work at reducing negative, judgmental self-talk by replacing it with realistic, positively oriented self-talk. Develop the habit of having your "positive self" argue with the judgmental self-talk of your "negative self." Make sure the positive self wins most of the time.

- Cultivate a positive outlook by adopting the practice of being thankful for all of your blessings. Make a list of all of the material and nonmaterial aspects of your life for which you are thankful, and regularly add to this list.

Use humor to increase your resiliency

Humor can be a wonderful addition in many situations. When used appropriately, humor has the power to draw people together, lighten a challenging situation, increase job satisfaction, keep people's attention, and relieve stress. When used inappropriately, it can backfire and pull people apart, create discomfort, increase stress, and even lead to arguments. Use the following suggestions to guide your use of humor:

- Spend time with friends and colleagues who display a good sense of humor. Note what they do and how they use humor. Incorporate effective methods into your work.

- Use humor when you need to "break the ice" or put people at ease, such as when you are attempting to build a new relationship or are beginning a presentation. Carefully watch reactions to humor, however, because humor is culture-specific.

- When you face an adverse situation, step back for a minute and look for a humorous angle. Humor can help you relax and allow ideas to flow.

- Ensure that your nonverbal behavior is in alignment with your humor. Humor can be ambiguous, so smiling and laughing will communicate to others that what you said was meant to be humorous. Conversely, a serious facial expression is likely to be confusing to others.

- Avoid humor that is based on the traits or stereotypes of a group of people. Humor used at the expense of others will, and should, backfire.

- Ask a trusted colleague to watch you over a period of time and give you feedback on your use of humor. Ask to be told what was considered both appropriate and inappropriate.

- Learn to laugh at yourself and take yourself less seriously.

- Collect a few humorous books, tapes, and videos. When you find yourself losing your sense of humor, rely on someone else's—take time to read a book or watch a video with family or friends.

PART 2: COPE EFFECTIVELY WITH STRESS AND PRESSURE

Emphasize focus, not life balance

Many people get caught up in trying to do it all when faced with the competing demands within and between work and personal life. When you encounter additional or changing demands, learn to use your core values and life goals to focus your time and energy. The following process will help you focus on what's most important:

1. First, take time to identify the values, principles, and life goals that are most important to you. Too often people get into trouble trying to do it all because they have not thought through what is most important to them. If you have difficulty completing this step, ask yourself, "What do I want my legacy to be?"

2. After identifying your critical goals and values, determine your most important priorities, both at work and in your personal life.

3. Next, use a "time finder" (below) to keep track of how you currently spend your time. A time finder is simply a grid with spaces for noting how you spend your time each hour of the day for seven days.

4. After tracking your time for a week, analyze the ways in which you spent your time. Identify the time spent on different areas of your life (work, family, leisure, spiritual, and so forth) and compare this with the values and goals you listed in the first step. Look for areas of inconsistency.

5. Create an action plan to further align your values and goals with how you are spending your time:
   - Once you have identified your values and goals, set your priorities accordingly. Then do your most important priorities first. You will get relief by not doing those things that are lower on your list of values.

ACTIVITIES

	DAY 1	DAY 2	DAY 3	DAY 4	DAY 5	DAY 6	DAY 7
6:00 AM							
7:00 AM							
8:00 AM							
ETC....							
6:00 PM							

- While difficult, cutting out lower-priority items is critical. Willingness to sacrifice less important items for those critical to your life values and goals only comes about when you are clear on what is most important and central to your life.
- Set aside time periodically to think and reflect so you will retain your focus in the long haul—life priorities and goals change over time.
- To increase your likelihood of longer-lasting change, approach this process as a gradual redesign rather than a major overhaul of your life.

Identify your stressors

People vary in what they find stressful. By increasing your awareness of the situations that are stressful for you, including the reasons for the stress, you can take steps to prepare yourself for and cope with these stressors. The following procedure will help you identify the reasons for your stress so you can begin to reduce it:

1. Identify situations that cause stress.

2. For each situation, list all of the circumstances and responsibilities that make you feel particularly tense and pressured in that situation. Assume, for example, that the situation is a group meeting. Circumstances that often cause stress in meetings include:
   - The need to speak in front of a group.
   - The presence of higher-level managers.
   - Lack of knowledge about the meeting topics.
   - Interpersonal conflict between you and another group member.

3. Examine the reasons for your stress, looking for patterns and themes across the different situations that you identified in step 2.

4. Based on your analysis, identify future situations that are likely to cause you stress and look for ways to reduce your stress. For example, if interpersonal conflict between you and another group member causes you to feel stressed in a group situation, you could get together with that person before the meeting to iron out your differences in private.

5. Consider the possibility that the cause of your stress is rooted in your need to develop in a certain skill area. For example, poor conflict-management or time-management skills are often cited as reasons for stress. If this is the case for you, create a plan to improve that skill area. Review Chapter 32: Practice Self-Development for suggestions on creating a plan.

Use a support network to cope with life's challenges

When you're feeling under pressure, talking with other people can help. Talking with others about problems can provide an outlet for stress energy and can help you generate solutions. Thus, it's important to have a strong support network for both personal and work related problems. The following procedure can help you evaluate and build your support network:

1. Evaluate your support network for both your work and personal life. Using the chart that follows, list the people on whom you can rely in each situation.

2. Review your list and determine whether your network is adequate. Do you have people who can help you in each area?

3. For areas in which you require a stronger network, create a plan for building your network:
   - Ask trusted friends and coworkers where they've found support and help.
   - Think of other ways in which you can build your network. For example:
     ○ To build a stronger network for support with work-related problems, think of people in your organization or other organizations who hold positions similar to yours. Professional organizations and meetings can be excellent places to meet these people.
     ○ To build a stronger network for support with personal problems, consider your church, community organizations, health clubs, and so forth.

Keep in mind that building long-lasting support relationships takes time and requires a lot of give-and-take.

WORK LIFE	PEOPLE WHO CAN PROVIDE SUPPORT	PERSONAL LIFE	PEOPLE WHO CAN PROVIDE SUPPORT
INFORMATION TRAINING		RELAXATION	
ADVICE		ADVICE	
RELIEF FROM OVERLOAD		RELIEF FROM OVERLOAD	
DISCUSSION OF ISSUES/VALUES/ PROBLEMS		COMPANIONSHIP	
OTHER		DISCUSSION OF PROBLEMS/ SHARING OF CONSEQUENCES	
OTHER		ROMANCE	

Use physical coping strategies to reduce stress

We all have automatic or habitual responses to stress. You probably are already aware of some of the ways in which your physical state affects your ability to handle stress. The next time you are stressed, consider the following suggestions:

• Concentrate on your breathing. Work to slow your breathing cycle, which will lead to relaxation.
  - Begin by paying attention to the breath leaving and entering your nostrils. Awareness of this pattern can help you slow your breathing cycle and make it smoother.
  - Next, pay attention to your nostrils during your breathing cycle (when inhaling and exhaling). Count each breath as it leaves your nostrils. Count to ten and then begin again very slowly, trying to breathe a little more slowly. As you do so, consciously begin to breathe gently and smoothly.

• Increase your level of physical activity. Physical exercise helps discharge built-up stress energy. Furthermore, when your body is in good shape, it's more efficient in using available energy.

• Limit your intake of caffeine, alcohol, and nicotine, all of which are ways of coping with stress in the short term, but which reduce your ability to effectively function in the long term.

Because of Caffeine I'm cutting back to one cup per day!

Relax through mental imagery

Mental imagery is very powerful. You can make yourself upset by imagining all of the possible negative aspects of a decision or an event. But you can also relax by using positive images. To relax through mental imagery, follow this procedure:

1. Find a comfortable place to sit or lie down. Then close your eyes and take four slow, deep breaths through your nose. Think of the place in which you relax as your personal sanctuary.

2. In your mind, construct a scene that is very pleasant and relaxing for you. This may be a scene from your past or an image you create just for this exercise. Solitary images work best for most people. For example, you might picture yourself fishing on a beautiful, calm lake or sitting in a comfortable chair in front of a warm fire on a cold winter day.

   The secret to using imagery is to develop as vivid a scenario as possible. Use all of your senses to imagine what it would be like in that situation—what it would look like, the sounds you would hear, and the diverse aromas in the air.

Set aside five minutes a day to take one of these "mental vacations."

RESOURCES

The resources for this chapter begin on page 682.

32
PRACTICE
SELF–DEVELOPMENT

PART 1: GET READY TO LEARN
- *An overview of PDI's Development FIRST™ process*
- *Create a road map*

PART 2: DECIDE WHERE TO FOCUS YOUR DEVELOPMENT
- *Gather information about your competency portfolio*
- *Analyze your competency portfolio (or GAPS Grid)*
- *Select your top-priority learning objectives*
- *Leverage your strengths*

PART 3: SPEND TIME EACH DAY ON YOUR DEVELOPMENT
- *Take just five minutes a day for your development*
- *Make your learning more efficient*
- *Get the most out of readings and seminars*
- *Anticipate roadblocks that could sidetrack your development*

PART 4: EXTRACT MAXIMUM LEARNING FROM YOUR EXPERIENCES
- *Reflect on what you have learned*
- *View mistakes as learning opportunities*

PART 5: LEARN FROM OTHERS' IDEAS AND PERSPECTIVES
- *Involve others in your development efforts*
- *Seek honest feedback from others*
- *Respond openly to feedback*
- *Use development partners to support your development*

PART 6: ADAPT AND PLAN FOR CONTINUED LEARNING
- *Transfer learning into next steps*

INTRODUCTION

We are what we repeatedly do. Excellence, then, is not an act, but a habit.

— Aristotle

As the pace of change intensifies in today's business environment, continued development of one's skills and knowledge is no longer optional. Career success now requires a serious commitment to ongoing learning and self-development. PDI's Development FIRST™ process can help you proactively drive your development and establish a cycle of continuous learning. The process includes these five strategies:

Focusing on your priorities

Implementing something every day

Reflecting on what happens

Seeking feedback and support

Transferring learning into next steps

Learning is like an insurance policy for success and survival in tomorrow's world. To help maintain your "policy" in good standing, this chapter presents a number of useful Development FIRST™ strategies and tactics.

VALUABLE TIPS

- Put your action step for your development goals on your daily "to do" list and make it the number-one priority.

- Visualize your goals so you have a clear picture of what success looks like. Then, to help sustain your motivation, imagine yourself attaining your goals.

- Find something you can learn from each person with whom you work.

- Do one thing every day, even if it is a small step, to move toward your goals.

- When you set goals, ensure that they reflect accomplishments you really want, not what others want or what you think you should want.

- Review your calendar daily. Identify at least one time in the day that you can practice a behavior or skill you are trying to learn or fine-tune.

- Learn to look at negative feedback and criticism as potentially useful information that you need to understand more fully.

- Approach each day with the same sense of discovery that you had when you were a child.

- Decide on a clear-cut, long-range goal for yourself. Then establish what you will need to do and what attitudes you will need to have in order to achieve it.

- Take more risks.

- Limit your focus. Genuine progress on your two or three most important goals is more meaningful and rewarding than negligible progress on a dozen less critical fronts.

- Keep a list of the things you want to learn in the next five, ten, and 20 years.

- Make some form of public commitment to your goals, so others can encourage you to reach them.

- When you make a mistake, learn from it.

- Examine what you do with the lessons you learn from feedback and experience. Observe how you change and adapt based on these lessons.

- Keep track of lessons learned; refer to them periodically to reinforce your learning.

- Be more willing to take personal criticism without showing defensiveness.

- Separate what you are learning from how you are performing. Ask, "What have I just learned?" rather than, "How did I just do?"

- Find ways to leverage your strengths.

- To help you stay the course during tough times, determine your incentives or payoffs for attaining your learning objective.

- Consider using a multi-rater or 360-degree feedback instrument to obtain comprehensive feedback on your skills from others.

- Learn for the sake of gaining wisdom, not just knowledge.

- Commit to being a lifelong learner. Approach every situation by asking yourself, "What can I learn?"

- Confront problems instead of avoiding them. When you put off dealing with a problem situation, ask yourself why. Learn to lean into your areas of discomfort to improve your skills and knowledge.

- Consider using PDI's eAdvisor™ or DevelopMentor®. Both tools provide a library of advice for self-development, including practical tips, exercises, resource lists, and development suggestions and ideas to help you improve and learn.

PART 1:
GET READY TO LEARN

An overview of PDI's Development FIRST™ process

Real learning seldom has a distinct beginning and end; rather it is an ongoing, cyclical process. PDI's Development FIRST™ process includes five simple strategies to drive your development and establish a cycle of continuous learning:

- *Focus on priorities: Identify your critical issues and goals.* It is important to focus on development goals that matter to both you and your organization. Focusing on one or two goals will help you concentrate your efforts so you can see real progress.

- *Implement something every day: Stretch your comfort zone.* Development goals and tactics need to be translated into daily action to make change a reality. Just as in a disciplined exercise program, you need to identify concrete opportunities for growth and address the emotions and external challenges that threaten to drive you off course.

- *Reflect on what happens: Extract maximum learning from your experiences.* Without pausing to consolidate and assimilate your learning experiences, your lessons will go to waste. You need to distill what worked well, what went awry, and what you plan to do differently next time.

- *Seek feedback and support: Learn from others' ideas and perspectives.* With the feedback and support of others, you can gather relevant information about your progress, sustain your motivation, and stay the course.

- *Transfer learning to the next level: Adapt and plan for continued learning.* Use the transfer strategy when you accomplish your objectives, when you are stuck, or when you need to step back and take stock of your progress. You can then cycle back to the first self-development strategy, *Focus*, to maintain a cycle of continuous, lifelong learning.

Create a road map

A basic plan or road map can help guide you to your destination on a variety of life's journeys. Certainly this is the case in the learning process.

A career plan, or longer-term road map, takes into account your vision and overall goals from both a personal and professional standpoint. A development plan is a medium-range plan that maps your strengths, development needs, and untested skills; charts your future roles in the organization; and defines how you will get there. A learning plan, the focus of this chapter, is a short-range plan that outlines your learning objectives and defines what you will actually do differently to change your behavior. A sample completed Learning Plan can be found on page xxii of the About This Book section of this handbook.

The format of your learning plan matters far less than its content and whether you use it. One possible format, modeled after PDI's Development FIRST™ process, is shown below. The following questions can help you create a learning plan useful to you:

1. Is your plan focused? Have you limited yourself to one or two learning goals?

2. Does your plan trigger daily action? Have you listed times, situations, and people who will trigger new behavior? Have you identified potential roadblocks and how you will overcome them?

3. Does your plan outline when and how you will take time to reflect and make your learning a conscious process?

4. Does your plan involve feedback and support from others?

5. Does your plan include how and when you will measure your success?

True development does not have a beginning and an end, but instead is an ongoing process in which goals are achieved and simultaneously updated and revised. Hence, a learning plan is not a static document but rather changes as you and your environment change.

PERSONAL LEARNING PLAN

Name_____ Date_____

1. FOCUS ON CRITICAL PRIORITIES.
What do I want to change or develop?
What development priorities give me the greatest leverage?

◇

2. IMPLEMENT SOMETHING EVERY DAY.

What situations, people, or events signal that right now is the time to put new behaviors into action?	What new behavior will I try? Where will I push my comfort zone?
Every time I see the following situation(s)...	*...I will take the following development action(s):*
1.	
2.	
3.	
4.	
5.	

3. REFLECT ON WHAT YOU HAVE LEARNED.
What will I do each day to consider what worked, what didn't work, and what I want to do next time?

◇

4. SEEK FEEDBACK AND SUPPORT.
How will I draw on other people to track my progress, gather advice and feedback, and support my learning?

◇

5. TRANSFER LEARNING TO THE NEXT LEVEL.
How will I periodically evaluate my progress?
Considering my goals and organizational priorities, how will I update my development strategy and learning plan? How will I leverage what I have already learned?

◇

PART 2:
DECIDE WHERE TO FOCUS YOUR DEVELOPMENT

Gather information about your competency portfolio

Before you can decide the direction of your learning and development, you need to update where you are now and where you need and want to go. By thinking about your Goals and Abilities and collecting information about the Perceptions and Success Factors of others—your "GAPS"—you will be able to make informed decisions about your development.

The GAPS grid shown below is a tool to help you collect information about your competency portfolio and prioritize your development. Use the questions that follow to complete your GAPS grid. Gather data from as many sources as you can.

GAPS GRID

	WHERE YOU ARE	WHERE YOU ARE GOING	
	ABILITIES: *How you see yourself.* What I already know: What I need to learn:	**GOALS AND VALUES:** *What matters to you.* What I already know: What I need to learn:	**YOUR VIEW**
	PERCEPTIONS: *How others see you.* What I already know: What I need to learn:	**STANDARDS AND SUCCESS FACTORS:** *What matters to others.* What I already know: What I need to learn:	**OTHERS' VIEWS**

Goals and Values: what you care most about, including your personal goals, interests, career aspirations, and values.

- What are your most important goals, values, and interests?
- What do you care most about in your work and life? Why?
- In what ways do you want to contribute at work?
- What do you want to do that you are not doing now?

Information sources for Goals and Values might include career and development planning discussions, personal goal setting, and values clarification.

Abilities: your view of your capabilities and performance.

- Where have you been successful? What skills contributed to that success?
- Where have you been least successful? Why?
- Based on appraisals of your work and your own perception of your track record, what do you see as your key strengths and weaknesses?
- In what areas do you turn to others for assistance? In what areas do others turn to you?

The information source for Abilities is your own self-assessment.

Perceptions: how others see your capabilities, including any interpretations and assumptions regarding their observations.

- Based on feedback from others and project debriefs, how do you think others see you?
- What do others say concerning your strengths and development needs?
- What is your reputation with different groups and at different levels in the organization?

Information sources for Perceptions might include direct feedback from others; 360-degree feedback; performance reviews; in-depth, objective assessment; and customer feedback.

Standards and Success Factors: others' expectations and goals, including expectations of you, your role, organizational core competency expectations, anticipated changes in those expectations.

- What are the criteria for success in your current job/position?

- Who is most valued and respected in your organization? Why?

- What competencies are in greatest demand in your organization right now? In the future?

Information sources for Standards and Success Factors might include competency models for your current and future roles; respected role models; organizational vision, values, strategies, and goals; and market demands.

Analyze your competency portfolio (or GAPS Grid)

After collecting your GAPS information, you are ready to interpret your competency portfolio. To do so, consider these suggestions:

- Look for common themes and patterns. For example, your GAPS grid might show that your interpersonal abilities match the perceptions of others and will be necessary for you to achieve your goals.

- Try to make sense of discrepancies, or "gaps," among the various cells. Ask yourself the following questions to better understand your gaps:
  - *Abilities and Goals:* Do I have the abilities I need to reach my goal?
  - *Goals and Success Factors:* Am I motivated to reach my goal?
  - *Perceptions and Success Factors:* Do others have confidence in my abilities?
  - *Abilities and Perceptions:* Do I have a blind spot, do I need to do something more frequently, or do I need to market my skills better?
  - *Goals and Goals:* Are my goals compatible? For example: How do I balance the fact that I want to be a senior vice president, which requires living near corporate headquarters, with the fact I do not want to move from the part of the country I am in?

- Realize that both you and your environment will change over time. Update your GAPS grid and reevaluate your portfolio at least every few years, or after any major learning experience or when significant changes occur in the organization and its expectations.

Select your top-priority learning objectives

Once you have created and analyzed your competency portfolio, you are ready to select one or two high-priority goals based on what is most valuable to you and your organization.

- Ask yourself:
  - What do I want to change, develop, or learn?
  - What development priorities will give me the most leverage?
  - Where will I get my best return on investment?

- Realize that it is unlikely you will have perfect clarity concerning what to develop. Some uncertainty is part of the development process.

- Limit your focus. Real progress in a couple of areas will be far more rewarding than minor changes in many less important areas.

- Choose learning objectives that require you to stretch yourself and take some risks, yet are still attainable.

- Use the following guidelines when writing your learning objectives:
  - Be specific. Make your objective clear enough so that someone will be able to tell whether you have achieved it.
  - State your objective in positive terms. What behavior or outcome would you like to see?
  - Focus on what will change in you, rather than on a business goal or objective.

Leverage your strengths

People succeed because of what they do well. Yet often people are so focused on improving their weaker areas that they ignore their strengths. To maximize your competency portfolio, it is at least as important to determine how you can capitalize on your strengths, or assets, as how to improve your weaknesses. Consider the following:

- Gain a greater understanding of your strengths by considering how you would answer the following questions in a job interview:
  - Why should we hire you?
  - What are you skilled at?
  - What special qualities and abilities would you bring to our organization?
  - What things have people praised you for?

- Redefine your current opportunities. First, identify parts of your job that you handle easily. Then add a new challenge by asking yourself:
  - How can I make this more strategic?
  - Can I teach this to others?
  - How can I streamline it and reduce cycle time?
  - How can I make it more effective?

- Seek experience in new, complex situations.

- Spend time with others who are more skilled than you. Benchmark yourself against the leaders in your field.

- Cross-train and pursue learning in related areas.

PART 3:
SPEND TIME EACH DAY ON YOUR DEVELOPMENT

Take just five minutes a day for your development

The most effective way to develop is to make it a regular part of your daily discipline. You are more likely to succeed if you chip away at your development in small, bite-sized pieces than if you attend one intensive training program a year. Even five minutes a day, used wisely, can make a tremendous difference. Consider the following suggestions for your five-minute daily dose of development:

- Make development routine. Set aside a regular time, such as at the beginning or end of each day, to act and reflect on your development goals.

- Make your development step your number-one task on your daily "to do" list.

- Link your goals with something you are already doing. Take a moment each day to examine the development opportunities that are right in front of you. Make sure your learning permeates your schedule.

- As you look at the day, figure out how you can practice the behavior you want to increase, improve, or fine-tune.

- Identify the situations, people, events, and other triggers that will remind you to try new behaviors related to your learning objective.

- Break out of your normal routine. When you are locked in to your comfortable habits, you are less able to adapt to changing situations. Search for innovative ways to approach the situations you deal with every day.

- Allow your employees to teach you. Spend time with all the people in your department who have the expertise and skills you need. Ask them questions.

- Be flexible and take advantage of opportunities as they arise. Some learning just happens without much planning or forethought.

- Consider using PDI's eAdvisor™ or DevelopMentor® to help make development plans and to find quick, on-the-job help on a daily basis. Both tools provide a library of advice for self-development, including practical tips, exercises, resource lists, and development suggestions and ideas to help you improve and learn. They also contain guidance for common problems encountered by leaders.

Make your learning more efficient

To progress in an organization, you need to continue learning. Sometimes the not-so-obvious experiences turn out to offer the most powerful learning opportunities. Training yourself to take advantage of a broad variety of experiences can accelerate your learning and development. To increase your "learning quotient," consider the following:

- Determine your own most effective learning style. Some people learn best from observing others; others learn best by trial and error; still others learn best by reading. Emphasize the style that works best for you.

- Get involved in a variety of experiences to maximize your development. High-quality learning most often comes from a wide range of life activities, not just a few.

- Admit your weaknesses and compensate for them by surrounding yourself with people who are skilled in those areas. For example, hire employees who have strengths that you lack. Not only can you learn from them, but your team will be more well-rounded and synergistic.

- View your strengths as development opportunities. Typically, your greatest successes will come from leveraging your strengths. Broaden and improve your strengths by finding new ways to use these skills, by teaching them to others, and by pursuing assignments that stretch your skills even further.

- Experiment and take intelligent risks each day. Seek out "high-voltage" situations, such as projects that are highly visible to others or ones that give you an opportunity to work with new people.

- Determine how effectively you handle your emotions by answering these questions:
  - Do I worry too much about what others think and, as a result, allow my actions to be unduly influenced by their opinions?
  - Do I tend to be out of touch with my emotions and take action without tuning in to my own feelings or considering the feelings of others?
  - Do I express too little or too much emotion?

  Successful learners effectively tune in to their emotions and use them to help guide their decisions and enhance their effectiveness.

Get the most out of readings and seminars

While the most powerful development experiences often occur on the job, readings and seminars are also good ways to gain knowledge and skills for your current and future job responsibilities. Use the following suggestions to ensure that you get the most out of readings and seminars:

- Rather than reading an entire book, scan the table of contents to determine which sections are most relevant. Then read just these sections.

- Search for one insight or application in everything you read. It is more beneficial to read one article and learn from it than to lightly skim five articles and take away nothing of substance. Work hard when you are reading by drawing conclusions and searching for meanings relevant to your development.

- Choose learning experiences that are relevant to your learning objectives and give you a chance to practice and apply new information and skills.

- Be open to new ideas and innovations. Determine how you can implement them in your own area. Refine your ideas by discussing them with colleagues and staff.

- Build in time to reflect on and apply to your job what you have learned. Your behavior will not change simply because you have learned something from a book or training program.

Therefore, always determine what you will do with your new information or insight. Set a new goal and work on it.

Anticipate roadblocks that could sidetrack your development

People have a natural tendency to learn. Yet there are many roadblocks that can derail progress. It's important to anticipate possible barriers to your development so you are better prepared to address them. Consider the following suggestions:

- Show your development plans and goals to others. This will increase your commitment to attaining the goals and will involve others in your development. Specifically, ask for support and feedback in the areas you find toughest to master.

- Keep the development process simple. Complexity can make development feel intimidating rather than motivational.

EXCUSE ME – I BELIEVE THAT'S MY CAREER PATH YOU'RE STANDING IN.

- Lean into your discomfort. Accept that change and development may feel frightening or ambiguous at times. Remind yourself that this feeling is only temporary.

- Be patient and realize that change takes time. Real behavioral change feels natural and easy only with persistence and practice.

- Be aware of what happens when your progress begins to slip. Keep track of situations that cause you difficulty and figure out how to address them.

- Redefine success by separating what you are learning from how you are performing. Ask, "What have I just learned?" rather than "How did I just do?"

PART 4:
EXTRACT MAXIMUM LEARNING FROM YOUR EXPERIENCES

Reflect on what you have learned

Development and change require both action and reflection. Focused reflection allows you to identify themes and patterns in your behavior to ensure that you continue to apply the lessons you have learned. Reflection makes learning a conscious process. Consider the following suggestions:

- Create a regular time for reflection. Take advantage of the following natural cycles for reflection:
  - Regular daily events, such as your commute to and from work, can be a good time to reflect on lessons of the day.
  - Periodic reviews, such as at the beginning of each month or quarter, provide an opportunity to consolidate your lessons over a period.
  - Major events, such as completion of a long-term assignment, offer opportunities to debrief what went well and what needed improvement. Reflection at the midpoint of a large assignment also makes sense, because you then still have a chance to make course corrections.

- Take stock of what happened. Ask yourself what went well, what did not go well, and how you will handle a similar situation in the future.

- Learn from your successes by examining them and determining exactly what you did to succeed. Then look for opportunities to transfer your behaviors and skills to other situations.

- Tune in to your emotions. Use negative emotions to motivate you, to draw your attention to something that may need changing, or to identify areas of future growth. Also pay attention to positive emotions, such as feelings of satisfaction, and think about what you did to experience them.

- Consider keeping a learning log to track and document your lessons and progress.

View mistakes as learning opportunities

Viewing mistakes and failures as learning opportunities builds a foundation for further learning. Mistakes often prompt people to look inward and evaluate their limitations and shortcomings, learning more about themselves in the process. Mistakes are a problem only if you repeat them or don't learn from them.

Try the following suggestions to turn your mistakes into learning opportunities:

- The next time you attempt something and fail, ask yourself, "What have I learned?" Write down what you learned, as well as possible ways to do things differently the next time.

- Share your mistakes. Talking through a mistake with others will increase your understanding of the situation. Solicit ideas on what you might do differently in the future. When you can openly share your mistakes with others, they will become more comfortable sharing their mistakes with you. You can also learn valuable lessons from others' mistakes.

- Focus on your role in the failure, rather than looking at what others did or didn't do. Avoid any temptation to blame others. Instead, examine what you did or failed to do so that you can learn from your actions to create more success in the future.

- When you make a mistake, ask yourself and others, if appropriate, if you have made a similar mistake in the past. You can gain powerful insights by studying patterns of behavior that have resulted in repeated mistakes, miscalculations, or misreading of a situation.

- If you have not made a mistake lately, ask yourself:
  - Am I challenging myself in my job and outside of work?
  - Am I requesting or hearing feedback from others?
  - Am I taking any risks?

PART 5:
LEARN FROM OTHERS' IDEAS AND PERSPECTIVES

Involve others in your development efforts

Effective development rarely happens in isolation. Rather, successful learning occurs through a continuous process of feedback and support from others. Consider the following suggestions for involving others in your learning pursuits:

- Realize that no single person will fill all of your development and feedback needs, so keep a diverse list of people who can support your development. Colleagues, direct reports, managers, team leaders, human resources staff, role models and mentors, and family and friends can all support your development in various ways.

- Involve other people in testing your assumptions and conclusions to ensure that you are on the right track. Choose people who will give you candid feedback and encourage you to take risks.

- Ask other people about significant events in their careers to understand the experiences and challenges you are likely to face as you assume greater responsibility.

- Observe others who are skilled or savvy in the areas you are attempting to develop. Note what they do well and what they don't do well. Integrate the positive aspects into your own behavior.

- Learn from people outside of work. Leaders from other professions or organizations, as well as community leaders, can serve as effective coaches and role models. They may be able to expose you to skills, styles, and techniques that you have not found in your current situation.

Seek honest feedback from others

Getting personal feedback is like finding your location on a map. While it's important to know where you've been and what is your destination, it's also critical to have an accurate picture of where you are now. Ongoing and honest feedback from others will allow you to continue to develop.

Many people are reluctant to give feedback, especially negative feedback. As a result, if you wait for others to offer their feedback, you may never get it. It's up to you to actively solicit the feedback you need to grow and develop. The following suggestions can help you do so:

- Before you solicit feedback from others, decide what to ask for. Ask questions that effectively uncover what you are trying to learn about yourself. For example, if you are just beginning to work on something, broad feedback is likely to be most helpful. Or, you may want feedback on different elements at different times. Let others know before they observe you what feedback will be most helpful, so they know what to look for.

- Actively seek feedback from your manager on a continuing basis. He or she can be a valuable source of feedback for self-improvement. Ask for specific comments, suggestions, and feedback in areas you are attempting to improve.

- Encourage your employees and peers to provide feedback. Ask them how you can be more effective in your job. Also ask what you might change to help them be more effective in their jobs.

- Cultivate key feedback sources. Identify two or three people from whom you can regularly seek feedback.

- Solicit feedback from others at the end of projects. Ask them what you did that was effective and what you did that was not effective. Once you have thought about the feedback and have decided how you'd like to do things differently the next time, ask them to observe you in this specific area on a future project and provide you with additional feedback.

- When someone gives you vague feedback, either positive or negative (for example, "nice job"), ask for specifics on what you did well or where your performance was lacking.

- Express your appreciation to those who give you feedback. Then put relevant feedback to visible use. If others see that you act on the feedback you receive, they will be more willing to give you constructive, honest feedback in the future.

- Obtain comprehensive feedback on your skills using multi-rater or 360-degree feedback instruments available through Personnel Decisions International or your organization.

Respond openly to feedback

Feedback, especially constructive or negative feedback, can evoke an automatic defensive response. Defensiveness, however, interferes with your ability to hear and understand the information others are giving you. More important, it can cause others to stop giving you honest feedback and information that you need to learn and grow.

The following suggestions can help you keep feedback channels open and overcome the tendency to be defensive:

- View defensiveness as your worst enemy. Don't argue, don't explain, and don't debate the feedback. If you become defensive, others will be reluctant to give you feedback in the future, and you will cut off a critical information source.

- Check your response patterns for phrases such as "Yes, but…" and eliminate them from your speech. Whenever you catch yourself explaining why, stop talking and listen. Explanations are often perceived as a defensive response.

- When you are feeling defensive, stop and ask yourself a fixed set of rational/ analytical questions, such as the following, to help diminish your defensiveness:
  - Do I understand exactly what is being said?
  - Is the criticism about a situation or behavior I could change if I wanted to?
  - What would happen if I acted on the feedback?

- Avoid seeking feedback when you are emotionally "on edge," when you are upset with the feedback giver, or when you do not intend to use the feedback.

- Use discretion when sharing your point of view. First, summarize the feedback to ensure that you fully heard and understood it. Second, share your point of view only if the other person has expressed an interest in hearing it.

- Ask trusted colleagues to tell you when you are appearing defensive. Eliminate or change the behavior they have labeled as defensive, even if you do not agree with their point of view. Their perception of your behavior is reality; it is what they believe to be true.

Use development partners to support your development

You need support to sustain your learning progress, to stay committed when your enthusiasm fades, and to persist when the going gets tough. A development support network can help keep your learning pursuits alive. Consider the following suggestions:

- Choose development partners who can help you learn and who care about your development. Actively search for development partners who:
  - Have access to resources you could use.
  - Know other people who could help you.
  - Are good at something you struggle with.
  - Can help keep you on track.
  - You trust.
  - Are willing to be candid with you.

- Share your goals, strengths, expectations, fears, and development strategies with your development partners.

- Find ways to provide mutual encouragement and accountability to each other.

- Consult your development partners when you find yourself straying off course.

PART 6:
ADAPT AND PLAN FOR CONTINUED LEARNING

Transfer learning into next steps

Even though the learning process is continuous, it is helpful to take a break and reflect on where you have been, where you are now, and where you want to go next. Periodically evaluating your progress, updating your development strategy and learning plan, and leveraging what you have already learned are effective ways to maintain strong momentum and keep your learning alive. The following suggestions can help you in this area:

- Evaluate your progress on a regular basis. Create success criteria for each learning objective so you can effectively measure your progress.

- Take time to celebrate and acknowledge your progress and accomplishments. Personal recognition builds self-confidence and feelings of personal worth, and provides renewed energy for your continued growth.

- Create additional opportunities to apply what you have learned. Using your new skills will ensure that you keep them sharp and up-to-date.

- Advance to the next level of mastery. For example, seek experience in a new, complex situation. Force yourself to face additional challenges that will push your limits.

- If you feel stuck or your development efforts have not been successful so far, regroup and correct your course. Revisit your learning plan and make necessary changes in your approach. Review your objectives and actions with others, and seek their candid feedback and advice.

- Take a break to recharge your batteries before your next development challenge. Take stock of what development strategies and tactics worked best so you can apply them in your future development efforts.

- Focus on new goals. Update your competency portfolio, or GAPS grid, to include your newly developed skills. Then reanalyze your portfolio to determine your next development priority.

RESOURCES

The resources begin on page 684.

RESOURCES
BY CHAPTER

Many of the books in this section are available in several languages other than English, through different publishers in various countries. Please contact the original publishers listed to find out if a book is available in a specific language.

Many of the seminars are also offered in languages other than English through customized programs offered within an organization (in-house). Please contact the vendors for more information.

**Chapter 1
Create Strategic
Advantage**

Gubman, Edward L. *The Talent Solution: Aligning Strategy and People to Achieve Extraordinary Results*. New York: McGraw-Hill, 1998.
ISBN: 0070251614
The economy is booming but companies are finding it harder to fill positions and keep good people. *The Talent Solution* holds the key to leveraging a company's most vital competitive advantage—its people. More than a quick fix, *The Talent Solution* enables managers to transform their organization into a world-class competitor.

Hamel, Gary, and Prahalad, C.K. *Competing for the Future.*
Boston: Harvard Business School Press, 1994.
ISBN: 0875844162
The authors postulate that managers in today's most successful firms are more interested in creating new competitive space than positioning themselves in the existing market. This book shows how to develop stretch goals and build core competencies to create advantage and new markets for the future.

Kaplan, Robert S., and Norton, David P. *Balanced Scorecard: Translating Strategy into Action.* Boston: Harvard Business School Press, 1996.
ISBN: 0875846513
The authors provide a framework for translating a company's visions and strategy into a coherent set of performance measures. In addition, they discuss how to channel employees' energies, abilities, and specific knowledge toward long-term goals.

Mintzberg, Henry, and Quinn, James B. *Readings in the Strategy Process.*
Englewood Cliffs, NJ: Prentice Hall, 1998.
ISBN: 0134949641
This collection of readings presents an up-to-date look at how actual companies act strategically and the research driving them. While retaining many of the classic articles, this edition includes new organization and strategy concepts to emerge in the last few years.

Porter, Michael E. *Competitive Strategy: Techniques for Analyzing Industries and Competitors.*
New York: Free Press, 1998.
ISBN: 0684841487
Porter's classic book outlines a comprehensive set of analytical techniques for understanding an organization and the behavior of its competitors. He presents techniques to help leaders anticipate and prepare for sudden competitor moves or shifts in industry structure.

Treacy, Michael, and Wiersma, Fred. *The Discipline of Market Leaders.*
Reading, MA: Perseus Books, 1997.
ISBN: 0201407191
This book highlights how companies that are market leaders have focused attention and resources on different things. Market leaders excel in one of the customer value disciplines: best cost, best product, or best solution. Focusing on one of these disciplines means knowing which one to choose, designing the organization around it, and offering better value year after year.

Ulrich, Dave, and Lake, Dale. *Organizational Capability.*
Reading, MA: Perseus Books, 1997.
ISBN: 0471618071
The authors go beyond the premise that the people of a company are its most important asset by introducing "organizational capability." This concept helps organizations realize their potential from the inside out. Based on the authors' extensive research and first-hand experience, this book offers both a strategic overview of organizational capability and precise guidelines for putting it into action.

SEMINARS

Creating Strategic Leverage
SLC Consultants, Inc.

This workshop provides the missing link between strategy theory and the operating decisions business managers make every day. Participants learn to exploit opportunities in any given market, avoid common mistakes, translate common planning tools into action, refocus resources from current tactical problems to future opportunities, and drive strategic thinking throughout.

Length: 2 days
Price: $1,595
Location: Chicago, IL
Tel: 312-346-7797
Fax: 312-346-9563
URL: http://www.slc-consultants.com/seminars/

Critical Thinking: A New Paradigm for Peak Performance
American Management Association

This three-day workshop teaches managers how to expand their thinking skills, how to fully consider all sides of an issue, and how to anticipate a broad range of possibilities. It presents a holistic process that can be applied to the day-to-day course of conducting business.

Length: 3 days
Price: $1,525
Location: See Web site for dates and locations.
Tel: 800-262-9699
Fax: 212-903-8168
URL: http://www.amanet.org

Return On People™
Personnel Decisions International

Through interactive sessions and exercises, participants in this program learn how to identify and increase the value of their organization's human capital. Skills covered include analyzing human capital value, identifying the economic impact of human capital investments, and building partnerships with other company functions. Customized and available for delivery within an organization.

Price: Call vendor.
Tel: 800-633-4410
Fax: 612-904-7120
URL: http://www.personneldecisions.com

Tools and Techniques for Thinking and Managing Strategically
American Management Association

A proving ground for strategic management ideas, this seminar leads participants through realistic business scenarios. Participants learn to analyze internal and external business factors to identify, manage, and adapt to the swift changes that characterize today's business climate.

Length: 3 days
Price: $1,525
Location: See Web site for dates and locations.
Tel: 800-262-9699
Fax: 212-903-8168
URL: http://www.amanet.org

**Chapter 2
Champion
Change and
Innovation**

Chopra, A. J. *Managing the People Side of Innovation: 8 Rules for Engaging Minds and Hearts.* West Hartford, CT: Kumerian Press, Inc., 1999.
ISBN: 1565490983
At the heart of Chopra's approach is the recognition of how important people's ideas are to their sense of themselves and of how, by doing the right thing with ideas, organizations can tap powerful sources of motivation. This book will greatly increase the effectiveness of anyone charged with making an innovation happen.

Grove, Andrew S. *Only the Paranoid Survive: How to Exploit the Crisis Points that Challenge Every Company and Career.* New York: Currency Doubleday, 1996.
ISBN: 0385482582
Grove, CEO of Intel, attributes much of his company's success to what he calls Strategic Inflection Points—moments when massive change occurs and all bets are off. SIPs can be set off by almost anything: mega-competition, change in regulations, or a change in technology. Managed right, a company can turn a SIP into a positive force to win in the marketplace and emerge stronger than ever.

Kodama, Fumio. *Emerging Patterns of Innovation, Sources of Japan's Technological Edge.* Boston: Harvard Business School Press, 1995.
ISBN: 0875844375
Kodama provides a well-substantiated model that sheds light on competition in technology across the globe. The author isolates six areas of constant change in business, and, using scientific methods, case studies, and historical perspective, illustrates the ways technology is changing business innovation.

Kotter, John P. *Leading Change.* Boston: Harvard Business School Press, 1996.
ISBN: 0875847471
One of the world's foremost experts on business leadership distills 25 years of experience and wisdom into this visionary guide. Kotter outlines what it will take to lead the organization of the 21st century.

Leonard-Barton, Dorothy, and Swap, Walter C. *When Sparks Fly: Igniting Creativity in Groups.* Boston: Harvard Business School Press, 1999.
ISBN: 0875848656
Group creativity is the key to success in many organizations. The authors provide a comprehensive look at developing creativity in a group setting, including their five-step process. The book includes examples of corporate innovation and a psychology-based look at human creativity.

Robinson, Alan G., and Stern, Sam. *Corporate Creativity: How Innovation and Improvement Actually Happen.* San Francisco: Barrett-Koehler Publishers, 1997.
ISBN: 1576750493
This book outlines six essential elements to a corporation's creative process. Using real-life corporate examples of their ideas in action, the authors show how imagination and originality can lead to improvements and breakthroughs.

SEMINARS

Breakthrough Performance: Driving Innovation by Unleashing Creativity in Your Organization
University of South Carolina, Daniel Management Center

This seminar is designed to help managers develop the competencies to become champions of innovation.
Length: 2 days
Price: $845
Location: Columbia, SC
Tel: 803-777-2231
Fax: 803-777-4447
URL: http://www.uscdmc.org

Leading Corporate Renewal
IMD

This program teaches participants to apply change-management concepts and frameworks to their own organization by exploring the key issues and best practices in implementing change. Participants work on their own organization's change issues and formulate a strategy for action.
Length: 2 weeks
Price: Fr14,000
Location: Lausanne, Switzerland
Tel: 41-21-618-0342
Fax: 41-21-618-0715
URL: http://www.imd.ch

Leading Organizational Change
University of Pennsylvania, Wharton Executive Education

This seminar shows change as a natural process that can be continuously nurtured within organizations. Through simulations, case studies, group presentations, and videotapes, participants develop and practice the skills needed to recognize, adjust to, and facilitate change.
Length: 6 days
Price: $6,950
Location: Philadelphia, PA
Tel: 800-255-3932 (U.S. and Canada) or 215-898-1776 (worldwide)
Fax: 215-898-2064
URL: http://www.wharton.upenn.edu/execed

Managing Technology and Strategic Innovation
Stanford University, Graduate School of Business

Participants in this program learn how to analyze strategies for managing innovation, explore ways to encourage creativity and change, assess the process of innovation within their organizations, and develop an action plan to improve that process.
Length: 1 week
Price: $5,700
Location: Stanford, CA
Tel: 650-723-3341
Fax: 650-723-3950
URL: http://www-gsb.stanford.edu/eep

**Chapter 3
Create
Customer Loyalty**

Heskett, James L.; Sasser, Earl W.; and Schlesinger, James L. *The Service Profit Chain: How Leading Companies Link Profit and Growth to Loyalty, Satisfaction, and Value.*
New York: Free Press, 1997.
ISBN: 0684832569
Directly linking profit and growth to customer loyalty and employee productivity, the authors present a step-by-step action plan for managing, marketing, hiring, delivering services, and assessing results. In-depth case examples and 50 line drawings demonstrate how the best companies have handled this challenge.

Hiebler, Robert, et al. *Best Practices: Building Your Business with Customer-Focused Solutions.*
New York: Simon & Schuster, 1998.
ISBN: 0684834537
Arthur Andersen shares its data and understanding of how companies worldwide focus on their customers, create growth, reduce cost, and increase profits. This book concentrates primarily on customers and how to involve them in everything from the design of products and services to marketing, selling, and product delivery.

Howe, Roger J.; Gaeddert, Dee; and Howe, Maynard A. *Quality on Trial.*
New York: McGraw-Hill, 1995.
ISBN: 0070305838
Based on the work and experience of Personnel Decisions International's Customer-Centered Solutions, this book focuses on just that—solutions that can reenergize companies with new business and committed customers. It explains how to manage customers in order to build and improve relationships, as well as solidify the relationships for the benefit of the company, its employees, and its future.

Peppers, Don, and Rogers, Martha. *Enterprise One to One: Tools for Competing in the Interactive Age.* New York: Currency Doubleday, 1999.
ISBN: 038548755X
Companies today need to harness technology for competitive advantage. The authors explain what strategies are applicable under what circumstances, how to retain customers and increase business, how to create entirely new markets of individual customers, and how to make the transition to the interactive age—all by taking advantage of new technology.

Reichheld, Frederick F. *The Loyalty Effect: The Hidden Force behind Growth, Profits, and Lasting Value.* Boston: Harvard Business School Press, 1996.
ISBN: 0875844480
U.S. corporations now lose half their customers in five years, half their employees in four, and half their investors in less than one. *The Loyalty Effect* reveals the secrets of successful companies that base their business strategies on loyal relationships. Reichheld lays out the principles that connect value creation, loyalty, growth, and profits, and shows how great companies have used these principles to build loyal customers, loyal employees, and loyal owners.

Zemke, Ron, and Woods, John A. *Best Practices in Customer Service.*
New York: AMACOM, 1998.
ISBN: 0814470289
Zemke and Woods have combined 35 articles that clarify the connection between great customer service and superior organizational performance. Readers will come to a better understanding of what consumers really want and how to create systems that will meet their demands.

SEMINARS

Achieving Breakthrough Service
Harvard Business School

Managers of service, retail, manufacturing, and information systems firms learn how to differentiate "merely good" from "breakthrough" service, helping them improve their companies' profitability and growth.

Length: 1 week
Price: $7,500
Location: Boston, MA
Tel: 617-495-6226
Fax: 617-495-6999
URL: http://www.exed.hbs.edu

Achieving Service Excellence
The Forum Corporation

This seminar is designed for anyone in an organization who serves internal or external customers. It teaches the participants to understand how to deliver excellent service, deal with customer relationships, improve teamwork, and close gaps in service quality.

Length: 2 days
Price: Call vendor.
Location: Boston, MA
Tel: 800-FORUM11 (800-367-8611)
URL: http://www.forum.com

Building Relationships with Customers
Personnel Decisions International

Designed to cover the basics of managing customer relationships, this program outlines techniques for dealing with and responding to customer requests and complaints. Participants practice skills in communicating with customers, maintaining exceptional customer service, and coaching others to reinforce and establish strong customer relationships. Customized and available for delivery within an organization.

Tel: 800-633-4410
Fax: 612-904-7120
URL: http://www.personneldecisions.com

The Disney Approach to Customer Loyalty
Walt Disney World

Participants learn the best practices and business strategies to win and retain loyal customers. Attendees will have the opportunity to see Disney's core philosophies in action in everyday business situations.

Length: 4 days
Price: $2,695
Location: Lake Buena Vista, FL
Tel: 407-828-1039
URL: http://www.disneyseminars.com

**Chapter 4
Promote Global
Perspective**

Bryan, Lowell L., et al. *Race for the World: Strategies to Build a Great Global Firm.*
Boston: Harvard Business School Press, 1999.
ISBN: 087584846X
Looking at the vast changes in the world's economy that are altering business, the authors assert that geographic barriers to business will virtually disappear over the next 30 years and that the implications for companies could be devastating—or incredibly rewarding. "Over time, the only class that matters will be world class," they write. "All others will be forced to restructure or go out of business."

Kanter, Rosabeth Moss. *World Class: Thriving Locally in the Global Economy.*
New York: Simon & Schuster, 1995.
ISBN: 0684611294
This book addresses how local companies and communities can reap profits and flourish by tapping into global business networks. The author presents a detailed action agenda for both business and community leaders that will enable them to achieve their mutually beneficial goals.

Mobley, William H.; Gessner, Jocelyne M.; and Arnold, Val. *Advances in Global Leadership, Vol. 1.* Stamford, CT: JAI Press, 1999.
ISBN: 0762305053
Individuals interested in global leadership will find the latest academic research on global leadership models and definitions in this book. The authors use a wide-ranging approach, including perspectives from multiple cultures, on such topics as international business and management, organizational behavior, and leadership development processes.

Morrison, Teresa C., et al. *Dun & Bradstreet's Guide to Doing Business around the World.*
Englewood Cliffs, NJ: Prentice Hall, 1997.
ISBN: 0135314844
This reference lays out the demographics for the 40 countries identified as America's top trading partners, covering everything from work standards to the religious, social, and political influences in each country. It also includes five cultural tips for each country that are vital to doing business there, as well as country ratings based on political risk, monetary and trade policy, protection of intellectual property rights, and foreign investment climate.

Root, Franklin R. *Entry Strategies for International Markets: Revised and Expanded.*
San Francisco: Jossey-Bass, 1998.
ISBN: 0787945714
Revised and expanded, this book represents the latest word on an evolving and complex subject. Root offers recent examples of company practices and greater detail on the complexities of global integration.

Rosen, Robert; Digh, Patricia; Singer, Marshall; and Phillips, Carl.
Global Literacies: Lessons on Business Leadership and National Cultures.
New York: Simon & Schuster, 2000.
ISBN: 0684859025
Over 1,000 senior executives around the globe weigh in on the universal leadership skills and cultural knowledge leaders need to survive in today's borderless, global marketplace. A team of researchers led by Robert Rosen, Ph.D., of Healthy Companies International, presents the exclusive results of in-depth interviews with CEOs of 78 companies representing 3.5 million employees in more than 200 countries.

SEMINARS

Financial Issues in Global Competition
Thunderbird Executive Education
This seminar gives mid- and upper-level managers a working knowledge of the financial, accounting, and control issues that arise as an organization becomes global. Topics covered include management of foreign exchange and interest rate risk, capital expenditure analysis, international performance measurement, and control systems.
Length: 1 week
Price: $4,300
Location: Glendale, AZ
Tel: 602-978-7634 or 7925
Fax: 602-439-4851 or 602-978-0362
URL: http://www.t-bird.edu

Globalization: Merging Strategy with Action
Thunderbird Executive Education
Corporate strategy, human resources management, cross-cultural communication, and operations management all have special characteristics in a globally competitive industry. Participants learn how to become better managers in a world where competition is global, complex, and intense.
Length: 1 week
Price: $4,300
Location: Glendale, AZ
Tel: 602-978-7634 or 7925
Fax: 602-439-4851 or 602-978-0362
URL: http://www.t-bird.edu

Managing International Expansions in Global Markets
University of Michigan Business School
Ideally suited for managers responsible for entering, developing, and operating business in foreign markets, this program teaches participants to analyze international economics and understand complex cultural, economic, and governmental influences in the global business environment. The course covers business operations in Latin America, Asia, and Europe.
Length: 5 days
Price: $5,320
Location: Ann Arbor, MI
Tel: 734-763-1003
Fax: 734-763-9467
URL: http://www.bus.umich.edu/execed

**Chapter 5
Analyze Issues**

Browne, M. Neil, and Keeley, Stuart M. *Asking the Right Questions: A Guide to Critical Thinking.* Englewood Cliffs, NJ: Prentice Hall, 1997.
ISBN: 0137581866
Focusing on the question-asking skills and techniques necessary for evaluating different types of evidence, this book addresses critical thinking as a skill with many applications while also emphasizing moral reasoning as an integral part of critical thinking. Illustrating the system of "right" questions, it provides extensive treatment of evidence while analyzing the biases that hinder critical thinking.

Chang, Richard Y., and Kelly, Keith P. *Step-by-Step Problem Solving: A Practical Guide to Ensure Problems Get (and Stay) Solved.*
Irvine, CA: Richard Chang Associates, 1999.
ISBN: 0787950785
Taking a common-sense approach to problem solving and providing a wealth of practical examples to apply on the job, this book helps the reader define problems, analyze causes, identify solutions, develop action plans, implement solutions, and evaluate progress. It includes reproducible forms.

Kepner, Charles H., and Iikubo, Hirotsugu. *Managing beyond the Ordinary.*
New York: AMACOM, 1996.
ISBN: 0814403360
Kepner and Iikubo supply the hands-on, how-to guidance every manager needs to master the principles and process of collaboration. The author's ten-step model will help readers understand problems, determine what is causing them, decide who needs to be involved in problem resolution, create a workable plan, and implement it.

Mitchell, Donald; Coles, Carol; and Metz, Robert. *The 2,000 Percent Solution: Free Your Organization from "Stalled" Thinking to Achieve Exponential Success.*
New York: AMACOM, 1999.
ISBN: 0814404766
The authors argue that organizations' ingrained habits, which often masquerade as efficient procedures, actually obstruct true growth. As a solution, they introduce "stallbusting," a process to help readers recognize stalled thinking and overcome it.

Mitroff, Ian I., and Linstone, Harold A. *The Unbounded Mind: Breaking the Chains of Traditional Business Thinking.* New York: Oxford University Press, 1996.
ISBN: 0195102886
Global markets, Japanese competition, the service economy, the sophisticated consumer—American business today faces challenges undreamed of just a few decades ago. In this groundbreaking work, two pioneering thinkers pinpoint the profound changes that must occur in the way executives think, make decisions, and solve problems in order for their businesses to remain competitive.

Newman, Victor. *Problem Solving for Results.*
Brookfield, VT: Ashgate Publishing Company, 1995.
ISBN: 0566075660
This book offers managers and team leaders a framework for solving problems on both the personal and organizational level, identifying eight stages of problem solving, and how to recognize which technique is appropriate to each stage. The author also discusses obstacles to developing a problem-solving style and managing stress.

SEMINARS

Critical Thinking: A New Paradigm for Peak Performance
American Management Association
This workshop teaches participants how to build and expand their thinking skills to fully consider all sides of an issue and anticipate a broader range of possibilities. Participants learn how to better assess and develop thinking preferences, optimal thinking time, and ability to influence others.
Length: 3 days
Price: $1,525
Location: See Web site for dates and locations.
Tel: 800-262-9699
Fax: 212-903-8168
URL: http://www.amanet.org

Critical Thinking
Management Concepts, Inc.
This seminar is designed for those who want to improve their ability to analyze ideas, evaluate information, and challenge assumptions. Participants learn how to analyze an argument, how to use deductive and inductive arguments, how to argue effectively, and how to work with diverse problem-solving styles.
Length: 1 day
Price: $185
Location: Vienna, VA
Tel: 703-790-9595 and press 4
Fax: 703-790-1371
URL: http://www.mgmtconcepts.com

Problem Solving and Decision Making
Viability Group Inc.
For managers at all levels, this step-by-step workshop shows how to confront unclear situations, short-term crises, long-term problems, people barriers, and interpersonal tensions. The workshop is based on a comprehensive six-stage formula, which shows how to reliably identify, define, unravel, analyze, and resolve recurring technical symptoms and tough people dilemmas.
Length: Call vendor.
Price: Call vendor.
Location: Call vendor.
Tel: 530-587-1317
Fax: 530-587-9056
URL: http://www.viabilitygroup.com

Six Thinking Hats®
Innova Training and Consulting, Inc.
This seminar is designed to help participants become more effective in solving problems, making decisions, and thinking creatively. Participants learn to use factual information, emotions and intuitions, positive perspective, caution and risk, creativity, and organization when solving problems.
Languages: Spanish, German, English, Portuguese, Turkish, French, Italian, Japanese, Mandarin, Thai, Dutch, Swedish, Finnish
Length: 1 or 2 days
Price: Call vendor, prices vary by location.
Location: See Web site for dates and locations.
Tel: 877-334-2687 or 515-334-2687
Fax: 515-278-2245
URL: http://www.innovatraining.com

**Chapter 6
Use Sound
Judgment**

Bazerman, Max H. *Judgment in Managerial Decision Making*.
New York: John Wiley & Sons, 1997.
ISBN: 0471178071
Decision making plays a crucial role in managerial life. But too often, our decisions are clouded by personal biases and uncertainty. This brief book shows readers how to identify their own biases in order to make better decisions. Experimental in approach, the book teaches decision making by involving the reader in decision quizzes.

Hammond, John. *Smart Choices: A Practical Guide to Making Better Decisions*.
Boston: Harvard Business School Press, 1998.
ISBN: 0875848575
Smart Choices outlines eight elements involved in making the right decision, including identifying exactly what the decision is, specifying objectives, considering risk tolerance, and looking at how today's decisions influence tomorrow's decisions.

Heller, Robert, and Hindle, Tom. *Essential Managers: Making Decisions (DK Business Guides)*. New York: DK Publishing, Inc., 1999.
ISBN: 078942889X
This innovative new series covers a wide range of business topics relevant to every manager's work environment, from large corporations to small businesses. Concise treatments of dozens of business techniques, approaches, skills, methods, and problems are presented with hundreds of photos, charts, and diagrams.

Klein, Gary. *Sources of Power: How People Make Decisions*.
Cambridge, MA: MIT Press, 1998.
ISBN: 0262112272
Klein presents an overview of naturalistic decision making and explains the strengths people bring to difficult tasks. His work is based on observations of people acting under real-life constraints such as time pressure, high stakes, personal responsibility, and shifting conditions.

Mitroff, Gary. *Smart Thinking for Crazy Times: The Art of Solving the Right Problems*.
San Francisco: Berrett-Koehler, 1998.
ISBN: 1576750205
Mitroff demonstrates that the majority of serious management errors can be traced to one fundamental flaw: solving the wrong problems. He introduces a process to help readers focus on the right problems, frame them correctly, and implement appropriate solutions.

Zambruski, Michael S. *The Business Analyzer and Planner: The Unique Process for Solving Problems, Finding Opportunities, and Making Better Decisions Every Day*.
New York: AMACOM, 1999.
ISBN: 0814479847
The seven-phase process outlined in this book helps readers get out of the rut of using guesswork, intuition, and habit to make decisions. The process explains how to perform a preliminary diagnosis of the situation, evaluate underlying business issues, determine necessary resources, select a realistic course of action, prepare a detailed business plan, monitor its success or failure, and develop backup plans.

SEMINARS

Critical Thinking: Real-World, Real-Time Decisions
University of Pennsylvania, Wharton Executive Education

Participants learn a sound process for framing problems and making decisions, including identifying the key elements of decisions, defining the right problem, and identifying tradeoffs and choices.

Length: 3 days
Price: $4,750
Location: Philadelphia, PA
Tel: 215-898-1775
Fax: 215-386-4304
URL: http://www.wharton.upenn.edu/execed

Problem Solving and Decision Making
Kepner Tregoe

The key topics of this seminar include solving critical problems, making decisions in unclear circumstances, anticipating problems and opportunities, managing complex issues, and applying proven principles to on-the-job concerns.

Languages: English, French in Montreal, and Spanish in Puerto Rico
Length: 3 days
Price: $1,495
Location: See Web site for dates and locations.
Tel: 609-921-2806 or 800-537-6378
URL: http://www.kepner-tregoe.com

Problem Solving and Decision Making: Good Decisions, Good Solutions
American Management Association

This program teaches participants how to strike a balance between logical soundness and intuition when making decisions. Topics include: differentiating between problem solving and decision making, balancing logic and experience with creativity, evaluating options, and setting up criteria to evaluate decisions and monitor results.

Length: 3 days
Price: $1,445
Location: See Web site for dates and locations.
Tel: 800-262-9699
Fax: 212-903-8168
URL: http://www.amanet.org

**Chapter 7
Think
Strategically**

Collins, James C., and Porras, Jerry I. *Built to Last: Successful Habits of Visionary Companies.*
Reading, MA: Perseus Books, 1997.
ISBN: 0887307396
Groundbreaking research lead to this book, which challenges ideas about long-term success.
Using such companies as 3M, Merck, Walt Disney, and General Electric as examples, the
book identifies each company's BHAGs—Big, Hairy, Audacious Goals—and examines the
flexibility, ideology, and strong sense of purpose that make them achievable.

Lasher, William R. *Strategic Thinking for Smaller Businesses and Divisions.*
Malden, MA: Blackwell, 1999.
ISBN: 0631208399
This books uses systematic strategic analysis to apply the principles of strategy to smaller
businesses. It uses research findings to bring order to the chaos of a small company.
Step-by-step grounding in practical aspects of strategic management for the smaller business
will show readers how to set up a workable business plan and successfully develop and
implement strategy.

Sanders, T. Irene. *Strategic Thinking and the New Science: Planning in the Midst of Chaos,
Complexity, and Change.* New York: Free Press, 1998.
ISBN: 0684842688
This book illustrates how managers gain insight into future business trends, innovations, and
inventions, and keep one step ahead of their competitors, by applying scientific concepts
to the business world.

Schwartz, Peter. *The Art of the Long View: Planning for the Future in an Uncertain
World.* New York: Doubleday, 1996.
ISBN: 0385267320
One of the world's leading futurists—a consultant to clients as diverse as Volvo and the
White House—presents a revolutionary guide to planning for the future. A powerful tool
for developing strategic vision, this book reveals how to navigate the future by applying
the intuitive skills used by artists and musicians.

Slywotzky, Adrian J. *Value Migration: How to Think Several Moves Ahead of the Competition.*
Boston: Harvard Business School Press, 1996.
ISBN: 0875846327
This book directs readers to ask the right questions about their customers, business, and
industry to be able to recognize patterns of shifting value and stay ahead of the competition.
The authors maintain that the key is to create a superior business design based on a strategic
understanding of customers' highest priorities.

Van Der Heijden, Kees. *Scenarios: The Art of Strategic Conversation.*
Chichester, England: New York: John Wiley & Sons, 1996.
ISBN: 0471966398
The author shows how to use scenarios—a powerful new approach to strategic planning—
to pilot your company profitably through unknown territory. After tackling external
forces, he shows you how to apply the logic of scenario planning to internal forces as well.

Wells, Stuart III. *Choosing the Future: The Power of Strategic Thinking.*
Boston: Butterworth-Heinemann, 1997
ISBN: 0750698764
This book discusses the two parts of the term "strategic planning." Strategy is thinking;
planning is doing. Readers will have an increased understanding of strategic thinking and
an ability to create well thought-out strategies and operational plans that will continue to
grow their business.

SEMINARS

Dynamics of Strategy
London Business School

This program is designed to give senior managers a new way of developing and implementing strategy. Participants will learn how to capture the resources and competencies of their enterprise, upgrade performance and protect against risks, and pull ahead of the competition.
Length: 5 days
Price: £4,350
Location: London, UK
Tel: 44-171-706-6835
Fax: 44-171-724-6051
URL: http://www.lbs.lon.ac.uk/execed/

Lateral Thinking™
Innova Training and Consulting, Inc.

This program asserts that creative thinking is not a talent, but a skill that can be learned. Participants in this program learn "lateral thinking," an unorthodox problem-solving method. This deliberate, systematic process builds on individual strengths to improve creativity and innovation, leading to increased productivity and profit.
Languages: Spanish, German, English, Portuguese, Turkish, French, Italian, Japanese, Mandarin, Thai, Dutch, Swedish, Finnish
Length: 2 days
Price: Call vendor, prices vary by location.
Location: See Web site for dates and locations.
Tel: 877-334-2687 or 515-334-2687
Fax: 515-278-2245
URL: http://www.innovatraining.com

Strategic Thinking and Management for Competitive Advantage
University of Pennsylvania, Wharton Executive Education

This program helps participants think strategically and use their resources more effectively. It is designed specifically to broaden one's perspective on how to make organizations more competitive.
Length: 1 week
Price: $6,950
Location: Philadelphia, PA
Tel: 215-898-1776
Fax: 215-386-4304
URL: http://www.wharton.upenn.edu/execed

CD-ROM

Serious Creativity
Advanced Practical Thinking Training®, Inc.

Access the innovative Lateral Thinking method for creative problem solving with a click of the mouse. This interactive tool outlines Dr. de Bono's systematic method of disrupting "vertical" logical thinking to arrive at unexpected solutions. Users learn the techniques and tools to leverage their own creativity for increased business success.
URL: http://www.aptt.com

**Chapter 8
Apply
Technical/
Functional
Expertise**

Celente, Gerald. *Trends 2000: How to Prepare for and Profit from the Changes of the 21st Century*. New York: Warner Books, 1998.
ISBN: 0446673315
This practical guide for the future details major trends in financial, environmental, political, sociological/sexual, communications/technological, medical, and artistic/philosophical areas, helping readers make sound business, career, and personal decisions.

Keen, Peter G. W., and Knapp, Ellen M. *Every Manager's Guide to Business Processes: A Glossary of Key Terms and Concepts for Today's Business Leader*.
Boston: Harvard Business School Press, 1995.
ISBN: 0875845754
Reengineering, total quality management, time-based competition—this is an invaluable reference to these and other process-based movements that have transformed business practices. Presented as a selective glossary of key business process concepts and terms, the book helps managers sort the hype from the reality and create business process advantages in their marketplace.

Silbiger, Steven. *The Ten-Day MBA: A Step-by-Step Guide to Mastering the Skills Taught in America's Top Business Schools*. New York: W. Morrow, 1999.
ISBN: 0688137881
Featuring chapters on finance, marketing, accounting, strategy, quantitative analysis, operations, economics, organizational behavior, and ethics, this guide helps readers master MBA jargon and theory.

SEMINARS

Enhancing Leadership Performance: The Leader as Teacher
University of Chicago, Graduate School of Business

Today's leaders are being called to build collaborative enterprises in which there are significant co-creating and sharing of information. In effect, colleagues are expected to regularly teach and learn from each other. This program will expand them to become leader and teacher.
Length: 1 week
Price: $4,650
Location: Chicago, IL
Tel: 312-464-8732
Fax: 312-464-8731
URL: http://gsb.uchicago.edu

General Management Program
Ashridge Management College

This program develops participants' ability to take a general management perspective in running the operational processes of their organization.
Length: 2 weeks
Price: £11,950 + VAT
Location: Berkhamsted, Hertfordshire, UK
Tel: 44-144-284-3491
Fax: 44-144-284-1209
URL: http://www.ashridge.org.uk

The Institute for Managerial Leadership for Engineers, Scientists, and Computer Professionals
University of Texas at Austin, Graduate School of Business

This program provides technical managers with an understanding of business strategy and corporate functions as well as skills for managing other professionals and communicating effectively. The participants are challenged to consider technology from a business perspective and to think strategically and globally about company goals.
Length: nine monthly sessions, 3 days/session
Price: $9,250
Location: Austin, TX, and Houston, TX
Tel: 512-471-5893
Fax: 512-471-0853
URL: http://www.bus.utexas.edu/execed

The Management Development Program
Asian Institute of Management

This program teaches leadership, teamwork, and communication skills needed to manage conflict and change, and provides participants with the opportunity to interact with a diverse group of executives from Asia and the rest of the world, thereby broadening their managerial perspectives.
Length: 8 weeks
Price: $6,095
Location: Makati City, Philippines
Tel: 632-892-4011
Fax: 632-817-9240
URL: http://www.aim.edu.ph

**Chapter 9
Use Financial
Acumen**

Fraser, Lyn M., and Ormiston, Aileen. *Understanding Financial Statements.*
Englewood Cliffs, NJ: Prentice Hall, 1997.
ISBN: 0136191150
A text on conceptual background and analytical tools for interpreting financial statements, this book covers the balance sheet, the income statement, retained earnings, statements of cash flow, and analysis of financial statements. Self-tests and answers, study questions and problems, and case studies are included in each chapter.

Helfert, Erich A. *Techniques of Financial Analysis: A Modern Approach (Techniques of Financial Analysis, 9th).* New York: McGraw-Hill, 1996.
ISBN: 0786311207
Helfert covers the most useful analytical tools and related financial concepts for making everyday financial decisions. He organizes the book according to types of financial decisions, making it easy to locate relevant information. It is written in a conversational style and includes self-study exercises.

Slywotzky, Adrian J., and Morrison, David J. *The Profit Zone: How Strategic Business Design Will Lead You to Tomorrow's Profits.* New York: Times Books, 1997.
ISBN: 0812929004
The Profit Zone looks at how profit happens in today's customer-driven economy. The authors demonstrate why market share often leads to a "no-profit zone" and identify 22 profit models that have helped dozens of companies make money. The book considers example after example of how the profit zone works, from Disney's theme parks to Schwab's marketing of mutual funds. The final chapter is a handbook that allows managers to apply the ideas to their own companies.

Tracy, John. *How to Read a Financial Report: Wringing Vital Signs Out of the Numbers.* New York: John Wiley & Sons, 1999.
ISBN: 0471329355
This book cuts through the maze of accounting information to reveal what those numbers really mean. It steers readers through the basic accounting concepts, with line-by-line explanations of the basic financial statement and visual guides to explain what balance sheets, income statements, and cash flow statements mean to their companies.

Tracy, John. *Budgeting a la Carte: Essential Tools for Harried Business Managers (Finance Fundamentals for Nonfinancial Managers Series).* New York: John Wiley & Sons, 1996.
ISBN: 0471109282
Budgeting is a tool to maximize financial performance and position. As a business manager, would you like to spend less time budgeting, and learn more from the budgeting you do? This book offers a menu of budgeting options that allows you to pick and choose only those items that suit your business situation.

SEMINARS

Basic Budgeting for Nonfinancial Managers
American Management Association

From the basics of budgeting through planning and implementation, participants in this workshop will develop the capability to identify the costs and characteristics of different budgeting systems.

Length: 3 days
Price: $1,425
Location: See Web site for dates and locations.
Tel: 800-262-9699
Fax: 212-903-8168
URL: http://www.amanet.org

Direct Costing, Flexible Budgeting, and Contribution Reporting
University of Wisconsin, School of Business

In this program, participants learn effective methods for performance reporting, pricing for profit, marketing and business-unit segmentation, and communicating financial information. Participants gain the tools necessary to integrate financial data with their operations.

Length: 3 days
Price: $1,395
Location: Madison, WI
Tel: 800-292-8964 or 608-262-2155
Fax: 608-265-3357
URL: http://uwexeced.com

Finance and Accounting for the Nonfinancial Manager
University of Pennsylvania, Wharton Executive Education

This seminar focuses on learning how to read, understand, and analyze financial data; becoming familiar with the rationale and content of different types of financial statements; learning the process that generates financial data; and obtaining a working knowledge of significant concepts and terminology in finance and accounting.

Length: 5 days
Price: $6,950
Location: Philadelphia, PA
Tel: 800-255-3932 (U.S. and Canada), 215-898-1776 (worldwide)
Fax: 215-898-2064
URL: http://www.wharton.upenn.edu/execed

Finance for the Nonfinancial Manager
University of Michigan, The Michigan Business School

Participants in this program learn how to improve communication with people in financial areas, develop financial policy, and better understand the impact of financial decisions on their organization's profitability.

Length: 5 days
Price: $5,520
Location: Ann Arbor, MI
Tel: 734-763-1003
Fax: 734-763-9467
URL: http://www.bus.umich.edu/execed

**Chapter 10
Manage
Technology**

Bates, Regis J. *Voice and Data Communications Handbook, 3rd edition.*
New York: McGraw-Hill, 2000.
ISBN: 0072122765
Industry veterans, the authors offer a comprehensive, jargon-free guide to the latest in telecommunications. The book guides readers through the basics of voice processing, telephone equipment and networks, transmissions, and traffic engineering. Also included are sections on the Internet, intranets, and extranets.

Duarte, Deborah L., and Snyder, Nancy T. *Mastering Virtual Teams: Strategies, Tools, and Techniques that Succeed.* San Francisco: Jossey-Bass, 1999.
ISBN: 0787941832
A practical toolkit for leaders and members of virtual and global teams, this book details solutions to the unique challenges of working cross-culturally and cross-functionally. It lays out specific guidelines, exercises, and strategies, to tackle the complex issues of managing across time, distance, business function, and culture.

Franson, Paul. *High Tech, High Hope: Turning Your Vision of Technology into Business Success.*
New York: John Wiley & Sons, 1998.
ISBN: 047123981X
Franson analyzes leading firms that have applied a range of new technology strategies to their businesses. Using Chrysler, Federal Express, and Hallmark as examples, he demonstrates how to apply technology solutions to problems in all functions, from operations and purchasing to marketing and sales.

Hodges, Susan M. *Computers: Systems, Terms, and Acronyms, 11th edition.*
Winter Park, FL: Semco Enterprises, 1999.
ISBN: 0966842227
Complete with real-world business examples and over 9,200 definitions of computer products, this reference explains computer technology in nontechnical terms and is useful for recruiters, salespeople, and administrators who work with computer professionals and products.

Martin, E. Wainright, and Dehayes, Daniel W. *Managing Information Technology: What Managers Need to Know.* Englewood Cliffs, NJ: Prentice Hall, 1999.
ISBN: 013860925X
This practical text gives managers the tools to best exploit information technology. Case studies and the explanation of key technology show how to evaluate information systems and how to manage the data in them. The authors also outline strategic use of information technology across an organization.

Petrozzo, Daniel P. *The Fast Forward MBA in Technology Management.*
New York: John Wiley & Sons, 1998.
ISBN: 0471239801
Petrozzo, vice president of Information Technology at Morgan Stanley, cuts through the hype to provide a clear, business-relevant picture of current and emerging information technology. His easy-to-follow guidelines and strategies help readers make technology work for their needs.

Szewczak, Edward, and Khosrowpour, Mehdi. *The Human Side of Information Technology Management.* Harrisburg, PA: Idea Group Publishing, 1996.
ISBN: 1878289330
Many experts feel that the human aspect of information technology has been widely ignored. The authors attempt to remedy this with an analysis of the human impact of our technology culture, examining such topics as user satisfaction with information systems, the impact of office automation on employees, and electronic communication.

SEMINARS

Computers: Systems, Terms, and Acronyms (CSTA)
SemCo

Forming the foundation upon which computer knowledge is built, this seminar defines five skill areas involved in every computer job: platforms, development tools and techniques, data management issues, online and networking knowledge, and applications software.
Length: 2 days
Price: $745
Location: See Web site for dates and locations.
Tel: 407-830-5400
Fax: 407-830-0016
URL: http://www.semcoenterprises.com

Forecasting, Planning, and Managing Technology
Technology Futures, Inc.

Managers and professionals who plan for new technologies and markets will find this interactive seminar helpful. A combination of formal instruction, group discussion, and practical exercises, it teaches participants how to conduct and assess technology forecasts and to integrate them into organizational planning.
Length: 3 days
Price: $1,095
Location: Austin, TX
Tel: 800-TEK-FUTR (inside U.S.) or 512-258-8898 (local or outside U.S.)
Fax: 512-258-0087
URL: http://www.tfi.com

Program for Technology Managers
University of North Carolina at Chapel Hill

This program is designed to help participants communicate effectively about technology and innovation, instill an understanding of the strategic significance of technology, and manage strategic alliances among corporations for new technology development.
Length: 2-week program, spaced format
Price: $9,300
Location: Chapel Hill, NC
Tel: 800-862-3932 (inside U.S.) or 919-962-1531
Fax: 919-962-1667
URL: http://www.bschool.unc.edu

Systems Analysis and Design for Information and Business Professionals
American Management Association

Participants in this program learn how to adapt their information systems to their organization and customers. Focusing on the Systems Development Life Cycle, the seminar covers current and emerging technology trends and teaches participants how to plan quality and reliability into a system from the start.
Length: 4 days
Price: $1,595
Location: See Web site for dates and locations.
Tel: 800-262-9699
Fax: 212-903-8168
URL: http://www.amanet.org

**Chapter 11
Promote
Corporate
Citizenship**

Bollier, David. *Aiming Higher: 25 Stories of How Companies Prosper by Combining Sound Management and Social Vision.* New York: AMACOM, 1996.
ISBN: 0814403190
Each year, The Business Enterprise Trust honors companies or individuals who have shown bold, creative leadership in combining sound business management with social conscience. *Aiming Higher* presents the stories of 25 of these honorees. These inspiring narratives illuminate the complicated, gritty challenges met and overcome by public-spirited business people.

Hesselbein, Frances; Goldsmith, Marshall; and Beckhard, Richard; editors. *The Organization of the Future (Drucker Foundation Future Series).* San Francisco: Jossey-Bass, 1997.
ISBN: 0787903035
Combining writings from best-selling authors, Fortune 500 CEOs, and management scholars, 28 new essays comprise the second title in the Drucker Foundation Future Series, which focuses on the challenges companies face as they build the organization of tomorrow.

McIntosh, Malcolm, et al. *Corporate Citizenship: Successful Strategies for Responsible Companies.* Englewood Cliffs, NJ: Prentice Hall, 1998.
ISBN: 0273631063
Describing the new contract between business and society, this book offers the first comprehensive guide to the issues, emerging best practices, and the new Social Accountability Standards—SA8000, set by the Council for Economic Priorities in 1998.

Stead, W. Edward, and Stead, Jean Garner. *Management for a Small Planet: Strategic Decision Making and the Environment.* Thousand Oaks, CA: Sage Publications, 1996.
ISBN: 0761902945
The authors argue that today's organizations need to recognize environmental concerns. The book presents topical environmental issues as they relate to business and management practice. The authors describe the social, scientific, and economic concepts related to making environmentally sensitive strategic decisions.

Tichy, Noel M., et al. *Corporate Global Citizenship: Doing Business in the Public Eye.* New York: Lexington Books, 1997.
ISBN: 0787910953
Thoroughly researched, this book is a cutting-edge study of how the world's largest multinational corporations—such as American Express, Merck & Company, and General Electric—create and implement programs that positively influence their communities. It also offers a penetrating look at the future prospects for global corporate citizenship initiative.

Wheeler, David; Sillanpaa, Maria; and Roddick, Anita. *The Stakeholder Corporation: The Body Shop: Blueprint for Maximizing Stakeholder Value.* Englewood Cliffs, NJ: Prentice Hall, 1998.
ISBN: 0273626612
The Body Shop has gained renown for combining a successful business idea with a concern for all its stakeholders—employees, shareholders, customers, suppliers, local communities, and the environment. Here, senior managers from The Body Shop lay out the case for the stakeholder corporation as a new model for responsible corporate growth.

SEMINARS

Executive Seminar
The Aspen Institute
Classic readings from Plato and Jefferson support this seminar's discussion of the forces at work in society and the global community. This values-based program focuses on enhancing leaders' qualities of vision and integrity. Participants will examine the origins of many current business issues to gain new perspectives as they manage change in their organizations.
Length: 1 week
Price: $6,200
Location: Aspen, CO
Tel: 800-525-6618 or 970-544-7915
URL: http://www.aspeninst.org

Managing Corporate Community Investment
Ashridge Management College
This program enables participants to develop strategies for the benefit for the community and their organizations. Areas covered include: understanding the business case for corporate community involvement (CCI), gaining an insight into best practice, and becoming part of a network.
Length: 3 days
Price: £1,600 + VAT
Location: Berkhamsted, Hertfordshire, UK
Tel: 44-144-284-3491
Fax: 44-144-284-1209
URL: http://www.ashridge.org.uk

Chapter 12
Establish Plans

Baker, Sunny, and Baker, Kim. *The Complete Idiot's Guide to Project Management.*
New York: Alpha Books, 1998.
ISBN: 0028617452
This guide provides instructions for managing all types of projects from original concept through completion and implementation. It includes tips and techniques for problem solving and a technical terms glossary.

Brassard, Michael, and Ritter, Diane. *Memory Jogger II: A Pocket Guide of Tools for Continuous Improvement and Effective Planning.* Salem, NH: Goal/QPC, 1994.
ISBN: 1879364441
This handy book describes tools for making continuous improvements in any organization. The charts, diagrams, and exercises help identify and solve problems, eliminate rework, streamline processes, improve communication, decrease costs, and measure results.

Kaufman, Roger. *Strategic Planning Plus.*
Thousand Oaks, CA: Sage Publications, 1992.
ISBN: 0803948050
The author discusses strategic planning at three levels—micro, macro, and mega—and describes in detail how to plan for the needs of any organization. Guidance on identifying the organization's direction, a six-step process for solving problems, and methods for evaluating progress and revising plans are also included.

Verzuh, Eric. *The Fast Forward MBA in Project Management.*
New York: John Wiley & Sons, 1999.
ISBN: 0471325465
This guide presents proven techniques for managing projects, from establishing project objectives to building realistic schedules and cost projections. Along with basic methods for defining, planning, and tracking a project, it also shows how to use these techniques to build stronger teams and work with all project participants, from the customer to management.

Williams, Paul B. *Getting a Project Done on Time: Managing People, Time, and Results.*
New York: AMACOM, 1996.
ISBN: 0814402844
This book provides guidelines on all the essential project management skills needed to complete projects on time. Using ready-to-use tools, checklists, and tips, the author helps readers succeed in all projects, from the simple to the complicated.

SEMINARS

Project Management
Kepner Tregoe
This hands-on, results-oriented program helps managers learn to complete projects on schedule, within budget, and with the desired results. It covers clarifying goals, specifying the needed resources, scheduling, and assigning responsibilities, monitoring the project during implementation, and evaluating success.
Languages: English, French in Montreal, and Spanish in Puerto Rico
Length: 3 days
Price: $1,395
Location: See Web site for dates and locations.
Tel: 800-537-6378
URL: http://www.kepner-tregoe.com

Project Scope, Time, and Cost
American Management Association
Vital to project success, scope, time, and cost must be well planned. Participants in this seminar learn how to gauge budget and timeframes, collaborate with management and clients, manage changes, track progress, and allocate resources.
Length: 3 days
Price: $1,545
Location: See Web site for dates and locations.
Tel: 800-262-9699
Fax: 212-903-8168
URL: http://www.amanet.org

Project Management: Planning, Scheduling, and Control
University of Wisconsin Business School
This workshop teaches managers how to design a project plan; estimate project costs, resources, and time; employ network scheduling and allocate time-critical resources; establish feedback systems for project control; and utilize project status reports.
Length: 3 days
Price: $1,275
Location: Madison, WI
Tel: 800-292-8964
Fax: 608-265-3357
URL: http://uwexeced.com

Strategic Planning
American Management Association
To help participants capitalize on today's changing business environment, this program shares the strategic planning processes necessary to translate vision into reality. Participants will learn how to build effective strategic teams, recognize and overcome barriers, capitalize on strengths, and implement change.
Length: 3 days
Price: $1,725
Location: See Web site for dates and locations.
Tel: 800-262-9699
Fax: 212-903-8168
URL: http://www.amanet.org

**Chapter 13
Manage and
Improve
Processes**

Burrill, Claude W.; Burrill, Claude C.; and Ledolter, Johannes. *Achieving Quality through Continual Improvement.* New York: John Wiley & Sons, 1998.
ISBN: 0471092207
The quality of goods and services depends on the underlying processes used in their creation. These processes must be designed, constructed, and continually improved. This book addresses the managerial aspects of process improvement in order to help organizations provide the quality goods and services demanded in today's marketplace.

Harrington, H. James, et al. *Business Process Improvement Workbook: Documentation, Analysis, Design, and Management of Business Process Improvement.*
New York: McGraw-Hill, 1997.
ISBN: 0070267790
This hands-on implementation guide tells how to document a company's processes, analyze current effectiveness, design new processes, and use system enablers. Lists, charts, and appendices are included.

Hunt, Daniel V. *Process Mapping: How to Reengineer Your Business Processes.*
New York: John Wiley & Sons, 1996.
ISBN: 0471132810
This practical blueprint for getting to market faster, cheaper and better is based on the experiences of successful companies, including IBM, General Electric, NASA, and Tandy Electronics. The guide outlines a 12-step program for successfully transforming the business processes of any company and contains useful how-to advice and numerous sample process maps.

Rummler, Geary A., and Brache, Alan P. *Improving Performance: How to Manage the White Space on the Organization Chart.* San Francisco: Jossey-Bass, 1995.
ISBN: 0787900907
This practical guide offers an integrated framework for achieving competitive advantage by managing organizations, processes, and jobs more effectively. The authors show how their approach can forge a stronger link between strategy and process design, create a foundation for continuous improvement, and overcome common pitfalls in process redesign.

Swanson, Richard A. *Analysis for Improving Performance.*
San Francisco: Berrett-Koehler, 1996.
ISBN: 1576750019
Analysis for Improving Performance details the front-end work essential to the success of any performance-improvement effort. Swanson shows how to do the rigorous preparatory analysis that defines and shapes successful performance-improvement efforts, and he maps out the critical steps necessary for a program to meet real business needs.

SEMINARS

Focus: Tools for Managing Sideways
Rummler-Brache Group

Every organization, and its managers, must practice process. Understanding how people, processes, and structure are intimately linked, knowing what tools are available, and having the skills to use them are key foundations for success in process improvement.
Length: 2 days
Price: $995
Location: See Web site for dates and locations.
Tel: 800-992-5922
Fax: 972-789-7979
URL: http://www.rummler-brache.com

Process Analysis and Redesign
Wizdom Systems, Inc.

This course focuses on the analysis and redesign of business processes to meet customer needs. It covers forecasting of potential problems and opportunities, as well as developing measures for tracking and redesigning processes.
Length: 1 day
Price: Call vendor.
Location: Call vendor.
Tel: 630-357-3000
URL: http://www.wizdomsystems.com

Process Improvement Techniques
Management Concepts, Inc.

Using practical exercises, this course compares and contrasts different process-improvement and implementation tools.
Length: 3 days
Price: $450
Location: See Web site for dates and locations.
Tel: 703-790-9595 and press 4
Fax: 703-790-1371
URL: http://www.mgmtconcepts.com

Process Mapping
APQC

This course teaches participants how to create process maps and use these maps to drive positive change and improvement in their organizations.
Length: 1 day
Price: $595
Location: See Web site for dates and locations.
Tel: 800-776-9676 (713-681-4020 outside the U.S.)
Fax: 713-681-8578
URL: http://www.apqc.org/training

**Chapter 14
Drive Execution**

Bens, Ingrid. *Facilitation at a Glance: A Pocket Guide of Tools and Techniques for Effective Meeting Facilitation.* Cincinnati, OH: Participative Dynamics, 1999.
ISBN: 1890416053
This pocket guide provides a comprehensive set of tools and techniques in simplified format for anyone required to facilitate meetings.

Doyle, Mike, and Strauss, David. *How to Make Meetings Work: The New Interaction Method.*
New York: Berkley Books, 1993.
ISBN: 0425138704
Tested on more than 10,000 participants, the method described in this book covers meeting design, facilitation, and management and provides a thorough explanation of the facilitator's role. Demonstrating how time and people can be better used in meetings, this thorough manual is useful in any organization—from large corporations to small.

Heller, Robert. *How to Delegate.*
New York: DK Publishing, 1998.
ISBN: 0789428903
Heller, a founding editor of *Management Today*, provides essential tips for power (and potential power) players. The book presents a concise treatment of hundreds of business issues, skills, methods, and problems, many illustrated with photos, charts, and diagrams.

Mackenzie, Alec. *The Time Trap.*
New York: AMACOM, 1997.
ISBN: 081447926X
Mackenzie has distilled years of studying people's work habits into a book filled with practical, easy-to-use tips and techniques for decision making, organization, delegation, and overcoming procrastination. His suggestions will help readers become more efficient at work and enable them to spend more time on high-priority activities.

Maddux, Robert B. *Delegating for Results.*
Menlo Park, CA: Crisp Publications, 1998.
ISBN: 1560524553
This book shows how to learn the process of management and make the full transition to successful manager.

Weaver, Richard G., and Farrell, John D. *Managers as Facilitators: A Practical Guide to Getting Work Done in a Changing Workplace.* San Francisco: Berrett-Koehler, 1999.
ISBN: 1564143635
This guide provides practical ideas for getting work done through a new model of facilitation. It includes how to clarify what needs to be done, personally assist in the work, improve productivity through group dynamics, effectively build work processes, and manage changes.

SEMINARS

Basic Skills for Mastering Meetings
Interaction Associates
This seminar aims to enhance participants' meeting leadership skills. Lectures, professional video presentations, and small group practice sessions demonstrate how to set up, conduct, and follow through on successful meetings.
Languages: in-house programs offered in languages other than English; call vendor for details.
Length: 2 days
Price: $995
Tel: 800-347-8352
Locations: See Web site for locations and dates.
URL: http://www.interactionassociates.com

Delegation and Team Effort: People and Performance
University of Michigan, The Michigan Business School
This program introduces the skills necessary for effective delegation and team leadership. Participants learn to manage in the team environment, design and create a context for high-performance teams, and overcome roadblocks to effective delegation.
Length: 5 days
Price: $5,320
Location: Ann Arbor, MI
Tel: 734-763-1000
Fax: 734-763-9467
URL: http://www.bus.umich.edu/execed

Time Management
American Management Association
Designed to help individuals at all levels make the best possible use of time, this seminar presents a systematic approach to time control. Participants learn how to take charge of their time, accomplish more with fewer meetings, and get their teams involved in time management.
Length: 2 days
Price: $1,195
Location: See Web site for dates and locations.
Tel: 800-262-9699
Fax: 212-903-8168
URL: http://www.amanet.org

**Chapter 15
Manage Change**

Barger, Nancy, and Kirby, Linda. *The Challenge of Change in Organizations: Helping Employees Thrive in the New Frontier*. Palo Alto, CA: Davies-Black, 1995.
ISBN: 0891060790
Presenting the frontier as a metaphor for understanding organizational change, Barger and Kirby explore the psychological impact of change on employees and provide managers with strategies necessary for successful transitions. The authors provide practical advice about management styles and how to help employees with different personalities deal with the difficulties of change.

Bridges, William. *Managing Transitions: Making the Most of Change*.
Reading, MA: Addison-Wesley, 1991.
ISBN: 0201550733
Business consultant William Bridges tackles an aspect of managing change that many companies avoid or do not even recognize—the human side of change. Aimed at managers in today's corporations, this book addresses the fact that it is people who carry out change, and, when the human side is neglected, change initiatives often fail.

D'Aprix, Roger. *Communicating for Change: Connecting the Workplace with the Marketplace*.
San Francisco: Jossey-Bass, 1996.
ISBN: 0787901997
Breakdowns in communication contribute to the confusion during times of change. D'Aprix shows why and where such breakdowns occur. His market-based, strategic communication model demonstrates how to align communication at all levels to help employees understand and commit to workplace change.

Skarke, Gary; Rogers, Bill; Holland, Dutch; and Landon, Diane. *Change Management Toolkit for Reengineering, Process Redesigner or Any Other Pragmatic Organizational Change*.
Houston, TX: WinHope Press, 1999.
ISBN: 0967140102
A guide to the methodology, forms, tools, and techniques for implementing change, this book provides a hands-on, practical roadmap. Garnered from experience with large corporations, government agencies, and nonprofit organizations, the book helps both beginning and experienced change agents to make concrete steps toward lasting change.

Smith, Douglas K. *Taking Charge of Change: 10 Principles for Managing People and Performance*. Reading, MA: Addison-Wesley, 1997.
ISBN: 0201916045
Cooking up great ideas of how things should be is easy. Getting things to actually change is a different matter, especially in large, complex organizations. This book provides the diagnostic tools to assess particular needs for change and the tool kit required to implement the changes a manager wants to see.

SEMINARS

Facilitating Change
Interaction Associates

This workshop offers guiding principles and techniques for facilitating multistakeholder projects. It also provides advanced training in collaborative problem solving and decision making.

Languages: in-house programs offered in languages other than English; call vendor for details.
Length: 4 days
Price: $2,095
Location: See Web site for dates and locations.
Tel: 800-347-8352
URL: http://www.interactionassociates.com

Leadership and Change
LMA, Inc.

Participants in this workshop learn how to develop and successfully implement positive changes that improve business results. Topics include making real change happen, building on strengths, implementing lasting improvements, and enhancing mind-sets around personal and organizational change.

Length: 3 days
Price: $1,500 ($1,250 if paid in advance)
Location: Merrimack, NH
Tel: 603-878-9000
Fax: 603-878-4500
URL: http://www.lma-thegrowthco.com

Leading and Managing People
Columbia University

This program emphasizes managing teams through times of change. Participants assess their personal leadership styles and explore ways of making them more effective. Topics include empowerment, communication, and group dynamics.

Length: 6 days
Price: $6,250
Location: Harriman, NY
Tel: 800-692-3932 (within the U.S.) or 212-854-3395 (outside the U.S.)
Fax: 212-316-1473
URL: http://www.columbia.edu/cu/business

**Chapter 16
Drive for Results**

Charles, C. Leslie. *Stick to It!: The Power of Positive Persistence.*
East Lansing, MI: Yes! Press, 1995.
ISBN: 0964462109
Charles offers a handy resource of quick inspirations and lasting ideas to help readers persist when the going gets rough.

Dawson, Roger. *The 13 Secrets of Power Performance.*
Englewood Cliffs, NJ: Prentice Hall, 1997.
ISBN: 0136714978
Dawson interviewed some of the world's most successful people, and has revealed their secrets of success in this book. These secret strategies include ways to create opportunities, overcome obstacles, unleash one's hidden energy, accomplish more, make better use of time, and eliminate inertia and anxiety.

Koch, Richard. *The 80/20 Principle: The Secret of Achieving More with Less.*
New York: Currency, 1998.
ISBN: 0385491700
The 80/20 principle—80 percent of results flow from just 20 percent of our efforts—is one of the great secrets of highly effective people and organizations. Koch shows how you can achieve much more with much less effort, time, and resources, simply by concentrating on the all-important 20 percent.

Kouzes, James M., and Posner, Barry Z. *The Leadership Challenge: How to Keep Getting Extraordinary Things Done in Organizations.* San Francisco: Jossey-Bass, 1996.
ISBN: 0787902691
Emphasizing the critical role of leadership in human organizations, this handbook offers guidelines for keeping the business momentum going in business, government, education, and community sectors.

Ulrich, Dave; Zenger, Jack; and Smallwood, Norm. *Results-Based Leadership.*
Boston: Harvard Business School Press, 1999.
ISBN: 0875848710
The authors show how leaders can deliver results in four specific areas: results for employees, the organization, its customers, and its investors. They provide action-oriented guidelines for developing and honing the reader's results-based leadership skills.

Zenger, John H. *22 Management Secrets to Achieve More with Less.*
New York: McGraw-Hill, 1997.
ISBN: 0070727171
This book provides managers with practical themes and tactics to "turbo-charge" their staff's performance and clear the obstacles to worker productivity.

SEMINARS

Dale Carnegie Training®
Dale Carnegie and Associates

Dale Carnegie Training® benefits people, at all levels in a company, who seek to maximize their performance, become stronger leaders, and add more value to the organization. The training offers practical new knowledge, skills, and tools—competitive resources employees can apply right away to make a dramatic difference in performance.

Languages: many languages offered in many countries; see Web site or call vendor for details.
Price: Call vendor.
Location: Call vendor.
Tel: 516-248-5100
Fax: 516-248-5817
URL: http://www.dale-carnegie.com

Increasing Human Effectiveness: Managing the Rapids of Change
Edge Learning Institute

This program provides participants with the tools to enable them to tap the wellspring of potential that exists within them, allowing for improved self-image, morale, productivity, and bottom line.

Length: 2 days
Price: $4,495
Location: Tacoma, WA
Tel: 800-858-1484 or 253-272-3103
Fax: 253-572-2668
URL: http://www.edgelearning.com

Motivation and Behavior
Menninger Leadership Center

Participants in this seminar gain an understanding of human behavior and motivation, take a critical look at their own strengths and weaknesses as managers, and develop plans for putting what they learn to work in their professional and personal lives.

Length: 3 days
Price: $4,100
Location: See Web site for dates and locations.
Tel: 800-288-5357
Fax: 913-648-3155
URL: http://www.menningerleadership.net

**Chapter 17
Lead
Courageously**

Gilley, Kay. *Leading from the Heart: Choosing Courage over Fear in the Workplace.*
Boston: Butterworth-Heinemann, 1996.
ISBN: 0750698357
According to Gilley, there are two paths in life: the path of fear and the path of courage.
The path of fear involves doing what friends, family, the culture, or others want. The path
of courage leads to knowing the essence of ourselves, ultimately resulting in success and
self-awareness.

Michelli, Dena. *Successful Assertiveness.*
Hauppauge, NY: Barron's, 1997.
ISBN: 0764100718
The author offers strategies for clear, honest communication, developing personal and
professional self-esteem, and building successful business and personal relationships.

Senge, Peter M. *The Fifth Discipline: The Art & Practice of the Learning Organization.*
New York: Doubleday/Currency, 1994.
ISBN: 0385260946
Senge offers the concept of the learning organization as an alternative to the traditional
authoritarian hierarchy. He argues that people are the only long-term competitive advantage
today due to the knowledge they bring to the enterprise. Their value can be maximized
through continuous opportunities for lifelong learning.

Terry, Robert W. *Authentic Leadership: Courage in Action.*
San Francisco: Jossey-Bass, 1993.
ISBN: 155542547X
Terry contends that authenticity is the core principle of leadership and that leadership is
essential to success. The book includes resources and techniques that one can use to further
everyday leadership actions.

SEMINARS

Assertiveness Training for Managers
American Management Association
This seminar teaches participants effective assertiveness techniques. Topics include: managing assertively, achieving your objectives, resolving conflicts, and developing a self-improvement plan.
Length: 3 days
Price: $1,475
Location: See Web site for dates and locations.
Tel: 800-262-9699
Fax: 212-903-8168
URL: http://www.amanet.org

Impact Leadership
Personnel Decisions International
Participants in this workshop will learn more about their assets as a leader, understand their organization and its changes, learn how to enlist others in their vision, and establish their own leadership agenda. Standard or customized programs are available for delivery within an organization. Call vendor for details.
Length: 5 1/2 days
Price: Call vendor.
Tel: 800-633-4410
Fax: 612-904-7120
URL: http://www.personneldecisions.com

The Leadership Challenge Workshop
Tom Peters Group
This intensive program focuses on the leadership practices required to get extraordinary things done and strengthens individuals' abilities and self-confidence to lead others in challenging situations. It is based on the award-winning book *The Leadership Challenge*, by Jim Kouzes.
Length: 2 or 3 days
Price: $1,995
Location: See Web site for dates and locations.
Tel: 800-333-8878
Fax: 650-326-7065
URL: http://www.tpgls.com

Leadership Essentials™
Personnel Decisions International
The leadership excellence training in this program focuses on four key areas: personal, people, business, and work. Through the use of PROFILOR® feedback, exercises, and coaching, participants learn how to evaluate their current leadership skills, improve their strategic organizational and interpersonal effectiveness, and achieve results through others. Standard or customized programs are available for delivery within an organization. Call vendor for details.
Length: 5 days
Price: Call vendor.
Tel: 800-633-4410
Fax: 612-904-7120
URL: http://www.personneldecisions.com

**Chapter 18
Influence Others**

Aubuchon, Norbert. *Anatomy of Persuasion: How to Pursuade Others to: Act on Your Ideas, Accept Your Proposals, Buy Your Products or Services, Hire You, Promote You.* New York: AMACOM, 1997.
ISBN: 0814479529
This book provides readers with a unique, proven, step-by-step analytical thinking process that anyone can use to analyze, organize, and present information in a persuasive way. Readers learn how to perceive the needs of others, create an error-free proposal, and more.

Charvet, Shelle Rose. *Words that Change Minds: Mastering the Language of Influence.* Dubuque, IA: Kendall/Hunt Publishing Company, 1997.
ISBN: 0787234796
Charvet teaches readers how to understand, predict, and influence behavior. She describes the type of language that will effectively reach particular kinds of people, and demonstrates how to communicate, sell, and manage, while respecting people at a deep level.

Cohen, Allen R., and Bradford, David L. *Influence without Authority.* New York: John Wiley & Sons, 1990.
ISBN: 0471622680
The authors discuss how people without official authority can command the resources, information, and support needed to get work done. They stress thinking of the interests of coworkers in order to gain collaboration, challenging tasks, and responsibility from above, laterally, and below.

Hogan, Kevin. *The Psychology of Persuasion: How to Persuade Others to Your Way of Thinking.* Gretna, LA: Pelican Pub. Co., 1996.
ISBN: 1565541464
Using techniques from hypnosis, neurolinguistic programming, and the Bible, Hogan teaches readers the skills of persuasion. Packed with the expertise of successful salespeople, this book shares the tools used by political candidates, television ministers, and corporate leaders to change the way others think.

Kozicki, Stephen. *Creative Negotiating: Proven Techniques for Getting What You Want from any Negotiation.* Holbrook, MA: Adams Media, 1998.
ISBN: 1558507973
This book is written in a friendly, approachable style that includes anecdotes, illustrations, and diagrams. The author focuses on flexibility, careful planning, and four basic rules: there are no rules, everything is negotiable, always ask for a better deal, and learn to say no.

SEMINARS

How to Influence without Direct Authority
University of Wisconsin, School of Business

Participants in this workshop examine characteristics and skills of influential people to understand the sources of their informal power. They analyze situations requiring influence and learn how to build effective relationships upward, downward, and laterally. They also learn practical influential strategies, trust-building skills, and the tools of team building, persuasion, conflict management, and negotiation.

Length: 3 days
Price: $1,275
Location: Madison, WI
Tel: 800-292-8964
Fax: 608-265-3357
URL: http://uwexeced.com

Negotiation and Influence Strategies
Stanford University, Graduate School of Business

This highly interactive program teaches participants how to implement negotiation strategies more effectively, and emphasizes coalitions, networks, relationships, and ethics.

Length: 5 days
Price: $6,300
Location: Stanford, CA
Tel: 650-723-9120
Fax: 650-723-3950
URL: http://www-gsb.stanford.edu/eep

Persuasion and Influencing Skills for Managers: Communication, Negotiation, Group Management
Vanderbilt University

This program is designed to increase participants' ability to sell their ideas, motivate individuals, and establish their credibility. Participants practice creating rapport and negotiating effectively, using new tools and knowledge about the influence process.

Length: 3 days
Price: $1,550
Location: Nashville, TN
Tel: 615-322-3932
Fax: 615-343-2293
URL: http://mba.vanderbilt.edu

Positive Power and Influence
Situation Management Systems, Inc.

The program focuses on developing and refining the skills required to influence people and events while building and maintaining beneficial relationships. Participants assess their current influencing styles, refine present skills, develop alternative styles, and apply the appropriate influence style to a given situation.

Languages: Afrikaan, Danish, Dutch, Australian-English, British-English, Finish, French, German, Korean, Norwegian, Portuguese, Swedish, 3 Spanish versions (Spain, Venezuela, Mexico)
Length: 2 or 3 days
Price: $1,295 or $1,675 (2 or 3 days)
Location: See Web site for dates and locations.
Tel: 781-826-4433
Fax: 781-826-2863
URL: http://www.smsinc.com

**Chapter 19
Build Talent Pools**

Harris, Jim, and Brannick, Joan. *Finding and Keeping Great Employees.*
New York: AMACOM, 1999.
ISBN: 0814404545
In today's tight labor market, finding employees that are "keepers" is critical to success. This book offers a powerful new action plan to help companies leverage their core purpose and corporate culture to attract and retain great employees.

Janz, Tom; Hellervik, Lowell; and Gilmor, David C. *Behavior Description Interviewing.*
Newton, MA: Allyn & Bacon, 1986.
ISBN: 0205085970
Behavior description interviewing improves on traditional approaches by systematically probing what applicants have done in the past in situations similar to those they will face on the job. This book is written for interviewers from many backgrounds who want to make the best, most scientific hiring decisions within the structure of an interview.

Kraut, Allen I., and Korman, Abraham K. *Evolving Practices in Human Resource Management: Responses to a Changing World of Work.* San Francisco: Jossey-Bass, 1999.
ISBN: 0787940127
During the last two decades, fundamental changes have taken place in the world of work. As a result, HR practices are being scrutinized for their ability to make companies competitive, flexible, and productive.

McCall, Morgan W. *High Flyers: Developing the Next Generation of Leaders.*
Boston: Harvard Business School Press, 1997.
ISBN: 0875843360
McCall presents a strategic framework for identifying and developing future executives. He believes leaders need to be open to continuous learning and be able to learn from their experiences. The key is finding the right experiences.

Schippman, Jeffery S. *Strategic Job Modeling: Working at the Core of Integrated Human Resources.* Mahwah, NJ: Lawrence Erlbaum, 1999.
ISBN: 0805830537
Based on a decade of job analysis research, this book shows readers how to create and strategically use models of workers, their competencies, and their work itself. The author provides practical advice grounded in sound human resources management and industrial psychology.

Wood, Robert, and Payne, Tim. *Competency-Based Recruitment and Selection.*
New York: John Wiley & Sons, 1998.
ISBN: 0471974730
Many professionals want to know how to use competencies to recruit and select staff. The authors offer a step-by-step guide to the process, discuss practical considerations, and utilize leading-edge methods developed in the field.

SEMINARS

Advanced Recruitment and Retention Strategies for a Tight Labor Market
American Management Association

This seminar will help organizations tap the tight labor market with methods that attract, retain, and better utilize talented employees. Topics include: creatively stretching your recruiting budget; gaining insight into the new workforce; and turning the new workforce into loyal, long-term members of your organization.
Length: 2 days
Price: $1,545
Location: See Web site for dates and locations.
Tel: 800-262-9699
Fax: 212-903-8168
URL: http://www.amanet.org

Interviewing: A Strategic Approach
University of Michigan, The Michigan Business School

This seminar is designed to provide participants with knowledge and skill in interviewing. Topics include: developing and using predictive questioning techniques; protecting an organization from liability regarding discrimination; forming judgments from interviewing data; and enhancing personal communication style in interviewing.
Length: 3 days
Price: $2,250
Location: Ann Arbor, MI
Tel: 734-763-1003
Fax: 734-763-9467
URL: http://www.bus.umich.edu/execed

Interviewing Skills
Communispond, Inc.

Designed for recruiters and managers, this seminar turns the art of interviewing into science. Proven strategies and effective questioning methods help participants gain the facts, probe for a candidate's achievements, and measure a candidate's qualifications against criteria. It also reviews EEO and ADA guidelines.
Length: Call vendor.
Price: Call vendor.
Tel: 212-486-2300
Fax: 212-486-2680
URL: http://communispond.com

Selecting for Success®
Personnel Decisions International

This workshop teaches the critical skills needed to get in-depth information from candidates and make the best hiring decisions. Topics include: predicting future performance, avoiding common interviewing errors, structuring and controlling interviews, and coordinating interview results with others. Standard or customized programs are available for delivery within an organization. Call vendor for details.
Length: 1 or 2 days
Price: Call vendor.
Tel: 800-633-4410
Fax: 612-904-7120
URL: http://www.personneldecisions.com

Chapter 20
Coach and
Develop People

Buckingham, Marcus, and Coffman, Curt. *First Break All the Rules: What the World's Greatest Managers Do Differently.* New York: Simon & Schuster, 1999.
ISBN: 0684852861
Buckingham and Coffman explain how the best managers select an employee for talent rather than skills or experience, set expectations for them, build on their unique strengths instead of trying to fix their weaknesses, and develop them.

Cook, Marshall J. *Effective Coaching.*
New York: McGraw-Hill, 1998.
ISBN: 0070718644
This book explains how to apply sound coaching methods in the workplace, encouraging top performance by working with employees, instead of over them. Cook shows readers how to understand the characteristics of an effective coach and apply them in the workplace.

Hargrove, Robert A. *Masterful Coaching: Extraordinary Results by Impacting People and the Way They Think and Work Together.* San Francisco: Jossey-Bass, 1995.
ISBN: 0893842818
This book emphasizes core coaching skills including sponsoring, counseling, acknowledging, teaching, and confronting others. The author provides inspirational and practical examples to help readers see the breakthrough results achievable through coaching.

Jacobs, Ronald L., and Jones, Michael J. *Structured On-the-Job Training.*
San Francisco: Berrett-Koehler, 1994.
ISBN: 0887306853
On-the-job training is often informal, incomplete, and an extra burden on colleagues. The answer to this problem is structured on-the-job training. The authors present a step-by-step plan for preparing, delivering, and evaluating structured training.

Peterson, David B., and Hicks, Mary Dee. *Leader as Coach: Strategies for Coaching and Developing Others.* Minneapolis, MN: Personnel Decisions International, 1996.
ISBN: 0938529145
Because people are an organization's most valuable asset, leaders must equip them with the tools, knowledge, and opportunities they need to develop themselves and become more effective. This book shows how purposeful coaching can direct energy and fuel systematic growth in the competencies your organization needs.

Whitworth, Laura; Sandahl, Phil; and House, Henry. *Co-Active Coaching: New Skills for Coaching People toward Success in Work and Life.*
Palo Alto, CA: Davies-Black Publishing, 1998.
ISBN: 0891061231
Co-Active Coaching presents a revolutionary collaborative approach for client and coach. The book offers a detailed look at the fundamental principles, skills, and practice critical to coaching success.

SEMINARS

Coaching for Improved Performance
Communispond, Inc.
Participants will improve organizational and individual effectiveness by learning to develop a "performance partnership" with their employees and peers, and help people change their behavior without resentment.
Length: 2 days
Price: $590
Location: See Web site for dates and locations.
Tel: 800-529-5925
Fax: 212-486-2680
URL: http://www.communispond.com

Coaching Foundations
Personnel Decisions International
Designed for more experienced coaches, this seminar covers how to build employees' skills to effectively and quickly achieve business results. Instructors share state-of-the art methods for guiding others' learning, and give participants a deeper understanding of what coaching is and how it works in today's business environment. Standard or customized programs are available for delivery within an organization. Call vendor for details.
Length: 1 day
Price: Call vendor.
Tel: 800-633-4410
Fax: 612-904-7120
URL: http://www.personneldecisions.com

Coaching Skills
Personnel Decisions International
Focusing on leveraging the strengths of employees and aligning them with the business, this seminar teaches beginning coaches these five strategies: forging a partnership, inspiring commitment, growing skills, promoting persistence, and shaping the environment.
Participants practice creating coaching plans, communicating, and observing and evaluating behavior. Standard or customized programs are available for delivery within an organization. Call vendor for details.
Length: 2 days
Price: Call vendor.
Tel: 800-633-4410
Fax: 612-904-7120
URL: http://www.personneldecisions.com

Effective Managerial Coaching and Counseling
University of Michigan, The Michigan Business School
This program will help participants distinguish between a coaching and a counseling situation; help them apply coaching and counseling techniques appropriately and effectively; and explore coaching and counseling as they relate to organizational growth and success.
Length: 3 days
Price: $2,600
Location: Ann Arbor, MI
Tel: 734-763-1003
Fax: 734-763-9467
URL: http://www.bus.umich.edu/execed

**Chapter 21
Engage and
Inspire People**

Belasco, James, and Stead, Jerre. *Soaring with the Phoenix: Renewing the Vision, Reviving the Spirit, and Re-Creating the Success of Your Company*. New York: Warner Books, 1999.
ISBN: 044652400X
The authors describe how to motivate employees, make learning an adventure, see the big picture, create a culture that celebrates performance and accountability, build a customer-focused, people-based organization, and leave a legacy that makes a difference.

Kelley, Robert E. *The Power of Followership: How to Create Leaders People Want to Follow, and Followers Who Lead Themselves*. New York: Doubleday/Currency, 1992.
ISBN: 0385413068
Arguing that followers are more important to getting work done than leaders, Kelley analyzes the different types of followers in successful organizations. Drawing lessons from cultures such as Germany and Japan, this book gives leaders the insight to effectively maximize their followers and learn to be good followers themselves.

Kerr, Steven, editor. *Ultimate Rewards: What Really Motivates People to Achieve*. Boston: Harvard Business School Press, 1997.
ISBN: 0875848087
This collection of *Harvard Business Review* articles identifies sources of motivation and offers managers insights on how to use rewards, job enhancement, and other methods to keep employees motivated.

Kouzes, James M., and Posner, Barry Z. *Encouraging the Heart: A Leader's Guide to Rewarding and Recognizing Others*. New York: Simon & Schuster, 1997.
ISBN: 0787941840
Kouzes and Posner delve into a core leadership principle they call "encouraging the heart." This includes building self-confidence through high expectations, connecting performance and rewards, using a variety of rewards, letting others find their voice, making people feel like heroes, and showing how leaders can genuinely love their people.

Matusak, Larraine R. *Finding Your Voice: Learning to Lead Anywhere You Want to Make a Difference*. San Francisco: Jossey-Bass, 1997.
ISBN: 0787903051
A tool for leaders in business, community, or nonprofit organizations, this book gives readers, even those without official authority, the skills needed to influence the world around them. Topics include sharing a common vision, communicating that vision, and appreciating diverse views.

Useem, Michael. *The Leadership Moment: Nine True Stories of Triumph and Disaster and Their Lessons for Us All*. New York: Times Business, 1998.
ISBN: 0812929357
The author, director of the Center for Leadership at the University of Pennsylvania's Wharton School, culls survival lessons for any leader from nine amazing stories, including an account of a dangerous mountain ascent and the struggles of tattered Civil War troops.

SEMINARS

Leadership for Extraordinary Performance
University of Virginia, Darden Executive Education
This program examines how to develop vision and leadership that inspire others to extraordinary performance. Participants learn how to gain support from key people and manage the fulfillment of individual and group commitments.
Length: 1 week
Price: $5,300
Location: Charlottesville, VA
Tel: 877-833-3974 (U.S. and Canada) or 804-924-3000 (worldwide)
Fax: 804-982-2833
URL: http://www.darden.virginia.edu/execed

Mobilizing People
IMD
This unique program will help managers mobilize others to meet corporate, divisional, team, or project objectives. Using intensive coaching and feedback, as well as some outdoor exercises, the program shows participants how to develop individual energy, lead successful teams, and ultimately mobilize the organization.
Length: 2 weeks
Price: Fr16,000
Location: Lausanne, Switzerland
Tel: 41 (0)21 618 01 11
Fax: 41 (0)21 618 07 07
URL: http://www.imd.ch

Motivating Employees for Improved Performance
Management Concepts, Inc.
This program is for supervisors, HR professionals, and anyone interested in motivating employees with alternative reward and recognition programs. Participants learn what truly motivates people and how to use this knowledge to attract and retain the best and brightest employees.
Length: 1 day
Price: $185
Location: Vienna, VA
Tel: 703-790-9595 and press 4
Fax: 703-790-1371
URL: http://www.mgmtconcepts.com

Motivating Others: Bringing Out the Best in People
American Management Association
Participants evaluate their own degree of motivation and learn how to set employees up for success, communicate directly and openly, provide feedback that motivates, and create an atmosphere that allows people to flourish.
Length: 3 days
Price: $1,475
Location: See Web site for dates and locations.
Tel: 800-262-9699
Fax: 212-903-8168
URL: http://www.amanet.org

**Chapter 22
Foster
Collaboration**

Bennis, Warren G., and Biederman, Patricia W. *Organizing Genius: Secrets of Creative Collaboration*. Reading, MA: Perseus Press, 1998.
ISBN: 0201339897
Bennis and Biederman explore the characteristics of groups that achieve great things and those that don't. Using anecdotes from Xerox innovation to the 1992 presidential campaign, they illustrate the distinctive collaboration and leadership approaches that achieve success, as well as those that derail the best of intentions.

Hargrove, Robert A. *Mastering the Art of Creative Collaboration*.
New York: McGraw-Hill, 1998.
ISBN: 0070264090
Creative collaboration makes the impossible possible. But all too often collaboration stifles creativity. This book offers tradition-shattering advice that gives readers the tools to make any collaborative activity creative, productive, and rewarding.

Harrington-MacKin, Deborah. *The Team Building Tool Kit: Tips, Tactics, and Rules for Effective Workplace Teams*. New York: AMACOM, 1993.
ISBN: 0814478263
Harrington-Mackin shows how to manage the human factors and nitty-gritty details that can hamper teamwork. She explains how to define roles and responsibilities, select team members, encourage positive behavior, maintain control, evaluate and reward teams, and more.

Hunter, Dale; Bailey, Anne; and Taylor, Bill. *The Art of Facilitation*.
Tuscon, AZ: Fisher Books, 1995.
ISBN: 155561101X
This guide reveals the secrets of group facilitation and equips group members to take on this role themselves. The authors also discuss the source of group empowerment and show how to create group synergy.

Lipmack, Jessica, and Stamps, Jeffrey. *Virtual Teams: Reaching across Space, Time, and Organizations with Technology*. New York: John Wiley & Sons, 1997.
ISBN: 0471165530
The authors address major issues of virtual teams, including team principles, linking people together via technology, enhancing communication, and increasing productivity. They include stories from companies who depend on virtual teams to execute their strategies, including Hewlett-Packard, Motorola, Bank of Boston, and Steelcase.

Zenger, John H., et al. *Leading Teams: Mastering the New Role*.
Homewood, Ill.: Business One Irwin, 1994.
ISBN: 1556238940
This book shows managers how to create an enduring and vital position for themselves in a team environment while helping their people make the transition to shared leadership.

SEMINARS

Delegation and Team Effort: Getting Results in the New Team Environment
University of Michigan, The Michigan Business School
This program is designed for managers who wish to enhance their managerial skills through delegation and effective team leadership.
Length: 5 days
Price: $5,320
Location: Ann Arbor, MI
Tel: 734-763-1003
Fax: 734-763-9467
URL: http://www.bus.umich.edu/execed

Managing Teams for Innovation and Success
Stanford University, Graduate School of Business
This program explores the key ingredients for successful, effective teams—composition, managing information flow, and achieving synergy—to give participants the distinctive skill sets necessary to make teams work.
Length: 1 week
Price: $6,300
Location: Stanford, CA
Tel: 650-723-3341
Fax: 650-723-3950
URL: http://www-gsb.stanford.edu/eep

Orchestrating Team Performance
Cahner's TRACOM Group
This program uses experiential exercises to help participants understand the different stages of team development and formation, apply the most effective leadership style for each stage, and build skills to improve team effectiveness.
Length: 3 days
Price: $495
Location: See Web site for dates and locations.
Tel: 800-221-2321 or 303-470-4900
Fax: 303-470-4901
URL: http://www.tracomcorp.com

The Skilled Facilitator Intensive Workshop
Center for the Study of Work Teams
The Skilled Facilitator approach focuses on creating highly effective groups and organizations. It begins with a set of core values and principles, then adds specific techniques and methods. Designed to facilitate fundamental change, the approach is central to creating empowered organizations, self-managing teams, and learning organizations.
Length: 5 days
Price: $2,395
Location: See Web site for dates and locations.
Tel: 940-565-3096
Fax: 940-565-4806
URL: http://www.workteams.unt.edu

**Chapter 23
Build
Relationships**

Block, Peter. *Stewardship: Choosing Service over Self-Interest.*
San Francisco: Berrett-Koehler, 1996.
ISBN: 1881052869
Block advocates replacing the traditional management tools of control and consistency with partnership and choice with both employees and customers. His book is a practical resource to guiding your organization through a redistribution of power.

Bolton, Robert H., and Bolton, Dorothy Grover. *People Styles at Work: Making Bad Relationships Good and Good Relationships Better.* New York: AMACOM, 1996.
ISBN: 0814477232
According to the authors, it is possible to overcome personality conflicts by understanding other people's differences instead of merely reacting to them emotionally. They present a comprehensive behavioral science model for understanding four different "people styles"—driver, analytical, amiable, and expressive.

Fairhurst, Gail T., and Saar, Robert A. *The Art of Framing: Managing the Language of Leadership.* San Francisco: Jossey-Bass, 1996.
ISBN: 0787901814
The authors demonstrate that leaders can influence how events are seen and interpreted, even when they cannot control the events. Dozens of real-life examples illustrate how people can skillfully frame events, ideas, and goals at every opportunity, including everyday conversations.

Fisher, Roger, and Sharp, Alan. *Getting It Done: How to Lead When You're Not in Charge.* New York: HarperBusiness, 1999.
ISBN: 0887309585
The authors believe lateral leadership can overcome the inertia that affects many companies. Lateral leadership consists of five elements: clarifying your purpose; harnessing the power of organized thought; integrating thinking with doing; getting yourself and your team engaged; and learning how to give feedback on what's been accomplished.

Mackay, Harvey. *Dig Your Well Before You're Thirsty: The Only Networking Book You'll Ever Need.* New York: Currency/Doubleday, 1997.
ISBN: 0385485468
Mackay reveals his techniques for cultivating useful contacts in business, including targeting the right people, staying in touch with them, and asking for favors.

SEMINARS

Cross-Functional Communication: Strategies for Workplace Effectiveness
American Management Association
This highly interactive seminar shows participants how to develop win/win professional relationships that lead to organizational effectiveness.
Length: 3 days
Price: $1,450
Location: See Web site for dates and locations.
Tel: 800-262-9699
Fax: 212-903-8168
URL: http://www.amanet.org

How to Work More Effectively with People
University of Wisconsin
This workshop is designed to teach managers how to develop positive relationships. Participants learn why self-esteem and self-confidence are such important elements in human motivation and performance, and how to tune in to the needs of others. Participants also learn how to understand and manage frustration, defensiveness, anger, hostility, and insensitivity in themselves and others.
Length: 3 days
Price: $1,275
Location: Madison, WI
Tel: 800-292-8964
Fax: 608-262-2155
URL: http://uwexeced.com/management/leadership

Leadership through People Skills
Psychological Associates
Participants learn the practical skills for becoming leader-managers, turning vision into reality, empowering people to act competently and confidently, and managing in all directions—upward with their manager, laterally with coworkers, and downward with direct reports.
Length: 3 1/2 days
Price: $1,375
Location: St. Louis, MO
Tel: 800-345-6525
URL: http://www.q4solutions.com

**Chapter 24
Manage Conflict**

Borisoff, Deborah, and Victor, David A. *Conflict Management: A Communication Skills Approach.* Newton, MA: Allyn & Bacon, 1997.
ISBN: 0205272940
This book offers clear, usable advice on how to manage conflicts that arise on the job and in personal relationships. The authors apply a model of approaching and analyzing interpersonal conflict to different topics, providing readers with a genuinely effective structure for working through differences with colleagues, friends, and others.

Folger, Joseph P.; Poole, Marshall Scott; and Stuttman, Randall. *Working through Conflict: Strategies for Relationships, Groups, and Organizations.*
Reading, MA: Addison Wesley, 1996.
ISBN: 0673997669
The authors focus on a wide range of conflict settings, using theory, case studies, and discussions of third party roles and cultural differences in conflict management.

Kiser, A. Glenn. *Masterful Facilitation: Becoming a Catalyst for Meaningful Change.*
New York: AMACOM, 1998.
ISBN: 0814403980
This book applies a systematic approach to facilitation, which helps group members articulate their purpose, determine desired results, and choose and apply the most efficient level of intervention to achieve organizational objectives. It offers specific techniques and tools to become an outstanding facilitator.

Rozakis, Laurie E., and Rozakis, Bo. *The Complete Idiot's Guide to Office Politics.*
New York, NY: Alpha Books, 1998.
ISBN: 0028623975
In a humorous manner, this book provides tips on maneuvering through company politics. Topics include: step-by-step instructions for working your way up without stepping on anyone's toes; valuable hints on getting into the boss's good graces; tips for surviving—and shining—in meetings; and sound advice on avoiding political cross-fire.

Ury, William L. *Getting to Peace: Transforming Conflict at Home, at Work, and in the World.*
New York: Viking Press, 1998.
ISBN: 0670887587
Ury suggests a powerful new approach for turning conflict into cooperation which he calls the "Third Side." He believes every dispute has not just two sides, but also a silent third side that can help bring about agreement. Practicing the ten roles of the third side can help people achieve fair and nonviolent conflict resolution.

SEMINARS

From Conflict to Collaboration
Personnel Decisions International
Managers not only need to resolve conflict, but build on it. Participants in this interactive program learn a positive approach to conflict that reduces tension, values differences of opinion, and builds cooperative relationships. Standard or customized programs are available for delivery within an organization. Call vendor for details.
Length: 2 days
Tel: 800-633-4410
Fax: 612-904-7120
URL: http://www.personneldecisions.com

Managing Differences and Agreement: Making Conflict Work for You
Designed Learning, Inc.
This seminar is designed to teach managers multiple options for successfully managing the opposition, conflict, clashes, discord, and other disagreements that arise when working with individuals and within teams.
Length: 3 days
Price: $850
Location: See Web site for dates and locations.
Tel: 908-889-0300
Fax: 908-889-4995
URL: http://www.designedlearning.com

Responding to Conflict: Strategies for Improved Communication
American Management Association
This program teaches strategies for resolving conflict and building trust. Participants learn how to establish clear outcomes for resolving conflict, deal with conflict in different types of situations, express anger in a constructive way, use effective nonverbal behavior, and understand gender differences and group dynamics that lead to conflict.
Length: 3 days
Price: $1,395
Location: See Web site for dates and locations.
Tel: 800-262-9699
Fax: 212-903-8168
URL: http://www.amanet.org

CD-ROMs

Dealing with Conflict and Confrontation
Skillsoft
Conflicts are inevitable. Anger, grudges, hurt, and blame are not. This program offers psychologically sound conflict solutions for many confrontational situations. The techniques will help participants relieve the tensions, anxiety, and fear that often come with conflict.
Product Number: MGMT0220-PDI
URL: http://www.skillsoft.com

**Chapter 25
Leverage
Individual and
Cultural Diversity**

Elashmawi, Farid, and Harris, Philip R. *Multicultural Management 2000: Essential Cultural Insights for Global Business Success (Managing Cultural Differences Series).* Houston, TX: Gulf Pub Co, 1998.
ISBN: 0884154947
This book explores the vast cultural differences between the Arabs, North Americans, Latin Americans, and Asians. It guides the reader through many real-life cross-cultural situations including personal introductions, telephone calls, meetings, presentations, training, and negotiations. Dialogues, examples, self-tests, checklists, reference charts, and case studies are included.

Gudykunst, William B. *Bridging Differences: Effective Intergroup Communication.* Thousand Oaks, CA: Sage Publications, 1998.
ISBN: 0761915117
One of the biggest challenges in today's organizations, in which most managers work with people from different cultural and ethnic backgrounds, is communication. Stereotypes impact how messages are received and interpreted. Gudykunst discusses how individuals can improve their intergroup communication.

Mead, Richard. *International Management: Cross-Cultural Dimensions.* Malden, MA: Blackwell Business, 1998.
ISBN: 0631200037
This comprehensive introduction explores how cultural factors influence workplace behavior. Numerous examples, drawn from the United States, Europe, and Asia, demonstrate practical applications of theory in issues such as negotiating, staffing, and planning.

Morrison, Ann M. *The New Leaders: Leadership Diversity in America.* San Francisco: Jossey-Bass, 1996.
ISBN: 0787901849
If diversity at the management level is important to organizations, why is it so difficult to achieve? Morrison outlines a step-by-step approach to designing and carrying out a diversity strategy, including effective practices used by progressive organizations.

Sonnenschein, William. *The Diversity Toolkit: How You Can Build and Benefit from a Diverse Workforce.* Lincolnwood, Chicago, IL : Contemporary Books, 2000.
ISBN: 0809228424
Diversity is a business reality. With the help of this book, readers can not only adapt to, but profit from workforce diversity. Featuring tips for improving communications skills, perfecting team relationships, and attaining leadership skills, this practical guide will help readers achieve tangible results.

Trompenaars, Alfons. *Riding the Waves of Culture: Understanding Cultural Diversity in Global Business.* Burr Ridge, IL: Irwin Professional Pub, 1998.
ISBN: 0786311258
This book shows international managers how to build the skills, sensitivity, and cultural awareness needed to establish and sustain management effectiveness across cultural borders.

SEMINARS

Cultures at Work: Understanding Global Corporations
The Intercultural Communication Institute
Participants discuss a wide range of topics, including defining a global corporation, identifying cultural biases that impede or facilitate success, leveraging cultural differences, assessing the impact of diversity on ethics, developing intercultural corporate skills, and assessing personal and corporate readiness to "go global."
Price: Call vendor.
Location: Portland, OR
Tel: 503-297-4622
Fax: 503-297-4695
URL: http://www.intercultural.org

Managing Inclusion
J. Howard and Associates, Inc.
This interactive workshop is designed to transform the challenge of diversity into the opportunity of inclusion. Participants explore the benefits of a learning environment for all employees and focus on developing skills to eliminate barriers to learning opportunities. The goal is to help managers engage a greater percentage of the work force in core business activities and increase productivity.
Length: 2 days
Price: Call vendor.
Location: Call vendor.
Tel: 781-862-8887
Fax: 781-862-9025
URL: http://www.jhoward.com

The Diverse Workforce
Management Concept, Inc.
This program teaches participants how to manage today's employees so that varied backgrounds and talents can enrich an organization. Topics include: recognizing the new work force, understanding and valuing differences, communicating across cultures, dealing with foreign languages on the job, using appropriate nonverbal communication, and building a positive culture.
Length: 2 days
Price: $300
Location: See Web site for dates and locations.
Tel: 703-790-9595 and press 4
Fax: 703-790-1371
URL: http://www.mgmtconcepts.com

Chapter 26
Foster Open
Communication

Armstrong, David. *Managing by Storying Around.*
New York: Doubleday, 1992.
ISBN: 0964802716
Armstrong has taken one of the oldest forms of communication—storytelling—and turned it into a powerful management tool. His method is simple and timeless yet effective for imparting information.

Goleman, Daniel. *Working with Emotional Intelligence.*
New York: Bantam Doubleday Dell, 1998.
ISBN: 0553104624
Goleman provides guidelines for cultivating self-awareness, self-confidence, and self-control. He also discusses commitment and integrity, the ability to communicate and influence, and the ability to initiate and accept change.

Isaacs, William. *Dialogue and the Art of Thinking Together: A Pioneering Approach to Communicating in Business and in Life.* New York: Doubleday, 1999.
ISBN: 0385479999
Founder of the Dialogue Project at MIT, the author shows how problems between managers and employees, and between companies or divisions, stem from an inability to conduct a successful dialogue. He demonstrates how to embrace different points of view to "think together" and bridge the communication gap.

Larkin, T.J., and Larkin, Sandar. *Communicating Change: How to Win Employee Support for New Business Directions.* New York: McGraw-Hill, 1994.
ISBN: 0070364524
Messages about organizational change must be successfully communicated. This book reveals how to implement changes and make them work by enlisting the support and cooperation of employees. Packed with checklists, sample communications, diagrams, and surveys, it provides a roadmap for successful change communication.

Ryan, Kathleen D.; Oestreich, Daniel K.; and Orr, George A. III. *The Courageous Messenger: How to Successfully Speak Up at Work.* San Francisco: Jossey-Bass, 1996.
ISBN: 0766942902
Many people hesitate to deliver tough news in the workplace. They are unwilling to confront others about unpleasant, unethical, or threatening behavior, and they are afraid that some day they will be punished for speaking their mind. Practical, easy-to-read, applicable tools and exercises will help you learn how to effectively communicate uncomfortable messages.

SEMINARS

Planning Communications to Support Organizational Objectives
Gavin Hodges Associates
Participants analyze and increase their conceptual understanding of planned communications processes, and learn specific skills for implementing communication plans based on operating objectives.
Length: 2 days
Price: $495
Location: See Web site for dates and locations.
Tel: 215-576-0606
Fax: 215-576-0303
URL: http://www.gavinhodges.com

Speaking Up: Assertiveness Skills
Management Concepts, Inc.
Participants learn to communicate their needs, negotiate to win, say "no," handle defensiveness, clear roadblocks, and avoid manipulation. They also assess their interpersonal style, develop goals, and learn the behaviors necessary to take charge, maintain control, and get more out of themselves and others.
Length: 1 day
Price: $185
Location: Vienna, VA
Tel: 703-790-9595 and press 4
Fax: 703-790-1371
URL: http://www.managementconcepts.com

Interpersonal Impact and Influence
Impact Training Associates, Inc.
In this seminar, participants learn how to improve their interpersonal and communication skills. Topics include: negotiating and marketing ideas; building rapport; strengthening relationships with people who have different personality styles and people at other organizational levels; dealing with tension in relationships; engaging in healthy conflict; and achieving consensus through collaboration.
Length: 2 days
Price: $895
Location: Glendale, CA
Tel: 800-848-8333
Fax: 818-241-4416
URL: http://impact-training.com

CD-ROM

Interpersonal Communication Skills
SkillSoft
This series will build your skills in communication—from meeting new people and networking, to increasing personal power and influence through vocabulary, to improving team communication. Experts today consider communication to be the backbone of any effective team or organization. Effective communication is essential to building collaboration and minimizing conflict in today's team-oriented workplace. It will help ensure that you and your group are "on the same wavelength" and shooting for the same goals.
Product Number: COMM0100-PDI
URL: http://www.skillsoft.com

**Chapter 27
Speak with
Impact**

Bailey, Edward P. *Plain English at Work: A Guide to Writing and Speaking.*
New York: Oxford University Press, 1996.
ISBN: 0195104498
Communication is key to success. Bailey encourages people to write as they speak, and discusses style, organization, and text layout. He also gives several practical tips for designing and delivering presentations, including how to use hand gestures and how to set up the room for the most impact.

Carpenter, Ronald H. *Choosing Powerful Words: Eloquence That Works.*
Newton, MA: Allyn & Bacon, 1999.
ISBN: 0205271243
Carpenter outlines the secrets of eloquence that underlie great persuasive speeches. Drawing on familiar presidential addresses and statements from an array of well-known public figures, he explains the tools and techniques by which people make their words effective and memorable.

Olson, Jeff. *The Agile Manager's Guide to Giving Great Presentations.*
Bristol, VT: Velocity Business Publications, 1997.
ISBN: 0965919315
Olson shows readers how to control their nerves, prepare a presentation that educates or moves people, craft robust openings and endings, use visual aids, rehearse to get the best results, handle the question-and-answer session, and deal with difficult situations.

Qubein, Nido R. *How to Be a Great Communicator: In Person, on Paper, and on the Podium.*
New York: John Wiley & Sons, 1996.
ISBN: 0471163147
The author gives you the knowledge you need to excel at all types of business communication. He shows that all successful business communication, whether a speech from a podium or a face-to-face conversation, stems from the same basic principles. By using his Five Keys to Successful Communication anyone can unlock the potential to become a great communicator in any medium.

Urech, Elizabeth. *Speaking Globally.*
London: Kogan Page Ltd., 1998.
ISBN: 0749422211
Many managers work with colleagues and customers in other countries and from other cultures. Urech shares a practical, step-by-step approach for making presentations to audiences across the globe. She includes country-specific guidelines and tips.

Wilder, Lilyan. *Seven Steps to Fearless Speaking.*
New York: John Wiley & Sons, 1999.
ISBN: 0471321591
This seven-step program for improving oral communication skills tells how to improve one's voice, structure a presentation, use props, and demonstrate conviction.

Yankelovich, Daniel. *The Magic of Dialogue: Transforming Conflict into Cooperation.*
New York: Simon & Schuster, 1999.
ISBN: 0684854570
Famed social scientist Daniel Yankelovich reinvents the ancient art of dialogue in a brief, practical form that suits our times. Drawing on decades of research, he shows how the discipline of dialogue can make individuals more effective managers, strengthen relationships, resolve problems, and achieve shared objectives.

SEMINARS

Effective Executive Speaking
American Management Association
Participants evaluate their strengths and development needs, give an impromptu talk, build ideas, use visual aids, and answer questions. This program includes videotaping.
Length: 3 days
Price: $1,475
Location: See Web site for dates and locations.
Tel: 800-262-9699
Fax: 212-903-8168
URL: http://www.amanet.org

Effective Presentation Skills for Technical Professionals
American Management Association
Participants learn how to give presentations to technical and nontechnical audiences, and how to communicate complex technical concepts.
Length: 3 days
Price: $1,445
Location: See Web site for dates and locations.
Tel: 800-262-9699
Fax: 212-903-8168

Speaking with Impact
Personnel Decisions International
Theory and practice come together in this program, in which participants receive personalized feedback on their skills. Topics include nonverbal style and impact, content, style and strategic considerations, visual aids, and handling the question-and-answer session. Standard or customized programs are available for delivery within an organization. Call vendor for details.
Length: 2 days
Price: Call vendor.
Tel: 800-633-4410
Fax: 612-904-7120
URL: http://www.personneldecisions.com

Toastmasters
Toastmasters International
This professional organization of volunteers meets in local groups for the purpose of fostering the speaking ability and self-confidence of its members.
Price: $16 new member fee, $18 dues every six months, other fees depend on location
Location: See Web site for group locations.
Tel: 800-993-7732 (voice-mail line) or 949-858-8255 (live operator)
Fax: 949-858-1207
URL: http://www.toastmasters.org

Chapter 28
Listen to Others

Bolton, Robert. *People Skills.*
New York: Simon & Schuster, 1986.
ISBN: 06__2248X
Communication can be improved through effective listening, assertiveness, and conflict resolution. Bolton describes the twelve most common communication barriers and how to overcome them. The reader will find practical suggestions that can be incorporated into everyday interactions.

Burley-Allen, Madelyn. *Listening: The Forgotten Skill (A Self-Teaching Guide).*
New York: John Wiley & Sons, 1995.
ISBN: 0471015873
The author shares techniques for overcoming language barriers, interpreting body language, asking constructive, nonthreatening questions, and more. The book includes worksheets, charts, and graphs, plus each chapter concludes with a self-test to check progress.

Dugger, Jim. *Listen Up: Hear What's Really Being Said.*
West Des Moines, IA: American Media, 1995.
ISBN: 1884926401
Dugger outlines five ways to improve listening skills, helps pinpoint strengths and weaknesses in listening, outlines how to interpret nonverbal communication, and gives examples of how to respond with nonjudgmental phrases.

Kratz, Dennis M., and Kratz, Abby Robinson. *Effective Listening Skills (Business Skills Express).* Chicago: Irwin Professional Pub., 1995.
ISBN: 0786301228
This book covers the essential listening skills everyone needs to succeed in business, including a basic understanding of the communication process, giving and receiving feedback, screening out distractions, listening critically for information and evidence, and being open, interested, and attentive.

Tannen, Deborah. *Talking from 9 to 5—Women and Men in the Workplace: Language, Sex, and Power.* New York: W. Morrow, 1995.
ISBN: 0380717832
Tannen's lively and insightful book takes a linguistic approach to understanding how men and women talk at work. Gender-based communication differences can determine raises, promotions, and favorable or unfavorable work assignments. Recognizing communication patterns will help the reader adjust his or her style to specific situations.

SEMINARS

Dynamic Listening Skills for Successful Communication
American Management Association
Listening is a core skill for managers. This seminar will help participants build their listening skills in the following areas: using encouragement and praise to build rapport, separating content from feelings, asking questions to expand knowledge and bring out new ideas, motivating people to share information, and strengthening staff trust and morale.
Length: 2 days
Price: $1,175
Location: See Web site for dates and locations.
Tel: 800-262-9699
Fax: 212-903-8168
URL: http://www.amanet.org

Listening and Writing: Building a Foundation for Better Communication
American Management Association
This practical seminar is designed to help managers communicate more effectively. Topics include: analyzing the situation and the audience, active and passive listening, listening for understanding, determining the proper channel/medium for communication, and organizing and writing concise, understandable messages.
Length: 2 days
Price: $1,175
Location: See Web site for dates and locations.
Tel: 800-262-9699
Fax: 212-903-8168
URL: http://www.amanet.org

People Skills
Ridge Associates
This seminar teaches the participant the skills involved in listening, reaching agreement, confronting problems, and managing conflict. Private coaching in instant-reply video sessions helps participants develop their skills and monitor their progress.
Length: 3-4 days
Price: $1,250 - $1,600
Location: See Web site for dates and locations.
Tel: 315-655-3393
Fax: 315-655-8726
URL: http://www.ridge.com

**Chapter 29
Write Effectively**

Corbett, Edward P.J., and Finkle, Sheryl L. *The Little English Handbook, 8th edition.*
Reading, MA: Addison-Wesley, 1998.
ISBN: 032104438X
This handbook covers basic grammar, style, punctuation, and mechanics of written prose.
It addresses the most common and persistent problems encountered in the writing
process. Well organized and annotated, it includes samples of letters, a resume, and a
research paper.

Hale, Constance. *Sin and Syntax: How to Craft Wickedly Effective Prose.*
New York: Broadway Books, 1999.
ISBN: 0767903080
Sin and Syntax is an essential guide for all people who want to improve their command
of the English language. Hale teaches writers when and how to effectively break the rules.
She includes numerous examples from traditional and nontraditional prose.

Joseph, Albert M. *Put It in Writing: Learn How to Write Clearly, Quickly, and
Persuasively.* New York: McGraw-Hill, 1998.
ISBN: 0070393087
This book shows readers how to write clearly, effectively, and quickly; improve letters and
reports; develop a pleasing style; project a positive personal and corporate image; avoid
common errors in grammar, spelling, and usage; beat deadlines; and use writing for career
advancement.

O'Conner, Patricia. *Woe Is I.*
New York: Riverhead Books, 1998.
ISBN: 1573226254
O'Conner, a copy editor at *The New York Times Book Review*, provides a witty,
nontechnical guide to English grammar and style. Examples are organized according to
specific problems.

Piotrowski, Maryann V. *Effective Business Writing: Strategies, Suggestion, and Examples:
A Guide for Those Who Write on the Job.* New York: HarperCollins, 1996.
ISBN: 0062733818
Many writers are uncertain about how to choose an appropriate format, style, and tone for
their message. Piotrowski discusses basic grammar, then moves on to topics such as overcoming
writer's block, organizing messages for maximum impact, achieving an easy-to-read style,
and finding an efficient writing system.

Williams, Joseph M., and Colomb, Gregory G. *Style: Toward Clarity and Grace.*
Chicago, IL: University of Chicago Press, 1995.
ISBN: 0226899152
Most people have received muddled, confusing memos, rambling letters without a main
point, or e-mails filled with jargon. Written for the general reader, Williams' book shows
readers how to clean up their prose to make it powerful, clear, and effective.

SEMINARS

How to Sharpen Your Business Writing Skills
American Management Association
This practice-based program teaches how to write in a conversational manner, ways to grab the reader's attention, how to organize writing, how to choose the most effective formats, and how to write personal memos.
Length: 4 days
Price: $1,575
Location: See Web site for dates and locations.
Tel: 800-262-9699
Fax: 212-903-8168
URL: http://www.amanet.org

Write to the Top: Writing for Corporate Success
Better Communication, Inc.
This practical, participative seminar offers techniques for improving writing speed and impact through a combination of individual attention, short lectures, exercises, and discussions.
Length: 2 days
Price: Call vendor.
Location: Call vendor.
Tel: 781-862-3800
Fax: 781-862-8383
URL: http://www.bettercom.com

Write Up Front
Communispond, Inc.
This innovative program shows participants how to improve the organization and style of their writing by developing effective formats for business documents, and making their writing more personal, powerful, and colorful. Fast-paced writing and editing exercises, followed by group discussion and feedback, also teach 12 ways to improve writing.
Length: 1 day
Price: $450
Location: See Web site for dates and locations.
Tel: 800-529-5925
Fax: 212-486-2680
URL: http://www.communispond.com

CD-ROM

Grammar for Professionals
SkillSoft
A thorough understanding of the often-confused rules of correct writing is necessary for a manager to become a high-confidence writing. This series focuses on how to write effective business communications through proper use of grammar.
Product Number: COMM0200-PDI
URL: http://www.skillsoft.com

Chapter 30
Inspire Trust

Covey, Stephen R. *The 7 Habits of Highly Effective People.*
New York: Simon & Schuster, 1993.
ISBN: 0671708635
Covey presents a holistic, integrated, principle-centered approach for solving personal and professional problems. His principles provide the security to adapt to change, the wisdom and power to take advantage of opportunities, and the ability to project this assurance to others.

Kouzes, James M., and Posner, Barry A. *Encouraging the Heart: A Leader's Guide to Rewarding and Recognizing Others.* San Francisco: Jossey-Bass, 1999.
ISBN: 0787941840
The authors reflect on one of the most elusive aspects of leadership—caring—and offer readers a deeper understanding of how and why it works. They extend a set of principles, practices, and examples that show how to energize people to excel. The book presents over 150 ways readers can reward and recognize their coworkers.

Posner, Barry Z.; Kouzes, James M.; and Peters, Tom. *Credibility: How Leaders Gain and Lose It, Why People Demand It.* San Francisco: Jossey-Bass, 1993.
ISBN: 155542550X
Kouzes and Posner show why credibility is the cornerstone of leadership. Rich examples demonstrate how leaders can encourage greater initiative, risk taking, and productivity by demonstrating trust in employees and resolving conflicts on the basis of principles, not positions.

Ryan, Kathleen, and Oestreich, Daniel K. *Driving Fear Out of the Workplace: Creating the High-Trust, High-Performance Organization.* San Francisco: Jossey-Bass, 1998.
ISBN: 0787939684
Left unaddressed, workplace anxieties can seriously inhibit individual performance and a company's ability to compete. Ryan and Oestreich confront the fears that permeate today's business environment so that companies can become the high-trust, high-performance organizations of tomorrow.

Shelton, Ken. *Integrity at Work.*
Provo, UT: Executive Excellence Publishing, 1999.
ISBN: 1890009326
This compilation features leaders who have made high ethical standards and honest business practices top priorities in their organizations. These leaders share their experience with fostering honest behavior, dealing with ethical dilemmas, and leading others by moral example.

Solomon, Robert C. *A Better Way to Think about Business: How Personal Integrity Leads to Corporate Success.* New York: Oxford University Press, 1999.
ISBN: 0195112385
Drawing on 20 years of consulting experience, Solomon clarifies difficult ethical choices, examines how deficient values destroy businesses, and debunks the pervasive myths that encourage unethical business practices.

SEMINARS

Foundations of Leadership
Center for Creative Leadership
This workshop assists first-level and middle-level managers with three areas of critical development: evaluating interpersonal effectiveness, understanding basic leadership principles, and developing the potential of others.
Length: 3 days
Price: $2,900
Location: See Web site for dates and locations.
Tel: 336-545-2810
Fax: 336-282-3284
URL: http://www.ccl.org

Making Managers into Leaders
Enlightened Leadership International
Providing an introduction to the skills that distinguish leaders from managers, this seminar teaches participants how to lift employee attitudes and build the trust necessary to lead in today's changing business climate. Learn how to create an atmosphere of trust that promotes open communication and banishes fear from the workplace.
Length: 1 day
Price: $199
Location: See Web site for dates and locations.
Tel: 800-780-7910 or 303-729-0540
Fax: 800-780-7914 or 303-729-0551
URL: http://www.enleadership.com

The Seven Habits of Highly Effective People®
Franklin Covey
This program is based on the principles of interpersonal relationships outlined in Stephen R. Covey's book of the same name. The program, based on the premise that effective leadership starts from the inside out, is designed to heighten the participant's total leadership potential.
Length: 3 days
Price: Call vendor.
Location: See Web site for dates and locations.
Tel: 800-655-1492
URL: http://www.franklincovey.com

**Chapter 31
Demonstrate
Adaptability**

Carlson, Richard. *Don't Sweat the Small Stuff at Work: Simple Ways to Minimize Stress and Conflict while Bringing Out the Best in Yourself and Others.* New York: Hyperion, 1998.
ISBN: 0786883367
Carlson shows readers how to interact more peaceably with colleagues, clients, and managers, and reveals tips to minimize stress and bring out the best in themselves and others.

Goulston, Mark, and Goldberg, Philip. *Get Out of Your Own Way: Overcoming Self-Defeating Behavior.* New York, NY: Berkley Pub. Group, 1996.
ISBN: 0399519904
The authors share practical advice to help readers overcome a range of self-defeating behaviors—including procrastination, obsession, self-pity, rebellion, and guilt—to effectively cope with the challenges of life.

Nierenberg, Gerard I. *Do It Right the First Time: A Short Guide to Learning from Your Most Memorable Errors, Mistakes, and Blunders.* New York: John Wiley & Sons, 1996.
ISBN: 047114889X
The author discusses how errors are made and provides techniques for substantially decreasing them. He offers advice on how readers can achieve their potential, focus their concentration, analyze errors, learn from others' mistakes, and boost accuracy.

Noer, David M. *Breaking Free: A Prescription for Personal and Organizational Change.* San Francisco: Jossey-Bass, 1996.
ISBN: 0787902675
As major organizations continue the trend of massive layoffs, Noer focuses on employees struggling with the new rules of today's workplace. The book discusses the employer-employee relationship and encourages workers to direct their own future.

Seligman, Martin E.P. *Learned Optimism.*
New York: Pocket Books, 1998.
ISBN: 0671019112
Seligman compiles scientific evidence that optimism is vital to overcoming defeat and exhibits how to learn the habit of positive thinking. The author includes a thorough psychological discussion of optimism, pessimism, and the behaviors they engender.

Wilson, Paul. *Calm at Work: Breeze through Your Day Feeling Calm, Relaxed, and in Control.* New York: Plume, 1999.
ISBN: 0452280427
The author offers simple, straightforward techniques for overcoming stress on the job and creating a more tranquil workplace. The book explores how to overcome anxiety, control time, handle coworkers, and deal with crises—all leading to lasting calm.

SEMINARS

Course in Creativity
Innova Training and Consulting, Inc.
Learn both the Six Thinking Hats® and Lateral Thinking™ approaches to creativity. This three-day course teaches participants how to separate thinking into six distinct categories, as well as a deliberate, systematic process that results in innovative thinking.
Length: 3 days
Price: $795
Location: See Web site for dates and locations.
Tel: 800-621-3366
Fax: 515-278-2245
URL: http://www.innovatraining.com
E-mail: info@aptt.com

Managing Emotion in the Workplace: Maintaining High Performance Under Pressure
American Management Association
Participants will learn to identify their personal trigger points, develop techniques for staying calm in tense situations, receive criticism in a positive manner, and reenergize themselves at the end of the day.
Length: 2 days
Price: $1,395
Location: See Web site for dates and locations.
Tel: 800-262-9699.
Fax: 212-903-8168
URL: http://www.amanet.org

**Chapter 32
Practice
Self-Development**

Hathway, Patti. *Giving and Receiving Feedback.*
Los Altos, CA: Crisp Publications, 1998.
ISBN: 1560524308
This updated guide shows how to eliminate negative overtones and use feedback communication as a vehicle for growth. The author uses case studies to illustrate feedback in light of gender, self-image, and criticism.

Jaworski, Joseph. *Synchronicity: The Inner Path of Leadership.*
San Francisco: Berrett-Koehler, 1998.
ISBN: 1576750310
The author provides a guide to developing an essential leadership capacity: how leaders can collectively shape the future. The author offers a new definition of leadership that applies to all types of leaders: community, regional, national, international, corporate, and political.

Peterson, David B., and Hicks, Mary Dee. *Development FIRST: Strategies for Self-Development.* Minneapolis, MN: Personnel Decisions International, 1995.
ISBN: 0938529137
This book is the first in a series dealing with practical approaches to individual and team development within the changing corporate environment. Its five concise development strategies enable readers to plan and execute their own development in a busy, demanding world.

Vaill, Peter B. *Learning as a Way of Being: Strategies for Survival in a World of Permanent White Water.* San Francisco: Jossey-Bass, 1996.
ISBN: 0787902462
Vaill argues that managers must adopt a discipline of learning if they are to survive the "permanent white water" of change in today's business environment. This learning includes strong self-direction, willingness to take risks, and learning from life experience.

Wick, Calhoun W., and Lean, Lu Stanton. *The Learning Edge: How Smart Managers and Smart Companies Stay Ahead.* New York: McGraw-Hill, 1996.
ISBN: 0070700834
Based on the authors' rigorous 12-year study, this guide provides a blueprint for bringing intentional learning to the workplace, both individually and company-wide. With the aid of charts, graphs, and personal action plans, the book reveals the five components essential to the learning process.

SEMINARS

Achieving Professional Excellence: Strategies for Self-Development
American Management Association
This seminar teaches participants how to set goals, build self-esteem, and reach higher levels of performance. Topics include taking responsibility; leaving one's comfort zone; and coping with stress, pressure, and change.
Length: 3 days
Price: $1,495
Location: See Web site for dates and locations.
Tel: 800-262-9699
Fax: 212-903-8168
URL: http://www.amanet.org

Development FIRST™
Personnel Decisions International
Today's rapidly changing workplace requires constant learning and improvement. Participants in this program learn practical strategies for creating a personal development plan, managing their development, and maintaining a cycle of continuous learning. Standard or customized programs are available for delivery within an organization. Call vendor for details.
Length: 1 day
Price: Call vendor.
Tel: 800-633-4410
Fax: 612-904-7120
URL: http://www.personneldecisions.com

Individual Coaching Services
Personnel Decisions International
This customized coaching program helps people develop critical skills such as leadership, interpersonal, communication, and organizational-influence skills. Through a tailored assessment to diagnose developmental needs, one-on-one skills training, and state-of-the-art techniques for behavior change, participants gain powerful self-insight and successfully learn new skills and behaviors to make them stronger performers. Call vendor for details.
Tel: 800-633-4410
Fax: 612-904-7120
URL: http://www.personneldecisions.com

Leadership Development Program
Center for Creative Leadership
This program teaches participants how to grow as leaders to become more productive in their work and personal lives. Drawn from 30 years of research and experience in individual development, the program blends coaching, change management, activity-based learning and individual feedback to help participants develop their capacity for total leadership.
Length: 5 days
Price: $5,200
Location: See Web site for dates and locations.
Tel: 336-545-2810
Fax: 336-282-3284
URL: http://www.ccl.org

RECOMMENDED WEB SITES FOR GENERAL BUSINESS INFORMATION:

http://mitsloan.mit.edu/smr/index.html — *Sloan Management Review*

http://www.businessweek.com — *Business Week*

http://www.fastcompany.com — *Fast Company Magazine*

http://www.acnielsen.com — consumer goods

http://www.hbsp.harvard.edu — Ideas@Work; from Harvard Business

http://www.strategy-business.com — strategy and business; Booz, Allen & Hamilton

http://www.va.gov/fedsbest/library.htm — The Interactive Benchmarking and Best Practices Council Library

http://www.wsj.com — *Wall Street Journal*.com

http://www.hardatwork.com — Hard@Work; communication about what's happening on the job, through interaction with mentors, discussion groups, and case studies

http://humanresources.about.com — About.com; human resources and related links

RECOMMENDED WEB SITES FOR SPECIFIC CHAPTERS:

Chapters 1: Create Strategic Advantage and Chapter 7: Think Strategically

http://www.strategy-business.com — strategy and business; Booz, Allen & Hamilton

Chapter 2: Champion Change and Innovation

http://www.thinksmart.com — The Innovation Network; corporate innovation and creativity

http://www.thetech.org — The Tech Museum of Innovation

http://www.infinn.com/toolbox.html — Innovation Toolbox

http://www.innovation.cc — *The Innovation Journal*

http://www.mmm.com — 3M Innovation Network

http://www.cordis.lu/innovation — The European Commission's Innovation Programme

Chapter 4: Promote Global Perspective

http://globalbusiness.about.com — About.com; global business information and links to related sites

http://www.glreach.com/gbc — Global Reach; a guide to Web sites around the world, arranged by language, in topic-specific directories

http://ciber.bus.msu.edu — Center for International Business Education and Research at Michigan State University

http:://www.webofculture.com — Web of Culture; provides research services on the topics of international business and cross-cultural communications and links to other related sites

Chapter 9: Use Financial Acumen

http://www.ft.com — *Financial Times*.com; editorial analysis of financial markets, industries, and companies around the globe

http://www.research.ml.com/marketing/content/frhowtor.pdf — Merrill Lynch's "How to Read a Financial Report" booklet

http://www.morevalue.com — specializes in business journal reprints and teaching materials, and provides links to archived news stories on finance

http://www.investorguide.com — provides tools to handle your own personal finance and investing decisions

Chapters 12: Establish Plans and Chapter 14: Drive Execution

http://www.pmi.org — The Project Management Institute

http://www.projectnet.co.uk — Project Net: "The World of Project Management"

Chapter 13: Manage and Improve Processes

http://www.apqc.org — The American Productivity and Quality Center

http://deming.eng.clemson.edu/onlineq.html — On-line Quality Resource Guide; provides links to quality-related sites

http://www.asq-qmd.org — The Quality Management Division of the American Society for Quality

http://www.goalqpc.com — Goal/QPC; provides products and services to continuously improve business processes through team problem solving, project management, planning, idea generation, and standardization

Chapter 25: Leverage Individual and Cultural Diversity

http://aad.english.ucsb.edu — Affirmative Action and Diversity Project

http://www.diversityinc.com — DiversityInc.com

Chapter 27: Speak with Impact

http://www.presentations.com — *Presentations* magazine

Chapter 29: Write Effectively

http://www.m-w.com/dictionary — WWWebster Dictionary

http://www.thesaurus.com — Thesaurus.com

http://www.theslot.com/contents.html#start — *The Curmudgeon's Stylebook*

Chapter 32: Practice Self-Development

http://www.careermag.com — *Career Magazine*

About Personnel Decisions International

Personnel Decisions International (PDI) is a global consulting firm based on organizational psychology. We use our expertise to define, measure, and develop the capabilities needed to make organizations successful by growing the talents of their people, improving customer relationships, and increasing organizational performance.

Founded in 1967, PDI has become an internationally recognized leader in applying behavioral sciences to building successful organizations. PDI delivers services with the highest professional standards to hundreds of corporations and organizations throughout the world, from *Fortune* 500 organizations to emerging companies.

We work closely with our clients to better understand and meet their special needs. PDI's growth has been guided by a firm commitment to maintaining and enhancing the expertise our clients require. As a result, we have won a reputation for both professional excellence and practical results.

There are more than 250 psychologists and consultants at Ph.D. and Masters levels at PDI who specialize in assessment-based development. Our expertise spans many disciplines of psychology, a broad mix of corporate backgrounds, and practical business experience. This diversity of staff experience and professional credentials gives PDI a depth and breadth unique in our field.

Services, products, and consulting from Personnel Decisions International provide solutions to virtually every area of concern in human resources development:

- Assessment—for selection and promotion of the most qualified people for key positions

- Management development—to build the effectiveness and leadership ability of managers and executives

- Organizational effectiveness—to maximize the potential of the entire group

- Career transitions and career development—to strengthen organizations and preserve individual dignity

For information on services and products, call or write Personnel Decisions International, 2000 Plaza VII Tower, 45 South Seventh Street, Minneapolis, Minnesota 55402-1608, USA. Telephone: 800.633.4410 or 920.997.6995. Visit our Web site at **www.personneldecisions.com.**

PDI OFFICES
www.personneldecisions.com

NORTH AMERICA

CORPORATE HEADQUARTERS
2000 Plaza VII Tower
45 South Seventh Street
Minneapolis, Minnesota 55402-1608
Phone 800 633 4410 Fax 612 904 7120

ATLANTA
Suite 560
1040 Crown Pointe Parkway
Atlanta, Georgia 30338
Phone 770 668 9908 Fax 770 668 9958

AUSTIN
Suite 190
8310 Capital of Texas Highway North
Austin, Texas 78731
Phone 512 346 2800 Fax 512 346 2467

BOSTON
Suite 401
Three Copley Place
Boston, Massachusetts 02116
Phone 617 236 6511 Fax 617 236 6569

CHICAGO
Suite 2270
225 West Wacker Drive
Chicago, Illinois 60606
Phone 312 251 4180 Fax 312 251 4454

DALLAS
Suite 1700 LB 142
600 East Las Colinas Boulevard
Irving, Texas 75039
Phone 972 401 3190 Fax 972 401 3193

DENVER
One DTC
5251 DTC Parkway, Suite 1045
Greenwood Village, Colorado 80111
Phone 303 740 1020 Fax 303 740 0390

DETROIT
Suite 390
100 West Big Beaver Road
Troy, Michigan 48084
Phone 248 619 9330 Fax 248 619 9016

HOUSTON
Suite 700
1300 Post Oak Boulevard
Houston, Texas 77056
Phone 713 499 7500 Fax 713 499 7557

LOS ANGELES
Suite 750
2029 Century Park East
Los Angeles, California 90067-2928
Phone 310 556 4860 Fax 310 556 4865

MINNEAPOLIS/ST. PAUL
2000 Plaza VII Tower
45 South Seventh Street
Minneapolis, Minnesota 55402-1608
Phone 612 339 0927 Fax 612 904 7120

NEW YORK
52nd Floor
405 Lexington Avenue
New York, New York 10174-5301
Phone 212 972 6633 Fax 212 692 3300

SAN FRANCISCO
Suite 310
999 Baker Way
San Mateo, California 94404
Phone 650 372 1090 Fax 650 372 1099

WASHINGTON, DC
Suite 1000
1300 Wilson Boulevard
Arlington, Virginia 22209
Phone 703 522 3519 Fax 703 524 6325

EUROPE

BRATISLAVA
WBB Slovensko S.R.O. - a PDI company
Tomásikova 14
SK - 820 09 Bratislava
Slovak Republic
Tel 421 2 4333 9368 Fax 421 2 4341 3977

BRUSSELS
Gulledelle 96
B-1200 Brussels
Belgium
Tel 32 2 777 70 20 Fax 32 2 777 70 30

BUCHAREST
WBB Romania S.R.L. - a PDI company
B-dul Corneliu Coposu nr. 3
Bl. 101, sc. 3, et. 7
ap. 61, sector 3
RO-70491 Bucharest
Romania
Tel 401 321 77 93 Fax 401 320 11 14

BUDAPEST
WBB Hungary Ltd. - a PDI company
Victor Hugo U. 11-15
1132 Budapest
Hungary
Tel 36 1 350 87 07 Fax 36 1 350 87 09

GENEVA
Immeuble Jean-Baptiste Say
13 Chemin du Levant
01210 Ferney-Voltaire
France
Tel 33 4 50 40 64 11 Fax 33 4 50 40 64 53

GÖTEBORG
Norra Liden 629
411 18 Göteborg
Sweden
Tel 46 031 701 82 12 Fax 46 031 701 82 89

LONDON
80 Wimpole Street
London W1M 7DB
UK
Tel 44 20 7487 5776 Fax 44 20 7487 5356

PARIS
6, square de l'Opéra-Louis-Jouvet
75009 Paris
France
Tel 33 1 43 12 92 92 Fax 33 1 47 42 13 55

PROSTĚJOV
WBB SPOL S.R.O. - a PDI company
Olomoucká 19
CZ - 79601 Prostějov
Czech Republic
Tel 420 508 33 63 26 Fax 420 508 33 63 26

STOCKHOLM
Kungsbroplan 3A
SE-112 27 Stockholm
Sweden
Tel 46 08 402 00 20 Fax 46 08 411 88 30

STUTTGART
WBB - a PDI company
Neue Strasse 7
D-72070 Tübingen
Germany
Tel 49 70 71 55 98 60 Fax 49 70 71 55 98 88

ASIA

HONG KONG
Personnel Decisions International Greater China
Suite 3705-6, 37/F
Tower II, Lippo Center
89 Queensway, Admiralty
Hong Kong
Tel 852 2572 2641 Fax 852 2572 2649

SHANGHAI
Personnel Decisions International Greater China
Room 810, Tomson Financial Building
710 Dong Fang Road, Pudong New Area
Shanghai 200122
China
Tel 86 21 5830 9993 Fax 86 21 5830 0907

SINGAPORE
Personnel Decisions International
#24-08 Orchard Towers
400 Orchard Road
Singapore 238875
Tel 65 6732 2252 Fax 65 6733 2252

TOKYO
Yebisu Garden Place Tower 18F
4-20-3, Ebisu, Shibuya-ku
Tokyo 150-6018
Japan
Phone 813 5798 3400 Fax 813 5798 3410

AUSTRALIA

MELBOURNE
Coyne Didsbury PDI, Pty Ltd
Level 4
398 Lonsdale Street
Melbourne Victoria 3000
Australia
Phone 61 3 9670 3833 Fax 61 3 9600 4001

SYDNEY
Coyne Didsbury PDI, Pty Ltd
Level 13
109 Pitt Street
Sydney New South Wales 2000
Australia
Phone 61 2 9235 1516 Fax 61 2 9235 1526

Development Products from PDI

SUCCESSFUL EXECUTIVE'S HANDBOOK

This book is the result of years of work with many successful Fortune 500 executives who lead today's high performance organizations. It is based on the same competency model as The PROFILOR® for Executives from PDI, which identifies the eight factors essential to executive success in every industry.

ISBN: 0-938529-15-3 $75.00 U.S.

DEVELOPMENT FIRST: STRATEGIES FOR SELF-DEVELOPMENT

This easy-to-read book walks people through proven, practical steps to development. It helps them assess what they should work on, pick the right approaches and tactics, and learn from their experiences.

ISBN: 0-938529-13-7 $16.95 U.S.

LEADER AS COACH: STRATEGIES FOR COACHING AND DEVELOPING OTHERS

Coaching improves the bottom line because it goes to the heart of what makes people productive. This book discusses five practical coaching strategies that will increase the potential of your people and your organization.

ISBN: 0-938529-14-5 $19.95 U.S.

PRESENTATIONS: HOW TO CALM DOWN, THINK CLEARLY, AND CAPTIVATE YOUR AUDIENCE

This proven approach helps people develop and fine-tune their presentation skills, from crafting a message to delivering it effectively.

ISBN: 0-938529-23-4 $19.95 U.S.

SUCCESSFUL MANAGER'S HANDBOOK

Over 850,000 copies in print, this 800-page reference book provides practical tips, on-the-job activities, and suggestions for improving managerial skills and effectiveness.

ISBN: 0-938529-20-X $59.95 U.S.

DEVELOPMENT FIRST WORKBOOK

Companion to the *Development FIRST* book, this workbook will help you create and implement a personal learning plan. The workbook comes with fill-in-the-blank templates and a completed sample.

ISBN: 0-938529-21-8 $13.95 U.S.

LEADER AS COACH WORKBOOK

Companion to the *Leader As Coach* book, this workbook offers targeted advice, exercises, and worksheets that will help you develop your coaching capabilities, whether you are a beginner or a seasoned veteran.

ISBN: 0-938529-22-6 $13.95 U.S.

Price Grid for Books Listed	
Quantity	% Discount
1-9	0%
10-24	10%
25-49	20%
50-199	25%
200+	30%
Plus Shipping and Handling Charges	

DEVELOPMENTOR® eADVISOR™

*e*Advisor is a Web-based, on-line library that contains targeted, comprehensive employee development and coaching information. It provides a cost-effective and time-sensitive way for people to self-develop and learn new skills to achieve personal or career goals.

eAdvisor Annual Subscription	
Quantity	U.S. Dollars
1-9	$59.95
10-24	$55.95
25-49	$51.95
50-99	$47.95
100-199	$43.95
200-499	$38.95
500+	Call

PDI ADVICE

On-line PDI development suggestions for managers in eight languages including Dutch, English (UK and US), French, German, Italian, Portuguese, Spanish, and Swedish.

Advice	
Quantity	U.S. Dollars
1-9	$49.95
10-24	$47.95
25-49	$45.95
50-99	$42.95
100-199	$39.95
200-499	$36.95
500+	Call